Survey of Economics Version 1.1

By
Libby Rittenberg

flat**world**
KNOWLEDGE

S-1658807-BW

9 781453 364963

Survey of Economics Version 1.1

Libby Rittenberg

Published by:

Flat World Knowledge, Inc.
1111 19th St NW, Suite 1180
Washington, DC 20036

Brief Contents

Contents

About the Authors

LIBBY RITTENBERG

Libby Rittenberg has been a Professor of Economics at Colorado College in Colorado Springs since 1989. She teaches principles of economics, intermediate macroeconomic theory, comparative economic systems, and international political economy. She received her B. A. in economics-mathematics and Spanish from Simmons College and her Ph.D. in economics from Rutgers University.

Prior to joining the faculty at Colorado College, she taught at Lafayette College and at the Rutgers University Graduate School of Management. She served as a Fulbright Scholar in Istanbul, Turkey, and as a research economist at Mathematica, Inc. in Princeton, New Jersey.

Dr. Rittenberg specializes in the internationally oriented areas of economics, with numerous articles in journals and books on comparative and development economics. Much of her work focuses on transition issues and on the Turkish economy.

She has been very involved in study abroad education and has directed programs in central Europe and Turkey.

TIM TREGARTHEN

There is one word that captures the essence of Dr. Timothy Tregarthen—inspiring. Tim was first diagnosed with multiple sclerosis (MS) in 1975. Yet, he continued a remarkable academic career of teaching and research. In 1996, he published the first edition of his principles of economics textbook to great acclaim, and it became widely used in colleges around the country. That same year, MS made him wheelchair-bound. The disease forced his retirement from teaching at the University of Colorado at Colorado Springs in 1998. He lost the use of his arms in 2001 and has been quadriplegic ever since. In 2002, Tim's doctor expected him to die.

He was placed in the Pikes Peak Hospice program and was twice given his last rites by his priest. UCCS Chancellor Shockley-Zalabak says, "I really thought that Tim would die in hospice. That's what the doctors told me, and I really believed that. I remember one day they called me and told me to try to come see him. They didn't expect him to live through the night."

Not only did he live through the night, but he eventually recovered to the point that he moved from hospice to a long-term care facility. There, he never let his disease get him down. In fact, he turned back to his love of writing and teaching for inspiration. He obtained a voice-activated computer, recruited a coauthor, Libby Rittenberg of Colorado College, and turned his attention to revising his principles of economics book. Flat World Knowledge is honored to publish a new, first edition relaunch of this wonderful book, and proud to bring Tim's incredible talents as a teacher back to life for future generations of students to learn from.

In addition to completing the rewrite of his textbook, Tim recently completed an autobiography about the thirty-two years he has had MS, titled *Suffering, Faith, and Wildflowers*. He is nearing completion of a novel, *Cool Luck*, based on the life of a friend. It is the story of a young couple facing the husband's diagnosis of ALS—Lou Gehrig's disease. Remarkably, in 2007, he was able to return to the classroom at UCCS, where he had taught economics for twenty-seven years. In January of 2009, Tim married Dinora Montenegro (now Dinora Tregarthen); the couple lives in San Gabriel, California.

Perhaps Tim's approach to life is best summed up by an observation by UCCS English Professor Thomas Naperierkowski: "One of the remarkable things is, heck, I can wake up with a headache and be a pretty grouchy character, but given his physical trials, which he faces every minute of his life these days, I've never seen him grouchy, I've never seen him cranky." Carry on, Tim.

Acknowledgments

The authors would like to thank the following individuals who reviewed the text and whose contributions were invaluable in shaping the final product:

Carlos Aguilar	El Paso Community College
Jeff Ankrom	Wittenberg University
Lee Ash	Skagit Valley Community College
Randall Bennett	Gonzaga University
Joseph Calhoun	Florida State University
Richard Cantrell	Western Kentucky University
Gregg Davis	Flathead Valley Community College
Kevin Dunagan	Oakton Community College
Mona El Shazly	Columbia College
Jose Esteban	Palomar College
Maurita Fawls	Portland Community College
Fred Foldvary	Santa Clara University
Richard Fowles	University of Utah
Doris Geide-Stevenson	Weber State University
Sarmila Ghosh	University of Scranton, Kania School of Management
David Gordon	Illinois Valley Community College
Clinton Greene	University of Missouri-St. Louis
James Holcomb	University of Texas at El Paso
Phil Holleran	Mitchell Community College
Yu Hsing	Southeastern Louisiana University
Thomas Hyclak	Lehigh University
Bruce Johnson	Centre College
James Kahiga	Georgia Perimeter College
Andrew Kohen	James Madison University
Mark Maier	Glendale Community College
David McClough	Bowling Green State University
Ann McPherren	Huntington University
John Min	Northern Virginia Community College
Kristen Monaco	California State University–Long Beach
Shahriar Mostashari	Campbell University, Lundy-Fetterman School of Business
Francis Mummery	Fullerton College
Robert Murphy	Boston College
Kathryn Nantz	Fairfield University
Paul Okello	Tarrant County College-South Campus
Nicholas Peppes	St. Louis Community College
Ramoo Ratha	Diablo Valley College
Teresa Riley	Youngstown State University
Michael Robinson	Mount Holyoke College
Anirban Sengupta	Texas A&M University

John Solow	The University of Iowa
John Somers	Portland Community College
Charles Staelin	Smith College
Richard Stratton	The University of Akron
Kay E. Strong	Bowling Green State University–Firelands
Della Sue	Marist College
John Vahaly	University of Louisville
Robert Whaples	Wake Forest University
Mark Wheeler	Western Michigan University
Leslie Wolfson	The Pingry School
Sourushe Zandvakili	University of Cincinnati

We would like to extend a special thank you to the following instructors who class tested the text in their courses:

Johnathan Millman	University of Massachusetts–Boston
John Min	Northern Virginia Community College
Kristen Monaco	California State University–Long Beach
Steve Skinner	Western Connecticut State University
Richard Stratton	University of Akron

Preface

Greek philosopher Heraclitus said over 2500 years ago that "Nothing endures but change." Forecasting is a tricky business, but this sentiment strikes us as being as safe a bet as one can make. Change—rapid change—underlies all our lives. As we were completing this textbook, the world entered a period of marked economic uncertainty that led many students, and indeed people from all walks of life, to tune into economic events as never before to try to understand the economic world around them. So, while we as economists have the public's attention, we see an opportunity to share economics principles and the economic way of thinking in a way that emphasizes their relevance to today's world. We use applications from sports, politics, campus life, current events, and other familiar settings to illustrate the links between theoretical principles and common experiences. Because of the increasingly global nature of economic activity, we also recognize the need for a clear and consistent international focus throughout an economics text. In addition, we have tried to provide a sense of the intellectual excitement of the field and an appreciation for the gains it has made, as well as an awareness of the challenges that lie ahead.

To ensure students realize that economics is a unified discipline and not a bewildering array of seemingly unrelated topics, we develop the presentation of microeconomics and of macroeconomics around integrating themes.

The integrating theme for microeconomics is the marginal decision rule, a simple approach to choices that maximize the value of some objective. Following its presentation in an early microeconomics chapter, the marginal decision rule becomes an integrating device throughout the discussion of microeconomics. Instead of a hodgepodge of rules for different market conditions, we give a single rule that can be applied within any market setting.

The integrating theme for macroeconomics is the model of aggregate demand and aggregate supply. Following its presentation in an early macroeconomics chapter, this model allows us to look at both short-run and long-run concepts and to address a variety of policy issues and debates.

Recognizing that a course in economics may seem daunting to some students, we have tried to make the writing clear and engaging. Clarity comes in part from the intuitive presentation style, but we have also integrated a number of pedagogical features that we believe make learning economic concepts and principles easier and more fun. These features are very student-focused.

The chapters themselves are written using a "modular" format. In particular, chapters generally consist of three main content sections that break down a particular topic into manageable parts. Each content section contains not only an exposition of the material at hand but also learning objectives, summaries, examples, and problems. Each chapter is introduced with a story to motivate the material and each chapter ends with a wrap-up and additional problems. Our goal is to encourage active learning by including many examples and many problems of different types.

A tour of the features available for each chapter may give a better sense of what we mean:

- Start Up—Chapter introductions set the stage for each chapter with an example that we hope will motivate readers to study the material that follows. These essays, on topics such as the value of a college degree in the labor market or how policy makers reacted to a particular economic recession, lend themselves to the type of analysis explained in the chapter. We often refer to these examples later in the text to demonstrate the link between theory and reality.

- Learning Objectives—These succinct statements are guides to the content of each section. Instructors can use them as a snapshot of the important points of the section. After completing the section, students can return to the learning objectives to check if they have mastered the material.

- Heads Up!—These notes throughout the text warn of common errors and explain how to avoid making them. After our combined teaching experience of more than fifty years, we have seen the same mistakes made by many students. This feature provides additional clarification and shows students how to navigate possibly treacherous waters.

- Key Takeaways—These statements review the main points covered in each content section.

- Key Terms—Defined within the text, students can review them in context, a process that enhances learning.

- Try It! questions—These problems, which appear at the end of each content section and which are answered completely in the text, give students the opportunity to be active learners. They are designed to give students a clear signal as to whether they understand the material before they go on to the next topic.

- Cases in Point—These essays included at the end of each content section illustrate the influence of economic forces on real issues and real people. Unlike other texts that use boxed features to present interesting new material or newspaper articles, we have written each case ourselves to integrate them more clearly with the rest of the text.

- Summary—In a few paragraphs, the information presented in the chapter is pulled together in a way that allows for a quick review of the material.

- End-of-chapter concept and numerical problems—These are bountiful and are intended to check understanding, to promote discussion of the issues raised in the chapter, and to engage students in critical thinking about the material. Included are not only general review questions to test basic understanding but also examples drawn from the news and from results of economics research. Some have students working with real-world data.
- Chapter quizzes—Each chapter also includes online, supplementary multiple choice questions that provide students with feedback on both correct and incorrect responses. These provide yet another way for students to test themselves on the material.

ADDITIONAL MATERIAL FOR INSTRUCTORS

The authors have been personally involved in the generation of a huge *Test Bank* that includes multiple choice, true/false, and short essays questions. These questions are scored in terms of level of difficulty and include multiple ways of testing the material.

The *Solutions Manual*, with which the authors were also involved, contains answers for all concept and numerical problems found at the end of each text chapter.

The *PowerPoint Slides* include all the exhibits contained in the text to allow ease of use in class.

We hope that users will find this text an engaging and enjoyable way of becoming acquainted with economics principles and that mastery of the material will lead to looking at the world in a deeper and more meaningful way. We welcome all feedback.

Libby Rittenberg

Timothy Tregarthen

CHAPTER 1
Economics: The Study of Choice

START UP: ECONOMICS IN THE NEWS

Economic issues dominated the news in 2011, just as they dominate news in most years. What happens to economic phenomena such as growth, unemployment, gasoline and food prices, house values, and the national debt matters—and these phenomena matter a great deal.

What causes the prices of some goods to rise while the prices of other goods fall? Price determination is one of the things that we will study in this book. We will consider factors that lead an economy to grow more or less rapidly, the determination of unemployment rates, and even the process through which governments make choices that can lead to the kind of dilemma the United States faced in 2011 as the national debt soared past the nation's debt limit.

While the investigation of these problems surely falls within the province of economics, economics encompasses a far broader range of issues. Ultimately, economics is the study of choice. Because choices range over every imaginable aspect of human experience, so does economics. Economists have investigated the nature of family life, the arts, education, crime, sports, law—the list is virtually endless because so much of our lives involves making choices.

Consider some of the choices you face. Would you like better grades? More time to relax? More time watching movies? Getting better grades probably requires more time studying, and perhaps less relaxation and entertainment. Not only must we make choices as individuals, we must make choices as a society. Do we want a cleaner environment? Faster economic growth? Both may be desirable, but efforts to clean up the environment may conflict with faster economic growth. Society must make choices.

Economics is defined less by the subjects economists investigate than by the way in which economists investigate them. Economists have a way of looking at the world that differs from the way scholars in other disciplines look at the world. It is the *economic way of thinking*; this chapter introduces that way of thinking.

1. DEFINING ECONOMICS

Economics is a social science that examines how people choose among the alternatives available to them. It is social because it involves people and their behavior. It is a science because it uses, as much as possible, a scientific approach in its investigation of choices.

1.1 Scarcity, Choice, and Cost

All choices mean that one alternative is selected over another. Selecting among alternatives involves three ideas central to economics: scarcity, choice, and opportunity cost.

Scarcity

Our resources are limited. At any one time, we have only so much land, so many factories, so much oil, so many people. But our wants, our desires for the things that we can produce with those resources, are unlimited. We would always like more and better housing, more and better education—more and better of practically everything.

If our resources were also unlimited, we could say yes to each of our wants—and there would be no economics. Because our resources are limited, we cannot say yes to everything. To say yes to one thing requires that we say no to another. Whether we like it or not, we must make choices.

Our unlimited wants are continually colliding with the limits of our resources, forcing us to pick some activities and to reject others. **Scarcity** is the condition of having to choose among alternatives. A **scarce good** is one for which the choice of one alternative use of the good requires that another be given up.

Consider a parcel of land. The parcel presents us with several alternative uses. We could build a house on it. We could put a gas station on it. We could create a small park on it. We could leave the land undeveloped in order to be able to make a decision later as to how it should be used.

Suppose we have decided the land should be used for housing. Should it be a large and expensive house or several modest ones? Suppose it is to be a large and expensive house. Who should live in the house? If the Lees live in it, the Nguyens cannot. There are alternative uses of the land both in the sense of the type of use and also in the sense of who gets to use it. The fact that land is scarce means that society must make choices concerning its use.

Virtually everything is scarce. Consider the air we breathe, which is available in huge quantity at no charge to us. Could it possibly be scarce?

The test of whether air is scarce is whether it has alternative uses. What uses can we make of the air? We breathe it. We pollute it when we drive our cars, heat our houses, or operate our factories. In effect, one use of the air is as a garbage dump. We certainly need the air to breathe. But just as certainly, we choose to dump garbage in it. Those two uses are clearly alternatives to each other. The more garbage we dump in the air, the less desirable—and healthy—it will be to breathe. If we decide we want to breathe cleaner air, we must limit the activities that generate pollution. Air is a scarce good because it has alternative uses.

Not all goods, however, confront us with such choices. A **free good** is one for which the choice of one use does not require that we give up another. One example of a free good is gravity. The fact that gravity is holding you to the earth does not mean that your neighbor is forced to drift up into space! One person's use of gravity is not an alternative to another person's use.

There are not many free goods. Outer space, for example, was a free good when the only use we made of it was to gaze at it. But now, our use of space has reached the point where one use can be an alternative to another. Conflicts have already arisen over the allocation of orbital slots for communications satellites. Thus, even parts of outer space are scarce. Space will surely become scarcer as we find new ways to use it. Scarcity characterizes virtually everything. Consequently, the scope of economics is wide indeed.

---

economics

A social science that examines how people choose among the alternatives available to them.

scarcity

The condition of having to choose among alternatives.

scarce good

A good for which the choice of one alternative requires that another be given up.

free good

A good for which the choice of one use does not require that another be given up.

Scarcity and the Fundamental Economic Questions

The choices we confront as a result of scarcity raise three sets of issues. Every economy must answer the following questions:

1. **What should be produced?** Using the economy's scarce resources to produce one thing requires giving up another. Producing better education, for example, may require cutting back on other services, such as health care. A decision to preserve a wilderness area requires giving up other uses of the land. Every society must decide what it will produce with its scarce resources.

2. **How should goods and services be produced?** There are all sorts of choices to be made in determining how goods and services should be produced. Should a firm employ a few skilled or a lot of unskilled workers? Should it produce in its own country or should it use foreign plants? Should manufacturing firms use new or recycled raw materials to make their products?

3. **For whom should goods and services be produced?** If a good or service is produced, a decision must be made about who will get it. A decision to have one person or group receive a good or service usually means it will not be available to someone else. For example, representatives of the poorest nations on earth often complain that energy consumption per person in the United States is many *times* greater than energy consumption per person in the world's scores of poorest countries. Critics argue that the world's energy should be more evenly allocated. Should it? That is a "for whom" question.

Every economy must determine what should be produced, how it should be produced, and for whom it should be produced. We shall return to these questions again and again.

Opportunity Cost

It is within the context of scarcity that economists define what is perhaps the most important concept in all of economics, the concept of opportunity cost. **Opportunity cost** is the value of the best alternative forgone in making any choice.

The opportunity cost to you of reading the remainder of this chapter will be the value of the best other use to which you could have put your time. If you choose to spend $20 on a potted plant, you have simultaneously chosen to give up the benefits of spending the $20 on pizzas or a paperback book or a night at the movies. If the book is the most valuable of those alternatives, then the opportunity cost of the plant is the value of the enjoyment you otherwise expected to receive from the book.

The concept of opportunity cost must not be confused with the purchase price of an item. Consider the cost of a college or university education. That includes the value of the best alternative use of money spent for tuition, fees, and books. But the most important cost of a college education is the value of the forgone alternative uses of time spent studying and attending class instead of using the time in some other endeavor. Students sacrifice that time in hopes of even greater earnings in the future or because they place a value on the opportunity to learn. Or consider the cost of going to the doctor. Part of that cost is the value of the best alternative use of the money required to see the doctor. But the cost also includes the value of the best alternative use of the time required to see the doctor. The essential thing to see in the concept of opportunity cost is found in the name of the concept. Opportunity cost is the value of the best opportunity forgone in a particular choice. It is not simply the amount spent on that choice.

The concepts of scarcity, choice, and opportunity cost are at the heart of economics. A good is scarce if the choice of one alternative requires that another be given up. The existence of alternative uses forces us to make choices. The opportunity cost of any choice is the value of the best alternative forgone in making it.

opportunity cost

The value of the best alternative forgone in making any choice.

KEY TAKEAWAYS

- Economics is a social science that examines how people choose among the alternatives available to them.
- Scarcity implies that we must give up one alternative in selecting another. A good that is not scarce is a free good.
- The three fundamental economic questions are: What should be produced? How should goods and services be produced? For whom should goods and services be produced?
- Every choice has an opportunity cost and opportunity costs affect the choices people make. The opportunity cost of any choice is the value of the best alternative that had to be forgone in making that choice.

Identify the elements of scarcity, choice, and opportunity cost in each of the following:

1. The Environmental Protection Agency is considering an order that a 500-acre area on the outskirts of a large city be preserved in its natural state, because the area is home to a rodent that is considered an endangered species. Developers had planned to build a housing development on the land.

2. The manager of an automobile assembly plant is considering whether to produce cars or sport utility vehicles (SUVs) next month. Assume that the quantities of labor and other materials required would be the same for either type of production.

3. A young man who went to work as a nurses' aide after graduating from high school leaves his job to go to college, where he will obtain training as a registered nurse.

Case in Point

Canadians Make a Choice

© Thinkstock

Canadian Prime Minister Stephen Harper, head of the Conservative Party, had walked a political tightrope for five years as the leader of a minority government in Canada's parliamentary system. His opponents, upset by policies such as a reduction in corporate tax rates, sought a no-confidence vote in Parliament in 2011. It passed Parliament overwhelmingly, toppling Harper's government and forcing national elections for a new Parliament.

The political victory was short-lived—the Conservative Party won the May 2011 election easily and emerged as the ruling party in Canada. This allowed Mr. Harper to continue to pursue a policy of deficit and tax reduction.

Canadian voters faced the kinds of choices we have been discussing. Opposition parties—the New Democratic Party (NDP) and the more moderate Liberal Party—sought higher corporate tax rates and less deficit reduction than those advocated by the Conservatives. Under Mr. Harper, the deficit had fallen by one-third in 2010. He promises a surplus budget by 2015, a plan the International Monetary Fund has termed "strong and credible."

Canada's unemployment rate in May, 2011 was 7.4 percent compared to a U.S. rate that month of 9.1 percent. GDP growth in Canada was 3.1 percent in 2010; the Bank of Canada projects 4.2 for its growth rate the first quarter of 2011, compared to a U.S. rate for that quarter of 1.8 percent.

Mr. Harper employed a stimulus package to battle the recession that began in Canada in 2008. He scaled back that effort in 2010 and 2011, producing substantial reductions in the deficit.

Writing on the eve of the election, *Wall Street Journal* columnist Mary Anastasia O'Grady termed the vote a "referendum on limited government." Whether or not that characterization was accurate, Canadians clearly made a choice that will result in lower taxes and less spending than the packages offered by the NDP and Liberal Party.

While the issue did not seem to figure prominently in the 2011 campaign, the NDP platform promised to reduce Canada's greenhouse gas emissions, which have increased with the development of huge oil deposits in Alberta, deposits that have put Canada in third place (behind Venezuela and Saudi Arabia) in the world in terms of oil reserves. Mr. Harper and the Conservatives have promised to proceed with this development as a key factor in Canada's growth, while the NDP would restrict it sharply. It is a classic case of the problem when choices are made between environmental quality and economic growth.

Sources: Kathleen Harris, "A Vote for the Economy," Canadian Business, 84(6), May 9, 2011; Nirmala Menon and Paul Vieira, "Canada's Conservatives Win Majority," The Wall Street Journal online, May 3, 2011; Paul Vieira, "Canada's Budget Deficit Shrinks on Strong Growth," The Wall Street Journal online, April 22, 2011; Mary Anastasia O'Grady, "Canada's Capitalism Referendum, The Wall Street Journal online, May 2, 2011. The platform of the NDP is available at http://xfer.ndp.ca/2011/2011-Platform/NDP-2011-Platform-En.pdf.

ANSWERS TO TRY IT! PROBLEMS

1. The 500-acre area is scarce because it has alternative uses: preservation in its natural state or a site for homes. A choice must be made between these uses. The opportunity cost of preserving the land in its natural state is the forgone value of the land as a housing development. The opportunity cost of using the land as a housing development is the forgone value of preserving the land.

2. The scarce resources are the plant and the labor at the plant. The manager must choose between producing cars and producing SUVs. The opportunity cost of producing cars is the profit that could be earned from producing SUVs; the opportunity cost of producing SUVs is the profit that could be earned from producing cars.

3. The man can devote his time to his current career or to an education; his time is a scarce resource. He must choose between these alternatives. The opportunity cost of continuing as a nurses' aide is the forgone benefit he expects from training as a registered nurse; the opportunity cost of going to college is the forgone income he could have earned working full-time as a nurses' aide.

2.   THE FIELD OF ECONOMICS

LEARNING OBJECTIVES

1. **Explain the distinguishing characteristics of the economic way of thinking.**
2. **Distinguish between microeconomics and macroeconomics.**

We have examined the basic concepts of scarcity, choice, and opportunity cost in economics. In this section, we will look at economics as a field of study. We begin with the characteristics that distinguish economics from other social sciences.

2.1   The Economic Way of Thinking

Economists study choices that scarcity requires us to make. This fact is not what distinguishes economics from other social sciences; all social scientists are interested in choices. An anthropologist might study the choices of ancient peoples; a political scientist might study the choices of legislatures; a psychologist might study how people choose a mate; a sociologist might study the factors that have led to a rise in single-parent households. Economists study such questions as well. What is it about the study of choices by economists that makes economics different from these other social sciences?

Three features distinguish the economic approach to choice from the approaches taken in other social sciences:

1. Economists give special emphasis to the role of opportunity costs in their analysis of choices.

2. Economists assume that individuals make choices that seek to maximize the value of some objective, and that they define their objectives in terms of their own self-interest.

3. Individuals maximize by deciding whether to do a little more or a little less of something. Economists argue that individuals pay attention to the consequences of small changes in the levels of the activities they pursue.

The emphasis economists place on opportunity cost, the idea that people make choices that maximize the value of objectives that serve their self-interest, and a focus on the effects of small changes are ideas of great power. They constitute the core of economic thinking. The next three sections examine these ideas in greater detail.

Opportunity Costs Are Important

If doing one thing requires giving up another, then the expected benefits of the alternatives we face will affect the ones we choose. Economists argue that an understanding of opportunity cost is crucial to the examination of choices.

As the set of available alternatives changes, we expect that the choices individuals make will change. A rainy day could change the opportunity cost of reading a book; we might expect more reading to get done in bad than in good weather. A high income can make it very costly to take a day off; we might expect highly paid individuals to work more hours than those who are not paid as well. If individuals are maximizing their level of satisfaction and firms are maximizing profits, then a change in the set of alternatives they face may affect their choices in a predictable way.

The emphasis on opportunity costs is an emphasis on the examination of alternatives. One benefit of the economic way of thinking is that it pushes us to think about the value of alternatives in each problem involving choice.

Individuals Maximize in Pursuing Self-Interest

What motivates people as they make choices? Perhaps more than anything else, it is the economist's answer to this question that distinguishes economics from other fields.

Economists assume that individuals make choices that they expect will create the maximum value of some objective, given the constraints they face. Furthermore, economists assume that people's objectives will be those that serve their own self-interest.

Economists assume, for example, that the owners of business firms seek to maximize profit. Given the assumed goal of profit maximization, economists can predict how firms in an industry will respond to changes in the markets in which they operate. As labor costs in the United States rise, for example, economists are not surprised to see firms moving some of their manufacturing operations overseas.

Similarly, economists assume that maximizing behavior is at work when they examine the behavior of consumers. In studying consumers, economists assume that individual consumers make choices aimed at maximizing their level of satisfaction. In the next chapter, we will look at the results of the shift from skiing to snowboarding; that is a shift that reflects the pursuit of self-interest by consumers and by manufacturers.

In assuming that people pursue their self-interest, economists are not assuming people are selfish. People clearly gain satisfaction by helping others, as suggested by the large charitable contributions people make. Pursuing one's own self-interest means pursuing the things that give one satisfaction. It need not imply greed or selfishness.

Choices Are Made at the Margin

margin

The current level of an activity.

choice at the margin

A decision to do a little more or a little less of something.

Economists argue that most choices are made "at the margin." The **margin** is the current level of an activity. Think of it as the edge from which a choice is to be made. A **choice at the margin** is a decision to do a little more or a little less of something.

Assessing choices at the margin can lead to extremely useful insights. Consider, for example, the problem of curtailing water consumption when the amount of water available falls short of the amount people now use. Economists argue that one way to induce people to conserve water is to raise its price. A common response to this recommendation is that a higher price would have no effect on water consumption, because water is a necessity. Many people assert that prices do not affect water consumption because people "need" water.

But choices in water consumption, like virtually all choices, are made at the margin. Individuals do not make choices about whether they should or should not consume water. Rather, they decide whether to consume a little more or a little less water. Household water consumption in the United States totals about 105 gallons per person per day. Think of that starting point as the edge from which a choice at the margin in water consumption is made. Could a higher price cause you to use less water brushing your teeth, take shorter showers, or water your lawn less? Could a higher price cause people to reduce their use, say, to 104 gallons per person per day? To 103? When we examine the choice to consume water at the margin, the notion that a higher price would reduce consumption seems much more plausible. Prices affect our consumption of water because choices in water consumption, like other choices, are made at the margin.

The elements of opportunity cost, maximization, and choices at the margin can be found in each of two broad areas of economic analysis: microeconomics and macroeconomics. Your economics course, for example, may be designated as a "micro" or as a "macro" course. We will look at these two areas of economic thought in the next section.

2.2 Microeconomics and Macroeconomics

The field of economics is typically divided into two broad realms: microeconomics and macroeconomics. It is important to see the distinctions between these broad areas of study.

Microeconomics is the branch of economics that focuses on the choices made by individual decision-making units in the economy—typically consumers and firms—and the impacts those choices have on individual markets. **Macroeconomics** is the branch of economics that focuses on the impact of choices on the total, or aggregate, level of economic activity.

Why do tickets to the best concerts cost so much? How does the threat of global warming affect real estate prices in coastal areas? Why do women end up doing most of the housework? Why do senior citizens get discounts on public transit systems? These questions are generally regarded as microeconomic because they focus on individual units or markets in the economy.

Is the total level of economic activity rising or falling? Is the rate of inflation increasing or decreasing? What is happening to the unemployment rate? These are the questions that deal with aggregates, or totals, in the economy; they are problems of macroeconomics. The question about the level of economic activity, for example, refers to the total value of all goods and services produced in the economy. Inflation is a measure of the rate of change in the average price level for the entire economy; it is a macroeconomic problem. The total levels of employment and unemployment in the economy represent the aggregate of all labor markets; unemployment is also a topic of macroeconomics.

Both microeconomics and macroeconomics give attention to individual markets. But in microeconomics that attention is an end in itself; in macroeconomics it is aimed at explaining the movement of major economic aggregates—the level of total output, the level of employment, and the price level.

microeconomics

The branch of economics that focuses on the choices made by consumers and firms and the impacts those choices have on individual markets.

macroeconomics

The branch of economics that focuses on the impact of choices on the total, or aggregate, level of economic activity.

KEY TAKEAWAYS

- Economists focus on the opportunity costs of choices, they assume that individuals make choices in a way that maximizes the value of an objective defined in terms of their own self-interest, and they assume that individuals make those choices at the margin.
- Economics is divided into two broad areas: microeconomics and macroeconomics.

TRY IT!

The Department of Agriculture estimated that the expenditures a middle-income, husband–wife family of three would incur to raise one additional child from birth in 2005 to age 17 would be $250,530. In what way does this estimate illustrate the economic way of thinking? Would the Department's estimate be an example of microeconomic or of macroeconomic analysis? Why?

Case in Point

Opportunity Cost with *The Simpsons*

© *Thinkstock*

In the animated television comedy *The Simpsons*, Homer's father, Grampa Simpson, faced a classic problem in the allocation of a scarce resource—his time. He wanted to spend the day with his girlfriend, Bea—it was, after all, her birthday. His alternative was to spend the day with Homer and the family, which he did not really want to do, partly because they never visited him anyway.

Homer and his family prevailed, however, and insisted on taking Grampa to "Discount Lion Safari," a local amusement park. The cost of Grampa's day with his family is the enjoyment he anticipated from spending time with Bea. It all ends up badly for Grampa anyway—Homer's car breaks down on the way to the park. As for the forgone alternative, Bea dies that day, possibly because of a broken heart from not being able to spend the day with Grampa.

Sources: R. Andrew Luccasen and M. Kathleen Thomas, "Simpsonomics: Teaching Economics Using Episodes of The Simpsons," The Journal of Economic Education, 41(2), Spring 2010, 136–149. The Simpsons, Episode no. 30, first broadcast 28 March 1991 by Fox, directed by David Silverman and written by Jay Kogen and Wallace Wolodarsky.

ANSWER TO TRY IT! PROBLEM

The information given suggests one element of the economic way of thinking: assessing the choice at the margin. The estimate reflects the cost of one more child for a family that already has one. It is not clear from the information given how close the estimate of cost comes to the economic concept of opportunity cost. The Department of Agriculture's estimate included such costs as housing, food, transportation, clothing, health care, child care, and education. An economist would add the value of the best alternative use of the additional time that would be required for the child. If the couple is looking far ahead, they may want to consider the opportunity cost of sending a child to college. And, if they are looking *very* far ahead, they may want to consider the fact that nearly half of all parents over the age of 50 support at least one child over the age of 21. This is a problem in microeconomic analysis, because it focuses on the choices of individual households.

3. THE ECONOMISTS' TOOL KIT

LEARNING OBJECTIVES

1. **Explain how economists test hypotheses, develop economic theories, and use models in their analyses.**
2. **Explain how the all-other-things unchanged (ceteris paribus) problem and the fallacy of false cause affect the testing of economic hypotheses and how economists try to overcome these problems.**
3. **Distinguish between normative and positive statements.**

Economics differs from other social sciences because of its emphasis on opportunity cost, the assumption of maximization in terms of one's own self-interest, and the analysis of choices at the margin. But certainly much of the basic methodology of economics and many of its difficulties are common to every social science—indeed, to every science. This section explores the application of the scientific method to economics.

variable

Something whose value can change.

constant

Something whose value does not change.

Researchers often examine relationships between variables. A **variable** is something whose value can change. By contrast, a **constant** is something whose value does not change. The speed at which a car is traveling is an example of a variable. The number of minutes in an hour is an example of a constant.

Research is generally conducted within a framework called the **scientific method**, a systematic set of procedures through which knowledge is created. In the scientific method, hypotheses are suggested and then tested. A **hypothesis** is an assertion of a relationship between two or more variables that could be proven to be false. A statement is not a hypothesis if no conceivable test could show it to be false. The statement "Plants like sunshine" is not a hypothesis; there is no way to test whether plants like sunshine or not, so it is impossible to prove the statement false. The statement "Increased solar radiation increases the rate of plant growth" is a hypothesis; experiments could be done to show the relationship between solar radiation and plant growth. If solar radiation were shown to be unrelated to plant growth or to retard plant growth, then the hypothesis would be demonstrated to be false.

If a test reveals that a particular hypothesis is false, then the hypothesis is rejected or modified. In the case of the hypothesis about solar radiation and plant growth, we would probably find that more sunlight increases plant growth over some range but that too much can actually retard plant growth. Such results would lead us to modify our hypothesis about the relationship between solar radiation and plant growth.

If the tests of a hypothesis yield results consistent with it, then further tests are conducted. A hypothesis that has not been rejected after widespread testing and that wins general acceptance is commonly called a **theory**. A theory that has been subjected to even more testing and that has won virtually universal acceptance becomes a **law**. We will examine two economic laws in the next two chapters.

Even a hypothesis that has achieved the status of a law cannot be proven true. There is always a possibility that someone may find a case that invalidates the hypothesis. That possibility means that nothing in economics, or in any other social science, or in any science, can ever be *proven* true. We can have great confidence in a particular proposition, but it is always a mistake to assert that it is "proven."

3.1   Models in Economics

All scientific thought involves simplifications of reality. The real world is far too complex for the human mind—or the most powerful computer—to consider. Scientists use models instead. A **model** is a set of simplifying assumptions about some aspect of the real world. Models are always based on assumed conditions that are simpler than those of the real world, assumptions that are necessarily false. A model of the real world cannot *be* the real world.

We will encounter an economic model in Chapter 2. For that model, we will assume that an economy can produce only two goods. Then we will explore the model of demand and supply. One of the assumptions we will make there is that all the goods produced by firms in a particular market are identical. Of course, real economies and real markets are not that simple. Reality is never as simple as a model; one point of a model is to simplify the world to improve our understanding of it.

Economists often use graphs to represent economic models. The appendix to this chapter provides a quick, refresher course, if you think you need one, on understanding, building, and using graphs.

Models in economics also help us to generate hypotheses about the real world. In the next section, we will examine some of the problems we encounter in testing those hypotheses.

3.2   Testing Hypotheses in Economics

Here is a hypothesis suggested by the model of demand and supply: an increase in the price of gasoline will reduce the quantity of gasoline consumers demand. How might we test such a hypothesis?

Economists try to test hypotheses such as this one by observing actual behavior and using empirical (that is, real-world) data. The average retail price of gasoline in the United States rose from an average of $2.12 per gallon on May 22, 2005 to $2.88 per gallon on May 22, 2006. The number of gallons of gasoline consumed by U.S. motorists rose 0.3% during that period.

The small increase in the quantity of gasoline consumed by motorists as its price rose is inconsistent with the hypothesis that an increased price will lead to a reduction in the quantity demanded. Does that mean that we should dismiss the original hypothesis? On the contrary, we must be cautious in assessing this evidence. Several problems exist in interpreting any set of economic data. One problem is that several things may be changing at once; another is that the initial event may be unrelated to the event that follows. The next two sections examine these problems in detail.

The All-Other-Things-Unchanged Problem

The hypothesis that an increase in the price of gasoline produces a reduction in the quantity demanded by consumers carries with it the assumption that there are no other changes that might also affect consumer demand. A better statement of the hypothesis would be: An increase in the price of gasoline will reduce the quantity consumers demand, ceteris paribus. **Ceteris paribus** is a Latin phrase that means "all other things unchanged."

---

scientific method

A systematic set of procedures through which knowledge is created.

hypothesis

An assertion of a relationship between two or more variables that could be proven to be false.

theory

A hypothesis that has not been rejected after widespread testing and that wins general acceptance.

law

A theory that has been subjected to even more testing and that has won virtually universal acceptance.

model

A set of simplifying assumptions about some aspect of the real world.

ceteris paribus

A Latin phrase that means, "all other things unchanged."

But things changed between May 2005 and May 2006. Economic activity and incomes rose both in the United States and in many other countries, particularly China, and people with higher incomes are likely to buy more gasoline. Employment rose as well, and people with jobs use more gasoline as they drive to work. Population in the United States grew during the period. In short, many things happened during the period, all of which tended to increase the quantity of gasoline people purchased.

Our observation of the gasoline market between May 2005 and May 2006 did not offer a conclusive test of the hypothesis that an increase in the price of gasoline would lead to a reduction in the quantity demanded by consumers. Other things changed and affected gasoline consumption. Such problems are likely to affect any analysis of economic events. We cannot ask the world to stand still while we conduct experiments in economic phenomena. Economists employ a variety of statistical methods to allow them to isolate the impact of single events such as price changes, but they can never be certain that they have accurately isolated the impact of a single event in a world in which virtually everything is changing all the time.

In laboratory sciences such as chemistry and biology, it is relatively easy to conduct experiments in which only selected things change and all other factors are held constant. The economists' laboratory is the real world; thus, economists do not generally have the luxury of conducting controlled experiments.

The Fallacy of False Cause

dependent variable

A variable that responds to change.

independent variable

A variable that induces a change.

Hypotheses in economics typically specify a relationship in which a change in one variable causes another to change. We call the variable that responds to the change the **dependent variable**; the variable that induces a change is called the **independent variable**. Sometimes the fact that two variables move together can suggest the false conclusion that one of the variables has acted as an independent variable that has caused the change we observe in the dependent variable.

Consider the following hypothesis: People wearing shorts cause warm weather. Certainly, we observe that more people wear shorts when the weather is warm. Presumably, though, it is the warm weather that causes people to wear shorts rather than the wearing of shorts that causes warm weather; it would be incorrect to infer from this that people cause warm weather by wearing shorts.

fallacy of false cause

The incorrect assumption that one event causes another because the two events tend to occur together.

Reaching the incorrect conclusion that one event causes another because the two events tend to occur together is called the **fallacy of false cause**. The accompanying essay on baldness and heart disease suggests an example of this fallacy.

Because of the danger of the fallacy of false cause, economists use special statistical tests that are designed to determine whether changes in one thing actually do cause changes observed in another. Given the inability to perform controlled experiments, however, these tests do not always offer convincing evidence that persuades all economists that one thing does, in fact, cause changes in another.

In the case of gasoline prices and consumption between May 2005 and May 2006, there is good theoretical reason to believe the price increase should lead to a reduction in the quantity consumers demand. And economists have tested the hypothesis about price and the quantity demanded quite extensively. They have developed elaborate statistical tests aimed at ruling out problems of the fallacy of false cause. While we cannot prove that an increase in price will, ceteris paribus, lead to a reduction in the quantity consumers demand, we can have considerable confidence in the proposition.

Normative and Positive Statements

positive statement

A statement of fact or a hypothesis.

Two kinds of assertions in economics can be subjected to testing. We have already examined one, the hypothesis. Another testable assertion is a statement of fact, such as "It is raining outside" or "Microsoft is the largest producer of operating systems for personal computers in the world." Like hypotheses, such assertions can be demonstrated to be false. Unlike hypotheses, they can also be shown to be correct. A statement of fact or a hypothesis is a **positive statement**.

normative statement

A statement that makes a value judgment.

Although people often disagree about positive statements, such disagreements can ultimately be resolved through investigation. There is another category of assertions, however, for which investigation can never resolve differences. A **normative statement** is one that makes a value judgment. Such a judgment is the opinion of the speaker; no one can "prove" that the statement is or is not correct. Here are some examples of normative statements in economics: "We ought to do more to help the poor." "People in the United States should save more." "Corporate profits are too high." The statements are based on the values of the person who makes them. They cannot be proven false.

Because people have different values, normative statements often provoke disagreement. An economist whose values lead him or her to conclude that we should provide more help for the poor will disagree with one whose values lead to a conclusion that we should not. Because no test exists for these values, these two economists will continue to disagree, unless one persuades the other to adopt a different set of values. Many of the disagreements among economists are based on such differences in values and therefore are unlikely to be resolved.

Case in Point

Does Baldness Cause Heart Disease?

© 2010 Jupiterimages Corporation

A website called embarrassingproblems.com received the following email:

> *Dear Dr. Margaret,*
>
> *I seem to be going bald. According to your website, this means I'm more likely to have a heart attack. If I take a drug to prevent hair loss, will it reduce my risk of a heart attack?*

What did Dr. Margaret answer? Most importantly, she did not recommend that the questioner take drugs to treat his baldness, because doctors do not think that the baldness causes the heart disease. A more likely explanation for the association between baldness and heart disease is that both conditions are affected by an underlying factor. While noting that more research needs to be done, one hypothesis that Dr. Margaret offers is that higher testosterone levels might be triggering both the hair loss and the heart disease. The good news for people with early balding (which is really where the association with increased risk of heart disease has been observed) is that they have a signal that might lead them to be checked early on for heart disease.

Source: Formerly available at http://www.embarrassingproblems.com/problems/problempage230701.htm.

4.   REVIEW AND PRACTICE

Summary

Choices are forced on us by scarcity; economists study the choices that people make. Scarce goods are those for which the choice of one alternative requires giving up another. The opportunity cost of any choice is the value of the best alternative forgone in making that choice.

Some key choices assessed by economists include what to produce, how to produce it, and for whom it should be produced. Economics is distinguished from other academic disciplines that also study choices by an emphasis on the central importance of opportunity costs in evaluating choices, the assumption of maximizing behavior that serves the interests of individual decision makers, and a focus on evaluating choices at the margin.

Economic analyses may be aimed at explaining individual choice or choices in an individual market; such investigations are largely the focus of microeconomics. The analysis of the impact of those individual choices on such aggregates as total output, the level of employment, and the price level is the concern of macroeconomics.

Working within the framework of the scientific method, economists formulate hypotheses and then test them. These tests can only refute a hypothesis; hypotheses in science cannot be proved. A hypothesis that has been widely tested often comes to be regarded as a theory; one that has won virtually universal acceptance is a law. Because of the complexity of the real world, economists rely on models that rest on a series of simplifying assumptions. The models are used to generate hypotheses about the economy that can be tested using real-world data.

Statements of fact and hypotheses are positive statements. Normative statements, unlike positive statements, cannot be tested and provide a source for potential disagreement.

PROBLEMS

1. Why does the fact that something is scarce require that we make choices?

2. Does the fact that something is abundant mean it is not scarce in the economic sense? Why or why not?

3. In some countries, such as Cuba and North Korea, the government makes most of the decisions about what will be produced, how it will be produced, and for whom. Does the fact that these choices are made by the government eliminate scarcity in these countries? Why or why not?

4. Explain what is meant by the opportunity cost of a choice.

5. What is the approximate dollar cost of the tuition and other fees associated with the economics course you are taking? Does this dollar cost fully reflect the opportunity cost to you of taking the course?

6. In the Case in Point "Canadians Make a Choice," what would be some of the things that would be included in an estimate of the opportunity cost of preserving part of northern Alberta Canada by prohibiting heavy crude oil extraction? Do you think that the increased extraction represents the best use of the land? Why or why not?

7. Indicate whether each of the following is a topic of microeconomics or macroeconomics:

    a. The impact of higher oil prices on the production of steel

    b. The increased demand in the last 15 years for exotic dietary supplements

    c. The surge in aggregate economic activity that hit much of Asia late in the early 2000s

    d. The sharp increases in U.S. employment and total output that occurred between 2003 and 2007

    e. The impact of preservation of wilderness areas on the logging industry and on the price of lumber

8. Determine whether each of the following raises a "what," "how," or "for whom" issue. Are the statements normative or positive?

    a. A requirement that aluminum used in cars be made from recycled materials will raise the price of automobiles.

    b. The federal government does not spend enough for children.

    c. An increase in police resources provided to the inner city will lower the crime rate.

    d. Automation destroys jobs.

    e. Efforts to improve the environment tend to reduce production and employment.

    f. Japanese firms should be more willing to hire additional workers when production rises and to lay off workers when production falls.

    g. Access to health care should not be limited by income.

9. Your time is a scarce resource. What if the quantity of time were increased, say to 48 hours per day, and everyone still lived as many days as before. Would time still be scarce?

10. Most college students are under age 25. Give two explanations for this—one based on the benefits people of different ages are likely to receive from higher education and one based on the opportunity costs of a college education to students of different ages.

11. Some municipal water companies charge customers a flat fee each month, regardless of the amount of water they consume. Others meter water use and charge according to the quantity of water customers use. Compare the way the two systems affect the cost of water use at the margin.

12. How might you test each of the following hypotheses? Suggest some problems that might arise in each test due to the ceteris paribus (all-other-things-unchanged) problem and the fallacy of false cause.

    a. Reducing the quantity of heroin available will increase total spending on heroin and increase the crime rate.

    b. Higher incomes make people happier.

    c. Higher incomes make people live longer.

13. Many models in physics and in chemistry assume the existence of a perfect vacuum (that is, a space entirely empty of matter). Yet we know that a perfect vacuum cannot exist. Are such models valid? Why are models based on assumptions that are essentially incorrect?

14. Suppose you were asked to test the proposition that publishing students' teacher evaluations causes grade inflation. What evidence might you want to consider? How would the inability to carry out controlled experiments make your analysis more difficult?

15. Referring to the Case in Point "Baldness and Heart Disease," explain the possible fallacy of false cause in concluding that baldness makes a person more likely to have heart disease.

16. In 2005 the Food and Drug Administration ordered that Vioxx and other popular drugs for treating the pain of arthritis be withdrawn from the market. The order resulted from a finding that people taking the drugs had an increased risk of cardiovascular problems. Some researchers criticized the government's action, arguing that concluding that the drugs caused the cardiovascular problems represented an example of the fallacy of false cause. Can you think of any reason why this might be the case?

CHAPTER 2
Confronting Scarcity: Choices in Production

START UP: AN ATTEMPT TO PRODUCE SAFER AIR TRAVEL

In the wake of the terrorist attacks on the United States on September 11, 2001, American taxpayers continue to give up a great deal of money, and airline passengers continue to give much of their time—and a great deal of their privacy—in an effort to ensure that other terrorists will not turn their flights into tragedies.

The U.S. effort is run by the Transportation Security Administration (TSA), a federal agency created in response to the 2001 attacks. TSA requirements became a bit more onerous after Richard Reid, an Englishman and member of al-Qaeda, tried in December of that same year to blow up an American Airlines flight with a bomb he had concealed in his shoe. Reid was unsuccessful, but passengers must now remove their shoes so TSA agents can check them for bombs.

TSA restrictions became dramatically more stringent after Umar Farouk Abdulmutallab, a jihadist from Nigeria, tried—again without success—to blow up a plane flying from Amsterdam to Detroit on Christmas Day, 2009, using a bomb concealed in his underwear. The subsequent tightening of TSA regulations, and the introduction of body-scan machines and "patdown inspections," were quick to follow. Each new procedure took additional money and time and further reduced passenger privacy. It was a production choice that has created many irate passengers but has also been successful, to date, in preventing subsequent terrorist attacks.

While the TSA procedures represent an unusual production choice, it is still a production choice—one that is being made all over the world as countries grapple with the danger of terrorist attacks. In this chapter we introduce our first model, the **production possibilities model**, to examine the nature of choices to produce more of some goods and less of others. As its name suggests, the production possibilities model shows the goods and services that an economy is capable of producing—its possibilities—given the factors of production and the technology it has available. The model specifies what it means to use resources fully and efficiently and suggests some important implications for international trade. We can also use the model to illustrate economic growth, a process that expands the set of production possibilities available to an economy.

We then turn to an examination of the type of economic system in which choices are made. An **economic system** is the set of rules that define how an economy's resources are to be owned and how decisions about their use are to be made. We will see that economic systems differ—primarily in the degree of government involvement—in terms of how they answer the fundamental economic questions. Many of the world's economic systems, including the systems that prevail in North America, Europe, much of Asia, and parts of Central and South America, rely on individuals operating in a market economy to make those choices. Other economic systems rely principally

production possibilities model

Shows the goods and services that an economy is capable of producing—its opportunities—given the factors of production and the technology it has available.

economic system

The set of rules that define how an economy's resources are to be owned and how decisions about their use are to be made.

on government to make these choices. Different economic systems result in different choices and thus different outcomes; that market economies generally outperform the others when it comes to providing more of the things that people want helps to explain the dramatic shift from government-dominated toward market-dominated economic systems that occurred throughout the world in the last two decades of the 20th century. The chapter concludes with an examination of the role of government in an economy that relies chiefly on markets to allocate goods and services.

1. FACTORS OF PRODUCTION

LEARNING OBJECTIVES

1. **Define the three factors of production—labor, capital, and natural resources.**
2. **Explain the role of technology and entrepreneurs in the utilization of the economy's factors of production.**
3. **Explain what a firm is and how different firms may be organized.**

factors of production

The resources available to the economy for the production of goods and services.

utility

The value, or satisfaction, that people derive from the goods and services they consume and the activities they pursue.

labor

The human effort that can be applied to the production of goods and services.

capital

A factor of production that has been produced for use in the production of other goods and services.

natural resources

The resources of nature that can be used for the production of goods and services.

human capital

The skills a worker has as a result of education, training, or experience that can be used in production.

Choices concerning what goods and services to produce are choices about an economy's use of its **factors of production**, the resources available to it for the production of goods and services. The value, or satisfaction, that people derive from the goods and services they consume and the activities they pursue is called **utility**. Ultimately, then, an economy's factors of production create utility; they serve the interests of people.

The factors of production in an economy are its labor, capital, and natural resources. **Labor** is the human effort that can be applied to the production of goods and services. People who are employed—or are available to be—are considered part of the labor available to the economy. **Capital** is a factor of production that has been produced for use in the production of other goods and services. Office buildings, machinery, and tools are examples of capital. **Natural resources** are the resources of nature that can be used for the production of goods and services.

In the next three sections, we will take a closer look at the factors of production we use to produce the goods and services we consume. The three basic building blocks of labor, capital, and natural resources may be used in different ways to produce different goods and services, but they still lie at the core of production. We will then look at the roles played by technology and entrepreneurs in putting these factors of production to work. As economists began to grapple with the problems of scarcity, choice, and opportunity cost more than two centuries ago, they focused on these concepts, just as they are likely to do two centuries hence.

1.1 Labor

Labor is the human effort that can be applied to production. People who work to repair tires, pilot airplanes, teach children, or enforce laws are all part of the economy's labor. People who would like to work but have not found employment—who are unemployed—are also considered part of the labor available to the economy.

In some contexts, it is useful to distinguish two forms of labor. The first is the human equivalent of a natural resource. It is the natural ability an untrained, uneducated person brings to a particular production process. But most workers bring far more. Skills a worker has as a result of education, training, or experience that can be used in production are called **human capital**. Students are acquiring human capital. Workers who are gaining skills through experience or through training are acquiring human capital.

The amount of labor available to an economy can be increased in two ways. One is to increase the total quantity of labor, either by increasing the number of people available to work or by increasing the average number of hours of work per time period. The other is to increase the amount of human capital possessed by workers.

1.2 Capital

Long ago, when the first human beings walked the earth, they produced food by picking leaves or fruit off a plant or by catching an animal and eating it. We know that very early on, however, they began shaping stones into tools, apparently for use in butchering animals. Those tools were the first capital because they were produced for use in producing other goods—food and clothing.

Modern versions of the first stone tools include saws, meat cleavers, hooks, and grinders; all are used in butchering animals. Tools such as hammers, screwdrivers, and wrenches are also capital. Transportation equipment, such as cars and trucks, is capital. Facilities such as roads, bridges, ports, and airports are capital. Buildings, too, are capital; they help us to produce goods and services.

Capital does not consist solely of physical objects. The score for a new symphony is capital because it will be used to produce concerts. Computer software used by business firms or government agencies to produce goods and services is capital. Capital may thus include physical goods and intellectual discoveries. Any resource is capital if it satisfies two criteria:

1. The resource must have been produced.
2. The resource can be used to produce other goods and services.

One thing that is not considered capital is money. A firm cannot use money directly to produce other goods, so money does not satisfy the second criterion for capital. Firms can, however, use money to acquire capital. Money is a form of financial capital. **Financial capital** includes money and other "paper" assets (such as stocks and bonds) that represent claims on future payments. These financial assets are not capital, but they can be used directly or indirectly to purchase factors of production or goods and services.

> **financial capital**
>
> Includes money and other "paper" assets (such as stocks and bonds) that represent claims on future payments.

1.3 Natural Resources

There are two essential characteristics of natural resources. The first is that they are found in nature—that no human effort has been used to make or alter them. The second is that they can be used for the production of goods and services. That requires knowledge; we must know how to use the things we find in nature before they become resources.

Consider oil. Oil in the ground is a natural resource because it is found (not manufactured) and can be used to produce goods and services. However, 250 years ago oil was a nuisance, not a natural resource. Pennsylvania farmers in the eighteenth century who found oil oozing up through their soil were dismayed, not delighted. No one knew what could be done with the oil. It was not until the mid-nineteenth century that a method was found for refining oil into kerosene that could be used to generate energy, transforming oil into a natural resource. Oil is now used to make all sorts of things, including clothing, drugs, gasoline, and plastic. It became a natural resource because people discovered and implemented a way to use it.

Defining something as a natural resource only if it can be used to produce goods and services does not mean that a tree has value only for its wood or that a mountain has value only for its minerals. If people gain utility from the existence of a beautiful wilderness area, then that wilderness provides a service. The wilderness is thus a natural resource.

The natural resources available to us can be expanded in three ways. One is the discovery of new natural resources, such as the discovery of a deposit of ore containing titanium. The second is the discovery of new uses for resources, as happened when new techniques allowed oil to be put to productive use or sand to be used in manufacturing computer chips. The third is the discovery of new ways to extract natural resources in order to use them. New methods of discovering and mapping oil deposits have increased the world's supply of this important natural resource.

1.4 Technology and the Entrepreneur

Goods and services are produced using the factors of production available to the economy. Two things play a crucial role in putting these factors of production to work. The first is **technology**, the knowledge that can be applied to the production of goods and services. The second is an individual who plays a key role in a market economy: the entrepreneur. An **entrepreneur** is a person who, operating within the context of a market economy, seeks to earn profits by finding new ways to organize factors of production. In non-market economies the role of the entrepreneur is played by bureaucrats and other decision makers who respond to incentives other than profit to guide their choices about resource allocation decisions.

The interplay of entrepreneurs and technology affects all our lives. Entrepreneurs put new technologies to work every day, changing the way factors of production are used. Farmers and factory workers, engineers and electricians, technicians and teachers all work differently than they did just a few years ago, using new technologies introduced by entrepreneurs. The music you enjoy, the books you read, the athletic equipment with which you play are produced differently than they were five years ago. The book you are reading was written and manufactured using technologies that did not exist ten years ago. We can dispute whether all the changes have made our lives better. What we cannot dispute is that they have made our lives different.

1.5 Organizing the Factors of Production

Organizations that combine factors of production to produce goods and services are called **firms**. A firm may be owned by one individual (a **sole proprietorship**), by several individuals (a **partnership**), or by shareholders who own stock in a firm (a **corporation**). Although most firms in the United States are sole proprietorships or partnerships, the bulk of the nation's total output (about 90%) is produced by corporations. Corporations also own most of the capital (machines, plants, buildings, and the like).

KEY TAKEAWAYS

- Factors of production are the resources the economy has available to produce goods and services.
- Labor is the human effort that can be applied to the production of goods and services. Labor's contribution to an economy's output of goods and services can be increased either by increasing the quantity of labor or by increasing human capital.
- Capital is a factor of production that has been produced for use in the production of other goods and services.
- Natural resources are those things found in nature that can be used for the production of goods and services.
- Two keys to the utilization of an economy's factors of production are technology and, in the case of a market economic system, the efforts of entrepreneurs.
- Firms are organizations that combine factors of production to produce goods and services. They can be sole proprietorships, partnerships, or corporations.

TRY IT!

Explain whether each of the following is labor, capital, or a natural resource.

1. An unemployed factory worker
2. A college professor
3. The library building on your campus
4. Yellowstone National Park
5. An untapped deposit of natural gas
6. The White House
7. The local power plant

Case in Point

Technology Cuts Costs and Boosts Productivity, Profits, and Utility

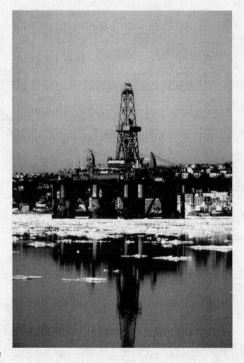

© 2010 Jupiterimages Corporation

Technology can seem like an abstract force in the economy—important, but invisible.

It is not invisible to the 130 people who work on a Shell Oil Company oil rig called Mars, located in the deep waters of the Gulf of Mexico, about 160 miles southwest of Pensacola, Florida. The name Mars reflects its otherworldly appearance—it extends 300 feet above the water's surface and has steel tendons that reach 3,000 feet down to extract the Gulf's oil deposits. This facility would not exist if it were not for the development of better oil discovery methods that include three-dimensional seismic mapping techniques, satellites that locate oil from space, and drills that can make turns as drilling foremen steer them by monitoring them on computer screens from the comfort of Mars. "We don't hit as many dry holes," commented Shell manager Miles Barrett. As a result of these new technologies, over the past two decades, the cost of discovering a barrel of oil dropped from $20 to under $5. And the technologies continue to improve. Three-dimensional surveys are being replaced with four-dimensional ones that allow geologists to see how the oil fields change over time.

The Mars project was destroyed by Hurricane Katrina in 2005. Royal Dutch Shell completed repairs in 2006, at a cost of $200 million. But the facility is again pumping 130,000 barrels of oil per day and 150 million cubic feet of natural gas, the energy equivalent of an additional 26,000 barrels of oil. Shell announced a new Mars-like project, Mars B Olympus, in 2010. The second Mars hub will be located 100 miles south of New Orleans and is expected to begin production in 2015.

Technology is doing more than helping energy companies track oil deposits. It is changing the way soft drinks and other grocery items are delivered to retail stores. For example, when a PepsiCo delivery driver arrives at a 7-Eleven, the driver keys into a handheld computer the store's inventory of soft drinks, chips, and other PepsiCo products. The information is transmitted to a main computer at the warehouse that begins processing the next order for that store. The result is that the driver can visit more stores in a day and PepsiCo can cover a given territory with fewer drivers and trucks.

New technology is even helping to produce more milk from cows. Ed Larsen, who owns a 1,200-cow dairy farm in Wisconsin, never gets up before dawn to milk the cows, the way he did as a boy. Rather, the cows are hooked up to electronic milkers. Computers measure each cow's output, and cows producing little milk are sent to a "hospital wing" for treatment. With the help of such technology, as well as better feed, today's dairy cows produce 50% more milk than cows did roughly 20 years ago. Even though the number of dairy cows in the United States in the last 20 years has fallen 17%, milk output has increased 25%.

Who benefits from technological progress? Consumers gain from lower prices and better service. Workers gain a greater ability to produce goods and services, which translates into higher wages. And firms gain lower production costs, which mean higher profits. Of course, some people lose as technology advances. Some jobs are eliminated, and some firms find their services are no longer needed. One can argue about whether particular technological changes have improved our lives, but they have clearly made—and will continue to make—them far different.

Sources: David Ballingrud, "Drilling in the Gulf: Life on Mars," St. Petersburg Times (Florida), August 5, 2001, p. 1A; Barbara Hagenbaugh, "Dairy Farms Evolve to Survive," USA Today, August 7, 2003, p. 1B; Del Jones and Barbara Hansen, "Special Report: A Who's Who of Productivity," USA Today, August 30, 2001, p. 1B; Christopher Helman, Shell Shocked, Forbes Online, July 27, 2006; "Shell Plans Second Deep Water Production Hub," September 9, 2010 at http://www.investorvillage.com/smbd.asp?mb=4288&mn=59408&pt=msg&mid=9575777.

ANSWERS TO TRY IT! PROBLEMS

1. An unemployed factory worker could be put to work; he or she counts as labor.
2. A college professor is labor.
3. The library building on your campus is part of capital.
4. Yellowstone National Park. Those areas of the park left in their natural state are a natural resource. Facilities such as visitors' centers, roads, and campgrounds are capital.
5. An untapped deposit of natural gas is a natural resource. Once extracted and put in a storage tank, natural gas is capital.
6. The White House is capital.
7. The local power plant is capital.

2. THE PRODUCTION POSSIBILITIES CURVE

LEARNING OBJECTIVES

1. **Explain the concept of the production possibilities curve and understand the implications of its downward slope and bowed-out shape.**
2. **Use the production possibilities model to distinguish between full employment and situations of idle factors of production and between efficient and inefficient production.**
3. **Understand specialization and its relationship to the production possibilities model and comparative advantage.**

production possibilities curve

A graphical representation of the alternative combinations of goods and services an economy can produce.

An economy's factors of production are scarce; they cannot produce an unlimited quantity of goods and services. A **production possibilities curve** is a graphical representation of the alternative combinations of goods and services an economy can produce. It illustrates the production possibilities model. In drawing the production possibilities curve, we shall assume that the economy can produce only two goods and that the quantities of factors of production and the technology available to the economy are fixed.

2.1 Constructing a Production Possibilities Curve

FIGURE 2.1 A Production Possibilities Curve

The table shows the combinations of pairs of skis and snowboards that Plant 1 is capable of producing each month. These are also illustrated with a production possibilities curve. Notice that this curve is linear.

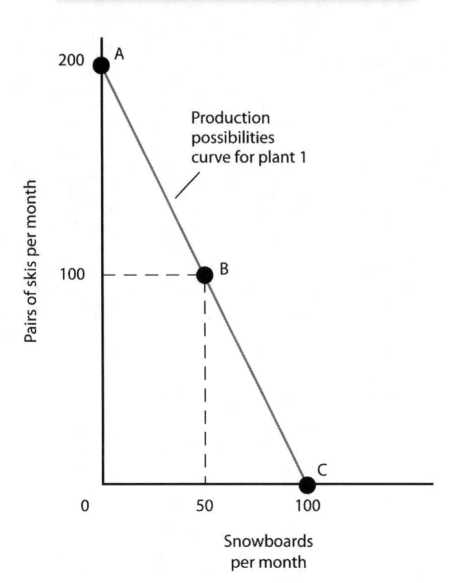

	Pairs of skis per month	Snowboards per month
A	200	0
B	100	50
C	0	100

To construct a production possibilities curve, we will begin with the case of a hypothetical firm, Alpine Sports, Inc., a specialized sports equipment manufacturer. Christie Ryder began the business 15 years ago with a single ski production facility near Killington ski resort in central Vermont. Ski sales grew, and she also saw demand for snowboards rising—particularly after snowboard competition events were included in the 2002 Winter Olympics in Salt Lake City. She added a second plant in a nearby town. The second plant, while smaller than the first, was designed to produce snowboards as well as skis. She also modified the first plant so that it could produce both snowboards and skis. Two years later she added a third plant in another town. While even smaller than the second plant, the third was primarily designed for snowboard production but could also produce skis.

We can think of each of Ms. Ryder's three plants as a miniature economy and analyze them using the production possibilities model. We assume that the factors of production and technology available to each of the plants operated by Alpine Sports are unchanged.

Suppose the first plant, Plant 1, can produce 200 pairs of skis per month when it produces only skis. When devoted solely to snowboards, it produces 100 snowboards per month. It can produce skis and snowboards simultaneously as well.

The table in Figure 2.1 gives three combinations of skis and snowboards that Plant 1 can produce each month. Combination A involves devoting the plant entirely to ski production; combination C means shifting all of the plant's resources to snowboard production; combination B involves the production of both goods. These values are plotted in a production possibilities curve for Plant 1. The curve is a downward-sloping straight line, indicating we have assumed that there is a linear, negative relationship between the production of the two goods.

Neither skis nor snowboards is an independent or a dependent variable in the production possibilities model; we can assign either one to the vertical or to the horizontal axis. Here, we have placed the number of pairs of skis produced per month on the vertical axis and the number of snowboards produced per month on the horizontal axis.

The negative slope of the production possibilities curve reflects the scarcity of the plant's capital and labor. Producing more snowboards requires shifting resources out of ski production and thus producing fewer skis. Producing more skis requires shifting resources out of snowboard production and thus producing fewer snowboards.

The slope of Plant 1's production possibilities curve measures the rate at which Alpine Sports must give up ski production to produce additional snowboards. Because the production possibilities curve for Plant 1 is linear, we can compute the slope between any two points on the curve and get the same result. Between points A and B, for example, the slope equals −2 pairs of skis/snowboard (equals −100 pairs of skis/50 snowboards). (Many students are helped when told to read this result as "−2 pairs of skis *per* snowboard.") We get the same value between points B and C, and between points A and C.

To see this relationship more clearly, examine Figure 2.2. Suppose Plant 1 is producing 100 pairs of skis and 50 snowboards per month at point B. Now consider what would happen if Ms. Ryder decided to produce 1 more snowboard per month. The segment of the curve around point B is magnified in Figure 2.2. The slope between points B and B′ is −2 pairs of skis/snowboard. Producing 1 additional snowboard at point B′ requires giving up 2 pairs of skis. We can think of this as the opportunity cost of producing an additional snowboard at Plant 1. This opportunity cost equals the absolute value of the slope of the production possibilities curve.

The absolute value of the slope of any production possibilities curve equals the opportunity cost of an additional unit of the good on the horizontal axis. It is the amount of the good on the vertical axis that must be given up in order to free up the resources required to produce one more unit of the good on the horizontal axis. We will make use of this important fact as we continue our investigation of the production possibilities curve.

FIGURE 2.2   The Slope of a Production Possibilities Curve

The slope of the linear production possibilities curve in Figure 2.1 is constant; it is −2 pairs of skis/snowboard. In the section of the curve shown here, the slope can be calculated between points B and B'. Expanding snowboard production to 51 snowboards per month from 50 snowboards per month requires a reduction in ski production to 98 pairs of skis per month from 100 pairs. The slope equals −2 pairs of skis/snowboard (that is, it must give up two pairs of skis to free up the resources necessary to produce one additional snowboard). To shift from B' to B", Alpine Sports must give up two more pairs of skis per snowboard. The absolute value of the slope of a production possibilities curve measures the opportunity cost of an additional unit of the good on the horizontal axis measured in terms of the quantity of the good on the vertical axis that must be forgone.

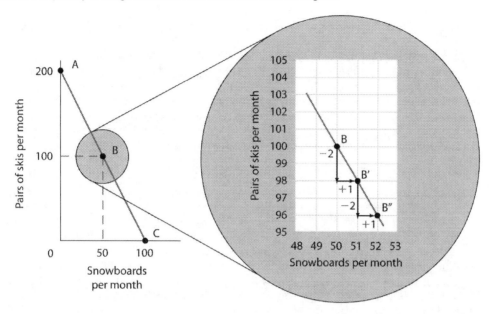

Figure 2.3 shows production possibilities curves for each of the firm's three plants. Each of the plants, if devoted entirely to snowboards, could produce 100 snowboards. Plants 2 and 3, if devoted exclusively to ski production, can produce 100 and 50 pairs of skis per month, respectively. The exhibit gives the slopes of the production possibilities curves for each plant. The opportunity cost of an additional snowboard at each plant equals the absolute values of these slopes (that is, the number of pairs of skis that must be given up per snowboard).

FIGURE 2.3   Production Possibilities at Three Plants

The slopes of the production possibilities curves for each plant differ. The steeper the curve, the greater the opportunity cost of an additional snowboard. Here, the opportunity cost is lowest at Plant 3 and greatest at Plant 1.

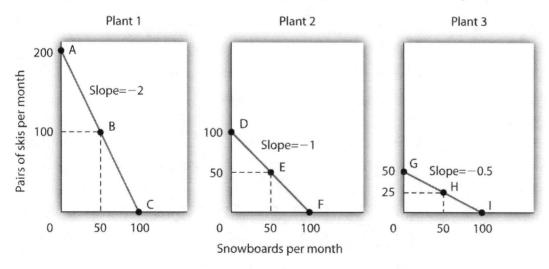

The exhibit gives the slopes of the production possibilities curves for each of the firm's three plants. The opportunity cost of an additional snowboard at each plant equals the absolute values of these slopes. More generally, the absolute value of the slope of any production possibilities curve at any point gives the opportunity cost of an additional unit of the good on the horizontal axis, measured in terms of the number of units of the good on the vertical axis that must be forgone.

The greater the absolute value of the slope of the production possibilities curve, the greater the opportunity cost will be. The plant for which the opportunity cost of an additional snowboard is greatest is the plant with the steepest production possibilities curve; the plant for which the opportunity cost is lowest is the plant with the flattest production possibilities curve. The plant with the lowest opportunity cost of producing snowboards is Plant 3; its slope of −0.5 means that Ms. Ryder's firm must give up half a pair of skis in that plant to produce an additional snowboard. In Plant 2, she must give up one pair of skis to gain one more snowboard. We have already seen that an additional snowboard requires giving up two pairs of skis in Plant 1.

2.2   Comparative Advantage and the Production Possibilities Curve

To construct a combined production possibilities curve for all three plants, we can begin by asking how many pairs of skis Alpine Sports could produce if it were producing only skis. To find this quantity, we add up the values at the vertical intercepts of each of the production possibilities curves in Figure 2.3. These intercepts tell us the maximum number of pairs of skis each plant can produce. Plant 1 can produce 200 pairs of skis per month, Plant 2 can produce 100 pairs of skis per month, and Plant 3 can produce 50 pairs. Alpine Sports can thus produce 350 pairs of skis per month if it devotes its resources exclusively to ski production. In that case, it produces no snowboards.

Now suppose the firm decides to produce 100 snowboards. That will require shifting one of its plants out of ski production. Which one will it choose to shift? The sensible thing for it to do is to choose the plant in which snowboards have the lowest opportunity cost—Plant 3. It has an advantage not because it can produce more snowboards than the other plants (all the plants in this example are capable of producing up to 100 snowboards per month) but because it is the least productive plant for making skis. Producing a snowboard in Plant 3 requires giving up just half a pair of skis.

Economists say that an economy has a **comparative advantage** in producing a good or service if the opportunity cost of producing that good or service is lower for that economy than for any other. Plant 3 has a comparative advantage in snowboard production because it is the plant for which the opportunity cost of additional snowboards is lowest. To put this in terms of the production possibilities curve, Plant 3 has a comparative advantage in snowboard production (the good on the horizontal axis) because its production possibilities curve is the flattest of the three curves.

comparative advantage

In producing a good or service, the situation that occurs if the opportunity cost of producing that good or service is lower for that economy than for any other.

FIGURE 2.4   The Combined Production Possibilities Curve for Alpine Sports

The curve shown combines the production possibilities curves for each plant. At point A, Alpine Sports produces 350 pairs of skis per month and no snowboards. If the firm wishes to increase snowboard production, it will first use Plant 3, which has a comparative advantage in snowboards.

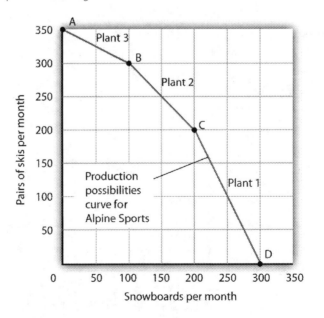

Plant 3's comparative advantage in snowboard production makes a crucial point about the nature of comparative advantage. It need not imply that a particular plant is especially good at an activity. In our example, all three plants are equally good at snowboard production. Plant 3, though, is the least efficient of the three in ski production. Alpine thus gives up fewer skis when it produces snowboards in

Plant 3. Comparative advantage thus can stem from a lack of efficiency in the production of an alternative good rather than a special proficiency in the production of the first good.

The combined production possibilities curve for the firm's three plants is shown in Figure 2.4. We begin at point A, with all three plants producing only skis. Production totals 350 pairs of skis per month and zero snowboards. If the firm were to produce 100 snowboards at Plant 3, ski production would fall by 50 pairs per month (recall that the opportunity cost per snowboard at Plant 3 is half a pair of skis). That would bring ski production to 300 pairs, at point B. If Alpine Sports were to produce still more snowboards in a single month, it would shift production to Plant 2, the facility with the next-lowest opportunity cost. Producing 100 snowboards at Plant 2 would leave Alpine Sports producing 200 snowboards and 200 pairs of skis per month, at point C. If the firm were to switch entirely to snowboard production, Plant 1 would be the last to switch because the cost of each snowboard there is 2 pairs of skis. With all three plants producing only snowboards, the firm is at point D on the combined production possibilities curve, producing 300 snowboards per month and no skis.

Notice that this production possibilities curve, which is made up of linear segments from each assembly plant, has a bowed-out shape; the absolute value of its slope increases as Alpine Sports produces more and more snowboards. This is a result of transferring resources from the production of one good to another according to comparative advantage. We shall examine the significance of the bowed-out shape of the curve in the next section.

2.3   The Law of Increasing Opportunity Cost

We see in Figure 2.4 that, beginning at point A and producing only skis, Alpine Sports experiences higher and higher opportunity costs as it produces more snowboards. The fact that the opportunity cost of additional snowboards increases as the firm produces more of them is a reflection of an important economic law. The **law of increasing opportunity cost** holds that as an economy moves along its production possibilities curve in the direction of producing more of a particular good, the opportunity cost of additional units of that good will increase.

We have seen the law of increasing opportunity cost at work traveling from point A toward point D on the production possibilities curve in Figure 2.4. The opportunity cost of each of the first 100 snowboards equals half a pair of skis; each of the next 100 snowboards has an opportunity cost of 1 pair of skis, and each of the last 100 snowboards has an opportunity cost of 2 pairs of skis. The law also applies as the firm shifts from snowboards to skis. Suppose it begins at point D, producing 300 snowboards per month and no skis. It can shift to ski production at a relatively low cost at first. The opportunity cost of the first 200 pairs of skis is just 100 snowboards at Plant 1, a movement from point D to point C, or 0.5 snowboards per pair of skis. We would say that Plant 1 has a comparative advantage in ski production. The next 100 pairs of skis would be produced at Plant 2, where snowboard production would fall by 100 snowboards per month. The opportunity cost of skis at Plant 2 is 1 snowboard per pair of skis. Plant 3 would be the last plant converted to ski production. There, 50 pairs of skis could be produced per month at a cost of 100 snowboards, or an opportunity cost of 2 snowboards per pair of skis.

The bowed-out shape of the production possibilities curve illustrates the law of increasing opportunity cost. Its downwards slope reflects scarcity.

Figure 2.5 illustrates a much smoother production possibilities curve. This production possibilities curve in Panel (a) includes 10 linear segments and is almost a smooth curve. As we include more and more production units, the curve will become smoother and smoother. In an actual economy, with a tremendous number of firms and workers, it is easy to see that the production possibilities curve will be smooth. We will generally draw production possibilities curves for the economy as smooth, bowed-out curves, like the one in Panel (b). This production possibilities curve shows an economy that produces only skis and snowboards. Notice the curve still has a bowed-out shape; it still has a negative slope. Notice also that this curve has no numbers. Economists often use models such as the production possibilities model with graphs that show the general shapes of curves but that do not include specific numbers.

law of increasing opportunity cost

As an economy moves along its production possibilities curve in the direction of producing more of a particular good, the opportunity cost of additional units of that good will increase.

FIGURE 2.5 Production Possibilities for the Economy

As we combine the production possibilities curves for more and more units, the curve becomes smoother. It retains its negative slope and bowed-out shape. In Panel (a) we have a combined production possibilities curve for Alpine Sports, assuming that it now has 10 plants producing skis and snowboards. Even though each of the plants has a linear curve, combining them according to comparative advantage, as we did with 3 plants in Figure 2.4, produces what appears to be a smooth, nonlinear curve, even though it is made up of linear segments. In drawing production possibilities curves for the economy, we shall generally assume they are smooth and "bowed out," as in Panel (b). This curve depicts an entire economy that produces only skis and snowboards.

2.4 Movements Along the Production Possibilities Curve

We can use the production possibilities model to examine choices in the production of goods and services. In applying the model, we assume that the economy can produce two goods, and we assume that technology and the factors of production available to the economy remain unchanged. In this section, we shall assume that the economy operates on its production possibilities curve so that an increase in the production of one good in the model implies a reduction in the production of the other.

We shall consider two goods and services: national defense and security and a category we shall call "all other goods and services." This second category includes the entire range of goods and services the economy can produce, aside from national defense and security. Clearly, the transfer of resources to the effort to enhance national security reduces the quantity of other goods and services that can be produced. In the wake of the 9/11 attacks in 2001, nations throughout the world increased their spending for national security. This spending took a variety of forms. One, of course, was increased defense spending. Local and state governments also increased spending in an effort to prevent terrorist attacks. Airports around the world hired additional agents to inspect luggage and passengers.

The increase in resources devoted to security meant fewer "other goods and services" could be produced. In terms of the production possibilities curve in Figure 2.6, the choice to produce more security and less of other goods and services means a movement from A to B. Of course, an economy cannot really *produce* security; it can only attempt to provide it. The attempt to provide it requires resources; it is in that sense that we shall speak of the economy as "producing" security.

At point A, the economy was producing S_A units of security on the vertical axis—defense services and various forms of police protection—and O_A units of other goods and services on the horizontal axis. The decision to devote more resources to security and less to other goods and services represents the choice we discussed in the chapter introduction. In this case we have categories of goods rather than specific goods. Thus, the economy chose to increase spending on security in the effort to defeat terrorism. Since we have assumed that the economy has a fixed quantity of available resources, the increased use of resources for security and national defense necessarily reduces the number of resources available for the production of other goods and services.

FIGURE 2.6 Spending More for Security

Here, an economy that can produce two categories of goods, security and "all other goods and services," begins at point A on its production possibilities curve. The economy produces S_A units of security and O_A units of all other goods and services per period. A movement from A to B requires shifting resources out of the production of all other goods and services and into spending on security. The increase in spending on security, to S_A units of security per period, has an opportunity cost of reduced production of all other goods and services. Production of all other goods and services falls by $O_A - O_B$ units per period.

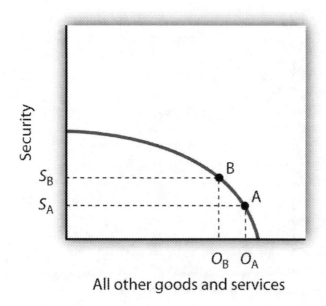

The law of increasing opportunity cost tells us that, as the economy moves along the production possibilities curve in the direction of more of one good, its opportunity cost will increase. We may conclude that, as the economy moved along this curve in the direction of greater production of security, the opportunity cost of the additional security began to increase. That is because the resources transferred from the production of other goods and services to the production of security had a greater and greater comparative advantage in producing things other than security.

The production possibilities model does not tell us where on the curve a particular economy will operate. Instead, it lays out the possibilities facing the economy. Many countries, for example, chose to move along their respective production possibilities curves to produce more security and national defense and less of all other goods in the wake of 9/11. We will see in the chapter on demand and supply how choices about what to produce are made in the marketplace.

2.5   Producing on Versus Producing Inside the Production Possibilities Curve

An economy that is operating inside its production possibilities curve could, by moving onto it, produce more of all the goods and services that people value, such as food, housing, education, medical care, and music. Increasing the availability of these goods would improve the standard of living. Economists conclude that it is better to be on the production possibilities curve than inside it.

Two things could leave an economy operating at a point inside its production possibilities curve. First, the economy might fail to use fully the resources available to it. Second, it might not allocate resources on the basis of comparative advantage. In either case, production within the production possibilities curve implies the economy could improve its performance.

Idle Factors of Production

Suppose an economy fails to put all its factors of production to work. Some workers are without jobs, some buildings are without occupants, some fields are without crops. Because an economy's production possibilities curve assumes the full use of the factors of production available to it, the failure to use some factors results in a level of production that lies inside the production possibilities curve.

full employment

Situation in which all the
factors of production that are
available for use under
current market conditions are
being utilized.

If all the factors of production that are available for use under current market conditions are being utilized, the economy has achieved **full employment**. An economy cannot operate on its production possibilities curve unless it has full employment.

FIGURE 2.7   Idle Factors and Production

The production possibilities curve shown suggests an economy that can produce two goods, food and clothing. As a result of a failure to achieve full employment, the economy operates at a point such as B, producing F_B units of food and C_B units of clothing per period. Putting its factors of production to work allows a move to the production possibilities curve, to a point such as A. The production of both goods rises.

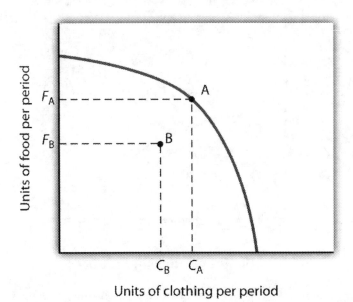

Units of clothing per period

Figure 2.7 shows an economy that can produce food and clothing. If it chooses to produce at point A, for example, it can produce F_A units of food and C_A units of clothing. Now suppose that a large fraction of the economy's workers lose their jobs, so the economy no longer makes full use of one factor of production: labor. In this example, production moves to point B, where the economy produces less food (F_B) and less clothing (C_B) than at point A. We often think of the loss of jobs in terms of the workers; they have lost a chance to work and to earn income. But the production possibilities model points to another loss: goods and services the economy could have produced that are not being produced.

Inefficient Production

Now suppose Alpine Sports is fully employing its factors of production. Could it still operate inside its production possibilities curve? Could an economy that is using all its factors of production still produce less than it could? The answer is "Yes," and the key lies in comparative advantage. An economy achieves a point on its production possibilities curve only if it allocates its factors of production on the basis of comparative advantage. If it fails to do that, it will operate inside the curve.

Suppose that, as before, Alpine Sports has been producing only skis. With all three of its plants producing skis, it can produce 350 pairs of skis per month (and no snowboards). The firm then starts producing snowboards. This time, however, imagine that Alpine Sports switches plants from skis to snowboards in numerical order: Plant 1 first, Plant 2 second, and then Plant 3. Figure 2.8 illustrates the result. Instead of the bowed-out production possibilities curve ABCD, we get a bowed-in curve, AB′C′D. Suppose that Alpine Sports is producing 100 snowboards and 150 pairs of skis at point B′. Had the firm based its production choices on comparative advantage, it would have switched Plant 3 to snowboards and then Plant 2, so it could have operated at a point such as C. It would be producing more snowboards and more pairs of skis—and using the same quantities of factors of production it was using at B′. Had the firm based its production choices on comparative advantage, it would have switched Plant 3 to snowboards and then Plant 2, so it would have operated at point C. It would be producing more snowboards and more pairs of skis—and using the same quantities of factors of production it was using at B′. When an economy is operating on its production possibilities curve, we say that it is engaging in **efficient production**. If it is using the same quantities of factors of production but is operating inside its production possibilities curve, it is engaging in **inefficient production**.

efficient production

When an economy is
operating on its production
possibilities curve.

inefficient production

Situation in which the
economy is using the same
quantities of factors of
production but is operating
inside its production
possibilities curve.

Inefficient production implies that the economy could be producing more goods without using any additional labor, capital, or natural resources.

Points on the production possibilities curve thus satisfy two conditions: the economy is making full use of its factors of production, and it is making efficient use of its factors of production. If there are idle or inefficiently allocated factors of production, the economy will operate inside the production possibilities curve. Thus, the production possibilities curve not only shows what can be produced; it provides insight into how goods and services should be produced. It suggests that to obtain efficiency in production, factors of production should be allocated on the basis of comparative advantage. Further, the economy must make full use of its factors of production if it is to produce the goods and services it is capable of producing.

Specialization

The production possibilities model suggests that specialization will occur. **Specialization** implies that an economy is producing the goods and services in which it has a comparative advantage. If Alpine Sports selects point C in Figure 2.8, for example, it will assign Plant 1 exclusively to ski production and Plants 2 and 3 exclusively to snowboard production.

Such specialization is typical in an economic system. Workers, for example, specialize in particular fields in which they have a comparative advantage. People work and use the income they earn to buy—perhaps import—goods and services from people who have a comparative advantage in doing other things. The result is a far greater quantity of goods and services than would be available without this specialization.

Think about what life would be like without specialization. Imagine that you are suddenly completely cut off from the rest of the economy. You must produce everything you consume; you obtain nothing from anyone else. Would you be able to consume what you consume now? Clearly not. It is hard to imagine that most of us could even survive in such a setting. The gains we achieve through specialization are enormous.

Nations specialize as well. Much of the land in the United States has a comparative advantage in agricultural production and is devoted to that activity. Hong Kong, with its huge population and tiny endowment of land, allocates virtually none of its land to agricultural use; that option would be too costly. Its land is devoted largely to nonagricultural use.

FIGURE 2.8 Efficient Versus Inefficient Production

When factors of production are allocated on a basis other than comparative advantage, the result is inefficient production. Suppose Alpine Sports operates the three plants we examined in Figure 2.3. Suppose further that all three plants are devoted exclusively to ski production; the firm operates at A. Now suppose that, to increase snowboard production, it transfers plants in numerical order: Plant 1 first, then Plant 2, and finally Plant 3. The result is the bowed-in curve AB'C'D. Production on the production possibilities curve ABCD requires that factors of production be transferred according to comparative advantage.

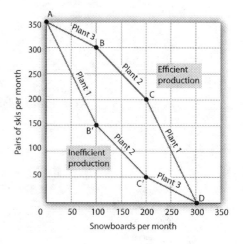

specialization

Situation in which an economy is producing the goods and services in which it has a comparative advantage.

KEY TAKEAWAYS

- A production possibilities curve shows the combinations of two goods an economy is capable of producing.
- The downward slope of the production possibilities curve is an implication of scarcity.
- The bowed-out shape of the production possibilities curve results from allocating resources based on comparative advantage. Such an allocation implies that the law of increasing opportunity cost will hold.
- An economy that fails to make full and efficient use of its factors of production will operate inside its production possibilities curve.
- Specialization means that an economy is producing the goods and services in which it has a comparative advantage.

TRY IT!

Suppose a manufacturing firm is equipped to produce radios or calculators. It has two plants, Plant R and Plant S, at which it can produce these goods. Given the labor and the capital available at both plants, it can produce the combinations of the two goods at the two plants shown.

Output per day, Plant R

Combination	Calculators	Radios
A	100	0
B	50	25
C	0	50

Output per day, Plant S

Combination	Calculators	Radios
D	50	0
E	25	50
F	0	100

Put calculators on the vertical axis and radios on the horizontal axis. Draw the production possibilities curve for Plant R. On a separate graph, draw the production possibilities curve for Plant S. Which plant has a comparative advantage in calculators? In radios? Now draw the combined curves for the two plants. Suppose the firm decides to produce 100 radios. Where will it produce them? How many calculators will it be able to produce? Where will it produce the calculators?

Case in Point

The Cost of the Great Depression

© 2010 Jupiterimages Corporation

The U.S. economy looked very healthy in the beginning of 1929. It had enjoyed seven years of dramatic growth and unprecedented prosperity. Its resources were fully employed; it was operating quite close to its production possibilities curve.

In the summer of 1929, however, things started going wrong. Production and employment fell. They continued to fall for several years. By 1933, more than 25% of the nation's workers had lost their jobs. Production had plummeted by almost 30%. The economy had moved well within its production possibilities curve.

Output began to grow after 1933, but the economy continued to have vast numbers of idle workers, idle factories, and idle farms. These resources were not put back to work fully until 1942, after the U.S. entry into World War II demanded mobilization of the economy's factors of production.

Between 1929 and 1942, the economy produced 25% fewer goods and services than it would have if its resources had been fully employed. That was a loss, measured in today's dollars, of well over $3 trillion. In material terms, the forgone output represented a greater cost than the United States would ultimately spend in World War II. The Great Depression was a costly experience indeed.

The production possibilities curves for the two plants are shown, along with the combined curve for both plants. Plant R has a comparative advantage in producing calculators. Plant S has a comparative advantage in producing radios, so, if the firm goes from producing 150 calculators and no radios to producing 100 radios, it will produce them at Plant S. In the production possibilities curve for both plants, the firm would be at M, producing 100 calculators at Plant R.

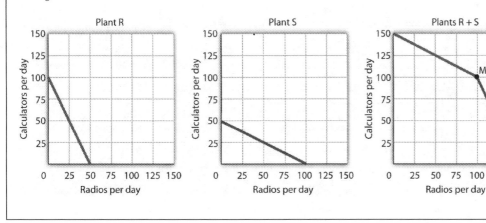

3.   APPLICATIONS OF THE PRODUCTION POSSIBILITIES MODEL

L E A R N I N G   O B J E C T I V E S

1. **Understand the argument for unrestricted international trade in terms of economic specialization and comparative advantage.**
2. **Define economic growth in terms of the production possibilities model and discuss factors that make such growth possible.**
3. **Explain the classification of economic systems, the role of government in different economic systems, and the strengths and weaknesses of different systems.**

The production possibilities curve gives us a model of an economy. The model provides powerful insights about the real world, insights that help us to answer some important questions: How does trade between two countries affect the quantities of goods available to people? What determines the rate at which production will increase over time? What is the role of economic freedom in the economy? In this section we explore applications of the model to questions of international trade, economic growth, and the choice of an economic system.

3.1   Comparative Advantage and International Trade

One of the most important implications of the concepts of comparative advantage and the production possibilities curve relates to international trade. We can think of different nations as being equivalent to Christie Ryder's plants. Each will have a comparative advantage in certain activities, and efficient world production requires that each nation specialize in those activities in which it has a comparative advantage. A failure to allocate resources in this way means that world production falls inside the production possibilities curve; more of each good could be produced by relying on comparative advantage.

If nations specialize, then they must rely on each other. They will sell the goods in which they specialize and purchase other goods from other nations. Suppose, for example, that the world consists of two continents that can each produce two goods: South America and Europe can produce food and computers. Suppose they can produce the two goods according to the tables in Panels (a) and (b) of Figure 2.9. We have simplified this example by assuming that each continent has a linear production possibilities curve; the curves are plotted below the tables in Panels (a) and (b). Each continent has a separate production possibilities curve; the two have been combined to illustrate a world production possibilities curve in Panel (c) of the exhibit.

FIGURE 2.9 Production Possibilities Curves and Trade

Suppose the world consists of two continents: South America and Europe. They can each produce two goods: food and computers. In this example, we assume that each continent has a linear production possibilities curve, as shown in Panels (a) and (b). South America has a comparative advantage in food production and Europe has a comparative advantage in computer production. With free trade, the world can operate on the bowed-out curve GHI, shown in Panel (c). If the continents refuse to trade, the world will operate inside its production possibilities curve. If, for example, each continent were to produce at the midpoint of its production possibilities curve, the world would produce 300 computers and 300 units of food per period at point Q. If each continent were to specialize in the good in which it has a comparative advantage, world production could move to a point such as H, with more of both goods produced.

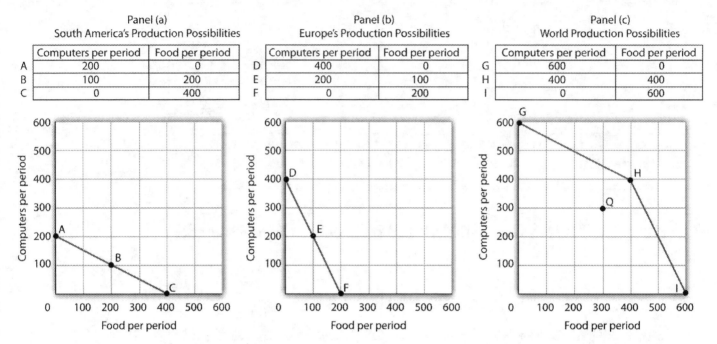

Panel (a)
South America's Production Possibilities

	Computers per period	Food per period
A	200	0
B	100	200
C	0	400

Panel (b)
Europe's Production Possibilities

	Computers per period	Food per period
D	400	0
E	200	100
F	0	200

Panel (c)
World Production Possibilities

	Computers per period	Food per period
G	600	0
H	400	400
I	0	600

The world production possibilities curve assumes that resources are allocated between computer and food production based on comparative advantage. Notice that, even with only two economies and the assumption of linear production possibilities curves for each, the combined curve still has a bowed-out shape. At point H, for example, South America specializes in food, while Europe produces only computers. World production equals 400 units of each good. In this situation, we would expect South America to export food to Europe while Europe exports computers to South America.

But suppose the regions refuse to trade; each insists on producing its own food and computers. Suppose further that each chooses to produce at the midpoint of its own production possibilities curve. South America produces 100 units of computers and 200 units of food per period, while Europe produces 200 units of computers and 100 units of food per period. World production thus totals 300 units of each good per period; the world operates at point Q in Figure 2.9. If the two continents were willing to move from isolation to trade, the world could achieve an increase in the production of both goods. Producing at point H requires no more resources, no more effort than production at Q. It does, however, require that the world's resources be allocated on the basis of comparative advantage.

The implications of our model for trade are powerful indeed. First, we see that trade allows the production of more of all goods and services. Restrictions on trade thus reduce production of goods and services. Second, we see a lesson often missed in discussions of trade: a nation's trade policy has nothing to do with its level of employment of its factors of production. In our example, when South America and Europe do not engage in trade and produce at the midpoints of each of their respective production possibilities curves, *they each have full employment*. With trade, the two nations still operate on their respective production possibilities curves: *they each have full employment*. Trade certainly redistributes employment in the two continents. In South America, employment shifts from computer production to food production. In Europe, it shifts from food production to computer production. Once the shift is made, though, there is no effect on employment in either continent.

Of course, this idealized example would have all of South America's computer experts becoming farmers while all of Europe's farmers become computer geeks! That is a bit much to swallow, but it is merely the result of assuming linear production possibilities curves and complete specialization. In the real world, production possibilities curves are concave, and the reallocation of resources required by trade is not nearly as dramatic. Still, free trade can require shifts in resources from one activity to another. These shifts produce enormous benefits, but they do not come without costs.

Nearly all economists agree that largely unrestricted trade between countries is desirable; restrictions on trade generally force the world to operate inside its production possibilities curve. In some cases restrictions on trade could be desirable, but in the main, free trade promotes greater production of goods and services for the world's people. The role of international trade is explored in greater detail in subsequent chapters of this book.

3.2   Economic Growth

An increase in the physical quantity or in the quality of factors of production available to an economy or a technological gain will allow the economy to produce more goods and services; it will shift the economy's production possibilities curve outward. The process through which an economy achieves an outward shift in its production possibilities curve is called **economic growth**. An outward shift in a production possibilities curve is illustrated in Figure 2.10. In Panel (a), a point such as N is not attainable; it lies outside the production possibilities curve. Growth shifts the curve outward, as in Panel (b), making previously unattainable levels of production possible.

economic growth

The process through which an economy achieves an outward shift in its production possibilities curve.

FIGURE 2.10 Economic Growth and the Production Possibilities Curve

An economy capable of producing two goods, A and B, is initially operating at point M on production possibilities curve OMR in Panel (a). Given this production possibilities curve, the economy could not produce a combination such as shown by point N, which lies outside the curve. An increase in the factors of production available to the economy would shift the curve outward to SNT, allowing the choice of a point such as N, at which more of both goods will be produced.

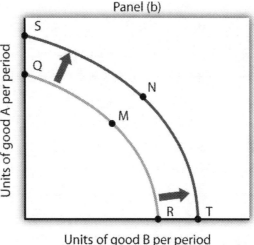

The Sources of Economic Growth

Economic growth implies an outward shift in an economy's production possibilities curve. Recall that when we draw such a curve, we assume that the quantity and quality of the economy's factors of production and its technology are unchanged. Changing these will shift the curve. Anything that increases the quantity or quality of the factors of production available to the economy or that improves the technology available to the economy contributes to economic growth.

Consider, for example, the dramatic gains in human capital that have occurred in the United States since the beginning of the past century. In 1900, about 3.5% of U.S. workers had completed a high school education. By 2009, that percentage rose almost to 92. Fewer than 1% of the workers in 1900 had graduated from college; as late as 1940 only 3.5% had graduated from college. By 2009, over 32% had graduated from college. In addition to being better educated, today's workers have received more and better training on the job. They bring far more economically useful knowledge and skills to their work than did workers a century ago.

Moreover, the technological changes that have occurred within the past 100 years have greatly reduced the time and effort required to produce most goods and services. Automated production has become commonplace. Innovations in transportation (automobiles, trucks, and airplanes) have made the movement of goods and people cheaper and faster. A dizzying array of new materials is available for manufacturing. And the development of modern information technology—including computers, software, and communications equipment—that seemed to proceed at breathtaking pace especially during the final years of the last century and continuing to the present has transformed the way we live and work.

Look again at the technological changes of the last few years described in the Case in Point on advances in technology. Those examples of technological progress through applications of computer technology—from new ways of mapping oil deposits to new methods of milking cows—helped propel the United States and other economies to dramatic gains in the ability to produce goods and services. They have helped shift the countries' production possibilities curve outward. They have helped fuel economic growth.

Table 2.1 summarizes the factors that have contributed to U.S. economic growth since 1960. When looking at the period of 1960–2007 as a whole we see that about 65% of economic growth stems from increases in quantities of capital and labor and about 35% from increases in qualities of the factors of production and improvements in technology or innovation. Looking at the three shorter subperiods (1960-1995, 1995-2000, and 2000-2007), we see that the share attributed to quantity increases declined (from 68% to 56% and then 50%), while the share attributed to improvement in the qualities of the factors of production and to technological improvement grew (from 32% to 44% and then to 50%).

TABLE 2.1 Sources of U.S. Economic Growth, 1960–2007

Total output for the period shown increased nearly fivefold. The chart shows the percentage of growth accounted for by increases in the quantity of labor and of capital and by increases in the quality of labor and of capital and improvements in technology.

Period	Percentage Contribution to Growth	Period Growth Rate
Years 1960–2007		3.45%
Increase in quantity of labor	0.74%	
Increase in quantity of capital	1.48%	
Increase in quality of labor	0.23%	
Increase in quality of capital	0.58%	
Improved technology	0.41%	
Years 1960–1995		3.42%
Increase in quantity of labor	0.80%	
Increase in quantity of capital	1.55%	
Increase in quality of labor	0.24%	
Increase in quality of capital	0.56%	
Improved technology	0.28%	
Years 1995–2000		4.52%
Increase in quantity of labor	1.09%	
Increase in quantity of capital	1.43%	
Increase in quality of labor	0.20%	
Increase in quality of capital	0.89%	
Improved technology	0.90%	
Years 2000–2007		2.78%
Increase in quantity of labor	0.17%	
Increase in quantity of capital	1.21%	
Increase in quality of labor	0.22%	
Increase in quality of capital	0.46%	
Improved technology	0.72%	

Source: Dale W. Jorgenson, Mun Ho, and Jon Samuels, "Information Technology and U.S. Productivity Growth: Evidence from a Prototype Industry Production Account," prepared for Matilde Mas and Robert Stehrer, Industrial Productivity in Europe: Growth and Crisis, November 19, 2010.

Another way of looking at these data is to note that while the contribution of improved technology has increased over time (from 8% for the 1960–1995 period, to 20% for the 1995–2000 period, and 26% for the 2000–2007 period), most growth comes from more and better-quality factors of production. The study by economists Dale Jorgenson, Mun Ho, and Jon Samuels, on which the data shown in Table 2.1 are derived, concludes that "the great preponderance of economic growth in the U.S. involves the replication of existing technologies through investment in equipment and software and expansion of the labour force. Replication generates economic growth with no increase in productivity. Productivity growth is the key economic indicator of innovation…Although innovation contributes only a modest portion of growth, this is vital to long-term gains in the American standard of living."[1]

Waiting for Growth

One key to growth is, in effect, the willingness to wait, to postpone current consumption in order to enhance future productive capability. When Stone Age people fashioned the first tools, they were spending time building capital rather than engaging in consumption. They delayed current consumption to enhance their future consumption; the tools they made would make them more productive in the future.

Resources society could have used to produce consumer goods are being used to produce new capital goods and new knowledge for production instead—all to enhance future production. An even more important source of growth in many nations has been increased human capital. Increases in human capital often require the postponement of consumption. If you are a college student, you are engaged in precisely this effort. You are devoting time to study that could have been spent working, earning income, and thus engaging in a higher level of consumption. If you are like most students, you are making this choice to postpone consumption because you expect it will allow you to earn more income, and thus enjoy greater consumption, in the future.

Think of an economy as being able to produce two goods, capital and consumer goods (those destined for immediate use by consumers). By focusing on the production of consumer goods, the people in the economy will be able to enjoy a higher standard of living today. If they reduce their consumption—and their standard of living—today to enhance their ability to produce goods and services in the future, they will be able to shift their production possibilities curve outward. That may allow them to produce even more consumer goods. A decision for greater growth typically involves the sacrifice of present consumption.

3.3   Arenas for Choice: A Comparison of Economic Systems

Under what circumstances will a nation achieve efficiency in the use of its factors of production? The discussion above suggested that Christie Ryder would have an incentive to allocate her plants efficiently because by doing so she could achieve greater output of skis and snowboards than would be possible from inefficient production. But why would she want to produce more of these two goods—or of any goods? Why would decision makers throughout the economy want to achieve such efficiency?

Economists assume that privately owned firms seek to maximize their profits. The drive to maximize profits will lead firms such as Alpine Sports to allocate resources efficiently to gain as much production as possible from their factors of production. But whether firms will seek to maximize profits depends on the nature of the economic system within which they operate.

Classifying Economic Systems

Each of the world's economies can be viewed as operating somewhere on a spectrum between market capitalism and command socialism. In a **market capitalist economy**, resources are generally owned by private individuals who have the power to make decisions about their use. A market capitalist system is often referred to as a free enterprise economic system. In a **command socialist economy**, the government is the primary owner of capital and natural resources and has broad power to allocate the use of factors of production. Between these two categories lie **mixed economies** that combine elements of market capitalist and of command socialist economic systems.

No economy represents a pure case of either market capitalism or command socialism. To determine where an economy lies between these two types of systems, we evaluate the extent of government ownership of capital and natural resources and the degree to which government is involved in decisions about the use of factors of production.

Figure 2.11 suggests the spectrum of economic systems. Market capitalist economies lie toward the left end of this spectrum; command socialist economies appear toward the right. Mixed economies lie in between. The market capitalist end of the spectrum includes countries such as the United States, the United Kingdom, and Chile. Hong Kong, though now part of China, has a long history as a market capitalist economy and is generally regarded as operating at the market capitalist end of the spectrum. Countries at the command socialist end of the spectrum include North Korea and Cuba.

market capitalist economy

Economy in which resources are generally owned by private individuals who have the power to make decisions about their use.

command socialist economy

Economy in which government is the primary owner of capital and natural resources and has broad power to allocate the use of factors of production.

mixed economies

Economy that combine elements of market capitalist and of command socialist economic systems.

FIGURE 2.11 Economic Systems

Some European economies, such as France, Germany, and Sweden, have a sufficiently high degree of regulation that we consider them as operating more toward the center of the spectrum. Russia and China, which long operated at the command socialist end of the spectrum, can now be considered mixed economies. Most economies in Latin America once operated toward the right end of the spectrum. While their governments did not exercise the extensive ownership of capital and natural resources that are one characteristic of command socialist systems, their governments did impose extensive regulations. Many of these nations are in the process of carrying out economic reforms that will move them further in the direction of market capitalism.

The global shift toward market capitalist economic systems that occurred in the 1980s and 1990s was in large part the result of three important features of such economies. First, the emphasis on individual ownership and decision-making power has generally yielded greater individual freedom than has been available under command socialist or some more heavily regulated mixed economic systems that lie toward the command socialist end of the spectrum. People seeking political, religious, and economic freedom have thus gravitated toward market capitalism. Second, market economies are more likely than other systems to allocate resources on the basis of comparative advantage. They thus tend to generate higher levels of production and income than do other economic systems. Third, market capitalist-type systems appear to be the most conducive to entrepreneurial activity.

Suppose Christie Ryder had the same three plants we considered earlier in this chapter but was operating in a mixed economic system with extensive government regulation. In such a system, she might be prohibited from transferring resources from one use to another to achieve the gains possible from comparative advantage. If she were operating under a command socialist system, she would not be the owner of the plants and thus would be unlikely to profit from their efficient use. If that were the case, there is no reason to believe she would make any effort to assure the efficient use of the three plants. Generally speaking, it is economies toward the market capitalist end of the spectrum that offer the greatest inducement to allocate resources on the basis of comparative advantage. They tend to be more productive and to deliver higher material standards of living than do economies that operate at or near the command socialist end of the spectrum.

FIGURE 2.12 Economic Freedom and Income

The graph shows the relationship between economic freedom and per capita income by region. Countries with higher degrees of economic freedom tended to have higher per capita incomes.

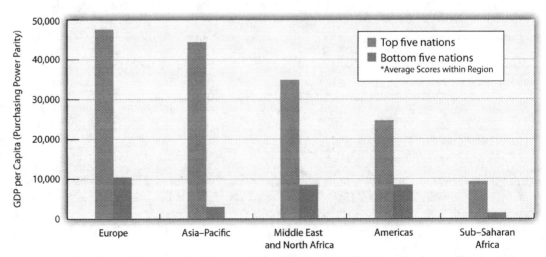

Source: Terry Miller and Kim R. Holmes, 2011 Index of Economic Freedom (Washington, D.C.: The Heritage Foundation and Dow Jones & Company, Inc., 2011), at www.heritage.org/index.

Market capitalist economies rely on economic freedom. Indeed, one way we can assess the degree to which a country can be considered market capitalist is by the degree of economic freedom it permits.

Several organizations have attempted to compare economic freedom in various countries. One of the most extensive comparisons is a joint annual effort by the Heritage Foundation and the *Wall Street Journal*. The 2011 rating was based on policies in effect in 183 nations early that year. The report ranks these nations on the basis of such things as the degree of regulation of firms, tax levels, and restrictions on international trade. Hong Kong ranked as the freest economy in the world. North Korea received the dubious distinction of being the least free.

One might expect that the greater the degree of economic freedom a country permits, the greater the amount of income per person it will generate. This proposition is illustrated in Figure 2.12. The study also found a positive association between the degree of economic freedom and overall well-being using a measure that takes into account such variables as health, education, security, and personal freedom. We must be wary of slipping into the fallacy of false cause by concluding from this evidence that economic freedom generates higher incomes. It could be that higher incomes lead nations to opt for greater economic freedom. But in this case, it seems reasonable to conclude that, in general, economic freedom does lead to higher incomes.

3.4 Government in a Market Economy

The production possibilities model provides a menu of choices among alternative combinations of goods and services. Given those choices, which combinations will be produced?

In a market economy, this question is answered in large part through the interaction of individual buyers and sellers. As we have already seen, government plays a role as well. It may seek to encourage greater consumption of some goods and discourage consumption of others. In the United States, for example, taxes imposed on cigarettes discourage smoking, while special treatment of property taxes and mortgage interest in the federal income tax encourages home ownership. Government may try to stop the production and consumption of some goods altogether, as many governments do with drugs such as heroin and cocaine. Government may supplement the private consumption of some goods by producing more of them itself, as many U.S. cities do with golf courses and tennis courts. In other cases, there may be no private market for a good or service at all. In the choice between security and defense versus all other goods and services outlined at the beginning of this chapter, government agencies are virtually the sole providers of security and national defense.

All nations also rely on government to provide defense, enforce laws, and redistribute income. Even market economies rely on government to regulate the activities of private firms, to protect the environment, to provide education, and to produce a wide range of other goods and services. Government's role may be limited in a market economy, but it remains fundamentally important.

KEY TAKEAWAYS

- The ideas of comparative advantage and specialization suggest that restrictions on international trade are likely to reduce production of goods and services.
- Economic growth is the result of increasing the quantity or quality of an economy's factors of production and of advances in technology.
- Policies to encourage growth generally involve postponing consumption to increase capital and human capital.
- Market capitalist economies have generally proved more productive than mixed or command socialist economies.
- Government plays a crucial role in any market economy.

TRY IT!

Draw a production possibilities curve for an economy that can produce two goods, CD players and jackets. You do not have numbers for this one—just draw a curve with the usual bowed-out shape. Put the quantity of CD players per period on the vertical axis and the quantity of jackets per period on the horizontal axis. Now mark a point A on the curve you have drawn; extend dotted lines from this point to the horizontal and vertical axes. Mark the initial quantities of the two goods as CD_A and J_A, respectively. Explain why, in the absence of economic growth, an increase in jacket production requires a reduction in the production of CD players. Now show how economic growth could lead to an increase in the production of both goods.

Case in Point

The Prospects for World Economic Growth

© *Thinkstock*

What will happen to world economic growth in the next 10 years? The prognosis, according to economists Dale W. Jorgenson of Harvard University and Khuong M. Vu of the National University of Singapore, suggests that world growth is likely to be somewhat slower in the next decade than it was in the last.

The two economists, who have written extensively on the problem of estimating world economic growth, estimate that the world economy (based on their sample of 122 countries that account for 95% of world GDP) grew at a rate of just 2.20% from 1990–1995. That increased to 3.37% per year from 1995–2000. During the period from 2000–2005 the annual growth rate accelerated again to 3.71%. Despite the recession and financial crisis that began in 2008, world growth slowed a bit but was still 3.06% from 2005 to 2009. Growth at 3% would double world economic income every 24 years. Think for a moment about what that implies—world income would quadruple in just 48 years. Growth at the 1990–1995 pace of 2.20% per year would take 33 years for income to double.

Might the world growth rates from 2000 to 2009 of above 3% be repeated during the next 10 years? Under their base-case scenario, the economists project the world growth rate between 2010 and 2020 to be about 3.37%.

What do they think the economic world will look like then? They predict that over the next 10-year period: the U.S. growth rate will slow down compared to the last two decades, primarily due to slower growth in labor quality, but the U.S. growth rate will still lead among the G7 countries (a group of seven large industrialized countries that includes Canada, France, Germany, Italy, Japan, the United Kingdom, and the United States); the overall growth in the G7 countries will continue to decline; and growth in the developing countries of Asia (Bangladesh Cambodia, China, Hong Kong, India, Indonesia, Malaysia, Nepal, Pakistan, Philippines, Singapore, South Korea, Sri Lanka, Taiwan, Thailand, and Vietnam) will slow a bit from the recent past but will be high enough that those countries' GDPs will comprise nearly 37% of world GDP in 2020, as compared to 29% in 2010. In terms of size of GDP in 2020, they predict the following new order: China, the United States, India, Japan, Russia, Germany, and Brazil. If their predictions are realized, it will mark the end of a period of more than a century in which the United States has been the world's largest economy.

Sources: Dale W. Jorgenson and Khoung M. Vu, "The Rise of Developing Asia and the New Economic Order," Journal of Policy Modeling 33:5 (September–October 2011), forthcoming.

Your first production possibilities curve should resemble the one in Panel (a). Starting at point A, an increase in jacket production requires a move down and to the right along the curve, as shown by the arrow, and thus a reduction in the production of CD players. Alternatively, if there is economic growth, it shifts the production possibilities curve outward, as in Panel (b). This shift allows an increase in production of both goods, as suggested by the arrow.

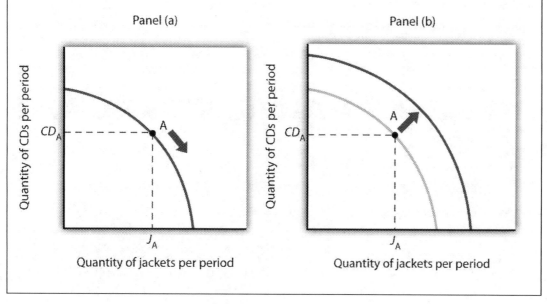

Panel (a)   Panel (b)

Quantity of CDs per period

Quantity of jackets per period

4.   REVIEW AND PRACTICE

Summary

Economics deals with choices. In this chapter we have examined more carefully the range of choices in production that must be made in any economy. In particular, we looked at choices involving the allocation of an economy's factors of production: labor, capital, and natural resources.

In addition, in any economy, the level of technology plays a key role in determining how productive the factors of production will be. In a market economy, entrepreneurs organize factors of production and act to introduce technological change. Firms are the basic unit of production.

The production possibilities model is a device that assists us in thinking about many of the choices about resource allocation in an economy. The model assumes that the economy has factors of production that are fixed in both quantity and quality. When illustrated graphically, the production possibilities model typically limits our analysis to two goods. Given the economy's factors of production and technology, the economy can produce various combinations of the two goods. If it uses its factors of production efficiently and has full employment, it will be operating on the production possibilities curve.

Two characteristics of the production possibilities curve are particularly important. First, it is downward sloping. This reflects the scarcity of the factors of production available to the economy; producing more of one good requires giving up some of the other. Second, the curve is bowed out. Another way of saying this is to say that the curve gets steeper as we move from left to right; the absolute value of its slope is increasing. Producing each additional unit of the good on the horizontal axis requires a greater sacrifice of the good on the vertical axis than did the previous units produced. This fact, called the law of increasing opportunity cost, is the inevitable result of efficient choices in production—choices based on comparative advantage.

The production possibilities model has important implications for international trade. It suggests that free trade will allow countries to specialize in the production of goods and services in which they have a comparative advantage. This specialization increases the production of all goods and services.

Increasing the quantity or quality of factors of production and/or improving technology will shift the production possibilities curve outward. This process is called economic growth. In the last 50 years, economic growth in the United States has resulted chiefly from increases in human capital and from technological advance.

Choices concerning the use of scarce resources take place within the context of a set of institutional arrangements that define an economic system. The principal distinctions between systems lie in the degree to which ownership of capital and natural resources and decision making authority over scarce resources are held by government or by private individuals. Economic systems include market capitalist, mixed, and command socialist economies. An increasing body of evidence suggests that market capitalist economies tend to be most productive; many command socialist and mixed economies are moving in the direction of market capitalist systems.

The presumption in favor of market-based systems does not preclude a role for government. Government is necessary to provide the system of laws on which market systems are founded. It may also be used to provide certain goods and services, to help individuals in need, and to regulate the actions of individuals and firms.

CONCEPT PROBLEMS

1. How does a college education increase one's human capital?

2. Why does the downward-sloping production possibilities curve imply that factors of production are scarce?

3. In what ways are the bowed-out shape of the production possibilities curve and the law of increasing opportunity cost related?

4. What is the relationship between the concept of comparative advantage and the law of increasing opportunity cost?

5. Suppose an economy can produce two goods, A and B. It is now operating at point E on production possibilities curve RT. An improvement in the technology available to produce good A shifts the curve to ST, and the economy selects point E'. How does this change affect the opportunity cost of producing an additional unit of good B?

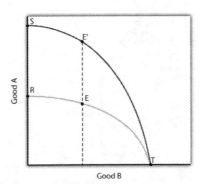

6. Could a nation's production possibilities curve ever shift inward? Explain what such a shift would mean, and discuss events that might cause such a shift to occur.

7. Suppose blue-eyed people were banned from working. How would this affect a nation's production possibilities curve?

8. Evaluate this statement: "The U.S. economy could achieve greater growth by devoting fewer resources to consumption and more to investment; it follows that such a shift would be desirable."

9. Two countries, Sportsland and Foodland, have similar total quantities of labor, capital, and natural resources. Both can produce two goods, figs and footballs. Sportsland's resources are particularly well suited to the production of footballs but are not very productive in producing figs. Foodland's resources are very productive when used for figs but are not capable of producing many footballs. In which country is the cost of additional footballs generally greater? Explain.

10. Suppose a country is committed to using its resources based on the reverse of comparative advantage doctrine: it first transfers those resources for which the cost is greatest, not lowest. Describe this country's production possibilities curve.

11. The U.S. Constitution bans states from restricting imports of goods and services from other states. Suppose this restriction did not exist and that states were allowed to limit imports of goods and services produced in other states. How do you think this would affect U.S. output? Explain.

12. By 1993, nations in the European Union (EU) had eliminated all barriers to the flow of goods, services, labor, and capital across their borders. Even such things as consumer protection laws and the types of plugs required to plug in appliances have been standardized to ensure that there will be no barriers to trade. How do you think this elimination of trade barriers affected EU output?

13. How did the technological changes described in the Case in Point "Technology Cuts Costs, Boosts Productivity and Profits" affect the production possibilities curve for the United States?

NUMERICAL PROBLEMS

1. Nathan can mow four lawns in a day or plant 20 trees in a day.

    a. Draw Nathan's production possibilities curve for mowing lawns and planting trees. Assume the production possibilities curve is linear and put the quantity of lawns mowed per day on the horizontal axis and the quantity of trees planted per day on the vertical axis.

    b. What is Nathan's opportunity cost of planting trees?

    c. What is Nathan's opportunity cost of mowing lawns?

2. David can mow four lawns in a day or plant four trees in a day.

    a. Draw David's production possibilities curve for mowing lawns and planting trees. Again, assume a linear production possibilities curve and put the quantity of lawns mowed per day on the horizontal axis.

    b. What is David's opportunity cost of planting trees?

    c. What is David's opportunity cost of mowing lawns?

3. Given the production information in problems 1 and 2 above, who has the comparative advantage in planting trees? Mowing lawns?

4. The exhibits below describe the production possibilities for Germany and Turkey.

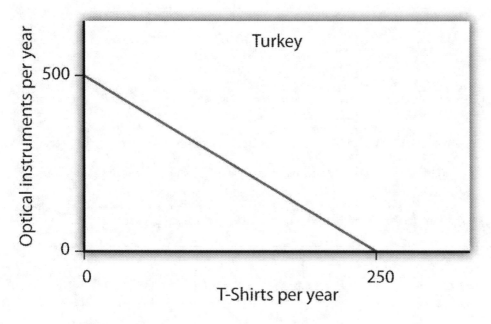

    a. What is the slope of Germany's production possibilities curve?

    b. What is the slope of Turkey's production possibilities curve?

    c. What is the opportunity cost of producing T-shirts in Germany?

    d. What is the opportunity cost of producing T-shirts in Turkey?

    e. What is the opportunity cost of producing optical instruments in Germany?

    f. What is the opportunity cost of producing optical instruments in Turkey?

    g. In which good does Germany have a comparative advantage?

    h. In which good does Turkey have a comparative advantage?

5. The nation of Leisureland can produce two goods, bicycles and bowling balls. The western region of Leisureland can, if it devotes all its resources to bicycle production, produce 100 bicycles per month. Alternatively, it could devote all its resources to bowling balls and produce 400 per month—or it could produce any combination of bicycles and bowling balls lying on a straight line between these two extremes.

    a. Draw a production possibilities curve for western Leisureland (with bicycles on the vertical axis).

    b. What is the opportunity cost of producing an additional bowling ball measured in terms of forgone bicycles in western Leisureland?

    c. Suppose that eastern Leisureland can, if it devotes all its resources to the production of bicycles, produce 400. If it devotes all its resources to bowling ball production, though, it can produce only 100. Draw the production possibilities curve for eastern Leisureland (again, assume it is linear and put bicycles on the vertical axis).

    d. What is the opportunity cost of producing an additional bowling ball measured in terms of forgone bicycles in eastern Leisureland?

    e. Explain the difference in opportunity cost between western and eastern Leisureland. Which region has a comparative advantage in producing bowling balls? Bicycles?

    f. Draw the production possibilities curve for Leisureland, one that combines the curves for western and eastern Leisureland.

    g. Suppose it is determined that 400 bicycles must be produced. How many bowling balls can be produced?

    h. Where will these goods be produced?

6. The table below shows the production possibilities schedule for an economy.

Production Alternatives	Capital goods per period	Consumer goods per period
A	0	40
B	1	36
C	2	28
D	3	16
E	4	0

    a. Putting capital goods per period on the horizontal axis and consumer goods per period on the vertical axis, graph the production possibilities curve for the economy.

    b. If the economy is producing at alternative B, what is the opportunity cost to it of producing at alternative C instead?

    c. If the economy is producing at alternative C, what is the opportunity cost to it of producing at alternative D instead?

    d. Is it possible for this economy to produce 30 units of consumer goods per period while producing 1 unit of capital goods? Would this combination of goods represent efficient or inefficient production? Explain.

    e. Which point, B or C, would lead to higher economic growth? Explain your answer.

7. The exhibit below shows the sources of growth in the United States between 1909 and 1929 and between 1950 and 1979, according to a study by Edward Denison.[2] (Note: The sources of economic growth are cumulative and, taken collectively, explain 100% of total growth over the period.)

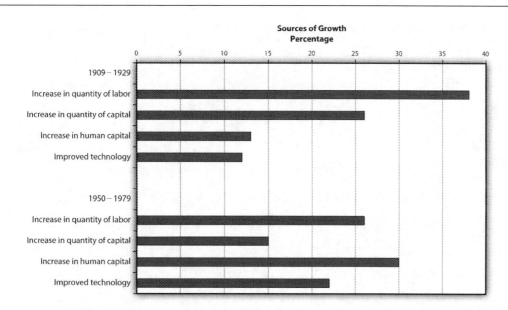

a. Approximately what percentage of U.S. growth between 1909 and 1929 was due to increases in quantities of factors of production?

b. Approximately what percentage of U.S. growth between 1909 and 1929 was due to increases in quality of factors of production and technological improvement?

c. Approximately what percentage of U.S. growth between 1950 and 1979 was due to increases in quantities of factors of production?

d. Approximately what percentage of U.S. growth between 1950 and 1979 was due to increases in quality of factors of production and technological improvement?

ENDNOTES

1. Dale W. Jorgenson, Mun Ho, and Jon Samuels, "Information Technology and U.S. Productivity Growth: Evidence from a Prototype Industry Production Account," in *Industrial Productivity in Europe: Growth and Crisis*, ed. Matilde Mas and Robert Stehrer (Gloucestershire, UK: Edward Elgar, forthcoming).

2. Edward Denison, *The Sources of Economic Growth in the United States* (New York: Committee for Economic Development, 1962) and Edward Denison, *Trends in American Growth 1929–1982* (Washington, D.C.: Brookings Institutions, 1985).

CHAPTER 3
Demand and Supply

START UP: CRAZY FOR COFFEE

Starbucks Coffee Company has revolutionized the coffee-drinking habits of millions of people all over the world. Starbucks, whose bright green-and-white logo is almost as familiar as the golden arches of McDonald's, began in Seattle in 1971. Fifteen years later it had grown into a chain of four stores in the Seattle area. Then in 1987 Howard Schultz, a former Starbucks employee, who had become intrigued by the culture of Italian coffee bars, bought the company from its founders for $3.8 million. In 2011, Americans were willingly paying $5 or more for a cappuccino or a latté, and Starbucks had grown to become an international chain, with approximately 17,000 stores in more than 50 countries.

The change in American consumers' taste for coffee and the profits raked in by Starbucks lured other companies to get into the game. Retailers such as Seattle's Best Coffee and Gloria Jean's Coffees entered the market, and today there are thousands of coffee bars, carts, drive-throughs, and kiosks in downtowns, malls, and airports all around the country. Even McDonald's began selling specialty coffees.

But over the last decade the price of coffee beans has been quite volatile, nearly doubling between 2009 and 2011, primarily due to bad harvests in Central America. Cappuccinos and lattés were suddenly more expensive.

Markets, the institutions that bring together buyers and sellers, are always responding to events such as bad harvests and changing consumer tastes that affect the prices and quantities of particular goods. The demand for some goods increases, while the demand for others decreases. The supply of some goods rises, while the supply of others falls. As such events unfold, prices adjust to keep markets in balance. This chapter explains how the market forces of demand and supply interact to determine equilibrium prices and equilibrium quantities of goods and services. We will see how prices and quantities adjust to changes in demand and supply and how changes in prices serve as signals to buyers and sellers.

> **markets**
> The institutions that bring together buyers and sellers.

The model of demand and supply that we shall develop in this chapter is one of the most powerful tools in economic analysis. You will be using it throughout your study of economics. We will first look at the variables that influence demand. Then we will turn to supply, and we will put demand and supply together to explore how the model of demand and supply operates. As we examine the model, bear in mind that demand is a representation of the behavior of buyers and that supply is a representation of the behavior of sellers. Buyers may be consumers purchasing groceries or producers purchasing iron ore to make steel. Sellers may be firms selling cars or households selling their labor services. We shall see that the ideas of demand and supply apply, whatever the identity of the buyers or sellers and whatever the good or service being exchanged in the market. In this chapter, we shall focus on buyers and sellers of goods and services.

Finally, we will look at situations in which price controls prevent markets from moving toward equilibrium. By legislating maximum and minimum prices, the government can keep the prices of certain goods below or above equilibrium. We will look at the arguments for direct government intervention in controlling prices as well as the consequences of such policies. As we shall see, preventing the price of a good from finding its own equilibrium often has consequences that may be at odds with the intentions of the policy makers who put the regulations in place.

1. DEMAND

> ### LEARNING OBJECTIVES
>
> 1. **Define the quantity demanded of a good or service and illustrate it using a demand schedule and a demand curve.**
> 2. **Distinguish between the following pairs of concepts: demand and quantity demanded, demand schedule and demand curve, movement along and shift in a demand curve.**
> 3. **Identify demand shifters and determine whether a change in a demand shifter causes the demand curve to shift to the right or to the left.**

How many pizzas will people eat this year? How many doctor visits will people make? How many houses will people buy?

Each good or service has its own special characteristics that determine the quantity people are willing and able to consume. One is the price of the good or service itself. Other independent variables that are important determinants of demand include consumer preferences, prices of related goods and services, income, demographic characteristics such as population size, and buyer expectations. The number of pizzas people will purchase, for example, depends very much on how much they like pizza. It also depends on the prices for alternatives such as hamburgers or spaghetti. The number of doctor visits is likely to vary with income—people with higher incomes are likely to see a doctor more often than people with lower incomes. The demands for pizza, for doctor visits, and for housing are certainly affected by the age distribution of the population and its size.

While different variables play different roles in influencing the demands for different goods and services, economists pay special attention to one: the price of the good or service. Given the values of all the other variables that affect demand, a higher price tends to reduce the quantity people demand, and a lower price tends to increase it. A medium pizza typically sells for $5 to $10. Suppose the price were $30. Chances are, you would buy fewer pizzas at that price than you do now. Suppose pizzas typically sold for $2 each. At that price, people would be likely to buy more pizzas than they do now.

We will discuss first how price affects the quantity demanded of a good or service and then how other variables affect demand.

1.1   Price and the Demand Curve

Because people will purchase different quantities of a good or service at different prices, economists must be careful when speaking of the "demand" for something. They have therefore developed some specific terms for expressing the general concept of demand.

quantity demanded

The quantity buyers are willing and able to buy of a good or service at a particular price during a particular period, all other things unchanged.

The **quantity demanded** of a good or service is the quantity buyers are willing and able to buy at a particular price during a particular period, all other things unchanged. (As we learned, we can substitute the Latin phrase "ceteris paribus" for "all other things unchanged.") Suppose, for example, that 100,000 movie tickets are sold each month in a particular town at a price of $8 per ticket. That quantity—100,000—is the quantity of movie admissions demanded per month at a price of $8. If the price were $12, we would expect the quantity demanded to be less. If it were $4, we would expect the quantity demanded to be greater. The quantity demanded at each price would be different if other things that might affect it, such as the population of the town, were to change. That is why we add the qualifier that other things have not changed to the definition of quantity demanded.

demand schedule

A table that shows the quantities of a good or service demanded at different prices during a particular period, all other things unchanged.

A **demand schedule** is a table that shows the quantities of a good or service demanded at different prices during a particular period, all other things unchanged. To introduce the concept of a demand schedule, let us consider the demand for coffee in the United States. We will ignore differences among types of coffee beans and roasts, and speak simply of coffee. The table in Figure 3.1 shows quantities of coffee that will be demanded each month at prices ranging from $9 to $4 per pound; the table is a demand schedule. We see that the higher the price, the lower the quantity demanded.

FIGURE 3.1   A Demand Schedule and a Demand Curve

The table is a demand schedule; it shows quantities of coffee demanded per month in the United States at particular prices, all other things unchanged. These data are then plotted on the demand curve. At point A on the curve, 25 million pounds of coffee per month are demanded at a price of $6 per pound. At point B, 30 million pounds of coffee per month are demanded at a price of $5 per pound.

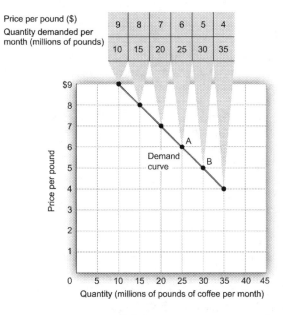

Price per pound ($)	9	8	7	6	5	4
Quantity demanded per month (millions of pounds)	10	15	20	25	30	35

The information given in a demand schedule can be presented with a **demand curve**, which is a graphical representation of a demand schedule. A demand curve thus shows the relationship between the price and quantity demanded of a good or service during a particular period, all other things unchanged. The demand curve in Figure 3.1 shows the prices and quantities of coffee demanded that are given in the demand schedule. At point A, for example, we see that 25 million pounds of coffee per month are demanded at a price of $6 per pound. By convention, economists graph price on the vertical axis and quantity on the horizontal axis.

Price alone does not determine the quantity of coffee or any other good that people buy. To isolate the effect of changes in price on the quantity of a good or service demanded, however, we show the quantity demanded at each price, assuming that those other variables remain unchanged. We do the same thing in drawing a graph of the relationship between any two variables; we assume that the values of other variables that may affect the variables shown in the graph (such as income or population) remain unchanged for the period under consideration.

A change in price, with no change in any of the other variables that affect demand, results in a movement *along* the demand curve. For example, if the price of coffee falls from $6 to $5 per pound, consumption rises from 25 million pounds to 30 million pounds per month. That is a movement from point A to point B along the demand curve in Figure 3.1. A movement along a demand curve that results from a change in price is called a **change in quantity demanded**. Note that a change in quantity demanded is not a change or shift in the demand curve; it is a movement *along* the demand curve.

The negative slope of the demand curve in Figure 3.1 suggests a key behavioral relationship in economics. All other things unchanged, the **law of demand** holds that, for virtually all goods and services, a higher price leads to a reduction in quantity demanded and a lower price leads to an increase in quantity demanded.

The law of demand is called a law because the results of countless studies are consistent with it. Undoubtedly, you have observed one manifestation of the law. When a store finds itself with an overstock of some item, such as running shoes or tomatoes, and needs to sell these items quickly, what does it do? It typically has a sale, expecting that a lower price will increase the quantity demanded. In general, we expect the law of demand to hold. Given the values of other variables that influence demand, a higher price reduces the quantity demanded. A lower price increases the quantity demanded. Demand curves, in short, slope downward.

demand curve

A graphical representation of a demand schedule.

change in quantity demanded

A movement along a demand curve that results from a change in price.

law of demand

For virtually all goods and services, a higher price leads to a reduction in quantity demanded and a lower price leads to an increase in quantity demanded.

1.2   Changes in Demand

Of course, price alone does not determine the quantity of a good or service that people consume. Coffee consumption, for example, will be affected by such variables as income and population. Preferences also play a role. The story at the beginning of the chapter illustrates how Starbucks "turned people on" to coffee. We also expect other prices to affect coffee consumption. People often eat donuts or bagels with their coffee, so a reduction in the price of donuts or bagels might induce people to drink more coffee. An alternative to coffee is tea, so a reduction in the price of tea might result in the consumption of more tea and less coffee. Thus, a change in any one of the variables held constant in constructing a demand schedule will change the quantities demanded at each price. The result will be a *shift* in the entire demand curve rather than a movement along the demand curve. A *shift* in a demand curve is called a **change in demand**.

Suppose, for example, that something happens to increase the quantity of coffee demanded at each price. Several events could produce such a change: an increase in incomes, an increase in population, or an increase in the price of tea would each be likely to increase the quantity of coffee demanded at each price. Any such change produces a new demand schedule. Figure 3.2 shows such a change in the demand schedule for coffee. We see that the quantity of coffee demanded per month is greater at each price than before. We show that graphically as a shift in the demand curve. The original curve, labeled D_1, shifts to the right to D_2. At a price of $6 per pound, for example, the quantity demanded rises from 25 million pounds per month (point A) to 35 million pounds per month (point A′).

FIGURE 3.2   An Increase in Demand

An increase in the quantity of a good or service demanded at each price is shown as an increase in demand. Here, the original demand curve D_1 shifts to D_2. Point A on D_1 corresponds to a price of $6 per pound and a quantity demanded of 25 million pounds of coffee per month. On the new demand curve D_2, the quantity demanded at this price rises to 35 million pounds of coffee per month (point A′).

Price	Old quantity demanded	New quantity demanded
$9	10	20
8	15	25
7	20	30
6	25	35
5	30	40
4	35	45

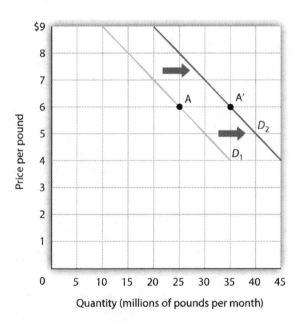

Just as demand can increase, it can decrease. In the case of coffee, demand might fall as a result of events such as a reduction in population, a reduction in the price of tea, or a change in preferences. For example, a definitive finding that the caffeine in coffee contributes to heart disease, which is currently being debated in the scientific community, could change preferences and reduce the demand for coffee.

A reduction in the demand for coffee is illustrated in Figure 3.3. The demand schedule shows that less coffee is demanded at each price than in Figure 3.1. The result is a shift in demand from the original curve D_1 to D_3. The quantity of coffee demanded at a price of $6 per pound falls from 25 million pounds per month (point A) to 15 million pounds per month (point A″). Note, again, that a change in quantity demanded, ceteris paribus, refers to a movement *along* the demand curve, while a change in demand refers to a *shift* in the demand curve.

FIGURE 3.3   A Reduction in Demand

A reduction in demand occurs when the quantities of a good or service demanded fall at each price. Here, the demand schedule shows a lower quantity of coffee demanded at each price than we had in Figure 3.1. The reduction shifts the demand curve for coffee to D_3 from D_1. The quantity demanded at a price of $6 per pound, for example, falls from 25 million pounds per month (point A) to 15 million pounds of coffee per month (point A").

Price	Old quantity demanded	New quantity demanded
$9	10	0
8	15	5
7	20	10
6	25	15
5	30	20
4	35	25

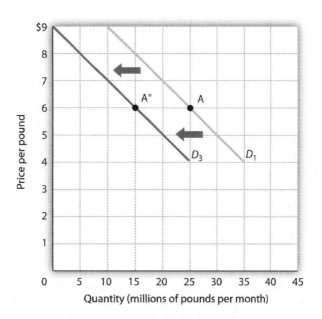

A variable that can change the quantity of a good or service demanded at each price is called a **demand shifter**. When these other variables change, the all-other-things-unchanged conditions behind the original demand curve no longer hold. Although different goods and services will have different demand shifters, the demand shifters are likely to include (1) consumer preferences, (2) the prices of related goods and services, (3) income, (4) demographic characteristics, and (5) buyer expectations. Next we look at each of these.

Preferences

Changes in preferences of buyers can have important consequences for demand. We have already seen how Starbucks supposedly increased the demand for coffee. Another example is reduced demand for cigarettes caused by concern about the effect of smoking on health. A change in preferences that makes one good or service more popular will shift the demand curve to the right. A change that makes it less popular will shift the demand curve to the left.

Prices of Related Goods and Services

Suppose the price of donuts were to fall. Many people who drink coffee enjoy dunking donuts in their coffee; the lower price of donuts might therefore increase the demand for coffee, shifting the demand curve for coffee to the right. A lower price for tea, however, would be likely to reduce coffee demand, shifting the demand curve for coffee to the left.

In general, if a reduction in the price of one good increases the demand for another, the two goods are called **complements**. If a reduction in the price of one good reduces the demand for another, the two goods are called **substitutes**. These definitions hold in reverse as well: two goods are complements if an increase in the price of one reduces the demand for the other, and they are substitutes if an increase in the price of one increases the demand for the other. Donuts and coffee are complements; tea and coffee are substitutes.

Complementary goods are goods used in conjunction with one another. Tennis rackets and tennis balls, eggs and bacon, and stationery and postage stamps are complementary goods. Substitute goods are goods used instead of one another. iPODs, for example, are likely to be substitutes for CD players. Breakfast cereal is a substitute for eggs. A file attachment to an e-mail is a substitute for both a fax machine and postage stamps.

demand shifter

A variable that can change the quantity of a good or service demanded at each price.

complements

Two goods for which an increase in price of one reduces the demand for the other.

substitutes

Two goods for which an increase in price of one increases the demand for the other.

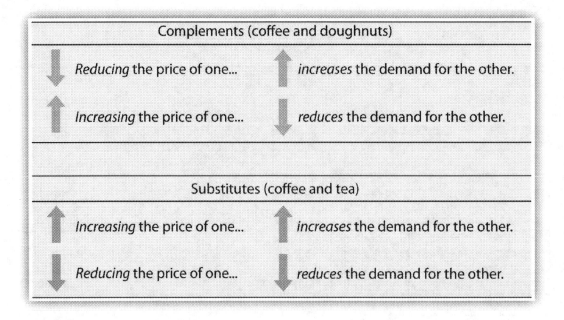

Income

As incomes rise, people increase their consumption of many goods and services, and as incomes fall, their consumption of these goods and services falls. For example, an increase in income is likely to raise the demand for gasoline, ski trips, new cars, and jewelry. There are, however, goods and services for which consumption falls as income rises—and rises as income falls. As incomes rise, for example, people tend to consume more fresh fruit but less canned fruit.

A good for which demand increases when income increases is called a **normal good**. A good for which demand decreases when income increases is called an **inferior good**. An increase in income shifts the demand curve for fresh fruit (a normal good) to the right; it shifts the demand curve for canned fruit (an inferior good) to the left.

Demographic Characteristics

The number of buyers affects the total quantity of a good or service that will be bought; in general, the greater the population, the greater the demand. Other demographic characteristics can affect demand as well. As the share of the population over age 65 increases, the demand for medical services, ocean cruises, and motor homes increases. The birth rate in the United States fell sharply between 1955 and 1975 but has gradually increased since then. That increase has raised the demand for such things as infant supplies, elementary school teachers, soccer coaches, in-line skates, and college education. Demand can thus shift as a result of changes in both the number and characteristics of buyers.

Buyer Expectations

The consumption of goods that can be easily stored, or whose consumption can be postponed, is strongly affected by buyer expectations. The expectation of newer TV technologies, such as high-definition TV, could slow down sales of regular TVs. If people expect gasoline prices to rise tomorrow, they will fill up their tanks today to try to beat the price increase. The same will be true for goods such as automobiles and washing machines: an expectation of higher prices in the future will lead to more purchases today. If the price of a good is expected to fall, however, people are likely to reduce their purchases today and await tomorrow's lower prices. The expectation that computer prices will fall, for example, can reduce current demand.

normal good

A good for which demand increases when income increases.

inferior good

A good for which demand decreases when income increases.

Heads Up!

It is crucial to distinguish between a change in quantity demanded, which is a movement along the demand curve caused by a change in price, and a change in demand, which implies a shift of the demand curve itself. A change in demand is caused by a change in a demand shifter. An increase in demand is a shift of the demand curve to the right. A decrease in demand is a shift in the demand curve to the left. This drawing of a demand curve highlights the difference.

KEY TAKEAWAYS

- The quantity demanded of a good or service is the quantity buyers are willing and able to buy at a particular price during a particular period, all other things unchanged.
- A demand schedule is a table that shows the quantities of a good or service demanded at different prices during a particular period, all other things unchanged.
- A demand curve shows graphically the quantities of a good or service demanded at different prices during a particular period, all other things unchanged.
- All other things unchanged, the law of demand holds that, for virtually all goods and services, a higher price induces a reduction in quantity demanded and a lower price induces an increase in quantity demanded.
- A change in the price of a good or service causes a change in the quantity demanded—a movement *along* the demand curve.
- A change in a demand shifter causes a change in demand, which is shown as a *shift* of the demand curve. Demand shifters include preferences, the prices of related goods and services, income, demographic characteristics, and buyer expectations.
- Two goods are substitutes if an increase in the price of one causes an increase in the demand for the other. Two goods are complements if an increase in the price of one causes a decrease in the demand for the other.
- A good is a normal good if an increase in income causes an increase in demand. A good is an inferior good if an increase in income causes a decrease in demand.

TRY IT!

All other things unchanged, what happens to the demand curve for DVD rentals if there is (a) an increase in the price of movie theater tickets, (b) a decrease in family income, or (c) an increase in the price of DVD rentals? In answering this and other "Try It!" problems in this chapter, draw and carefully label a set of axes. On the horizontal axis of your graph, show the quantity of DVD rentals. It is necessary to specify the time period to which your quantity pertains (e.g., "per period," "per week," or "per year"). On the vertical axis show the price per DVD rental. Since you do not have specific data on prices and quantities demanded, make a "free-hand" drawing of the curve or curves you are asked to examine. Focus on the general shape and position of the curve(s) before and after events occur. Draw new curve(s) to show what happens in each of the circumstances given. The curves could shift to the left or to the right, or stay where they are.

Case in Point

Solving Campus Parking Problems Without Adding More Parking Spaces

© 2010 Jupiterimages Corporation

Unless you attend a "virtual" campus, chances are you have engaged in more than one conversation about how hard it is to find a place to park on campus. Indeed, according to Clark Kerr, a former president of the University of California system, a university is best understood as a group of people "held together by a common grievance over parking."

Clearly, the demand for campus parking spaces has grown substantially over the past few decades. In surveys conducted by Daniel Kenney, Ricardo Dumont, and Ginger Kenney, who work for the campus design company Sasaki and Associates, it was found that 7 out of 10 students own their own cars. They have interviewed "many students who confessed to driving from their dormitories to classes that were a five-minute walk away," and they argue that the deterioration of college environments is largely attributable to the increased use of cars on campus and that colleges could better service their missions by not adding more parking spaces.

Since few universities charge enough for parking to even cover the cost of building and maintaining parking lots, the rest is paid for by all students as part of tuition. Their research shows that "for every 1,000 parking spaces, the median institution loses almost $400,000 a year for surface parking, and more than $1,200,000 for structural parking." Fear of a backlash from students and their parents, as well as from faculty and staff, seems to explain why campus administrators do not simply raise the price of parking on campus.

While Kenney and his colleagues do advocate raising parking fees, if not all at once then over time, they also suggest some subtler, and perhaps politically more palatable, measures—in particular, shifting the demand for parking spaces to the left by lowering the prices of substitutes.

Two examples they noted were at the University of Washington and the University of Colorado at Boulder. At the University of Washington, car poolers may park for free. This innovation has reduced purchases of single-occupancy parking permits by 32% over a decade. According to University of Washington assistant director of transportation services Peter Dewey, "Without vigorously managing our parking and providing commuter alternatives, the university would have been faced with adding approximately 3,600 parking spaces, at a cost of over $100 million…The university has created opportunities to make capital investments in buildings supporting education instead of structures for cars." At the University of Colorado, free public transit has increased use of buses and light rail from 300,000 to 2 million trips per year over the last decade. The increased use of mass transit has allowed the university to avoid constructing nearly 2,000 parking spaces, which has saved about $3.6 million annually.

Sources: Daniel R. Kenney, "How to Solve Campus Parking Problems Without Adding More Parking," The Chronicle of Higher Education, March 26, 2004, Section B, pp. B22-B23.

ANSWER TO TRY IT! PROBLEM

Since going to the movies is a substitute for watching a DVD at home, an increase in the price of going to the movies should cause more people to switch from going to the movies to staying at home and renting DVDs. Thus, the demand curve for DVD rentals will shift to the right when the price of movie theater tickets increases [Panel (a)].

A decrease in family income will cause the demand curve to shift to the left if DVD rentals are a normal good but to the right if DVD rentals are an inferior good. The latter may be the case for some families, since staying at home and watching DVDs is a cheaper form of entertainment than taking the family to the movies. For most others, however, DVD rentals are probably a normal good [Panel (b)].

An increase in the price of DVD rentals does not shift the demand curve for DVD rentals at all; rather, an increase in price, say from P_1 to P_2, is a movement upward to the left along the demand curve. At a higher price, people will rent fewer DVDs, say Q_2 instead of Q_1, ceteris paribus [Panel (c)].

2. SUPPLY

LEARNING OBJECTIVES

1. Define the quantity supplied of a good or service and illustrate it using a supply schedule and a supply curve.
2. Distinguish between the following pairs of concepts: supply and quantity supplied, supply schedule and supply curve, movement along and shift in a supply curve.
3. Identify supply shifters and determine whether a change in a supply shifter causes the supply curve to shift to the right or to the left.

What determines the quantity of a good or service sellers are willing to offer for sale? Price is one factor; ceteris paribus, a higher price is likely to induce sellers to offer a greater quantity of a good or service. Production cost is another determinant of supply. Variables that affect production cost include the prices of factors used to produce the good or service, returns from alternative activities, technology, the expectations of sellers, and natural events such as weather changes. Still another factor affecting the quantity of a good that will be offered for sale is the number of sellers—the greater the number of sellers of a particular good or service, the greater will be the quantity offered at any price per time period.

2.1 Price and the Supply Curve

The **quantity supplied** of a good or service is the quantity sellers are willing to sell at a particular price during a particular period, all other things unchanged. Ceteris paribus, the receipt of a higher price increases profits and induces sellers to increase the quantity they supply.

In general, when there are many sellers of a good, an increase in price results in an increase in quantity supplied, and this relationship is often referred to as the law of supply. We will see, though, through our exploration of microeconomics, that there are a number of exceptions to this relationship. There are cases in which a higher price will not induce an increase in quantity supplied. Goods that cannot be produced, such as additional land on the corner of Park Avenue and 56th Street in Manhattan, are fixed in supply—a higher price cannot induce an increase in the quantity supplied. There are

quantity supplied

The quantity sellers are willing to sell of a good or service at a particular price during a particular period, all other things unchanged.

even cases, which we investigate in microeconomic analysis, in which a higher price induces a reduction in the quantity supplied.

Generally speaking, however, when there are many sellers of a good, an increase in price results in a greater quantity supplied. The relationship between price and quantity supplied is suggested in a **supply schedule**, a table that shows quantities supplied at different prices during a particular period, all other things unchanged. Figure 3.4 gives a supply schedule for the quantities of coffee that will be supplied per month at various prices, ceteris paribus. At a price of $4 per pound, for example, producers are willing to supply 15 million pounds of coffee per month. A higher price, say $6 per pound, induces sellers to supply a greater quantity—25 million pounds of coffee per month.

supply schedule

A table that shows quantities supplied at different prices during a particular period, all other things unchanged.

FIGURE 3.4 A Supply Schedule and a Supply Curve

The supply schedule shows the quantity of coffee that will be supplied in the United States each month at particular prices, all other things unchanged. The same information is given graphically in the supply curve. The values given here suggest a positive relationship between price and quantity supplied.

Price per pound ($)	4	5	6	7	8	9
Quantity supplied per month (millions of pounds)	15	20	25	30	35	40

supply curve

A graphical representation of a supply schedule.

A **supply curve** is a graphical representation of a supply schedule. It shows the relationship between price and quantity supplied during a particular period, all other things unchanged. Because the relationship between price and quantity supplied is generally positive, supply curves are generally upward sloping. The supply curve for coffee in Figure 3.4 shows graphically the values given in the supply schedule.

change in quantity supplied

Movement along the supply curve caused by a change in price.

A change in price causes a movement *along* the supply curve; such a movement is called a **change in quantity supplied**. As is the case with a change in quantity demanded, a change in quantity supplied does not shift the supply curve. By definition, it is a movement along the supply curve. For example, if the price rises from $6 per pound to $7 per pound, the quantity supplied rises from 25 million pounds per month to 30 million pounds per month. That's a movement from point A to point B along the supply curve in Figure 3.4.

2.2 Changes in Supply

change in supply

A shift in the supply curve.

When we draw a supply curve, we assume that other variables that affect the willingness of sellers to supply a good or service are unchanged. It follows that a change in any of those variables will cause a **change in supply**, which is a shift in the supply curve. A change that increases the quantity of a good or service supplied at each price shifts the supply curve to the right. Suppose, for example, that the price of fertilizer falls. That will reduce the cost of producing coffee and thus increase the quantity of coffee producers will offer for sale at each price. The supply schedule in Figure 3.5 shows an increase in the quantity of coffee supplied at each price. We show that increase graphically as a shift in the supply curve from S_1 to S_2. We see that the quantity supplied at each price increases by 10 million pounds of coffee per month. At point A on the original supply curve S_1, for example, 25 million pounds of coffee per month are supplied at a price of $6 per pound. After the increase in supply, 35 million pounds per month are supplied at the same price (point A' on curve S_2).

FIGURE 3.5 An Increase in Supply

If there is a change in supply that increases the quantity supplied at each price, as is the case in the supply schedule here, the supply curve shifts to the right. At a price of $6 per pound, for example, the quantity supplied rises from the previous level of 25 million pounds per month on supply curve S_1 (point A) to 35 million pounds per month on supply curve S_2 (point A').

Price	Old quantity supplied	New quantity supplied
$4	15	25
5	20	30
6	25	35
7	30	40
8	35	45
9	40	50

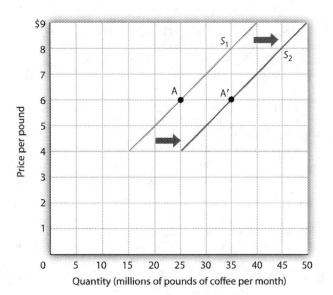

An event that reduces the quantity supplied at each price shifts the supply curve to the left. An increase in production costs and excessive rain that reduces the yields from coffee plants are examples of events that might reduce supply. Figure 3.6 shows a reduction in the supply of coffee. We see in the supply schedule that the quantity of coffee supplied falls by 10 million pounds of coffee per month at each price. The supply curve thus shifts from S_1 to S_3.

FIGURE 3.6 A Reduction in Supply

A change in supply that reduces the quantity supplied at each price shifts the supply curve to the left. At a price of $6 per pound, for example, the original quantity supplied was 25 million pounds of coffee per month (point A). With a new supply curve S_3, the quantity supplied at that price falls to 15 million pounds of coffee per month (point A").

Price	Old quantity supplied	New quantity supplied
$4	15	5
5	20	10
6	25	15
7	30	20
8	35	25
9	40	30

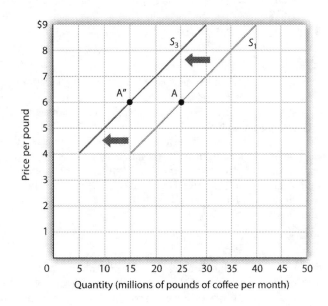

supply shifter

A variable that can change
the quantity of a good or
service supplied at each price.

A variable that can change the quantity of a good or service supplied at each price is called a **supply shifter**. Supply shifters include (1) prices of factors of production, (2) returns from alternative activities, (3) technology, (4) seller expectations, (5) natural events, and (6) the number of sellers. When these other variables change, the all-other-things-unchanged conditions behind the original supply curve no longer hold. Let us look at each of the supply shifters.

Prices of Factors of Production

A change in the price of labor or some other factor of production will change the cost of producing any given quantity of the good or service. This change in the cost of production will change the quantity that suppliers are willing to offer at any price. An increase in factor prices should decrease the quantity suppliers will offer at any price, shifting the supply curve to the left. A reduction in factor prices increases the quantity suppliers will offer at any price, shifting the supply curve to the right.

Suppose coffee growers must pay a higher wage to the workers they hire to harvest coffee or must pay more for fertilizer. Such increases in production cost will cause them to produce a smaller quantity at each price, shifting the supply curve for coffee to the left. A reduction in any of these costs increases supply, shifting the supply curve to the right.

Returns from Alternative Activities

To produce one good or service means forgoing the production of another. The concept of opportunity cost in economics suggests that the value of the activity forgone is the opportunity cost of the activity chosen; this cost should affect supply. For example, one opportunity cost of producing eggs is not selling chickens. An increase in the price people are willing to pay for fresh chicken would make it more profitable to sell chickens and would thus increase the opportunity cost of producing eggs. It would shift the supply curve for eggs to the left, reflecting a decrease in supply.

Technology

A change in technology alters the combinations of inputs or the types of inputs required in the production process. An improvement in technology usually means that fewer and/or less costly inputs are needed. If the cost of production is lower, the profits available at a given price will increase, and producers will produce more. With more produced at every price, the supply curve will shift to the right, meaning an increase in supply.

Impressive technological changes have occurred in the computer industry in recent years. Computers are much smaller and are far more powerful than they were only a few years ago—and they are much cheaper to produce. The result has been a huge increase in the supply of computers, shifting the supply curve to the right.

While we usually think of technology as enhancing production, declines in production due to problems in technology are also possible. Outlawing the use of certain equipment without pollution-control devices has increased the cost of production for many goods and services, thereby reducing profits available at any price and shifting these supply curves to the left.

Seller Expectations

All supply curves are based in part on seller expectations about future market conditions. Many decisions about production and selling are typically made long before a product is ready for sale. Those decisions necessarily depend on expectations. Changes in seller expectations can have important effects on price and quantity.

Consider, for example, the owners of oil deposits. Oil pumped out of the ground and used today will be unavailable in the future. If a change in the international political climate leads many owners to expect that oil prices will rise in the future, they may decide to leave their oil in the ground, planning to sell it later when the price is higher. Thus, there will be a decrease in supply; the supply curve for oil will shift to the left.

Natural Events

Storms, insect infestations, and drought affect agricultural production and thus the supply of agricultural goods. If something destroys a substantial part of an agricultural crop, the supply curve will shift to the left. The terrible cyclone that killed more than 50,000 people in Myanmar in 2008 also destroyed some of the country's prime rice growing land. That shifted the supply curve for rice to the left. If there is an unusually good harvest, the supply curve will shift to the right.

The Number of Sellers

The supply curve for an industry, such as coffee, includes all the sellers in the industry. A change in the number of sellers in an industry changes the quantity available at each price and thus changes supply. An increase in the number of sellers supplying a good or service shifts the supply curve to the right; a reduction in the number of sellers shifts the supply curve to the left.

The market for cellular phone service has been affected by an increase in the number of firms offering the service. Over the past decade, new cellular phone companies emerged, shifting the supply curve for cellular phone service to the right.

Heads Up!

There are two special things to note about supply curves. The first is similar to the Heads Up! on demand curves: it is important to distinguish carefully between changes in supply and changes in quantity supplied. A change in supply results from a change in a supply shifter and implies a shift of the supply curve to the right or left. A change in price produces a change in quantity supplied and induces a movement along the supply curve. A change in price does not shift the supply curve.

The second caution relates to the interpretation of increases and decreases in supply. Notice that in Figure 3.5 an increase in supply is shown as a shift of the supply curve to the right; the curve shifts in the direction of increasing quantity with respect to the horizontal axis. In Figure 3.6 a reduction in supply is shown as a shift of the supply curve to the left; the curve shifts in the direction of decreasing quantity with respect to the horizontal axis.

Because the supply curve is upward sloping, a shift to the right produces a new curve that in a sense lies "below" the original curve. It is easy to make the mistake of thinking of such a shift as a shift "down" and therefore as a reduction in supply. Similarly, it is easy to make the mistake of showing an increase in supply with a new curve that lies "above" the original curve. But that is a reduction in supply!

To avoid such errors, focus on the fact that an increase in supply is an increase in the quantity supplied at each price and shifts the supply curve in the direction of increased quantity on the horizontal axis. Similarly, a reduction in supply is a reduction in the quantity supplied at each price and shifts the supply curve in the direction of a lower quantity on the horizontal axis.

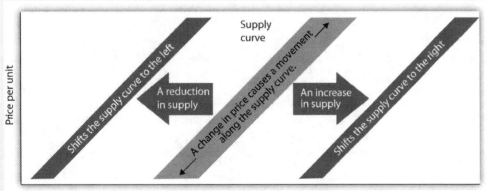

KEY TAKEAWAYS

- The quantity supplied of a good or service is the quantity sellers are willing to sell at a particular price during a particular period, all other things unchanged.
- A supply schedule shows the quantities supplied at different prices during a particular period, all other things unchanged. A supply curve shows this same information graphically.
- A change in the price of a good or service causes a change in the quantity supplied—a movement *along* the supply curve.
- A change in a supply shifter causes a change in supply, which is shown as a *shift* of the supply curve. Supply shifters include prices of factors of production, returns from alternative activities, technology, seller expectations, natural events, and the number of sellers.
- An increase in supply is shown as a shift to the right of a supply curve; a decrease in supply is shown as a shift to the left.

If all other things are unchanged, what happens to the supply curve for DVD rentals if there is (a) an increase in wages paid to DVD rental store clerks, (b) an increase in the price of DVD rentals, or (c) an increase in the number of DVD rental stores? Draw a graph that shows what happens to the supply curve in each circumstance. The supply curve can shift to the left or to the right, or stay where it is. Remember to label the axes and curves, and remember to specify the time period (e.g., "DVDs rented per week").

Case in Point

The Monks of St. Benedict's Get Out of the Egg Business

© 2010 Jupiterimages Corporation

It was cookies that lured the monks of St. Benedict's out of the egg business, and now private retreat sponsorship is luring them away from cookies.

St. Benedict's is a Benedictine monastery, nestled on a ranch high in the Colorado Rockies, about 20 miles down the road from Aspen. The monastery's 20 monks operate the ranch to support themselves and to provide help for poor people in the area. They lease out about 3,500 acres of their land to cattle and sheep grazers, produce cookies, and sponsor private retreats. They used to produce eggs.

Attracted by potential profits and the peaceful nature of the work, the monks went into the egg business in 1967. They had 10,000 chickens producing their Monastery Eggs brand. For a while, business was good. Very good. Then, in the late 1970s, the price of chicken feed started to rise rapidly.

"When we started in the business, we were paying $60 to $80 a ton for feed—delivered," recalls the monastery's abbot, Father Joseph Boyle. "By the late 1970s, our cost had more than doubled. We were paying $160 to $200 a ton. That really hurt, because feed represents a large part of the cost of producing eggs."

The monks adjusted to the blow. "When grain prices were lower, we'd pull a hen off for a few weeks to molt, then return her to laying. After grain prices went up, it was 12 months of laying and into the soup pot," Fr. Joseph says.

Grain prices continued to rise in the 1980s and increased the costs of production for all egg producers. It caused the supply of eggs to fall. Demand fell at the same time, as Americans worried about the cholesterol in eggs. Times got tougher in the egg business.

"We were still making money in the financial sense," Fr. Joseph says. "But we tried an experiment in 1985 producing cookies, and it was a success. We finally decided that devoting our time and energy to the cookies would pay off better than the egg business, so we quit the egg business in 1986."

The mail-order cookie business was good to the monks. They sold 200,000 ounces of Monastery Cookies in 1987.

By 1998, however, they had limited their production of cookies, selling only locally and to gift shops. Since 2000, they have switched to "providing private retreats for individuals and groups—about 40 people per month," according to Fr. Micah Schonberger.

The monks' calculation of their opportunity costs revealed that they would earn a higher return through sponsorship of private retreats than in either cookies or eggs. This projection has proved correct.

And there is another advantage as well.

"The chickens didn't stop laying eggs on Sunday," Fr. Joseph chuckles. "When we shifted to cookies we could take Sundays off. We weren't hemmed in the way we were with the chickens." The move to providing retreats is even better in this regard. Since guests provide their own meals, most of the monastery's effort goes into planning and scheduling, which frees up even more of their time for other worldly as well as spiritual pursuits.

Source: Personal interviews and the monastery's website at http://www.snowmass.org.

ANSWER TO TRY IT! PROBLEM

DVD rental store clerks are a factor of production in the DVD rental market. An increase in their wages raises the cost of production, thereby causing the supply curve of DVD rentals to shift to the left [Panel (a)]. (*Caution:* It is possible that you thought of the wage increase as an increase in income, a demand shifter, that would lead to an increase in demand, but this would be incorrect. The question refers only to wages of DVD rental store clerks. They may rent some DVD, but their impact on total demand would be negligible. Besides, we have no information on what has happened overall to incomes of people who rent DVDs. We do know, however, that the cost of a factor of production, which is a supply shifter, increased.)

An increase in the price of DVD rentals does not shift the supply curve at all; rather, it corresponds to a movement upward to the right along the supply curve. At a higher price of P_2 instead of P_1, a greater quantity of DVD rentals, say Q_2 instead of Q_1, will be supplied [Panel (b)].

An increase in the number of stores renting DVDs will cause the supply curve to shift to the right [Panel (c)].

3.   DEMAND, SUPPLY, AND EQUILIBRIUM

LEARNING OBJECTIVES

1. **Use demand and supply to explain how equilibrium price and quantity are determined in a market.**
2. **Understand the concepts of surpluses and shortages and the pressures on price they generate.**
3. **Explain the impact of a change in demand or supply on equilibrium price and quantity.**

In this section we combine the demand and supply curves we have just studied into a new model. The **model of demand and supply** uses demand and supply curves to explain the determination of price and quantity in a market.

model of demand and supply

Model that uses demand and supply curves to explain the determination of price and quantity in a market.

3.1   The Determination of Price and Quantity

The logic of the model of demand and supply is simple. The demand curve shows the quantities of a particular good or service that buyers will be willing and able to purchase at each price during a specified period. The supply curve shows the quantities that sellers will offer for sale at each price during that same period. By putting the two curves together, we should be able to find a price at which the quantity buyers are willing and able to purchase equals the quantity sellers will offer for sale.

Figure 3.7 combines the demand and supply data introduced in Figure 3.1 and Figure 3.4 Notice that the two curves intersect at a price of $6 per pound—at this price the quantities demanded and supplied are equal. Buyers want to purchase, and sellers are willing to offer for sale, 25 million pounds of coffee per month. The market for coffee is in equilibrium. Unless the demand or supply curve shifts, there will be no tendency for price to change. The **equilibrium price** in any market is the price at which quantity demanded equals quantity supplied. The equilibrium price in the market for coffee is thus $6 per pound. The **equilibrium quantity** is the quantity demanded and supplied at the equilibrium price. At a price above the equilibrium, there is a natural tendency for the price to fall. At a price below the equilibrium, there is a tendency for the price to rise.

With an upward-sloping supply curve and a downward-sloping demand curve, there is only a single price at which the two curves intersect. This means there is only one price at which equilibrium is achieved. It follows that at any price other than the equilibrium price, the market will not be in equilibrium. We next examine what happens at prices other than the equilibrium price.

equilibrium price

The price at which quantity demanded equals quantity supplied.

equilibrium quantity

The quantity demanded and supplied at the equilibrium price.

FIGURE 3.7 The Determination of Equilibrium Price and Quantity

When we combine the demand and supply curves for a good in a single graph, the point at which they intersect identifies the equilibrium price and equilibrium quantity. Here, the equilibrium price is $6 per pound. Consumers demand, and suppliers supply, 25 million pounds of coffee per month at this price.

Surpluses

Figure 3.8 shows the same demand and supply curves we have just examined, but this time the initial price is $8 per pound of coffee. Because we no longer have a balance between quantity demanded and quantity supplied, this price is not the equilibrium price. At a price of $8, we read over to the demand curve to determine the quantity of coffee consumers will be willing to buy—15 million pounds per month. The supply curve tells us what sellers will offer for sale—35 million pounds per month. The difference, 20 million pounds of coffee per month, is called a surplus. More generally, a **surplus** is the amount by which the quantity supplied exceeds the quantity demanded at the current price. There is, of course, no surplus at the equilibrium price; a surplus occurs only if the current price exceeds the equilibrium price.

A surplus in the market for coffee will not last long. With unsold coffee on the market, sellers will begin to reduce their prices to clear out unsold coffee. As the price of coffee begins to fall, the quantity of coffee supplied begins to decline. At the same time, the quantity of coffee demanded begins to rise. Remember that the reduction in quantity supplied is a movement *along* the supply curve—the curve itself does not shift in response to a reduction in price. Similarly, the increase in quantity demanded is a movement *along* the demand curve—the demand curve does not shift in response to a reduction in price. Price will continue to fall until it reaches its equilibrium level, at which the demand and supply curves intersect. At that point, there will be no tendency for price to fall further. In general, surpluses in the marketplace are short-lived. The prices of most goods and services adjust quickly, eliminating the surplus. Later on, we will discuss some markets in which adjustment of price to equilibrium may occur only very slowly or not at all.

surplus

The amount by which the quantity supplied exceeds the quantity demanded at the current price.

FIGURE 3.8 A Surplus in the Market for Coffee

At a price of $8, the quantity supplied is 35 million pounds of coffee per month and the quantity demanded is 15 million pounds per month; there is a surplus of 20 million pounds of coffee per month. Given a surplus, the price will fall quickly toward the equilibrium level of $6.

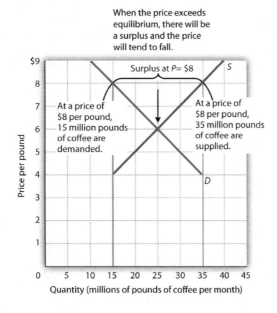

Shortages

Just as a price above the equilibrium price will cause a surplus, a price below equilibrium will cause a shortage. A **shortage** is the amount by which the quantity demanded exceeds the quantity supplied at the current price.

Figure 3.9 shows a shortage in the market for coffee. Suppose the price is $4 per pound. At that price, 15 million pounds of coffee would be supplied per month, and 35 million pounds would be demanded per month. When more coffee is demanded than supplied, there is a shortage.

shortage

The amount by which the quantity demanded exceeds the quantity supplied at the current price.

FIGURE 3.9 A Shortage in the Market for Coffee

At a price of $4 per pound, the quantity of coffee demanded is 35 million pounds per month and the quantity supplied is 15 million pounds per month. The result is a shortage of 20 million pounds of coffee per month.

In the face of a shortage, sellers are likely to begin to raise their prices. As the price rises, there will be an increase in the quantity supplied (but not a change in supply) and a reduction in the quantity demanded (but not a change in demand) until the equilibrium price is achieved.

3.2 Shifts in Demand and Supply

A change in one of the variables (shifters) held constant in any model of demand and supply will create a change in demand or supply. A shift in a demand or supply curve changes the equilibrium price and equilibrium quantity for a good or service. Figure 3.10 combines the information about changes in the demand and supply of coffee presented in Figure 3.2, Figure 3.3, Figure 3.5, and Figure 3.6 In each case, the original equilibrium price is $6 per pound, and the corresponding equilibrium quantity is 25 million pounds of coffee per month. Figure 3.10 shows what happens with an increase in demand, a reduction in demand, an increase in supply, and a reduction in supply. We then look at what happens if both curves shift simultaneously. Each of these possibilities is discussed in turn below.

FIGURE 3.10 Changes in Demand and Supply

A change in demand or in supply changes the equilibrium solution in the model. Panels (a) and (b) show an increase and a decrease in demand, respectively; Panels (c) and (d) show an increase and a decrease in supply, respectively.

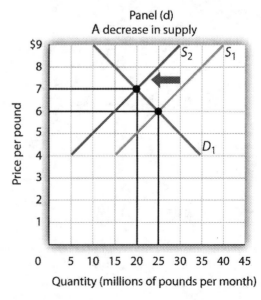

An Increase in Demand

An increase in demand for coffee shifts the demand curve to the right, as shown in Panel (a) of Figure 3.10. The equilibrium price rises to $7 per pound. As the price rises to the new equilibrium level, the quantity supplied increases to 30 million pounds of coffee per month. Notice that the supply curve does not shift; rather, there is a movement along the supply curve.

Demand shifters that could cause an increase in demand include a shift in preferences that leads to greater coffee consumption; a lower price for a complement to coffee, such as donuts; a higher price for a substitute for coffee, such as tea; an increase in income; and an increase in population. A change in buyer expectations, perhaps due to predictions of bad weather lowering expected yields on coffee plants and increasing future coffee prices, could also increase current demand.

A Decrease in Demand

Panel (b) of Figure 3.10 shows that a decrease in demand shifts the demand curve to the left. The equilibrium price falls to $5 per pound. As the price falls to the new equilibrium level, the quantity supplied decreases to 20 million pounds of coffee per month.

Demand shifters that could reduce the demand for coffee include a shift in preferences that makes people want to consume less coffee; an increase in the price of a complement, such as donuts; a reduction in the price of a substitute, such as tea; a reduction in income; a reduction in population; and a change in buyer expectations that leads people to expect lower prices for coffee in the future.

An Increase in Supply

An increase in the supply of coffee shifts the supply curve to the right, as shown in Panel (c) of Figure 3.10. The equilibrium price falls to $5 per pound. As the price falls to the new equilibrium level, the quantity of coffee demanded increases to 30 million pounds of coffee per month. Notice that the demand curve does not shift; rather, there is movement along the demand curve.

Possible supply shifters that could increase supply include a reduction in the price of an input such as labor, a decline in the returns available from alternative uses of the inputs that produce coffee, an improvement in the technology of coffee production, good weather, and an increase in the number of coffee-producing firms.

A Decrease in Supply

Panel (d) of Figure 3.10 shows that a decrease in supply shifts the supply curve to the left. The equilibrium price rises to $7 per pound. As the price rises to the new equilibrium level, the quantity demanded decreases to 20 million pounds of coffee per month.

Possible supply shifters that could reduce supply include an increase in the prices of inputs used in the production of coffee, an increase in the returns available from alternative uses of these inputs, a decline in production because of problems in technology (perhaps caused by a restriction on pesticides used to protect coffee beans), a reduction in the number of coffee-producing firms, or a natural event, such as excessive rain.

Heads Up!

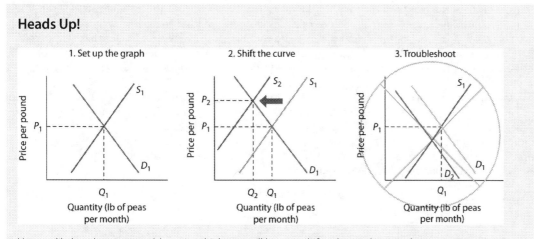

You are likely to be given problems in which you will have to shift a demand or supply curve.

Suppose you are told that an invasion of pod-crunching insects has gobbled up half the crop of fresh peas, and you are asked to use demand and supply analysis to predict what will happen to the price and quantity of peas demanded and supplied. Here are some suggestions.

Put the quantity of the good you are asked to analyze on the horizontal axis and its price on the vertical axis. Draw a downward-sloping line for demand and an upward-sloping line for supply. The initial equilibrium price is determined by the intersection of the two curves. Label the equilibrium solution. You may find it helpful to use a number for the equilibrium price instead of the letter "P." Pick a price that seems plausible, say, 79¢ per pound. Do not worry about the precise positions of the demand and supply curves; you cannot be expected to know what they are.

Step 2 can be the most difficult step; the problem is to decide which curve to shift. The key is to remember the difference between a change in demand or supply and a change in quantity demanded or supplied. At each price, ask yourself whether the given event would change the quantity demanded. Would the fact that a bug has attacked the pea crop change the quantity demanded at a price of, say, 79¢ per pound? Clearly not; none of the demand shifters have changed. The event would, however, reduce the quantity supplied at this price, and the supply curve would shift to the left. There is a change in supply and a reduction in the quantity demanded. There is no change in demand.

Next check to see whether the result you have obtained makes sense. The graph in Step 2 makes sense; it shows price rising and quantity demanded falling.

It is easy to make a mistake such as the one shown in the third figure of this Heads Up! One might, for example, reason that when fewer peas are available, fewer will be demanded, and therefore the demand curve will shift to the left. This suggests the price of peas will fall—but that does not make sense. If only half as many fresh peas were available, their price would surely rise. The error here lies in confusing a change in quantity demanded with a change in demand. Yes, buyers will end up buying fewer peas. But no, they will not demand fewer peas at each price than before; the demand curve does not shift.

Simultaneous Shifts

As we have seen, when *either* the demand or the supply curve shifts, the results are unambiguous; that is, we know what will happen to both equilibrium price and equilibrium quantity, so long as we know whether demand or supply increased or decreased. However, in practice, several events may occur at around the same time that cause *both* the demand and supply curves to shift. To figure out what happens to equilibrium price and equilibrium quantity, we must know not only in which direction the demand and supply curves have shifted but also the relative amount by which each curve shifts. Of course, the demand and supply curves could shift in the same direction or in opposite directions, depending on the specific events causing them to shift.

For example, all three panels of Figure 3.11 show a decrease in demand for coffee (caused perhaps by a decrease in the price of a substitute good, such as tea) and a simultaneous decrease in the supply of coffee (caused perhaps by bad weather). Since reductions in demand and supply, considered separately, each cause the equilibrium quantity to fall, the impact of both curves shifting simultaneously to the left means that the new equilibrium quantity of coffee is less than the old equilibrium quantity. The effect on the equilibrium price, though, is ambiguous. Whether the equilibrium price is higher, lower, or unchanged depends on the extent to which each curve shifts.

If the demand curve shifts farther to the left than does the supply curve, as shown in Panel (a) of Figure 3.11, then the equilibrium price will be lower than it was before the curves shifted. In this case the new equilibrium price falls from $6 per pound to $5 per pound. If the shift to the left of the supply curve is greater than that of the demand curve, the equilibrium price will be higher than it was before, as shown in Panel (b). In this case, the new equilibrium price rises to $7 per pound. In Panel (c), since both curves shift to the left by the same amount, equilibrium price does not change; it remains $6 per pound.

Regardless of the scenario, changes in equilibrium price and equilibrium quantity resulting from two different events need to be considered separately. If both events cause equilibrium price or quantity to move in the same direction, then clearly price or quantity can be expected to move in that direction. If one event causes price or quantity to rise while the other causes it to fall, the extent by which each curve shifts is critical to figuring out what happens. Figure 3.12 summarizes what may happen to equilibrium price and quantity when demand and supply both shift.

FIGURE 3.11 Simultaneous Decreases in Demand and Supply

Both the demand and the supply of coffee decrease. Since decreases in demand and supply, considered separately, each cause equilibrium quantity to fall, the impact of both decreasing simultaneously means that a new equilibrium quantity of coffee must be less than the old equilibrium quantity. In Panel (a), the demand curve shifts farther to the left than does the supply curve, so equilibrium price falls. In Panel (b), the supply curve shifts farther to the left than does the demand curve, so the equilibrium price rises. In Panel (c), both curves shift to the left by the same amount, so equilibrium price stays the same.

As demand and supply curves shift, prices adjust to maintain a balance between the quantity of a good demanded and the quantity supplied. If prices did not adjust, this balance could not be maintained.

Notice that the demand and supply curves that we have examined in this chapter have all been drawn as linear. This simplification of the real world makes the graphs a bit easier to read without sacrificing the essential point: whether the curves are linear or nonlinear, demand curves are downward sloping and supply curves are generally upward sloping. As circumstances that shift the demand curve or the supply curve change, we can analyze what will happen to price and what will happen to quantity.

FIGURE 3.12 Simultaneous Shifts in Demand and Supply

If simultaneous shifts in demand and supply cause equilibrium price or quantity to move in the same direction, then equilibrium price or quantity clearly moves in that direction. If the shift in one of the curves causes equilibrium price or quantity to rise while the shift in the other curve causes equilibrium price or quantity to fall, then the relative amount by which each curve shifts is critical to figuring out what happens to that variable.

KEY TAKEAWAYS

- The equilibrium price is the price at which the quantity demanded equals the quantity supplied. It is determined by the intersection of the demand and supply curves.
- A surplus exists if the quantity of a good or service supplied exceeds the quantity demanded at the current price; it causes downward pressure on price. A shortage exists if the quantity of a good or service demanded exceeds the quantity supplied at the current price; it causes upward pressure on price.
- An increase in demand, all other things unchanged, will cause the equilibrium price to rise; quantity supplied will increase. A decrease in demand will cause the equilibrium price to fall; quantity supplied will decrease.
- An increase in supply, all other things unchanged, will cause the equilibrium price to fall; quantity demanded will increase. A decrease in supply will cause the equilibrium price to rise; quantity demanded will decrease.
- To determine what happens to equilibrium price and equilibrium quantity when both the supply and demand curves shift, you must know in which direction each of the curves shifts and the extent to which each curve shifts.

TRY IT!

What happens to the equilibrium price and the equilibrium quantity of DVD rentals if the price of movie theater tickets increases and wages paid to DVD rental store clerks increase, all other things unchanged? Be sure to show all possible scenarios, as was done in Figure 3.11. Again, you do not need actual numbers to arrive at an answer. Just focus on the general position of the curve(s) before and after the events occurred.

Case in Point

Demand, Supply, and Obesity

© 2010 Jupiterimages Corporation

Why are so many Americans fat? Put so crudely, the question may seem rude, but, indeed, the number of obese Americans has increased by more than 50% over the last generation, and obesity may now be the nation's number one health problem. According to Sturm Roland in a recent RAND Corporation study, "Obesity appears to have a stronger association with the occurrence of chronic medical conditions, reduced physical health-related quality of life and increased health care and medication expenditures than smoking or problem drinking."

Many explanations of rising obesity suggest higher demand for food. What more apt picture of our sedentary life style is there than spending the afternoon watching a ballgame on TV, while eating chips and salsa, followed by a dinner of a lavishly topped, take-out pizza? Higher income has also undoubtedly contributed to a rightward shift in the demand curve for food. Plus, any additional food intake translates into more weight increase because we spend so few calories preparing it, either directly or in the process of earning the income to buy it. A study by economists Darius Lakdawalla and Tomas Philipson suggests that about 60% of the recent growth in weight may be explained in this way—that is, demand has shifted to the right, leading to an increase in the equilibrium quantity of food consumed and, given our less strenuous life styles, even more weight gain than can be explained simply by the increased amount we are eating.

What accounts for the remaining 40% of the weight gain? Lakdawalla and Philipson further reason that a rightward shift in demand would by itself lead to an increase in the quantity of food as well as an increase in the price of food. The problem they have with this explanation is that over the post–World War II period, the relative price of food has declined by an average of 0.2 percentage points per year. They explain the fall in the price of food by arguing that agricultural innovation has led to a substantial rightward shift in the supply curve of food. As shown, lower food prices and a higher equilibrium quantity of food have resulted from simultaneous rightward shifts in demand and supply and that the rightward shift in the supply of food from S_1 to S_2 has been substantially larger than the rightward shift in the demand curve from D_1 to D_2.

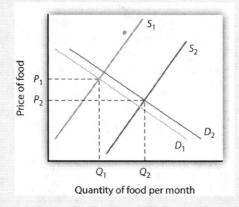

Sources: Roland, Sturm, "The Effects of Obesity, Smoking, and Problem Drinking on Chronic Medical Problems and Health Care Costs," Health Affairs, 2002; 21(2): 245–253. Lakdawalla, Darius and Tomas Philipson, "The Growth of Obesity and Technological Change: A Theoretical and Empirical Examination," National Bureau of Economic Research Working Paper no. w8946, May 2002.

An increase in the price of movie theater tickets (a substitute for DVD rentals) will cause the demand curve for DVD rentals to shift to the right. An increase in the wages paid to DVD rental store clerks (an increase in the cost of a factor of production) shifts the supply curve to the left. Each event taken separately causes equilibrium price to rise. Whether equilibrium quantity will be higher or lower depends on which curve shifted more.

If the demand curve shifted more, then the equilibrium quantity of DVD rentals will rise [Panel (a)].

If the supply curve shifted more, then the equilibrium quantity of DVD rentals will fall [Panel (b)].

If the curves shifted by the same amount, then the equilibrium quantity of DVD rentals would not change [Panel (c)].

Panel (a)

Panel (b)

Panel (c)

4. GOVERNMENT INTERVENTION IN MARKET PRICES: PRICE FLOORS AND PRICE CEILINGS

L E A R N I N G   O B J E C T I V E S

1. **Use the model of demand and supply to explain what happens when the government imposes price floors or price ceilings.**
2. **Discuss the reasons why governments sometimes choose to control prices and the consequences of price control policies.**

So far in this chapter, we have learned that markets tend to move toward their equilibrium prices and quantities. Surpluses and shortages of goods are short-lived as prices adjust to equate quantity demanded with quantity supplied.

In some markets, however, governments have been called on by groups of citizens to intervene to keep prices of certain items higher or lower than what would result from the market finding its own equilibrium price. In this section we will examine agricultural markets and apartment rental markets—two markets that have often been subject to price controls. Through these examples, we will identify the effects of controlling prices. In each case, we will look at reasons why governments have chosen to control prices in these markets and the consequences of these policies.

4.1 Agricultural Price Floors

Governments often seek to assist farmers by setting price floors in agricultural markets. A minimum allowable price set above the equilibrium price is a **price floor**. With a price floor, the government forbids a price below the minimum. (Notice that, if the price floor were for whatever reason set below the equilibrium price, it would be irrelevant to the determination of the price in the market since nothing would prohibit the price from rising to equilibrium.) A price floor that is set above the equilibrium price creates a surplus.

Figure 3.13 shows the market for wheat. Suppose the government sets the price of wheat at P_F. Notice that P_F is above the equilibrium price of P_E. At P_F, we read over to the demand curve to find that the quantity of wheat that buyers will be willing and able to purchase is W_1 bushels. Reading over to the supply curve, we find that sellers will offer W_2 bushels of wheat at the price floor of P_F. Because P_F is above the equilibrium price, there is a surplus of wheat equal to $(W_2 - W_1)$ bushels. The surplus persists because the government does not allow the price to fall.

Why have many governments around the world set price floors in agricultural markets? Farming has changed dramatically over the past two centuries. Technological improvements in the form of new equipment, fertilizers, pesticides, and new varieties of crops have led to dramatic increases in crop output per acre. Worldwide production capacity has expanded markedly. As we have learned, technological improvements cause the supply curve to shift to the right, reducing the price of food. While such price reductions have been celebrated in computer markets, farmers have successfully lobbied for government programs aimed at keeping their prices from falling.

While the supply curve for agricultural goods has shifted to the right, the demand has increased with rising population and with rising income. But as incomes rise, people spend a smaller and smaller fraction of their incomes on food. While the demand for food has increased, that increase has not been nearly as great as the increase in supply. Figure 3.14 shows that the supply curve has shifted much farther to the right, from S_1 to S_2, than the demand curve has, from D_1 to D_2. As a result, equilibrium quantity has risen dramatically, from Q_1 to Q_2, and equilibrium price has fallen, from P_1 to P_2.

On top of this long-term historical trend in agriculture, agricultural prices are subject to wide swings over shorter periods. Droughts or freezes can sharply reduce supplies of particular crops, causing sudden increases in prices. Demand for agricultural goods of one country can suddenly dry up if the government of another country imposes trade restrictions against its products, and prices can fall. Such dramatic shifts in prices and quantities make incomes of farmers unstable.

The Great Depression of the 1930s led to a major federal role in agriculture. The Depression affected the entire economy, but it hit farmers particularly hard. Prices received by farmers plunged nearly two-thirds from 1930 to 1933. Many farmers had a tough time keeping up mortgage payments. By 1932, more than half of all farm loans were in default.

Farm legislation passed during the Great Depression has been modified many times, but the federal government has continued its direct involvement in agricultural markets. This has meant a variety of government programs that guarantee a minimum price for some types of agricultural products. These programs have been accompanied by government purchases of any surplus, by requirements to restrict acreage in order to limit those surpluses, by crop or production restrictions, and the like.

To see how such policies work, look back at Figure 3.13. At P_F, W_2 bushels of wheat will be supplied. With that much wheat on the market, there is market pressure on the price of wheat to fall. To prevent price from falling, the government buys the surplus of $(W_2 - W_1)$ bushels of wheat, so that only W_1 bushels are actually available to private consumers for purchase on the market. The government can store the surpluses or find special uses for them. For example, surpluses generated in the United States have been shipped to developing countries as grants-in-aid or distributed to local school lunch programs. As a variation on this program, the government can require farmers who want to participate in the price support program to reduce acreage in order to limit the size of the surpluses.

After 1973, the government stopped buying the surpluses (with some exceptions) and simply guaranteed farmers a "target price." If the average market price for a crop fell below the crop's target price, the government paid the difference. If, for example, a crop had a market price of $3 per unit and a target price of $4 per unit, the government would give farmers a payment of $1 for each unit sold. Farmers would thus receive the market price of $3 plus a government payment of $1 per unit. For farmers to receive these payments, they had to agree

price floor

A minimum allowable price set above the equilibrium price.

FIGURE 3.13 Price Floors in Wheat Markets

A price floor for wheat creates a surplus of wheat equal to $(W_2 - W_1)$ bushels.

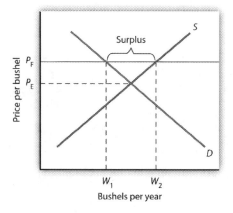

FIGURE 3.14 Supply and Demand Shifts for Agricultural Products

A relatively large increase in the supply of agricultural products, accompanied by a relatively small increase in demand, has reduced the price received by farmers and increased the quantity of agricultural goods.

to remove acres from production and to comply with certain conservation provisions. These restrictions sought to reduce the size of the surplus generated by the target price, which acted as a kind of price floor.

What are the effects of such farm support programs? The intention is to boost and stabilize farm incomes. But, with price floors, consumers pay more for food than they would otherwise, and governments spend heavily to finance the programs. With the target price approach, consumers pay less, but government financing of the program continues. U.S. federal spending for agriculture averaged well over $22 billion per year between 2003 and 2007, roughly $70 per person.

Help to farmers has sometimes been justified on the grounds that it boosts incomes of "small" farmers. However, since farm aid has generally been allotted on the basis of how much farms produce rather than on a per-farm basis, most federal farm support has gone to the largest farms. If the goal is to eliminate poverty among farmers, farm aid could be redesigned to supplement the incomes of small or poor farmers rather than to undermine the functioning of agricultural markets.

In 1996, the U.S. Congress passed the Federal Agriculture Improvement and Reform Act of 1996, or FAIR. The thrust of the new legislation was to do away with the various programs of price support for most crops and hence provide incentives for farmers to respond to market price signals. To protect farmers through a transition period, the act provided for continued payments that were scheduled to decline over a seven-year period. However, with prices for many crops falling in 1998, the U.S. Congress passed an emergency aid package that increased payments to farmers. In 2008, as farm prices reached record highs, Congress passed a farm bill that increased subsidy payments to $40 billion. It did, however, for the first time limit payments to the wealthiest farmers. Individual farmers whose farm incomes exceed $750,000 (or $1.5 million for couples) would be ineligible for some subsidy programs.

4.2   Rental Price Ceilings

The purpose of rent control is to make rental units cheaper for tenants than they would otherwise be. Unlike agricultural price controls, rent control in the United States has been largely a local phenomenon, although there were national rent controls in effect during World War II. Currently, about 200 cities and counties have some type of rent control provisions, and about 10% of rental units in the United States are now subject to price controls. New York City's rent control program, which began in 1943, is among the oldest in the country. Many other cities in the United States adopted some form of rent control in the 1970s. Rent controls have been pervasive in Europe since World War I, and many large cities in poorer countries have also adopted rent controls.

Rent controls in different cities differ in terms of their flexibility. Some cities allow rent increases for specified reasons, such as to make improvements in apartments or to allow rents to keep pace with price increases elsewhere in the economy. Often, rental housing constructed after the imposition of the rent control ordinances is exempted. Apartments that are vacated may also be decontrolled. For simplicity, the model presented here assumes that apartment rents are controlled at a price that does not change.

Figure 3.15 shows the market for rental apartments. Notice that the demand and supply curves are drawn to look like all the other demand and supply curves you have encountered so far in this text: the demand curve is downward-sloping and the supply curve is upward-sloping.

The demand curve shows that a higher price (rent) reduces the quantity of apartments demanded. For example, with higher rents, more young people will choose to live at home with their parents. With lower rents, more will choose to live in apartments. Higher rents may encourage more apartment sharing; lower rents would induce more people to live alone.

The supply curve is drawn to show that as rent increases, property owners will be encouraged to offer more apartments to rent. Even though an aerial photograph of a city would show apartments to be fixed at a point in time, owners of those properties will decide how many to rent depending on the amount of rent they anticipate. Higher rents may also induce some homeowners to rent out apartment space. In addition, renting out apartments implies a certain level of service to renters, so that low rents may lead some property owners to keep some apartments vacant.

FIGURE 3.15 Effect of a Price Ceiling on the Market for Apartments

A price ceiling on apartment rents that is set below the equilibrium rent creates a shortage of apartments equal to ($A_2 - A_1$) apartments.

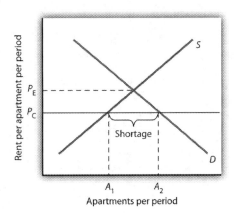

Rent control is an example of a **price ceiling**, a maximum allowable price. With a price ceiling, the government forbids a price above the maximum. A price ceiling that is set below the equilibrium price creates a shortage that will persist.

price ceiling

A maximum allowable price.

Suppose the government sets the price of an apartment at P_C in Figure 3.15. Notice that P_C is below the equilibrium price of P_E. At P_C, we read over to the supply curve to find that sellers are willing to offer A_1 apartments. Reading over to the demand curve, we find that consumers would like to rent A_2 apartments at the price ceiling of P_C. Because P_C is below the equilibrium price, there is a shortage of apartments equal to $(A_2 - A_1)$. (Notice that if the price ceiling were set above the equilibrium price it would have no effect on the market since the law would not prohibit the price from settling at an equilibrium price that is lower than the price ceiling.)

If rent control creates a shortage of apartments, why do some citizens nonetheless clamor for rent control and why do governments often give in to the demands? The reason generally given for rent control is to keep apartments affordable for low- and middle-income tenants.

But the reduced quantity of apartments supplied must be rationed in some way, since, at the price ceiling, the quantity demanded would exceed the quantity supplied. Current occupants may be reluctant to leave their dwellings because finding other apartments will be difficult. As apartments do become available, there will be a line of potential renters waiting to fill them, any of whom is willing to pay the controlled price of P_C or more. In fact, reading up to the demand curve in Figure 3.16 from A_1 apartments, the quantity available at P_C, you can see that for A_1 apartments, there are potential renters willing and able to pay P_B. This often leads to various "backdoor" payments to apartment owners, such as large security deposits, payments for things renters may not want (such as furniture), so-called "key" payments ("The monthly rent is $500 and the key price is $3,000"), or simple bribes.

In the end, rent controls and other price ceilings often end up hurting some of the people they are intended to help. Many people will have trouble finding apartments to rent. Ironically, some of those who do find apartments may actually end up paying more than they would have paid in the absence of rent control. And many of the people that the rent controls do help (primarily current occupants, regardless of their income, and those lucky enough to find apartments) are not those they are intended to help (the poor). There are also costs in government administration and enforcement.

Because New York City has the longest history of rent controls of any city in the United States, its program has been widely studied. There is general agreement that the rent control program has reduced tenant mobility, led to a substantial gap between rents on controlled and uncontrolled units, and favored long-term residents at the expense of newcomers to the city.[1] These distortions have grown over time, another frequent consequence of price controls.

A more direct means of helping poor tenants, one that would avoid interfering with the functioning of the market, would be to subsidize their incomes. As with price floors, interfering with the market mechanism may solve one problem, but it creates many others at the same time.

FIGURE 3.16 The Unintended Consequences of Rent Control

Controlling apartment rents at P_C creates a shortage of $(A_2 - A_1)$ apartments. For A_1 apartments, consumers are willing and able to pay P_B, which leads to various "backdoor" payments to apartment owners.

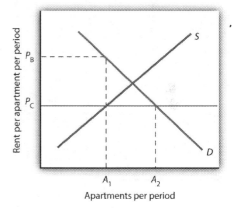

KEY TAKEAWAYS

- Price floors create surpluses by fixing the price above the equilibrium price. At the price set by the floor, the quantity supplied exceeds the quantity demanded.
- In agriculture, price floors have created persistent surpluses of a wide range of agricultural commodities. Governments typically purchase the amount of the surplus or impose production restrictions in an attempt to reduce the surplus.
- Price ceilings create shortages by setting the price below the equilibrium. At the ceiling price, the quantity demanded exceeds the quantity supplied.
- Rent controls are an example of a price ceiling, and thus they create shortages of rental housing.
- It is sometimes the case that rent controls create "backdoor" arrangements, ranging from requirements that tenants rent items that they do not want to outright bribes, that result in rents higher than would exist in the absence of the ceiling.

A minimum wage law is another example of a price floor. Draw demand and supply curves for unskilled labor. The horizontal axis will show the quantity of unskilled labor per period and the vertical axis will show the hourly wage rate for unskilled workers, which is the price of unskilled labor. Show and explain the effect of a minimum wage that is above the equilibrium wage.

Case in Point

Corn: It Is Not Just Food Any More

© 2010 Jupiterimages Corporation

Government support for corn dates back to the Agricultural Act of 1938 and, in one form or another, has been part of agricultural legislation ever since. Types of supports have ranged from government purchases of surpluses to target pricing, land set asides, and loan guarantees. According to one estimate, the U.S. government spent nearly $42 billion to support corn between 1995 and 2004.

Then, during the period of rising oil prices of the late 1970s and mounting concerns about dependence on foreign oil from volatile regions in the world, support for corn, not as a food, but rather as an input into the production of ethanol—an alternative to oil-based fuel—began. Ethanol tax credits were part of the Energy Act of 1978. Since 1980, a tariff of 50¢ per gallon against imported ethanol, even higher today, has served to protect domestic corn-based ethanol from imported ethanol, in particular from sugar-cane-based ethanol from Brazil.

The Energy Policy Act of 2005 was another milestone in ethanol legislation. Through loan guarantees, support for research and development, and tax credits, it mandated that 4 billion gallons of ethanol be used by 2006 and 7.5 billion gallons by 2012. Ethanol production had already reached 6.5 billion gallons by 2007, so new legislation in 2007 upped the ante to 15 billion gallons by 2015.

Beyond the increased amount the government is spending to support corn and corn-based ethanol, criticism of the policy has three major prongs:

1. Corn-based ethanol does little to reduce U.S. dependence on foreign oil because the energy required to produce a gallon of corn-based ethanol is quite high. A 2006 National Academy of Sciences paper estimated that one gallon of ethanol is needed to bring 1.25 gallons of it to market. Other studies show an even less favorable ratio.

2. Biofuels, such as corn-based ethanol, are having detrimental effects on the environment, with increased deforestation, stemming from more land being used to grow fuel inputs, contributing to global warming.

3. The diversion of corn and other crops from food to fuel is contributing to rising food prices and an increase in world hunger. C. Ford Runge and Benjamin Senauer wrote in *Foreign Affairs* that even small increases in prices of food staples have severe consequences on the very poor of the world, and "Filling the 25-gallon tank of an SUV with pure ethanol requires over 450 pounds of corn—which contains enough calories to feed one person for a year."

Some of these criticisms may be contested as exaggerated: Will the ratio of energy-in to energy-out improve as new technologies emerge for producing ethanol? Did not other factors, such as weather and rising food demand worldwide, contribute to higher grain prices? Nonetheless, it is clear that corn-based ethanol is no free lunch. It is also clear that the end of government support for corn is nowhere to be seen.

Sources: Alexei Barrionuevo, "Mountains of Corn and a Sea of Farm Subsidies," New York Times, November 9, 2005, online version; David Freddoso, "Children of the Corn," National Review Online, May 6, 2008; C. Ford Runge and Benjamin Senauer, "How Biofuels Could Starve the Poor," Foreign Affairs, May/June 2007, online version; Michael Grunwald, "The Clean Energy Scam," Time 171:14 (April 7, 2008): 40–45.

ANSWER TO TRY IT! PROBLEM

A minimum wage (W_{min}) that is set above the equilibrium wage would create a surplus of unskilled labor equal to ($L_2 - L_1$). That is, L_2 units of unskilled labor are offered at the minimum wage, but companies only want to use L_1 units at that wage. Because unskilled workers are a substitute for a skilled workers, forcing the price of unskilled workers higher would increase the demand for skilled labor and thus increase their wages.

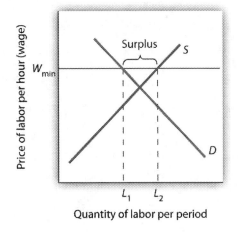

5. REVIEW AND PRACTICE

Summary

In this chapter we have examined the model of demand and supply. We found that a demand curve shows the quantity demanded at each price, all other things unchanged. The law of demand asserts that an increase in price reduces the quantity demanded and a decrease in price increases the quantity demanded, all other things unchanged. The supply curve shows the quantity of a good or service that sellers will offer at various prices, all other things unchanged. Supply curves are generally upward sloping: an increase in price generally increases the quantity supplied, all other things unchanged.

The equilibrium price occurs where the demand and supply curves intersect. At this price, the quantity demanded equals the quantity supplied. A price higher than the equilibrium price increases the quantity supplied and reduces the quantity demanded, causing a surplus. A price lower than the equilibrium price increases the quantity demanded and reduces the quantity supplied, causing a shortage. Usually, market surpluses and shortages are short-lived. Changes in demand or supply, caused by changes in the determinants of demand and supply otherwise held constant in the analysis, change the equilibrium price and output.

We then examined markets in which some form of government price control keeps price permanently above or below equilibrium. A price floor leads to persistent surpluses because it is set above the equilibrium price, whereas a price ceiling, because it is set below the equilibrium price, leads to persistent shortages. We saw that interfering with the market mechanism may solve one problem but also creates other problems at the same time. We discussed what some of these unintended consequences might be. For example, agricultural price floors aimed at boosting farm income have also raised prices for consumers and cost taxpayers dearly, and the bulk of government payments have gone to large farms. Rent controls have lowered rents, but they have also reduced the quantity of rental housing supplied, created shortages, and sometimes led to various forms of "backdoor" payments, which sometimes force the price of rental housing above what would exist in the absence of controls.

CONCEPT PROBLEMS

1. What do you think happens to the demand for pizzas during the Super Bowl? Why?

2. Which of the following goods are likely to be classified as normal goods or services? Inferior? Defend your answer.

   a. Beans
   b. Tuxedos
   c. Used cars
   d. Used clothing
   e. Computers
   f. Books reviewed in *The New York Times*
   g. Macaroni and cheese
   h. Calculators
   i. Cigarettes
   j. Caviar
   k. Legal services

3. Which of the following pairs of goods are likely to be classified as substitutes? Complements? Defend your answer.

   a. Peanut butter and jelly
   b. Eggs and ham
   c. Nike brand and Reebok brand sneakers
   d. IBM and Apple Macintosh brand computers
   e. Dress shirts and ties
   f. Airline tickets and hotels
   g. Gasoline and tires
   h. Beer and wine
   i. Faxes and first-class mail
   j. Cereal and milk
   k. Cereal and eggs

4. A study found that lower airfares led some people to substitute flying for driving to their vacation destinations. This reduced the demand for car travel and led to reduced traffic fatalities, since air travel is safer per passenger mile than car travel. Using the logic suggested by that study, suggest how each of the following events would affect the number of highway fatalities in any one year.

   a. An increase in the price of gasoline
   b. A large reduction in rental rates for passenger vans
   c. An increase in airfares

5. Children under age 2 are now allowed to fly free on U.S. airlines; they usually sit in their parents' laps. Some safety advocates have urged that they be required to be strapped in infant seats, which would mean their parents would have to purchase tickets for them. Some economists have argued that such a measure would actually increase infant fatalities. Can you say why?

6. The following graphs show four possible shifts in demand or in supply that could occur in particular markets. Relate each of the following described events to one of them.

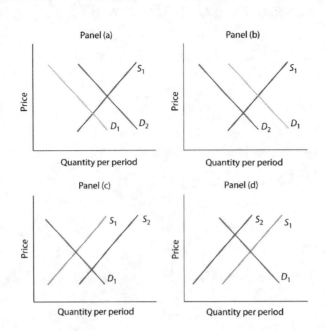

Panel (a)   Panel (b)   Panel (c)   Panel (d)

a. How did the heavy rains in South America in 1997 affect the market for coffee?

b. The Surgeon General decides french fries are not bad for your health after all and issues a report endorsing their use. What happens to the market for french fries?

c. How do you think rising incomes affect the market for ski vacations?

d. A new technique is discovered for manufacturing computers that greatly lowers their production cost. What happens to the market for computers?

e. How would a ban on smoking in public affect the market for cigarettes?

7. As low-carb diets increased in popularity, egg prices rose sharply. How might this affect the monks' supply of cookies or private retreats? (See the Case in Point on the Monks of St. Benedict's.)

8. Gasoline prices typically rise during the summer, a time of heavy tourist traffic. A "street talk" feature on a radio station sought tourists' reactions to higher gasoline prices. Here was one response: "I don't like 'em [the higher prices] much. I think the gas companies just use any excuse to jack up prices, and they're doing it again now." How does this tourist's perspective differ from that of economists who use the model of demand and supply?

9. The introduction to the chapter argues that preferences for coffee changed in the 1990s and that excessive rain hurt yields from coffee plants. Show and explain the effects of these two circumstances on the coffee market.

10. With preferences for coffee remaining strong in the early part of the century, Vietnam entered the market as a major exporter of coffee. Show and explain the effects of these two circumstances on the coffee market.

11. The study on the economics of obesity discussed in the Case in Point in this chapter on that topic also noted that another factor behind rising obesity is the decline in cigarette smoking as the price of cigarettes has risen. Show and explain the effect of higher cigarette prices on the market for food. What does this finding imply about the relationship between cigarettes and food?

12. In 2004, *The New York Times* reported that India might be losing its outsourcing edge due to rising wages[2]. The reporter noted that a recent report "projected that if India continued to produce college graduates at the current rate, demand would exceed supply by 20% in the main outsourcing markets by 2008." Using the terminology you learned in this chapter, explain what he meant to say was happening in the market for Indian workers in outsourcing jobs. In particular, is demand for Indian workers increasing or decreasing? Is the supply of Indian workers increasing or decreasing? Which is shifting faster? How do you know?

13. For more than a century, milk producers have produced skim milk, which contains virtually no fat, along with regular milk, which contains 4% fat. But a century ago, skim milk accounted for only about 1% of total production, and much of it was fed to hogs. Today, skim and other reduced-fat milks make up the bulk of milk sales. What curve shifted, and what factor shifted it?

14. During World War II, there was a freeze on wages, and corporations found they could evade the freeze by providing other fringe benefits such as retirement funds and health insurance for their employees. The Office of Price Administration, which administered the wage freeze, ruled that the offer of retirement funds and health literature was not a violation of the freeze. The Internal Revenue Service went along with this and ruled that employer-financed retirement and health insurance plans were not taxable income. Was the wage freeze an example of a price floor or a price ceiling? Use the model of demand and supply to explain why employers began to offer such benefits to their employees.

15. People often argue that there is a "shortage" of child care. Using the model of demand and supply, evaluate whether this argument is likely to be correct.

16. "During most of the past 50 years the United States has had a surplus of farmers, and this has been the root of the farm problem." Comment.

17. Suppose the Department of Agriculture ordered all farmers to reduce the acreage they plant by 10%. Would you expect a 10% reduction in food production? Why or why not?

NUMERICAL PROBLEMS

Problems 1–5 are based on the following graph.

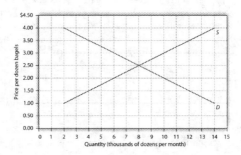

1. At a price of $1.50 per dozen, how many bagels are demanded per month?
2. At a price of $1.50 per dozen, how many bagels are supplied per month?
3. At a price of $3.00 per dozen, how many bagels are demanded per month?
4. At a price of $3.00 per dozen, how many bagels are supplied per month?
5. What is the equilibrium price of bagels? What is the equilibrium quantity per month?

Problems 6–9 are based on the model of demand and supply for coffee as shown in Figure 3.10. You can graph the initial demand and supply curves by using the following values, with all quantities in millions of pounds of coffee per month:

Price	Quantity demanded	Quantity supplied
$3	40	10
4	35	15
5	30	20
6	25	25
7	20	30
8	15	35
9	10	40

6. Suppose the quantity demanded rises by 20 million pounds of coffee per month at each price. Draw the initial demand and supply curves based on the values given in the table above. Then draw the new demand curve given by this change, and show the new equilibrium price and quantity.

7. Suppose the quantity demanded falls, relative to the values given in the above table, by 20 million pounds per month at prices between $4 and $6 per pound; at prices between $7 and $9 per pound, the quantity demanded becomes zero. Draw the new demand curve and show the new equilibrium price and quantity.

8. Suppose the quantity supplied rises by 20 million pounds per month at each price, while the quantities demanded retain the values shown in the table above. Draw the new supply curve and show the new equilibrium price and quantity.

9. Suppose the quantity supplied falls, relative to the values given in the table above, by 20 million pounds per month at prices above $5; at a price of $5 or less per pound, the quantity supplied becomes zero. Draw the new supply curve and show the new equilibrium price and quantity.

Problems 10–15 are based on the following demand and supply schedules for gasoline (all quantities are in thousands of gallons per week):

Price per gallon	Quantity demanded	Quantity supplied
$1	8	0
2	7	1
3	6	2
4	5	3
5	4	4
6	3	5
7	2	6
8	1	7

10. Graph the demand and supply curves and show the equilibrium price and quantity.

11. At a price of $3 per gallon, would there be a surplus or shortage of gasoline? How much would the surplus or shortage be? Indicate the surplus or shortage on the graph.

12. At a price of $6 per gallon, would there be a surplus or shortage of gasoline? How much would the surplus or shortage be? Show the surplus or shortage on the graph.

13. Suppose the quantity demanded increased by 2,000 gallons per month at each price. At a price of $3 per gallon, how much would the surplus or shortage be? Graph the demand and supply curves and show the surplus or shortage.

14. Suppose the quantity supplied decreased by 2,000 gallons per month at each price for prices between $4 and $8 per gallon. At prices less than $4 per gallon the quantity supplied becomes zero, while the quantities demanded retain the values shown in the table. At a price of $4 per gallon, how much would the surplus or shortage be? Graph the demand and supply curves and show the surplus or shortage.

15. If the demand curve shifts as in problem 13 and the supply curve shifts as in problem 14, without drawing a graph or consulting the data, can you predict whether equilibrium price increases or decreases? What about equilibrium quantity? Now draw a graph that shows what the new equilibrium price and quantity are.

Problems 16–19 are based on the following demand and supply schedules for corn (all quantities are in millions of bushels per year).

Price per bushel	Quantity demanded	Quantity supplied
$0	6	0
1	5	1
2	4	2
3	3	3
4	2	4
5	1	5
6	0	6

16. Draw the demand and supply curves for corn. What is the equilibrium price? The equilibrium quantity?

17. Suppose the government now imposes a price floor at $4 per bushel. Show the effect of this program graphically. How large is the surplus of corn?

18. With the price floor, how much do farmers receive for their corn? How much would they receive if there were no price floor?

19. If the government buys all the surplus wheat, how much will it spend?

Problems 20–24 are based on the following hypothetical demand and supply curves for apartments.

Rent/Month	Number of Apts. Demanded/Month	Number of Apts. Supplied/Month
$0	120,000	0
200	100,000	20,000
400	80,000	40,000
600	60,000	60,000
800	40,000	80,000
1000	20,000	100,000
1200	0	120,000

20. Draw the demand and supply curves for apartments.

21. What is the equilibrium rent per month? At this rent, what is the number of apartments demanded and supplied per month?

22. Suppose a ceiling on rents is set at $400 per month. Characterize the situation that results from this policy.

23. At the rent ceiling, how many apartments are demanded? How many are supplied?

24. How much are people willing to pay for the number of apartments supplied at the ceiling? Describe the arrangements to which this situation might lead.

ENDNOTES

1. Richard Arnott, "Time for Revisionism on Rent Control," *Journal of Economic Perspectives* 9(1) (Winter, 1995): 99–120.

2. Noam Scheiber, "As a Center for Outsourcing, India Could Be Losing Its Edge," *New York Times*, May 9, 2004, p. BU3.

CHAPTER 4
Elasticity: A Measure of Response

START UP: RAISE FARES? LOWER FARES? WHAT'S A PUBLIC TRANSIT MANAGER TO DO?

Imagine that you are the manager of the public transportation system for a large metropolitan area. Operating costs for the system have soared in the last few years, and you are under pressure to boost revenues. What do you do?

An obvious choice would be to raise fares. That will make your customers angry, but at least it will generate the extra revenue you need—or will it? The law of demand says that raising fares will reduce the number of passengers riding on your system. If the number of passengers falls only a little, then the higher fares that your remaining passengers are paying might produce the higher revenues you need. But what if the number of passengers falls by so much that your higher fares actually reduce your revenues? If that happens, you will have made your customers mad and your financial problem worse!

Maybe you should recommend *lower* fares. After all, the law of demand also says that lower fares will increase the number of passengers. Having more people use the public transportation system could more than offset a lower fare you collect from each person. But it might not. What *will* you do?

Your job and the fiscal health of the public transit system are riding on your making the correct decision. To do so, you need to know just how responsive the quantity demanded is to a price change. You need a measure of responsiveness.

Economists use a measure of responsiveness called elasticity. **Elasticity** is the ratio of the percentage change in a dependent variable to a percentage change in an independent variable. If the dependent variable is y, and the independent variable is x, then the elasticity of y with respect to a change in x is given by:

$$e_{y,\, x} = \frac{\%\ \text{change in } y}{\%\ \text{change in } x}$$

A variable such as y is said to be more elastic (responsive) if the percentage change in y is large relative to the percentage change in x. It is less elastic if the reverse is true.

As manager of the public transit system, for example, you will want to know how responsive the number of passengers on your system (the dependent variable) will be to a change in fares (the independent variable). The concept of elasticity will help you solve your public transit pricing problem and a great many other issues in economics. We will examine several elasticities in this chapter—all will tell us how responsive one variable is to a change in another.

elasticity

The ratio of the percentage change in a dependent variable to a percentage change in an independent variable.

1.   THE PRICE ELASTICITY OF DEMAND

LEARNING OBJECTIVES

1. **Explain the concept of price elasticity of demand and its calculation.**
2. **Explain what it means for demand to be price inelastic, unit price elastic, price elastic, perfectly price inelastic, and perfectly price elastic.**
3. **Explain how and why the value of the price elasticity of demand changes along a linear demand curve.**
4. **Understand the relationship between total revenue and price elasticity of demand.**
5. **Discuss the determinants of price elasticity of demand.**

We know from the law of demand how the quantity demanded will respond to a price change: it will change in the opposite direction. But how *much* will it change? It seems reasonable to expect, for example, that a 10% change in the price charged for a visit to the doctor would yield a different percentage change in quantity demanded than a 10% change in the price of a Ford Mustang. But how much is this difference?

price elasticity of demand

The percentage change in quantity demanded of a particular good or service divided by the percentage change in the price of that good or service, all other things unchanged.

To show how responsive quantity demanded is to a change in price, we apply the concept of elasticity. The **price elasticity of demand** for a good or service, e_D, is the percentage change in quantity demanded of a particular good or service divided by the percentage change in the price of that good or service, all other things unchanged. Thus we can write

EQUATION 4.1

$$e_D = \frac{\% \text{ change in quantity demanded}}{\% \text{ change in price}}$$

Because the price elasticity of demand shows the responsiveness of quantity demanded to a price change, assuming that other factors that influence demand are unchanged, it reflects movements *along* a demand curve. With a downward-sloping demand curve, price and quantity demanded move in opposite directions, so the price elasticity of demand is always negative. A positive percentage change in price implies a negative percentage change in quantity demanded, and vice versa. Sometimes you will see the absolute value of the price elasticity measure reported. In essence, the minus sign is ignored because it is expected that there will be a negative (inverse) relationship between quantity demanded and price. In this text, however, we will retain the minus sign in reporting price elasticity of demand and will say "the absolute value of the price elasticity of demand" when that is what we are describing.

Heads Up!

Be careful not to confuse elasticity with slope. The slope of a line is the change in the value of the variable on the vertical axis divided by the change in the value of the variable on the horizontal axis between two points. Elasticity is the ratio of the percentage changes. The slope of a demand curve, for example, is the ratio of the change in price to the change in quantity between two points on the curve. The price elasticity of demand is the ratio of the percentage change in quantity to the percentage change in price. As we will see, when computing elasticity at different points on a linear demand curve, the slope is constant—that is, it does not change—but the value for elasticity will change.

1.1   Computing the Price Elasticity of Demand

Finding the price elasticity of demand requires that we first compute percentage changes in price and in quantity demanded. We calculate those changes between two points on a demand curve.

Figure 4.1 shows a particular demand curve, a linear demand curve for public transit rides. Suppose the initial price is $0.80, and the quantity demanded is 40,000 rides per day; we are at point A on the curve. Now suppose the price falls to $0.70, and we want to report the responsiveness of the quantity demanded. We see that at the new price, the quantity demanded rises to 60,000 rides per day (point B). To compute the elasticity, we need to compute the percentage changes in price and in quantity demanded between points A and B.

FIGURE 4.1 Responsiveness and Demand

The demand curve shows how changes in price lead to changes in the quantity demanded. A movement from point A to point B shows that a $0.10 reduction in price increases the number of rides per day by 20,000. A movement from B to A is a $0.10 increase in price, which reduces quantity demanded by 20,000 rides per day.

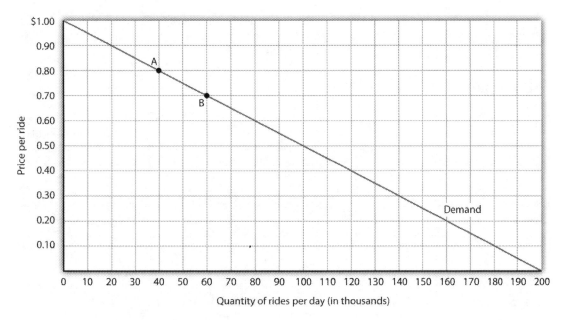

We measure the percentage change between two points as the change in the variable divided by the *average* value of the variable between the two points. Thus, the percentage change in quantity between points A and B in Figure 4.1 is computed relative to the *average* of the quantity values at points A and B: (60,000 + 40,000)/2 = 50,000. The percentage change in quantity, then, is 20,000/50,000, or 40%. Likewise, the percentage change in price between points A and B is based on the *average* of the two prices: ($0.80 + $0.70)/2 = $0.75, and so we have a percentage change of −0.10/0.75, or −13.33%. The price elasticity of demand between points A and B is thus 40%/(−13.33%) = −3.00.

This measure of elasticity, which is based on percentage changes relative to the average value of each variable between two points, is called **arc elasticity**. The arc elasticity method has the advantage that it yields the same elasticity whether we go from point A to point B or from point B to point A. It is the method we shall use to compute elasticity.

For the arc elasticity method, we calculate the price elasticity of demand using the average value of price, $\overline{P}$, and the average value of quantity demanded, $\overline{Q}$. We shall use the Greek letter Δ to mean "change in," so the change in quantity between two points is ΔQ and the change in price is ΔP. Now we can write the formula for the price elasticity of demand as

arc elasticity

Measure of elasticity based on percentage changes relative to the average value of each variable between two points.

EQUATION 4.2

$$e_D = \frac{\Delta Q \,/\, \overline{Q}}{\Delta P \,/\, \overline{P}}$$

The price elasticity of demand between points A and B is thus:

$$e_D = \frac{\dfrac{20,000}{(40,000 + 60,000)/2}}{\dfrac{-\$0.10}{(\$0.80 + \$0.70)/2}} = \frac{40\%}{-13.33\%} = -3.00$$

With the arc elasticity formula, the elasticity is the same whether we move from point A to point B or from point B to point A. If we start at point B and move to point A, we have:

$$e_D = \frac{\dfrac{-20,000}{(60,000 + 40,000)/2}}{\dfrac{0.10}{(\$0.70 + \$0.80)/2}} = \frac{-40\%}{13.33\%} = -3.00$$

The arc elasticity method gives us an estimate of elasticity. It gives the value of elasticity at the midpoint over a range of change, such as the movement between points A and B. For a precise computation of elasticity, we would need to consider the response of a dependent variable to an extremely small change in an independent variable. The fact that arc elasticities are approximate suggests an important practical rule in calculating arc elasticities: we should consider only small changes in independent variables. We cannot apply the concept of arc elasticity to large changes.

Another argument for considering only small changes in computing price elasticities of demand will become evident in the next section. We will investigate what happens to price elasticities as we move from one point to another along a linear demand curve.

Heads Up!

Notice that in the arc elasticity formula, the method for computing a percentage change differs from the standard method with which you may be familiar. That method measures the percentage change in a variable relative to its original value. For example, using the standard method, when we go from point A to point B, we would compute the percentage change in quantity as 20,000/40,000 = 50%. The percentage change in price would be −$0.10/$0.80 = −12.5%. The price elasticity of demand would then be 50%/(−12.5%) = −4.00. Going from point B to point A, however, would yield a different elasticity. The percentage change in quantity would be −20,000/60,000, or −33.33%. The percentage change in price would be $0.10/$0.70 = 14.29%. The price elasticity of demand would thus be −33.33%/14.29% = −2.33. By using the average quantity and average price to calculate percentage changes, the arc elasticity approach avoids the necessity to specify the direction of the change and, thereby, gives us the same answer whether we go from A to B or from B to A.

1.2   Price Elasticities Along a Linear Demand Curve

What happens to the price elasticity of demand when we travel along the demand curve? The answer depends on the nature of the demand curve itself. On a linear demand curve, such as the one in Figure 4.2, elasticity becomes smaller (in absolute value) as we travel downward and to the right.

FIGURE 4.2   Price Elasticities of Demand for a Linear Demand Curve

The price elasticity of demand varies between different pairs of points along a linear demand curve. The lower the price and the greater the quantity demanded, the lower the absolute value of the price elasticity of demand.

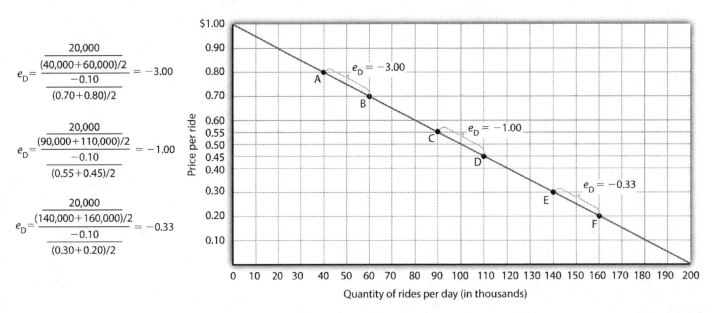

Figure 4.2 shows the same demand curve we saw in Figure 4.1. We have already calculated the price elasticity of demand between points A and B; it equals −3.00. Notice, however, that when we use the same method to compute the price elasticity of demand between other sets of points, our answer varies. For each of the pairs of points shown, the changes in price and quantity demanded are the same (a $0.10 decrease in price and 20,000 additional rides per day, respectively). But at the high prices and low quantities on the upper part of the demand curve, the percentage change in quantity is relatively large, whereas the percentage change in price is relatively small. The absolute value of the price elasticity of demand is thus relatively large. As we move down the demand curve, equal changes in quantity

represent smaller and smaller percentage changes, whereas equal changes in price represent larger and larger percentage changes, and the absolute value of the elasticity measure declines. Between points C and D, for example, the price elasticity of demand is −1.00, and between points E and F the price elasticity of demand is −0.33.

On a linear demand curve, the price elasticity of demand varies depending on the interval over which we are measuring it. For any linear demand curve, the absolute value of the price elasticity of demand will fall as we move down and to the right along the curve.

1.3   The Price Elasticity of Demand and Changes in Total Revenue

Suppose the public transit authority is considering raising fares. Will its total revenues go up or down? **Total revenue** is the price per unit times the number of units sold.[1] In this case, it is the fare times the number of riders. The transit authority will certainly want to know whether a price increase will cause its total revenue to rise or fall. In fact, determining the impact of a price change on total revenue is crucial to the analysis of many problems in economics.

We will do two quick calculations before generalizing the principle involved. Given the demand curve shown in Figure 4.2, we see that at a price of $0.80, the transit authority will sell 40,000 rides per day. Total revenue would be $32,000 per day ($0.80 times 40,000). If the price were lowered by $0.10 to $0.70, quantity demanded would increase to 60,000 rides and total revenue would increase to $42,000 ($0.70 times 60,000). The reduction in fare *increases* total revenue. However, if the initial price had been $0.30 and the transit authority reduced it by $0.10 to $0.20, total revenue would *decrease* from $42,000 ($0.30 times 140,000) to $32,000 ($0.20 times 160,000). So it appears that the impact of a price change on total revenue depends on the initial price and, by implication, the original elasticity. We generalize this point in the remainder of this section.

The problem in assessing the impact of a price change on total revenue of a good or service is that a change in price always changes the quantity demanded in the opposite direction. An increase in price reduces the quantity demanded, and a reduction in price increases the quantity demanded. The question is how much. Because total revenue is found by multiplying the price per unit times the quantity demanded, it is not clear whether a change in price will cause total revenue to rise or fall.

We have already made this point in the context of the transit authority. Consider the following three examples of price increases for gasoline, pizza, and diet cola.

Suppose that 1,000 gallons of gasoline per day are demanded at a price of $4.00 per gallon. Total revenue for gasoline thus equals $4,000 per day (=1,000 gallons per day times $4.00 per gallon). If an increase in the price of gasoline to $4.25 reduces the quantity demanded to 950 gallons per day, total revenue rises to $4,037.50 per day (=950 gallons per day times $4.25 per gallon). Even though people consume less gasoline at $4.25 than at $4.00, total revenue rises because the higher price more than makes up for the drop in consumption.

Next consider pizza. Suppose 1,000 pizzas per week are demanded at a price of $9 per pizza. Total revenue for pizza equals $9,000 per week (=1,000 pizzas per week times $9 per pizza). If an increase in the price of pizza to $10 per pizza reduces quantity demanded to 900 pizzas per week, total revenue will still be $9,000 per week (=900 pizzas per week times $10 per pizza). Again, when price goes up, consumers buy less, but this time there is no change in total revenue.

Now consider diet cola. Suppose 1,000 cans of diet cola per day are demanded at a price of $0.50 per can. Total revenue for diet cola equals $500 per day (=1,000 cans per day times $0.50 per can). If an increase in the price of diet cola to $0.55 per can reduces quantity demanded to 880 cans per month, total revenue for diet cola falls to $484 per day (=880 cans per day times $0.55 per can). As in the case of gasoline, people will buy less diet cola when the price rises from $0.50 to $0.55, but in this example total revenue drops.

In our first example, an increase in price increased total revenue. In the second, a price increase left total revenue unchanged. In the third example, the price rise reduced total revenue. Is there a way to predict how a price change will affect total revenue? There is; the effect depends on the price elasticity of demand.

total revenue

A firm's output multiplied by the price at which it sells that output.

Elastic, Unit Elastic, and Inelastic Demand

price elastic

Situation in which the absolute value of the price elasticity of demand is greater than 1.

unit price elastic

Situation in which the absolute value of the price elasticity of demand is equal to 1.

price inelastic

Situation in which the absolute value of the price of elasticity of demand is less than 1.

To determine how a price change will affect total revenue, economists place price elasticities of demand in three categories, based on their absolute value. If the absolute value of the price elasticity of demand is greater than 1, demand is termed **price elastic**. If it is equal to 1, demand is **unit price elastic**. And if it is less than 1, demand is **price inelastic**.

Relating Elasticity to Changes in Total Revenue

When the price of a good or service changes, the quantity demanded changes in the opposite direction. Total revenue will move in the direction of the variable that changes by the larger percentage. If the variables move by the same percentage, total revenue stays the same. If quantity demanded changes by a larger percentage than price (i.e., if demand is price elastic), total revenue will change in the direction of the quantity change. If price changes by a larger percentage than quantity demanded (i.e., if demand is price inelastic), total revenue will move in the direction of the price change. If price and quantity demanded change by the same percentage (i.e., if demand is unit price elastic), then total revenue does not change.

When demand is price inelastic, a given percentage change in price results in a smaller percentage change in quantity demanded. That implies that total revenue will move in the direction of the price change: a reduction in price will reduce total revenue, and an increase in price will increase it.

Consider the price elasticity of demand for gasoline. In the example above, 1,000 gallons of gasoline were purchased each day at a price of $4.00 per gallon; an increase in price to $4.25 per gallon reduced the quantity demanded to 950 gallons per day. We thus had an average quantity of 975 gallons per day and an average price of $4.125. We can thus calculate the arc price elasticity of demand for gasoline:

Percentage change in quantity demanded = −50 / 975 = −5.1%
Percentage change in price = 0.25 / 4.125 = 6.06%
Price elasticity of demand = −5.1% / 6.06% = −0.84

The demand for gasoline is price inelastic, and total revenue moves in the direction of the price change. When price rises, total revenue rises. Recall that in our example above, total spending on gasoline (which equals total revenues to sellers) rose from $4,000 per day (=1,000 gallons per day times $4.00) to $4037.50 per day (=950 gallons per day times $4.25 per gallon).

When demand is price inelastic, a given percentage change in price results in a smaller percentage change in quantity demanded. That implies that total revenue will move in the direction of the price change: an increase in price will increase total revenue, and a reduction in price will reduce it.

Consider again the example of pizza that we examined above. At a price of $9 per pizza, 1,000 pizzas per week were demanded. Total revenue was $9,000 per week (=1,000 pizzas per week times $9 per pizza). When the price rose to $10, the quantity demanded fell to 900 pizzas per week. Total revenue remained $9,000 per week (=900 pizzas per week times $10 per pizza). Again, we have an average quantity of 950 pizzas per week and an average price of $9.50. Using the arc elasticity method, we can compute:

Percentage change in quantity demanded = − 100 / 950 = − 10.5%
Percentage change in price = $1.00 / $9.50 = 10.5%
Price elasticity of demand = − 10.5% / 10.5% = − 1.0

Demand is unit price elastic, and total revenue remains unchanged. Quantity demanded falls by the same percentage by which price increases.

Consider next the example of diet cola demand. At a price of $0.50 per can, 1,000 cans of diet cola were purchased each day. Total revenue was thus $500 per day (=$0.50 per can times 1,000 cans per day). An increase in price to $0.55 reduced the quantity demanded to 880 cans per day. We thus have an average quantity of 940 cans per day and an average price of $0.525 per can. Computing the price elasticity of demand for diet cola in this example, we have:

Percentage change in quantity demanded = − 120 / 940 = − 12.8%
Percentage change in price = $0.05 / $0.525 = 9.5%
Price elasticity of demand = − 12.8% / 9.5% = − 1.3

The demand for diet cola is price elastic, so total revenue moves in the direction of the quantity change. It falls from $500 per day before the price increase to $484 per day after the price increase.

A demand curve can also be used to show changes in total revenue. Figure 4.3 shows the demand curve from Figure 4.1 and Figure 4.2. At point A, total revenue from public transit rides is given by the area of a rectangle drawn with point A in the upper right-hand corner and the origin in the lower left-hand corner. The height of the rectangle is price; its width is quantity. We have already seen that total revenue at point A is $32,000 ($0.80 × 40,000). When we reduce the price and move to point B, the rectangle showing total revenue becomes shorter and wider. Notice that the area gained in moving to the rectangle at B is greater than the area lost; total revenue rises to $42,000 ($0.70 × 60,000). Recall from Figure 4.2 that demand is elastic between points A and B. In general, demand is elastic in the upper half of any linear demand curve, so total revenue moves in the direction of the quantity change.

FIGURE 4.3 Changes in Total Revenue and a Linear Demand Curve

Moving from point A to point B implies a reduction in price and an increase in the quantity demanded. Demand is elastic between these two points. Total revenue, shown by the areas of the rectangles drawn from points A and B to the origin, rises. When we move from point E to point F, which is in the inelastic region of the demand curve, total revenue falls.

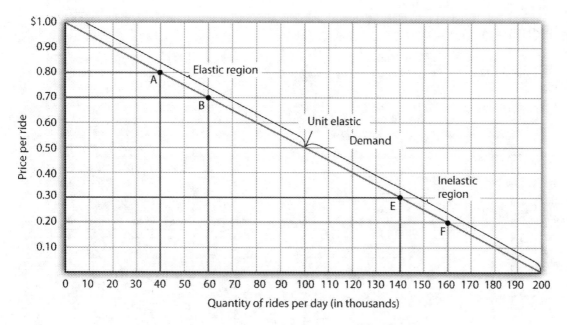

A movement from point E to point F also shows a reduction in price and an increase in quantity demanded. This time, however, we are in an inelastic region of the demand curve. Total revenue now moves in the direction of the price change—it falls. Notice that the rectangle drawn from point F is smaller in area than the rectangle drawn from point E, once again confirming our earlier calculation.

We have noted that a linear demand curve is more elastic where prices are relatively high and quantities relatively low and less elastic where prices are relatively low and quantities relatively high. We can be even more specific. *For any linear demand curve, demand will be price elastic in the upper half of the*

curve and price inelastic in its lower half. At the midpoint of a linear demand curve, demand is unit price elastic.

1.4 Constant Price Elasticity of Demand Curves

perfectly inelastic

Situation in which the price elasticity of demand is zero.

Figure 4.4 shows four demand curves over which price elasticity of demand is the same at all points. The demand curve in Panel (a) is vertical. This means that price changes have no effect on quantity demanded. The numerator of the formula given in Equation 4.1 for the price elasticity of demand (percentage change in quantity demanded) is zero. The price elasticity of demand in this case is therefore zero, and the demand curve is said to be **perfectly inelastic**. This is a theoretically extreme case, and no good that has been studied empirically exactly fits it. A good that comes close, at least over a specific price range, is insulin. A diabetic will not consume more insulin as its price falls but, over some price range, will consume the amount needed to control the disease.

FIGURE 4.4 Demand Curves with Constant Price Elasticities

The demand curve in Panel (a) is perfectly inelastic. The demand curve in Panel (b) is perfectly elastic. Price elasticity of demand is −1.00 all along the demand curve in Panel (c), whereas it is −0.50 all along the demand curve in Panel (d).

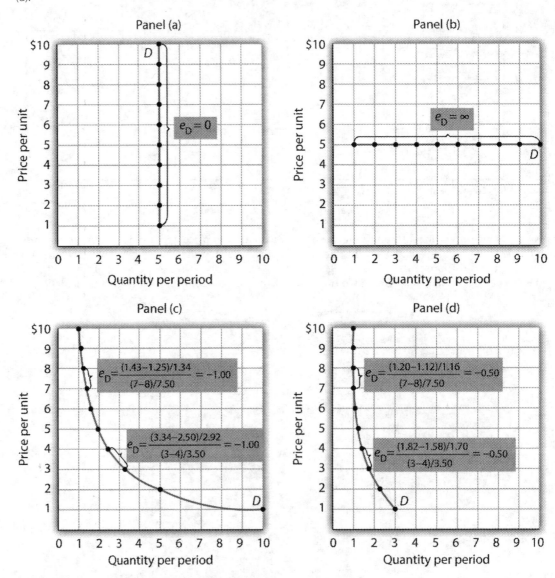

perfectly elastic

Situation in which the price elasticity of demand is infinite.

As illustrated in Figure 4.4, several other types of demand curves have the same elasticity at every point on them. The demand curve in Panel (b) is horizontal. This means that even the smallest price changes have enormous effects on quantity demanded. The denominator of the formula given in Equation 4.1 for the price elasticity of demand (percentage change in price) approaches zero. The price elasticity of demand in this case is therefore infinite, and the demand curve is said to be **perfectly elastic**.[2] This is the type of demand curve faced by producers of standardized products such as wheat. If the wheat of other farms is selling at \$4 per bushel, a typical farm can sell as much wheat as it wants to at \$4 but nothing at a higher price and would have no reason to offer its wheat at a lower price.

The nonlinear demand curves in Panels (c) and (d) have price elasticities of demand that are negative; but, unlike the linear demand curve discussed above, the value of the price elasticity is constant all along each demand curve. The demand curve in Panel (c) has price elasticity of demand equal to −1.00 throughout its range; in Panel (d) the price elasticity of demand is equal to −0.50 throughout its range. Empirical estimates of demand often show curves like those in Panels (c) and (d) that have the same elasticity at every point on the curve.

Heads Up!

Do not confuse price inelastic demand and perfectly inelastic demand. Perfectly inelastic demand means that the change in quantity is zero for any percentage change in price; the demand curve in this case is vertical. Price inelastic demand means only that the percentage change in quantity is less than the percentage change in price, not that the change in quantity is zero. With price inelastic (as opposed to perfectly inelastic) demand, the demand curve itself is still downward sloping.

1.5   Determinants of the Price Elasticity of Demand

The greater the absolute value of the price elasticity of demand, the greater the responsiveness of quantity demanded to a price change. What determines whether demand is more or less price elastic? The most important determinants of the price elasticity of demand for a good or service are the availability of substitutes, the importance of the item in household budgets, and time.

Availability of Substitutes

The price elasticity of demand for a good or service will be greater in absolute value if many close substitutes are available for it. If there are lots of substitutes for a particular good or service, then it is easy for consumers to switch to those substitutes when there is a price increase for that good or service. Suppose, for example, that the price of Ford automobiles goes up. There are many close substitutes for Fords—Chevrolets, Chryslers, Toyotas, and so on. The availability of close substitutes tends to make the demand for Fords more price elastic.

If a good has no close substitutes, its demand is likely to be somewhat less price elastic. There are no close substitutes for gasoline, for example. The price elasticity of demand for gasoline in the intermediate term of, say, three–nine months is generally estimated to be about −0.5. Since the absolute value of price elasticity is less than 1, it is price inelastic. We would expect, though, that the demand for a particular brand of gasoline will be much more price elastic than the demand for gasoline in general.

Importance in Household Budgets

One reason price changes affect quantity demanded is that they change how much a consumer can buy; a change in the price of a good or service affects the purchasing power of a consumer's income and thus affects the amount of a good the consumer will buy. This effect is stronger when a good or service is important in a typical household's budget.

A change in the price of jeans, for example, is probably more important in your budget than a change in the price of pencils. Suppose the prices of both were to double. You had planned to buy four pairs of jeans this year, but now you might decide to make do with two new pairs. A change in pencil prices, in contrast, might lead to very little reduction in quantity demanded simply because pencils are not likely to loom large in household budgets. The greater the importance of an item in household budgets, the greater the absolute value of the price elasticity of demand is likely to be.

Time

Suppose the price of electricity rises tomorrow morning. What will happen to the quantity demanded?

The answer depends in large part on how much time we allow for a response. If we are interested in the reduction in quantity demanded by tomorrow afternoon, we can expect that the response will be very small. But if we give consumers a year to respond to the price change, we can expect the response to be much greater. We expect that the absolute value of the price elasticity of demand will be greater when more time is allowed for consumer responses.

Consider the price elasticity of crude oil demand. Economist John C. B. Cooper estimated short- and long-run price elasticities of demand for crude oil for 23 industrialized nations for the period 1971–2000. Professor Cooper found that for virtually every country, the price elasticities were negative, and the long-run price elasticities were generally much greater (in absolute value) than were the short-run price elasticities. His results are reported in Table 4.1. As you can see, the research was reported in a journal published by OPEC (Organization of Petroleum Exporting Countries), an organization whose members have profited greatly from the inelasticity of demand for their product. By restricting supply, OPEC, which produces about 45% of the world's crude oil, is able to put upward pressure on the price of crude. That increases OPEC's (and all other oil producers') total revenues and reduces total costs.

TABLE 4.1 Short- and Long-Run Price Elasticities of the Demand for Crude Oil in 23 Countries
For most countries, price elasticity of demand for crude oil tends to be greater (in absolute value) in the long run than in the short run.

Country	Short-Run Price Elasticity of Demand	Long-Run Price Elasticity of Demand
Australia	−0.034	−0.068
Austria	−0.059	−0.092
Canada	−0.041	−0.352
China	0.001	0.005
Denmark	−0.026	−0.191
Finland	−0.016	−0.033
France	−0.069	−0.568
Germany	−0.024	−0.279
Greece	−0.055	−0.126
Iceland	−0.109	−0.452
Ireland	−0.082	−0.196
Italy	−0.035	−0.208
Japan	−0.071	−0.357
Korea	−0.094	−0.178
Netherlands	−0.057	−0.244
New Zealand	−0.054	−0.326
Norway	−0.026	−0.036
Portugal	0.023	0.038
Spain	−0.087	−0.146
Sweden	−0.043	−0.289
Switzerland	−0.030	−0.056
United Kingdom	−0.068	−0.182
United States	−0.061	−0.453

Source: John C. B. Cooper, "Price Elasticity of Demand for Crude Oil: Estimates from 23 Countries," OPEC Review: Energy Economics & Related Issues 27:1 (March 2003): 4. The estimates are based on data for the period 1971–2000, except for China and South Korea, where the period is 1979–2000. While the price elasticities for China and Portugal were positive, they were not statistically significant.

KEY TAKEAWAYS

- The price elasticity of demand measures the responsiveness of quantity demanded to changes in price; it is calculated by dividing the percentage change in quantity demanded by the percentage change in price.

- Demand is price inelastic if the absolute value of the price elasticity of demand is less than 1; it is unit price elastic if the absolute value is equal to 1; and it is price elastic if the absolute value is greater than 1.

- Demand is price elastic in the upper half of any linear demand curve and price inelastic in the lower half. It is unit price elastic at the midpoint.

- When demand is price inelastic, total revenue moves in the direction of a price change. When demand is unit price elastic, total revenue does not change in response to a price change. When demand is price elastic, total revenue moves in the direction of a quantity change.

- The absolute value of the price elasticity of demand is greater when substitutes are available, when the good is important in household budgets, and when buyers have more time to adjust to changes in the price of the good.

TRY IT!

You are now ready to play the part of the manager of the public transit system. Your finance officer has just advised you that the system faces a deficit. Your board does not want you to cut service, which means that you cannot cut costs. Your only hope is to increase revenue. Would a fare increase boost revenue?

You consult the economist on your staff who has researched studies on public transportation elasticities. She reports that the estimated price elasticity of demand for the first few months after a price change is about −0.3, but that after several years, it will be about −1.5.

1. Explain why the estimated values for price elasticity of demand differ.
2. Compute what will happen to ridership and revenue over the next few months if you decide to raise fares by 5%.
3. Compute what will happen to ridership and revenue over the next few years if you decide to raise fares by 5%.
4. What happens to total revenue now and after several years if you choose to raise fares?

Case in Point

Elasticity and Stop Lights

© 2010 Jupiterimages Corporation

We all face the situation every day. You are approaching an intersection. The yellow light comes on. You know that you are supposed to slow down, but you are in a bit of a hurry. So, you speed up a little to try to make the light. But the red light flashes on just before you get to the intersection. Should you risk it and go through?

Many people faced with that situation take the risky choice. In 1998, 2,000 people in the United States died as a result of drivers running red lights at intersections. In an effort to reduce the number of drivers who make such choices, many areas have installed cameras at intersections. Drivers who run red lights have their pictures taken and receive citations in the mail. This enforcement method, together with recent increases in the fines for driving through red lights at intersections, has led to an intriguing application of the concept of elasticity. Economists Avner Bar-Ilan of the University of Haifa in Israel and Bruce Sacerdote of Dartmouth University have estimated what is, in effect, the price elasticity for driving through stoplights with respect to traffic fines at intersections in Israel and in San Francisco.

In December 1996, Israel sharply increased the fine for driving through a red light. The old fine of 400 shekels (this was equal at that time to $122 in the United States) was increased to 1,000 shekels ($305). In January 1998, California raised its fine for the offense from $104 to $271. The country of Israel and the city of San Francisco installed cameras at several intersections. Drivers who ignored stoplights got their pictures taken and automatically received citations imposing the new higher fines.

We can think of driving through red lights as an activity for which there is a demand—after all, ignoring a red light speeds up one's trip. It may also generate satisfaction to people who enjoy disobeying traffic laws. The concept of elasticity gives us a way to show just how responsive drivers were to the increase in fines.

Professors Bar-Ilan and Sacerdote obtained information on all the drivers cited at 73 intersections in Israel and eight intersections in San Francisco. For Israel, for example, they defined the period January 1992 to June 1996 as the "before" period. They compared the number of violations during the before period to the number of violations from July 1996 to December 1999—the "after" period—and found there was a reduction in tickets per driver of 31.5 per cent. Specifically, the average number of tickets per driver was 0.073 during the period before the increase; it fell to 0.050 after the increase. The increase in the fine was 150 per cent. (Note that, because they were making a "before" and "after" calculation, the authors used the standard method described in the Heads Up! on computing a percentage change—i.e., they computed the percentage changes in comparison to the original values instead of the average value of the variables.) The elasticity of citations with respect to the fine was thus −0.21 (= **−31.5%/150%**).

The economists estimated elasticities for particular groups of people. For example, young people (age 17–30) had an elasticity of −0.36; people over the age of 30 had an elasticity of −0.16. In general, elasticities fell in absolute value as income rose. For San Francisco and Israel combined, the elasticity was between −0.26 and −0.33.

In general, the results showed that people responded rationally to the increases in fines. Increasing the price of a particular behavior reduced the frequency of that behavior. The study also points out the effectiveness of cameras as an enforcement technique. With cameras, violators can be certain they will be cited if they ignore a red light. And reducing the number of people running red lights clearly saves lives.

Source: Avner Bar-Ilan and Bruce Sacerdote. "The Response of Criminals and Non-Criminals to Fines." Journal of Law and Economics, 47:1 (April 2004): 1–17.

ANSWERS TO TRY IT! PROBLEMS

1. The absolute value of price elasticity of demand tends to be greater when more time is allowed for consumers to respond. Over time, riders of the commuter rail system can organize car pools, move, or otherwise adjust to the fare increase.

2. Using the formula for price elasticity of demand and plugging in values for the estimate of price elasticity (−0.5) and the percentage change in price (5%) and then rearranging terms, we can solve for the percentage change in quantity demanded as $e_D = \%\Delta$ in $Q/\%\Delta$ in P; $-0.5 = \%\Delta$ in $Q/5\%$; $(-0.5)(5\%) = \%\Delta$ in $Q = -2.5\%$. Ridership falls by 2.5% in the first few months.

3. Using the formula for price elasticity of demand and plugging in values for the estimate of price elasticity over a few years (−1.5) and the percentage change in price (5%), we can solve for the percentage change in quantity demanded as $e_D = \%\Delta$ in $Q/\%\Delta$ in P; $-1.5 = \%\Delta$ in $Q/5\%$; $(-1.5)(5\%) = \%\Delta$ in $Q = -7.5\%$. Ridership falls by 7.5% over a few years.

4. Total revenue rises immediately after the fare increase, since demand over the immediate period is price inelastic. Total revenue falls after a few years, since demand changes and becomes price elastic.

2. RESPONSIVENESS OF DEMAND TO OTHER FACTORS

LEARNING OBJECTIVES

1. **Explain the concept of income elasticity of demand and its calculation.**
2. **Classify goods as normal or inferior depending on their income elasticity of demand.**
3. **Explain the concept of cross price elasticity of demand and its calculation.**
4. **Classify goods as substitutes or complements depending on their cross price elasticity of demand.**

Although the response of quantity demanded to changes in price is the most widely used measure of elasticity, economists are interested in the response to changes in the demand shifters as well. Two of the most important measures show how demand responds to changes in income and to changes in the prices of related goods and services.

2.1   Income Elasticity of Demand

We saw in the chapter that introduced the model of demand and supply that the demand for a good or service is affected by income. We measure the **income elasticity of demand**, e_Y, as the percentage change in quantity demanded *at a specific price* divided by the percentage change in income that produced the demand change, all other things unchanged:

EQUATION 4.3

$$e_Y = \frac{\text{\% change in quantity demanded}}{\text{\% change in income}}$$

The symbol Y is often used in economics to represent income. Because income elasticity of demand reports the responsiveness of quantity demanded to a change in income, all other things unchanged (including the price of the good), it reflects a shift in the demand curve at a given price. Remember that price elasticity of demand reflects movements *along* a demand curve in response to a change in price.

A positive income elasticity of demand means that income and demand move in the same direction—an increase in income increases demand, and a reduction in income reduces demand. As we learned, a good whose demand rises as income rises is called a normal good.

Studies show that most goods and services are normal, and thus their income elasticities are positive. Goods and services for which demand is likely to move in the same direction as income include housing, seafood, rock concerts, and medical services.

If a good or service is inferior, then an increase in income reduces demand for the good. That implies a negative income elasticity of demand. Goods and services for which the income elasticity of demand is likely to be negative include used clothing, beans, and urban public transit. For example, the studies we have already cited concerning the demands for urban public transit in France and in Madrid found the long-run income elasticities of demand to be negative (−0.23 in France and −0.25 in Madrid).[3]

When we compute the income elasticity of demand, we are looking at the change in the quantity demanded at a specific price. We are thus dealing with a change that shifts the demand curve. An increase in income shifts the demand for a normal good to the right; it shifts the demand for an inferior good to the left.

2.2   Cross Price Elasticity of Demand

The demand for a good or service is affected by the prices of related goods or services. A reduction in the price of salsa, for example, would increase the demand for chips, suggesting that salsa is a complement of chips. A reduction in the price of chips, however, would reduce the demand for peanuts, suggesting that chips are a substitute for peanuts.

income elasticity of demand

The percentage change in quantity demanded at a specific price divided by the percentage change in income that produced the demand change, all other things unchanged.

The measure economists use to describe the responsiveness of demand for a good or service to a change in the price of another good or service is called the **cross price elasticity of demand**, $e_{A, B}$. It equals the percentage change in the quantity demanded of one good or service *at a specific price* divided by the percentage change in the price of a related good or service. We are varying the price of a related good when we consider the cross price elasticity of demand, so the response of quantity demanded is shown as a shift in the demand curve.

The cross price elasticity of the demand for good A with respect to the price of good B is given by:

EQUATION 4.4

$$e_{A, B} = \frac{\%\ \text{change in quantity demanded of good A}}{\%\ \text{change in price of good B}}$$

Cross price elasticities of demand define whether two goods are substitutes, complements, or unrelated. If two goods are substitutes, an increase in the price of one will lead to an increase in the demand for the other—the cross price elasticity of demand is positive. If two goods are complements, an increase in the price of one will lead to a reduction in the demand for the other—the cross price elasticity of demand is negative. If two goods are unrelated, a change in the price of one will not affect the demand for the other—the cross price elasticity of demand is zero.

An examination of the demand for local television advertising with respect to the price of local radio advertising revealed that the two goods are clearly substitutes. A 10 per cent increase in the price of local radio advertising led to a 10 per cent increase in demand for local television advertising, so that the cross price elasticity of demand for local television advertising with respect to changes in the price of radio advertising was 1.0.[4]

Heads Up!

Notice that with income elasticity of demand and cross price elasticity of demand we are primarily concerned with whether the measured value of these elasticities is positive or negative. In the case of income elasticity of demand this tells us whether the good or service is normal or inferior. In the case of cross price elasticity of demand it tells us whether two goods are substitutes or complements. With price elasticity of demand we were concerned with whether the measured absolute value of this elasticity was greater than, less than, or equal to 1, because this gave us information about what happens to total revenue as price changes. The terms elastic and inelastic apply to price elasticity of demand. They are not used to describe income elasticity of demand or cross price elasticity of demand.

KEY TAKEAWAYS

- The income elasticity of demand reflects the responsiveness of demand to changes in income. It is the percentage change in quantity demanded *at a specific price* divided by the percentage change in income, ceteris paribus.
- Income elasticity is positive for normal goods and negative for inferior goods.
- The cross price elasticity of demand measures the way demand for one good or service responds to changes in the price of another. It is the percentage change in the quantity demanded of one good or service *at a specific price* divided by the percentage change in the price of another good or service, all other things unchanged.
- Cross price elasticity is positive for substitutes, negative for complements, and zero for goods or services whose demands are unrelated.

TRY IT!

Suppose that when the price of bagels rises by 10%, the demand for cream cheese falls by 3% at the current price, and that when income rises by 10%, the demand for bagels increases by 1% at the current price. Calculate the cross price elasticity of demand for cream cheese with respect to the price of bagels and tell whether bagels and cream cheese are substitutes or complements. Calculate the income elasticity of demand and tell whether bagels are normal or inferior.

Case in Point

Various Demand Elasticities for Conventional and Organic Milk

© *Thinkstock*

Peruse the milk display at any supermarket and you will see a number of items that you would not have seen a decade ago. Choices include fat content; with or without lactose; animal milks or milk substitutes, such as soy or almond milk; flavors; and organic or conventional milk. Whereas in the 1990s only specialty stores stocked organic milk, today it is readily available in most supermarkets. In fact, the market share for organic milk has grown, as sales of conventional milk have been fairly constant while sales of organic milk have increased.

Professors Pedro Alviola and Oral Capps have estimated various demand elasticities associated with conventional and organic milk, based on a study of 38,000 households. Their results are summarized in the following table.

Elasticity Measure	Organic Milk	Conventional Milk
Own-price elasticity	−2.00	−0.87
Cross-price elasticity	0.70	0.18
Income elasticity	0.27	−0.01

Organic milk is price elastic, while conventional milk is price inelastic. Both cross-price elasticities are positive, indicating that these two kinds of milk are substitutes but their estimated values differ. In particular, a 1% increase in the price of conventional milk leads to a 0.70% increase in the quantity demanded of organic milk, while a 1% increase in the price of organic milk leads to an increase in the quantity demanded of conventional milk of only 0.18%. This asymmetry suggests that organic milk consumers have considerable reluctance in switching back to what they may perceive as a lower-quality product. Finally, the income elasticity estimates suggest that organic milk is a normal good, while conventional milk is an inferior good. As might be expected, in the sample used in the study, purchasers of organic milk are more affluent as a group than are purchasers of conventional milk.

Being a fairly new product, organic milk studies are just becoming available and the authors point out that other researchers using different data sets have calculated different values for these elasticities. Over time, as more data become available and various studies are compared, this type of work is likely to influence milk marketing and pricing.

Source: Pedro A. Alviola IV and Oral Capps Jr., "Household Demand Analysis of Organic and Conventional Fluid Milk in the United States Based on the 2004 Nielsen Homescan Panel," Agribusiness 26:3 (2010): 369–388.

ANSWER TO TRY IT! PROBLEM

Using the formula for cross price elasticity of demand, we find that $e_{AB} = (-3\%)/(10\%) = -0.3$. Since the e_{AB} is negative, bagels and cream cheese are complements. Using the formula for income elasticity of demand, we find that $e_Y = (+1\%)/(10\%) = +0.1$. Since e_Y is positive, bagels are a normal good.

3. PRICE ELASTICITY OF SUPPLY

LEARNING OBJECTIVES

1. **Explain the concept of elasticity of supply and its calculation.**
2. **Explain what it means for supply to be price inelastic, unit price elastic, price elastic, perfectly price inelastic, and perfectly price elastic.**
3. **Explain why time is an important determinant of price elasticity of supply.**
4. **Apply the concept of price elasticity of supply to the labor supply curve.**

The elasticity measures encountered so far in this chapter all relate to the demand side of the market. It is also useful to know how responsive quantity supplied is to a change in price.

Suppose the demand for apartments rises. There will be a shortage of apartments at the old level of apartment rents and pressure on rents to rise. All other things unchanged, the more responsive the quantity of apartments supplied is to changes in monthly rents, the lower the increase in rent required to eliminate the shortage and to bring the market back to equilibrium. Conversely, if quantity supplied is less responsive to price changes, price will have to rise more to eliminate a shortage caused by an increase in demand.

This is illustrated in Figure 4.5. Suppose the rent for a typical apartment had been R_0 and the quantity Q_0 when the demand curve was D_1 and the supply curve was either S_1 (a supply curve in which quantity supplied is less responsive to price changes) or S_2 (a supply curve in which quantity supplied is more responsive to price changes). Note that with either supply curve, equilibrium price and quantity are initially the same. Now suppose that demand increases to D_2, perhaps due to population growth. With supply curve S_1, the price (rent in this case) will rise to R_1 and the quantity of apartments will rise to Q_1. If, however, the supply curve had been S_2, the rent would only have to rise to R_2 to bring the market back to equilibrium. In addition, the new equilibrium number of apartments would be higher at Q_2. Supply curve S_2 shows greater responsiveness of quantity supplied to price change than does supply curve S_1.

We measure the **price elasticity of supply** (e_S) as the ratio of the percentage change in quantity supplied of a good or service to the percentage change in its price, all other things unchanged:

EQUATION 4.5

$$e_S = \frac{\% \text{ change in quantity supplied}}{\% \text{ change in price}}$$

Because price and quantity supplied usually move in the same direction, the price elasticity of supply is usually positive. The larger the price elasticity of supply, the more responsive the firms that supply the good or service are to a price change.

Supply is price elastic if the price elasticity of supply is greater than 1, unit price elastic if it is equal to 1, and price inelastic if it is less than 1. A vertical supply curve, as shown in Panel (a) of Figure 4.6, is perfectly inelastic; its price elasticity of supply is zero. The supply of Beatles' songs is perfectly inelastic because the band no longer exists. A horizontal supply curve, as shown in Panel (b) of Figure 4.6, is perfectly elastic; its price elasticity of supply is infinite. It means that suppliers are willing to supply any amount at a certain price.

FIGURE 4.5 Increase in Apartment Rents Depends on How Responsive Supply Is

The more responsive the supply of apartments is to changes in price (rent in this case), the less rents rise when the demand for apartments increases.

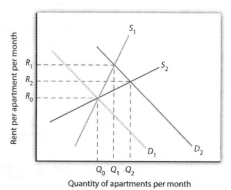

price elasticity of supply

The ratio of the percentage change in quantity supplied of a good or service to the percentage change in its price, all other things unchanged.

FIGURE 4.6 Supply Curves and Their Price Elasticities

The supply curve in Panel (a) is perfectly inelastic. In Panel (b), the supply curve is perfectly elastic.

3.1 Time: An Important Determinant of the Elasticity of Supply

Time plays a very important role in the determination of the price elasticity of supply. Look again at the effect of rent increases on the supply of apartments. Suppose apartment rents in a city rise. If we are looking at a supply curve of apartments over a period of a few months, the rent increase is likely to induce apartment owners to rent out a relatively small number of additional apartments. With the higher rents, apartment owners may be more vigorous in reducing their vacancy rates, and, indeed, with more people looking for apartments to rent, this should be fairly easy to accomplish. Attics and basements are easy to renovate and rent out as additional units. In a short period of time, however, the supply response is likely to be fairly modest, implying that the price elasticity of supply is fairly low. A supply curve corresponding to a short period of time would look like S_1 in Figure 4.5. It is during such periods that there may be calls for rent controls.

If the period of time under consideration is a few years rather than a few months, the supply curve is likely to be much more price elastic. Over time, buildings can be converted from other uses and new apartment complexes can be built. A supply curve corresponding to a longer period of time would look like S_2 in Figure 4.5.

3.2 Elasticity of Labor Supply: A Special Application

The concept of price elasticity of supply can be applied to labor to show how the quantity of labor supplied responds to changes in wages or salaries. What makes this case interesting is that it has sometimes been found that the measured elasticity is negative, that is, that an increase in the wage rate is associated with a reduction in the quantity of labor supplied.

In most cases, labor supply curves have their normal upward slope: higher wages induce people to work more. For them, having the additional income from working more is preferable to having more leisure time. However, wage increases may lead some people in very highly paid jobs to cut back on the number of hours they work because their incomes are already high and they would rather have more time for leisure activities. In this case, the labor supply curve would have a negative slope. The reasons for this phenomenon are explained more fully in a later chapter. The Case in Point in this section gives another example where an increase in the wage may reduce the number of hours of work.

KEY TAKEAWAYS

- The price elasticity of supply measures the responsiveness of quantity supplied to changes in price. It is the percentage change in quantity supplied divided by the percentage change in price. It is usually positive.
- Supply is price inelastic if the price elasticity of supply is less than 1; it is unit price elastic if the price elasticity of supply is equal to 1; and it is price elastic if the price elasticity of supply is greater than 1. A vertical supply curve is said to be perfectly inelastic. A horizontal supply curve is said to be perfectly elastic.
- The price elasticity of supply is greater when the length of time under consideration is longer because over time producers have more options for adjusting to the change in price.
- When applied to labor supply, the price elasticity of supply is usually positive but can be negative. If higher wages induce people to work more, the labor supply curve is upward sloping and the price elasticity of supply is positive. In some very high-paying professions or other unusual circumstances, the labor supply curve may have a negative slope, which leads to a negative price elasticity of supply.

TRY IT!

In the late 1990s, it was reported on the news that the high-tech industry was worried about being able to find enough workers with computer-related expertise. Job offers for recent college graduates with degrees in computer science went with high salaries. It was also reported that more undergraduates than ever were majoring in computer science. Compare the price elasticity of supply of computer scientists at that point in time to the price elasticity of supply of computer scientists over a longer period of, say, 1999 to 2009.

Case in Point

Child Labor in Pakistan

© *Thinkstock*

Professor Sonia Bhalotra investigated the role of household poverty in child labor. Imagine a household with two parents and two children, a boy and a girl. If only the parents work, the family income may be less than an amount required for subsistence. In order to at least raise the income of the family to subsistence, will the labor of both children be added? If only one child will work, will it be the boy or the girl? How do the motivations of parents to send their children to work affect the design of policies to encourage education? Will a program that reduces school fees or improves school quality lead to more education or would a program that provides cash or food to households who send their children to school work better?

Using information on over 3,000 children in an area of rural Pakistan where their labor force participation is high, child wage labor is common, and gender differences in education and work of children prevail, Professor Bhalotra specifically estimated how changes in wages for boys and girls affect the number of hours they work. She focused on wage work outside the home because it usually involves more hours and less flexibility than, say, work on one's own farm, which essentially rules out going to school.

She argues that if the work of a child is geared toward the family hitting a target level of income, then an increase in the wage will lead to fewer hours of work. That is, the labor supply elasticity will be negative and the labor supply curve will have a negative slope. For boys, she finds that the wage elasticity is about −0.5. For girls, she finds that the wage elasticity is about 0, meaning the labor supply curve is vertical. To further her hypothesis that the labor supply decision for boys but not for girls is compelled by household poverty, she notes that separate estimates show that the income of the family from sources other than having their children work reduces the amount that boys work but has no effect on the amount that girls work. Other research she has undertaken on labor supply of children on household-run farms provides further support for these gender differences: Girls from families that own relatively larger farms were both more likely to work and less likely to go to school than girls from households with farms of smaller acreage.

Why the gender differences and how do these findings affect drafting of policies to encourage schooling? For boys, cash or food given to households could induce parents to send their sons to school. For girls, household poverty reduction may not work. Their relatively lower level of participating in schooling may be related to an expected low impact of education on their future wages. Expectations about when they will get married and whether or not they should work as adults, especially if it means moving to other areas, may also play a role. For girls, policies that alter attitudes toward girls' education and in the longer term affect educated female adult earnings may be more instrumental in increasing their educational attainment.

Source: Sonia Bhalotra, "Is Child Work Necessary?" Oxford Bulletin of Economics and Statistics 69:1 (2007): 29–55.

While at a point in time the supply of people with degrees in computer science is very price inelastic, over time the elasticity should rise. That more students were majoring in computer science lends credence to this prediction. As supply becomes more price elastic, salaries in this field should rise more slowly.

4. REVIEW AND PRACTICE

Summary

This chapter introduced a new tool: the concept of elasticity. Elasticity is a measure of the degree to which a dependent variable responds to a change in an independent variable. It is the percentage change in the dependent variable divided by the percentage change in the independent variable, all other things unchanged.

The most widely used elasticity measure is the price elasticity of demand, which reflects the responsiveness of quantity demanded to changes in price. Demand is said to be price elastic if the absolute value of the price elasticity of demand is greater than 1, unit price elastic if it is equal to 1, and price inelastic if it is less than 1. The price elasticity of demand is useful in forecasting the response of quantity demanded to price changes; it is also useful for predicting the impact a price change will have on total revenue. Total revenue moves in the direction of the quantity change if demand is price elastic, it moves in the direction of the price change if demand is price inelastic, and it does not change if demand is unit price elastic. The most important determinants of the price elasticity of demand are the availability of substitutes, the importance of the item in household budgets, and time.

Two other elasticity measures commonly used in conjunction with demand are income elasticity and cross price elasticity. The signs of these elasticity measures play important roles. A positive income elasticity tells us that a good is normal; a negative income elasticity tells us the good is inferior. A positive cross price elasticity tells us that two goods are substitutes; a negative cross price elasticity tells us they are complements.

Elasticity of supply measures the responsiveness of quantity supplied to changes in price. The value of price elasticity of supply is generally positive. Supply is classified as being price elastic, unit price elastic, or price inelastic if price elasticity is greater than 1, equal to 1, or less than 1, respectively. The length of time over which supply is being considered is an important determinant of the price elasticity of supply.

CONCEPT PROBLEMS

1. Explain why the price elasticity of demand is generally a negative number, except in the cases where the demand curve is perfectly elastic or perfectly inelastic. What would be implied by a positive price elasticity of demand?

2. Explain why the sign (positive or negative) of the cross price elasticity of demand is important.

3. Explain why the sign (positive or negative) of the income elasticity of demand is important.

4. Economists Dale Heien and Cathy Roheim Wessells found that the price elasticity of demand for fresh milk is −0.63 and the price elasticity of demand for cottage cheese is −1.1.[5] Why do you think the elasticity estimates differ?

5. The price elasticity of demand for health care has been estimated to be −0.2. Characterize this demand as price elastic, unit price elastic, or price inelastic. The text argues that the greater the importance of an item in consumer budgets, the greater its elasticity. Health-care costs account for a relatively large share of household budgets. How could the price elasticity of demand for health care be such a small number?

6. Suppose you are able to organize an alliance that includes all farmers. They agree to follow the group's instructions with respect to the quantity of agricultural products they produce. What might the group seek to do? Why?

7. Suppose you are the chief executive officer of a firm, and you have been planning to reduce your prices. Your marketing manager reports that the price elasticity of demand for your product is −0.65. How will this news affect your plans?

8. Suppose the income elasticity of the demand for beans is −0.8. Interpret this number.

9. Transportation economists generally agree that the cross price elasticity of demand for automobile use with respect to the price of bus fares is about 0. Explain what this number means.

10. Suppose the price elasticity of supply of tomatoes as measured on a given day in July is 0. Interpret this number.

11. The price elasticity of supply for child-care workers has been estimated to be quite high, about 2. What will happen to the wages of child-care workers as demand for them increases, compared to what would happen if the measured price elasticity of supply were lower?

12. Studies suggest that a higher tax on cigarettes would reduce teen smoking and premature deaths. Should cigarette taxes therefore be raised?

NUMERICAL PROBLEMS

1. Economist David Romer found that in introductory economics classes a 10% increase in class attendance is associated with a 4% increase in course grade.[6] What is the elasticity of course grade with respect to class attendance?

2. Refer to Figure 4.2 and

   a. Using the arc elasticity of demand formula, compute the price elasticity of demand between points B and C.

   b. Using the arc elasticity of demand formula, compute the price elasticity of demand between points D and E.

   c. How do the values of price elasticity of demand compare? Why are they the same or different?

   d. Compute the slope of the demand curve between points B and C.

   e. Computer the slope of the demand curve between points D and E.

   f. How do the slopes compare? Why are they the same or different?

3. Consider the following quote from *The Wall Street Journal:* "A bumper crop of oranges in Florida last year drove down orange prices. As juice marketers' costs fell, they cut prices by as much as 15%. That was enough to tempt some value-oriented customers: unit volume of frozen juices actually rose about 6% during the quarter."

   a. Given these numbers, and assuming there were no changes in demand shifters for frozen orange juice, what was the price elasticity of demand for frozen orange juice?

   b. What do you think happened to total spending on frozen orange juice? Why?

4. Suppose you are the manager of a restaurant that serves an average of 400 meals per day at an average price per meal of $20. On the basis of a survey, you have determined that reducing the price of an average meal to $18 would increase the quantity demanded to 450 per day.

   a. Compute the price elasticity of demand between these two points.

   b. Would you expect total revenues to rise or fall? Explain.

   c. Suppose you have reduced the average price of a meal to $18 and are considering a further reduction to $16. Another survey shows that the quantity demanded of meals will increase from 450 to 500 per day. Compute the price elasticity of demand between these two points.

   d. Would you expect total revenue to rise or fall as a result of this second price reduction? Explain.

   e. Compute total revenue at the three meal prices. Do these totals confirm your answers in (b) and (d) above?

5. The text notes that, for any linear demand curve, demand is price elastic in the upper half and price inelastic in the lower half. Consider the following demand curves:

The table gives the prices and quantities corresponding to each of the points shown on the two demand curves.

	Demand curve D_1 [Panel (a)]			Demand curve D_2 [Panel (b)]	
	Price	Quantity		Price	Quantity
A	80	2	E	8	20
B	70	3	F	7	30
C	30	7	G	3	70
D	20	8	H	2	80

a. Compute the price elasticity of demand between points A and B and between points C and D on demand curve D_1 in Panel (a). Are your results consistent with the notion that a linear demand curve is price elastic in its upper half and price inelastic in its lower half?

b. Compute the price elasticity of demand between points E and F and between points G and H on demand curve D_2 in Panel (b). Are your results consistent with the notion that a linear demand curve is price elastic in its upper half and price inelastic in its lower half?

c. Compare total spending at points A and B on D_1 in Panel (a). Is your result consistent with your finding about the price elasticity of demand between those two points?

d. Compare total spending at points C and D on D_1 in Panel (a). Is your result consistent with your finding about the price elasticity of demand between those two points?

e. Compare total spending at points E and F on D_2 in Panel (b). Is your result consistent with your finding about the price elasticity of demand between those two points?

f. Compare total spending at points G and H on D_2 in Panel (b). Is your result consistent with your finding about the price elasticity of demand between those two points?

6. Suppose Janice buys the following amounts of various food items depending on her weekly income:

Weekly Income	Hamburgers	Pizza	Ice Cream Sundaes
$500	3	3	2
$750	4	2	2

a. Compute Janice's income elasticity of demand for hamburgers.

b. Compute Janice's income elasticity of demand for pizza.

c. Compute Janice's income elasticity of demand for ice cream sundaes.

d. Classify each good as normal or inferior.

7. Suppose the following table describes Jocelyn's weekly snack purchases, which vary depending on the price of a bag of chips:

Price of bag of chips	Bags of chips	Containers of salsa	Bags of pretzels	Cans of soda
$1.00	2	3	1	4
$1.50	1	2	2	4

a. Compute the cross price elasticity of salsa with respect to the price of a bag of chips.

b. Compute the cross price elasticity of pretzels with respect to the price of a bag of chips.

c. Compute the cross price elasticity of soda with respect to the price of a bag of chips.

d. Are chips and salsa substitutes or complements? How do you know?

e. Are chips and pretzels substitutes or complements? How do you know?

f. Are chips and soda substitutes or complements? How do you know?

8. The table below describes the supply curve for light bulbs:

Price per light bulb	Quantity supplied per day
$1.00	500
1.50	3,000
2.00	4,000
2.50	4,500
3.00	4,500

Compute the price elasticity of supply and determine whether supply is price elastic, price inelastic, perfectly elastic, perfectly inelastic, or unit elastic:

    a. when the price of a light bulb increases from $1.00 to $1.50.

    b. when the price of a light bulb increases from $1.50 to $2.00.

    c. when the price of a light bulb increases from $2.00 to $2.50.

    d. when the price of a light bulb increases from $2.50 to $3.00.

ENDNOTES

1. Notice that since the number of units sold of a good is the same as the number of units bought, the definition for total revenue could also be used to define total spending. Which term we use depends on the question at hand. If we are trying to determine what happens to revenues of sellers, then we are asking about total revenue. If we are trying to determine how much consumers spend, then we are asking about total spending.

2. Division by zero results in an undefined solution. Saying that the price elasticity of demand is infinite requires that we say the denominator "approaches" zero.

3. See Georges Bresson, Joyce Dargay, Jean-Loup Madre, and Alain Pirotte, "Economic and Structural Determinants of the Demand for French Transport: An Analysis on a Panel of French Urban Areas Using Shrinkage Estimators." *Transportation Research: Part A* 38: 4 (May 2004): 269–285. See also Anna Matas. "Demand and Revenue Implications of an Integrated Transport Policy: The Case of Madrid." *Transport Reviews* 24:2 (March 2004): 195–217.

4. Robert B. Ekelund, S. Ford, and John D. Jackson. "Are Local TV Markets Separate Markets?" *International Journal of the Economics of Business* 7:1 (2000): 79–97.

5. Dale M. Heien and Cathy Roheim Wessels, "The Demand for Dairy Products: Structure, Prediction, and Decomposition," *American Journal of Agricultural Economics* 70:2 (May 1988): 219–228.

6. David Romer, "Do Students Go to Class? Should They?" *Journal of Economic Perspectives* 7:3 (Summer 1993): 167–174.

CHAPTER 5
Markets, Maximizers, and Efficiency

START UP: A DRIVE IN THE COUNTRY

Suppose you decide to take a drive. For purposes of this example, we will assume that you have a car available, that the weather is pleasant, and that there is an area nearby that will be perfect for your drive.

Your decision to take this drive is a choice. Since economics deals with choices, we can put economics to work in thinking about it. Economists assume that people make choices that maximize the value of some objective. You are a consumer; we assume that taking a drive is a choice that maximizes your utility—the satisfaction you obtain from your use of goods and services and from the activities you pursue.

You certainly plan to enjoy the drive; that enjoyment is the benefit you expect from it. But you will give up some things as well. Your drive will take some time, time you could have spent doing something else. It will take some gasoline; what you spend for the gasoline could have been used for something else. The drive will also generate some wear and tear on your car. That will cost you the price of repair and maintenance and reduced resale value of your car. The opportunity cost of your drive will thus include the value of the best other use of your time and the value of the best other use of the funds your drive will require. To maximize utility you will weigh the benefits of the drive against the cost of the drive and maximize the difference between those benefits and costs.

This chapter introduces the method through which maximizing choices can be made. This method applies not just to your decision to take a drive, but also to Wal-Mart's decision to hire extra workers and to USX Corporation's to produce extra steel. The method we will learn can be applied to the analysis of any choice; we will use it throughout our investigation of microeconomics.

We will also see how maximizing choices by individuals and by firms can lead to an allocation of resources that generates the greatest gains possible for the economy as a whole. In this analysis, we will put a new item in our tool kit, the method through which individuals and firms maximize, together with demand and supply analysis, to see how the marketplace can guide resources to their best uses.

We will also examine cases in which maximizing choices do not guide resources to their best uses. That possibility is suggested by another aspect of your choice to take a drive. In addition to the costs you will consider, there will be costs imposed on others. Your drive will pollute the air, so part of the opportunity cost of the drive will be the value of the slightly cleaner air people in your area might have had. Resources such as the air we breathe will almost certainly be misallocated as the result of maximizing choices. We will see just how misallocation of an economy's resources can occur and how this misallocation could be fixed.

1. THE LOGIC OF MAXIMIZING BEHAVIOR

LEARNING OBJECTIVES

1. Explain the maximization assumption that economists make in explaining the behavior of consumers and firms.
2. Explain and illustrate the concepts of marginal benefit and marginal cost and apply them to understanding the marginal decision rule.

economic profit

The difference between total revenue and total cost.

To say that individuals maximize is to say that they pick some objective and then seek to maximize its value. A sprinter might want to maximize his or her speed; a politician might want to maximize the probability that he or she will win the next election. Economists pay special attention to two groups of maximizers: consumers and firms. We assume that consumers seek to maximize utility and that firms seek to maximize **economic profit**, which is the difference between total revenue and total cost. The costs involved in this concept of economic profit are computed in the economic sense—as the opportunity costs, or value of the best opportunity forgone.

The assumption of maximizing behavior lies at the heart of economic analysis. As we explore its implications, however, we must keep in mind the distinction between models and the real world. Our model assumes that individuals make choices in a way that achieves a maximum value for some clearly defined objective. In using such a model, economists do not assume that people actually go through the calculations we will describe. What economists do argue is that people's behavior is broadly consistent with such a model. People may not consciously seek to maximize anything, but they behave as though they do.

1.1   The Analysis of Maximizing Behavior

net benefit

The total benefit of an activity minus its opportunity cost.

The activities of consumers and firms have benefits, and they also have opportunity costs. We assume that given these benefits and costs, consumers and firms will make choices that maximize the **net benefit** of each activity—the total benefit of the activity minus its opportunity cost. The specific measures of benefit and cost vary with the kind of choice being made. In the case of a firm's choices in production, for example, the total benefit of production is the revenue a firm receives from selling the product; the total cost is the opportunity cost the firm incurs by producing it. The net benefit is thus total revenue minus total opportunity cost, or economic profit.

Economists maintain that in order to maximize net benefit, consumers and firms evaluate each activity at the margin—they consider the additional benefit and the additional cost of another unit of the activity. Should you "supersize" your order at McDonald's? Will the additional beverage and the additional french fries be worth the extra cost? Should a firm hire one more worker? Will the benefits to the firm of hiring this worker be worth the additional cost of hiring him or her?

marginal benefit

The amount by which an additional unit of an activity increases its total benefit.

marginal cost

The amount by which an additional unit of an activity increases its total cost.

marginal decision rule

If the marginal benefit of an additional unit of an activity exceeds the marginal cost, the quantity of the activity should be increased. If the marginal benefit is less than the marginal cost, the quantity should be reduced.

The **marginal benefit** is the amount by which an additional unit of an activity increases its total benefit. It is the amount by which the extra french fries increase your satisfaction, or the extra revenue the firm expects to bring in by hiring another worker. The **marginal cost** is the amount by which an additional unit of an activity increases its total cost. You will pay more to supersize your McDonald's order; the firm's labor costs will rise when it hires another worker.

To determine the quantity of any activity that will maximize its net benefit, we apply the **marginal decision rule**: If the marginal benefit of an additional unit of an activity exceeds the marginal cost, the quantity of the activity should be increased. If the marginal benefit is less than the marginal cost, the quantity should be reduced. Net benefit is maximized at the point at which marginal benefit equals marginal cost. The marginal decision rule is at the heart of the economic way of thinking. The rule basically says this: If the additional benefit of one more unit exceeds the extra cost, do it; if not, do not. This simple logic gives us a powerful tool for the analysis of choice. Perhaps more than any other rule in economic analysis, the marginal decision rule typifies the way in which economists analyze problems. We shall apply it in every chapter that follows in the microeconomics portion of this text.

Maximizing choices must be made within the parameters imposed by some **constraint**, which is a boundary that limits the range of choices that can be made. We assume that a consumer seeks the greatest satisfaction possible within the limits of his or her income or budget. A firm cannot produce beyond the limits of its production capacity at a point in time.

The marginal decision rule forms the foundation for the structure economists use to analyze all choices. At first glance, it may seem that a consumer seeking satisfaction from, say, pizza has little in common with an entrepreneur seeking profit from the production of custom-designed semiconductors. But maximizing choices always follow the marginal decision rule—and that rule holds regardless of what is being maximized or who is doing the maximizing.

To see how the logic of maximizing choices works, we will examine a specific problem. We will then extend that problem to the general analysis of maximizing choices.

A Problem in Maximization

Suppose a college student, Laurie Phan, faces two midterms tomorrow, one in economics and another in accounting. She has already decided to spend 5 hours studying for the two examinations. This decision imposes a constraint on the problem. Suppose that Ms. Phan's goal is to allocate her 5 hours of study so that she increases her total score for the two exams by as much as possible.

Ms. Phan expects the relationship between the time she spends studying for the economics exam and the total gain in her score to be as given by the second row of the table in Panel (a) of Figure 5.1. We interpret the expected total gain in her score as the total benefit of study. She expects that 1 hour of study will raise her score by 18 points; 2 hours will raise it by 32 points, and so on. These values are plotted in Panel (b). Notice that the total benefit curve rises, but by smaller and smaller amounts, as she studies more and more. The slope of the curve, which in this case tells us the rate at which her expected score rises with increased study time, falls as we travel up and to the right along the curve.

Now look at the third row in the table in Panel (a). It tells us the amount by which each additional hour of study increases her expected score; it gives the marginal benefit of studying for the economics exam. Marginal benefit equals the amount by which total benefit rises with each additional hour of study. Because these marginal benefits are given by the changes in total benefits from additional hours of study, they equal the slope of the total benefit curve. We see this in the relationship between Panels (b) and (c) of Figure 5.1. The decreasing slope of the total benefit curve in Panel (b) gives us the downward-sloping marginal benefit curve in Panel (c).

The marginal benefit curve tells us what happens when we pass from one point to another on the total benefit curve, so we have plotted marginal benefits at the midpoints of the hourly intervals in Panel (c). For example, the total benefit curve in Panel (b) tells us that, when Ms. Phan increases her time studying for the economics exam from 2 hours to 3 hours, her total benefit rises from 32 points to 42 points. The increase of 10 points is the marginal benefit of increasing study time for the economics exam from 2 hours to 3 hours. We mark the point for a marginal benefit of 10 points midway between 2 and 3 hours. Because marginal values tell us what happens as we pass from one quantity to the next, we shall always plot them at the midpoints of intervals of the variable on the horizontal axis.

constraint

A boundary that limits the range of choices that can be made.

FIGURE 5.1 The Benefits of Studying Economics

The table in Panel (a) shows the total benefit and marginal benefit of the time Laurie Phan spends studying for her economics exam. Panel (b) shows the total benefit curve. Panel (c) shows the marginal benefit curve, which is given by the slope of the total benefit curve in Panel (b).

Panel (a)

Hours studying economics	0	1	2	3	4	5
Expected total point gain in test score (total benefit)	0	18	32	42	48	50
Marginal benefit		18	14	10	6	2

We can perform the same kind of analysis to obtain the marginal benefit curve for studying for the accounting exam. Figure 5.2 presents this curve. Like the marginal benefit curve for studying economics, it slopes downward. Once again, we have plotted marginal values at the midpoints of the intervals. Increasing study time in accounting from 0 to 1 hour increases Ms. Phan's expected accounting score by 14 points.

FIGURE 5.2 The Marginal Benefits of Studying Accounting

The marginal benefit Laurie Phan expects from studying for her accounting exam is shown by the marginal benefit curve. The first hour of study increases her expected score by 14 points, the second hour by 10 points, the third by 6 points, and so on.

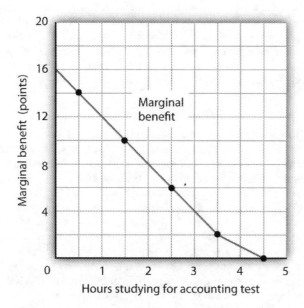

Ms. Phan's marginal benefit curves for studying typify a general phenomenon in economics. Marginal benefit curves for virtually all activities, including the activities of consumers and of firms, slope downward. Think about your own experience with studying. On a given day, the first hour spent studying a certain subject probably generates a greater marginal benefit than the second, and the second hour probably generates a greater marginal benefit than the third. You may reach a point at which an extra hour of study is unlikely to yield any benefit at all. Of course, our example of Laurie Phan's expected exam scores is a highly stylized one. One could hardly expect a student to have a precise set of numbers to guide him or her in allocating study time. But it is certainly the case that students have a rough idea of the likely payoff of study time in different subjects. If you were faced with exams in two subjects, it is likely that you would set aside a certain amount of study time, just as Ms. Phan did in our example. And it is likely that your own experience would serve as a guide in determining how to allocate that time. Economists do not assume that people have numerical scales in their heads with which to draw marginal benefit and marginal cost curves. They merely assume that people act as if they did.

The nature of marginal benefits can change with different applications. For a restaurant, the marginal benefit of serving one more meal can be defined as the revenue that meal produces. For a consumer, the marginal benefit of one more slice of pizza can be considered in terms of the additional satisfaction the pizza will create. But whatever the nature of the benefit, marginal benefits generally fall as quantities increase.

Ms. Phan's falling marginal benefit from hours spent studying accounting has special significance for our analysis of her choice concerning how many hours to devote to economics. In our problem, she had decided to devote 5 hours to studying the two subjects. That means that the opportunity cost of an hour spent studying economics equals the benefit she would have gotten spending that hour studying accounting.

Suppose, for example, that she were to consider spending all 5 hours studying accounting. The marginal benefit curve for studying for her accounting exam tells us that she expects that the fifth hour will add nothing to her score. Shifting that hour to economics would cost nothing. We can say that the marginal cost of the first hour spent studying economics is zero. We obtained this value from the marginal benefit curve for studying accounting in Figure 5.2.

Similarly, we can find the marginal cost of the second hour studying economics. That requires giving up the fourth hour spent on accounting. Figure 5.2 tells us that the marginal benefit of that hour equals 2—that is the marginal cost of spending the second hour studying economics.

Figure 5.3 shows the marginal cost curve of studying economics. We see that at first, time devoted to studying economics has a low marginal cost. As time spent studying economics increases, however, it requires her to give up study time in accounting that she expects will be more and more productive.

The marginal cost curve for studying economics can thus be derived from the marginal benefit curve for studying accounting. Figure 5.3 also shows the marginal benefit curve for studying economics that we derived in Panel (b) of Figure 5.1.

FIGURE 5.3 The Marginal Benefits and Marginal Costs of Studying Economics

The marginal benefit curve from Panel (c) of Figure 5.1 is shown together with the marginal costs of studying economics. The marginal cost curve is derived from the marginal benefit curve for studying accounting shown in Figure 5.2.

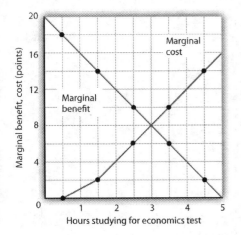

Just as marginal benefit curves generally slope downward, marginal cost curves generally slope upward, as does the one in Figure 5.3. In the case of allocating time, the phenomenon of rising marginal cost results from the simple fact that, the more time a person devotes to one activity, the less time is available for another. And the more one reduces the second activity, the greater the forgone marginal benefits are likely to be. That means the marginal cost curve for that first activity rises.

Because we now have marginal benefit and marginal cost curves for studying economics, we can apply the marginal decision rule. This rule says that, to maximize the net benefit of an activity, a decision maker should increase an activity up to the point at which marginal benefit equals marginal cost. That occurs where the marginal benefit and marginal cost curves intersect, with 3 hours spent studying economics and 2 hours spent studying accounting.

Using Marginal Benefit and Marginal Cost Curves to Find Net Benefits

We can use marginal benefit and marginal cost curves to show the total benefit, the total cost, and the net benefit of an activity. We will see that equating marginal benefit to marginal cost does, indeed, maximize net benefit. We will also develop another tool to use in interpreting marginal benefit and cost curves.

Panel (a) of Figure 5.4 shows the marginal benefit curve we derived in Panel (c) of Figure 5.1. The corresponding point on the marginal benefit curve gives the marginal benefit of the first hour of study for the economics exam, 18 points. This same value equals the area of the rectangle bounded by 0 and 1 hour of study and the marginal benefit of 18. Similarly, the marginal benefit of the second hour, 14 points, is shown by the corresponding point on the marginal benefit curve and by the area of the shaded rectangle bounded by 1 and 2 hours of study. The total benefit of 2 hours of study equals the sum of the areas of the first two rectangles, 32 points. We continue this procedure through the fifth hour of studying economics; the areas for each of the shaded rectangles are shown in the graph.

FIGURE 5.4 The Benefits and Costs of Studying Economics

Panel (a) shows the marginal benefit curve of Figure 5.1. The total benefit of studying economics at any given quantity of study time is given approximately by the shaded area below the marginal benefit curve up to that level of study. Panel (b) shows the marginal cost curve from Figure 5.3. The total cost of studying economics at any given quantity of study is given approximately by the shaded area below the marginal cost curve up to that level of study.

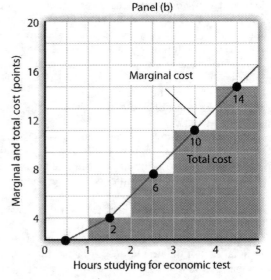

Two features of the curve in Panel (a) of Figure 5.4 are particularly important. First, note that the sum of the areas of the five rectangles, 50 points, equals the total benefit of 5 hours of study given in the table in Panel (a) of Figure 5.1. Second, notice that the shaded areas are approximately equal to the area under the marginal benefit curve between 0 and 5 hours of study. We can pick any quantity of study time, and the total benefit of that quantity equals the sum of the shaded rectangles between zero and that quantity. Thus, the total benefit of 2 hours of study equals 32 points, the sum of the areas of the first two rectangles.

Now consider the marginal cost curve in Panel (b) of Figure 5.4. The areas of the shaded rectangles equal the values of marginal cost. The marginal cost of the first hour of study equals zero; there is thus no rectangle under the curve. The marginal cost of the second hour of study equals 2 points; that is the area of the rectangle bounded by 1 and 2 hours of study and a marginal cost of 2. The marginal cost of the third hour of study is 6 points; this is the area of the shaded rectangle bounded by 2 and 3 hours of study and a marginal cost of 6.

Looking at the rectangles in Panel (b) over the range of 0 to 5 hours of study, we see that the areas of the five rectangles total 32, the total cost of spending all 5 hours studying economics. And looking at the rectangles, we see that their area is approximately equal to the area under the marginal cost curve between 0 and 5 hours of study.

We have seen that the areas of the rectangles drawn with Laurie Phan's marginal benefit and marginal cost curves equal the total benefit and total cost of studying economics. We have also seen that these areas are roughly equal to the areas under the curves themselves. We can make this last statement much stronger. Suppose, instead of thinking in intervals of whole hours, we think in terms of smaller intervals, say, of 12 minutes. Then each rectangle would be only one-fifth as wide as the rectangles we drew in Figure 5.4. Their areas would still equal the total benefit and total cost of study, and the sum of those areas would be closer to the area under the curves. We have done this for Ms. Phan's marginal benefit curve in Figure 5.5; notice that the areas of the rectangles closely approximate the area under the curve. They still "stick out" from either side of the curve as did the rectangles we drew in Figure 5.4, but you almost need a magnifying glass to see that. The smaller the interval we choose, the closer the areas under the marginal benefit and marginal cost curves will be to total benefit and total cost. For purposes of our model, we can imagine that the intervals are as small as we like. Over a particular range of quantity, the area under a marginal benefit curve equals the total benefit of that quantity, and the area under the marginal cost curve equals the total cost of that quantity.

FIGURE 5.5 The Marginal Benefit Curve and Total Benefit

When the increments used to measure time allocated to studying economics are made smaller, in this case 12 minutes instead of whole hours, the area under the marginal benefit curve is closer to the total benefit of studying that amount of time.

deadweight loss

The loss in net benefits resulting from a failure to carry out an activity at the most efficient level.

Panel (a) of Figure 5.6 shows marginal benefit and marginal cost curves for studying economics, this time without numbers. We have the usual downward-sloping marginal benefit curve and upward-sloping marginal cost curve. The marginal decision rule tells us to choose D hours studying economics, the quantity at which marginal benefit equals marginal cost at point C. We know that the total benefit of study equals the area under the marginal benefit curve over the range from A to D hours of study, the area ABCD. Total cost equals the area under the marginal cost curve over the same range, or ACD. The difference between total benefit and total cost equals the area between marginal benefit and marginal cost between A and D hours of study; it is the green-shaded triangle ABC. This difference is the net benefit of time spent studying economics. Panel (b) of Figure 5.6 introduces another important concept. If an activity is carried out at a level less than the efficient level, then net benefits are forgone. The loss in net benefits resulting from a failure to carry out an activity at the efficient level is called a **deadweight loss**.

FIGURE 5.6 Using Marginal Benefit and Marginal Cost Curves to Determine Net Benefit

In Panel (a) net benefits are given by the difference between total benefits (as measured by the area under the marginal benefit curve up to any given level of activity) and total costs (as measured by the area under the marginal cost curve up to any given level of activity). Maximum net benefits are found where the marginal benefit curve intersects the marginal cost curve at activity level D. Panel (b) shows that if the level of the activity is restricted to activity level E, net benefits are reduced from the light-green shaded triangle ABC in Panel (a) to the smaller area ABGF. The forgone net benefits, or deadweight loss, is given by the purple-shaded area FGC. If the activity level is increased from D to J, as shown in Panel (c), net benefits declined by the deadweight loss measured by the area CHI.

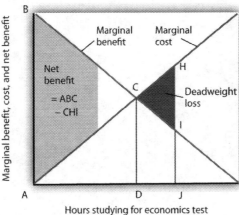

Now suppose a person increases study time from D to J hours as shown in Panel (c). The area under the marginal cost curve between D and J gives the total cost of increasing study time; it is DCHJ. The total benefit of increasing study time equals the area under the marginal benefit curve between D and J; it is DCIJ. The cost of increasing study time in economics from D hours to J hours exceeds the benefit. This gives us a deadweight loss of CHI. The net benefit of spending J hours studying economics equals the net benefit of studying for D hours less the deadweight loss, or ABC *minus* CHI. Only by studying up to the point at which marginal benefit equals marginal cost do we achieve the maximum net benefit shown in Panel (a).

We can apply the marginal decision rule to the problem in Figure 5.6 in another way. In Panel (b), a person studies economics for E hours. Reading up to the marginal benefit curve, we reach point G. Reading up to the marginal cost curve, we reach point F. Marginal benefit at G exceeds marginal cost at F; the marginal decision rule says economics study should be increased, which would take us toward the intersection of the marginal benefit and marginal cost curves. Spending J hours studying economics, as shown in Panel (c), is too much. Reading up to the marginal benefit and marginal cost curves, we see that marginal cost exceeds marginal benefit, suggesting that study time be reduced.

This completes our introduction to the marginal decision rule and the use of marginal benefit and marginal cost curves. We will spend the remainder of the chapter applying the model.

Heads Up!

It is easy to make the mistake of assuming that if an activity is carried out up to the point where marginal benefit equals marginal cost, then net benefits must be zero. Remember that following the marginal decision rule and equating marginal benefits and costs *maximizes* net benefits. It makes the *difference* between total benefits and total cost as large as possible.

KEY TAKEAWAYS

- Economists assume that decision makers make choices in the way that maximizes the value of some objective.
- Maximization involves determining the change in total benefit and the change in total cost associated with each unit of an activity. These changes are called marginal benefit and marginal cost, respectively.
- If the marginal benefit of an activity exceeds the marginal cost, the decision maker will gain by increasing the activity.
- If the marginal cost of an activity exceeds the marginal benefit, the decision maker will gain by reducing the activity.
- The area under the marginal benefit curve for an activity gives its total benefit; the area under the marginal cost curve gives the activity's total cost. Net benefit equals total benefit less total cost.
- The marginal benefit rule tells us that we can maximize the net benefit of any activity by choosing the quantity at which marginal benefit equals marginal cost. At this quantity, the net benefit of the activity is maximized.

TRY IT!

Suppose Ms. Phan still faces the exams in economics and in accounting, and she still plans to spend a total of 5 hours studying for the two exams. However, she revises her expectations about the degree to which studying economics and accounting will affect her scores on the two exams. She expects studying economics will add somewhat less to her score, and she expects studying accounting will add more. The result is the table below of expected total benefits and total costs of hours spent studying economics. Notice that several values in the table have been omitted. Fill in the missing values in the table. How many hours of study should Ms. Phan devote to economics to maximize her net benefit?

Hours studying economics	0	1	2	3	4	5
Total benefit	0	14	24	30		32
Total cost	0	2	8		32	50
Net benefit	0	12		12	0	−18

Now compute the marginal benefits and costs of hours devoted to studying economics, completing the table below.

Hours studying economics	0	1	2	3	4	5
Total benefit	0	14	24	30		32
Marginal benefit		___	___	___	___	___
Total cost	0	2	8		32	50
Marginal cost		___	___	___	___	___

Draw the marginal benefit and marginal cost curves for studying economics (remember to plot marginal values at the midpoints of the respective hourly intervals). Do your curves intersect at the "right" number of hours of study—the number that maximizes the net benefit of studying economics?

Case in Point

Preventing Oil Spills

© 2010 Jupiterimages Corporation

Do we spill enough oil in our oceans and waterways? It is a question that perhaps only economists would ask—and, as economists, we should ask it.

There is, of course, no virtue in an oil spill. It destroys wildlife and fouls shorelines. Cleanup costs can be tremendous. However, preventing oil spills has costs as well: greater enforcement expenditures and higher costs to shippers of oil and, therefore, higher costs of goods such as gasoline to customers. The only way to prevent oil spills completely is to stop drilling for and shipping oil. That is a cost few people would accept. But what is the right balance between environmental protection and the satisfaction of consumer demand for oil?

Vanderbilt University economist Mark Cohen examined the U.S. Coast Guard's efforts to reduce oil spills when transporting oil through its enforcement of shipping regulations in coastal waters and on rivers. He focused on the costs and benefits resulting from the Coast Guard's enforcement efforts in 1981. On the basis of the frequency of oil spills before the Coast Guard began its enforcement, Mr. Cohen estimated that the Coast Guard prevented 1,159,352 gallons of oil from being spilled in 1981.

Given that there was a total of 824,921 gallons of oil actually spilled in 1981, should the Coast Guard have attempted to prevent even more spillage? Mr. Cohen estimated that the marginal benefit of preventing one more gallon from being spilled was $7.27 ($3.42 in cleanup costs, $3 less in environmental damage, and $0.85 worth of oil saved). The marginal cost of preventing one more gallon from being spilled was $5.50. Mr. Cohen suggests that because the marginal benefit of more vigorous enforcement exceeded the marginal cost, more vigorous Coast Guard efforts would have been justified.

More vigorous efforts have, indeed, been pursued. In 1989, the Exxon oil tanker Exxon Valdez ran aground, spilling 10.8 million gallons of oil off the coast of Alaska. The spill damaged the shoreline of a national forest, four national wildlife refuges, three national parks, five state parks, four critical habitat areas, and a state game refuge. Exxon was ordered to pay $900 million in damages; a federal jury found Exxon and the captain guilty of criminal negligence and imposed an additional $5 billion in punitive damages. In 2008, The Supreme Court reduced the assessment of punitive damages to $507 million, with the majority arguing that the original figure was too high in comparison to the compensatory damages for a case in which the actions of the defendant, Exxon, were "reprehensible" but not intentional.

Perhaps the most important impact of the Exxon Valdez disaster was the passage of the Oil Pollution Act of 1990. It increased shipper liability from $14 million to $100 million. It also required double-hulled tankers for shipping oil.

The European Union (EU) has also strengthened its standards for oil tankers. The 2002 breakup of the oil tanker Prestige off the coast of Spain resulted in the spillage of 3.2 million gallons of oil. The EU had planned to ban single-hulled tankers, phasing in the ban between 2003 and 2015. The sinking of the Prestige led the EU to move up that deadline.

Tanker spill crises have led both the United States and the European Union to tighten up their regulations of oil tankers. The result has been a reduction in the quantity of oil spilled, which was precisely what economic research had concluded was needed. Whereas the total quantity of oil spilled from tankers in the 1970s was over 3 million tons, for the decade of the 2000s the total was 212,000 tons—a decline of over 90%—even as the amount of oil shipped rose dramatically.

The year 2010 saw another kind of major oil spill resulting from offshore drilling. The explosion of the Deepwater Horizon oil rig in the Gulf of Mexico on April 20, 2010, in which 11 workers were killed and 17 injured, led to a spill of 4.1 million barrels into the Gulf over a 3-month period. This spill was about 40% larger than the second largest offshore drilling spill off the U.S. coast and 19 times bigger than the Exxon Valdez spill. So far, no major legislation affecting oil drilling has passed, though, after a five-month drilling moratorium, the U.S. Department of the Interior has made changes to its enforcement practices.

Whether or not new legislation concerning offshore oil drilling is needed and how it should be constructed is being hotly debated. A preliminary study by Alan Krupnick, Sarah Campbell, Mark A. Cohen, and Ian W. H. Parry for the organization Resources for the Future estimated the annual benefits of preventing a catastrophic spill to be between $16.1 billion and $29.5 billion. The annual costs of a ban they estimate to be about $65 billion, from which they conclude that cost-benefit analysis does not justify a ban. On the other hand, they argue that regulation that would increase the costs of extraction by 10% or $11 billion annually would pass a cost-benefit analysis test and that regulation that raises extraction cost by 20% or $22 billion would pass the test at the upper end of the benefits estimate only. It should be noted that the Oil Pollution Act of 1990 was passed about a year and a half after the Exxon Valdez incident.

Sources: Mark A. Cohen, "The Costs and Benefits of Oil Spill Prevention and Enforcement," Journal of Environmental Economics and Management 13:2 (June 1986): 167–188; International Tanker Owners Pollution Federation Limited, Oil Tanker Spill Statistics 2010, available at http://www.itopf.com; Alan Krupnick, Sarah Campbell, Mark A. Cohen, and Ian W. H. Parry, "Understanding the Costs and Benefits of Deepwater Oil Drilling Regulation," Discussion Paper Resources for the Future RFF DP 10–62 (January 2011); Rick S. Kurtz, "Coastal Oil Pollution: Spills, Crisis, and Policy Change," Review of Policy Research, 21:2 (March 2004): 201–219; David S. Savage, "Justices Slash Exxon Valdez Verdict," Los Angeles Times, June 26, 2008, p. A1; Gerard Shields, "Gulf Oil Disaster: One Year Later," The Advocate (Baton Rouge, Louisiana), April 20, 2011, p. 1; and Edwin Unsworth, "Europe Gets Tougher on Aging Oil Tankers," Business Insurance, 36:48 (December 2, 2002): 33–34.

ANSWER TO TRY IT! PROBLEM

Here are the completed data table and the table showing total and marginal benefit and cost.

(a)

Hours studying for economics test

(b)

Hours studying economics	0	1	2	3	4	5
Total benefit	0	14	24	30	32	32
Marginal benefit		14	10	6	2	0
Total cost	0	2	8	18	32	50
Marginal cost		2	6	10	14	18

Ms. Phan maximizes her net benefit by reducing her time studying economics to 2 hours. The change in her expectations reduced the benefit and increased the cost of studying economics. The completed graph of marginal benefit and marginal cost is at the far left. Notice that answering the question using the marginal decision rule gives the same answer.

2. MAXIMIZING IN THE MARKETPLACE

LEARNING OBJECTIVES

1. **Explain what is meant by an efficient allocation of resources in an economy and describe the market conditions that must exist to achieve this goal.**
2. **Define consumer and producer surplus.**
3. **Discuss the relationship between efficiency and equity.**

In perhaps the most influential book in economics ever written, *An Inquiry into the Nature and Causes of the Wealth of Nations*, published in 1776, Adam Smith argued that the pursuit of self-interest in a marketplace would promote the general interest. He said resources would be guided, as if by an "invisible hand," to their best uses. That invisible hand was the marketplace.

Smith's idea was radical for its time; he saw that the seemingly haphazard workings of the marketplace could promote the common good. In this section, we will use the tools we have developed thus far to see the power of Smith's invisible hand. Efforts by individuals to maximize their own net benefit can maximize net benefit for the economy as a whole.

When the net benefits of all economic activities are maximized, economists say the allocation of resources is **efficient**. This concept of efficiency is broader than the notion of efficient production that we encountered when discussing the production possibilities curve. There, we saw that the economy's factors of production would be efficient *in production* if they were allocated according to the principle of comparative advantage. That meant producing as much as possible with the factors of production available. The concept of an efficient allocation of resources incorporates production, as in that discussion, but it includes efficiency in the consumption of goods and services as well.

efficient

The allocation of resources when the net benefits of all economic activities are maximized.

2.1 Achieving Efficiency

Imagine yourself arriving at the store to purchase some food. In your choice, you will weigh your own benefits and costs to maximize your net benefit. The farmers, the distributors, and the grocer have sought to maximize their net benefits as well. How can we expect that all those efforts will maximize net benefits for the economy as a whole? How can we expect the marketplace to achieve an efficient allocation of food, or of anything else?

One condition that must be met if the market's allocation is to be efficient is that the marketplace must be competitive or function as if it were. We will have a great deal more to say about competitive markets versus less competitive ones in subsequent chapters. For now, we can simply note that a competitive market is one with many buyers and sellers in each market and in which entry and exit are fairly easy. No one controls the price; the forces of demand and supply determine price.

The second condition that must hold if the market is to achieve an efficient allocation concerns property rights. We turn to that topic in the next section.

The Role of Property Rights

property rights

A set of rules that specify the ways in which an owner can use a resource.

A smoothly functioning market requires that producers possess property rights to the goods and services they produce and that consumers possess property rights to the goods and services they buy. **Property rights** are a set of rules that specify the ways in which an owner can use a resource.

Consider the tomato market. Farmers who grow tomatoes have clearly defined rights to their land and to the tomatoes they produce and sell. Distributors who purchase tomatoes from farmers and sell them to grocers have clear rights to the tomatoes until they sell them to grocers. The grocers who purchase the tomatoes retain rights to them until they sell them to consumers. When you buy a tomato, you have the exclusive right to its use.

A system of property rights forms the basis for all market exchange. Before exchange can begin, there must be a clear specification of who owns what. The system of property rights must also show what purchasers are acquiring when they buy rights to particular resources. Because property rights must exist if exchange is to occur, and because exchange is the process through which economic efficiency is achieved, a system of property rights is essential to the efficient allocation of resources.

Imagine what would happen in the market for tomatoes if property rights were not clearly defined. Suppose, for example, that grocers could not legally prevent someone from simply grabbing some tomatoes and leaving without paying for them. If that were the case, grocers would not be likely to offer tomatoes for sale. If it were the case for all grocery items, there would not be grocery stores at all.

Although property rights vary for different resources, two characteristics are required if the marketplace is to achieve an efficient allocation of resources:

exclusive property right

A property right that allows its owner to prevent others from using the resource.

transferable property right

A property right that allows the owner of a resource to sell or lease it to someone else.

1. Property rights must be exclusive. An **exclusive property right** is one that allows its owner to prevent others from using the resource. The owner of a house, for example, has the right to exclude others from the use of the house. If this right did not exist, ownership would have little value; it is not likely that the property could be exchanged in a market. And the inability to sell property would limit the incentive of owners to maintain it.

2. Property rights must be transferable. A **transferable property right** is one that allows the owner of a resource to sell or lease it to someone else. In the absence of transferability, no exchange could occur.

Markets and the Efficiency Condition

efficiency condition

A situation that requires a competitive market with well-defined and transferable property rights.

A competitive market with well-defined and transferable property rights satisfies the **efficiency condition**. If met, we can assume that the market's allocation of resources will be efficient.

Consider again your purchase of tomatoes. Suppose the curves of demand and supply for tomatoes are those given in Figure 5.7; the equilibrium price equals $1.50 per pound. Suppose further that the market satisfies the efficiency condition. With that assumption, we can relate the model of demand and supply to our analysis of marginal benefits and costs.

FIGURE 5.7 Demand and Supply and the Efficiency Condition

In a competitive market with exclusive and transferable property rights, such as the market for tomatoes, the efficiency condition is met. Buyers and sellers are faced with all of the relevant benefits and costs, and the equilibrium price equals the marginal cost to society of producing that good, here $2.50 per pound. We can interpret the market demand and supply curve as marginal benefit and marginal cost curves, respectively.

The demand curve tells us that the last pound of tomatoes was worth $1.50; we can think of that as the marginal benefit of the last pound of tomatoes since that is how much consumers were willing to pay. We can say that about any price on a market demand curve; a demand curve can be considered as a marginal benefit curve. Similarly, the supply curve can be considered the marginal cost curve. In the case of the tomato market, for example, the price tells us that the marginal cost of producing the last pound of tomatoes is $1.50. This marginal cost is considered in the economic sense—other goods and services worth $1.50 were not produced in order to make an additional pound of tomatoes available.

On what basis can we presume that the price of a pound of tomatoes equals its marginal cost? The answer lies in our marginal decision rule. Profit-maximizing tomato producers will produce more tomatoes as long as their marginal benefit exceeds their marginal cost. What is the marginal benefit to a producer of an extra pound of tomatoes? It is the price that the producer will receive. What is the marginal cost? It is the value that must be given up to produce an extra pound of tomatoes.

Producers maximize profit by expanding their production up to the point at which their marginal cost equals their marginal benefit, which is the market price. The price of $1.50 thus reflects the marginal cost to society of making an additional pound of tomatoes available.

At the equilibrium price and output of tomatoes, then, the marginal benefit of tomatoes to consumers, as reflected by the price they are willing to pay, equals the marginal cost of producing tomatoes. Where marginal benefit equals marginal cost, net benefit is maximized. The equilibrium quantity of tomatoes, as determined by demand and supply, is efficient.

2.2 Producer and Consumer Surplus

Think about the last thing you purchased. You bought it because you expected that its benefits would exceed its opportunity cost; you expected that the purchase would make you better off. The seller sold it

consumer surplus

The amount by which the total benefits to consumers from consuming a good exceed their total expenditures on the good.

to you because he or she expected that the money you paid would be worth more than the value of keeping the item. The seller expected to be better off as a result of the sale. Exchanges in the market-place have a remarkable property: Both buyers and sellers expect to emerge from the transaction better off.

Panel (a) of Figure 5.8 shows a market demand curve for a particular good. Suppose the price equals OB and the quantity equals OE. The area under the demand curve over the range of quantities from the origin at O to the quantity at E equals the total benefit of consuming OE units of the good. It is the area OCDE. Consumers pay for this benefit; their total expenditures equal the rectangle OBDE, which is the dark shaded region in the graph. Because the total benefits exceed total expenditures, there is a consumer surplus given by the triangle BCD. **Consumer surplus** is the amount by which the total benefits to consumers from consuming a good exceed their total expenditures on the good.

FIGURE 5.8 Consumer and Producer Surplus

Consumer surplus [Panel (a)] measures the difference between total benefit of consuming a given quantity of output and the total expenditures consumers pay to obtain that quantity. Here, total benefits are given by the shaded area OCDE; total expenditures are given by the rectangle OBDE. The difference, shown by the triangle BCD, is consumer surplus. Producer surplus [Panel (b)] measures the difference between total revenue received by firms at a given quantity of output and the total cost of producing it. Here, total revenue is given by the rectangle OBDE, and total costs are given by the area OADE. The difference, shown by the triangle ABD is producer surplus.

Now consider the sellers' side of transactions. Panel (b) of Figure 5.8 shows a market supply curve; re-call that it gives us marginal cost. Suppose the market price equals OB and quantity supplied is OE; those are the same values we had in Panel (a). The price times the quantity equals the total revenue received by sellers. It is shown as the shaded rectangle OBDE. The total revenue received by sellers equals total expenditures by consumers.

The total cost to sellers is the area under the marginal cost curve; it is the area OADE. That cost is less than revenue. The difference between the total revenue received by sellers and their total cost is called **producer surplus**. In Panel (b) it is the light-shaded triangle ABD.

We put the demand and supply curves of Figure 5.8 Panels (a) and (b) together in Figure 5.9. The intersection of the two curves determines the equilibrium price, OB, and the equilibrium quantity, OE. The shaded regions give us consumer and producer surplus. The sum of these two surpluses is net benefit. This net benefit is maximized where the demand and supply curves intersect.

producer surplus

The difference between the total revenue received by sellers and their total cost.

FIGURE 5.9 Net Benefit: The Sum of Consumer and Producer Surplus

The sum of consumer surplus and producer surplus measures the net benefit to society of any level of economic activity. Net benefit is maximized when production and consumption are carried out at the level where the demand and supply curves intersect. Here, the net benefit to society equals the area ACD. It is the sum of consumer surplus, BCD, and producer surplus, ABD.

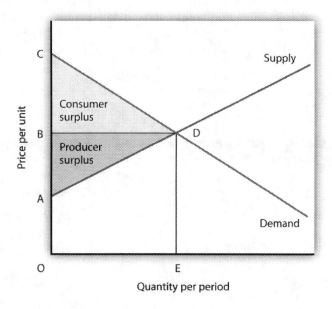

2.3 Efficiency and Equity

Consumer demands are affected by incomes. Demand, after all, reflects ability as well as willingness to pay for goods and services. The market will be more responsive to the preferences of people with high incomes than to those of people with low incomes.

In a market that satisfies the efficiency condition, an efficient allocation of resources will emerge from any particular distribution of income. Different income distributions will result in different, but still efficient, outcomes. For example, if 1% of the population controls virtually all the income, then the market will efficiently allocate virtually all its production to those same people.

What is a fair, or equitable, distribution of income? What is an unfair distribution? Should everyone have the same income? Is the current distribution fair? Should the rich have less and the poor have more? Should the middle class have more? Equity is very much in the mind of the observer. What may seem equitable to one person may seem inequitable to another. There is, however, no test we can apply to determine whether the distribution of income is or is not equitable. That question requires a normative judgment.

Determining whether the allocation of resources is or is not efficient is one problem. Determining whether the distribution of income is fair is another. The governments of all nations act in some way to redistribute income. That fact suggests that people generally have concluded that leaving the distribution of income solely to the market would not be fair and that some redistribution is desirable. This may take the form of higher taxes for people with higher incomes than for those with lower incomes. It may take the form of special programs, such as welfare programs, for low-income people.

Whatever distribution society chooses, an efficient allocation of resources is still preferred to an inefficient one. Because an efficient allocation maximizes net benefits, the gain in net benefits could be distributed in a way that leaves all people better off than they would be at any inefficient allocation. If an efficient allocation of resources seems unfair, it must be because the distribution of income is unfair.

KEY TAKEAWAYS

- In a competitive system in which the interaction of demand and supply determine prices, the corresponding demand and supply curves can be considered marginal benefit and marginal cost curves, respectively.

- An efficient allocation of resources is one that maximizes the net benefit of each activity. We expect it to be achieved in markets that satisfy the efficiency condition, which requires a competitive market and well-defined, transferable property rights.

- Consumer surplus is the amount by which the total benefit to consumers from some activity exceeds their total expenditures for it.

- Producer surplus is the amount by which the total revenues of producers exceed their total costs.

- An inequitable allocation of resources implies that the distribution of income and wealth is inequitable. Judgments about equity are normative judgments.

TRY IT!

Draw hypothetical demand and supply curves for a typical product, say coffee. Now show the areas of consumer and producer surplus. Under what circumstances is the market likely to be efficient?

Case in Point

Bah Humbug!

© *Thinkstock*

Professor Joel Waldfogel, in his book *Scroogenomics*, derides Christmas gift giving as only an economist would. Based on repeated surveys from students in his classes (which asked them to compare value and price of gifts they received and of items they bought for themselves) and estimates of annual Christmas spending in the United States of $66 billion in 2007, he concludes that $12 billion, roughly 18% of the total, constituted deadweight loss. And that doesn't count the 2.8 billion hours collectively spent shopping for the stuff.

The crux of his argument is that when you buy something for yourself, the price you pay is at least equal to the value of the satisfaction you get from the item. For some items, the consumer surplus (the difference between the value to you of the item and the price you pay), may be small or even zero, but for other items it may be large. One example he gives where consumer surplus may be huge is the purchase of a $20 antibiotic for your child with an ear infection who has been screaming all night. But what are the chances that consumer surplus will be positive for an item you receive as a gift? "Relative to how much satisfaction their [gift givers] expenditures could have given us, their choices destroy value. Take that, Santa," writes Professor Waldfogel.

Doesn't sentimental value make up for the differences between the price of an item you receive, say a $50 sweater, and the value you attach to it, say $25? If you attach $50 in sentimental value to the sweater, then it is really worth $75 to you, which is more than the $50 price paid by the gift giver. The problem with this line of argument is that if the gift giver had chosen a sweater for you that you actually liked—one that you valued at least at the purchase price of $50—its total value to you would then have been $100. Compared to giving you a sweater you actually liked, giving you the one you did not much care for destroyed value.

The surveys have also questioned the relationship of the gift giver to the gift recipient to see if giver knowledge of the recipient leads to more gift giving efficiency. The results are as one might expect. Gifts from aunts, uncles, and grandparents generated between 75 and 80 cents of satisfaction per dollar spent. Friends generated 91 cents, parents 97 cents, siblings 99 cents, and significant others 102 cents of satisfaction per dollar spent. In general, frequency of contact between giver and receiver increases the yield of a gift.

While acknowledging that there are some situations in which gifts may create value for recipients beyond what they could have purchased for themselves, such as when a recipient receives a CD of a band he or she was unfamiliar with but turns out to love, overall Waldfogel's estimates reveal a great loss for society. What to do about it? Giving cash would work but there seems to be a stigma associated with doing so, especially for certain kinds of relationships between givers and receivers. Gift registries solve the problem for newlyweds and could do so for Christmas gifts if that idea caught on. Since outside of your immediate circle you are unlikely to select a gift that does not destroy value, he suggests giving cash, if that is not too uncomfortable, or gift cards, possibly ones for charitable causes. Of course, people often forget to use their gift cards. When that happens, the benefit is not lost but rather goes to the retailer, which was not likely the intention of the gift giver. He thus suggests that retailers team up with charities so that any amount not redeemed after a certain time period goes to a charity stated on the gift card.

Parodying Karl Marx's *Communist Manifesto*, he concludes, "A specter has been haunting the rich economies of the West, and that specter is wasteful gift giving. Gift givers of the world unite. You have nothing to lose but deadweight loss and a world of satisfaction to gain."

Source: Joel Waldfogel, Scroogenomics: Why You Shouldn't Buy Presents for the Holidays (Princeton: Princeton University Press, 2009).

ANSWER TO TRY IT! PROBLEM

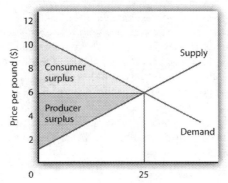

On the assumption that the coffee market is competitive and that it is characterized by well-defined exclusive and transferable property rights, the coffee market meets the efficiency condition. That means that the allocation of resources shown at the equilibrium will be the one that maximizes the net benefit of all activities. The net benefit is shared by coffee consumers (as measured by consumer surplus) and coffee producers (as measured by producer surplus).

3.   MARKET FAILURE

market failure

The failure of private decisions in the marketplace to achieve an efficient allocation of scarce resources.

Private decisions in the marketplace may not be consistent with the maximization of the net benefit of a particular activity. The failure of private decisions in the marketplace to achieve an efficient allocation of scarce resources is called **market failure**. Markets will not generate an efficient allocation of resources if they are not competitive or if property rights are not well defined and fully transferable. Either condition will mean that decision makers are not faced with the marginal benefits and costs of their choices.

Think about the drive that we had you take at the beginning of this chapter. You faced some, but not all, of the opportunity costs involved in that choice. In particular, your choice to go for a drive would increase air pollution and might increase traffic congestion. That means that, in weighing the marginal benefits and marginal costs of going for a drive, not all of the costs would be counted. As a result, the net benefit of the allocation of resources such as the air might not be maximized.

3.1   Noncompetitive Markets

The model of demand and supply assumes that markets are competitive. No one in these markets has any power over the equilibrium price; each consumer and producer takes the market price as given and responds to it. Under such conditions, price is determined by the intersection of demand and supply.

In some markets, however, individual buyers or sellers are powerful enough to influence the market price. In subsequent chapters, we will study cases in which producers or consumers are in a position to affect the prices they charge or must pay, respectively. We shall find that when individual firms or groups of firms have market power, which is the ability to change the market price, the price will be distorted—it will not equal marginal cost.

3.2   Public Goods

public good

A good for which the cost of exclusion is prohibitive and for which the marginal cost of an additional user is zero.

private good

A good for which exclusion is possible and for which the marginal cost of another user is positive.

Some goods are unlikely to be produced and exchanged in a market because of special characteristics of the goods themselves. The benefits of these goods are such that exclusion is not feasible. Once they are produced, anyone can enjoy them; there is no practical way to exclude people who have not paid for them from consuming them. Furthermore, the marginal cost of adding one more consumer is zero. A good for which the cost of exclusion is prohibitive and for which the marginal cost of an additional user is zero is a **public good**. A good for which exclusion is possible and for which the marginal cost of another user is positive is a **private good**.

National defense is a public good. Once defense is provided, it is not possible to exclude people who have not paid for it from its consumption. Further, the cost of an additional user is zero—an army does not cost any more if there is one more person to be protected. Other examples of public goods include law enforcement, fire protection, and efforts to preserve species threatened with extinction.

Free Riders

Suppose a private firm, Terror Alert, Inc., develops a completely reliable system to identify and intercept 98% of any would-be terrorists that might attempt to enter the United States from anywhere in the world. This service is a public good. Once it is provided, no one can be excluded from the system's protection on grounds that he or she has not paid for it, and the cost of adding one more person to the group protected is zero. Suppose that the system, by eliminating a potential threat to U.S. security, makes the average person in the United States better off; the benefit to each household from the added security is worth $40 per month (about the same as an earthquake insurance premium). There are roughly 113 million households in the United States, so the total benefit of the system is $4.5 billion per month. Assume that it will cost Terror Alert, Inc., $1 billion per month to operate. The benefits of the system far outweigh the cost.

Suppose that Terror Alert installs its system and sends a bill to each household for $20 for the first month of service—an amount equal to half of each household's benefit. If each household pays its bill, Terror Alert will enjoy a tidy profit; it will receive revenues of more than $2.25 billion per month.

But will each household pay? Once the system is in place, each household would recognize that it will benefit from the security provided by Terror Alert whether it pays its bill or not. Although some households will voluntarily pay their bills, it seems unlikely that very many will. Recognizing the opportunity to consume the good without paying for it, most would be free riders. **Free riders** are people or firms that consume a public good without paying for it. Even though the total benefit of the system is $4.5 billion, Terror Alert will not be faced by the marketplace with a signal that suggests that the system is worthwhile. It is unlikely that it will recover its cost of $1 billion per month. Terror Alert is not likely to get off the ground.

The bill for $20 from Terror Alert sends the wrong signal, too. An efficient market requires a price equal to marginal cost. But the marginal cost of protecting one more household is zero; adding one more household adds nothing to the cost of the system. A household that decides not to pay Terror Alert anything for its service is paying a price equal to its marginal cost. But doing that, being a free rider, is precisely what prevents Terror Alert from operating.

Because no household can be excluded and because the cost of an extra household is zero, the efficiency condition will not be met in a private market. What is true of Terror Alert, Inc., is true of public goods in general: they simply do not lend themselves to private market provision.

Public Goods and the Government

Because many individuals who benefit from public goods will not pay for them, private firms will produce a smaller quantity of public goods than is efficient, if they produce them at all. In such cases, it may be desirable for government agencies to step in. Government can supply a greater quantity of the good by direct provision, by purchasing the public good from a private agency, or by subsidizing consumption. In any case, the cost is financed through taxation and thus avoids the free-rider problem.

Most public goods are provided directly by government agencies. Governments produce national defense and law enforcement, for example. Private firms under contract with government agencies produce some public goods. Park maintenance and fire services are public goods that are sometimes produced by private firms. In other cases, the government promotes the private consumption or production of public goods by subsidizing them. Private charitable contributions often support activities that are public goods; federal and state governments subsidize these by allowing taxpayers to reduce their tax payments by a fraction of the amount they contribute.

While the market will produce some level of public goods in the absence of government intervention, we do not expect that it will produce the quantity that maximizes net benefit. Figure 5.10 illustrates the problem. Suppose that provision of a public good such as national defense is left entirely to private firms. It is likely that some defense services would be produced; suppose that equals Q_1 units per period. This level of national defense might be achieved through individual contributions. But it is very unlikely that contributions would achieve the correct level of defense services. The efficient quantity occurs where the demand, or marginal benefit, curve intersects the marginal cost curve, at Q^*. The deadweight loss is the shaded area ABC; we can think of this as the net benefit of government intervention to increase the production of national defense from Q_1 up to the efficient quantity, Q^*.

> ### Heads Up!
>
> Note that the definitions of public and private goods are based on characteristics of the goods themselves, not on whether they are provided by the public or the private sector. Postal services are a private good provided by the public sector. The fact that these goods are produced by a government agency does not make them a public good.

FIGURE 5.10 Public Goods and Market Failure

Because free riders will prevent firms from being able to require consumers to pay for the benefits received from consuming a public good, output will be less than the efficient level. In the case shown here, private donations achieved a level of the public good of Q_1 per period. The efficient level is Q^*. The deadweight loss is shown by the triangle ABC.

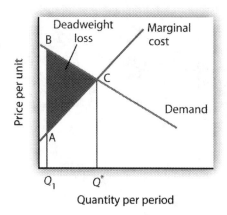

3.3 External Costs and Benefits

external cost

A cost imposed on others outside of any market exchange.

Suppose that in the course of production, the firms in a particular industry generate air pollution. These firms thus impose costs on others, but they do so outside the context of any market exchange—no agreement has been made between the firms and the people affected by the pollution. The firms thus will not be faced with the costs of their action. A cost imposed on others outside of any market exchange is an **external cost**.

We saw an example of an external cost in our imaginary decision to go for a drive. Here is another: violence on television, in the movies, and in video games. Many critics argue that the violence that pervades these media fosters greater violence in the real world. By the time a child who spends the average amount of time watching television finishes elementary school, he or she will have seen 100,000 acts of violence, including 8,000 murders, according to the American Psychological Association. Thousands of studies of the relationship between violence in the media and behavior have concluded that there is a link between watching violence and violent behaviors. Video games are a major element of the problem, as young children now spend hours each week playing them. Fifty percent of fourth-grade graders say that their favorite video games are the "first person shooter" type.[1]

Any tendency of increased violence resulting from increased violence in the media constitutes an external cost of such media. The American Academy of Pediatrics reported in 2001 that homicides were the fourth leading cause of death among children between the ages of 10 and 14 and the second leading cause of death for people aged 15 to 24 and has recommended a reduction in exposure to media violence.[2] It seems reasonable to assume that at least some of these acts of violence can be considered an external cost of violence in the media.

external benefit

An action taken by a person or firm that creates benefits for others in the absence of any market agreement.

An action taken by a person or firm can also create benefits for others, again in the absence of any market agreement; such a benefit is called an **external benefit**. A firm that builds a beautiful building generates benefits to everyone who admires it; such benefits are external.

External Costs and Efficiency

FIGURE 5.11 External Costs

When firms in an industry generate external costs, the supply curve S_1 reflects only their private marginal costs, MC_p. Forcing firms to pay the external costs they impose shifts the supply curve to S_2, which reflects the full marginal cost of the firms' production, MC_e. Output is reduced and price goes up. The deadweight loss that occurs when firms are not faced with the full costs of their decisions is shown by the shaded area in the graph.

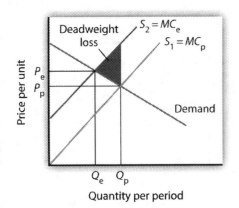

The case of the polluting firms is illustrated in Figure 5.11. The industry supply curve S_1 reflects private marginal costs, MC_p. The market price is P_p for a quantity Q_p. This is the solution that would occur if firms generating external costs were not forced to pay those costs. If the external costs generated by the pollution were added, the new supply curve S_2 would reflect higher marginal costs, MC_e. Faced with those costs, the market would generate a lower equilibrium quantity, Q_e. That quantity would command a higher price, P_e. The failure to confront producers with the cost of their pollution means that consumers do not pay the full cost of the good they are purchasing. The level of output and the level of pollution are therefore higher than would be economically efficient. If a way could be found to confront producers with the full cost of their choices, then consumers would be faced with a higher cost as well. Figure 5.11 shows that consumption would be reduced to the efficient level, Q_e, at which demand and the full marginal cost curve (MC_e) intersect. The deadweight loss generated by allowing the external cost to be generated with an output of Q_p is given as the shaded region in the graph.

External Costs and Government Intervention

If an activity generates external costs, the decision makers generating the activity will not be faced with its full costs. Agents who impose these costs will carry out their activities beyond the efficient level; those who consume them, facing too low a price, will consume too much. As a result, producers and consumers will carry out an excessive quantity of the activity. In such cases, government may try to intervene to reduce the level of the activity toward the efficient quantity. In the case shown in Figure 5.11, for example, firms generating an external cost have a supply curve S_1 that reflects their private marginal costs, MC_p. A per-unit pollution fee imposed on the firms would increase their marginal costs to MC_e, thus shifting the supply curve to S_2, and the efficient level of production would emerge. Taxes or other restrictions may be imposed on the activity that generates the external cost in an effort to confront decision makers with the costs that they are imposing. In many areas, firms and consumers that pollute rivers and lakes are required to pay fees based on the amount they pollute. Firms in many areas are required to purchase permits in order to pollute the air; the requirement that permits be purchased serves to confront the firms with the costs of their choices.

Another approach to dealing with problems of external costs is direct regulation. For example, a firm may be ordered to reduce its pollution. A person who turns his or her front yard into a garbage dump may be ordered to clean it up. Participants at a raucous party may be told to be quiet. Alternative ways of dealing with external costs are discussed later in the text.

3.4 Common Property Resources

Common property resources[3] are resources for which no property rights have been defined. The difficulty with common property resources is that individuals may not have adequate incentives to engage in efforts to preserve or protect them. Consider, for example, the relative fates of cattle and buffalo in the United States in the nineteenth century. Cattle populations increased throughout the century, while the buffalo nearly became extinct. The chief difference between the two animals was that exclusive property rights existed for cattle but not for buffalo.

Owners of cattle had an incentive to maintain herd sizes. A cattle owner who slaughtered all of his or her cattle without providing for replacement of the herd would not have a source of future income. Cattle owners not only maintained their herds but also engaged in extensive efforts to breed high-quality livestock. They invested time and effort in the efficient management of the resource on which their livelihoods depended.

Buffalo hunters surely had similar concerns about the maintenance of buffalo herds, but they had no individual stake in doing anything about them—the animals were a common property resource. Thousands of individuals hunted buffalo for a living. Anyone who cut back on hunting in order to help to preserve the herd would lose income—and face the likelihood that other hunters would go on hunting at the same rate as before.

Today, exclusive rights to buffalo have been widely established. The demand for buffalo meat, which is lower in fat than beef, has been increasing, but the number of buffalo in the United States is rising rapidly. If buffalo were still a common property resource, that increased demand, in the absence of other restrictions on hunting of the animals, would surely result in the elimination of the animal. Because there are exclusive, transferable property rights in buffalo and because a competitive market brings buyers and sellers of buffalo and buffalo products together, we can be reasonably confident in the efficient management of the animal.

When a species is threatened with extinction, it is likely that no one has exclusive property rights to it. Whales, condors, grizzly bears, elephants in Central Africa—whatever the animal that is threatened—are common property resources. In such cases a government agency may impose limits on the killing of the animal or destruction of its habitat. Such limits can prevent the excessive private use of a common property resource. Alternatively, as was done in the case of the buffalo, private rights can be established, giving resource owners the task of preservation.

common property resource

Resources for which no property rights have been defined.

KEY TAKEAWAYS

- Public sector intervention to increase the level of provision of public goods may improve the efficiency of resource allocation by overcoming the problem of free riders.
- Activities that generate external costs are likely to be carried out at levels that exceed those that would be efficient; the public sector may seek to intervene to confront decision makers with the full costs of their choices.
- Some private activities generate external benefits.
- A common property resource is unlikely to be allocated efficiently in the marketplace.

TRY IT!

The manufacture of memory chips for computers generates pollutants that generally enter rivers and streams. Use the model of demand and supply to show the equilibrium price and output of chips. Assuming chip manufacturers do not have to pay the costs these pollutants impose, what can you say about the efficiency of the quantity of chips produced? Show the area of deadweight loss imposed by this external cost. Show how a requirement that firms pay these costs as they produce the chips would affect the equilibrium price and output of chips. Would such a requirement help to satisfy the efficiency condition? Explain.

Case in Point

Protecting Wildlife by Establishing Private Property Rights

© *Thinkstock*

Imagine that you are a rural landowner in Kenya. You grow crops, sell them, and earn a return. You raise livestock, sell them, and earn a return on them as well. Wild animals, from birds to elephants, are also found on your property, but you are severely restricted in terms of what you can do with them. In Kenya, wildlife ownership and user rights are largely the property of the state (i.e., wildlife is owned by all the citizens of Kenya). But if wild animals kill some of your cattle, the loss is entirely yours, as the state will not compensate you. And do not seriously think about offering wildlife viewing on your property because that is restricted by the state to about 5% of the rangelands where the wildlife are found. If crops and livestock were treated in the same way as wildlife in Kenya, how much of their production would continue in these areas?

Mike Norton-Griffiths, a long-time resident of Kenya and researcher of conservation and land use policy, argues that the lack of private property rights for wildlife explains why wild animal populations there have been dwindling. Since 1977, when Kenya banned all sport hunting and all other consumptive uses of wildlife, the large animal wildlife population there has fallen by 60 to 70%. Over the same period, human population has grown by more than 3% per year, crop production by more than 8% per year, and livestock population has been stable.

To reverse the decline in wildlife population, Norton-Griffiths argues that property rights for wildlife should be changed so that returns to wildlife become competitive with returns to crops and livestock. This would mean that rural landowners would be allowed to generate income from wildlife from activities such as sales of wildlife between landowners and to the public sector, ranching for local and overseas and local trade, sales of wildlife products, tanning, making of trophies and curios, and sport hunting.

Private property rights for wildlife (sometimes referred to as private sector conservation) have been established in much of southern Africa (South Africa, Botswana, Namibia, and Zimbabwe). In those countries, there exist over 9,000 private game ranches and 1,100 private nature reserves. These private areas engage in wildlife viewing services, sport hunting, live game sales, and bush meat production.

The bounce back in wildlife population in the southern African countries is remarkable, even though the animals may move from property to property. For example, the wildlife population on private game ranches in Namibia has increased by about 70%. Similarly in Europe, rural landowners have invested in raising game birds, even though the birds can move freely from property to property, because they can sell the rights to game bird hunting on their property.

Peter Kareiva, the chief scientist for the Nature Conservancy, and Michélle Marvier, a professor at Santa Clara University, support a conservation-for-people approach. They argue that it does not make sense to pit people against nature. Rather, human well-being should become a part of biodiversity conservation efforts. If humans can benefit from managing wildlife, the wildlife may benefit as well.

Sources: Peter Kareiva and Michael Marvier, "Conservation for the People," Scientific American 297:4 (October 2007): 50–57; Mike Norton-Griffiths, "How Many Wildebeest Do You Need?" World Economics, 8:2 (April–June 2007): 41–64.

ANSWER TO TRY IT! PROBLEM

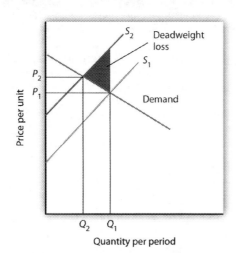

In the absence of any regulation, chip producers are not faced with the costs of the pollution their operations generate. The market price is thus P_1 and the quantity Q_1. The efficiency condition is not met; the price is lower and the quantity greater than would be efficient. If producers were forced to face the cost of their pollution as well as other production costs, the supply curve would shift to S_2, the price would rise to P_2, and the quantity would fall to Q_2. The new solution satisfies the efficiency condition.

4.   REVIEW AND PRACTICE

Summary

Economists insist that individuals do not make choices willy-nilly. Rather, economists assume that individuals make choices in a purposeful way, one that seeks the maximum value for some objective. We assume that consumers seek to maximize utility and that firms seek to maximize profits.

Whatever is being maximized, choices are based on the marginal decision rule. Following this rule results in an allocation that achieves the greatest degree of utility or profit possible.

If utility- and profit-maximizing choices are made in the context of a price system that confronts decision makers with all of the costs and all of the benefits of their choices, the allocation of resources will be efficient. An efficient allocation is one that maximizes the net benefit of every activity. The concepts of consumer and producer surplus show us how this net benefit is shared. Equity is a separate issue, one that calls for a normative evaluation of the fairness of the distribution of income.

The allocation of resources will be inefficient in the absence of competitive markets. It will also be inefficient if property rights are not exclusive and transferable. These two conditions break down when there are public goods, common property resources, or external benefits or costs. In each of these cases, public sector intervention may improve the efficiency of resource allocation. When a market fails to achieve the efficient solution, net benefit falls short of the maximum possible. Deadweight loss is the amount by which net benefit falls below the net benefit possible at the efficient solution.

CONCEPT PROBLEMS

1. What is achieved by selecting the quantity of an activity at which marginal benefit equals marginal cost?

2. Suppose the marginal benefit of an activity exceeds the marginal cost. What does the marginal decision rule say a maximizing decision maker will do?

3. Suppose you are a discus hurler and your goal is to maximize the distance you achieve. You "produce" discus hurls by practicing. The total benefit of practice is distance achieved, and the input that achieves this distance is hours of practice. Describe the total benefit curve of practice. What point on the curve would you select?

4. This chapter argues that consumers maximize utility and firms maximize profits. What do you suppose each of the following might be presumed to maximize?

     a. A minister or rabbi

     b. A United States Senator

     c. The manager of a major league baseball team

     d. The owner of a major league baseball team

     e. The director of a charitable organization

5. For each of the following goods, indicate whether exclusive, transferable property rights exist and whether the good poses a problem for public policy. If it does, does the problem relate to a problem of property rights?

     a. Clean air

     b. Tomatoes

     c. Housing

     d. Blue whales

6. The dry-cleaning industry is a major source of air pollution. What can you conclude about the price and output of dry-cleaning services?

7. Economists often recommend that polluters such as dry-cleaning establishments be charged fees for the pollution they emit. Critics of this idea respond that the establishments would simply respond by passing these charges on to their customers, leaving the level of pollution unchanged. Comment on this objection.

8. Government agencies often require that children be inoculated against communicable diseases such as polio and measles. From the standpoint of economic efficiency, is there any justification for such a requirement?

9. Which of the following goods or services are public? Why or why not?

     a. Libraries

     b. Fire protection

     c. Television programs

     d. Health care

     e. Water for household consumption

10. If a village in Botswana is granted several licenses to kill elephants, how does this give it an incentive to preserve elephants and increase the size of the herd? How does the international ban on ivory sales affect the incentive in Botswana to preserve the elephant?

11. The number of fish caught in the ocean has fallen in recent years partly as a result of more intensive fishing efforts and the use of more sophisticated equipment. Fish in the ocean are a common property resource. How might this fact be related to declining fish catches? How do you think this drop in the catch affects the price of seafood?

NUMERICAL PROBLEMS

1. Joe Higgins is thinking about how much time to spend studying for a biology exam tomorrow. Using "utility units" he measures the benefits and costs of study; his calculations are shown in the following table.

Hours spent studying	0	1	2	3	4	5	6
Total benefit	0	100	180	240	280	300	300
Total cost	0	50	100	150	200	250	300
Net benefit							

    a. Fill in the fourth row for net benefit in the table. Use the midpoint convention to emphasize that the net benefit is a marginal value showing the gain as hours spent increase by one-hour increments.

    b. Using a graph similar to Panel (a) of Figure 5.1 show the marginal benefit curve and verify that the area under the curve at 3 hours of study corresponds to the total benefit of that much study. (Hint: Remember that marginal values are plotted at the midpoints of the corresponding intervals on the horizontal axis.)

    c. Use a graph similar to Panel (b) of Figure 5.1 to show the marginal cost curve and verify that the area under the curve at 3 hours of study corresponds to the total cost of that much study.

    d. Use a graph similar to Panel (a) of Figure 5.6 to combine the marginal benefit and marginal cost curves you drew in parts (a) and (b).

    e. Based on the marginal decision rule, how many hours should Joe spend studying for his biology exam?

2. Now suppose some friends of Joe's call to say they are having a party tonight. Joe calculates that the party is now his best alternative to study, and he increases his estimate of the cost of each hour of study. One hour of study now costs 70; two hours cost 140; three hours 210, four hours 280; five hours 350; and six hours 470.

    a. Draw the new marginal benefit and marginal cost curves as in Problem 1, part (d):

    b. Based on the marginal decision rule, identify the new solution that maximizes the net benefit of study time.

3. The local gasoline market in a particular city has demand and supply curves given by the following data. (All quantities are in millions of gallons per month.)

Price per gallon	$1.00	$1.50	$2.00	$2.50	$3.00	$3.50	$4.00
Quantity demanded	6	5	4	3	2	1	0
Quantity supplied	0	1	2	3	4	5	6

    a. Plot the demand and supply curves, and determine the equilibrium price and quantity.

    b. Show the areas of consumer and producer surplus.

    c. Now suppose that the community determines that each gallon of gasoline consumed imposes $0.50 in pollution costs. Accordingly, a $0.50-per-gallon tax is imposed. The tax is imposed on sellers of gasoline, and it has the effect of increasing by $0.50 the price required to induce the quantities supplied in the table. For example, a price of $2.00 is now required for a quantity of 1 million gallons to be supplied each month. Plot the new supply curve.

    d. Approximate the new equilibrium price and output.

    e. Does the price increase by the full amount of the tax? If not, explain why.

    f. Would your answer be different if the demand for gasoline were perfectly inelastic?

4. The flu vaccination market has the demand and supply curves given by the following data. (All quantities are in thousands.)

Price per vaccination	$10	$15	$20	$25	$30
Quantity demanded	90	80	70	60	50
Quantity supplied	50	60	70	80	90

a. Plot the demand and supply curves, and determine the equilibrium price and quantity.

b. Show the areas of consumer and producer surplus.

c. Now suppose that each vaccination given generates an external benefit, as those who do not get vaccinated are less likely to get the flu when others do get vaccinated. As a result, suppliers receive a $10 subsidy from the government for each vaccine. For example, if consumers pay $10 per vaccination, suppliers receive $20, so only $10 from consumers is required to induce suppliers to offer 70,000 vaccinations per month. Plot the new supply curve.

d. Determine the new equilibrium price and quantity.

e. Does the price fall by the full amount of the subsidy? If not, explain why.

f. What is the total amount that consumers now pay for the new equilibrium quantity of vaccinations?

g. What is the total subsidy that suppliers receive from the government at the new equilibrium quantity of vaccinations?

5. Given the following information about the supply of and demand for apples:

Price per pound	Quantity demanded (pounds per month)	Quantity Supplied (pounds per month)
$0.50	12,000	0
0.75	10,000	2,000
1.00	8,000	4,000
1.25	6,000	6,000
1.50	4,000	8,000
1.75	2,000	10,000
2.00	0	12,000

a. Draw a graph similar to Figure 5.9

b. Assuming the market for apples meets the efficiency condition, show the equilibrium price and quantity that maximizes net benefit to society.

c. Identify the area of consumer surplus and the area of producer surplus.

ENDNOTES

1. See Report of the Committee on Commerce, Science, and Transportation, *Children's Protection From Violent Programming Act*, Senate Report 106–509 (October 26, 2000), Washington, D.C.: U.S. Government Printing Office, 2000, and Michael Rich, "Violent Video Games Testimony," Chicago City Council, October 30, 2000, at http://www.cwrl.utexas.edu/~bacon/Archives/VideoGames/Rich.pdf.

2. Mark Rosenberg, "Successful State Strategies," Adolescent Health Leadership Forum, December 6, 2003, at http://pediatrics.aappublications.org/content/124/5/1495.full.

3. Common property resources are sometimes referred to as open access resources.

CHAPTER 6
Production, Cost, and Market Models

START UP: STREET CLEANING AROUND THE WORLD

It is dawn in Shanghai, China. Already thousands of Chinese are out cleaning the city's streets. They are using brooms.

On the other side of the world, night falls in Washington, D.C., where the streets are also being cleaned—by a handful of giant street-sweeping machines driven by a handful of workers.

The difference in method is not the result of a greater knowledge of modern technology in the United States—the Chinese know perfectly well how to build street-sweeping machines. It is a production decision based on costs in the two countries. In China, where wages are relatively low, an army of workers armed with brooms is the least expensive way to produce clean streets. In Washington, where labor costs are high, it makes sense to use more machinery and less labor.

All types of production efforts require choices in the use of factors of production. In this chapter we examine such choices. Should a good or service be produced using relatively more labor and less capital? Or should relatively more capital and less labor be used? What about the use of natural resources?

In this chapter we see why firms make the production choices they do and how their costs affect their choices. We will apply the marginal decision rule to the production process and see how this rule ensures that production is carried out at the lowest cost possible. We will examine the nature of production and costs in order to gain a better understanding of supply. In producing goods and services, firms combine the factors of production—labor, capital, and natural resources—to produce various products.

Economists assume that firms engage in production in order to earn a profit and that they seek to make this profit as large as possible. That is, economists assume that firms apply the marginal decision rule as they seek to maximize their profits. Whether we consider the operator of a shoe-shine stand at an airport or the firm that produces airplanes, we will find there are basic relationships between the use of factors of production and output levels, and between output levels and costs, that apply to all production. The production choices of firms and their associated costs are at the foundation of supply.

Firms' production decisions also depend on the type of market in which they operate. The final section of this chapter presents an overview of models of market organization that economists have developed.

1.   PRODUCTION CHOICES AND COSTS: THE SHORT RUN

LEARNING OBJECTIVES

1. Understand the terms associated with the short-run production function—total product, average product, and marginal product—and explain and illustrate how they are related to each other.
2. Explain the concepts of increasing, diminishing, and negative marginal returns and explain the law of diminishing marginal returns.
3. Understand the terms associated with costs in the short run—total variable cost, total fixed cost, total cost, average variable cost, average fixed cost, average total cost, and marginal cost—and explain and illustrate how they are related to each other.
4. Explain and illustrate how the product and cost curves are related to each other and to determine in what ranges on these curves marginal returns are increasing, diminishing, or negative.

short run

A planning period over which the managers of a firm must consider one or more of their factors of production as fixed in quantity.

Our analysis of production and cost begins with a period economists call the short run. The **short run** in this microeconomic context is a planning period over which the managers of a firm must consider one or more of their factors of production as fixed in quantity. For example, a restaurant may regard its building as a fixed factor over a period of at least the next year. It would take at least that much time to find a new building or to expand or reduce the size of its present facility. Decisions concerning the operation of the restaurant during the next year must assume the building will remain unchanged. Other factors of production could be changed during the year, but the size of the building must be regarded as a constant.

fixed factor of production

A factor of production whose quantity cannot be changed during a particular period.

variable factor of production

A factor of production whose quantity can be changed during a particular period.

When the quantity of a factor of production cannot be changed during a particular period, it is called a **fixed factor of production**. For the restaurant, its building is a fixed factor of production for at least a year. A factor of production whose quantity can be changed during a particular period is called a **variable factor of production**; factors such as labor and food are examples.

While the managers of the restaurant are making choices concerning its operation over the next year, they are also planning for longer periods. Over those periods, managers may contemplate alternatives such as modifying the building, building a new facility, or selling the building and leaving the restaurant business. The planning period over which a firm can consider *all* factors of production as variable is called the **long run**.

long run

The planning period over which a firm can consider all factors of production as variable.

At any one time, a firm will be making both short-run and long-run choices. The managers may be planning what to do for the next few weeks and for the next few years. Their decisions over the next few weeks are likely to be short-run choices. Decisions that will affect operations over the next few years may be long-run choices, in which managers can consider changing every aspect of their operations. Our analysis in this section focuses on the short run. We examine long-run choices later in this chapter.

1.1   The Short-Run Production Function

production function

The relationship between factors of production and the output of a firm.

A firm uses factors of production to produce a product. The relationship between factors of production and the output of a firm is called a **production function**. Our first task is to explore the nature of the production function.

Consider a hypothetical firm, Acme Clothing, a shop that produces jackets. Suppose that Acme has a lease on its building and equipment. During the period of the lease, Acme's capital is its fixed factor of production. Acme's variable factors of production include things such as labor, cloth, and electricity. In the analysis that follows, we shall simplify by assuming that labor is Acme's *only* variable factor of production.

Total, Marginal, and Average Products

Figure 6.1 shows the number of jackets Acme can obtain with varying amounts of labor (in this case, tailors) and its given level of capital. A **total product curve** shows the quantities of output that can be obtained from different amounts of a variable factor of production, assuming other factors of production are fixed.

Notice what happens to the slope of the total product curve in Figure 6.1. Between 0 and 3 units of labor per day, the curve becomes steeper. Between 3 and 7 workers, the curve continues to slope upward, but its slope diminishes. Beyond the seventh tailor, production begins to decline and the curve slopes downward.

We measure the slope of any curve as the vertical change between two points divided by the horizontal change between the same two points. The slope of the total product curve for labor equals the change in output (ΔQ) divided by the change in units of labor (ΔL):

$$\text{Slope of the total product curve } = \Delta Q / \Delta L$$

The slope of a total product curve for any variable factor is a measure of the change in output associated with a change in the amount of the variable factor, with the quantities of all other factors held constant. The amount by which output rises with an additional unit of a variable factor is the **marginal product** of the variable factor. Mathematically, marginal product is the ratio of the change in output to the change in the amount of a variable factor. The **marginal product of labor** (MP_L), for example, is the amount by which output rises with an additional unit of labor. It is thus the ratio of the change in output to the change in the quantity of labor ($\Delta Q/\Delta L$), all other things unchanged. It is measured as the slope of the total product curve for labor.

EQUATION 6.1

$$MP_L = \Delta Q / \Delta L$$

In addition we can define the **average product** of a variable factor. It is the output per unit of variable factor. The **average product of labor** (AP_L), for example, is the ratio of output to the number of units of labor (Q/L).

EQUATION 6.2

$$AP_L = Q / L$$

The concept of average product is often used for comparing productivity levels over time or in comparing productivity levels among nations. When you read in the newspaper that productivity is rising or falling, or that productivity in the United States is nine times greater than productivity in China, the report is probably referring to some measure of the average product of labor.

The total product curve in Panel (a) of Figure 6.2 is repeated from Figure 6.1. Panel (b) shows the marginal product and average product curves. Notice that marginal product is the slope of the total product curve, and that marginal product rises as the slope of the total product curve increases, falls as the slope of the total product curve declines, reaches zero when the total product curve achieves its maximum value, and becomes negative as the total product curve slopes downward. As in other parts of this text, marginal values are plotted at the midpoint of each interval. The marginal product of the fifth unit of labor, for example, is plotted between 4 and 5 units of labor. Also notice that the marginal product curve intersects the average product curve at the maximum point on the average product curve. When marginal product is above average product, average product is rising. When marginal product is below average product, average product is falling.

total product curve

Graph that shows the quantities of output that can be obtained from different amounts of a variable factor of production, assuming other factors of production are fixed.

FIGURE 6.1 Acme Clothing's Total Product Curve

The table gives output levels per day for Acme Clothing Company at various quantities of labor per day, assuming the firm's capital is fixed. These values are then plotted graphically as a total product curve.

Point on graph	A	B	C	D	E	F	G	H	I
Units of labor per day	0	1	2	3	4	5	6	7	8
Jackets per day	0.0	1.0	3.0	7.0	9.0	10.0	10.7	11.0	10.5

marginal product

The amount by which output rises with an additional unit of a variable factor.

marginal product of labor

The amount by which output rises with an additional unit of labor.

average product

The output per unit of variable factor.

average product of labor

The ratio of output to the number of units of labor (Q/L).

FIGURE 6.2 From Total Product to the Average and Marginal Product of Labor

The first two rows of the table give the values for quantities of labor and total product from Figure 6.1. Marginal product, given in the third row, is the change in output resulting from a one-unit increase in labor. Average product, given in the fourth row, is output per unit of labor. Panel (a) shows the total product curve. The slope of the total product curve is marginal product, which is plotted in Panel (b). Values for marginal product are plotted at the midpoints of the intervals. Average product rises and falls. Where marginal product is above average product, average product rises. Where marginal product is below average product, average product falls. The marginal product curve intersects the average product curve at the maximum point on the average product curve.

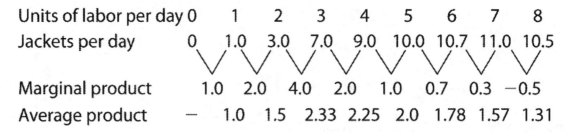

Units of labor per day	0	1	2	3	4	5	6	7	8
Jackets per day	0	1.0	3.0	7.0	9.0	10.0	10.7	11.0	10.5
Marginal product		1.0	2.0	4.0	2.0	1.0	0.7	0.3	−0.5
Average product	—	1.0	1.5	2.33	2.25	2.0	1.78	1.57	1.31

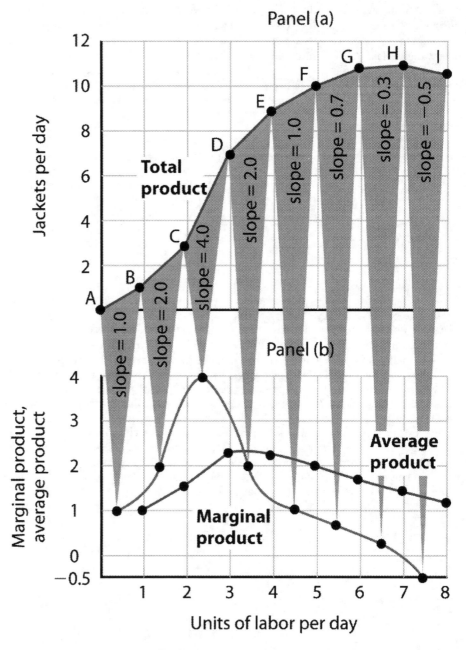

As a student you can use your own experience to understand the relationship between marginal and average values. Your grade point average (GPA) represents the average grade you have earned in all your course work so far. When you take an additional course, your grade in that course represents the marginal grade. What happens to your GPA when you get a grade that is higher than your previous average? It rises. What happens to your GPA when you get a grade that is lower than your previous average? It falls. If your GPA is a 3.0 and you earn one more B, your marginal grade equals your GPA and your GPA remains unchanged.

The relationship between average product and marginal product is similar. However, unlike your course grades, which may go up and down willy-nilly, marginal product always rises and then falls, for reasons we will explore shortly. As soon as marginal product falls below average product, the average product curve slopes downward. While marginal product is above average product, whether marginal product is increasing or decreasing, the average product curve slopes upward.

As we have learned, maximizing behavior requires focusing on making decisions at the margin. For this reason, we turn our attention now toward increasing our understanding of marginal product.

Increasing, Diminishing, and Negative Marginal Returns

Adding the first worker increases Acme's output from 0 to 1 jacket per day. The second tailor adds 2 jackets to total output; the third adds 4. The marginal product goes up because when there are more workers, each one can specialize to a degree. One worker might cut the cloth, another might sew the seams, and another might sew the buttonholes. Their increasing marginal products are reflected by the increasing slope of the total product curve over the first 3 units of labor and by the upward slope of the marginal product curve over the same range. The range over which marginal products are increasing is called the range of **increasing marginal returns**. Increasing marginal returns exist in the context of a total product curve for labor, so we are holding the quantities of other factors constant. Increasing marginal returns may occur for any variable factor.

The fourth worker adds less to total output than the third; the marginal product of the fourth worker is 2 jackets. The data in Figure 6.2 show that marginal product continues to decline after the fourth worker as more and more workers are hired. The additional workers allow even greater opportunities for specialization, but because they are operating with a fixed amount of capital, each new worker adds less to total output. The fifth tailor adds only a single jacket to total output. When each additional unit of a variable factor adds less to total output, the firm is experiencing **diminishing marginal returns**. Over the range of diminishing marginal returns, the marginal product of the variable factor is positive but falling. Once again, we assume that the quantities of all other factors of production are fixed. Diminishing marginal returns may occur for any variable factor. Panel (b) shows that Acme experiences diminishing marginal returns between the third and seventh workers, or between 7 and 11 jackets per day.

After the seventh unit of labor, Acme's fixed plant becomes so crowded that adding another worker actually reduces output. When additional units of a variable factor reduce total output, given constant quantities of all other factors, the company experiences **negative marginal returns**. Now the total product curve is downward sloping, and the marginal product curve falls below zero. Figure 6.3 shows the ranges of increasing, diminishing, and negative marginal returns. Clearly, a firm will never intentionally add so much of a variable factor of production that it enters a range of negative marginal returns.

The idea that the marginal product of a variable factor declines over some range is important enough, and general enough, that economists state it as a law. The **law of diminishing marginal returns** holds that the marginal product of any variable factor of production will eventually decline, assuming the quantities of other factors of production are unchanged.

increasing marginal returns

The range over which each additional unit of a variable factor adds more to total output than the previous unit.

diminishing marginal returns

The range over which each additional unit of a variable factor adds less to total output than the previous unit.

negative marginal returns

The range over which additional units of a variable factor reduce total output, given constant quantities of all other factors.

law of diminishing marginal returns

The marginal product of any variable factor of production will eventually decline, assuming the quantities of other factors of production are unchanged.

Heads Up!

It is easy to confuse the concept of diminishing marginal returns with the idea of negative marginal returns. To say a firm is experiencing diminishing marginal returns is not to say its output is falling. Diminishing marginal returns mean that the marginal product of a variable factor is declining. Output is still increasing as the variable factor is increased, but it is increasing by smaller and smaller amounts. As we saw in Figure 6.2 and Figure 6.3, the range of diminishing marginal returns was between the third and seventh workers; over this range of workers, output rose from 7 to 11 jackets. Negative marginal returns started after the seventh worker.

To see the logic of the law of diminishing marginal returns, imagine a case in which it does not hold. Say that you have a small plot of land for a vegetable garden, 10 feet by 10 feet in size. The plot itself is a fixed factor in the production of vegetables. Suppose you are able to hold constant all other factors—water, sunshine, temperature, fertilizer, and seed—and vary the amount of labor devoted to the garden. How much food could the garden produce? Suppose the marginal product of labor kept increasing or was constant. Then you could grow an *unlimited* quantity of food on your small plot—enough to feed the entire world! You could add an unlimited number of workers to your plot and still increase output at a constant or increasing rate. If you did not get enough output with, say, 500 workers, you could use 5 million; the five-millionth worker would add at least as much to total output as the first. If diminishing marginal returns to labor did not occur, the total product curve would slope upward at a constant or increasing rate.

FIGURE 6.3 Increasing Marginal Returns, Diminishing Marginal Returns, and Negative Marginal Returns

This graph shows Acme's total product curve from Figure 6.1 with the ranges of increasing marginal returns, diminishing marginal returns, and negative marginal returns marked. Acme experiences increasing marginal returns between 0 and 3 units of labor per day, diminishing marginal returns between 3 and 7 units of labor per day, and negative marginal returns beyond the 7th unit of labor.

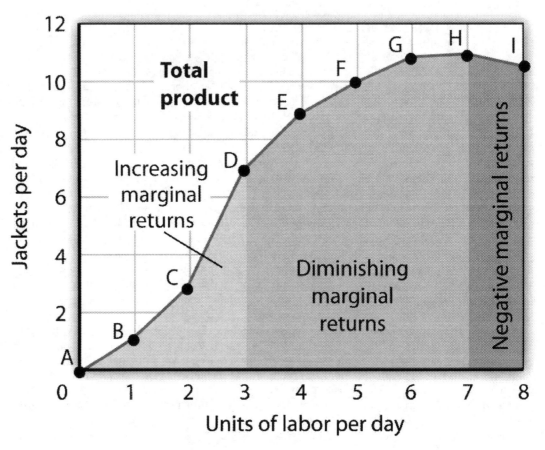

The shape of the total product curve and the shape of the resulting marginal product curve drawn in Figure 6.2 are typical of *any* firm for the short run. Given its fixed factors of production, increasing the use of a variable factor will generate increasing marginal returns at first; the total product curve for the variable factor becomes steeper and the marginal product rises. The opportunity to gain from increased specialization in the use of the variable factor accounts for this range of increasing marginal returns. Eventually, though, diminishing returns will set in. The total product curve will become flatter, and the marginal product curve will fall.

1.2   Costs in the Short Run

A firm's costs of production depend on the quantities and prices of its factors of production. Because we expect a firm's output to vary with the firm's use of labor in a specific way, we can also expect the firm's costs to vary with its output in a specific way. We shall put our information about Acme's product curves to work to discover how a firm's costs vary with its level of output.

We distinguish between the costs associated with the use of variable factors of production, which are called **variable costs**, and the costs associated with the use of fixed factors of production, which are called **fixed costs**. For most firms, variable costs includes costs for raw materials, salaries of production workers, and utilities. The salaries of top management may be fixed costs; any charges set by contract over a period of time, such as Acme's one-year lease on its building and equipment, are likely to be fixed costs. A term commonly used for fixed costs is *overhead*. Notice that fixed costs exist only in the short run. In the long run, the quantities of all factors of production are variable, so that all long-run costs are variable.

Total variable cost (TVC) is cost that varies with the level of output. **Total fixed cost (TFC)** is cost that does not vary with output. **Total cost (TC)** is the sum of total variable cost and total fixed cost:

EQUATION 6.3

$$TVC + TFC = TC$$

From Total Production to Total Cost

Next we illustrate the relationship between Acme's total product curve and its total costs. Acme can vary the quantity of labor it uses each day, so the cost of this labor is a variable cost. We assume capital is a fixed factor of production in the short run, so its cost is a fixed cost.

Suppose that Acme pays a wage of $100 per worker per day. If labor is the only variable factor, Acme's total variable costs per day amount to $100 times the number of workers it employs. We can use the information given by the total product curve, together with the wage, to compute Acme's total variable costs.

FIGURE 6.4 Computing Variable Costs

The points shown give the variable costs of producing the quantities of jackets given in the total product curve in Figure 6.1 and Figure 6.2. Suppose Acme's workers earn $100 per day. If Acme produces 0 jackets, it will use no labor—its variable cost thus equals $0 (Point A'). Producing 7 jackets requires 3 units of labor; Acme's variable cost equals $300 (Point D').

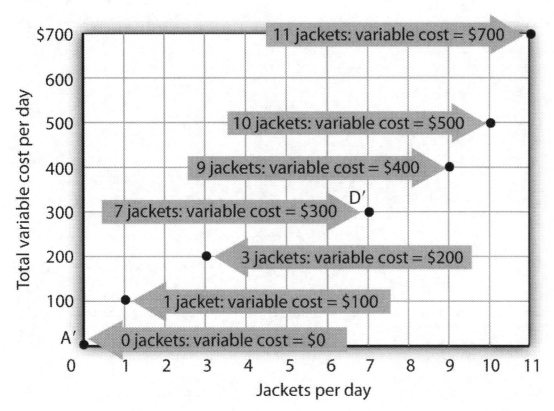

We know from Figure 6.1 that Acme requires 1 worker working 1 day to produce 1 jacket. The total variable cost of a jacket thus equals $100. Three units of labor produce 7 jackets per day; the total variable cost of 7 jackets equals $300. Figure 6.4 shows Acme's total variable costs for producing each of the output levels given in Figure 6.1.

---

variable costs

The costs associated with the use of variable factors of production.

fixed costs

The costs associated with the use of fixed factors of production.

total variable cost

Cost that varies with the level of output.

total fixed cost

Cost that does not vary with output.

total cost

The sum of total variable cost and total fixed cost.

Figure 6.4 gives us costs for several quantities of jackets, but we need a bit more detail. We know, for example, that 7 jackets have a total variable cost of $300. What is the total variable cost of 6 jackets?

We can estimate total variable costs for other quantities of jackets by inspecting the total product curve in Figure 6.1. Reading over from a quantity of 6 jackets to the total product curve and then down suggests that the Acme needs about 2.8 units of labor to produce 6 jackets per day. Acme needs 2 full-time and 1 part-time tailors to produce 6 jackets. Figure 6.5 gives the precise total variable costs for quantities of jackets ranging from 0 to 11 per day. The numbers in boldface type are taken from Figure 6.4; the other numbers are estimates we have assigned to produce a total variable cost curve that is consistent with our total product curve. You should, however, be certain that you understand how the numbers in boldface type were found.

FIGURE 6.5   The Total Variable Cost Curve

Total variable costs for output levels shown in Acme's total product curve were shown in Figure 6.4. To complete the total variable cost curve, we need to know the variable cost for each level of output from 0 to 11 jackets per day. The variable costs and quantities of labor given in Figure 6.4 are shown in boldface in the table here and with black dots in the graph. The remaining values were estimated from the total product curve in Figure 6.1 and Figure 6.2. For example, producing 6 jackets requires 2.8 workers, for a variable cost of $280.

Quantity/day	0	1.0	2.0	3.0	4.0	5.0	6.0	7.0	8.0	9.0	10.0	11.0
Labor/day	0	**1.00**	1.63	**2.00**	2.33	2.58	2.80	**3.00**	3.38	**4.00**	**5.00**	**7.00**
Total variable cost	$0	**$100**	$163	**$200**	$233	$258	$280	**$300**	$338	**$400**	**$500**	**$700**

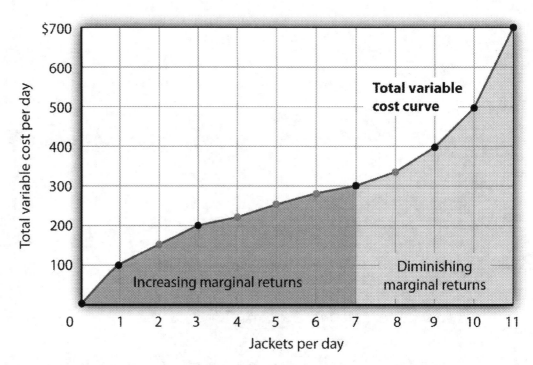

Suppose Acme's present plant, including the building and equipment, is the equivalent of 20 units of capital. Acme has signed a long-term lease for these 20 units of capital at a cost of $200 per day. In the short run, Acme cannot increase or decrease its quantity of capital—it must pay the $200 per day no matter what it does. Even if the firm cuts production to zero, it must still pay $200 per day in the short run.

Acme's total cost is its total fixed cost of $200 plus its total variable cost. We add $200 to the total variable cost curve in Figure 6.5 to get the total cost curve shown in Figure 6.6.

FIGURE 6.6   From Variable Cost to Total Cost

We add total fixed cost to the total variable cost to obtain total cost. In this case, Acme's total fixed cost equals $200 per day.

Notice something important about the shapes of the total cost and total variable cost curves in Figure 6.6. The total cost curve, for example, starts at $200 when Acme produces 0 jackets—that is its total fixed cost. The curve rises, but at a decreasing rate, up to the seventh jacket. Beyond the seventh jacket, the curve becomes steeper and steeper. The slope of the total variable cost curve behaves in precisely the same way.

Recall that Acme experienced increasing marginal returns to labor for the first three units of labor—or the first seven jackets. Up to the third worker, each additional worker added more and more to Acme's output. Over the range of increasing marginal returns, each additional jacket requires less and less additional labor. The first jacket required one tailor; the second required the addition of only a part-time tailor; the third required only that Acme boost that part-time tailor's hours to a full day. Up to the seventh jacket, each additional jacket requires less and less additional labor, and thus costs rise at a decreasing rate; the total cost and total variable cost curves become flatter over the range of increasing marginal returns.

Acme experiences diminishing marginal returns beyond the third unit of labor—or the seventh jacket. Notice that the total cost and total variable cost curves become steeper and steeper beyond this level of output. In the range of diminishing marginal returns, each additional unit of a factor adds less and less to total output. That means each additional unit of output requires larger and larger increases in the variable factor, and larger and larger increases in costs.

Marginal and Average Costs

average total cost

Total cost divided by quantity; it is the firm's total cost per unit of output.

Marginal and average cost curves, which will play an important role in the analysis of the firm, can be derived from the total cost curve. *Marginal cost* shows the additional cost of each additional unit of output a firm produces. This is a specific application of the general concept of marginal cost presented earlier. Given the marginal decision rule's focus on evaluating choices at the margin, the marginal cost curve takes on enormous importance in the analysis of a firm's choices. The second curve we shall derive shows the firm's average total cost at each level of output. **Average total cost (ATC)** is total cost divided by quantity; it is the firm's total cost per unit of output:

EQUATION 6.4

$$ATC = TC / Q$$

average variable cost

Total variable cost divided by quantity; it is the firm's total variable cost per unit of output.

We shall also discuss **average variable cost**s *(AVC)*, which is the firm's variable cost per unit of output; it is total variable cost divided by quantity:

EQUATION 6.5

$$AVC = TVC / Q$$

average fixed cost

Total fixed cost divided by quantity.

We are still assessing the choices facing the firm in the short run, so we assume that at least one factor of production is fixed. Finally, we will discuss **average fixed cost** *(AFC)*, which is total fixed cost divided by quantity:

EQUATION 6.6

$$AFC = TFC / Q$$

Marginal cost *(MC)* is the amount by which total cost rises with an additional unit of output. It is the ratio of the change in total cost to the change in the quantity of output:

EQUATION 6.7

$$MC = \Delta TC / \Delta Q$$

It equals the slope of the total cost curve. Figure 6.7 shows the same total cost curve that was presented in Figure 6.6. This time the slopes of the total cost curve are shown; these slopes equal the marginal cost of each additional unit of output. For example, increasing output from 6 to 7 units ($\Delta Q = 1$) increases total cost from $480 to $500 ($\Delta TC = \$20$). The seventh unit thus has a marginal cost of $20 ($\Delta TC / \Delta Q = \$20 / 1 = \$20$). Marginal cost falls over the range of increasing marginal returns and rises over the range of diminishing marginal returns.

Heads Up!

Notice that the various cost curves are drawn with the quantity of output on the horizontal axis. The various product curves are drawn with quantity of a factor of production on the horizontal axis. The reason is that the two sets of curves measure different relationships. Product curves show the relationship between output and the quantity of a factor; they therefore have the factor quantity on the horizontal axis. Cost curves show how costs vary with output and thus have output on the horizontal axis.

FIGURE 6.7 Total Cost and Marginal Cost

Marginal cost in Panel (b) is the slope of the total cost curve in Panel (a).

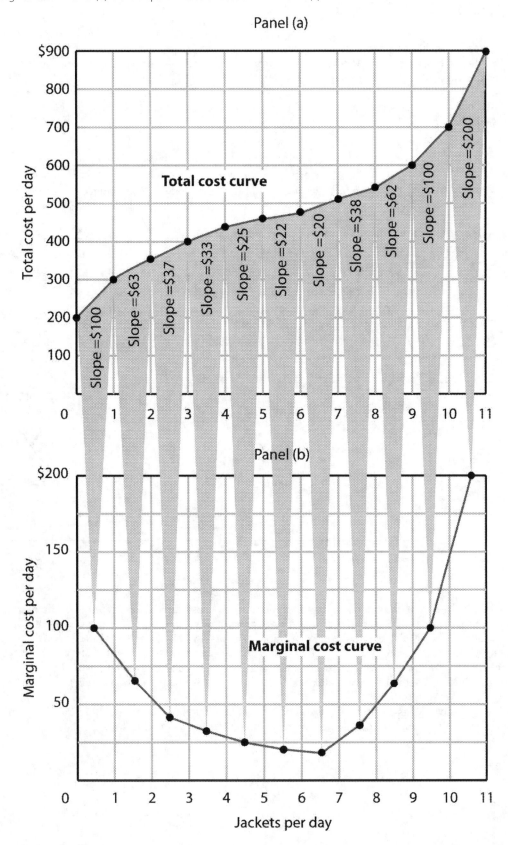

Figure 6.8 shows the computation of Acme's short-run average total cost, average variable cost, and average fixed cost and graphs of these values. Notice that the curves for short-run average total cost and average variable cost fall, then rise. We say that these cost curves are U-shaped. Average fixed cost keeps falling as output increases. This is because the fixed costs are spread out more and more as

output expands; by definition, they do not vary as labor is added. Since average total cost (*ATC*) is the sum of average variable cost (*AVC*) and average fixed cost (*AFC*), i.e.,

EQUATION 6.8

$$AVC + AFC = ATC$$

the distance between the *ATC* and *AVC* curves keeps getting smaller and smaller as the firm spreads its overhead costs over more and more output.

FIGURE 6.8 Marginal Cost, Average Fixed Cost, Average Variable Cost, and Average Total Cost in the Short Run

Total cost figures for Acme Clothing are taken from Figure 6.7. The other values are derived from these. Average total cost (*ATC*) equals total cost divided by quantity produced; it also equals the sum of the average fixed cost (*AFC*) and average variable cost (*AVC*) (exceptions in table are due to rounding to the nearest dollar); average variable cost is variable cost divided by quantity produced. The marginal cost (*MC*) curve (from Figure 6.7) intersects the *ATC* and *AVC* curves at the lowest points on both curves. The *AFC* curve falls as quantity increases.

Quantity/day	0	1	2	3	4	5	6	7	8	9	10	11
Total cost	$200	$300	$363	$400	$433	$458	$480	$500	$538	$600	$700	$900
AFC		$200	$100	$67	$50	$40	$33	$29	$25	$22	$20	$18
AVC		$100	$82	$67	$58	$52	$47	$43	$42	$44	$50	$64
ATC		$300	$182	$133	$108	$92	$80	$71	$67	$67	$70	$82
MC		$100	$63	$37	$33	$25	$22	$20	$38	$62	$100	$200

Figure 6.8 includes the marginal cost data and the marginal cost curve from Figure 6.7. The marginal cost curve intersects the average total cost and average variable cost curves at their lowest points. When marginal cost is below average total cost or average variable cost, the average total and average variable cost curves slope downward. When marginal cost is greater than short-run average total cost or average variable cost, these average cost curves slope upward. The logic behind the relationship between marginal cost and average total and variable costs is the same as it is for the relationship between marginal product and average product.

We turn next in this chapter to an examination of production and cost in the long run, a planning period in which the firm can consider changing the quantities of any or all factors.

KEY TAKEAWAYS

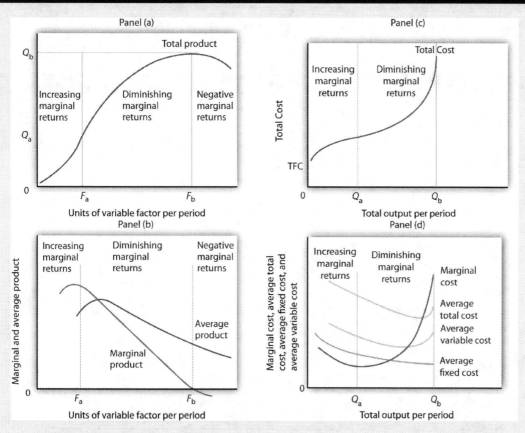

- In Panel (a), the total product curve for a variable factor in the short run shows that the firm experiences increasing marginal returns from zero to F_a units of the variable factor (zero to Q_a units of output), diminishing marginal returns from F_a to F_b (Q_a to Q_b units of output), and negative marginal returns beyond F_b units of the variable factor.

- Panel (b) shows that marginal product rises over the range of increasing marginal returns, falls over the range of diminishing marginal returns, and becomes negative over the range of negative marginal returns. Average product rises when marginal product is above it and falls when marginal product is below it.

- In Panel (c), total cost rises at a decreasing rate over the range of output from zero to Q_a. This was the range of output that was shown in Panel (a) to exhibit increasing marginal returns. Beyond Q_a, the range of diminishing marginal returns, total cost rises at an increasing rate. The total cost at zero units of output (shown as the intercept on the vertical axis) is total fixed cost.

- Panel (d) shows that marginal cost falls over the range of increasing marginal returns, then rises over the range of diminishing marginal returns. The marginal cost curve intersects the average total cost and average variable cost curves at their lowest points. Average fixed cost falls as output increases. Note that average total cost equals average variable cost plus average fixed cost.

- Assuming labor is the variable factor of production, the following definitions and relations describe production and cost in the short run:

$$MP_L = \Delta Q \, / \, \Delta L$$

$$AP_L = Q \, / \, L$$

$$TVC + TFC = TC$$

$$ATC = TC \, / \, Q$$

$$AVC = TVC \, / \, Q$$

$$AFC = TFC \, / \, Q$$

$$MC = \Delta TC / \Delta Q$$

TRY IT!

1. Suppose Acme gets some new equipment for producing jackets. The table below gives its new production function. Compute marginal product and average product and fill in the bottom two rows of the table. Referring to Figure 6.2, draw a graph showing Acme's new total product curve. On a second graph, below the one showing the total product curve you drew, sketch the marginal and average product curves. Remember to plot marginal product at the midpoint between each input level. On both graphs, shade the regions where Acme experiences increasing marginal returns, diminishing marginal returns, and negative marginal returns.

Units of labor per day	0	1	2	3	4	5	6	7	8
Jackets per day	0	2	5.5	9.5	12	14	15	15.5	15
Marginal product									
Average product									

2. Draw the points showing total variable cost at daily outputs of 0, 1, 3, 7, 9, 10, and 11 jackets per day when Acme faced a wage of $100 per day. (Use Figure 6.5 as a model.) Sketch the total variable cost curve as shown in Figure 6.4. Now suppose that the wage rises to $125 per day. On the same graph, show the new points and sketch the new total variable cost curve. Explain what has happened. What will happen to Acme's marginal cost curve? Its average total, average variable, and average fixed cost curves? Explain.

Case in Point

The Production of Fitness

How much should an athlete train?

Sports physiologists often measure the "total product" of training as the increase in an athlete's aerobic capacity—the capacity to absorb oxygen into the bloodstream. An athlete can be thought of as producing aerobic capacity using a fixed factor (his or her natural capacity) and a variable input (exercise). The chart shows how this aerobic capacity varies with the number of workouts per week. The curve has a shape very much like a total product curve—which, after all, is precisely what it is.

The data suggest that an athlete experiences increasing marginal returns from exercise for the first three days of training each week; indeed, over half the total gain in aerobic capacity possible is achieved. A person can become even more fit by exercising more, but the gains become smaller with each added day of training. The law of diminishing marginal returns applies to training.

The increase in fitness that results from the sixth and seventh workouts each week is small. Studies also show that the costs of daily training, in terms of increased likelihood of injury, are high. Many trainers and coaches now recommend that athletes—at all levels of competition—take a day or two off each week.

Source: Jeff Galloway, Galloway's Book on Running (Bolinas, CA: Shelter Publications, 2002), p. 56.

ANSWERS TO TRY IT! PROBLEMS

Units of labor per day	0	1	2	3	4	5	6	7	8
Jackets per day	0	2	5.5	9.5	12	14	15	15.5	15
Marginal product		2	3.5	4.0	2.5	2.0	1.0	0.5	−0.5
Average product		2	2.75	3.17	3	2.8	2.5	2.21	1.88

1. The increased wage will shift the total variable cost curve upward; the old and new points and the corresponding curves are shown at the right.

2. The total variable cost curve has shifted upward because the cost of labor, Acme's variable factor, has increased. The marginal cost curve shows the additional cost of each additional unit of output a firm produces. Because an increase in output requires more labor, and because labor now costs more, the marginal cost curve will shift upward. The increase in total variable cost will increase total cost; average total and average variable costs will rise as well. Average fixed cost will not change.

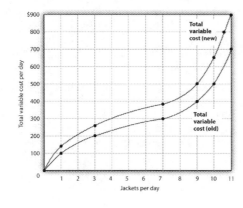

2. PRODUCTION CHOICES AND COSTS: THE LONG RUN

LEARNING OBJECTIVES

1. Apply the marginal decision rule to explain how a firm chooses its mix of factors of production in the long run.
2. Define the long-run average cost curve and explain how it relates to economies and diseconomies of scale.

In a long-run planning perspective, a firm can consider changing the quantities of *all* its factors of production. That gives the firm opportunities it does not have in the short run. First, the firm can select the mix of factors it wishes to use. Should it choose a production process with lots of labor and not much capital, like the street sweepers in China? Or should it select a process that uses a great deal of capital and relatively little labor, like street sweepers in the United States? The second thing the firm can select is the scale (or overall size) of its operations. In the short run, a firm can increase output only by increasing its use of a variable factor. But in the long run, all factors are variable, so the firm can expand the use of all of its factors of production. The question facing the firm in the long run is: How much of an expansion or contraction in the scale of its operations should it undertake? Alternatively, it could choose to go out of business.

In its long-run planning, the firm not only regards all factors as variable, but it regards all costs as variable as well. There are no fixed costs in the long run. Because all costs are variable, the structure of costs in the long run differs somewhat from what we saw in the short run.

2.1 Choosing the Factor Mix

How shall a firm decide what mix of capital, labor, and other factors to use? We can apply the marginal decision rule to answer this question.

Suppose a firm uses capital and labor to produce a particular good. It must determine how to produce the good and the quantity it should produce. We address the question of how much the firm should produce in subsequent chapters, but certainly the firm will want to produce whatever quantity it chooses at as low a cost as possible. Another way of putting that goal is to say that the firm seeks the maximum output possible at every level of total cost.

At any level of total cost, the firm can vary its factor mix. It could, for example, substitute labor for capital in a way that leaves its total cost unchanged. In terms of the marginal decision rule, we can think of the firm as considering whether to spend an additional $1 on one factor, hence $1 less on another. The marginal decision rule says that a firm will shift spending among factors as long as the marginal benefit of such a shift exceeds the marginal cost.

What is the marginal benefit, say, of an additional $1 spent on capital? An additional unit of capital produces the marginal product of capital. To determine the marginal benefit of $1 spent on capital, we divide capital's marginal product by its price: MP_K/P_K. The price of capital is the "rent" paid for the use of a unit of capital for a given period. If the firm already owns the capital, then this rent is an opportunity cost; it represents the return the firm could get by renting the capital to another user or by selling it and earning interest on the money thus gained.

If capital and labor are the only factors, then spending an additional $1 on capital while holding total cost constant means taking $1 out of labor. The cost of that action will be the output lost from cutting back $1 worth of labor. That cost equals the ratio of the marginal product of labor to the price of labor, MP_L/P_L, where the price of labor is the wage.

Suppose that a firm's marginal product of labor is 15 and the price of labor is $5 per unit; the firm gains 3 units of output by spending an additional $1 on labor. Suppose further that the marginal product of capital is 50 and the price of capital is $50 per unit, so the firm would lose 1 unit of output by spending $1 less on capital.

$$\frac{MP_L}{P_L} > \frac{MP_K}{P_K}$$

$$\frac{15}{5} > \frac{50}{50}$$

The firm achieves a net gain of 2 units of output, without any change in cost, by transferring $1 from capital to labor. It will continue to transfer funds from capital to labor as long as it gains more output from the additional labor than it loses in output by reducing capital. As the firm shifts spending in this fashion, however, the marginal product of labor will fall and the marginal product of capital will rise. At some point, the ratios of marginal product to price will be equal for the two factors. At this point, the firm will obtain the maximum output possible for a given total cost:

EQUATION 6.9

$$\frac{MP_L}{P_L} = \frac{MP_K}{P_K}$$

Suppose that a firm that uses capital and labor is satisfying Equation 6.9 when suddenly the price of labor rises. At the current usage levels of the factors, a higher price of labor (P_L') lowers the ratio of the marginal product of labor to the price of labor:

$$\frac{MP_L}{P_L'} < \frac{MP_K}{P_K}$$

The firm will shift funds out of labor and into capital. It will continue to shift from labor to capital until the ratios of marginal product to price are equal for the two factors. In general, a profit-maximizing firm will seek a combination of factors such that

EQUATION 6.10

$$\frac{MP_1}{P_1} = \frac{MP_2}{P_2} = ... = \frac{MP_n}{P_n} \qquad ,$$

When a firm satisfies the condition given in Equation 6.10 for efficient use, it produces the greatest possible output for a given cost. To put it another way, the firm achieves the lowest possible cost for a given level of output.

As the price of labor rises, the firm will shift to a factor mix that uses relatively more capital and relatively less labor. As a firm increases its ratio of capital to labor, we say it is becoming more **capital intensive**. A lower price for labor will lead the firm to use relatively more labor and less capital, reducing its ratio of capital to labor. As a firm reduces its ratio of capital to labor, we say it is becoming more **labor intensive**. The notions of labor-intensive and capital-intensive production are purely relative; they imply only that a firm has a higher or lower ratio of capital to labor.

Sometimes economists speak of labor-intensive versus capital-intensive countries in the same manner. One implication of the marginal decision rule for factor use is that firms in countries where labor is relatively expensive, such as the United States, will use capital-intensive production methods. Less developed countries, where labor is relatively cheap, will use labor-intensive methods.

Now that we understand how to apply the marginal decision rule to the problem of choosing the mix of factors, we can answer the question that began this chapter: Why does the United States employ a capital-intensive production process to clean streets while China chooses a labor-intensive process? Given that the same technology—know-how—is available, both countries could, after all, use the same production process. Suppose for a moment that the relative prices of labor and capital are the same in China and the United States. In that case, China and the United States can be expected to use the same method to clean streets. But the price of labor relative to the price of capital is, in fact, far lower in China than in the United States. A lower relative price for labor increases the ratio of the marginal product of labor to its price, making it efficient to substitute labor for capital. China thus finds it cheaper to clean streets with lots of people using brooms, while the United States finds it efficient to clean streets with large machines and relatively less labor.

Maquiladoras, plants in Mexico where processing is done using low-cost workers and labor-intensive methods, allow some U.S. firms to have it both ways. They complete part of the production process in the United States, using capital-intensive methods. They then ship the unfinished goods to *maquiladoras*. For example, many U.S. clothing manufacturers produce cloth at U.S. plants on large high-speed looms. They then ship the cloth to Mexico, where it is fashioned into clothing by workers using sewing machines. Another example is plastic injection molding, which requires highly skilled labor and is made in the U.S. The parts are molded in Texas border towns and are then shipped to *maquiladoras* and used in cars and computers. The resulting items are shipped back to the United States, labeled "Assembled in Mexico from U.S. materials." Overall maquiladoras import 97% of the components they use, of which 80 to 85% come from the U.S.

The *maquiladoras* have been a boon to workers in Mexico, who enjoy a higher demand for their services and receive higher wages as a result. The system also benefits the U.S. firms that participate and U.S. consumers who obtain less expensive goods than they would otherwise. It works because different factor prices imply different mixes of labor and capital. Companies are able to carry out the capital-intensive side of the production process in the United States and the labor-intensive side in Mexico. [1]

capital intensive

Situation in which a firm has a high ratio of capital to labor.

labor intensive

Situation in which a firm has a high ratio of labor to capital.

2.2   Costs in the Long Run

As in the short run, costs in the long run depend on the firm's level of output, the costs of factors, and the quantities of factors needed for each level of output. The chief difference between long- and short-run costs is there are no fixed factors in the long run. There are thus no fixed costs. All costs are variable, so we do not distinguish between total variable cost and total cost in the long run: total cost *is* total variable cost.

The long-run average cost (*LRAC*) curve shows the firm's lowest cost per unit at each level of output, assuming that all factors of production are variable. The *LRAC* curve assumes that the firm has chosen the optimal factor mix, as described in the previous section, for producing any level of output. The costs it shows are therefore the lowest costs possible for each level of output. It is important to note, however, that this does not mean that the minimum points of each short-run ATC curves lie on the *LRAC* curve. This critical point is explained in the next paragraph and expanded upon even further in the next section.

Figure 6.9 shows how a firm's *LRAC* curve is derived. Suppose Lifetime Disc Co. produces compact discs (CDs) using capital and labor. We have already seen how a firm's average total cost curve can be drawn in the short run for a given quantity of a particular factor of production, such as capital. In the short run, Lifetime Disc might be limited to operating with a given amount of capital; it would face one of the short-run average total cost curves shown in Figure 6.9. If it has 30 units of capital, for example, its average total cost curve is ATC_{30}. In the long run the firm can examine the average total cost curves associated with varying levels of capital. Four possible short-run average total cost curves for Lifetime Disc are shown in Figure 6.9 for quantities of capital of 20, 30, 40, and 50 units. The relevant curves are labeled ATC_{20}, ATC_{30}, ATC_{40}, and ATC_{50} respectively. The *LRAC* curve is derived from this set of short-run curves by finding the lowest average total cost associated with each level of output. Again, notice that the U-shaped *LRAC* curve is an envelope curve that surrounds the various short-run ATC curves. With the exception of ATC_{40}, in this example, the lowest cost per unit for a particular level of output in the long run is not the minimum point of the relevant short-run curve.

FIGURE 6.9   Relationship Between Short-Run and Long-Run Average Total Costs

The *LRAC* curve is found by taking the lowest average total cost curve at each level of output. Here, average total cost curves for quantities of capital of 20, 30, 40, and 50 units are shown for the Lifetime Disc Co. At a production level of 10,000 CDs per week, Lifetime minimizes its cost per CD by producing with 20 units of capital (point A). At 20,000 CDs per week, an expansion to a plant size associated with 30 units of capital minimizes cost per unit (point B). The lowest cost per unit is achieved with production of 30,000 CDs per week using 40 units of capital (point C). If Lifetime chooses to produce 40,000 CDs per week, it will do so most cheaply with 50 units of capital (point D).

Economies and Diseconomies of Scale

Notice that the long-run average cost curve in Figure 6.9 first slopes downward and then slopes upward. The shape of this curve tells us what is happening to average cost as the firm changes its scale of operations. A firm is said to experience **economies of scale** when long-run average cost declines as the firm expands its output. A firm is said to experience **diseconomies of scale** when long-run average cost increases as the firm expands its output. **Constant returns to scale** occur when long-run average cost stays the same over an output range.

Why would a firm experience economies of scale? One source of economies of scale is gains from specialization. As the scale of a firm's operation expands, it is able to use its factors in more specialized ways, increasing their productivity. Another source of economies of scale lies in the economies that can be gained from mass production methods. As the scale of a firm's operation expands, the company can begin to utilize large-scale machines and production systems that can substantially reduce cost per unit.

Why would a firm experience diseconomies of scale? At first glance, it might seem that the answer lies in the law of diminishing marginal returns, but this is not the case. The law of diminishing marginal returns, after all, tells us how output changes as a single factor is increased, with all other factors of production held constant. In contrast, diseconomies of scale describe a situation of rising average cost even when the firm is free to vary any or all of its factors as it wishes. Diseconomies of scale are generally thought to be caused by management problems. As the scale of a firm's operations expands, it becomes harder and harder for management to coordinate and guide the activities of individual units of the firm. Eventually, the diseconomies of management overwhelm any gains the firm might be achieving by operating with a larger scale of plant, and long-run average costs begin rising. Firms experience constant returns to scale at output levels where there are neither economies nor diseconomies of scale. For the range of output over which the firm experiences constant returns to scale, the long-run average cost curve is horizontal.

Firms are likely to experience all three situations, as shown in Figure 6.10. At very low levels of output, the firm is likely to experience economies of scale as it expands the scale of its operations. There may follow a range of output over which the firm experiences constant returns to scale—empirical studies suggest that the range over which firms experience constant returns to scale is often very large. And certainly there must be some range of output over which diseconomies of scale occur; this phenomenon is one factor that limits the size of firms. A firm operating on the upward-sloping part of its *LRAC* curve is likely to be undercut in the market by smaller firms operating with lower costs per unit of output.

The Size Distribution of Firms

Economies and diseconomies of scale have a powerful effect on the sizes of firms that will operate in any market. Suppose firms in a particular industry experience diseconomies of scale at relatively low levels of output. That industry will be characterized by a large number of fairly small firms. The restaurant market appears to be such an industry. Barbers and beauticians are another example.

If firms in an industry experience economies of scale over a very wide range of output, firms that expand to take advantage of lower cost will force out smaller firms that have higher costs. Such industries are likely to have a few large firms instead of many small ones. In the refrigerator industry, for example, the size of firm necessary to achieve the lowest possible cost per unit is large enough to limit the market to only a few firms. In most cities, economies of scale leave room for only a single newspaper.

One factor that can limit the achievement of economies of scale is the demand facing an individual firm. The scale of output required to achieve the lowest unit costs possible may require sales that exceed the demand facing a firm. A grocery store, for example, could minimize unit costs with a large store and a large volume of sales. But the demand for groceries in a small, isolated community may not be able to sustain such a volume of sales. The firm is thus limited to a small scale of operation even though this might involve higher unit costs.

economies of scale

Situation in which the long-run average cost declines as the firm expands its output.

diseconomies of scale

Situation in which the long-run average cost increases as the firm expands its output.

constant returns to scale

Situation in which the long-run average cost stays the same over an output range.

FIGURE 6.10 Economies and Diseconomies of Scale and Long-Run Average Cost

The downward-sloping region of the firm's *LRAC* curve is associated with economies of scale. There may be a horizontal range associated with constant returns to scale. The upward-sloping range of the curve implies diseconomies of scale.

Output per period

KEY TAKEAWAYS

- A firm chooses its factor mix in the long run on the basis of the marginal decision rule; it seeks to equate the ratio of marginal product to price for all factors of production. By doing so, it minimizes the cost of producing a given level of output.
- The long-run average cost (LRAC) curve is derived from the average total cost curves associated with different quantities of the factor that is fixed in the short run. The LRAC curve shows the lowest cost per unit at which each quantity can be produced when all factors of production, including capital, are variable.
- A firm may experience economies of scale, constant returns to scale, or diseconomies of scale. Economies of scale imply a downward-sloping long-run average cost (LRAC) curve. Constant returns to scale imply a horizontal LRAC curve. Diseconomies of scale imply an upward-sloping LRAC curve.
- A firm's ability to exploit economies of scale is limited by the extent of market demand for its products.
- The range of output over which firms experience economies of scale, constant return to scale, or diseconomies of scale is an important determinant of how many firms will survive in a particular market.

TRY IT!

1. Suppose Acme Clothing is operating with 20 units of capital and producing 9 units of output at an average total cost of $67, as shown in Figure 6.8. How much labor is it using?
2. Suppose it finds that, with this combination of capital and labor, $MP_K/P_K > MP_L/P_L$. What adjustment will the firm make in the long run? Why does it not make this same adjustment in the short run?

Case in Point

Telecommunications Equipment, Economies of Scale, and Outage Risk

© 2010 Jupiterimages Corporation

How big should the call switching equipment a major telecommunications company uses be? Having bigger machines results in economies of scale but also raises the risk of larger outages that will affect more customers.

Verizon Laboratories economist Donald E. Smith examined both the economies of scale available from larger equipment and the greater danger of more widespread outages. He concluded that companies should not use the largest machines available because of the outage danger and that they should not use the smallest size because that would mean forgoing the potential gains from economies of scale of larger sizes.

Switching machines, the large computers that handle calls for telecommunications companies, come in four basic "port matrix sizes." These are measured in terms of Digital Cross-Connects (DCCs). The four DCS sizes available are 6,000; 12,000; 24,000; and 36,000 ports. Different machine sizes are made with the same components and thus have essentially the same probability of breaking down. Because larger machines serve more customers, however, a breakdown in a large machine has greater consequences for the company.

The costs of an outage have three elements. The first is lost revenue from calls that would otherwise have been completed. Second, the FCC requires companies to provide a credit of one month of free service after any outage that lasts longer than one minute. Finally, an outage damages a company's reputation and inevitably results in dissatisfied customers—some of whom may switch to other companies.

But, there are advantages to larger machines. A company has a "portfolio" of switching machines. Having larger machines lowers costs in several ways. First, the initial acquisition of the machine generates lower cost per call completed the greater the size of the machine. When the company must make upgrades to the software, having fewer—and larger—machines means fewer upgrades and thus lower costs.

In deciding on matrix size companies should thus compare the cost advantages of a larger matrix with the disadvantages of the higher outage costs associated with those larger matrixes.

Mr. Smith concluded that the economies of scale outweigh the outage risks as a company expands beyond 6,000 ports but that 36,000 ports is "too big" in the sense that the outage costs outweigh the advantage of the economies of scale. The evidence thus suggests that a matrix size in the range of 12,000 to 24,000 ports is optimal.

Source: Donald E. Smith, "How Big Is Too Big? Trading Off the Economies of Scale of Larger Telecommunications Network Elements Against the Risk of Larger Outages," European Journal of Operational Research, 173 (1) (August 2006): 299–312.

ANSWERS TO TRY IT! PROBLEMS

1. To produce 9 jackets, Acme uses 4 units of labor.
2. In the long run, Acme will substitute capital for labor. It cannot make this adjustment in the short run, because its capital is fixed in the short run.

3. AN OVERVIEW OF MODELS OF MARKET ORGANIZATION

LEARNING OBJECTIVES

1. **Define the four models of market organization.**
2. **Explain the difference between being a price taker or a price setter.**

Firms use production and cost information to decide how they will respond to market forces. In all cases, economists assume that firms will be attempting to maximize profits by applying the marginal decision rule. How that plays out in both the short run and in the long run, though, depends on the environment in which the firm is operating. For example, some markets are characterized by many, many firms selling the same product, while other markets may be dominated by a single firm. Many markets lie between these two extremes.

Instead of listing each firm on a continuum, economists have developed four models of market organization that characterize industries according to how many firms there are in the industry, how much control the firms in the industry have over the prices of their products, whether the firms in the industry are selling the same or somewhat differentiated products, and how easy or difficult it is to enter and exit from the market.

Perfect competition is a model of the market based on the assumption that a large number of firms produce identical goods consumed by a large number of buyers. Because there are many buyers and sellers, no individual buyer or seller has any influence over the market price of the products such firms are selling. Individuals or firms who must take the market price as given are called **price takers**.

At the other end of the spectrum, a **monopoly** is a firm that is the only producer of a good or service for which there are no close substitutes and for which entry by potential rivals is prohibitively difficult. A monopoly does not take the market price as given. Rather, it is a **price setter**, a firm that sets or picks price based on its output decision.

Two other market models lie between these two extremes. **Imperfect competition** is a market structure with more than one firm in an industry in which at least one firm is a price setter. There are two broad categories of imperfectly competitive markets.

Monopolistic competition is a model characterized by many firms producing similar but differentiated products in a market with easy entry and exit. Restaurants are a monopolistically competitive sector; in most areas there are many firms, each is different, and entry and exit are fairly easy. Each restaurant has many close substitutes—these may include other restaurants, fast-food outlets, and the deli and frozen-food sections at local supermarkets. Other industries that engage in monopolistic competition include retail stores, barber and beauty shops, auto-repair shops, and law and accounting firms. Firms in a monopolistically competitive industry have some power to set price, but their ability is limited by the availability of close substitutes.

The second form of imperfect competition is oligopoly. In an **oligopoly**, the market is dominated by a few firms, selling similar or differentiated products, each of which recognizes that its own actions will produce a response from its rivals and that those responses will affect it. Examples of oligopolistic industries include the automobile and cigarette industries. With few rivals, firms in oligopolistic industries also have some control over the price at which they sell their products; they are considered price setters.

In this text we will focus in depth on the behavior of firms under the assumptions of perfect competition and monopoly. By comparison, we will be able to draw some conclusions about firms in imperfectly competitive industries.

---

perfect competition

Model of the market based on the assumption that a large number of firms produce identical goods consumed by a large number of buyers.

price takers

Individuals or firms who must take the market price as given.

monopoly

A firm that is the only producer of a good or service for which there are no close substitutes and for which entry by potential rivals is prohibitively difficult.

price setter

A firm that sets or picks price based on its output decision.

imperfect condition

A market structure with more than one firm in an industry in which at least one firm is a price setter.

monopolistic competition

A model characterized by many firms producing similar but differentiated products in a market with easy entry and exit.

oligopoly

Situation in which a market is dominated by a few firms, each of which recognizes that its own actions will produce a response from its rivals and that those responses will affect it.

KEY TAKEAWAYS

- The four models of market organization are perfect competition, monopoly, monopolistic competition, and oligopoly.
- In perfectly competitive markets, firms are price takers. Firms in other types of market structures have at least some power to set price.

Which model of market organization do you think would best describe each of the following goods and services?

1. Accountants
2. Wheat
3. Astrologists
4. Coca-Cola and Pepsi
5. A local electric utility company

Case in Point

Craft Brewers: The Rebirth of a Monopolistically Competitive Industry

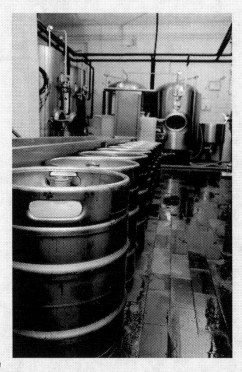

© 2010 Jupiterimages Corporation

In the early 1900s, there were about 2,000 local beer breweries across America. Prohibition in the 1920s squashed the industry; after the repeal of Prohibition, economies of scale eliminated smaller breweries. By the early 1980s, only about 40 remained in existence.

But the American desire for more variety has led to the rebirth of the nearly defunct industry. To be sure, large, national beer companies dominated the overall ale market in 1980 and they still do today—with 43 large national and regional breweries sharing about 85% of the U.S. market for beer. But their emphasis on similarly tasting, light lagers (at least, until they felt threatened enough by the new craft brewers to come up with their own specialty brands) left many niches to be filled. One niche was filled by imports, accounting for about 12% of the U.S. market. That leaves 3 to 4% of the national market for the domestic specialty or "craft" brewers.

The new craft brewers, which include contract brewers, regional specialty brewers, microbreweries, and brewpubs, offer choice. As Neal Leathers at Big Sky Brewing Company in Missoula, Montana, put it, "We sort of convert people. If you haven't had very many choices, and all of a sudden you get choices—especially if those choices involve a lot of flavor and quality—it's hard to go back."

Aided by the recent legalization in most states of brewpubs, establishments where beers are manufactured and retailed on the same premises, the number of microbreweries grew substantially over the last 25 years. A recent telephone book in Colorado Springs, a city with a population of about a half million and the home of the authors of your textbook, listed nine microbreweries and brewpubs; more exist but prefer to be listed as restaurants.

To what extent does this industry conform to the model of monopolistic competition? Clearly, the microbreweries sell differentiated products, giving them some degree of price-setting power. A sample of four brewpubs in the downtown area of Colorado Springs revealed that the price of a house beer ranged from 13 to 22 cents per ounce.

Entry into the industry seems fairly easy, judging from the phenomenal growth of the industry. After more than a decade of explosive growth and then a period of leveling off, the number of craft breweries, as they are referred to by the Brewers Association, stood at 1,716 in 2010. The start-up cost ranges from $100,000 to $400,000, according to Kevin Head, the owner of the Rhino Bar, also in Missoula.

The model of monopolistic competition also predicts that exit will be fairly easy. The reasons for leaving the industry will vary, but some of the firms that exit will do so because competitors have taken customers away from them. In the combined microbrewery and brewpub subsectors of the craft beer industry in 2010, for example, there were 152 openings and 43 closings.

Sources: Jim Ludwick, "The Art of Zymurgy—It's the Latest Thing: Microbrewers Are Tapping into the New Specialty Beer Market," Missoulian (November 29, 1996): p. A1; Brewers Association, "2010 Craft Brewing Statistics," http://www.brewersassociation.org/pages/business-tools/craft-brewing-statistics/number-of-breweries.

ANSWERS TO TRY IT! PROBLEMS

1. Monopolistic competition
2. Perfect competition
3. Monopolistic competition
4. Oligopoly
5. Monopoly

4. REVIEW AND PRACTICE

Summary

In this chapter we first concentrated on the production and cost relationships facing firms in the short run and in the long run.

In the short run, a firm has at least one factor of production that it cannot vary. This fixed factor limits the firm's range of factor choices. As a firm uses more and more of a variable factor (with fixed quantities of other factors of production), it is likely to experience at first increasing, then diminishing, then negative marginal returns. Thus, the short-run total cost curve has a positive value at a zero level of output (the firm's total fixed cost), then slopes upward at a decreasing rate (the range of increasing marginal returns), and then slopes upward at an increasing rate (the range of diminishing marginal returns).

In addition to short-run total product and total cost curves, we derived a firm's marginal product, average product, average total cost, average variable cost, average fixed cost, and marginal cost curves.

If the firm is to maximize profit in the long run, it must select the cost-minimizing combination of factors for its chosen level of output. Thus, the firm must try to use factors of production in accordance with the marginal decision rule. That is, it will use factors so that the ratio of marginal product to factor price is equal for all factors of production.

A firm's long-run average cost (*LRAC*) curve includes a range of economies of scale, over which the curve slopes downward, and a range of diseconomies of scale, over which the curve slopes upward. There may be an intervening range of output over which the firm experiences constant returns to scale; its *LRAC* curve will be horizontal over this range. The size of operations necessary to reach the lowest point on the *LRAC* curve has a great deal to do with determining the relative sizes of firms in an industry.

We concluded the chapter by describing the various models of market organization Knowledge of the nature of production processes and the costs associated with them as well as the type of market in which a firm operates form the basis for understanding the behavior of firms and the decisions they make concerning supply of goods and services.

CONCEPT PROBLEMS

1. Which of the following would be considered long-run choices? Which are short-run choices?

    a. A dentist hires a new part-time dental hygienist.

    b. The local oil refinery plans a complete restructuring of its production processes, including relocating the plant.

    c. A farmer increases the quantity of water applied to his or her fields.

    d. A law partnership signs a 3-year lease for an office complex.

    e. The university hires a new football coach on a 3-year contract.

2. "There are no fixed costs in the long run." Explain.

3. Business is booming at the local McDonald's restaurant. It is contemplating adding a new grill and french-fry machine, but the day supervisor suggests simply hiring more workers. How should the manager decide which alternative to pursue?

4. Suppose that the average age of students in your economics class is 23.7 years. If a new 19-year-old student enrolls in the class, will the average age in the class rise or fall? Explain how this relates to the relationship between average and marginal values.

5. Barry Bond's career home run average in his first 15 years in major league baseball (through 1997) was 33 home runs per season. In 2001, he hit 73 home runs. What happened to his career home run average? What effect did his performance in 2001 have on his career home run average? Explain how this relates to the relationship between average and marginal values.

6. Suppose a firm is operating at the minimum point of its short-run average total cost curve, so that marginal cost equals average total cost. Under what circumstances would it choose to alter the size of its plant? Explain.

7. What happens to the difference between average total cost and average variable cost as a firm's output expands? Explain.

8. How would each of the following affect average total cost, average variable cost, and marginal cost?

    a. An increase in the cost of the lease of the firm's building

    b. A reduction in the price of electricity

    c. A reduction in wages

    d. A change in the salary of the president of the company

9. Consider the following types of firms. For each one, the long-run average cost curve eventually exhibits diseconomies of scale. For which firms would you expect diseconomies of scale to set in at relatively low levels of output? Why?

    a. A copy shop

    b. A hardware store

    c. A dairy

    d. A newspaper

    e. An automobile manufacturer

    f. A restaurant

10. As car manufacturers incorporate more sophisticated computer technology in their vehicles, auto-repair shops require more computerized testing equipment, which is quite expensive, in order to repair newer cars. How is this likely to affect the shape of these firms' long-run average total cost curves? How is it likely to affect the number of auto-repair firms in any market?

11. What are the major distinctions between a monopolistically competitive industry and an oligopolistic industry?

12. What is the difference between a price taker and a price setter? Which do you think a firm would prefer to be? Why?

NUMERICAL PROBLEMS

1. The table below shows how the number of university classrooms cleaned in an evening varies with the number of janitors:

Janitors per evening	0	1	2	3	4	5	6	7
Classrooms cleaned per evening	0	3	7	12	16	17	17	16

   a. What is the marginal product of the second janitor?

   b. What is the average product of four janitors?

   c. Is the addition of the third janitor associated with increasing, diminishing, or negative marginal returns? Explain.

   d. Is the addition of the fourth janitor associated with increasing, diminishing, or negative marginal returns? Explain.

   e. Is the addition of the seventh janitor associated with increasing, diminishing, or negative marginal returns? Explain.

   f. Draw the total product, average product, and marginal product curves and shade the regions corresponding to increasing marginal returns, decreasing marginal returns, and negative marginal returns.

   g. Calculate the slope of the total product curve as each janitor is added.

   h. Characterize the nature of marginal returns in the region where

      1. The slope of the total product curve is positive and increasing.

      2. The slope of the total product curve is positive and decreasing.

      3. The slope of the total product curve is negative.

2. Suppose a firm is producing 1,000 units of output. Its average fixed costs are $100. Its average variable costs are $50. What is the total cost of producing 1,000 units of output?

3. The director of a nonprofit foundation that sponsors 8-week summer institutes for graduate students analyzed the costs and expected revenues for the next summer institute and recommended that the session be canceled. In her analysis she included a share of the foundation's overhead—the salaries of the director and staff and costs of maintaining the office—to the program. She estimated costs and revenues as follows:

Projected revenues (from tuition and fees)	$300,000
Projected costs	
Overhead	$ 50,000
Room and board for students	$100,000
Costs for faculty and miscellaneous	$175,000
Total costs	$325,000

   What was the error in the director's recommendation?

4. The table below shows the total cost of cleaning classrooms:

Classrooms cleaned per evening	0	3	7	12	16	17
Total cost	$100	$200	$300	$400	$500	$600

   a. What is the average fixed cost of cleaning three classrooms?

   b. What is the average variable cost of cleaning three classrooms?

   c. What is the average fixed cost of cleaning seven classrooms?

   d. What is the average variable cost of cleaning seven classrooms?

   e. What is the marginal cost of cleaning the seventeenth classroom?

   f. What is the average total cost of cleaning twelve classrooms?

5. The average total cost for printing 10,000 copies of an issue of a magazine is $0.45 per copy. For 20,000 copies, the average total cost is $0.35 apiece; for 30,000, the average total cost is $0.30 per copy. The average total cost continues to decline slightly over every level of output that the publishers of the magazine have considered. Sketch the approximate shapes of the average and marginal cost curves. What are some variable costs of publishing magazines? Some fixed costs?

6. The information in the table explains the production of socks. Assume that the price per unit of the variable factor of production (L) is $20 and the price per unit of the fixed factor of production (K) is $5.

Units of Fixed Factor (K)	Units of Variable Factor (L)	Total Product (Q)
10	0	0
10	1	2
10	2	5
10	3	12
10	4	15
10	5	16

    a. Add columns to the table and calculate the values for : Marginal Product of Labor (MP_L), Total Variable Cost (*TVC*), Total Fixed Cost (*TFC*), Total Cost (*TC*), Average Variable Cost (*AVC*), Average Fixed Cost (*AFC*), Average Total Cost (*ATC*), and Marginal Cost (*MC*).

    b. On two sets of axes, graph the Total Product and Marginal Product curves. Be sure to label curves and axes and remember to plot marginal product using the midpoint convention. Indicate the point on each graph at which diminishing marginal returns appears to begin.

    c. Graph Total Variable Cost, Total Fixed Cost, and Total Cost on another set of axes. Indicate the point on the graph at which diminishing marginal returns appears to begin.

    d. Graph the Average Fixed Cost, Average Variable Cost, Average Total Cost, and Marginal Cost curves on another set of axes. Indicate the point at which diminishing marginal returns appears to begin.

7. The table below shows the long-run average cost of producing knives:

Knives per hour	1,000	2,000	3,000	4,000	5,000	6,000
Cost per knife	$2	$1.50	$1.00	$1.00	$1.20	$1.30

    a. Draw the long-run average cost curve for knives.

    b. Shade the regions corresponding to economies of scale, constant returns to scale, and diseconomies of scale.

    c. In the region of the long-run average cost curve that corresponds to economies of scale, what is happening to the cost per knife?

    d. In the region of the long-run average cost curve that corresponds to constant returns to scale, what is happening to the cost per knife?

    e. In the region of the long-run average cost curve that corresponds to diseconomies of scale, what is happening to the cost per knife?

8. Suppose a firm finds that the marginal product of capital is 60 and the marginal product of labor is 20. If the price of capital is $6 and the price of labor is $2.50, how should the firm adjust its mix of capital and labor? What will be the result?

9. A firm minimizes its costs by using inputs such that the marginal product of labor is 10 and the marginal product of capital is 20. The price of capital is $10 per unit. What must the price of labor be?

10. Suppose that the price of labor is $10 per unit and the price of capital is $20 per unit.

    a. Assuming the firm is minimizing its cost, if the marginal product of labor is 50, what must the marginal product of capital be?

    b. Suppose the price of capital increases to $25 per unit, while the price of labor stays the same. To minimize the cost of producing the same level of output, would the firm become more capital-intensive or labor-intensive? Explain.

ENDNOTES

1. Lucinda Vargas, "Maquiladoras: Impact on Texas Border Cities," in *The Border Economy*, Federal Reserve Bank of Dallas (June 2001): 25–29; William C. Gruben, "Have Mexico's Maquiladoras Bottomed Out?", Southwest Economy, Federal Reserve Bank of Dallas (January/February, 2004), pp. 14–15.

CHAPTER 7

Competitive Markets for Goods and Services

START UP: LIFE ON THE FARM

They produce a commodity that is essential to our daily lives, one for which the demand is virtually assured. And yet many—even as farm prices are reaching record highs—seem to live on the margin of failure. Thousands are driven out of business each year. We provide billions of dollars in aid for them, but still we hear of the hardships many of them face. They are our nation's farmers.

What is it about farmers, and farming, that arouses our concern? Much of the answer probably lies in our sense that farming is fundamental to the American way of life. Our country was built, in large part, by independent men and women who made their living from the soil. Many of us perceive their plight as our plight. But part of the answer lies in the fact that farmers do, in fact, face a difficult economic environment. Most of them operate in highly competitive markets—markets that tolerate few mistakes and generally offer small rewards. Finally, perhaps our concern is stirred by our recognition that the farmers' plight is our blessing. The low prices that make life difficult for farmers are the low prices we enjoy as consumers of food.

What keeps the returns to farming as low as they are? What holds many farmers in a situation in which they always seem to be just getting by? In this chapter we shall see that prices just high enough to induce firms to continue to produce are precisely what we would expect to prevail in a competitive market. We will examine a model of how competitive markets work. Not only does this model help to explain the situation facing farmers, but it will also help us to understand the determination of price and output in a wide range of markets. A farm is a firm, and our analysis of such a firm in a competitive market will give us the tools to analyze the choices of all firms operating in competitive markets.

We will put the concepts of marginal cost, average variable cost, and average total cost to work to see how firms in a competitive market respond to market forces. We will see how firms adjust to changes in demand and supply in the short run and in the long run. In all of this, we will be examining how firms use the marginal decision rule.

1. PERFECT COMPETITION: A MODEL

Virtually all firms in a market economy face competition from other firms. In this chapter, we will be working with a model of a highly idealized form of competition called "perfect" by economists.

Perfect competition is a model of the market based on the assumption that a large number of firms produce identical goods consumed by a large number of buyers. The model of perfect competition also assumes that it is easy for new firms to enter the market and for existing ones to leave. And finally, it assumes that buyers and sellers have complete information about market conditions.

As we examine these assumptions in greater detail, we will see that they allow us to work with the model more easily. No market fully meets the conditions set out in these assumptions. As is always the case with models, our purpose is to understand the way things work, not to describe them. And the model of perfect competition will prove enormously useful in understanding the world of markets.

1.1 Assumptions of the Model

The assumptions of the model of perfect competition, taken together, imply that individual buyers and sellers in a perfectly competitive market accept the market price as given. No one buyer or seller has any influence over that price. Individuals or firms who must take the market price as given are called price takers. A consumer or firm that takes the market price as given has no ability to influence that price. A price-taking firm or consumer is like an individual who is buying or selling stocks. He or she looks up the market price and buys or sells at that price. The price is determined by demand and supply in the market—not by individual buyers or sellers. In a perfectly competitive market, each firm and each consumer is a price taker. A price-taking consumer assumes that he or she can purchase any quantity at the market price—without affecting that price. Similarly, a price-taking firm assumes it can sell whatever quantity it wishes at the market price without affecting the price.

You are a price taker when you go into a store. You observe the prices listed and make a choice to buy or not. Your choice will not affect that price. Should you sell a textbook back to your campus bookstore at the end of a course, you are a price-taking seller. You are confronted by a market price and you decide whether to sell or not. Your decision will not affect that price.

To see how the assumptions of the model of perfect competition imply price-taking behavior, let us examine each of them in turn.

Identical Goods

In a perfectly competitive market for a good or service, one unit of the good or service cannot be differentiated from any other on any basis. A bushel of, say, hard winter wheat is an example. A bushel produced by one farmer is identical to that produced by another. There are no brand preferences or consumer loyalties.

The assumption that goods are identical is necessary if firms are to be price takers. If one farmer's wheat were perceived as having special properties that distinguished it from other wheat, then that farmer would have some power over its price. By assuming that all goods and services produced by firms in a perfectly competitive market are identical, we establish a necessary condition for price-taking behavior. Economists sometimes say that the goods or services in a perfectly competitive market are *homogeneous*, meaning that they are all alike. There are no brand differences in a perfectly competitive market.

A Large Number of Buyers and Sellers

How many buyers and sellers are in our market? The answer rests on our presumption of price-taking behavior. There are so many buyers and sellers that none of them has any influence on the market price regardless of how much any of them purchases or sells. A firm in a perfectly competitive market can react to prices, but cannot affect the prices it pays for the factors of production or the prices it receives for its output.

Ease of Entry and Exit

The assumption that it is easy for other firms to enter a perfectly competitive market implies an even greater degree of competition. Firms in a market must deal not only with the large number of competing firms but also with the possibility that still more firms might enter the market.

Later in this chapter, we will see how ease of entry is related to the sustainability of economic profits. If entry is easy, then the promise of high economic profits will quickly attract new firms. If entry is difficult, it won't.

The model of perfect competition assumes easy exit as well as easy entry. The assumption of easy exit strengthens the assumption of easy entry. Suppose a firm is considering entering a particular market. Entry may be easy, but suppose that getting out is difficult. For example, suppliers of factors of production to firms in the industry might be happy to accommodate new firms but might require that they sign long-term contracts. Such contracts could make leaving the market difficult and costly. If that were the case, a firm might be hesitant to enter in the first place. Easy exit helps make entry easier.

Complete Information

We assume that all sellers have complete information about prices, technology, and all other knowledge relevant to the operation of the market. No one seller has any information about production methods that is not available to all other sellers. If one seller had an advantage over other sellers, perhaps special information about a lower-cost production method, then that seller could exert some control over market price—the seller would no longer be a price taker.

We assume also that buyers know the prices offered by every seller. If buyers did not know about prices offered by different firms in the market, then a firm might be able to sell a good or service for a price other than the market price and thus could avoid being a price taker.

The availability of information that is assumed in the model of perfect competition implies that information can be obtained at low cost. If consumers and firms can obtain information at low cost, they are likely to do so. Information about the marketplace may come over the internet, over the airways in a television commercial, or over a cup of coffee with a friend. Whatever its source, we assume that its low cost ensures that consumers and firms have enough of it so that everyone buys or sells goods and services at market prices determined by the intersection of demand and supply curves.

The assumptions of the perfectly competitive model ensure that each buyer or seller is a price taker. The market, not individual consumers or firms, determines price in the model of perfect competition. No individual has enough power in a perfectly competitive market to have any impact on that price.

1.2 Perfect Competition and the Real World

The assumptions of identical products, a large number of buyers, easy entry and exit, and perfect information are strong assumptions. The notion that firms must sit back and let the market determine price seems to fly in the face of what we know about most real firms, which is that firms customarily do set prices. Yet this is the basis for the model of demand and supply, the power of which you have already seen.

When we use the model of demand and supply, we assume that market forces determine prices. In this model, buyers and sellers respond to the market price. They are price takers. The assumptions of the model of perfect competition underlie the assumption of price-taking behavior. Thus we are using the model of perfect competition whenever we apply the model of demand and supply.

We can understand most markets by applying the model of demand and supply. Even though those markets do not fulfill all the assumptions of the model of perfect competition, the model allows us to understand some key features of these markets.

Changes within your lifetime have made many markets more competitive. Falling costs of transportation, together with dramatic advances in telecommunications, have opened the possibility of entering markets to firms all over the world. A company in South Korea can compete in the market for steel in the United States. A furniture maker in New Mexico can compete in the market for furniture in Japan. A firm can enter the world market simply by creating a web page to advertise its products and to take orders.

In the remaining sections of this chapter, we will learn more about the response of firms to market prices. We will see how firms respond, in the short run and in the long run, to changes in demand and to changes in production costs. In short, we will be examining the forces that constitute the supply side of the model of demand and supply.

We will also see how competitive markets work to serve consumer interests and how competition acts to push economic profits down, sometimes eliminating them entirely. When we have finished we will have a better understanding of the market conditions facing farmers and of the conditions that prevail in any competitive industry.

Case in Point

Entering and Exiting the Burkha Industry

© 2010 Jupiterimages Corporation

Muhammed Ibrahim Islamadin was driving a cab in Kabul, Afghanistan, when the Taliban took over the country. He foresaw the repression that would follow and sensed an opportunity.

He sold his taxicab and set up a shop for sewing and selling burkhas, the garments required of all women under the Taliban's rule. Mr. Islamadin had an easy task selling, as women caught outdoors with exposed skin were routinely beaten by the Taliban's religious police. He told *The Wall Street Journal*, "This was very bad for them, but it was good for me."

Of course, Mr. Islamadin was not the only producer to get into the industry. Other Afghani merchants, as well as merchants from Pakistan and China, also jumped at the opportunity.

The entry of new firms exemplifies an important characteristic of perfect competition. Whenever there is an opportunity to earn economic profits—even an unexpected opportunity—new firms will enter, provided that entry is easy.

The model of perfect competition also assumes that exit will be easy if and when a firm experiences economic losses. When the Taliban rulers were ousted by the United States and its allies in 2001, Mr. Islamadin expected that the demand for burkhas would begin to fall. It did. The sales fell 50% almost immediately. Prices fell as well, generally by about 20%.

It was simple for Mr. Islamadin to leave the industry. He gave his remaining stock of burkhas to a brother who was producing them in the countryside where women continued to wear them. As for Mr. Islamadin, he has made plans to go into the glassware business. He expects the demand for glass teacups to be strong whatever happens in Afghanistan's critical future.

Source: Andrew Higgins, "With Islamic Dress, Out Goes the Guy Who Sold Burkhas," The Wall Street Journal, December 19, 2001, p. A1.

ANSWERS TO TRY IT! PROBLEMS

1. Not perfectly competitive—There are few sellers in this market (Fedex, UPS, and the United States Postal Services are the main ones in the United States) probably because of the difficulty of entry and exit. To provide these services requires many outlets and a large transportation fleet, for example.

2. Perfectly competitive—There are many firms producing a largely homogeneous product and there is good information about prices. Entry and exit is also fairly easy as firms can switch among a variety of crops.

3. Not perfectly competitive—The main reason is that goods are not identical.

2.   OUTPUT DETERMINATION IN THE SHORT RUN

LEARNING OBJECTIVES

1. **Show graphically how an individual firm in a perfectly competitive market can use total revenue and total cost curves or marginal revenue and marginal cost curves to determine the level of output that will maximize its economic profit.**

2. **Explain when a firm will shut down in the short run and when it will operate even if it is incurring economic losses.**

3. **Derive the firm's supply curve from the firm's marginal cost curve and the industry supply curve from the supply curves of individual firms.**

Our goal in this section is to see how a firm in a perfectly competitive market determines its output level in the short run—a planning period in which at least one factor of production is fixed in quantity. We shall see that the firm can maximize economic profit by applying the marginal decision rule and increasing output up to the point at which the marginal benefit of an additional unit of output is just equal to the marginal cost. This fact has an important implication: over a wide range of output, the firm's marginal cost curve is its supply curve.

2.1   Price and Revenue

Each firm in a perfectly competitive market is a price taker; the equilibrium price and industry output are determined by demand and supply. Figure 7.1 shows how demand and supply in the market for radishes, which we shall assume are produced under conditions of perfect competition, determine total output and price. The equilibrium price is $0.40 per pound; the equilibrium quantity is 10 million pounds per month.

FIGURE 7.1 The Market for Radishes

Price and output in a competitive market are determined by demand and supply. In the market for radishes, the equilibrium price is $0.40 per pound; 10 million pounds per month are produced and purchased at this price.

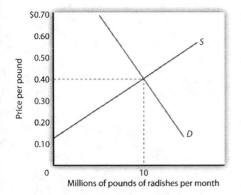

total revenue

A firm's output multiplied by the price at which it sells that output.

Because it is a price taker, each firm in the radish industry assumes it can sell all the radishes it wants at a price of $0.40 per pound. No matter how many or how few radishes it produces, the firm expects to sell them all at the market price.

The assumption that the firm expects to sell all the radishes it wants at the market price is crucial. If a firm did not expect to sell all of its radishes at the market price—if it had to lower the price to sell some quantities—the firm would not be a price taker. And price-taking behavior is central to the model of perfect competition.

Radish growers—and perfectly competitive firms in general—have no reason to charge a price lower than the market price. Because buyers have complete information and because we assume each firm's product is identical to that of its rivals, firms are unable to charge a price higher than the market price. For perfectly competitive firms, the price is very much like the weather: they may complain about it, but in perfect competition there is nothing any of them can do about it.

Total Revenue

While a firm in a perfectly competitive market has no influence over its price, it does determine the output it will produce. In selecting the quantity of that output, one important consideration is the revenue the firm will gain by producing it.

A firm's **total revenue** is found by multiplying its output by the price at which it sells that output. For a perfectly competitive firm, total revenue (TR) is the market price (P) times the quantity the firm produces (Q), or

EQUATION 7.1

$$TR = P \times Q$$

The relationship between market price and the firm's total revenue curve is a crucial one. Panel (a) of Figure 7.2 shows total revenue curves for a radish grower at three possible market prices: $0.20, $0.40, and $0.60 per pound. Each total revenue curve is a linear, upward-sloping curve. At any price, the greater the quantity a perfectly competitive firm sells, the greater its total revenue. Notice that the greater the price, the steeper the total revenue curve is.

FIGURE 7.2 Total Revenue, Marginal Revenue, and Average Revenue

Panel (a) shows different total revenue curves for three possible market prices in perfect competition. A total revenue curve is a straight line coming out of the origin. The slope of a total revenue curve is *MR*; it equals the market price (*P*) and *AR* in perfect competition. Marginal revenue and average revenue are thus a single horizontal line at the market price, as shown in Panel (b). There is a different marginal revenue curve for each price.

Price, Marginal Revenue, and Average Revenue

The slope of a total revenue curve is particularly important. It equals the change in the vertical axis (total revenue) divided by the change in the horizontal axis (quantity) between any two points. The slope measures the rate at which total revenue increases as output increases. We can think of it as the increase in total revenue associated with a 1-unit increase in output. The increase in total revenue from a 1-unit increase in quantity is **marginal revenue**. Thus marginal revenue (*MR*) equals the slope of the total revenue curve.

> **marginal revenue**
> The increase in total revenue from a one-unit increase in quantity.

How much additional revenue does a radish producer gain from selling one more pound of radishes? The answer, of course, is the market price for 1 pound. Marginal revenue equals the market price. Because the market price is not affected by the output choice of a single firm, the marginal revenue the firm gains by producing one more unit is always the market price. The marginal revenue curve shows the relationship between marginal revenue and the quantity a firm produces. For a perfectly competitive firm, the marginal revenue curve is a horizontal line at the market price. If the market price of a pound of radishes is $0.40, then the marginal revenue is $0.40. Marginal revenue curves for prices of $0.20, $0.40, and $0.60 are given in Panel (b) of Figure 7.2. In perfect competition, a firm's marginal revenue curve is a horizontal line at the market price.

Price also equals **average revenue**, which is total revenue divided by quantity. Equation 7.1 gives total revenue, *TR*. To obtain average revenue (*AR*), we divide total revenue by quantity, *Q*. Because total revenue equals price (*P*) times quantity (*Q*), dividing by quantity leaves us with price.

> **average revenue**
> Total revenue divided by quantity.

EQUATION 7.2

$$AR = \frac{TR}{Q} = \frac{P \times Q}{Q} = P$$

The marginal revenue curve is a horizontal line at the market price, and average revenue equals the market price. The average and marginal revenue curves are given by the same horizontal line. This is consistent with what we have learned about the relationship between marginal and average values. When the marginal value exceeds the average value, the average value will be rising. When the marginal value is less than the average value, the average value will be falling. What happens when the average and marginal values do not change, as in the horizontal curves of Panel (b) of Figure 7.2? The marginal value must equal the average value; the two curves coincide.

Marginal Revenue, Price, and Demand for the Perfectly Competitive Firm

We have seen that a perfectly competitive firm's marginal revenue curve is simply a horizontal line at the market price and that this same line is also the firm's average revenue curve. For the perfectly competitive firm, $MR = P = AR$. The marginal revenue curve has another meaning as well. It is the demand curve facing a perfectly competitive firm.

Consider the case of a single radish producer, Tony Gortari. We assume that the radish market is perfectly competitive; Mr. Gortari runs a perfectly competitive firm. Suppose the market price of radishes is $0.40 per pound. How many pounds of radishes can Mr. Gortari sell at this price? The answer comes from our assumption that he is a price taker: He can sell *any* quantity he wishes at this price. How many pounds of radishes will he sell if he charges a price that exceeds the market price? None. His radishes are identical to those of every other firm in the market, and everyone in the market has complete information. That means the demand curve facing Mr. Gortari is a horizontal line at the market price as illustrated in Figure 7.3. Notice that the curve is labeled *d* to distinguish it from the market demand curve, *D*, in Figure 7.1. The horizontal line in Figure 7.3 is also Mr. Gortari's marginal revenue curve, *MR*, and his average revenue curve, *AR*. It is also the market price, *P*.

Of course, Mr. Gortari could charge a price below the market price, but why would he? We assume he can sell all the radishes he wants at the market price; there would be no reason to charge a lower price. Mr. Gortari faces a demand curve that is a horizontal line at the market price. In our subsequent analysis, we shall refer to the horizontal line at the market price simply as marginal revenue. We should remember, however, that this same line gives us the market price, average revenue, and the demand curve facing the firm.

FIGURE 7.3 Price, Marginal Revenue, and Demand

A perfectly competitive firm faces a horizontal demand curve at the market price. Here, radish grower Tony Gortari faces demand curve *d* at the market price of $0.40 per pound. He could sell q_1 or q_2—or any other quantity—at a price of $0.40 per pound.

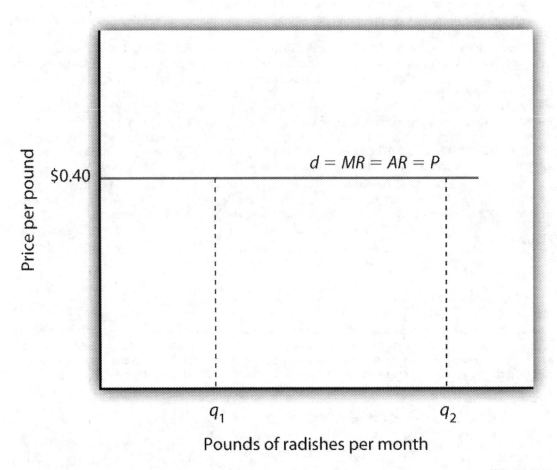

More generally, we can say that *any* perfectly competitive firm faces a horizontal demand curve at the market price. We saw an example of a horizontal demand curve in the chapter on elasticity. Such a curve is perfectly elastic, meaning that any quantity is demanded at a given price.

2.2 Economic Profit in the Short Run

A firm's economic profit is the difference between total revenue and total cost. Recall that total cost is the opportunity cost of producing a certain good or service. When we speak of economic profit we are speaking of a firm's total revenue less the total opportunity cost of its operations.

As we learned, a firm's total cost curve in the short run intersects the vertical axis at some positive value equal to the firm's total fixed costs. Total cost then rises at a decreasing rate over the range of increasing marginal returns to the firm's variable factors. It rises at an increasing rate over the range of diminishing marginal returns. Figure 7.4 shows the total cost curve for Mr. Gortari, as well as the total revenue curve for a price of $0.40 per pound. Suppose that his total fixed cost is $400 per month. For any given level of output, Mr. Gortari's economic profit is the vertical distance between the total revenue curve and the total cost curve at that level.

FIGURE 7.4   Total Revenue, Total Cost, and Economic Profit

Economic profit is the vertical distance between the total revenue and total cost curves (revenue minus costs). Here, the maximum profit attainable by Tony Gortari for his radish production is $938 per month at an output of 6,700 pounds.

Let us examine the total revenue and total cost curves in Figure 7.4 more carefully. At zero units of output, Mr. Gortari's total cost is $400 (his total fixed cost); total revenue is zero. Total cost continues to exceed total revenue up to an output of 1,500 pounds per month, at which point the two curves intersect. At this point, economic profit equals zero. As Mr. Gortari expands output above 1,500 pounds per month, total revenue becomes greater than total cost. We see that at a quantity of 1,500 pounds per month, the total revenue curve is steeper than the total cost curve. Because revenues are rising faster than costs, profits rise with increased output. As long as the total revenue curve is steeper than the total cost curve, profit increases as the firm increases its output.

The total revenue curve's slope does not change as the firm increases its output. But the total cost curve becomes steeper and steeper as diminishing marginal returns set in. Eventually, the total cost and total revenue curves will have the same slope. That happens in Figure 7.4 at an output of 6,700 pounds of radishes per month. Notice that a line drawn tangent to the total cost curve at that quantity has the same slope as the total revenue curve.

As output increases beyond 6,700 pounds, the total cost curve continues to become steeper. It becomes steeper than the total revenue curve, and profits fall as costs rise faster than revenues. At an output slightly above 8,000 pounds per month, the total revenue and cost curves intersect again, and economic profit equals zero. Mr. Gortari achieves the greatest profit possible by producing 6,700 pounds of radishes per month, the quantity at which the total cost and total revenue curves have the same slope. More generally, we can conclude that a perfectly competitive firm maximizes economic profit at the output level at which the total revenue curve and the total cost curve have the same slope.

2.3   Applying the Marginal Decision Rule

The slope of the total revenue curve is marginal revenue; the slope of the total cost curve is marginal cost. Economic profit, the difference between total revenue and total cost, is maximized where marginal revenue equals marginal cost. This is consistent with the marginal decision rule, which holds that a profit-maximizing firm should increase output until the marginal benefit of an additional unit equals the marginal cost. The marginal benefit of selling an additional unit is measured as marginal revenue.

Finding the output at which marginal revenue equals marginal cost is thus an application of our marginal decision rule.

Figure 7.5 shows how a firm can use the marginal decision rule to determine its profit-maximizing output. Panel (a) shows the market for radishes; the market demand curve (D), and supply curve (S) that we had in Figure 7.1; the market price is $0.40 per pound. In Panel (b), the MR curve is given by a horizontal line at the market price. The firm's marginal cost curve (MC) intersects the marginal revenue curve at the point where profit is maximized. Mr. Gortari maximizes profits by producing 6,700 pounds of radishes per month. That is, of course, the result we obtained in Figure 7.4, where we saw that the firm's total revenue and total cost curves differ by the greatest amount at the point at which the slopes of the curves, which equal marginal revenue and marginal cost, respectively, are equal.

FIGURE 7.5 Applying the Marginal Decision Rule

The market price is determined by the intersection of demand and supply. As always, the firm maximizes profit by applying the marginal decision rule. It takes the market price, $0.40 per pound, as given and selects an output at which MR equals MC. Economic profit per unit is the difference between ATC and price (here, $0.14 per pound); economic profit is profit per unit times the quantity produced ($0.14 × 6,700 = $938).

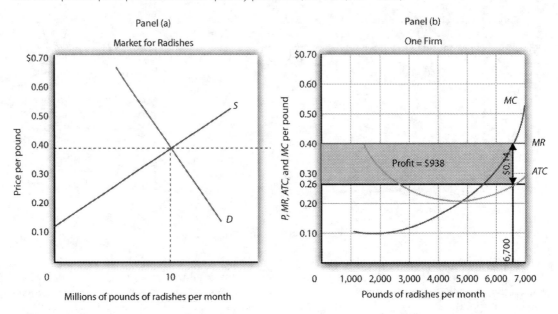

economic profit per unit

The difference between price and average total cost.

We can use the graph in Figure 7.5 to compute Mr. Gortari's economic profit. **Economic profit per unit** is the difference between price and average total cost. At the profit-maximizing output of 6,700 pounds of radishes per month, average total cost (ATC) is $0.26 per pound, as shown in Panel (b). Price is $0.40 per pound, so economic profit per unit is $0.14. Economic profit is found by multiplying economic profit per unit by the number of units produced; the firm's economic profit is thus $938 ($0.14 × 6,700). It is shown graphically by the area of the shaded rectangle in Panel (b); this area equals the vertical distance between marginal revenue (MR) and average total cost (ATC) at an output of 6,700 pounds of radishes times the number of pounds of radishes produced, 6,700, in Figure 7.5.

Heads Up!

Look carefully at the rectangle that shows economic profit in Panel (b) of Figure 7.5. It is found by taking the profit-maximizing quantity, 6,700 pounds, then reading up to the ATC curve and the firm's demand curve at the market price. Economic profit per unit equals price minus average total cost (P − ATC).

The firm's economic profit equals economic profit per unit times the quantity produced. It is found by extending horizontal lines from the ATC and MR curve to the vertical axis and taking the area of the rectangle formed.

There is no reason for the profit-maximizing quantity to correspond to the lowest point on the ATC curve; it does not in this case. Students sometimes make the mistake of calculating economic profit as the difference between the price and the lowest point on the ATC curve. That gives us the maximum economic profit per unit, but we assume that firms maximize economic profit, not economic profit per unit. The firm's economic profit equals economic profit per unit times quantity. The quantity that maximizes economic profit is determined by the intersection of ATC and MR.

2.4 Economic Losses in the Short Run

economic loss

The amount by which a firm's total cost exceeds its total revenue.

In the short run, a firm has one or more inputs whose quantities are fixed. That means that in the short run the firm cannot leave its industry. Even if it cannot cover *all* of its costs, including both its variable and fixed costs, going entirely out of business is not an option in the short run. The firm may close its doors, but it must continue to pay its fixed costs. It is forced to accept an **economic loss**, the amount by which its total cost exceeds its total revenue.

Suppose, for example, that a manufacturer has signed a 1-year lease on some equipment. It must make payments for this equipment during the term of its lease, whether it produces anything or not. During the period of the lease, the payments represent a fixed cost for the firm.

A firm that is experiencing economic losses—whose economic profits have become negative—in the short run may either continue to produce or shut down its operations, reducing its output to zero. It will choose the option that minimizes its losses. The crucial test of whether to operate or shut down lies in the relationship between price and average variable cost.

Producing to Minimize Economic Loss

Suppose the demand for radishes falls to D_2, as shown in Panel (a) of Figure 7.6. The market price for radishes plunges to $0.18 per pound, which is below average total cost. Consequently Mr. Gortari experiences negative economic profits—a loss. Although the new market price falls short of average total cost, it still exceeds average variable cost, shown in Panel (b) as AVC. Therefore, Mr. Gortari should continue to produce an output at which marginal cost equals marginal revenue. These curves (labeled MC and MR_2) intersect in Panel (b) at an output of 4,444 pounds of radishes per month.

When producing 4,444 pounds of radishes per month, Mr. Gortari faces an average total cost of $0.23 per pound. At a price of $0.18 per pound, he loses a nickel on each pound produced. Total economic losses at an output of 4,444 pounds per month are thus $222.20 per month (=4,444×$0.05).

No producer likes a loss (that is, negative economic profit), but the loss solution shown in Figure 7.6 is the best Mr. Gortari can attain. Any level of production other than the one at which marginal cost equals marginal revenue would produce even greater losses.

Suppose Mr. Gortari were to shut down and produce no radishes. Ceasing production would reduce variable costs to zero, but he would still face fixed costs of $400 per month (recall that $400 was the vertical intercept of the total cost curve in Figure 7.4). By shutting down, Mr. Gortari would lose $400 per month. By continuing to produce, he loses only $222.20.

Mr. Gortari is better off producing where marginal cost equals marginal revenue because at that output price exceeds average variable cost. Average variable cost is $0.14 per pound, so by continuing to produce he covers his variable costs, with $0.04 per pound left over to apply to fixed costs. Whenever price is greater than average variable cost, the firm maximizes economic profit (or minimizes economic loss) by producing the output level at which marginal revenue and marginal cost curves intersect.

FIGURE 7.6 Suffering Economic Losses in the Short Run

Tony Gortari experiences a loss when price drops below *ATC*, as it does in Panel (b) as a result of a reduction in demand. If price is above *AVC*, however, he can minimize his losses by producing where *MC* equals MR_2. Here, that occurs at an output of 4,444 pounds of radishes per month. The price is $0.18 per pound, and average total cost is $0.23 per pound. He loses $0.05 per pound, or $222.20 per month.

Shutting Down to Minimize Economic Loss

Suppose price drops below a firm's average variable cost. Now the best strategy for the firm is to shut down, reducing its output to zero. The minimum level of average variable cost, which occurs at the intersection of the marginal cost curve and the average variable cost curve, is called the **shutdown point**. Any price below the minimum value of average variable cost will cause the firm to shut down. If the firm were to continue producing, not only would it lose its fixed costs, but it would also face an additional loss by not covering its variable costs.

FIGURE 7.7 Shutting Down

The market price of radishes drops to $0.10 per pound, so MR_3 is below Mr. Gortari's *AVC*. Thus he would suffer a greater loss by continuing to operate than by shutting down. Whenever price falls below average variable cost, the firm will shut down, reducing its production to zero.

Figure 7.7 shows a case where the price of radishes drops to $0.10 per pound. Price is less than average variable cost, so Mr. Gortari not only would lose his fixed cost but would also incur additional losses by producing. Suppose, for example, he decided to operate where marginal cost equals marginal revenue, producing 1,700 pounds of radishes per month. Average variable cost equals $0.14 per pound, so he would lose $0.04 on each pound he produces ($68) plus his fixed cost of $400 per month. He would lose $468 per month. If he shut down, he would lose only his fixed cost. Because the price of $0.10 falls below his average variable cost, his best course would be to shut down.

Shutting down is not the same thing as going out of business. A firm shuts down by closing its doors; it can reopen them whenever it expects to cover its variable costs. We can even think of a firm's decision to close at the end of the day as a kind of shutdown point; the firm makes this choice because it does not anticipate that it will be able to cover its variable cost overnight. It expects to cover those costs the next morning when it reopens its doors.

2.5   Marginal Cost and Supply

In the model of perfect competition, we assume that a firm determines its output by finding the point where the marginal revenue and marginal cost curves intersect. Provided that price exceeds average variable cost, the firm produces the quantity determined by the intersection of the two curves.

A supply curve tells us the quantity that will be produced at each price, and that is what the firm's marginal cost curve tells us. The firm's supply curve in the short run is its marginal cost curve for prices above the average variable cost. At prices below average variable cost, the firm's output drops to zero.

Panel (a) of Figure 7.8 shows the average variable cost and marginal cost curves for a hypothetical astrologer, Madame LaFarge, who is in the business of providing astrological consultations over the telephone. We shall assume that this industry is perfectly competitive. At any price below $10 per call, Madame LaFarge would shut down. If the price is $10 or greater, however, she produces an output at which price equals marginal cost. The marginal cost curve is thus her supply curve at all prices greater than $10.

FIGURE 7.8 Marginal Cost and Supply

The supply curve for a firm is that portion of its *MC* curve that lies above the *AVC* curve, shown in Panel (a). To obtain the short-run supply curve for the industry, we add the outputs of each firm at each price. The industry supply curve is given in Panel (b).

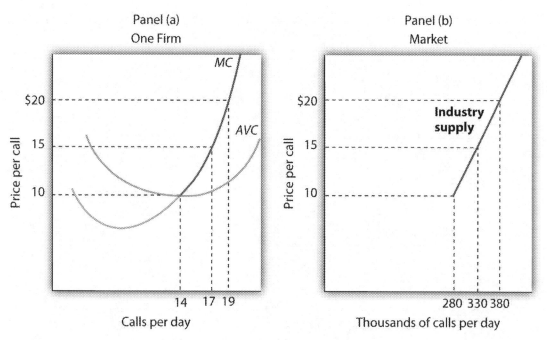

Now suppose that the astrological forecast industry consists of Madame LaFarge and thousands of other firms similar to hers. The market supply curve is found by adding the outputs of each firm at each price, as shown in Panel (b) of Figure 7.8. At a price of $10 per call, for example, Madame LaFarge supplies 14 calls per day. Adding the quantities supplied by all the other firms in the market, suppose we get a quantity supplied of 280,000. Notice that the market supply curve we have drawn is linear; throughout the book we have made the assumption that market demand and supply curves are linear in order to simplify our analysis.

Looking at Figure 7.8, we see that profit-maximizing choices by firms in a perfectly competitive market will generate a market supply curve that reflects marginal cost. Provided there are no external benefits or costs in producing a good or service, a perfectly competitive market satisfies the efficiency condition.

KEY TAKEAWAYS

- Price in a perfectly competitive industry is determined by the interaction of demand and supply.

- In a perfectly competitive industry, a firm's total revenue curve is a straight, upward-sloping line whose slope is the market price. Economic profit is maximized at the output level at which the slopes of the total revenue and total cost curves are equal, provided that the firm is covering its variable cost.

- To use the marginal decision rule in profit maximization, the firm produces the output at which marginal cost equals marginal revenue. Economic profit per unit is price minus average total cost; total economic profit equals economic profit per unit times quantity.

- If price falls below average total cost, but remains above average variable cost, the firm will continue to operate in the short run, producing the quantity where $MR = MC$ doing so minimizes its losses.

- If price falls below average variable cost, the firm will shut down in the short run, reducing output to zero. The lowest point on the average variable cost curve is called the shutdown point.

- The firm's supply curve in the short run is its marginal cost curve for prices greater than the minimum average variable cost.

TRY IT!

Assume that Acme Clothing, the firm introduced in the chapter on production and cost, produces jackets in a perfectly competitive market. Suppose the demand and supply curves for jackets intersect at a price of $81. Now, using the marginal cost and average total cost curves for Acme shown here:

Estimate Acme's profit-maximizing output per day (assume the firm selects a whole number). What are Acme's economic profits per day?

Case in Point

Not Out of Business 'Til They Fall from the Sky

© 2010 Jupiterimages Corporation

The 66 satellites were poised to start falling from the sky. The hope was that the pieces would burn to bits on their way down through the atmosphere, but there was the chance that a building or a person would take a direct hit.

The satellites were the primary communication devices of Iridium's satellite phone system. Begun in 1998 as the first truly global satellite system for mobile phones—providing communications across deserts, in the middle of oceans, and at the poles—Iridium expected five million subscribers to pay $7 a minute to talk on $3,000 handsets. In the climate of the late 1990s, users opted for cheaper, though less secure and less comprehensive, cell phones. By the end of the decade, Iridium had declared bankruptcy, shut down operations, and was just waiting for the satellites to start plunging from their orbits around 2007.

The only offer for Iridium's $5 billion system came from an ex-CEO of a nuclear reactor business, Dan Colussy, and it was for a measly $25 million. "It's like picking up a $150,000 Porsche 911 for $750," wrote *USA Today* reporter, Kevin Maney.

The purchase turned into a bonanza. In the wake of September 11, 2001, and then the wars in Afghanistan and Iraq, demand for secure communications in remote locations skyrocketed. New customers included the U.S. and British militaries, as well as reporters in Iraq, who, when traveling with the military have been barred from using less secure systems that are easier to track. The nonprofit organization Operation Call Home has bought time to allow members of the 81st Armor Brigade of the Washington National Guard to communicate with their families at home. Airlines and shipping lines have also signed up.

As the new Iridium became unburdened from the debt of the old one and technology improved, the lower fixed and variable costs have contributed to Iridium's revival, but clearly a critical element in the turnaround has been increased demand. The launching of an additional seven spare satellites and other tinkering have extended the life of the system to at least 2014. The firm was temporarily shut down but, with its new owners and new demand for its services, has come roaring back.

Why did Colussy buy Iridium? A top executive in the new firm said that Colussy just found the elimination of the satellites a terrible waste. Perhaps he had some niche uses in mind, as even before September 11, 2001, he had begun to enroll some new customers, such as the Colombian national police, who no doubt found the system useful in the fighting drug lords. But it was in the aftermath of 9/11 that its subscriber list really began to grow and its re-opening was deemed a stroke of genius. Today Iridium's customers include ships at sea (which account for about half of its business), airlines, military uses, and a variety of commercial and humanitarian applications.

Sources: Kevin Maney, "Remember Those 'Iridium's Going to Fail' Jokes? Prepare to Eat Your Hat," USA Today, April 9, 2003: p. 3B. Michael Mecham, "Handheld Comeback: A Resurrected Iridium Counts Aviation, Antiterrorism Among Its Growth Fields," Aviation Week and Space Technology, 161: 9 (September 6, 2004): p. 58. Iridium's webpage can be found at Iridium.com.

ANSWER TO TRY IT! PROBLEM

At a price of $81, Acme's marginal revenue curve is a horizontal line at $81. The firm produces the output at which marginal cost equals marginal revenue; the curves intersect at a quantity of 9 jackets per day. Acme's average total cost at this level of output equals $67, for an economic profit per jacket of $14. Acme's economic profit per day equals about $126.

3.   PERFECT COMPETITION IN THE LONG RUN

LEARNING OBJECTIVES

1. Distinguish between economic profit and accounting profit.
2. Explain why in long-run equilibrium in a perfectly competitive industry firms will earn zero economic profit.
3. Describe the three possible effects on the costs of the factors of production that expansion or contraction of a perfectly competitive industry may have and illustrate the resulting long-run industry supply curve in each case.
4. Explain why under perfection competition output prices will change by less than the change in production cost in the short run, but by the full amount of the change in production cost in the long run.
5. Explain the effect of a change in fixed cost on price and output in the short run and in the long run under perfect competition.

In the long run, a firm is free to adjust all of its inputs. New firms can enter any market; existing firms can leave their markets. We shall see in this section that the model of perfect competition predicts that, at a long-run equilibrium, production takes place at the lowest possible cost per unit and that all economic profits and losses are eliminated.

3.1   Economic Profit and Economic Loss

Economic profits and losses play a crucial role in the model of perfect competition. The existence of economic profits in a particular industry attracts new firms to the industry in the long run. As new firms enter, the supply curve shifts to the right, price falls, and profits fall. Firms continue to enter the industry until economic profits fall to zero. If firms in an industry are experiencing economic losses, some will leave. The supply curve shifts to the left, increasing price and reducing losses. Firms continue to leave until the remaining firms are no longer suffering losses—until economic profits are zero.

Before examining the mechanism through which entry and exit eliminate economic profits and losses, we shall examine an important key to understanding it: the difference between the accounting and economic concepts of profit and loss.

Economic Versus Accounting Concepts of Profit and Loss

Economic profit equals total revenue minus total cost, where cost is measured in the economic sense as opportunity cost. An economic loss (negative economic profit) is incurred if total cost exceeds total revenue.

Accountants include only explicit costs in their computation of total cost. **Explicit costs** include charges that must be paid for factors of production such as labor and capital, together with an estimate of depreciation. Profit computed using only explicit costs is called **accounting profit**. It is the measure of profit firms typically report; firms pay taxes on their accounting profits, and a corporation reporting its profit for a particular period reports its accounting profits. To compute his accounting profits, Mr. Gortari, the radish farmer, would subtract explicit costs, such as charges for labor, equipment, and other supplies, from the revenue he receives.

Economists recognize costs in addition to the explicit costs listed by accountants. If Mr. Gortari were not growing radishes, he could be doing something else with the land and with his own efforts. Suppose the most valuable alternative use of his land would be to produce carrots, from which Mr. Gortari could earn $250 per month in accounting profits. The income he forgoes by not producing carrots is an opportunity cost of producing radishes. This cost is not explicit; the return Mr. Gortari could get from producing carrots will not appear on a conventional accounting statement of his accounting profit. A cost that is included in the economic concept of opportunity cost, but that is not an explicit cost, is called an **implicit cost**.

The Long Run and Zero Economic Profits

Given our definition of economic profits, we can easily see why, in perfect competition, they must always equal zero in the long run. Suppose there are two industries in the economy, and that firms in Industry A are earning economic profits. By definition, firms in Industry A are earning a return greater

---

explicit costs

Charges that must be paid for factors of production such as labor and capital.

accounting profit

Profit computed using only explicit costs.

implicit cost

A cost that is included in the economic concept of opportunity cost but that is not an explicit cost.

than the return available in Industry B. That means that firms in Industry B are earning less than they could in Industry A. Firms in Industry B are experiencing economic losses.

Given easy entry and exit, some firms in Industry B will leave it and enter Industry A to earn the greater profits available there. As they do so, the supply curve in Industry B will shift to the left, increasing prices and profits there. As former Industry B firms enter Industry A, the supply curve in Industry A will shift to the right, lowering profits in A. The process of firms leaving Industry B and entering A will continue until firms in both industries are earning zero economic profit. That suggests an important long-run result: *Economic profits in a system of perfectly competitive markets will, in the long run, be driven to zero in all industries.*

Eliminating Economic Profit: The Role of Entry

The process through which entry will eliminate economic profits in the long run is illustrated in Figure 7.9, which is based on the situation presented in Figure 7.5. The price of radishes is $0.40 per pound. Mr. Gortari's average total cost at an output of 6,700 pounds of radishes per month is $0.26 per pound. Profit per unit is $0.14 ($0.40 − $0.26). Mr. Gortari thus earns a profit of $938 per month (=$0.14 × 6,700).

FIGURE 7.9   Eliminating Economic Profits in the Long Run

If firms in an industry are making an economic profit, entry will occur in the long run. In Panel (b), a single firm's profit is shown by the shaded area. Entry continues until firms in the industry are operating at the lowest point on their respective average total cost curves, and economic profits fall to zero.

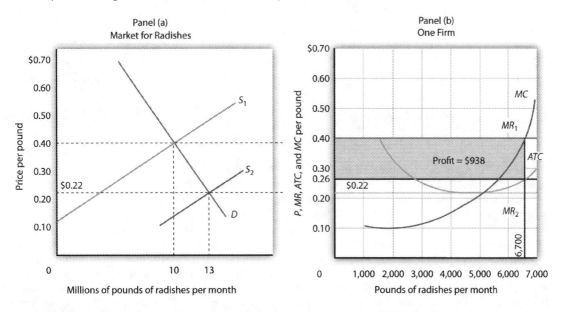

Profits in the radish industry attract entry in the long run. Panel (a) of Figure 7.9 shows that as firms enter, the supply curve shifts to the right and the price of radishes falls. New firms enter as long as there are economic profits to be made—as long as price exceeds ATC in Panel (b). As price falls, marginal revenue falls to MR_2 and the firm reduces the quantity it supplies, moving along the marginal cost (MC) curve to the lowest point on the ATC curve, at $0.22 per pound and an output of 5,000 pounds per month. Although the output of individual firms falls in response to falling prices, there are now more firms, so industry output rises to 13 million pounds per month in Panel (a).

Eliminating Losses: The Role of Exit

Just as entry eliminates economic profits in the long run, exit eliminates economic losses. In Figure 7.10, Panel (a) shows the case of an industry in which the market price P_1 is below ATC. In Panel (b), at price P_1 a single firm produces a quantity q_1, assuming it is at least covering its average variable cost. The firm's losses are shown by the shaded rectangle bounded by its average total cost C_1 and price P_1 and by output q_1.

Because firms in the industry are losing money, some will exit. The supply curve in Panel (a) shifts to the left, and it continues shifting as long as firms are suffering losses. Eventually the supply curve shifts all the way to S_2, price rises to P_2, and economic profits return to zero.

FIGURE 7.10 Eliminating Economic Losses in the Long Run

Panel (b) shows that at the initial price P_1, firms in the industry cannot cover average total cost (MR_1 is below ATC). That induces some firms to leave the industry, shifting the supply curve in Panel (a) to S_2, reducing industry output to Q_2 and raising price to P_2. At that price (MR_2), firms earn zero economic profit, and exit from the industry ceases. Panel (b) shows that the firm increases output from q_1 to q_2; total output in the market falls in Panel (a) because there are fewer firms. Notice that in Panel (a) quantity is designated by uppercase Q, while in Panel (b) quantity is designated by lowercase q. This convention is used throughout the text to distinguish between the quantity supplied in the market (Q) and the quantity supplied by a typical firm (q).

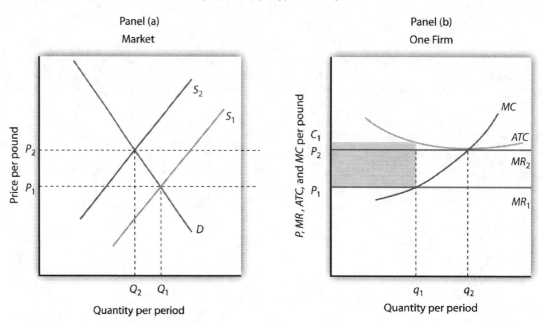

Entry, Exit, and Production Costs

constant-cost industry

Industry in which expansion does not affect the prices of factors of production.

In our examination of entry and exit in response to economic profit or loss in a perfectly competitive industry, we assumed that the ATC curve of a single firm does not shift as new firms enter or existing firms leave the industry. That is the case when expansion or contraction does not affect prices for the factors of production used by firms in the industry. When expansion of the industry does not affect the prices of factors of production, it is a **constant-cost industry**. In some cases, however, the entry of new firms may affect input prices.

As new firms enter, they add to the demand for the factors of production used by the industry. If the industry is a significant user of those factors, the increase in demand could push up the market price of factors of production for all firms in the industry. If that occurs, then entry into an industry will boost average costs at the same time as it puts downward pressure on price. Long-run equilibrium will still occur at a zero level of economic profit and with firms operating on the lowest point on the ATC curve, but that cost curve will be somewhat higher than before entry occurred. Suppose, for example, that an increase in demand for new houses drives prices higher and induces entry. That will increase the demand for workers in the construction industry and is likely to result in higher wages in the industry, driving up costs.

increasing-cost industry

Industry in which the entry of new firms bids up the prices of factors of production and thus increases production costs.

An industry in which the entry of new firms bids up the prices of factors of production and thus increases production costs is called an **increasing-cost industry**. As such an industry expands in the long run, its price will rise.

Some industries may experience reductions in input prices as they expand with the entry of new firms. That may occur because firms supplying the industry experience economies of scale as they increase production, thus driving input prices down. Expansion may also induce technological changes that lower input costs. That is clearly the case of the computer industry, which has enjoyed falling input costs as it has expanded. An industry in which production costs fall as firms enter in the long run is a **decreasing-cost industry**.

decreasing-cost industry

Industry in which production costs fall in the long run as firms enter.

Just as industries may expand with the entry of new firms, they may contract with the exit of existing firms. In a constant-cost industry, exit will not affect the input prices of remaining firms. In an increasing-cost industry, exit will reduce the input prices of remaining firms. And, in a decreasing-cost industry, input prices may rise with the exit of existing firms.

The behavior of production costs as firms in an industry expand or reduce their output has important implications for the **long-run industry supply curve**, a curve that relates the price of a good or service to the quantity produced after all long-run adjustments to a price change have been completed. Every point on a long-run supply curve therefore shows a price and quantity supplied at which firms in the industry are earning zero economic profit. Unlike the short-run market supply curve, the long-run industry supply curve does not hold factor costs and the number of firms unchanged.

Figure 7.11 shows three long-run industry supply curves. In Panel (a), S_{CC} is a long-run supply curve for a constant-cost industry. It is horizontal. Neither expansion nor contraction by itself affects market price. In Panel (b), S_{IC} is a long-run supply curve for an increasing-cost industry. It rises as the industry expands. In Panel (c), S_{DC} is a long-run supply curve for a decreasing-cost industry. Its downward slope suggests a falling price as the industry expands.

long-run industry supply curve

A curve that relates the price of a good or service to the quantity produced after all long-run adjustments to a price change have been completed.

FIGURE 7.11 Long-Run Supply Curves in Perfect Competition

The long-run supply curve for a constant-cost, perfectly competitive industry is a horizontal line, S_{CC}, shown in Panel (a). The long-run curve for an increasing-cost industry is an upward-sloping curve, S_{IC}, as in Panel (b). The downward-sloping long-run supply curve, S_{DC}, for a decreasing cost industry is given in Panel (c).

3.2 Changes in Demand and in Production Cost

The primary application of the model of perfect competition is in predicting how firms will respond to changes in demand and in production costs. To see how firms respond to a particular change, we determine how the change affects demand or cost conditions and then see how the profit-maximizing solution is affected in the short run and in the long run. Having determined how the profit-maximizing firms of the model would respond, we can then predict firms' responses to similar changes in the real world.

In the examples that follow, we shall assume, for simplicity, that entry or exit do not affect the input prices facing firms in the industry. That is, we assume a constant-cost industry with a horizontal long-run industry supply curve similar to S_{CC} in Figure 7.11. We shall assume that firms are covering their average variable costs, so we can ignore the possibility of shutting down.

Changes in Demand

Changes in demand can occur for a variety of reasons. There may be a change in preferences, incomes, the price of a related good, population, or consumer expectations. A change in demand causes a change in the market price, thus shifting the marginal revenue curves of firms in the industry.

Let us consider the impact of a change in demand for oats. Suppose new evidence suggests that eating oats not only helps to prevent heart disease, but also prevents baldness in males. This will, of course, increase the demand for oats. To assess the impact of this change, we assume that the industry is perfectly competitive and that it is initially in long-run equilibrium at a price of $1.70 per bushel. Economic profits equal zero.

The initial situation is depicted in Figure 7.12. Panel (a) shows that at a price of $1.70, industry output is Q_1 (point A), while Panel (b) shows that the market price constitutes the marginal revenue, MR_1, facing a single firm in the industry. The firm responds to that price by finding the output level at which the MC and MR_1 curves intersect. That implies a level of output q_1 at point A′.

The new medical evidence causes demand to increase to D_2 in Panel (a). That increases the market price to $2.30 (point B), so the marginal revenue curve for a single firm rises to MR_2 in Panel (b). The firm responds by increasing its output to q_2 in the short run (point B′). Notice that the firm's average total cost is slightly higher than its original level of $1.70; that is because of the U shape of the curve. The firm is making an economic profit shown by the shaded rectangle in Panel (b). Other firms in the industry will earn an economic profit as well, which, in the long run, will attract entry by new firms.

New entry will shift the supply curve to the right; entry will continue as long as firms are making an economic profit. The supply curve in Panel (a) shifts to S_2, driving the price down in the long run to the original level of $1.70 per bushel and returning economic profits to zero in long-run equilibrium. A single firm will return to its original level of output, q_1 (point A′) in Panel (b), but because there are more firms in the industry, industry output rises to Q_3 (point C) in Panel (a).

FIGURE 7.12   Short-Run and Long-Run Adjustments to an Increase in Demand

The initial equilibrium price and output are determined in the market for oats by the intersection of demand and supply at point A in Panel (a). An increase in the market demand for oats, from D_1 to D_2 in Panel (a), shifts the equilibrium solution to point B. The price increases in the short run from $1.70 per bushel to $2.30. Industry output rises to Q_2. For a single firm, the increase in price raises marginal revenue from MR_1 to MR_2; the firm responds in the short run by increasing its output to q_2. It earns an economic profit given by the shaded rectangle. In the long run, the opportunity for profit attracts new firms. In a constant-cost industry, the short-run supply curve shifts to S_2; market equilibrium now moves to point C in Panel (a). The market price falls back to $1.70. The firm's demand curve returns to MR_1, and its output falls back to the original level, q_1. Industry output has risen to Q_3 because there are more firms.

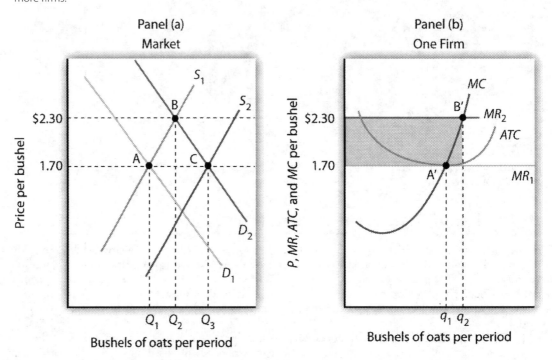

A reduction in demand would lead to a reduction in price, shifting each firm's marginal revenue curve downward. Firms would experience economic losses, thus causing exit in the long run and shifting the supply curve to the left. Eventually, the price would rise back to its original level, assuming changes in industry output did not lead to changes in input prices. There would be fewer firms in the industry, but each firm would end up producing the same output as before.

Changes in Production Cost

A firm's costs change if the costs of its inputs change. They also change if the firm is able to take advantage of a change in technology. Changes in production cost shift the ATC curve. If a firm's variable costs are affected, its marginal cost curves will shift as well. Any change in marginal cost produces a similar change in industry supply, since it is found by adding up marginal cost curves for individual firms.

Suppose a reduction in the price of oil reduces the cost of producing oil changes for automobiles. We shall assume that the oil-change industry is perfectly competitive and that it is initially in long-run equilibrium at a price of $27 per oil change, as shown in Panel (a) of Figure 7.13. Suppose that the reduction in oil prices reduces the cost of an oil change by $3.

FIGURE 7.13 A Reduction in the Cost of Producing Oil Changes

The initial equilibrium price, $27, and quantity, Q_1, of automobile oil changes are determined by the intersection of market demand, D_1, and market supply, S_1 in Panel (a). The industry is in long-run equilibrium; a typical firm, shown in Panel (b), earns zero economic profit. A reduction in oil prices reduces the marginal and average total costs of producing an oil change by $3. The firm's marginal cost curve shifts to MC_2, and its average total cost curve shifts to ATC_2. The short-run industry supply curve shifts down by $3 to S_2. The market price falls to $26; the firm increases its output to q_2 and earns an economic profit given by the shaded rectangle. In the long run, the opportunity for profit shifts the industry supply curve to S_3. The price falls to $24, and the firm reduces its output to the original level, q_1. It now earns zero economic profit once again. Industry output in Panel (a) rises to Q_3 because there are more firms; price has fallen by the full amount of the reduction in production costs.

A reduction in production cost shifts the firm's cost curves down. The firm's average total cost and marginal cost curves shift down, as shown in Panel (b). In Panel (a) the supply curve shifts from S_1 to S_2. The industry supply curve is made up of the marginal cost curves of individual firms; because each of them has shifted downward by $3, the industry supply curve shifts downward by $3.

Notice that price in the short run falls to $26; it does not fall by the $3 reduction in cost. That is because the supply and demand curves are sloped. While the supply curve shifts downward by $3, its intersection with the demand curve falls by less than $3. The firm in Panel (b) responds to the lower price and lower cost by increasing output to q_2, where MC_2 and MR_2 intersect. That leaves firms in the industry with an economic profit; the economic profit for the firm is shown by the shaded rectangle in Panel (b). Profits attract entry in the long run, shifting the supply curve to the right to S_3 in Panel (a) Entry will continue as long as firms are making an economic profit—it will thus continue until the price falls by the full amount of the $3 reduction in cost. The price falls to $24, industry output rises to Q_3, and the firm's output returns to its original level, q_1.

An increase in variable costs would shift the average total, average variable, and marginal cost curves upward. It would shift the industry supply curve upward by the same amount. The result in the short run would be an increase in price, but by less than the increase in cost per unit. Firms would experience economic losses, causing exit in the long run. Eventually, price would increase by the full amount of the increase in production cost.

Some cost increases will not affect marginal cost. Suppose, for example, that an annual license fee of $5,000 is imposed on firms in a particular industry. The fee is a fixed cost; it does not affect marginal cost. Imposing such a fee shifts the average total cost curve upward but causes no change in marginal cost. There is no change in price or output in the short run. Because firms are suffering economic losses, there will be exit in the long run. Prices ultimately rise by enough to cover the cost of the fee, leaving the remaining firms in the industry with zero economic profit.

Price will change to reflect whatever change we observe in production cost. A change in variable cost causes price to change in the short run. In the long run, any change in average total cost changes price by an equal amount.

The message of long-run equilibrium in a competitive market is a profound one. The ultimate beneficiaries of the innovative efforts of firms are consumers. Firms in a perfectly competitive world earn zero profit in the long-run. While firms can earn accounting profits in the long-run, they cannot earn economic profits.

KEY TAKEAWAYS

- The economic concept of profit differs from accounting profit. The accounting concept deals only with explicit costs, while the economic concept of profit incorporates explicit and implicit costs.
- The existence of economic profits attracts entry, economic losses lead to exit, and in long-run equilibrium, firms in a perfectly competitive industry will earn zero economic profit.
- The long-run supply curve in an industry in which expansion does not change input prices (a constant-cost industry) is a horizontal line. The long-run supply curve for an industry in which production costs increase as output rises (an increasing-cost industry) is upward sloping. The long-run supply curve for an industry in which production costs decrease as output rises (a decreasing-cost industry) is downward sloping.
- In a perfectly competitive market in long-run equilibrium, an increase in demand creates economic profit in the short run and induces entry in the long run; a reduction in demand creates economic losses (negative economic profits) in the short run and forces some firms to exit the industry in the long run.
- When production costs change, price will change by less than the change in production cost in the short run. Price will adjust to reflect fully the change in production cost in the long run.
- A change in fixed cost will have no effect on price or output in the short run. It will induce entry or exit in the long run so that price will change by enough to leave firms earning zero economic profit.

TRY IT!

Consider Acme Clothing's situation in "Try It!". Suppose this situation is typical of firms in the jacket market. Explain what will happen in the market for jackets in the long run, assuming nothing happens to the prices of factors of production used by firms in the industry. What will happen to the equilibrium price? What is the equilibrium level of economic profits?

Case in Point

Competition in the Market for Generic Prescription Drugs

© 2010 Jupiterimages Corporation

Generic prescription drugs are essentially identical substitutes for more expensive brand-name prescription drugs. Since the passage of the Drug Competition and Patent Term Restoration Act of 1984 (commonly referred to as the Hatch-Waxman Act) made it easier for manufacturers to enter the market for generic drugs, the generic drug industry has taken off. Generic drugs represented 19% of the prescription drug industry in 1984 and today represent more than two-thirds of the industry. U.S. generic sales were $29 billion in 1995 and soared to $176 billion in 2009. In 2009, the average price of a branded prescription was $155 compared to $40 for a generic prescription.

A study by David Reiffen and Michael R. Ward published in 2005 showed that entry into the generic drug industry has been the key to this price differential. As shown in the table, when there are one to three manufacturers selling generic copies of a given branded drug, the ratio of the generic price to the branded price is about 83%. The ratio falls to 76% when there are four to six competitors, 72.1% when there are seven to nine competitors, 69% when there are ten competitors, and 68% when there are eleven or more competitors.

They also found that the extent to which prices approach competitive levels depends on the potential revenue in the market for a drug. So long as markets are sufficiently large, entry of generic competitors leads to prices that are close to marginal cost (i.e., at near-competitive pricing levels).

The generic drug industry is largely characterized by the attributes of a perfectly competitive market. Competitors have good information about the product and sell identical products. The 1984 legislation eased entry into this market. And as the model of perfect competition predicts, entry has driven prices down, benefiting consumers to the tune of tens of billions of dollars each year.

TABLE 7.1 Price Comparison of Generic and Branded Drugs, by Number of Competitors

Number of Generic Competitors	Ratio of Average Generic Price to Pre-expiry Branded Drug Price
1 to 3	0.831
4 to 6	0.762
7 to 9	0.721
10	0.690
11 or more	0.675

Sources: David Reiffen and Michael R. Ward, "Generic Drug Industry Dynamics," Review of Economics and Statistics 87:1 (February 2005): 37–49; 2011 Statistical Abstract of the United States, Table 155.

ANSWER TO TRY IT! PROBLEM

The availability of economic profits will attract new firms to the jacket industry in the long run, shifting the market supply curve to the right. Entry will continue until economic profits are eliminated. The price will fall; Acme's marginal revenue curve shifts down. The equilibrium level of economic profits in the long run is zero.

4. REVIEW AND PRACTICE

Summary

The assumptions of the model of perfect competition ensure that every decision maker is a price taker—the interaction of demand and supply in the market determines price. Although most firms in real markets have some control over their prices, the model of perfect competition suggests how changes in demand or in production cost will affect price and output in a wide range of real-world cases.

A firm in perfect competition maximizes profit in the short run by producing an output level at which marginal revenue equals marginal cost, provided marginal revenue is at least as great as the minimum value of average variable cost. For a perfectly competitive firm, marginal revenue equals price and average revenue. This implies that the firm's marginal cost curve is its short-run supply curve for values greater than average variable cost. If price drops below average variable cost, the firm shuts down.

If firms in an industry are earning economic profit, entry by new firms will drive price down until economic profit achieves its long-run equilibrium value of zero. If firms are suffering economic losses, exit by existing firms will continue until price rises to eliminate the losses and economic profits are zero. A long-run equilibrium may be changed by a change in demand or in production cost, which would affect supply. The adjustment to the change in the short run is likely to result in economic profits or losses; these will be eliminated in the long run by entry or by exit.

CONCEPT PROBLEMS

1. Explain how each of the assumptions of perfect competition contributes to the fact that all decision makers in perfect competition are price takers.

2. If the assumptions of perfect competition are not likely to be met in the real world, how can the model be of any use?

3. Explain the difference between marginal revenue, average revenue, and price in perfect competition.

4. Suppose the only way a firm can increase its sales is to lower its price. Is this a perfectly competitive firm? Why or why not?

5. Consider the following goods and services. Which are the most likely to be produced in a perfectly competitive industry? Which are not? Explain why you made the choices you did, relating your answer to the assumptions of the model of perfect competition.

   a. Coca-Cola and Pepsi

   b. Potatoes

   c. Private physicians in your local community

   d. Government bonds and corporate stocks

   e. Taxicabs in Lima, Peru—a city that does not restrict entry or the prices drivers can charge

   f. Oats

6. Explain why an economic profit of zero is acceptable to a firm.

7. Explain why a perfectly competitive firm whose average total cost exceeds the market price may continue to operate in the short run. What about the long run?

8. You have decided to major in biology rather than computer science. A news report suggests that the salaries of computer science majors are increasing. How does this affect the opportunity cost of your choice?

9. Explain how each of the following events would affect the marginal cost curves of firms and thus the supply curve in a perfectly competitive market in the short run.

   a. An increase in wages

   b. A tax of $1 per unit of output imposed on the seller

   c. The introduction of cost-cutting technology

   d. The imposition of an annual license fee of $1,000

10. In a perfectly competitive market, who benefits from an event that lowers production costs for firms?

11. Dry-cleaning establishments generate a considerable amount of air pollution in producing cleaning services. Suppose these firms are allowed to pollute without restriction and that reducing their pollution would add significantly to their production costs. Who benefits from the fact that they pollute the air? Now suppose the government requires them to reduce their pollution. Who will pay for the cleanup? (Assume dry cleaning is a perfectly competitive industry, and answer these questions from a long-run perspective.)

12. The late columnist William F. Buckley, commenting on a strike by the Teamsters Union against UPS in 1997, offered this bit of economic analysis to explain how UPS had succeeded in reducing its average total cost: "UPS has done this by 'economies of scale.' Up to a point (where the marginal cost equals the price of the marginal unit), the larger the business, the less the per-unit cost." Use the concept of economies of scale, together with the information presented in this chapter, to explain the error in Mr. Buckley's statement. [1]

13. Suppose that a perfectly competitive industry is in long-run equilibrium and experiences an increase in production cost. Who will bear the burden of the increase? Is this fair?

14. Economists argue that the ultimate beneficiaries of the efforts of perfectly competitive firms are consumers. In what sense is this the case? Do the owners of perfectly competitive firms derive any long-run benefit from their efforts?

15. Explain carefully why a fixed license fee does not shift a firm's marginal cost curve in the short run. What about the long run?

NUMERICAL PROBLEMS

1. The graph below provides revenue and cost information for a perfectly competitive firm producing paper clips.

Output	Total Revenue	Total Variable Cost	Total Fixed Cost
1	$1,000	$1,500	$500
2	$2,000	$2,000	$500
3	$3,000	$2,600	$500
4	$4,000	$3,900	$500
5	$5,000	$5,000	$500

    a. How much are total fixed costs?

    b. About how much are total variable costs if 5,000 paper clips are produced?

    c. What is the price of a paper clip?

    d. What is the average revenue from producing paper clips?

    e. What is the marginal revenue of producing paper clips?

    f. Over what output range will this firm earn economic profits?

    g. Over what output range will this firm incur economic losses?

    h. What is the slope of the total revenue curve?

    i. What is the slope of the total cost curve at the profit-maximizing number of paper clips per hour?

    j. At about how many paper clips per hour do economic profits seem to be at a maximum?

2. Suppose rocking-chair manufacturing is a perfectly competitive industry in which there are 1,000 identical firms. Each firm's total cost is related to output per day as follows:

Quantity	Total cost	Quantity	Total cost
0	$500	5	$2,200
1	$1,000	6	$2,700
2	$1,300	7	$3,300
3	$1,500	8	$4,400
4	$1,800		

    a. Prepare a table that shows total variable cost, average total cost, and marginal cost at each level of output.

    b. Plot the average total cost, average variable cost, and marginal cost curves for a single firm (remember that values for marginal cost are plotted at the midpoint of the respective intervals).

    c. What is the firm's supply curve? How many chairs would the firm produce at prices of $350, $450, $550, and $650? (In computing quantities, assume that a firm produces a certain number of completed chairs each day; it does not produce fractions of a chair on any one day.)

    d. Suppose the demand curve in the market for rocking chairs is given by the following table:

Price	Quantity of chairs Demanded/day	Price	Quantity of chairs Demanded/day
$650	5,000	$450	7,000
$550	6,000	$350	8,000

    Plot the market demand curve for chairs. Compute and plot the market supply curve, using the information you obtained for a single firm in part (c). What is the equilibrium price? The equilibrium quantity?

    e. Given your solution in part (d), plot the total revenue and total cost curves for a single firm. Does your graph correspond to your solution in part (c)? Explain.

3. The following table shows the total output, total revenue, total variable cost, and total fixed cost of a firm. What level of output should the firm produce? Should it shut down? Should it exit the industry? Explain.

Output	Total revenue	Total variable cost	Total fixed cost
1	$1,000	$1,500	$500
2	$2,000	$2,000	$500
3	$3,000	$2,600	$500
4	$4,000	$3,900	$500
5	$5,000	$5,000	$500

4. Suppose a rise in fuel costs increases the cost of producing oats by $0.50 per bushel. Illustrate graphically how this change will affect the oat market and a single firm in the market in the short run and in the long run.

5. Suppose the demand for car washes in Collegetown falls as a result of a cutback in college enrollment. Show graphically how the price and output for the market and for a single firm will be affected in the short run and in the long run. Assume the market is perfectly competitive and that it is initially in long-run equilibrium at a price of $12 per car wash. Assume also that input prices don't change as the market responds to the change in demand.

6. Suppose that the market for dry-erase pens is perfectly competitive and that the pens cost $1 each. The industry is in long-run equilibrium. Now suppose that an increase in the cost of ink raises the production cost of the pens by $.25 per pen.

    a. Using a graph that shows the market as a whole and a typical firm in this market, illustrate the short run effects of the change.

    b. Is the price likely to rise by $.25? Why or why not?

    c. If it doesn't, are firms likely to continue to operate in the short run? Why or why not?

    d. What is likely to happen in the long run? Illustrate your results with a large, clearly labeled graph.

ENDNOTES

1. William F. Buckley, "Carey Took on 'Greed' as His Battle Cry," *The Gazette*, 22 August 1997, News 7 (a Universal Press Syndicate column).

CHAPTER 8
Monopoly and Its Regulation

START UP: SURROUNDED BY MONOPOLIES

If your college or university is like most, you spend a lot of time, and money, dealing with firms that face very little competition. Your campus bookstore is likely to be the only local firm selling the texts that professors require you to read. Your school may have granted an exclusive franchise to a single firm for food service and to another firm for vending machines. A single firm may provide your utilities—electricity, natural gas, and water.

Unlike the individual firms we have previously studied that operate in a competitive market, taking the price, which is determined by demand and supply, as given, in this chapter we investigate the behavior of firms that have their markets all to themselves. As the only suppliers of particular goods or services, they face the downward-sloping market demand curve alone.

We will find that firms that have their markets all to themselves behave in a manner that is in many respects quite different from the behavior of firms in perfect competition. Such firms continue to use the marginal decision rule in maximizing profits, but their freedom to select from the price and quantity combinations given by the market demand curve affects the way in which they apply this rule.

We will show that a monopoly firm is likely to produce less and charge more for what it produces than firms in a competitive industry. As a result, a monopoly solution is likely to be inefficient from society's perspective. We will compare monopoly to other forms of market organization and explore the policy alternatives available to government agencies dealing with monopoly firms and with other firms that have price-setting power. First, though, we will look at characteristics of monopoly and at conditions that give rise to monopolies in the first place.

1. THE NATURE OF MONOPOLY

LEARNING OBJECTIVES

1. Explain what economists mean by monopoly and describe the relationship between price setting and monopoly power.
2. List and explain the sources of monopoly power and how they can change over time.
3. Define what is meant by a natural monopoly.

Monopoly is at the opposite end of the spectrum of market models from perfect competition. A monopoly firm has no rivals. It is the only firm in its industry. There are no close substitutes for the good or service a monopoly produces. Not only does a monopoly firm have the market to itself, but it also need not worry about other firms entering. In the case of monopoly, entry by potential rivals is prohibitively difficult.

A monopoly does not take the market price as given; it determines its own price. It selects from its demand curve the price that corresponds to the quantity the firm has chosen to produce in order to earn the maximum profit possible. The entry of new firms, which eliminates profit in the long run in a competitive market, cannot occur in the monopoly model.

monopoly power

The ability to act as a price setter.

A firm that sets or picks price based on its output decision is called a price setter. A firm that acts as a price setter possesses **monopoly power**. Monopolies are not the only firms that have this power; however, the absence of rivals in monopoly gives it much more price-setting power.

As was the case when we discussed perfect competition in the previous chapter, the assumptions of the monopoly model are rather strong. In assuming there is one firm in a market, we assume there are no other firms producing goods or services that could be considered part of the same market as that of the monopoly firm. In assuming blocked entry, we assume, for reasons we will discuss below, that no other firm can enter that market. Such conditions are rare in the real world. As always with models, we make the assumptions that define monopoly in order to simplify our analysis, not to describe the real world. The result is a model that gives us important insights into the nature of the choices of firms and their impact on the economy.

1.1 Sources of Monopoly Power

Why are some markets dominated by single firms? What are the sources of monopoly power? Economists have identified a number of conditions that, individually or in combination, can lead to domination of a market by a single firm and create barriers that prevent the entry of new firms.

barriers to entry

Characteristic of a particular market that block the entry of new firms in a monopoly market.

Barriers to entry are characteristics of a particular market that block new firms from entering it. They include economies of scale, special advantages of location, high sunk costs, a dominant position in the ownership of some of the inputs required to produce the good, and government restrictions. These barriers may be interrelated, making entry that much more formidable. Although these barriers might allow one firm to gain and hold monopoly control over a market, there are often forces at work that can erode this control.

Economies of Scale

Scale economies and diseconomies define the shape of a firm's long-run average cost (*LRAC*) curve as it increases its output. If long-run average cost declines as the level of production increases, a firm is said to experience *economies of scale*.

natural monopoly

A firm that confronts economies of scale over the entire range of outputs demanded in its industry.

A firm that confronts economies of scale over the entire range of outputs demanded in its industry is a **natural monopoly**. Utilities that distribute electricity, water, and natural gas to some markets are examples. In a natural monopoly, the *LRAC* of any one firm intersects the market demand curve where long-run average costs are falling or are at a minimum. If this is the case, one firm in the industry will expand to exploit the economies of scale available to it. Because this firm will have lower unit costs than its rivals, it can drive them out of the market and gain monopoly control over the industry.

FIGURE 8.1 Economies of Scale Lead to Natural Monopoly

A firm with falling *LRAC* throughout the range of outputs relevant to existing demand (*D*) will monopolize the industry. Here, one firm operating with a large plant (*ATC₂*) produces 240 units of output at a lower cost than the $7 cost per unit of the 12 firms operating at a smaller scale (*ATC₁*), and producing 20 units of output each.

Suppose there are 12 firms, each operating at the scale shown by ATC_1 (average total cost) in Figure 8.1. A firm that expanded its scale of operation to achieve an average total cost curve such as ATC_2 could produce 240 units of output at a lower cost than could the smaller firms producing 20 units each. By cutting its price below the minimum average total cost of the smaller plants, the larger firm could drive the smaller ones out of business. In this situation, the industry demand is not large enough to support more than one firm. If another firm attempted to enter the industry, the natural monopolist would always be able to undersell it.

Location

Sometimes monopoly power is the result of location. For example, sellers in markets isolated by distance from their nearest rivals have a degree of monopoly power. The local movie theater in a small town has a monopoly in showing first-run movies. Doctors, dentists, and mechanics in isolated towns may also be monopolists.

Sunk Costs

The greater the cost of establishing a new business in an industry, the more difficult it is to enter that industry. That cost will, in turn, be greater if the outlays required to start a business are unlikely to be recovered if the business should fail.

Suppose, for example, that entry into a particular industry requires extensive advertising to make consumers aware of the new brand. Should the effort fail, there is no way to recover the expenditures for such advertising. An expenditure that has already been made and that cannot be recovered is called a **sunk cost**.

If a substantial fraction of a firm's initial outlays will be lost upon exit from the industry, exit will be costly. Difficulty of exit can make for difficulty of entry. The more firms have to lose from an unsuccessful effort to penetrate a particular market, the less likely they are to try. The potential for high sunk costs could thus contribute to the monopoly power of an established firm by making entry by other firms more difficult.

sunk cost
An expenditure that has already been made and that cannot be recovered.

Restricted Ownership of Raw Materials and Inputs

In very few cases the source of monopoly power is the ownership of strategic inputs. If a particular firm owns all of an input required for the production of a particular good or service, then it could emerge as the only producer of that good or service.

The Aluminum Company of America (ALCOA) gained monopoly power through its ownership of virtually all the bauxite mines in the world (bauxite is the source of aluminum). The International Nickel Company of Canada at one time owned virtually all the world's nickel. De Beers acquired rights to nearly all the world's diamond production, giving it enormous power in the market for diamonds. With new diamond supplies in Canada, Australia, and Russia being developed and sold independently of De Beers, however, this power has declined, and today De Beers controls a substantially smaller percentage of the world's supply.

Government Restrictions

Another important basis for monopoly power consists of special privileges granted to some business firms by government agencies. State and local governments have commonly assigned exclusive franchises—rights to conduct business in a specific market—to taxi and bus companies, to cable television companies, and to providers of telephone services, electricity, natural gas, and water, although the trend in recent years has been to encourage competition for many of these services. Governments might also regulate entry into an industry or a profession through licensing and certification requirements. Governments also provide patent protection to inventors of new products or production methods in order to encourage innovation; these patents may afford their holders a degree of monopoly power during the 17-year life of the patent.

Patents can take on extra importance when network effects are present. **Network effects** arise in situations where products become more useful the larger the number of users of the product. For example, one advantage of using the Windows computer operating system is that so many other people use it. That has advantages in terms of sharing files and other information.

network effects
Situations where products become more useful the larger the number of users of the product.

KEY TAKEAWAYS

- An industry with a single firm, in which entry is blocked, is called a monopoly.
- A firm that sets or picks price depending on its output decision is called a price setter. A price setter possesses monopoly power.
- The sources of monopoly power include economies of scale, locational advantages, high sunk costs associated with entry, restricted ownership of key inputs, and government restrictions, such as exclusive franchises, licensing and certification requirements, and patents.
- A firm that confronts economies of scale over the entire range of output demanded in an industry is a natural monopoly.

TRY IT!

What is the source of monopoly power—if any—in each of the following situations?

1. The U.S. Food and Drug Administration granted Burroughs Wellcome exclusive rights until 2005 to manufacture and distribute AZT, a drug used in the treatment of AIDS.
2. John and Mary Doe run the only shoe repair shop in town.
3. One utility company distributes residential electricity in your town.
4. The widespread use of automatic teller machines (ATMs) has proven a boon to Diebold, the principal manufacturer of the machines.

Case in Point

The Ambassador Bridge Fights to Maintain Its Monopoly

© 2010 Jupiterimages Corporation

Matty Moroun was quietly enjoying his monopoly power. He is the owner of the 80-year-old Ambassador Bridge, a suspension bridge that is the only connection between Detroit, Michigan, and Windsor, Ontario. He purchased the bridge from Warren Buffet in 1974 for $30 million. *Forbes* estimates that it is now worth more than $500 million. Mr. Moroun oversees the artery over which $100 billion of goods—one-quarter of U.S. trade with Canada and 40% of all truck shipments from the United States—make their way between the two countries.

Despite complaints of high and rising tolls—he has more than doubled fares for cars and tripled fares for trucks—Mr. Moroun has so far held on. Kenneth Davies, a lawyer who often battles Mr. Moroun in court, is a grudging admirer. "He's very intelligent and very aggressive. His avarice and greed are just American capitalism at work," he told *Forbes*.

What are the sources of his monopoly power? With the closest alternative bridge across the Detroit River two hours away, location is a big plus. In addition, the cost of creating a new transportation link is high. A group that is considering converting an old train tunnel to truck use and boring a new train tunnel some distance away is facing a $600 million price tag for the project. In addition to having entry by potential competitors blocked, he has a status not shared by most other monopolists. The Michigan Supreme Court ruled in 2008 that the city of Detroit cannot regulate his business because of the bridge's international nature. Canadian courts have barred any effort by Canadian authorities to regulate him. He will not even allow inspectors from the government of the United States to set foot on his bridge.

Increased security since 9/11 has caused delays, but Mr. Moroun has eased these by increasing his own spending on security to $50,000 a week and by building additional inspection stations and gifting them to the U.S. inspection agency, the General Services Administration. Even a monopolist understands the importance of keeping his customers content! Mr. Moroun has even proposed building a new bridge just next to the existing bridge.

Because of the terrorist attacks on 9/11 and the concern about vulnerability and security, calls to deal with this monopoly have increased. Some people argue that the government should buy what is the most important single international arterial in North America, while others have called for more regulatory oversight. The Canadian and Michigan governments have been discussing the possibility of building a publicly funded bridge nearby. Time will tell whether Mr. Moroun can hold onto what *Forbes* writers Stephane Fitch and Joann Muller dubbed "the best monopoly you never heard of."

Sources: Stephane Fitch and Joann Muller, "The Troll Under the Bridge," Forbes 174:10 (November 15, 2004): 134–139; John Gallagher, "Plan Uses Parkway to Ease Ambassador Bridge Traffic," Detroit Free Press, May 1, 2008; "State Supreme Court Sides With Ambassador Bridge in Dispute," Detroit News, May 7, 2008; and "A Floating Detroit River Bridge?" The Toronto Star, July 30, 2010.

ANSWERS TO TRY IT! PROBLEMS

1. The government's grant of an exclusive franchise to the drug gave the firm monopoly power.
2. While John and Mary have the only shop in town, this is an easy entry business. Further, there may be competitors in the nearby town. John and Mary probably have monopoly power, but they do not have a monopoly.
3. Natural monopoly.
4. Patent with strong network effects.

2. THE MONOPOLY MODEL

LEARNING OBJECTIVES

1. **Explain the relationship between price and marginal revenue when a firm faces a downward-sloping demand curve.**
2. **Explain the relationship between marginal revenue and elasticity along a linear demand curve.**
3. **Apply the marginal decision rule to explain how a monopoly maximizes profit.**

Analyzing choices is a more complex challenge for a monopoly firm than for a perfectly competitive firm. After all, a competitive firm takes the market price as given and determines its profit-maximizing output. Because a monopoly has its market all to itself, it can determine not only its output but its price as well. What kinds of price and output choices will such a firm make?

We will answer that question in the context of the marginal decision rule: a firm will produce additional units of a good until marginal revenue equals marginal cost. To apply that rule to a monopoly firm, we must first investigate the special relationship between demand and marginal revenue for a monopoly.

2.1   Monopoly and Market Demand

Because a monopoly firm has its market all to itself, it faces the market demand curve. Figure 8.2 compares the demand situations faced by a monopoly and a perfectly competitive firm. In Panel (a), the equilibrium price for a perfectly competitive firm is determined by the intersection of the demand and supply curves. The market supply curve is found simply by summing the supply curves of individual firms. Those, in turn, consist of the portions of marginal cost curves that lie above the average variable cost curves. The marginal cost curve, *MC*, for a single firm is illustrated. Notice the break in the horizontal axis indicating that the quantity produced by a single firm is a trivially small fraction of the whole. In the perfectly competitive model, one firm has *nothing* to do with the determination of the market price. Each firm in a perfectly competitive industry faces a horizontal demand curve defined by the market price.

FIGURE 8.2 Perfect Competition Versus Monopoly

Panel (a) shows the determination of equilibrium price and output in a perfectly competitive market. A typical firm with marginal cost curve MC is a price taker, choosing to produce quantity q at the equilibrium price P. In Panel (b) a monopoly faces a downward-sloping market demand curve. As a profit maximizer, it determines its profit-maximizing output. Once it determines that quantity, however, the price at which it can sell that output is found from the demand curve. The monopoly firm can sell additional units only by lowering price. The perfectly competitive firm, by contrast, can sell any quantity it wants at the market price.

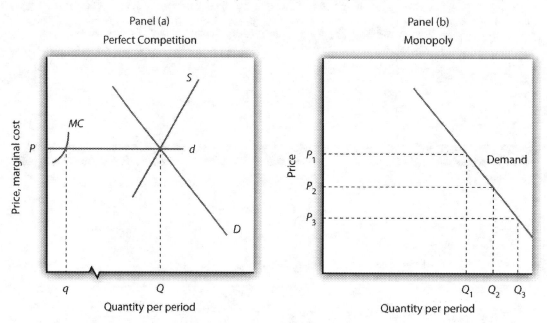

Contrast the situation shown in Panel (a) with the one faced by the monopoly firm in Panel (b). Because it is the only supplier in the industry, the monopolist faces the downward-sloping market demand curve alone. It may choose to produce any quantity. But, unlike the perfectly competitive firm, which can sell all it wants at the going market price, a monopolist can sell a greater quantity only by cutting its price.

Suppose, for example, that a monopoly firm can sell quantity Q_1 units at a price P_1 in Panel (b). If it wants to increase its output to Q_2 units—and sell that quantity—it must reduce its price to P_2. To sell quantity Q_3 it would have to reduce the price to P_3. The monopoly firm may choose its price and output, but it is restricted to a combination of price and output that lies on the demand curve. It could not, for example, charge price P_1 and sell quantity Q_3. To be a price setter, a firm must face a downward-sloping demand curve.

2.2 Total Revenue and Price Elasticity

A firm's elasticity of demand with respect to price has important implications for assessing the impact of a price change on total revenue. Also, the price elasticity of demand can be different at different points on a firm's demand curve. In this section, we shall see why a monopoly firm will always select a price in the elastic region of its demand curve.

Suppose the demand curve facing a monopoly firm is given by Equation 8.1, where Q is the quantity demanded per unit of time and P is the price per unit:

EQUATION 8.1

$$Q = 10 - P$$

This demand equation implies the demand schedule shown in Figure 8.3. Total revenue for each quantity equals the quantity times the price at which that quantity is demanded. The monopoly firm's total revenue curve is given in Panel (b). Because a monopolist must cut the price of every unit in order to increase sales, total revenue does not always increase as output rises. In this case, total revenue reaches a maximum of $25 when 5 units are sold. Beyond 5 units, total revenue begins to decline.

FIGURE 8.3   Demand, Elasticity, and Total Revenue

Suppose a monopolist faces the downward-sloping demand curve shown in Panel (a). In order to increase the quantity sold, it must cut the price. Total revenue is found by multiplying the price and quantity sold at each price. Total revenue, plotted in Panel (b), is maximized at $25, when the quantity sold is 5 units and the price is $5. At that point on the demand curve, the price elasticity of demand equals −1.

Price	$10	9	8	7	6	5	4	3	2	1	0
Quantity	0	1	2	3	4	5	6	7	8	9	10
Total revenue	$ 0	9	16	21	24	25	24	21	16	9	0

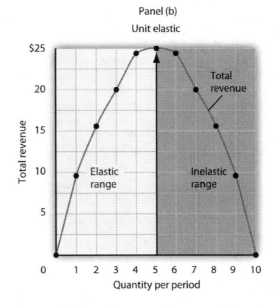

The demand curve in Panel (a) of Figure 8.3 shows ranges of values of the price elasticity of demand. We have learned that price elasticity varies along a linear demand curve in a special way: Demand is price elastic at points in the upper half of the demand curve and price inelastic in the lower half of the demand curve. If demand is price elastic, a price reduction increases total revenue. To sell an additional unit, a monopoly firm must lower its price. The sale of one more unit will increase revenue because the percentage increase in the quantity demanded exceeds the percentage decrease in the price. The elastic range of the demand curve corresponds to the range over which the total revenue curve is rising in Panel (b) of Figure 8.3.

If demand is price inelastic, a price reduction reduces total revenue because the percentage increase in the quantity demanded is less than the percentage decrease in the price. Total revenue falls as the firm sells additional units over the inelastic range of the demand curve. The downward-sloping portion of the total revenue curve in Panel (b) corresponds to the inelastic range of the demand curve.

Finally, recall that the midpoint of a linear demand curve is the point at which demand becomes unit price elastic. That point on the total revenue curve in Panel (b) corresponds to the point at which total revenue reaches a maximum.

The relationship among price elasticity, demand, and total revenue has an important implication for the selection of the profit-maximizing price and output: A monopoly firm will never choose a price and output in the inelastic range of the demand curve. Suppose, for example, that the monopoly firm represented in Figure 8.3 is charging $3 and selling 7 units. Its total revenue is thus $21. Because this combination is in the inelastic portion of the demand curve, the firm could increase its total revenue by raising its price. It could, at the same time, reduce its total cost. Raising price means reducing output; a reduction in output would reduce total cost. If the firm is operating in the inelastic range of its demand curve, then it is not maximizing profits. The firm could earn a higher profit by raising price and reducing output. It will continue to raise its price until it is in the elastic portion of its demand curve. A profit-maximizing monopoly firm will therefore select a price and output combination in the elastic range of its demand curve.

Of course, the firm could choose a point at which demand is unit price elastic. At that point, total revenue is maximized. But the firm seeks to maximize profit, not total revenue. A solution that maximizes total revenue will not maximize profit unless marginal cost is zero.

2.3   Demand and Marginal Revenue

In the perfectly competitive case, the additional revenue a firm gains from selling an additional unit—its marginal revenue—is equal to the market price. The firm's demand curve, which is a horizontal line at the market price, is also its marginal revenue curve. But a monopoly firm can sell an additional unit only by lowering the price. That fact complicates the relationship between the monopoly's demand curve and its marginal revenue.

Suppose the firm in Figure 8.3 sells 2 units at a price of $8 per unit. Its total revenue is $16. Now it wants to sell a third unit and wants to know the marginal revenue of that unit. To sell 3 units rather than 2, the firm must lower its price to $7 per unit. Total revenue rises to $21. The marginal revenue of the third unit is thus $5. But the *price* at which the firm sells 3 units is $7. Marginal revenue is less than price.

To see why the marginal revenue of the third unit is less than its price, we need to examine more carefully how the sale of that unit affects the firm's revenues. The firm brings in $7 from the sale of the third unit. But selling the third unit required the firm to charge a price of $7 instead of the $8 the firm was charging for 2 units. Now the firm receives less for the first 2 units. The marginal revenue of the third unit is the $7 the firm receives for that unit *minus* the $1 reduction in revenue for each of the first two units. The marginal revenue of the third unit is thus $5. (In this chapter we assume that the monopoly firm sells all units of output at the same price. In the next chapter, we will look at cases in which firms charge different prices to different customers.)

Marginal revenue is less than price for the monopoly firm. Figure 8.4 shows the relationship between demand and marginal revenue, based on the demand curve introduced in Figure 8.3. As always, we follow the convention of plotting marginal values at the midpoints of the intervals.

FIGURE 8.4 Demand and Marginal Revenue

The marginal revenue curve for the monopoly firm lies below its demand curve. It shows the additional revenue gained from selling an additional unit. Notice that, as always, marginal values are plotted at the midpoints of the respective intervals.

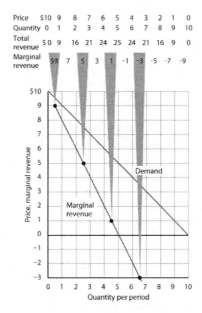

When the demand curve is linear, as in Figure 8.4, the marginal revenue curve can be placed according to the following rules: the marginal revenue curve is always below the demand curve and the marginal revenue curve will bisect any horizontal line drawn between the vertical axis and the demand curve. To put it another way, the marginal revenue curve will be twice as steep as the demand curve. The demand curve in Figure 8.4 is given by the equation $Q = 10 - P$, which can be written $P = 10 - Q$. The marginal revenue curve is given by $P = 10 - 2Q$, which is twice as steep as the demand curve.

The marginal revenue and demand curves in Figure 8.4 follow these rules. The marginal revenue curve lies below the demand curve, and it bisects any horizontal line drawn from the vertical axis to the demand curve. At a price of $6, for example, the quantity demanded is 4. The marginal revenue curve passes through 2 units at this price. At a price of 0, the quantity demanded is 10; the marginal revenue curve passes through 5 units at this point.

Just as there is a relationship between the firm's demand curve and the price elasticity of demand, there is a relationship between its marginal revenue curve and elasticity. Where marginal revenue is positive, demand is price elastic. Where marginal revenue is negative, demand is price inelastic. Where marginal revenue is zero, demand is unit price elastic.

When marginal revenue is …	then demand is …
positive,	price elastic.
negative,	price inelastic.
zero,	unit price elastic.

A firm would not produce an additional unit of output with negative marginal revenue. And, assuming that the production of an additional unit has some cost, a firm would not produce the extra unit if it has zero marginal revenue. Because a monopoly firm will generally operate where marginal revenue is positive, we see once again that it will operate in the elastic range of its demand curve.

2.4 Monopoly Equilibrium: Applying the Marginal Decision Rule

Profit-maximizing behavior is always based on the marginal decision rule: Additional units of a good should be produced as long as the marginal revenue of an additional unit exceeds the marginal cost. The maximizing solution occurs where marginal revenue equals marginal cost. As always, firms seek to maximize economic profit, and costs are measured in the economic sense of opportunity cost.

Figure 8.5 shows a demand curve and an associated marginal revenue curve facing a monopoly firm. The marginal cost curve is like those we derived earlier; it falls over the range of output in which the firm experiences increasing marginal returns, then rises as the firm experiences diminishing marginal returns.

FIGURE 8.5 The Monopoly Solution

The monopoly firm maximizes profit by producing an output Q_m at point G, where the marginal revenue and marginal cost curves intersect. It sells this output at price P_m.

To determine the profit-maximizing output, we note the quantity at which the firm's marginal revenue and marginal cost curves intersect (Q_m in Figure 8.5). We read up from Q_m to the demand curve to find the price P_m at which the firm can sell Q_m units per period. The profit-maximizing price and output are given by point E on the demand curve.

Thus we can determine a monopoly firm's profit-maximizing price and output by following three steps:

   1. Determine the demand, marginal revenue, and marginal cost curves.

2. Select the output level at which the marginal revenue and marginal cost curves intersect.

3. Determine from the demand curve the price at which that output can be sold.

FIGURE 8.6 Computing Monopoly Profit

A monopoly firm's profit per unit is the difference between price and average total cost. Total profit equals profit per unit times the quantity produced. Total profit is given by the area of the shaded rectangle ATC_mP_mEF.

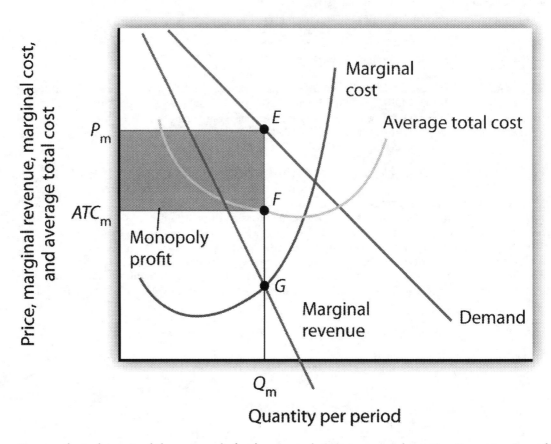

Once we have determined the monopoly firm's price and output, we can determine its economic profit by adding the firm's average total cost curve to the graph showing demand, marginal revenue, and marginal cost, as shown in Figure 8.6. The average total cost (ATC) at an output of Q_m units is ATC_m. The firm's profit per unit is thus P_m - ATC_m. Total profit is found by multiplying the firm's output, Q_m, by profit per unit, so total profit equals $Q_m(P_m$ - $ATC_m)$—the area of the shaded rectangle in Figure 8.6.

Heads Up!

Dispelling Myths About Monopoly

Three common misconceptions about monopoly are:

1. Because there are no rivals selling the products of monopoly firms, they can charge whatever they want.
2. Monopolists will charge whatever the market will bear.
3. Because monopoly firms have the market to themselves, they are guaranteed huge profits.

As Figure 8.5 shows, once the monopoly firm decides on the number of units of output that will maximize profit, the price at which it can sell that many units is found by "reading off" the demand curve price associated with that many units. If it tries to sell Q_m units of output for more than P_m, some of its output will go unsold. The monopoly firm can set its price, but is restricted to price and output combinations that lie on its demand curve. It cannot just "charge whatever it wants." And if it charges "all the market will bear," it will sell either 0 or, at most, 1 unit of output.

Neither is the monopoly firm guaranteed a profit. Consider Figure 8.6. Suppose the average total cost curve, instead of lying below the demand curve for some output levels as shown, were instead everywhere above the demand curve. In that case, the monopoly will incur losses no matter what price it chooses, since average total cost will always be greater than any price it might charge. As is the case for perfect competition, the monopoly firm can keep producing in the short run so long as price exceeds average variable cost. In the long run, it will stay in business only if it can cover all of its costs.

KEY TAKEAWAYS

- If a firm faces a downward-sloping demand curve, marginal revenue is less than price.
- Marginal revenue is positive in the elastic range of a demand curve, negative in the inelastic range, and zero where demand is unit price elastic.
- If a monopoly firm faces a linear demand curve, its marginal revenue curve is also linear, lies below the demand curve, and bisects any horizontal line drawn from the vertical axis to the demand curve.
- To maximize profit or minimize losses, a monopoly firm produces the quantity at which marginal cost equals marginal revenue. Its price is given by the point on the demand curve that corresponds to this quantity.

TRY IT!

The Troll Road Company is considering building a toll road. It estimates that its linear demand curve is as shown below. Assume that the fixed cost of the road is $0.5 million per year. Maintenance costs, which are the only other costs of the road, are also given in the table.

Tolls per trip	$1.00	0.90	0.80	0.70	0.60	0.50
Number of trips per year (in millions)	1	2	3	4	5	6
Maintenance cost per year (in millions)	$0.7	1.2	1.8	2.9	4.2	6.0

1. Using the midpoint convention, compute the profit-maximizing level of output.
2. Using the midpoint convention, what price will the company charge?
3. What is marginal revenue at the profit-maximizing output level? How does marginal revenue compare to price?

Case in Point

Profit-Maximizing Sports Teams

© 2010 Jupiterimages Corporation

Love of the game? Love of the city? Are those the factors that influence owners of professional sports teams in setting admissions prices? Four economists at the University of Vancouver have what they think is the answer for one group of teams: professional hockey teams set admission prices at levels that maximize their profits. They regard hockey teams as monopoly firms and use the monopoly model to examine the team's behavior.

The economists, Donald G. Ferguson, Kenneth G. Stewart, John Colin H. Jones, and Andre Le Dressay, used data from three seasons to estimate demand and marginal revenue curves facing each team in the National Hockey League. They found that demand for a team's tickets is affected by population and income in the team's home city, the team's standing in the National Hockey League, and the number of superstars on the team.

Because a sports team's costs do not vary significantly with the number of fans who attend a given game, the economists assumed that marginal cost is zero. The profit-maximizing number of seats sold per game is thus the quantity at which marginal revenue is zero, provided a team's stadium is large enough to hold that quantity of fans. This unconstrained quantity is labeled Q_u, with a corresponding price P_u in the graph.

Stadium size and the demand curve facing a team might prevent the team from selling the profit-maximizing quantity of tickets. If its stadium holds only Q_c fans, for example, the team will sell that many tickets at price P_c; its marginal revenue is positive at that quantity. Economic theory thus predicts that the marginal revenue for teams that consistently sell out their games will be positive, and the marginal revenue for other teams will be zero.

The economists' statistical results were consistent with the theory. They found that teams that do not typically sell out their games operate at a quantity at which marginal revenue is about zero and that teams with sellouts have positive marginal revenue. "It's clear that these teams are very sophisticated in their use of pricing to maximize profits," Mr. Ferguson said.

Not all studies of sporting event pricing have confirmed this conclusion. While a study of major league baseball ticket pricing by Leo Kahane and Stephen Shmanske and one of baseball spring training game tickets by Michael Donihue, David Findlay, and Peter Newberry suggested that tickets are priced where demand is unit elastic, some other studies of ticket pricing of sporting events have found that tickets are priced in the inelastic region of the demand curve. On its face, this would mean that team owners were not maximizing profits. Why would team owners do this? Are they really charging too little? To fans, it certainly may not seem so!

While some have argued that owners want to please fans by selling tickets for less than the profit-maximizing price, others argue they do so for possible political considerations, for example, keeping prices below the profit-maximizing level could help when they are asking for subsidies for building new stadiums. In line with the notion that team owners do behave like other profit-maximizing firms, another line of research, for example, proposed by Anthony Krautmann and David Berri, has been to recognize that owners also get revenue from selling concessions so that getting more fans at the game may boost revenue from other sources.

Sources: Michael R. Donihue, David W. Findlay, and Peter W. Newberry, "An Analysis of Attendance at Major League Baseball Spring Games," Journal of Sports Economics 8:1 (February 2007): 39–61; Donald G. Ferguson et al., "The Pricing of Sports Events: Do Teams Maximize Profit?" Journal of Industrial Economics 39:3 (March 1991): 297–310 and personal interview; Leo Kahane and Stephen Shmanske, "Team Roster Turnover and Attendance in Major League Baseball," Applied Economics 29 (1997): 425–431; and Anthony C. Krautmann and David J. Berri, "Can We Find It at the Concessions?" Journal of Sports Economics 8:2 (April 2007): 183–191.

ANSWERS TO TRY IT! PROBLEMS

Maintenance costs constitute the variable costs associated with building the road. In order to answer the first four parts of the question, you will need to compute total revenue, marginal revenue, and marginal cost, as shown at right:

1. Using the "midpoint" convention, the profit-maximizing level of output is 2.5 million trips per year. With that number of trips, marginal revenue ($0.60) equals marginal cost ($0.60).
2. Again, we use the "midpoint" convention. The company will charge a toll of $0.85.
3. The marginal revenue is $0.60, which is less than the $0.85 toll (price).

Price per trip	$1.00	0.90	0.80	0.70	0.60	0.50
Number of trips per year (in millions)	1	2	3	4	5	6
Total variable costs per year (in millions)	$0.7	1.2	1.8	2.9	4.2	6.0
Total revenue (in millions)	$1.00	1.80	2.40	2.80	3.00	3.00
Marginal revenue		$0.80	0.60	0.40	0.20	0.00
Marginal cost		$0.50	0.60	1.10	1.30	1.80

3. COMPARING MONOPOLY TO OTHER FORMS OF MARKET ORGANIZATION

LEARNING OBJECTIVES

1. **Explain and illustrate that a monopoly firm produces an output that is less than the efficient level and explain why this results in a deadweight loss to society.**
2. **Explain and illustrate how the higher price that a monopoly charges, compared to an otherwise identical perfectly competitive firm, transfers part of consumer surplus to the monopolist and raises questions of equity.**
3. **Considering both advantages and disadvantages, discuss the potential effects that a monopoly may have on consumer choices, price, quality of products, and technological innovations.**
4. **Compare monopoly to the other forms of market organization.**

We have seen that for monopolies pursuing profit maximization, the outcome differs from the case of perfect competition. Does this matter to society? In this section, we will focus on the differences that stem from market structure and assess their implications.

3.1 Efficiency, Equity, and Concentration of Power

A monopoly firm determines its output by setting marginal cost equal to marginal revenue. It then charges the price at which it can sell that output, a price determined by the demand curve. That price exceeds marginal revenue; it therefore exceeds marginal cost as well. That contrasts with the case in perfect competition, in which price and marginal cost are equal. The higher price charged by a monopoly firm may allow it a profit—in large part at the expense of consumers, whose reduced options may give them little say in the matter. The monopoly solution thus raises problems of efficiency, equity, and the concentration of power.

Monopoly and Efficiency

The fact that price in monopoly exceeds marginal cost suggests that the monopoly solution violates the basic condition for economic efficiency, that the price system must confront decision makers with all of the costs and all of the benefits of their choices. Efficiency requires that consumers confront prices that equal marginal costs. Because a monopoly firm charges a price greater than marginal cost, consumers will consume less of the monopoly's good or service than is economically efficient.

To contrast the efficiency of the perfectly competitive outcome with the inefficiency of the monopoly outcome, imagine a perfectly competitive industry whose solution is depicted in Figure 8.7. The short-run industry supply curve is the summation of individual marginal cost curves; it may be regarded as the marginal cost curve for the industry. A perfectly competitive industry achieves equilibrium at point C, at price P_c and quantity Q_c.

Now, suppose that all the firms in the industry merge and a government restriction prohibits entry by any new firms. Our perfectly competitive industry is now a monopoly. Assume the monopoly continues to have the same marginal cost and demand curves that the competitive industry did. The monopoly firm faces the same market demand curve, from which it derives its marginal revenue curve. It maximizes profit at output Q_m and charges price P_m. Output is lower and price higher than in the competitive solution.

FIGURE 8.7 Perfect Competition, Monopoly, and Efficiency

Given market demand and marginal revenue, we can compare the behavior of a monopoly to that of a perfectly competitive industry. The marginal cost curve may be thought of as the supply curve of a perfectly competitive industry. The perfectly competitive industry produces quantity Q_c and sells the output at price P_c. The monopolist restricts output to Q_m and raises the price to P_m. Reorganizing a perfectly competitive industry as a monopoly results in a deadweight loss to society given by the shaded area GRC. It also transfers a portion of the consumer surplus earned in the competitive case to the monopoly firm.

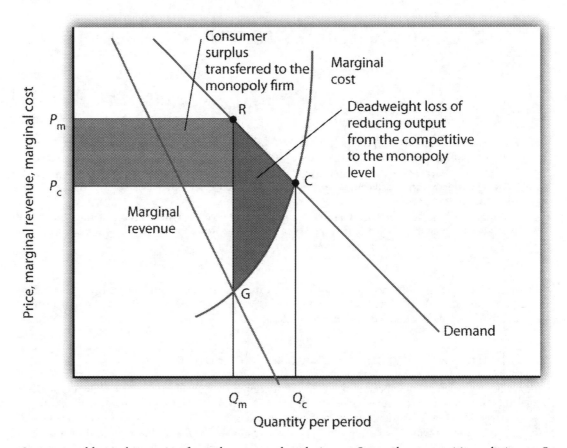

Society would gain by moving from the monopoly solution at Q_m to the competitive solution at Q_c. The benefit to consumers would be given by the area under the demand curve between Q_m and Q_c; it is the area Q_mRCQ_c. An increase in output, of course, has a cost. Because the marginal cost curve measures the cost of each additional unit, we can think of the area under the marginal cost curve over some range of output as measuring the total cost of that output. Thus, the total cost of increasing output from Q_m to Q_c is the area under the marginal cost curve over that range—the area Q_mGCQ_c. Subtracting this cost from the benefit gives us the net gain of moving from the monopoly to the competitive solution; it is the shaded area GRC. That is the potential gain from moving to the efficient solution. The area GRC is a deadweight loss.

Monopoly and Equity

The monopoly solution raises issues not just of efficiency but also of equity. Figure 8.7 shows that the monopolist charges price P_m rather than the competitive price P_c; the higher price charged by the monopoly firm reduces consumer surplus. Consumer surplus is the difference between what consumers are willing to pay for a good and what they actually pay. It is measured by the area under the demand curve and above the price of the good over the range of output produced.

If the industry were competitive, consumer surplus would be the area below the demand curve and above P_cC. With monopoly, consumer surplus would be the area below the demand curve and above P_mR. Part of the reduction in consumer surplus is the area under the demand curve between Q_c and Q_m; it is contained in the deadweight loss area GRC. But consumers also lose the area of the rectangle bounded by the competitive and monopoly prices and by the monopoly output; this lost consumer surplus is transferred to the monopolist.

The fact that society suffers a deadweight loss due to monopoly is an efficiency problem. But the transfer of a portion of consumer surplus to the monopolist is an equity issue. Is such a transfer legitimate? After all, the monopoly firm enjoys a privileged position, protected by barriers to entry from competition. Should it be allowed to extract these gains from consumers? We will see that public policy suggests that the answer is no. Regulatory efforts imposed in monopoly cases often seek to reduce the degree to which monopoly firms extract consumer surplus from consumers by reducing the prices these firms charge.

Monopoly and the Concentration of Power

The objections to monopoly run much deeper than worries over economic efficiency and high prices. Because it enjoys barriers that block potential rivals, a monopoly firm wields considerable market power. For many people, that concentration of power is objectionable. A decentralized, competitive market constantly tests the ability of firms to satisfy consumers, pushes them to find new products and new and better production methods, and whittles away economic profits. Firms that operate in the shelter of monopoly may be largely immune to such pressures. Consumers are likely to be left with fewer choices, higher costs, and lower quality.

Perhaps more important in the view of many economists is the fact that the existence of economic profits provides both an incentive and the means for monopolists to aggressively protect their position and extend it if possible. These economists point out that monopolists may be willing to spend their economic profits in attempts to influence political leaders and public authorities (including regulatory authorities) who can help them maintain or enhance their monopoly position. Graft and corruption may be the result, claim these critics. Indeed, Microsoft has been accused by its rivals of bullying computer manufacturers into installing its web browser, Internet Explorer, exclusively on their computers.

Attitudes about Microsoft reflect these concerns. Even among people who feel that its products are good and fairly priced, there is uneasiness about our seeming dependence on them. And once it has secured its dominant position, will it charge more for its products? Will it continue to innovate?

At the same time, though, we must be careful to avoid the mistake of simply assuming that competition is the alternative to monopoly, that every monopoly can and should be replaced by a competitive market. One key source of monopoly power, after all, is economics of scale. In the case of natural monopoly, the alternative to a single firm is many small, high-cost producers. We may not like having only one local provider of water, but we might like even less having dozens of providers whose costs—and prices—are higher. Where monopolies exist because economies of scale prevail over the entire range of market demand, they may serve a useful economic role. We might want to regulate their production and pricing choices, but we may not want to give up their cost advantages. Another source of monopoly power is the patent system. Would we want to forgo the technological innovation patents encourage in order to decrease the market power they afford to the patent holders?

3.2 Comparing Monopoly and Perfect Competition

Pulling together what we have learned in this chapter on monopoly and previously on perfect competition, Table 8.1 summarizes the differences between the models of perfect competition and monopoly. Most importantly we note that whereas the perfectly competitive firm is a price taker, the monopoly firm is a price setter. Because of this difference, we can object to monopoly on grounds of economic efficiency; monopolies produce too little and charge too much. Also, the high price and persistent profits strike many as inequitable. Others may simply see monopoly as an unacceptable concentration of power.

TABLE 8.1 Characteristics of Perfect Competition and Monopoly

Characteristic or Event	Perfect Competition	Monopoly
Market	Large number of sellers and buyers producing a homogeneous good or service, easy entry.	Large number of buyers, one seller. Entry is blocked.
Demand and marginal revenue curves	The firm's demand and marginal revenue curve is a horizontal line at the market price.	The firm faces the market demand curve; marginal revenue is below market demand.
Price	Determined by demand and supply; each firm is a price taker. Price equals marginal cost.	The monopoly firm determines price; it is a price setter. Price is greater than marginal cost.
Profit maximization	Firms produce where marginal cost equals marginal revenue	Firms produce where marginal cost equals marginal revenue and charge the corresponding price on the demand curve.
Profit	Entry forces economic profit to zero in the long run.	Because entry is blocked, a monopoly firm can sustain an economic profit in the long run.
Efficiency	The equilibrium solution is efficient because price equals marginal cost.	The equilibrium solution is inefficient because price is greater than marginal cost.

3.3 How Imperfect Competition Compares to Monopoly and Perfect Competition

Besides perfect competition and monopoly, there are two other models of market organization—monopolistic competition and oligopoly. Together these are referred to as models of imperfect competition. While we will not analyze them in detail, we can draw some general conclusions that will give a sense of how they compare to the two models we have studied in depth.

A monopolistically competitive industry, such as the restaurant industry, is similar to perfect competition in that there are a large number of firms and entry and exit is easy. It is different from perfect competition in that firms sell differentiated products, and thus each firm is a price setter rather than a price taker. Similar to monopoly, then, price and marginal revenue are not the same. Each firm faces a downward-sloping demand curve that is a portion of total market demand. In the short run, monopolistically competitive firms choose to produce the output where marginal revenue equals marginal cost and set price according to the demand curves they face. In the long run, however, any economic profits or losses will be eliminated by entry or exit, leaving firms with zero economic profits. The equilibrium solution is not efficient because price is greater than marginal cost but entry and exit make the inefficiency less than what would likely prevail under monopoly. Also, consumers are receiving the benefits of some choice among products in the industry. Finally, with many firms in an industry, power is not concentrated and, with zero economic profits in the long run, the ability to influence political leaders and public authorities is limited. In general, monopolistically competitive industries have not received much attention in terms of public policy initiatives.

In contrast, the other form of imperfect competition, oligopoly, is under the purview of antitrust laws, described in the next section of this chapter. Unlike the other models of market organization, economists have not developed a single model of how firms in an oligopolistic market will operate. This is because the small number of firms means that each will take into account that its own actions will produce a response from its rivals and that those responses will affect it. This interdependence has led to the development of a variety of models to describe different strategies that firms might take. Even without a single formal model, though, the difficulty of entry and exit suggests the possibility of a fairly large divergence between price and marginal cost (i.e., an equilibrium solution that is inefficient) and considerable market power and concentration. That economic profits are possible even in the long run also means that firms in the industry may attempt to influence government decision making. Thus antitrust laws are aimed at oligopolies as well as at monopolies. The next section provides a look at antitrust laws and their interpretation.

KEY TAKEAWAYS

- A monopoly firm produces an output that is less than the efficient level. The result is a deadweight loss to society, given by the area between the demand and marginal cost curves over the range of output between the output chosen by the monopoly firm and the efficient output.

- The higher price charged by the monopoly firm compared to the perfectly competitive firm reduces consumer surplus, part of which is transferred to the monopolist. This transfer generates an equity issue.

- The monopoly firm's market power reduces consumers' choices and may result in higher prices, but there may be advantages to monopoly as well, such as economies of scale and technological innovations encouraged by the patent system.

- Monopolistic competition and oligopoly fall in between perfect competition and monopoly on the spectrum of market organization models. As such, they can be compared to the two models that we have covered in more depth.

TRY IT!

Do the following statements better describe a firm operating in a perfectly competitive market or a firm that is a monopoly?

1. The demand curve faced by the firm is downward-sloping.
2. The demand curve and the marginal revenue curves are the same.
3. Entry and exit are relatively difficult.
4. The firm is likely to be concerned about antitrust laws.
5. Consumer surplus would be increased if the firm produced more output.

Case in Point

Technological Change, Public Policy, and Competition in Telecommunications

© 2010 Jupiterimages Corporation

Back in the olden days—before 1984—to use a telephone in the United States almost certainly meant being a customer of AT&T. Ma Bell, as the company was known, provided local and long-distance service to virtually every U.S. household. AT&T was clearly a monopoly.

The Justice Department began its battle with AT&T in the 1970s, charging it with monopolizing the industry. The case culminated in a landmark 1984 ruling that broke the company up into seven "Baby Bells" that would provide local telephone service. AT&T would continue to provide long-distance service.

In effect, the ruling replaced a single national monopoly with seven regional monopolies in local telephone service. AT&T maintained its monopoly position in long-distance service—for a while. The turmoil that has followed illustrates the fragility of monopoly power.

Technological developments in the industry have brought dramatic changes. Companies found ways to challenge AT&T's monopoly position in long-distance telephone service. Cable operators sprang up, typically developing monopoly power over the provision of cable television in their regional markets but also offering phone service. Mobile phone service, provided by AT&T, and others such as Verizon and Sprint, has led many consumers to do without land-line phone service entirely. Companies that had traditionally been telephone companies have begun providing cable services as well as Internet access. The ready availability of video services on the Internet threatens to make cable providers outmoded middlemen.

What is the status of AT&T today? While no longer a monopoly, it is a major player in all of the areas related to telecommunications and larger than all of its competitors in the United States. In 2011, it began the process of buying T-Mobile USA, a mobile service provider focused on the youth market. By the end of that year, however, in the face of strong opposition from the Department of Justice and the Federal Communications Commission on the grounds that the merger would stifle competition in the industry, AT&T announced that it was dropping the deal. Does AT&T have market power today? Undoubtedly. Is it a monopoly? Not anymore.

Source: Company Monitor, USA Telecommunication Report, Q2 2011: 69–79.

ANSWERS TO TRY IT! PROBLEMS

1. monopoly
2. perfect competition
3. monopoly
4. monopoly
5. monopoly

4. ANTITRUST LAWS AND THEIR INTERPRETATION

LEARNING OBJECTIVES

1. **Define antitrust policies and tell when and why they were introduced in the United States.**
2. **Discuss highlights in the history of antitrust policies in the United States, focusing on major issues.**

Antitrust policy

Policy by which government attempts to prevent the acquisition and exercise of monopoly power and to encourage competition in the marketplace.

In the decades after the Civil War, giant corporations and cartels began to dominate railroads, oil, banking, meat packing, and a dozen other industries. These businesses were led by entrepreneurs who, rightly or wrongly, have come to be thought of as "robber barons" out to crush their competitors, monopolize their markets, and gouge their customers. The term "robber baron" was associated with such names as J.P. Morgan and Andrew Carnegie in the steel industry, Philip Armour and Gustavas and Edwin Swift in meat packing, James P. Duke in tobacco, and John D. Rockefeller in the oil industry. They gained their market power through cartels and other business agreements aimed at restricting competition. Some formed *trusts*, a combination of corporations designed to consolidate, coordinate, and control the operations and policies of several companies. It was in response to the rise of these cartels and giant firms that antitrust policy was created in the United States. **Antitrust policy** refers to government attempts to prevent the acquisition and exercise of monopoly power and to encourage competition in the marketplace.

4.1 A Brief History of Antitrust Policy

The final third of the nineteenth century saw two major economic transitions. The first was industrialization—a period in which U.S. firms became far more capital intensive. The second was the emergence of huge firms able to dominate whole industries. In the oil industry, for example, Standard Oil of Ohio (after 1899, the Standard Oil Company of New Jersey) began acquiring smaller firms, eventually controlling 90% of U.S. oil-refining capacity. American Tobacco gained control of up to 90% of the market for most tobacco products, excluding cigars.

Public concern about the monopoly power of these giants led to a major shift in U.S. policy. What had been an economic environment in which the government rarely intervened in the affairs of private firms was gradually transformed into an environment in which government agencies took on a much more vigorous role. The first arena of intervention was antitrust policy, which authorized the federal government to challenge the monopoly power of firms head-on. The application of this policy, however, has followed a wandering and rocky road.

The Sherman Antitrust Act

The Sherman Antitrust Act of 1890 remains the cornerstone of U.S. antitrust policy. The Sherman Act outlawed contracts, combinations, and conspiracies in restraint of trade.

An important issue in the interpretation of the Sherman Act concerns which actions by firms are **illegal per se**, meaning illegal in and of itself without regard to the circumstances under which it occurs. Shoplifting, for example, is illegal per se; courts do not inquire whether shoplifters have a good reason for stealing something in determining whether their acts are illegal. One key question of interpretation is whether it is illegal per se to control a large share of a market. Another is whether a merger that is likely to produce substantial monopoly power is illegal per se.

Two landmark Supreme Court cases in 1911 in which the Sherman Act was effectively used to break up Standard Oil and American Tobacco enunciated the **rule of reason**, which holds that whether or not a particular business practice is illegal depends on the circumstances surrounding the action. In both cases, the companies held dominant market positions, but the Court made it clear that it was their specific "unreasonable" behaviors that the breakups were intended to punish. In determining what was illegal and what was not, emphasis was placed on the conduct, not the structure or size, of the firms.

In the next 10 years, the Court threw out antitrust suits brought by government prosecutors against Eastman Kodak, International Harvester, United Shoe Machinery, and United States Steel. The Court determined that none of them had used unreasonable means to achieve their dominant positions in the industry. Rather, they had successfully exploited economies of scale to reduce costs below competitors' costs and had used reasonable means of competition to reap the rewards of efficiency.

The rule of reason suggests that "bigness" is no offense if it has been achieved through legitimate business practices. This precedent, however, was challenged in 1945 when the U.S. Court of Appeals ruled against the Aluminum Company of America (Alcoa). The court acknowledged that Alcoa had been able to capture over 90% of the aluminum industry through reasonable business practices. Nevertheless, the court held that by sheer size alone, Alcoa was in violation of the prohibition against monopoly.

In a landmark 1962 court case involving a proposed merger between United Shoe Machinery and the Brown Shoe Company, one of United's competitors, the Supreme Court blocked the merger because the resulting firm would have been so efficient that it could have undersold all of its competitors. The Court recognized that lower shoe prices would have benefited consumers, but chose to protect competitors instead.

The Alcoa case and the Brown Shoe case, along with many other antitrust cases in the 1950s and 1960s, added confusion and uncertainty to the antitrust environment by appearing to reinvoke the doctrine of per se illegality. In the government's case against Visa and MasterCard, the government argued successfully that the behavior of the two firms was a per se violation of the Sherman Act.

The Sherman Act also aimed, in part, to prevent **price-fixing**, in which two or more firms agree to set prices or to coordinate their pricing policies. For example, in the 1950s General Electric, Westinghouse, and several other manufacturers colluded to fix prices. They agreed to assign market segments in which one firm would sell at a lower price than the others. In 1961, the General Electric–Westinghouse agreement was declared illegal. The companies paid a multimillion-dollar fine, and their officers served brief jail sentences. In 2008, three manufacturers of liquid crystal display panels—the flat screens used in televisions, cell phones, personal computers, and such—agreed to pay $585 million in fines for price fixing, with LG Display paying $400 million, Sharp Corporation paying $120 million, and Chunghwa Picture Tubes paying $65 million. The $400 million fine to LG is still less than the record single fine of $500 million paid in 1999 by F. Hoffman-LaRoche, the Swiss pharmaceutical company, in a case involving fixing prices of vitamin supplements.

Other Antitrust Legislation

Concerned about the continued growth of monopoly power, in 1914 Congress created the Federal Trade Commission (FTC), a five-member commission that, along with the antitrust division of the Justice Department, has the power to investigate firms that use illegal business practices.

In addition to establishing the FTC, Congress enacted new antitrust laws intended to strengthen the Sherman Act. The Clayton Act (1914) clarifies the illegal per se provision of the Sherman Act by prohibiting the purchase of a rival firm if the purchase would substantially decrease competition, and outlawing interlocking directorates, in which there are the same people sitting on the boards of directors of competing firms. More significantly, the act prohibits price discrimination that is designed to lessen competition or that tends to create a monopoly and exempts labor unions from antitrust laws.

illegal per se

Actions taken by firms that are illegal in and of themselves without regard to the circumstances under which they occur.

rule of reason

Rule stating that whether or not a particular business practice is illegal depends on the circumstances surrounding the action.

price-fixing

Situation in which two or more firms agree to set prices or to coordinate their pricing policies.

horizontal merger

The consolidation of two or more producers of the same good or service.

vertical merger

Mergers between firms at different stages in the production and distribution of a product.

contestable

Open to entry by potential rivals.

The Sherman and Clayton acts, like other early antitrust legislation, were aimed at preventing mergers that reduce the number of firms in a single industry. The consolidation of two or more producers of the same good or service is called a **horizontal merger**. Such mergers increase concentration and, therefore, the likelihood of collusion among the remaining firms.

The Celler–Kefauver Act of 1950 extended the antitrust provisions of earlier legislation by blocking **vertical mergers**, which are mergers between firms at different stages in the production and distribution of a product if a reduction in competition will result. For example, the acquisition by Ford Motor Company of a firm that supplies it with steel would be a vertical merger.

4.2   U.S. Antitrust Policy Today

The "bigness is badness" doctrine dominated antitrust policy from 1945 to the 1970s. But the doctrine always had its critics. If a firm is more efficient than its competitors, why should it be punished? Critics of the antitrust laws point to the fact that of the 500 largest companies in the United States in 1950, over 100 no longer exist. New firms, including such giants as Walmart, Microsoft, and Federal Express, have taken their place. The critics argue that the emergence of these new firms is evidence of the dynamism and competitive nature of the modern corporate scene.

There is no evidence to suggest, for example, that the degree of concentration across all industries has increased over the past 25 years. Global competition and the use of the internet as a marketing tool have increased the competitiveness of a wide range of industries. Moreover, critics of antitrust policy argue that it is not necessary that an industry be perfectly competitive to achieve the benefits of competition. It need merely be **contestable**—open to entry by potential rivals. A large firm may be able to prevent small firms from competing, but other equally large firms may enter the industry in pursuit of the high profits earned by the initial large firm. For example, Time Warner, primarily a competitor in the publishing and entertainment industries, has in recent years become a main competitor in the cable television market.

In the 1980s both the courts and the Justice Department held that bigness did not necessarily translate into badness, and corporate mergers proliferated. Merger activity waxed and waned (particularly during recessions) over the ensuing years. It has been substantial in most years.

When mergers are proposed, the Justice Department, defining the relevant market based on how high the cross price elasticity of demand is and using numerical tests of concentration, looks at the extent to which a merger affects how concentrated an industry will be post-merger. If it deems the industry would become too concentrated, it may block the merger, as it did in 2011 when AT&T and T-Mobile USA proposed merging. In many other cases, proposed mergers are allowed to go through.

KEY TAKEAWAYS

- The government uses antitrust policies to maintain competitive markets in the economy.
- The Sherman Antitrust Act of 1890 and subsequent legislation defined illegal business practices, but these acts are subject to widely varying interpretations by government agencies and by the courts.
- Although price-fixing is illegal per se, most business practices that may lessen competition are interpreted under the rule of reason.
- The Justice Department determines whether mergers should be challenged in particular industries.

TRY IT!

According to what basic principle did the U.S. Supreme Court find Eastman Kodak not guilty of violating antitrust laws? According to what basic principle did the Court block the merger of Brown Shoe Company and one of its competitors, United Shoe Machinery? Do you agree or disagree with the Court's choices?

Case in Point

Does Antitrust Policy Help Consumers?

© 2010 Jupiterimages Corporation

The Department of Justice and the Federal Trade Commission spend a great deal of money enforcing U.S. antitrust laws. Firms defending themselves may spend even more.

The government's first successful use of the Sherman Act came in its action against Standard Oil in 1911. The final decree broke Standard into 38 independent companies. Did the breakup make consumers better off?

In 1899, Standard controlled 88% of the market for refined oil products. But, by 1911, its share of the market had fallen to 64%. New discoveries of oil had sent gasoline prices down in the years before the ruling. After the ruling, gasoline prices began rising. It does not appear that the government's first major victory in an antitrust case had a positive impact on consumers.

In general, antitrust cases charging monopolization take so long to be resolved that, by the time a decree is issued, market conditions are likely to have changed in a way that makes the entire effort seem somewhat frivolous. For example, the government charged IBM with monopolization in 1966. That case was finally dropped in 1982 when the market had changed so much that the original premise of the case was no longer valid. In 1998, the Department of Justice began a case against Microsoft, accusing it of monopolizing the market for Internet browsers by bundling the browser with its operating system, Windows. A trial in 2000 ended with a judgment that Microsoft be split in two with one company having the operating system and another having applications. An appeals court overturned that decision a year later.

Actions against large firms such as Microsoft are politically popular. However, neither policy makers nor economists have been able to establish that they serve consumer interests.

We have seen that the Department of Justice and the Federal Trade Commission have a policy of preventing mergers in industries that are highly concentrated. But, mergers often benefit consumers by achieving reductions in cost. Perhaps the most surprising court ruling involving such a merger came in 1962 when the Supreme Court ruled that a merger in shoe manufacturing would achieve lower costs to consumers. The Court prevented the merger on grounds that the new company would be able to charge a lower price than its rivals! Clearly, the Court chose to protect firms rather than to enhance consumer welfare.

What about actions against price-fixing? The Department of Justice investigates roughly 100 price-fixing cases each year. In many cases, these investigations result in indictments. Those cases would, if justified, result in lower prices for consumers. But, economist Michael F. Sproul, in an examination of 25 price-fixing cases for which adequate data were available, found that prices actually *rose* in the four years following most indictments.

Economists Robert W. Crandall and Clifford Winston have asked a very important question: Has all of this effort enhanced consumer welfare? They conclude that the Department of Justice and the Federal Trade Commission would best serve the economy by following a policy of benign neglect in cases of monopolization, proposed mergers, and efforts by firms to exploit technological gains by lowering price. The economists conclude that antitrust actions should be limited to the most blatant cases of price-fixing or mergers that would result in monopolies. In contrast, law professor Jonathan Baker argued in the same journal that such a minimalist approach could be harmful to consumer welfare. One argument he makes is that antitrust laws and their enforcement create a deterrence effect.

A recent paper by Orley Ashenfelter and Daniel Hosken analyzed the impact of five mergers in the consumer products industry that seemed to be most problematic for antitrust enforcement agencies. In four of the five cases prices rose following the mergers and in the fifth case the merger had little effect on price. While they do not conclude that this small study should be used to determine the appropriate level of government enforcement of antitrust policy, they state that those who advocate less intervention should note that the price effects were not negative, as they would have been if these mergers were producing cost decreases and passing them on to consumers. Those advocating more intervention should note that the price increases they observed after these mergers were not very large.

Sources: Orley Ashenfelter and Daniel Hosken, "The Effect of Mergers on Consumer Prices: Evidence from Five Selected Cases," National Bureau of Economic Research Working Paper 13859, March 2008; James B. Baker, "The Case for Antitrust Enforcement," Journal of Economic Perspectives, 17:4 (Fall 2003): 27–50; Robert W. Crandall and Clifford Winston, "Does Antitrust Policy Improve Consumer Welfare? Assessing the Evidence," Journal of Economic Perspectives, 17:4 (Fall 2003): 3–26; Michael F. Sproul, "Antitrust and Prices," Journal of Political Economy, 101 (August 1993): 741–54.

ANSWER TO TRY IT! PROBLEM

In the case of Eastman Kodak, the Supreme Court argued that the rule of reason be applied. Even though the company held a dominant position in the film industry, its conduct was deemed reasonable. In the proposed merger between United Shoe Machinery and Brown Shoe, the court clearly chose to protect the welfare of firms in the industry rather than the welfare of consumers.

5. REVIEW AND PRACTICE

Summary

This chapter has examined the profit-maximizing behavior of monopoly firms. Monopoly occurs if an industry consists of a single firm and entry into that industry is blocked.

Potential sources of monopoly power include the existence of economies of scale over the range of market demand, locational advantages, high sunk costs associated with entry, restricted ownership of raw materials and inputs, and government restrictions such as licenses or patents. Network effects for certain products further increase the market power that patents afford.

Because the demand curve faced by the monopolist is downward-sloping, the firm is a price setter. It will maximize profits by producing the quantity of output at which marginal cost equals marginal revenue. The profit-maximizing price is then found on the demand curve for that quantity.

Because a typical monopolist holds market price above marginal cost, the major impact of monopoly is a reduction in efficiency. Compared to a competitive market, the monopoly is characterized by more centralized power, potential higher profits, and less pressure to be responsive to consumer preferences. Public policy toward monopoly includes antitrust laws and, in the case of natural monopolies, regulation of price and other aspects of the firm's behavior.

We saw that antitrust policy has evolved from a view that big business was bad business to an attempt to assess how the behavior of firms and the structure of markets affect social welfare and the public interest. The rule of reason rather than per se illegality guides most antitrust policy today, but because there is considerable debate concerning the appropriate role of government antitrust policy and regulation, application of the rule of reason in specific cases is uneven. Prosecution and enforcement of the nation's antitrust laws has varied over time.

CONCEPT PROBLEMS

1. Consider the following firms. Would you regard any of them as a monopoly? Why or why not? Could you use the monopoly model in analyzing the choices of any of them? Explain.

   a. the best restaurant in town

   b. your barber or beautician

   c. your local telephone company

   d. your campus bookstore

   e. Microsoft

   f. Amtrak

   g. the United States Postal Service

2. Explain the difference between the demand curve facing a monopoly firm and the demand curve facing a perfectly competitive firm.

3. What are the necessary conditions for a monopoly position in the market to be established?

4. A monopoly firm is free to charge any price it wishes. What constrains its choice of a price?

5. Suppose the government were to impose an annual license fee on a monopolist that just happened to be equal to its economic profits for a particular year. How would such a fee affect price and output? Do you think that such a fee would be appropriate? Why or why not?

6. Name one monopoly firm you deal with. What is the source of its monopoly power? Do you think it seeks to maximize its profits?

7. "A monopolist will never produce so much output as to operate in the inelastic portion of the demand curve." Explain.

8. "A monopoly is not efficient, and its pricing behavior leads to losses to society." What does this statement mean? Should society ban monopolies?

9. A small town located 30 miles from the nearest town has only one service station. Is the service station a monopoly? Why or why not?

10. Explain why under monopoly price is greater than marginal revenue, while under perfect competition price is equal to marginal revenue.

11. In what sense can the monopoly equilibrium be considered inequitable?

12. What is a natural monopoly? Should a natural monopoly be allowed to exist?

13. Give some examples of industries in which you think natural monopoly conditions are likely to prevail. Why do you think so?

14. People often blame the high prices for events such as professional football and basketball and baseball games on the high salaries of professional athletes. Assuming one of these teams is a monopoly, use the model to refute this argument.

15. How do the following events affect a monopoly firm's price and output? How does each affect the firm's profits? Illustrate your answers graphically.

    a. an increase in labor costs in the market in which the firm operates

    b. a reduction in the price of gasoline

    c. the firm's Chief Executive Officer persuades the Board to increase his or her annual salary

    d. demand for the firm's product falls

    e. demand for the firm's product rises

    f. the price of a substitute for the firm's product rises

16. What are the major distinctions between a monopolistically competitive industry and an oligopolistic industry?

17. What is the difference between a price taker and a price setter? Which do you think a firm would prefer to be? Why?

18. Apex Manufacturing charges Zenith Manufacturing with predatory pricing (that is, selling below cost). What do you think the antitrust authorities will want to consider before they determine whether to prosecute Zenith for unfair practices in restraint of trade?

19. What is so bad about price-fixing? Why does the government prohibit it?

20. The Case in Point on the efficacy of antitrust enforcement painted a rather negative view of antitrust enforcement. Do you agree with this assessment? Why or why not?

NUMERICAL PROBLEMS

1. A university football team estimates that it faces the demand schedule shown for tickets for each home game it plays. The team plays in a stadium that holds 60,000 fans. It estimates that its marginal cost of attendance, and thus for tickets sold, is zero.

Price per ticket	Tickets per game
$100	0
80	20,000
60	40,000
40	60,000
20	80,000
0	100,000

   a. Draw the demand and marginal revenue curves. Compute the team's profit-maximizing price and the number of tickets it will sell at that price.

   b. Determine the price elasticity of demand at the price you determined in part (a).

   c. How much total revenue will the team earn?

   d. Now suppose the city in which the university is located imposes a $10,000 annual license fee on all suppliers of sporting events, including the University. How does this affect the price of tickets?

   e. Suppose the team increases its spending for scholarships for its athletes. How will this affect ticket prices, assuming that it continues to maximize profit?

   f. Now suppose that the city imposes a tax of $10 per ticket sold. How would this affect the price charged by the team?

2. A monopoly firm faces a demand curve given by the following equation: $P = \$500 - 10Q$, where Q equals quantity sold per day. Its marginal cost curve is $MC = \$100$ per day. Assume that the firm faces no fixed cost.

   a. How much will the firm produce?

   b. How much will it charge?

   c. Can you determine its profit per day? (Hint: you can; state how much it is.)

   d. Suppose a tax of $1,000 per day is imposed on the firm. How will this affect its price?

   e. How would the $1,000 per day tax affect its output per day?

   f. How would the $1,000 per day tax affect its profit per day?

   g. Now suppose a tax of $100 per unit is imposed. How will this affect the firm's price?

   h. How would a $100 per unit tax affect the firm's profit maximizing output per day?

   i. How would the $100 per unit tax affect the firm's profit per day?

CHAPTER 9
Wages and Employment in Perfect Competition

START UP: COLLEGE PAYS

On NBC's 2005 television series, *The Apprentice: Street Smarts vs. Book Smarts*, the contestants without college degrees who were chosen for the program were earning three times as much as those with college degrees. The two sides fought valiantly against each other, and the final episode pitted 37 year old, "street smart" Tana, a top-selling sales woman for Mary Kay, against 26 year old, "book smart" Kendra, a real estate agent. At the end of the Apprentice series, it was Kendra, the college graduate, to whom Donald Trump shouted, "You're hired!" As the array of contestants in the series demonstrates, not every college graduate earns more than every high school graduate, but on average, that is certainly the case.

One way of measuring the payoff from college is to compare the extent to which the wages of college-trained workers exceed the wages of high school–trained workers. In the United States the payoff from college has soared over the last 30 years.

In 1979, male college graduates 25 years of age and older earned 30% more than male high school graduates in the same age bracket. By 2009 the gap had increased more than two and a half times—male college graduates earned a stunning 79% more than male high school graduates. Female college graduates gained as well. Female college graduates 25 years of age and older earned 56% more than their high school–educated counterparts in 1979; that gap increased to a whopping 96% by 2009.

The dramatic widening of the wage gap between workers with different levels of education reflects the operation of demand and supply in the market for labor. For reasons we will explore in this chapter, the demand for college graduates was increasing while the demand for high school graduates—particularly male high school graduates—was slumping.

Why would the demand curves for different kinds of labor shift? What determines the demand for labor? What about the supply? How do changes in demand and supply affect wages and employment? In this chapter we will answer those questions in the context of a perfectly competitive market for labor. Analyses of markets for other factors of production or for labor when the market is not perfectly competitive are beyond the scope of this book.

FIGURE 9.1 Labor's Share of U.S. Income, 1960–2010

Workers have accounted for 70% of all the income earned in the United States since 1960. The remaining income was generated by capital and natural resources.

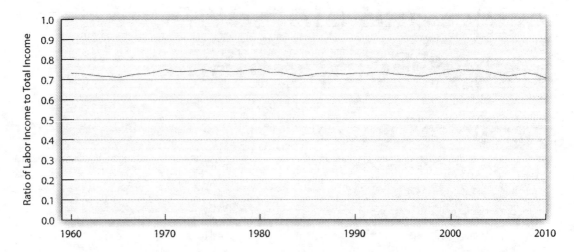

Labor generates considerably more income in the economy than all other factors of production combined. Figure 9.1 shows the share of total income earned annually by workers in the United States since 1960. Labor accounts for roughly 71% of the income earned in the U.S. economy. The rest is generated by owners of capital and of natural resources.

We calculate the total income earned by workers by multiplying their average wage times the number of workers employed. We can view the labor market as a single market, as suggested in Panel (a) of Figure 9.2. Here we assume that all workers are identical, that there is a single market for them, and that they all earn the same wage, W; the level of employment is L. Although the assumption of a single labor market flies wildly in the face of reality, economists often use it to highlight broad trends in the market. For example, if we want to show the impact of an increase in the demand for labor throughout the economy, we can show labor as a single market in which the increase in demand raises wages and employment.

But we can also use demand and supply analysis to focus on the market for a particular group of workers. We might examine the market for plumbers, beauticians, or chiropractors. We might even want to focus on the market for, say, clerical workers in the Boston area. In such cases, we would examine the demand for and the supply of a particular segment of workers, as suggested by the graphs in Panel (b) of Figure 9.2.

Macroeconomic analysis typically makes use of the highly aggregated approach to labor-market analysis illustrated in Panel (a), where labor is viewed as a single market. Microeconomic analysis typically assesses particular markets for labor, as suggested in Panel (b).

When we use the model of demand and supply to analyze the determination of wages and employment, we are assuming that market forces, not individuals, determine wages in the economy. The model says that equilibrium wages are determined by the intersection of the demand and supply curves for labor in a particular market. Workers and firms in the market are thus price takers; they take the market-determined wage as given and respond to it. We are, in this instance, assuming that perfect competition prevails in the labor market. Just as there are some situations in the analysis of markets for goods and services for which such an assumption is inappropriate, so there are some cases in which the assumption is inappropriate for labor markets. In this chapter, however, we will find that the assumption of perfect competition can give us important insights into the forces that determine wages and employment levels for workers.

FIGURE 9.2 Alternative Views of the Labor Market

One way to analyze the labor market is to assume that it is a single market with identical workers, as in Panel (a). Alternatively, we could examine specific pieces of the market, focusing on particular job categories or even on job categories in particular regions, as the graphs in Panel (b) suggest.

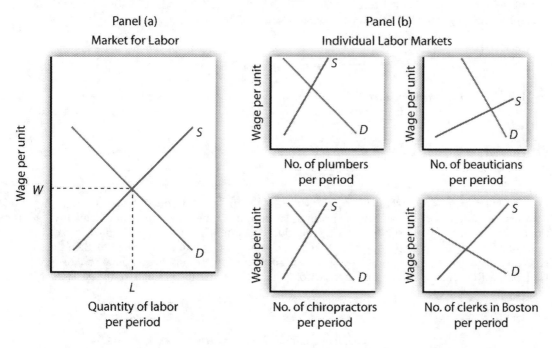

We will begin our analysis of labor markets in the next section by looking at the forces that influence the demand for labor. In the following section we will turn to supply. In the final section, we will use what we have learned to look at labor markets at work.

1. THE DEMAND FOR LABOR

LEARNING OBJECTIVES

1. Apply the marginal decision rule to determine the quantity of labor that a firm in a perfectly competitive market will demand and illustrate this quantity graphically using the marginal revenue product and marginal factor cost curves.
2. Describe how to find the market demand curve for labor and discuss the factors that can cause the market demand curve for labor to shift.

A firm must have labor to produce goods and services. But how much labor will the firm employ? A profit-maximizing firm will base its decision to hire additional units of labor on the marginal decision rule: If the extra output that is produced by hiring one more unit of labor adds more to total revenue than it adds to total cost, the firm will increase profit by increasing its use of labor. It will continue to hire more and more labor up to the point that the extra revenue generated by the additional labor no longer exceeds the extra cost of the labor.

For example, if a computer software company could increase its annual total revenue by $50,000 by hiring a programmer at a cost of $49,000 per year, the marginal decision rule says that it should do so. Since the programmer will add $49,000 to total cost and $50,000 to total revenue, hiring the programmer will increase the company's profit by $1,000. If still another programmer would increase annual total revenue by $48,000 but would also add $49,000 to the firm's total cost, that programmer should not be hired because he or she would add less to total revenue than to total cost and would reduce profit.

1.1 Marginal Revenue Product and Marginal Factor Cost

marginal revenue product

The amount that an additional unit of a factor adds to a firm's total revenue during a period.

The amount that an additional unit of a factor adds to a firm's total revenue during a period is called the **marginal revenue product (MRP)** of the factor. An additional unit of a factor of production adds to a firm's revenue in a two-step process: first, it increases the firm's output. Second, the increased output increases the firm's total revenue. We find marginal revenue product by multiplying the marginal product *(MP)* of the factor by the marginal revenue *(MR)*.

EQUATION 9.1

$$MRP = MP \times MR$$

In a perfectly competitive market the marginal revenue a firm receives equals the market-determined price *P*. Therefore, for firms in perfect competition, we can express marginal revenue product as follows:

EQUATION 9.2

$$\text{In perfect competition, } MRP = MP \times P$$

The marginal revenue product of labor (MRP_L) is the marginal product of labor (MP_L) times the marginal revenue (which is the same as price under perfect competition) the firm obtains from additional units of output that result from hiring the additional unit of labor. If an additional worker adds 4 units of output per day to a firm's production, and if each of those 4 units sells for $20, then the worker's marginal revenue product is $80 per day. With perfect competition, the marginal revenue product for labor, MRP_L, equals the marginal product of labor, MP_L, times the price, *P*, of the good or service the labor produces:

EQUATION 9.3

$$\text{In perfect competition, } MRP_L = MP_L \times P$$

The law of diminishing marginal returns tells us that if the quantity of a factor is increased while other inputs are held constant, its marginal product will eventually decline. If marginal product is falling, marginal revenue product must be falling as well.

Suppose that an accountant, Stephanie Lancaster, has started an evening call-in tax advisory service. Between the hours of 7 p.m. and 10 p.m., customers can call and get advice on their income taxes. Ms. Lancaster's firm, TeleTax, is one of several firms offering similar advice; the going market price is $10 per call. Ms. Lancaster's business has expanded, so she hires other accountants to handle the calls. She must determine how many accountants to hire.

As Ms. Lancaster adds accountants, her service can take more calls. The table in Figure 9.3 gives the relationship between the number of accountants available to answer calls each evening and the number of calls TeleTax handles. Panel (a) shows the increase in the number of calls handled by each additional accountant—that accountant's marginal product. The first accountant can handle 13 calls per evening. Adding a second accountant increases the number of calls handled by 20. With two accountants, a degree of specialization is possible if each accountant takes calls dealing with questions about which he or she has particular expertise. Hiring the third accountant increases TeleTax's output per evening by 23 calls.

Suppose the accountants share a fixed facility for screening and routing calls. They also share a stock of reference materials to use in answering calls. As more accountants are added, the firm will begin to experience diminishing marginal returns. The fourth accountant increases output by 20 calls. The marginal product of additional accountants continues to decline after that. The marginal product curve shown in Panel (a) of Figure 9.3 thus rises and then falls.

Each call TeleTax handles increases the firm's revenues by $10. To obtain marginal revenue product, we multiply the marginal product of each accountant by $10; the marginal revenue product curve is shown in Panel (b) of Figure 9.3.

FIGURE 9.3   Marginal Product and Marginal Revenue Product

The table gives the relationship between the number of accountants employed by TeleTax each evening and the total number of calls handled. From these values we derive the marginal product and marginal revenue product curves.

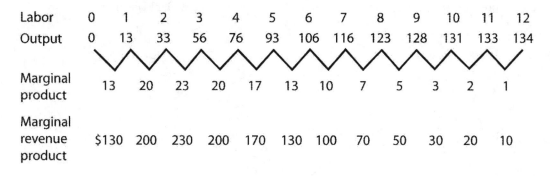

Labor	0	1	2	3	4	5	6	7	8	9	10	11	12
Output	0	13	33	56	76	93	106	116	123	128	131	133	134
Marginal product		13	20	23	20	17	13	10	7	5	3	2	1
Marginal revenue product		$130	200	230	200	170	130	100	70	50	30	20	10

Panel (a)

Panel (b)

At a price of $10 per call, the marginal revenue product of labor is found by multiplying the marginal product of each unit of labor by $10.

We can use Ms. Lancaster's marginal revenue product curve to determine the quantity of labor she will hire. Suppose accountants in her area are available to offer tax advice for a nightly fee of $150. Each additional accountant Ms. Lancaster hires thus adds $150 per night to her total cost. The amount a factor adds to a firm's total cost per period is called its **marginal factor cost (MFC)**. Marginal factor cost (MFC) is the change in total cost (ΔTC) divided by the change in the quantity of the factor (Δf):

marginal factor cost

The amount that an additional unit of a factor adds to a firm's total cost per period.

EQUATION 9.4

$$MFC = \frac{\Delta TC}{\Delta f}$$

The marginal factor cost to TeleTax of additional accountants ($150 per night) is shown as a horizontal line in Figure 9.4. It is simply the market wage (i.e., the price per unit of labor).

FIGURE 9.4 Marginal Revenue Product and Demand

The downward-sloping portion of a firm's marginal revenue product curve is its demand curve for a variable factor. At a marginal factor cost of $150, TeleTax hires the services of five accountants.

TeleTax will maximize profit by hiring additional units of labor up to the point where the downward-sloping portion of the marginal revenue product curve intersects the marginal factor cost curve; we see in Figure 9.4 that it will hire five accountants. Based on the information given in the table in Figure 9.3, we know that the five accountants will handle a total of 93 calls per evening; TeleTax will earn total revenue of $930 per evening. The firm pays $750 for the services of the five accountants—that leaves $180 to apply to the fixed cost associated with the tax advice service and the implicit cost of Stephanie Lancaster's effort in organizing the service. Recall that these implicit costs include the income forgone (that is, opportunity cost) by not shifting her resources, including her own labor, to her next best alternative.

If TeleTax had to pay a higher price for accountants, it would face a higher marginal factor cost curve and would hire fewer accountants. If the price were lower, TeleTax would hire more accountants. The downward-sloping portion of TeleTax's marginal revenue product curve shows the number of accountants it will hire at each price for accountants; it is thus the firm's demand curve for accountants. It is the portion of the curve that exhibits diminishing returns, and a firm will always seek to operate in the range of diminishing returns to the factors it uses.

It may seem counterintuitive that firms do not operate in the range of increasing returns, which would correspond to the upward-sloping portion of the marginal revenue product curve. However, to do so would forgo profit-enhancing opportunities. For example, in Figure 9.4, adding the second accountant adds $200 to revenue but only $150 to cost, so hiring that accountant clearly adds to profit. But why stop there? What about hiring a third accountant? That additional hire adds even more to revenue ($230) than to cost. In the region of increasing returns, marginal revenue product rises. With marginal factor cost constant, not to continue onto the downward-sloping part of the marginal revenue curve would be to miss out on profit-enhancing opportunities. The firm continues adding accountants until doing so no longer adds more to revenue than to cost, and that necessarily occurs where the marginal revenue product curve slopes downward.

In general, then, we can interpret the downward-sloping portion of a firm's marginal revenue product curve for a factor as its demand curve for that factor.[1] We find the market demand for labor by adding the demand curves for individual firms.

Heads Up!

The Two Rules Lead to the Same Outcome

In the chapter on competitive output markets we learned that profit-maximizing firms will increase output so long as doing so adds more to revenue than to cost, or up to the point where marginal revenue, which in perfect competition is the same as the market-determined price, equals marginal cost. In this chapter we have learned that profit-maximizing firms will hire labor up to the point where marginal revenue product equals marginal factor cost. Is it possible that a firm that follows the marginal decision rule for hiring labor would end up producing a different quantity of output compared to the quantity of output it would choose if it followed the marginal decision rule for deciding directly how much output to produce? Is there a conflict between these two marginal decision rules?

The answer is no. These two marginal decision rules are really just two ways of saying the same thing: one rule is in terms of quantity of output and the other in terms of the quantity of factors required to produce that quantity of output. Hiring an additional unit of a factor means producing a certain amount of additional output.

Using the example of TeleTax, at $150 per accountant per night, we found that Ms. Lancaster maximizes profit by hiring five accountants. The MP_L of the fifth accountant is ΔQ; it is 17. At five accountants, the marginal cost of a call is $\Delta TC/\Delta Q = \$150/17 = \$8.82$, which is less than the price of $10 per call, so hiring that accountant adds to her profit. At six accountants, the marginal cost of a call would be $150/13 = \$11.54$, which is greater than the $10 price, so hiring a sixth accountant would lower profit. The profit-maximizing output of 93 calls, found by comparing marginal cost and price, is thus consistent with the profit-maximizing quantity of labor of five accountants, found by comparing marginal revenue product and marginal factor cost.

1.2   Shifts in Labor Demand

The fact that a firm's demand curve for labor is given by the downward-sloping portion of its marginal revenue product of labor curve provides a guide to the factors that will shift the curve. In perfect competition, marginal revenue product equals the marginal product of labor times the price of the good that the labor is involved in producing; anything that changes either of those two variables will shift the curve. The marginal revenue product of labor will change when there is a change in the quantities of other factors employed. It will also change as a result of a change in technology, a change in the price of the good being produced, or a change in the number of firms hiring the labor.

Changes in the Use of Other Factors of Production

As a firm changes the quantities of different factors of production it uses, the marginal product of labor may change. Having more reference manuals, for example, is likely to make additional accountants more productive—it will increase their marginal product. That increase in their marginal product would increase the demand for accountants. When an increase in the use of one factor of production increases the demand for another, the two factors are **complementary factors of production**.

One important complement of labor is human capital, the set of skills and abilities workers bring to the production of goods and services. When workers gain additional human capital, their marginal product rises. The demand for them by firms thus increases. This is perhaps one reason why you have decided to pursue a college education.

Other inputs may be regarded as substitutes for each other. A robot, for example, may substitute for some kinds of assembly-line labor. Two factors are **substitute factors of production** if the increased use of one lowers the demand for the other.

Changes in Technology

Technological changes can increase the demand for some workers and reduce the demand for others. The production of a more powerful computer chip, for example, may increase the demand for software engineers. It may also allow other production processes to be computerized and thus reduce the demand for workers who had been employed in those processes.

Technological changes have significantly increased the economy's output over the past century. The application of sophisticated technologies to production processes has boosted the marginal products of workers who have the skills these technologies require. That has increased the demand for skilled workers. The same technologies have been a substitute for less-skilled workers, and the demand for those workers has fallen. As the Case in Point on the impact of computer technology implies, envisioning the impact of technological change on demand for different kinds of labor may be something to

complementary factors of production

Factors of production for which an increase in the use of one increases the demand for the other.

substitute factors of production

Factors of production for which an increase in the use of one decreases the demand for the other.

keep in mind as you consider educational options. As you consider your major, for example, you should keep in mind that some occupations may benefit from technological changes; others may not.

Changes in Product Demand

derived demand

Refers to the idea that demand for factors of production depends on the demand for the products that use the factors of production.

A change in demand for a final product changes its price, at least in the short run. An increase in the demand for a product increases its price and increases the demand for factors that produce the product. A reduction in demand for a product reduces its price and reduces the demand for the factors used in producing it. Because the demand for factors that produce a product depends on the demand for the product itself, factor demand is said to be **derived demand**. That is, factor demand is derived from the demand for the product that uses the factor in its production.

Suppose, for example, that the demand for airplanes increases. The price and quantity of airplanes available will go up. A higher price for airplanes increases the marginal revenue product of labor of airplane-assembly workers and thus increases the demand for these workers.

Just as increases in the demand for particular goods or services increase the demand for the workers that produce them, so reductions in demand for particular goods or services will reduce the demand for the workers that produce them. An example is the relationship between the demand for train travel and the demand for conductors. Over the years, the fall in demand for train travel has reduced the demand for railroad conductors.

Changes in the Number of Firms

We can determine the demand curve for any factor by adding the demand for that factor by each of the firms using it. If more firms employ the factor, the demand curve shifts to the right. A reduction in the number of firms shifts the demand curve to the left. For example, if the number of restaurants in an area increases, the demand for waiters and waitresses in the area goes up. We expect to see local wages for these workers rise as a result.

KEY TAKEAWAYS

- In using the model of demand and supply to examine labor markets, we assume in this chapter that perfect competition exists—that all workers and employers are price takers.
- A firm's demand curve for a factor is the downward-sloping portion of the marginal revenue product curve of the factor.
- The market demand for labor is found by adding the demand curves for labor of individual firms.
- The market demand for labor will change as a result of a change in the use of a complementary input or a substitute input, a change in technology, a change in the price of the good produced by labor, or a change in the number of firms that employ the labor.

TRY IT!

How would each of the following affect the demand for labor by the accounting advice service, TeleTax, described in this chapter?

1. A reduction in the market price for a tax advice call
2. An increase in the market fee for the accountants that TeleTax hires
3. An increase in the marginal product of each accountant due to an expansion of the facility for screening and routing calls and an increase in the number of reference materials available to the accountants

Case in Point

Computer Technology Increases the Demand for Some Workers and Reduces the Demand for Others

© 2010 Jupiterimages Corporation

"…[M]oving an object, performing a calculation, communicating a piece of information or resolving a discrepancy…[W]hich of these tasks can be performed by a computer?" ask economists David H. Autor, Frank Levy, and Richard J. Murname.

In general, computers are good at performing routine tasks and substitute for labor that had performed such tasks in the past. Conversely, computers are complements for workers performing nonroutine tasks, i.e., tasks that require such attributes as creativity, flexibility, and problem-solving. As the price of computers has fallen in recent decades, the demand for labor performing nonroutine tasks, usually college-educated workers, has grown, while the demand for labor performing routine tasks has fallen. The chart below illustrates how computerization likely affects demand for different kinds of labor.

	Routine Tasks	Nonroutine Tasks
Analytic and Interactive Tasks		
Examples:	• Record-keeping • Calculation • Repetitive customer service (e.g., bank teller)	• Forming/testing hypotheses • Medical diagnosis • Legal writing • Persuading/selling • Managing others
Computer Impact:	• Substantial substitution	• Strong complementarities
Manual Tasks		
Examples:	• Picking or sording • Repetitive assembly	• Janitorial services • Truck driving
Computer Impact:	• Substantial substitution	• Limited opportunities for substitution or complementary

In studying the impact of computerization on labor demand, the study's authors have also noted that changes in the nature of certain tasks ("task-shifting") stemming from computerization have markedly changed what an occupation encompasses.

For example, the Department of Labor's *Occupation Outlook Handbook* in 1976 described what secretaries do as: "Secretaries relieve their employers of routine duties so they can work on more important matters. Although most secretaries type, take shorthand, and deal with callers, the time spent on these duties varies in different types of organizations." In contrast, the 2000 edition of the *Handbook* describes the work of secretaries quite differently: "As technology continues to expand in offices across the Nation, the role of the secretary has greatly evolved. Office automation and organizational restructuring have led secretaries to assume a wide range of new responsibilities once reserved for managerial and professional staff. Many secretaries now provide training and orientation to new staff, conduct research on the Internet, and learn to operate new office technologies." The authors find that this task-shifting within occupations, away from routine tasks and towards nonroutine tasks, is pervasive.

Source: David H. Autor, Frank Levy, and Richard J. Murname, "The Skill Content of Recent Technological Change: An Empirical Exploration," Quarterly Journal of Economics, 118: 4 (November 2003): 1279–1333.

ANSWERS TO TRY IT! PROBLEMS

1. A reduction in market price would decrease the marginal revenue product of labor. Since the demand for labor is the downward-sloping portion of the marginal revenue product curve, the demand for labor by TeleTax would shift to the left.

2. An increase in the market fee that TeleTax pays the accountants it hires corresponds to an increase in marginal factor cost. TeleTax's demand curve would not shift; rather TeleTax would move up along its same demand curve for accountants. As a result, TeleTax would hire fewer accountants.

3. An increase in the marginal product of each accountant corresponds to a rightward shift in the marginal revenue product curve and hence a rightward shift in TeleTax's demand curve for accountants.

2. THE SUPPLY OF LABOR

LEARNING OBJECTIVES

1. **Explain the shape of the labor supply curve.**
2. **Discuss the factors that can cause the supply curve for labor to shift.**

The demand for labor is one determinant of the equilibrium wage and equilibrium quantity of labor in a perfectly competitive market. The supply of labor, of course, is the other.

Economists think of the supply of labor as a problem in which individuals weigh the opportunity cost of various activities that can fill an available amount of time and choose how to allocate it. Everyone has 24 hours in a day. There are lots of uses to which we can put our time: we can raise children, work, sleep, play, or participate in volunteer efforts. To simplify our analysis, let us assume that there are two ways in which an individual can spend his or her time: in work or in leisure. Leisure is a type of consumption good; individuals gain utility directly from it. Work provides income that, in turn, can be used to purchase goods and services that generate utility.

The more work a person does, the greater his or her income, but the smaller the amount of leisure time available. An individual who chooses more leisure time will earn less income than would otherwise be possible. There is thus a tradeoff between leisure and the income that can be earned from work. We can think of the supply of labor as the flip side of the demand for leisure. The more leisure people demand, the less labor they supply.

Two aspects of the demand for leisure play a key role in understanding the supply of labor. First, leisure is a normal good. All other things unchanged, an increase in income will increase the demand for leisure. Second, the opportunity cost or "price" of leisure is the wage an individual can earn. A worker who can earn $10 per hour gives up $10 in income by consuming an extra hour of leisure. The $10 wage is thus the price of an hour of leisure. A worker who can earn $20 an hour faces a higher price of leisure.

2.1 Wage Changes and the Slope of the Supply Curve

Suppose wages rise. The higher wage increases the price of leisure. To put it another way, *ceteris paribus*, the higher wage induces the individual to supply a greater quantity of labor.

But the higher wage also affects income. An increased wage means a higher income, and since leisure is a normal good, the quantity of leisure demanded will go up. And that means a *reduction* in the quantity of labor supplied. With these two forces working in opposite directions, it is not clear whether a wage increase will increase or decrease the quantity of labor supplied—or leave it unchanged.

Figure 9.5 illustrates the opposite pull of these two forces of a wage change facing an individual worker. A janitor, Meredith Wilson, earns $10 per hour. She now works 42 hours per week, on average, earning $420.

FIGURE 9.5 The Effects of a Wage Change

At a wage of $10 per hour, she supplies 42 hours of work per week (point A). At $15 per hour, on the one hand, she wants to substitute more labor for labor, which pulls in the direction of an increased quantity of labor supplied. On the other hand, though, the higher income from the wage increase pulls in the opposite direction.

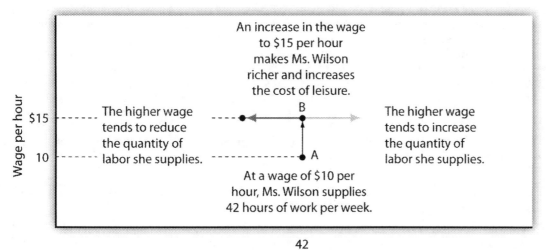

Now suppose Ms. Wilson receives a $5 raise to $15 per hour. As shown in Figure 9.5, on the one hand, the effect of the wage change induces her to increase the quantity of labor she supplies; she substitutes some of her leisure time for additional hours of work. But she is richer now; she can afford more leisure. At a wage of $10 per hour, she was earning $420 per week. She could earn that same amount at the higher wage in just 28 hours. With her higher income, she can certainly afford more leisure time. Looking only at the effect on income, the quantity of labor supplied falls. The effect of the wage increase on the quantity of labor Ms. Wilson actually supplies depends on the relative strength of these two forces.

FIGURE 9.6 A Backward-Bending Supply Curve for Labor

As the wage rate increases from $10 to $15 per hour, the quantity of labor Meredith Wilson supplies increases from 42 to 48 hours per week. As the wage rises above $15, Ms. Wilson's supply curve becomes a vertical line between points B and C. As the wage rises above $20, the supply curve bends backward between points C and D.

What would any one individual's supply curve for labor look like? Figure 9.6 shows Meredith Wilson's supply curve for labor. At a wage of $10 per hour, she supplies 42 hours of work per week (point A). An increase in her wage to $15 per hour boosts her quantity supplied to 48 hours per week (point B). Over this range of wages, she is more strongly pulled by the higher wage to increase the number of hours she works than she is lured by the higher income that wage allows to consume more leisure.

It is possible that beyond some wage rate, these two forces could just offset each other; over that range, a higher wage would have no effect on the quantity of labor supplied. That possibility is illustrated between points B and C on the supply curve in Figure 9.6; Ms. Wilson's supply curve is vertical. As wages continue to rise, the pull of higher income becomes even stronger, and additional increases in the wage reduce the quantity of labor she supplies. The supply curve illustrated here bends backward beyond point C and thus assumes a negative slope. The supply curve for labor can thus slope upward over part of its range, become vertical, and then bend backward.

It is quite likely that some individuals have backward-bending supply curves for labor—beyond some point, a higher wage induces those individuals to work less, not more. However, supply curves for labor in specific labor markets are generally upward sloping. As wages in one industry rise relative to wages in other industries, workers shift their labor to the relatively high-wage one. An increased quantity of labor is supplied in that industry. While some exceptions have been found, the mobility of labor between competitive labor markets is likely to prevent the total number of hours worked from falling as the wage rate increases. Thus we shall assume that supply curves for labor in particular markets are upward sloping.

2.2   Shifts in Labor Supply

What events shift the supply curve for labor? People supply labor in order to increase their utility—just as they demand goods and services in order to increase their utility. The supply curve for labor will shift in response to changes in the same set of factors that shift demand curves for goods and services.

Changes in Preferences

A change in attitudes toward work and leisure can shift the supply curve for labor. If people decide they value leisure more highly, they will work fewer hours at each wage, and the supply curve for labor will shift to the left. If they decide they want more goods and services, the supply curve is likely to shift to the right.

Changes in Income

An increase in income will increase the demand for leisure, reducing the supply of labor. We must be careful here to distinguish movements along the supply curve from shifts of the supply curve itself. An income change resulting from a change in wages is shown by a movement along the curve; it produces the income and substitution effects we already discussed. But suppose income is from some other source: a person marries and has access to a spouse's income, or receives an inheritance, or wins a lottery. Those nonlabor increases in income are likely to reduce the supply of labor, thereby shifting the supply curve for labor of the recipients to the left.

Changes in the Prices of Related Goods and Services

Several goods and services are complements of labor. If the cost of child care (a complement to work effort) falls, for example, it becomes cheaper for workers to go to work, and the supply of labor tends to increase. If recreational activities (which are a substitute for work effort) become much cheaper, individuals might choose to consume more leisure time and supply less labor.

Changes in Population

An increase in population increases the supply of labor; a reduction lowers it. Labor organizations have generally opposed increases in immigration because their leaders fear that the increased number of workers will shift the supply curve for labor to the right and put downward pressure on wages.

Changes in Expectations

One change in expectations that could have an effect on labor supply is life expectancy. Another is confidence in the availability of Social Security. Suppose, for example, that people expect to live longer yet become less optimistic about their likely benefits from Social Security. That could induce an increase in labor supply.

Labor Supply in Specific Markets

The supply of labor in particular markets could be affected by changes in any of the variables we have already examined—changes in preferences, incomes, prices of related goods and services, population, and expectations. In addition to these variables that affect the supply of labor in general, there are changes that could affect supply in specific labor markets.

A change in wages in related occupations could affect supply in another. A sharp reduction in the wages of surgeons, for example, could induce more physicians to specialize in, say, family practice, increasing the supply of doctors in that field. Improved job opportunities for women in other fields appear to have decreased the supply of nurses, shifting the supply curve for nurses to the left.

The supply of labor in a particular market could also shift because of a change in entry requirements. Most states, for example, require barbers and beauticians to obtain training before entering the profession. Elimination of such requirements would increase the supply of these workers. Financial planners have, in recent years, sought the introduction of tougher licensing requirements, which would reduce the supply of financial planners.

Worker preferences regarding specific occupations can also affect labor supply. A reduction in willingness to take risks could lower the supply of labor available for risky occupations such as farm work (the most dangerous work in the United States), law enforcement, and fire fighting. An increased desire to work with children could raise the supply of child-care workers, elementary school teachers, and pediatricians.

KEY TAKEAWAYS

- A higher wage increases the opportunity cost or price of leisure and increases worker incomes. The effects of these two changes pull the quantity of labor supplied in opposite directions.

- Thus an individual's supply curve of labor may be positively or negatively sloped or may have sections that are positively sloped, sections that are negatively sloped, and vertical sections. While some exceptions have been found, the labor supply curves for specific labor markets are generally upward sloping.

- The supply curve for labor will shift as a result of a change in worker preferences, a change in nonlabor income, a change in the prices of related goods and services, a change in population, or a change in expectations.

- In addition to the effects on labor supply of the variables just cited, other factors that can change the supply of labor in particular markets are changes in wages in related markets or changes in entry requirements.

TRY IT!

Economists Laura Duberstein and Karen Oppenheim Mason analyzed the labor-supply decisions of 1,383 mothers with preschool-aged children in the Detroit Metropolitan area.[2]

They found that respondents were more likely to work the higher the wage, less likely to work if they preferred a traditional family structure with a husband as the primary breadwinner, less likely to work if they felt that care provided by others was strongly inferior to a mother's care, and less likely to work if child-care costs were higher. Given these findings, explain how each of the following would affect the labor supply of mothers with preschool-aged children.

1. An increase in the wage
2. An increase in the preference for a traditional family structure
3. An increased sense that child care is inferior to a mother's care
4. An increase in the cost of child care

(Remember to distinguish between movements along the curve and shifts of the curve.) Is the labor supply curve positively or negatively sloped?

Case in Point

An Airline Pilot's Lament

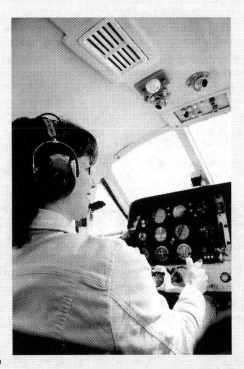

© 2010 Jupiterimages Corporation

Arguably, no single sector of the U.S. economy was hit harder by the events of 9/11 than the airline industry. By the time passengers did start returning, though, more than just the routine of getting through airport security had changed. Rather, the structure of the industry had begun to shift from domination by large national carriers—such as Delta, American, and United—operating according to the hub-and-spoke model, to increased competition from lower-cost regional carriers offering point-to-point service. Efforts by the large carriers in the early 2000s to reign in their costs and restore their financial health led to agreements with their labor unions that resulted in lower wages for most categories of airline workers.

How have airline employees responded to lower wages? Some categories of workers, such as mechanics, have little flexibility in deciding how many hours to work, but others, such as pilots, do. The following is an explanation of the impact of wages cuts on the labor supply from a female pilot who works for a major airline:

We were normally scheduled for anywhere from 15 to 18 days a month, which translated into 80 to 95 hours of flying and around 280 hours of duty time. Duty time includes flight planning, preflighting, crew briefing, boarding, preflight checks of the airplane, etc. We bid for a monthly schedule that would fall somewhere in that range. After we were assigned our schedule for a month, we usually had the flexibility to drop or trade trips within certain constraints. Without going into the vast complexities of our contract, I can tell you that, in general, we were allowed to drop down to 10 days a month, provided the company could cover the trips we wanted to drop, and still be considered a full-time employee. Generally, at that time, my goal was to work a minimum of 10 to 12 days a month and a maximum of 15 days a month.

After the first round of pay cuts, the typical month became 16 to 20 days of flying. With that round of pay cuts, my general goal became to work a minimum of 15 days a month and a maximum of 17 days a month. I imagine that with another round of cuts my goal would be to keep my pay as high as I possibly can.

Basically, I have a target income in mind. Anything above that was great, but I chose to have more days at home rather than more pay. As my target income became more difficult to achieve, I chose to work more days and hours to keep close to my target income…When total compensation drops by more than 50% it is difficult to keep your financial head above water no matter how well you have budgeted.

Source: personal interview.

ANSWER TO TRY IT! PROBLEM

The first question is about willingness to work as the wage rate changes. It thus refers to movement along the labor supply curve. That mothers of preschool-age children are more willing to work the higher the wage implies an upward-sloping labor supply curve. The other three questions refer to factors that cause the labor supply curve to shift. In all three cases, the circumstances imply that the labor supply curve would shift to the left.

3.   LABOR MARKETS AT WORK

LEARNING OBJECTIVES

1. **Explain and illustrate how wage and employment levels are determined in a perfectly competitive market and for an individual firm within that market.**
2. **Describe the forces that can raise or lower the equilibrium wage in a competitive market and illustrate these processes.**
3. **Describe the ways that government can increase wages and incomes.**

We have seen that a firm's demand for labor depends on the marginal product of labor and the price of the good the firm produces. We add the demand curves of individual firms to obtain the market demand curve for labor. The supply curve for labor depends on variables such as population and worker preferences. Supply in a particular market depends on variables such as worker preferences, the skills and training a job requires, and wages available in alternative occupations. Wages are determined by the intersection of demand and supply.

Once the wage in a particular market has been established, individual firms in perfect competition take it as given. Because each firm is a price taker, it faces a horizontal supply curve for labor at the market wage. For one firm, changing the quantity of labor it hires does not change the wage. In the context of the model of perfect competition, buyers and sellers are price takers. That means that a firm's choices in hiring labor do not affect the wage.

The operation of labor markets in perfect competition is illustrated in Figure 9.7. The wage W_1 is determined by the intersection of demand and supply in Panel (a). Employment equals L_1 units of labor per period. An individual firm takes that wage as given; it is the supply curve s_1 facing the firm. This wage also equals the firm's marginal factor cost. The firm hires l_1 units of labor, a quantity determined by the intersection of its marginal revenue product curve for labor MRP_1 and the supply curve s_1. We use lowercase letters to show quantity for a single firm and uppercase letters to show quantity in the market.

FIGURE 9.7 Wage Determination and Employment in Perfect Competition

Wages in perfect competition are determined by the intersection of demand and supply in Panel (a). An individual firm takes the wage W_1 as given. It faces a horizontal supply curve for labor at the market wage, as shown in Panel (b). This supply curve s_1 is also the marginal factor cost curve for labor. The firm responds to the wage by employing l_1 units of labor, a quantity determined by the intersection of its marginal revenue product curve MRP_1 and its supply curve s_1.

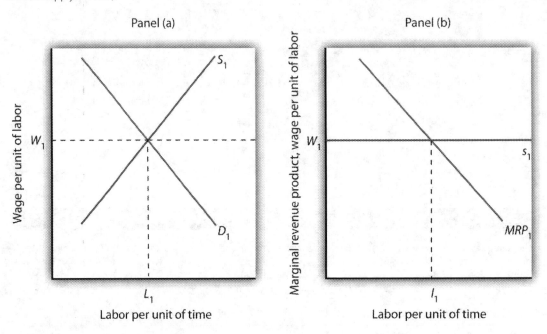

3.1 Changes in Demand and Supply

If wages are determined by demand and supply, then changes in demand and supply should affect wages. An increase in demand or a reduction in supply will raise wages; an increase in supply or a reduction in demand will lower them.

Panel (a) of Figure 9.8 shows how an increase in the demand for labor affects wages and employment. The shift in demand to D_2 pushes the wage to W_2 and boosts employment to L_2. Such an increase implies that the marginal product of labor has increased, that the number of firms has risen, or that the price of the good the labor produces has gone up. As we have seen, the marginal product of labor could rise because of an increase in the use of other factors of production, an improvement in technology, or an increase in human capital.

FIGURE 9.8   Changes in the Demand for and Supply of Labor

Panel (a) shows an increase in demand for labor; the wage rises to W_2 and employment rises to L_2. A reduction in labor demand, shown in Panel (b), reduces employment and the wage level. An increase in the supply of labor, shown in Panel (c), reduces the wage to W_2 and increases employment to L_2. Panel (d) shows the effect of a reduction in the supply of labor; wages rise and employment falls.

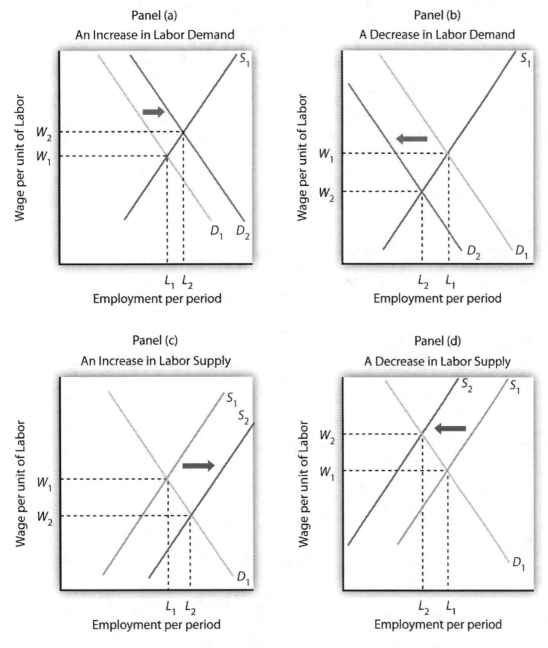

Clearly, a rising demand for labor has been the dominant trend in the market for U.S. labor through most of the nation's history. Wages and employment have generally risen as the availability of capital and other factors of production have increased, as technology has advanced, and as human capital has increased. All have increased the productivity of labor, and all have acted to increase wages.

Panel (b) of Figure 9.8 shows a reduction in the demand for labor to D_2. Wages and employment both fall. Given that the demand for labor in the aggregate is generally increasing, reduced labor demand is most often found in specific labor markets. For example, a slump in construction activity in a particular community can lower the demand for construction workers. Technological changes can reduce as well as increase demand. The Case in Point on wages and technology suggests that technological changes since the late 1970s have tended to reduce the demand for workers with only a high school education while increasing the demand for those with college degrees.

Panel (c) of Figure 9.8 shows the impact of an increase in the supply of labor. The supply curve shifts to S_2, pushing employment to L_2 and cutting the wage to W_2. For labor markets as a whole, such a supply increase could occur because of an increase in population or an increase in the amount of work people are willing to do. For individual labor markets, supply will increase as people move into a particular market.

Just as the demand for labor has increased throughout much of the history of the United States, so has the supply of labor. Population has risen both through immigration and through natural increases. Such increases tend, all other determinants of wages unchanged, to reduce wages. The fact that wages have tended to rise suggests that demand has, in general, increased more rapidly than supply. Still, the more supply rises, the smaller the increase in wages will be, even if demand is rising.

Finally, Panel (d) of Figure 9.8 shows the impact of a reduction in labor supply. One dramatic example of a drop in the labor supply was caused by a reduction in population after the outbreak of bubonic plague in Europe in 1348—the so-called Black Death. The plague killed about one-third of the people of Europe within a few years, shifting the supply curve for labor sharply to the left. Wages doubled during the period.[3]

The fact that a reduction in the supply of labor tends to increase wages explains efforts by some employee groups to reduce labor supply. Members of certain professions have successfully promoted strict licensing requirements to limit the number of people who can enter the profession—U.S. physicians have been particularly successful in this effort. Unions often seek restrictions in immigration in an effort to reduce the supply of labor and thereby boost wages.

3.2   Competitive Labor Markets and the Minimum Wage

The Case in Point on technology and the wage gap points to an important social problem. Changes in technology boost the demand for highly educated workers. In turn, the resulting wage premium for more highly educated workers is a signal that encourages people to acquire more education. The market is an extremely powerful mechanism for moving resources to the areas of highest demand. At the same time, however, changes in technology seem to be leaving less educated workers behind. What will happen to people who lack the opportunity to develop the skills that the market values highly or who are unable to do so?

FIGURE 9.9 Alternative Responses to Low Wages

Government can respond to a low wage by imposing a minimum wage of W_m in Panel (a). This increases the quantity of labor supplied and reduces the quantity demanded. It does, however, increase the income of those who keep their jobs. Another way the government can boost wages is by raising the demand for labor in Panel (b). Both wages and employment rise.

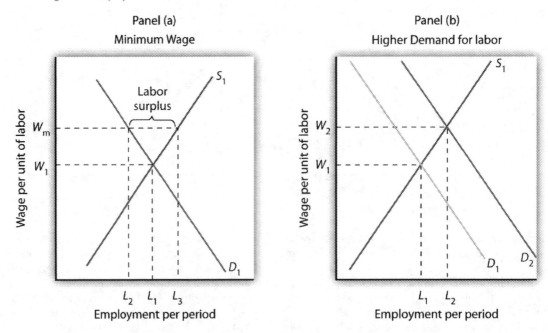

In order to raise wages of workers whose wages are relatively low, governments around the world have imposed minimum wages. A minimum wage works like other price floors. The impact of a minimum wage is shown in Panel (a) of Figure 9.9. Suppose the current equilibrium wage of unskilled workers is W_1, determined by the intersection of the demand and supply curves of these workers. The government determines that this wage is too low and orders that it be increased to W_m, a minimum wage. This strategy reduces employment from L_1 to L_2, but it raises the incomes of those who continue to work. The higher wage also increases the quantity of labor supplied to L_3. The gap between the quantity of labor supplied and the quantity demanded, $L_3 - L_2$, is a surplus—a surplus that increases unemployment.

Some economists oppose increases in the minimum wage on grounds that such increases boost unemployment. Other economists argue that the demand for unskilled labor is relatively inelastic, so a higher minimum wage boosts the incomes of unskilled workers as a group. That gain, they say, justifies the policy, even if it increases unemployment.

An alternative approach to imposing a legal minimum is to try to boost the demand for labor. Such an approach is illustrated in Panel (b). An increase in demand to D_2 pushes the wage to W_2 and at the same time increases employment to L_2. Public sector training programs that seek to increase human capital are examples of this policy.

Still another alternative is to subsidize the wages of workers whose incomes fall below a certain level. Providing government subsidies—either to employers who agree to hire unskilled workers or to workers themselves in the form of transfer payments—enables people who lack the skills—and the ability to acquire the skills—needed to earn a higher wage to earn more without the loss of jobs implied by a higher minimum wage. Such programs can be costly. They also reduce the incentive for low-skilled workers to develop the skills that are in greater demand in the marketplace.

KEY TAKEAWAYS

- Wages in a competitive market are determined by demand and supply.
- An increase in demand or a reduction in supply will increase the equilibrium wage. A reduction in demand or an increase in supply will reduce the equilibrium wage.
- The government may respond to low wages for some workers by imposing the minimum wage, by attempting to increase the demand for those workers, or by subsidizing the wages of workers whose incomes fall below a certain level.

TRY IT!

Assuming that the market for construction workers is perfectly competitive, illustrate graphically how each of the following would affect the demand or supply for construction workers. What would be the impact on wages and on the number of construction workers employed?

1. The demand for new housing increases as more people move into the community.
2. Changes in societal attitudes lead to more women wanting to work in construction.
3. Improved training makes construction workers more productive.
4. New technology allows much of the framing used in housing construction to be built by robots at a factory and then shipped to construction sites.

Case in Point

Technology and the Wage Gap

© 2010 Jupiterimages Corporation

Economist Daron Acemoglu's research begins by noting that the college premium, defined as the average wages of college graduates relative to that of high school graduates, rose 25% between 1979 and 1995 in the United States. Also, during essentially the same period, wage inequality rose. Whereas in the early 1970s, a person in the 90th percentile of the wage distribution earned 266% more than a person in the 10th percentile earned, 25 years later the gap had increased to 366%. The consensus view maintains that the increase in the college premium and in wage inequality stem primarily from skill-biased technological change. Skill-biased technological change means that, in general, newly developed technologies have favored the hiring of workers with better education and more skills.

But while technological advances *may* increase the demand for skilled workers, the opposite can also occur. For example, the rise of factories, assembly lines, and interchangeable parts in the nineteenth century reduced the demand for skilled artisans such as weavers and watchmakers. So, the twentieth century skill-bias of technological change leads researchers to ask why recent technological change has taken the form it has.

Acemoglu's answer is that, at least in part, the character of technological change itself constitutes a response to profit incentives:

> *The early nineteenth century was characterized by skill-replacing developments because the increased supply of unskilled workers in the English cities (resulting from migration from rural areas and from Ireland) made the introduction of these technologies profitable. In contrast, the twentieth century has been characterized by skill-biased technical change because the rapid increase in the supply of skilled workers has induced the development of skill-complementary technologies. (p. 9)*

In general, technological change in this model is *endogenous*—that is, its character is shaped by any incentives that firms face.

Of course, an increase in the supply of skilled labor, as has been occurring relentlessly in the United States over the past century, would, other things unchanged, lead to a fall in the wage premium. Acemoglu and others argue that the increase in the demand for skilled labor has simply outpaced the increase in supply.

But this also begs the *why* question. Acemoglu's answer again relies on the profit motive:

The development of skill-biased technologies will be more profitable when they have a larger market size—i.e., when there are more skilled workers. Therefore, the equilibrium degree of skill bias could be an increasing function of the relative supply of skilled workers. An increase in the supply of skills will then lead to skill-biased technological change. Furthermore, acceleration in the supply of skills can lead to acceleration in the demand for skill. (p. 37)

It follows from this line of reasoning that the rapid increase in the supply of college-educated workers led to more skill-biased technologies that in turn led to a higher college premium.

While these ideas explain the college premium, they do not address why the real wages of low-skilled workers have fallen in recent decades. Popular explanations include the decreased role of labor unions, the increased role of international trade, and immigration. Many studies, though, have concluded that the direct impacts of these factors have been limited. For example, in both the United States and United Kingdom, rising wage inequality preceded the decline of labor unions. Concerning the impact of trade and immigration on inequality, most research concludes that changes in these areas have not been large enough, despite how much they figure into the public's imagination. For example, according to economists Aaron Steelman and John Weinberg, immigration accounted for a 2 million person increase in the labor force in the 1970s, when the baby boom and increased labor force participation of women added 20 million workers. During the 1980s, immigration was relatively high but still only accounted for a one percentage point increase, from 7 to 8%, in immigrant share of the total labor supply. While Acemoglu accepts those conclusions, he argues that labor market institutions and trade may have interacted with technological change to magnify technological change's direct effect on inequality. For example, skill-biased technological change makes wage compression that unions tend to advocate more costly for skilled workers and thus weakens the "coalition between skilled and unskilled work that maintains unions" (p. 52). Likewise, trade expansion with less developed countries may have led to more skill-biased technological change than otherwise would have occurred.

Acemoglu recognizes that more research is needed to determine whether these indirect effects are operating and, if they are, the sizes of these effects, but looking at how technological change responds to economic conditions may begin to solve some heretofore puzzling aspects of recent labor market changes.

What is to be done, if anything, about widening inequality? Steelman and Weinberg argue, "First, do no harm." They state,

Increased trade with LDCs and immigration from abroad likely have had little effect on wage inequality, while almost certainly adding to the strength and vitality of the American economy. Efforts to slow the growth of foreign goods or labor coming to our shores would be costly to Americans as a whole, as well as to those people who seem to be hurt by globalization at present. (p. 11)

However, they do suggest that policies to promote acquisition of skills, especially in early education where the return seems especially high, may be useful.

Sources: Daron Acemoglu, "Technical Change, Inequality, and the Labor Market," Journal of Economic Literature 40:1 (March 2002): 7–73; Aaron Steelman and John A. Weinberg, "What's Driving Wage Inequality," Federal Reserve Bank of Richmond Economic Quarterly 91:3 (Summer 2005): 1–17.

ANSWERS TO TRY IT! PROBLEMS

1. An increase in the demand for new housing would shift the demand curve for construction workers to the right, as shown in Figure 9.8, Panel (a). Both the wage rate and the employment in construction rise.

2. A larger number of women wanting to work in construction means an increase in labor supply, as shown in Figure 9.8, Panel (c). An increase in the supply of labor reduces the wage rate and increases employment.

3. Improved training would increase the marginal revenue product of construction workers and hence increase demand for them. Wages and employment would rise, as shown in Figure 9.8, Panel (a).

4. The robots are likely to serve as a substitute for labor. That will reduce demand, wages, and employment of construction workers, as shown in Panel (b).

4. REVIEW AND PRACTICE

Summary

In this chapter we have extended our understanding of the operation of perfectly competitive markets by looking at the market for labor. We found that the common sense embodied in the marginal decision rule is alive and well. A firm should hire additional labor up to the point at which the marginal benefit of doing so equals the marginal cost.

The demand curve for labor is given by the downward-sloping portion of the marginal revenue product (*MRP*) curve of labor. A profit-maximizing firm will hire labor up to the point at which its marginal revenue product equals its marginal factor cost. The demand for labor shifts whenever there is a change in (1) related factors of production, including investment in human capital; (2) technology; (3) product demand; and (4) the number of firms.

The quantity of labor supplied is closely linked to the demand for leisure. As more hours are worked, income goes up, but the marginal cost of work, measured in terms of forgone leisure, also increases. Because these two forces pull the quantity of labor supplied in opposite directions, it is possible that, above some wage, an individual's supply curve for labor is backward bending. Supply curves for labor in individual markets, however, are likely to be upward sloping.

Because competitive labor markets generate wages equal to marginal revenue product, workers who add little to the value of a firm's output will receive low wages. The public sector can institute a minimum wage, seek to improve these workers' human capital, or subsidize their wages.

CONCEPT PROBLEMS

1. Explain the difference between the marginal product of a factor and the marginal revenue product of a factor. What factors would change a factor's marginal product? Its marginal revenue product?

2. In perfectly competitive input markets, the factor price and the marginal factor cost are the same. True or false? Explain.

3. Many high school vocational education programs are beginning to shift from an emphasis on training students to perform specific tasks to training students to learn new tasks. Students are taught, for example, how to read computer manuals so that they can more easily learn new systems. Why has this change occurred? Do you think the change is desirable?

4. How would an increase in the prices of crops of fresh produce that must be brought immediately to market—so-called truck crops—affect the wages of workers who harvest those crops? How do you think it would affect the quantity of labor supplied?

5. If individual labor supply curves of all individuals are backward bending, does this mean that a market supply curve for labor in a particular industry will also be backward bending? Why or why not?

6. There was an unprecedented wave of immigration to the United States during the latter third of the nineteenth century. Wages, however, rose at a rapid rate throughout the period. Why was the increase in wages surprising in light of rising immigration, and what probably caused it?

7. Suppose you were the economic adviser to the president of a small underdeveloped country. What advice would you give him or her with respect to how the country could raise the productivity of its labor force? (*Hint:* What factors increase labor productivity?)

8. The text argues that the effect of a minimum wage on the incomes of workers depends on whether the demand for their services is elastic or inelastic. Explain why.

9. How would a successful effort to increase the human capital of unskilled workers affect their wage? Why?

10. Do you think that bank tellers and automatic tellers are substitutes or complements? Explain.

11. What does the airline pilot's supply curve in the Case in Point on how she has dealt with wage cutbacks look like?

12. Given the evidence cited in the Case in Point on the increasing wage gap between workers with college degrees and those who have only completed high school, how has the greater use by firms of high-tech capital affected the marginal products of workers with college degrees? How has it affected their marginal revenue product?

13. Explain how each of the following events would affect wages in a particular labor market:

    a. an increase in labor productivity in the market.

    b. an increase in the supply of labor in the market.

    c. an increase in wages in another labor market that can be easily entered by workers in the first labor market.

    d. a reduction in wages in another market whose workers can easily enter the first market.

    e. an increase in the price of the good labor in the market produces.

14. How can a supply curve for labor be backward bending? Suppose the equilibrium wage occurs in the downward-sloping portion of the curve. How would an increase in the demand for labor in the market affect the wage? How would this affect the quantity of labor supplied?

15. How do you think a wage increase would affect the quantity of labor supplied by each of the following speakers?

    a. "I want to earn as much money as possible."

    b. "I am happy with my current level of income and want to maintain it."

    c. "I love my work; the wage I'm paid has nothing to do with the amount of work I want to do."

    d. "I would work the same number of hours regardless of the wage I am paid."

NUMERICAL PROBLEMS

1. Felicia Álvarez, a bakery manager, faces the total product curve shown, which gives the relationship between the number of bakers she hires each day and the number of loaves of bread she produces, assuming all other factors of production are given.

Number of bakers per day	Loaves of bread per day
0	0
1	400
2	700
3	900
4	1,025
5	1,100
6	1,150

Assume that bakers in the area receive a wage of $100 per day and that the price of bread is $1.00 per loaf.

   a. Plot the bakery's marginal revenue product curve (remember that marginal values are plotted at the mid-points of the respective intervals).

   b. Plot the bakery's marginal factor cost curve on the same graph.

   c. How many bakers will Ms. Álvarez employ per day?

   d. Suppose that the price of bread falls to $.80 per loaf. How will this affect the marginal revenue product curve for bakers at the firm? Plot the new curve.

   e. How will the change in (d) above affect the number of bakers Ms. Álvarez hires?

   f. Suppose the price of bread rises to $1.20 per loaf. How will this affect the marginal revenue product curve for bakers? Plot the new curve.

   g. How will the development in (f) above affect the number of bakers that Ms. Álvarez employs?

2. Suppose that wooden boxes are produced under conditions of perfect competition and that the price of a box is $10. The demand and supply curves for the workers who make these boxes are given in the table.

Wage per day	Workers demanded	Workers supplied
$100	6,000	12,000
80	7,000	10,000
60	8,000	8,000
40	9,000	6,000
20	10,000	4,000

Plot the demand and supply curves for labor, and determine the equilibrium wage for box makers.

3. Assume that the market for nurses is perfectly competitive, and that the initial equilibrium wage for registered nurses is $30 per hour. Illustrate graphically how each of the following events will affect the demand or supply for nurses. State the impact on wages and on the number of nurses employed (in terms of the direction of the changes that will occur).

   a. New hospital instruments reduce the amount of time physicians must spend with patients in intensive care and increase the care that nurses can provide.

   b. The number of doctors increases.

   c. Changes in the labor market lead to greater demand for the services of women in a wide range of occupations. The demand for nurses, however, does not change.

   d. New legislation establishes primary-care facilities in which nurses care for patients with minor medical problems. No supervision by physicians is required in the facilities.

   e. The wage for nurses rises.

4. Plot the supply curves for labor implied by each of the following statements. In this problem, actual numbers are not important; rather you should think about the shape of the curve.

   a. "I'm sorry, kids, but now that I'm earning more, I just can't afford to come home early in the afternoon, so I won't be there when you get home from school."

   b. "They can pay me a lot or they can pay me a little. I'll still put in my 8 hours a day."

   c. "Wow! With the raise the boss just gave me, I can afford to knock off early each day."

5. At an hourly wage of $10 per hour, Marcia Fanning is willing to work 36 hours per week. Between $30 and $40 per hour, she is willing to work 40 hours per week. At $50 per hour, she is willing to work 35 hours per week.

    a. Assuming her labor supply curve is linear between the data points mentioned, draw Ms. Fanning's labor supply curve.

    b. Given her labor supply curve, how much could she earn per week at the wage of $10 per hour? $30 per hour? $40 per hour? $50 per hour?

    c. How much would she earn at each hypothetical wage rate?

6. The following table describes the perfectly competitive market for dishwashers.

Wage per day	Quantity demanded per day (in thousands)	Quantity supplied per day (in thousands)
$50	4.0	1.0
100	3.5	2.0
150	3.0	3.0
200	2.5	4.0
250	2.0	5.0

    a. Draw the demand and supply curves for dishwashers.

    b. What is the equilibrium daily wage rate and quantity of dishwashers?

    c. What is the total (i.e., cumulative) daily income of dishwashers at the equilibrium daily wage?

    d. At a minimum daily wage of $200 per day, how many dishwashers will be employed? How many will be unemployed? What will be the total daily income of dishwashers?

    e. At a minimum wage of $250 per day, how many dishwashers will be employed? How many will be unemployed? What will be the total daily income of dishwashers?

ENDNOTES

1. Strictly speaking, it is only that part of the downward-sloping portion over which variable costs are at least covered. This is the flip-side of what you learned about a firm's supply curve in the chapter on competitive output markets: Only the portion of the rising marginal cost curve that lies above the minimum point of the average variable cost curve constitutes the supply curve of a perfectly competitive firm.

2. Laura Duberstein and Karen Oppenheim Mason, "Do Child Care Costs Influence Women's Work Plans? Analysis for a Metropolitan Area," Research Report, Population Studies Center, University of Michigan, Ann Arbor, July 1991.

3. Carlo M. Cipolla, *Before the Industrial Revolution: European Society and Economy, 1000–1700*, 2nd ed. (New York: Norton, 1980), pp. 200–202. The doubling in wages was a doubling in real terms, meaning that the purchasing power of an average worker's wage doubled.

CHAPTER 10
Inequality, Poverty, and Discrimination

START UP: OCCUPY WALL STREET AND THE WORLD

It all began September 17, 2011, with a march by thousands of demonstrators unhappy with all sorts of things about the United States—the distribution of income, with rallying cries on behalf of the 99%; "greed" on Wall Street; the bailout of many banks; capitalism in general; and a variety of other perceived ills, from hostility to certain nonfinancial companies such as Walmart and Starbucks to calls for the United States to pull out of military operations around the world and to abolish the Federal Reserve Bank. The symbol of the movement became the occupation of a small park in the neighborhood of Wall Street—Zuccotti Park. Two months later, the park continued to be jammed with demonstrators using it as a campground, after which New York City Mayor Michael Bloomberg shut it down as a place for overnight lodging.

Well before then, the "Occupy Wall Street" movement had become a national phenomenon and then an international phenomenon. The *Economist* in mid-October reported demonstrations in more than 900 cities and in more than 80 countries. The demonstrators generally rejected the entire concept of making specific demands, preferring instead to protest in support of an ill-defined, but clearly compelling, message—whatever that message might have been.

Who were the demonstrators? Douglas Schoen, who once worked as a pollster for President Bill Clinton, had his survey firm interview about 200 protesters occupying Zuccotti Park in mid-October of 2011 about their views. According to Schoen's survey, the Zuccotti Park demonstrators were committed to a radical redistribution of income and sharp increases in government regulation of the economy, with 98% of them supporting civil disobedience to further their aims and 31% advocating violent measures to achieve their goals. A Pew survey at about the same time found Americans divided in their opinion about the "Occupy Wall Street" movement, with nearly 40% in support and about 35% opposed. At the same time, support and opposition for the Tea Party were running 32% in favor and 44% opposed.[1]

Whatever the makeup of the groups demonstrating throughout the world, they clearly brought the issues examined in this chapter—poverty, discrimination, and the distribution of income—to the forefront of public attention. It was not obvious why inequality and related complaints had suddenly become an important issue. As we will see on this chapter, inequality in the U.S. distribution of income had begun increasing in 1967; it has continued to rise ever since.

At about the same time as the movement was in the news, the poverty rate in the United States reached its highest level since 1993. The number of people below the U.S. poverty line in 2010—an annual income of $22,314 for a family of four—rose to 15.1% of the population. The number of people considered to be below the poverty level rose to 46.2 million, the highest number ever recorded in the history of the United States. Those statistics came more than four decades after President Lyndon B. Johnson stood before the Congress of the United States to make his first State of the Union address in 1964 to declare a new kind of war, a War on Poverty. "This administration today here and now declares unconditional war on poverty in America," the President said. "Our aim is not only to relieve the symptoms of poverty but to cure it; and, above, all, to prevent it." In the United States that year, 35.1 million people, about 22% of the population, were, by the official definition, poor.

The President's plan included stepped-up federal aid to low-income people, an expanded health-care program for the poor, new housing subsidies, expanded federal aid to education, and job training programs. The proposal became law later that same year. More than four decades and trillions of dollars in federal antipoverty spending later, the nation seems to have made little progress toward the President's goal.

In this chapter, we shall also explore the problem of discrimination. Being at the lower end of the income distribution and being poor are more prevalent among racial minorities and among women than among white males. To a degree, this situation may reflect discrimination. We shall investigate the economics of discrimination and its consequences for the victims and for the economy. We shall also assess efforts by the public sector to eliminate discrimination.

Questions of fairness often accompany discussions of income inequality, poverty, and discrimination. Answering them ultimately involves value judgments; they are normative questions, not positive ones. You must decide for yourself if a particular distribution of income is fair or if society has made adequate progress toward reducing poverty or discrimination. The material in this chapter will not answer those questions for you; rather, in order for you to have a more informed basis for making your own value judgments, it will shed light on what economists have learned about these issues through study and testing of hypotheses.

1. INCOME INEQUALITY

LEARNING OBJECTIVES

1. **Explain how the Lorenz curve and the Gini coefficient provide information on a country's distribution of income.**
2. **Discuss and evaluate the factors that have been looked at to explain changes in the distribution of income in the United States.**

Income inequality in the United States has soared in the last half century. According to the Congressional Budget Office, between 1979 and 2007, real average household income—taking into account government transfers and federal taxes—rose 62%. For the top 1% of the population, it grew 275%. For others in the top 20% of the population, it grew 65%. For the 60% of the population in the middle, it grew a bit under 40% and for the 20% of the population at the lowest end of the income distribution, it grew about 18%.[2]

Increasingly, education is the key to a better material life. The gap between the average annual incomes of high school graduates and those with a bachelor's degree increased substantially over the last half century. A recent study undertaken at the Georgetown University Center on Education and the Workforce concluded that people with a bachelor's degree earn 84% more over a lifetime than do people who are high school graduates only. That college premium is up from 75% in 1999.[3] Moreover, education is not an equal opportunity employer. A student from a family in the upper end of the income distribution is much more likely to get a college degree than a student whose family is in the lower end of the income distribution.

That inequality perpetuates itself. College graduates marry other college graduates and earn higher incomes. Those who do not go to college earn lower incomes. Some may have children out of wedlock—an almost sure route to poverty. That does not, of course, mean that young people who go to college are assured high incomes while those who do not are certain to experience poverty, but the odds certainly push in that direction.

We shall learn in this section how the degree of inequality can be measured. We shall examine the sources of rising inequality and consider what policy measures, if any, are suggested. In this section on inequality we are essentially focusing the way the economic pie is shared, while setting aside the important fact that the size of the economic pie has certainly grown over time.

1.1 A Changing Distribution of Income

We have seen that the income distribution has become more unequal. This section describes a graphical approach to measuring the equality, or inequality, of the distribution of income.

Measuring Inequality

The primary evidence of growing inequality is provided by census data. Households are asked to report their income, and they are ranked from the household with the lowest income to the household with the highest income. The Census Bureau then reports the percentage of total income earned by those households ranked among the bottom 20%, the next 20%, and so on, up to the top 20%. Each 20% of households is called a quintile. The bureau also reports the share of income going to the top 5% of households.

Income distribution data can be presented graphically using a **Lorenz curve**, a curve that shows cumulative shares of income received by individuals or groups. It was developed by economist Max O. Lorenz in 1905. To plot the curve, we begin with the lowest quintile and mark a point to show the percentage of total income those households received. We then add the next quintile and its share and mark a point to show the share of the lowest 40% of households. Then, we add the third quintile, and then the fourth. Since the share of income received by all the quintiles will be 100%, the last point on the curve always shows that 100% of households receive 100% of the income.

> **Lorenz curve**
>
> A curve that shows cumulative shares of income received by individuals or groups.

FIGURE 10.1 The Distribution of U.S. Income, 1968 and 2010

The distribution of income among households in the United States became more unequal from 1968 to 2010. The shares of income received by each of the first four quintiles fell, while the share received by the top 20% rose sharply. The Lorenz curve for 2010 was more bowed out than was the curve for 1968. (Mean income adjusted for inflation and reported in 2010 dollars; percentages do not sum to 100% due to rounding.)

Quintile	1968 mean income	1968 income share	2010 mean income	2010 income share
Lowest 20%	$9,919	4.2	$11,034	3.3
Second 20%	26,594	11.1	28,636	8.5
Third 20%	42,181	17.6	49,309	14.6
Fourth 20%	58,839	24.5	79,040	23.4
Highest 20%	102,244	42.6	169,633	50.2
Top 5%		16.6		21.7

Household income of selected percentile	1968	2010
Lowest 20%—upper limit	$18,251.00	$20,000
Second 20%—upper limit	34,601	38,043
Third 20%—upper limit	49,595	61,735
Fourth 20%—upper limit	69,686	100,065
Top 5%—lower limit	108,022	180,810

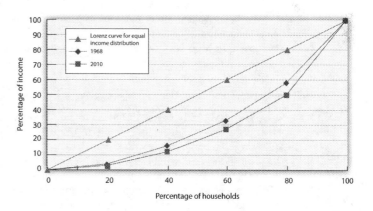

Sources: Carmen DeNavas-Walt, Bernadette D. Proctor, and Jessica C. Smith, U.S. Census Bureau, Current Population Reports, P60-239, Income, Poverty, and Health Insurance Coverage in the United States: 2010, U.S. Government Printing Office, Washington, DC, 2011, Table A-3; U.S. Census Bureau, Current Population Survey, 2010 Annual Social and Economic Supplement, Table HINC-05.

If every household in the United States received the same income, the Lorenz curve would coincide with the 45-degree line drawn in Figure 10.1. The bottom 20% of households would receive 20% of income; the bottom 40% would receive 40%, and so on. If the distribution of income were completely unequal, with one household receiving all the income and the rest zero, then the Lorenz curve would be shaped like a backward L, with a horizontal line across the bottom of the graph at 0% income and a vertical line up the right-hand side. The vertical line would show, as always, that 100% of families still receive 100% of income. Actual Lorenz curves lie between these extremes. The closer a Lorenz curve lies to the 45-degree line, the more equal the distribution. The more bowed out the curve, the less equal the distribution. We see in Figure 10.1 that the Lorenz curve for the United States became more bowed out between 1968 and 2010.

The degree of inequality is often measured with a **Gini coefficient**, the ratio between the Lorenz curve and the 45° line and the total area under the 45° line. The smaller the Gini coefficient, the more equal the income distribution. Larger Gini coefficients mean more unequal distributions. The Census Bureau reported that the Gini coefficient was 0.359 in 1968 and 0.457 in 2010.[4]

Gini coefficient

A measure of inequality expressed as the ratio of the area between the Lorenz curve and a 45° line and the total area under the 45° line.

Mobility and Income Distribution

When we speak of the bottom 20% or the middle 20% of families, we are not speaking of a static group. Some families who are in the bottom quintile one year move up to higher quintiles in subsequent years; some families move down. Because people move up and down the distribution, we get a quite different picture of income change when we look at the incomes of a fixed set of persons over time rather than comparing average incomes for a particular quintile at a particular point in time, as was done in Figure 10.1.

Addressing the question of mobility requires that researchers follow a specific group of families over a long period of time. Since 1968, the Panel Survey of Income Dynamics (PSID) at the University of Michigan has followed more than 5,000 families and their descendents. The effort has produced a much deeper understanding of changes in income inequality than it is possible to obtain from census data, which simply take a snapshot of incomes at a particular time.

Based on the University of Michigan's data, Federal Reserve Bank of Boston economist Katharine Bradbury compared mobility over the decades through 2005. She concluded that on most mobility measures, family income mobility was significantly lower in the 1990s and early 2000s than in earlier periods. Moreover, when families move out of a quintile, they move less. Finally, she notes that for the recent decades moving across quintiles has become harder to achieve precisely because of the increased income inequality.[5]

1.2   Explaining Inequality

Everyone agrees that the distribution of income in the United States generally became more equal during the first two decades after World War II and that it has become more unequal since 1968. While some people conclude that this increase in inequality suggests the latter period was unfair, others want to know why the distribution changed. We shall examine some of the explanations.

Family Structure

Clearly, an important source of rising inequality since 1968 has been the sharp increase in the number of families headed by women. In 2010, the median income of families headed by married couples was 2.5 times that of families headed by women without a spouse. The percentage of families headed by women with no spouse present has nearly doubled since 1968 and is thus contributing to increased inequality across households.

Technological and Managerial Change

Technological change has affected the demand for labor. One of the most dramatic changes since the late 1970s has been an increase in the demand for skilled labor and a reduction in the demand for unskilled labor.

The result has been an increase in the gap between the wages of skilled and unskilled workers. That has produced a widening gap between college- and high-school-trained workers.

Technological change has meant the integration of computers into virtually every aspect of production. And that has increased the demand for workers with the knowledge to put new methods to work—and to adapt to the even more dramatic changes in production likely to come. At the same time, the demand for workers who do not have that knowledge has fallen.

Along with new technologies that require greater technical expertise, firms are adopting new management styles that require stronger communication skills. The use of production teams, for example, shifts decision-making authority to small groups of assembly-line workers. That means those workers need more than the manual dexterity that was required of them in the past. They need strong communication skills. They must write effectively, speak effectively, and interact effectively with other workers. Workers who cannot do so simply are not in demand to the degree they once were.

The "intellectual wage gap" seems likely to widen as we move even further into the twenty-first century. That is likely to lead to an even higher degree of inequality and to pose a challenge to public policy for decades to come. Increasing education and training could lead to reductions in inequality. Indeed, individuals seem to have already begun to respond to this changing market situation, since the percentage who graduate from high school and college is rising.

Tax Policy

Did tax policy contribute to rising inequality over the past four decades? The tax changes most often cited in the fairness debate are the Reagan tax cuts introduced in 1981 and the Bush tax cuts introduced in 2001, 2002, and 2003.

An analysis of the Bush tax cuts by the Tax Foundation combines the three Bush tax cuts and assumes they occurred in 2003. Table 10.1 gives the share of total income tax liability for each quintile before and after the Bush tax cuts. It also gives the share of the Bush tax cuts received by each quintile.

TABLE 10.1 Income Tax Liability Before and After the Bush Tax Cuts

The share of total tax relief received by the first four quintiles was modest, while those in the top quintile received more than two-thirds of the total benefits of the three tax cuts. However, the share of income taxes paid by each of the first four quintiles fell as a result of the tax cuts, while the share paid by the top quintile rose.

Quintile	Share of income tax liability before tax cuts	Share of income tax liability after tax cuts	Share of total tax relief
First quintile	0.5%	0.3%	1.2%
Second quintile	2.3%	1.9%	4.2%
Third quintile	5.9%	5.2%	9.4%
Fourth quintile	12.6%	11.6%	17.5%
Top quintile	78.7%	81.0%	67.7%

Source: William Ahean, "Comparing the Kennedy, Reagan, and Bush Tax Cuts," Tax Foundation Fiscal Facts, August 24, 2004.

Tax cuts under George W. Bush were widely criticized as being tilted unfairly toward the rich. And certainly, Table 10.1 shows that the share of total tax relief received by the first four quintiles was modest, while those in the top quintile garnered more than two-thirds of the total benefits of the three tax cuts. Looking at the second and third columns of the table, however, gives a different perspective. The share of income taxes paid by each of the first four quintiles fell as a result of the tax cuts, while the share paid by the top quintile rose. Further, we see that each of the first four quintiles paid a very small share of income taxes before and after the tax cuts, while those in the top quintile ended up shouldering more than 80% of the total income tax burden. We saw in Figure 10.1 that those in the top quintile received just over half of total income. After the Bush tax cuts, they paid 81% of income taxes. Others are quick to point out that those same tax cuts were accompanied by reductions in expenditures for some social service programs designed to help lower income families. Still others point out that the tax cuts contributed to an increase in the federal deficit and, therefore, are likely to have distributional effects over many years and across several generations. Whether these changes increased or decreased fairness in the society is ultimately a normative question.

Methodology

The method by which the Census Bureau computes income shares has been challenged by some observers. For example, quintiles of households do not contain the same number of people. Rea Hederman of the Heritage Foundation, a conservative think tank, notes that the top 20% of households contains about 25% of the population. Starting in 2006, the Census Bureau report began calculating a measure called "equivalence-adjusted income" to take into account family size. The Gini coefficient for 2010 using this adjustment fell slightly from 0.469 to 0.457. The trend over time in the two Gini coefficients is similar. Two other flaws pointed out by Mr. Hederman are that taxes and benefits from non-cash programs that help the poor are not included. While some Census studies attempt to take these into account and report lower inequality, other studies do not receive as much attention as the main Census annual report.[6]

Even studies that look at incomes over a decade may not capture lifetime income. For example, people in retirement may have a low income but their consumption may be bolstered by drawing on their savings. Younger people may be borrowing to go to school, buy a house, or for other things. The annual income approach of the Census data does not capture this and even the ten-year look in the mobility study mentioned above is too short a period.

This suggests that more precise measurements may provide more insight into explaining inequality.

KEY TAKEAWAYS

- The distribution of income can be illustrated with a Lorenz curve. If all households had the same income, the Lorenz curve would be a 45° line. In general, the more equal the distribution of income, the closer the Lorenz curve will be to the 45° line. A more bowed out curves shows a less equal distribution. The Gini coefficient is another method for describing the distribution of income.
- The distribution of income has, according to the Census Bureau, become somewhat more unequal in the United States during the past 40 years.
- The degree of mobility up and down the distribution of income appears to have declined in recent years.
- Among the factors explaining increased inequality have been changes in family structure and changes in the demand for labor that have rewarded those with college degrees and have penalized unskilled workers.

TRY IT!

The accompanying Lorenz curves show the distribution of income in a country before taxes and welfare benefits are taken into account (curve *A*) and after taxes and welfare benefits are taken into account (curve *B*). Do taxes and benefits serve to make the distribution of income in the country more equal or more unequal?

Case in Point

Attitudes and Inequality

© 2010 Jupiterimages Corporation

In a fascinating examination of attitudes in the United States and in continental Western Europe, economists Alberto Alesina of Harvard University and George-Marios Angeletos of the Massachusetts Institute of Technology suggest that attitudes about the nature of income earning can lead to quite different economic systems and outcomes concerning the distribution of income.

The economists cite survey evidence from the World Values Survey, which concludes that 71% of Americans, and only 40% of Europeans, agree with the proposition: *"The poor could become rich if they worked hard enough."* Further, Americans are much more likely to attribute material success to hard work, while Europeans tend to attribute success to factors such as luck, connections, and even corruption. The result, according to Professors Alesina and Angeletos, is that Americans select a government that is smaller and engages in less redistributive activity than is selected by Europeans. Government in continental Western Europe is 50% larger than in the United States, the tax system in Europe is much more progressive than in the United States, regulation of labor and product markets is more extensive in Europe, and redistributive programs are more extensive in Europe than in the United States. As a result, the income distribution in Europe is much more equal than in the United States.

People get what they expect. The economists derive two sets of equilibria. Equilibrium in a society in which people think incomes are a result of luck, connections, and corruption turns out to be precisely that. And, in a society in which people believe incomes are chiefly the result of effort and skill, they are. In the latter society, people work harder and invest more. In the United States, the average worker works 1,600 hours per year. In Europe, the average worker works 1,200 hours per year.

So, who is right—Americans with their "you get what you deserve" or Europeans with their "you get what luck, connections, and corruption bring you" attitude? The two economists show that people get, in effect, what they expect. European values and beliefs produce societies that are more egalitarian. American values and beliefs produce the American result: a society in which the distribution of income is more unequal, the government smaller, and redistribution relatively minor. Professors Alesina and Angeletos conclude that Europeans tend to underestimate the degree to which people can improve their material well-being through hard work, while Americans tend to overestimate that same phenomenon.

Source: Alberto Alesina and George-Marios Angeletos, "Fairness and Redistribution," American Economic Review 95:4 (September, 2005) 960–80.

ANSWER TO TRY IT! PROBLEM

The Lorenz curve showing the distribution of income after taxes and benefits are taken into account is less bowed out than the Lorenz curve showing the distribution of income before taxes and benefits are taken into account. Thus, income is more equally distributed after taking them into account.

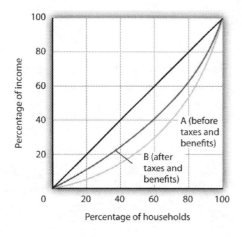

2. THE ECONOMICS OF POVERTY

LEARNING OBJECTIVES

1. **Distinguish between relative and absolute measures of poverty and discuss the uses and merits of each.**
2. **Describe the demographics of poverty in the United States.**
3. **Describe the forms of welfare programs in the United States and the reform of welfare in the mid-1990s.**
4. **Discuss the factors that have been looked at to explain the persistence of poverty in the United States.**

Poverty in the United States is something of a paradox. Per capita incomes in this country are among the highest on earth. Yet, the United States has a greater percentage of its population below the official poverty line than in the other industrialized nations. How can a nation that is so rich have so many people who are poor?

There is no single answer to the question of why so many people are poor. But we shall see that there are economic factors at work that help to explain poverty. We shall also examine the nature of the government's response to poverty and the impact that response has. First, however, we shall examine the definition of poverty and look at some characteristics of the poor in the United States.

2.1 Defining Poverty

Suppose you were asked to determine whether a particular family was poor or not poor. How would you do it?

You might begin by listing the goods and services that would be needed to provide a minimum standard of living and then finding out if the family's income was enough to purchase those items. If it were not, you might conclude that the family was poor. Alternatively, you might examine the family's income relative to the incomes of other families in the community or in the nation. If the family was on the low end of the income scale, you might classify it as poor.

These two approaches represent two bases on which poverty is defined. The first is an **absolute income test**, which sets a specific income level and defines a person as poor if his or her income falls below that level. The second is a **relative income test**, in which people whose incomes fall at the bottom of the income distribution are considered poor. For example, we could rank households according to income as we did in the previous section on income inequality and define the lowest one-fifth of households as poor. In 2010, any U.S. household with an annual income below $20,000 fell in this category.

In contrast, to determine who is poor according to the absolute income test, we define a specific level of income, independent of how many households fall above or below it. The federal government defines a household as poor if the household's annual income falls below a dollar figure called the **poverty line**. In 2010 the poverty line for a family of four was an income of $22,314. Figure 10.2 shows the poverty line for various family sizes.

absolute income test

Income test that sets a specific income level and defines a person as poor if his or her income falls below that level.

relative income test

Income test in which people whose incomes fall at the bottom of the income distribution are considered poor.

poverty line

Amount of annual income below which the federal government defines a household as poor.

FIGURE 10.2 Weighted Average Poverty Thresholds in 2010, by Size of Family

The Census Bureau uses a set of 48 money income thresholds that vary by family size and composition to determine who is in poverty. The "Weighted Average Poverty Thresholds" in the accompanying table is a summary of the 48 thresholds used by the census bureau. It provides a general sense of the "poverty line" based on the relative number of families by size and composition.

Number of people in household	Poverty Line
One person	$11,139
Two people	14,218
Three people	17,374
Four people	22,314
Five people	26,439
Six people	29,897
Seven people	34,009
Eight people	37,934
Nine people or more	45,220

Source: DeNavas-Walt, Carmen, Bernadette D. Proctor, and Jessica Smith, U.S. Census Bureau, Current Population Reports, P60-239, Income, Poverty, and Health Insurance Coverage in the United States: 2010, U.S. Government Printing Office, Washington, D.C., 2011; p. 61.

The concept of a poverty line grew out of a Department of Agriculture study in 1955 that found families spending one-third of their incomes on food. With the one-third figure as a guide, the Department then selected food plans that met the minimum daily nutritional requirements established by the federal government. The cost of the least expensive plan for each household size was multiplied by three to determine the income below which a household would be considered poor. The government used this method to count the number of poor people from 1959 to 1969. The poverty line was adjusted each year as food prices changed. Beginning in 1969, the poverty line was adjusted annually by the average percentage price change for all consumer goods, not just changes in the price of food.

There is little to be said for this methodology for defining poverty. No attempt is made to establish an income at which a household could purchase basic necessities. Indeed, no attempt is made in the definition to establish what such necessities might be. The day has long passed when the average household devoted one-third of its income to food purchases; today such purchases account for less than one-seventh of household income. Still, it is useful to have some threshold that is consistent from one year to the next so that progress—or the lack thereof—in the fight against poverty can be assessed. In addition, the U.S. Census Bureau and the Bureau of Labor Statistics have begun working on more broad-based alternative measures of poverty. The new Supplemental Poverty Measure is based on expenses for food, clothing, shelter, and utilities; adjusts for geographic differences; adds in various in-kind benefits such as school lunches, housing subsidies, and energy assistance; includes tax credits; and then subtracts out taxes, work expenses, and out-of-pocket medical expenses.[7]

The percentage of the population that falls below the poverty line is called the **poverty rate**. Figure 10.3 shows both the number of people and the percentage of the population that fell below the poverty line each year since 1959.

poverty rate

The percentage of the population that falls below the poverty line.

FIGURE 10.3   The Poverty Rate in the United States, 1959–2010

The curve shows the percentage of people who lived in households that fell below the poverty line in each year from 1959 to 2010. The poverty rate fell through the 1960s and since has been hovering between about 12% and 15%. It tends to rise during recessions.

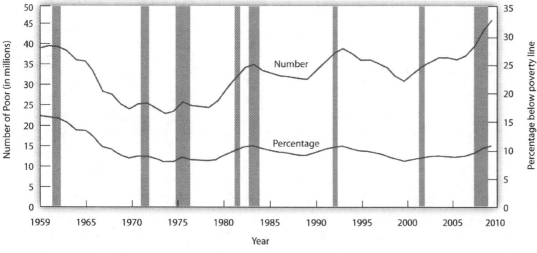

Source: DeNavas-Walt, Carmen, Bernadette D. Proctor, and Jessica Smith, U.S. Census Bureau, Current Population Reports P60-239, Income, Poverty, and Health Insurance Coverage in the United States: 2010, U.S. Government Printing Office, Washington DC, 2011; Figure 4, p. 14.

Despite its shortcomings, measuring poverty using an absolute measure allows for the possibility of progress in reducing it; using a relative measure of poverty does not, since there will always be a lowest 1/5, or 1/10 of the population. But relative measures do make an important point: Poverty is in large measure a relative concept. In the United States, people defined as poor have much higher incomes than most of the world's people or even than average Americans did as recently as the early 1970s. By international and historical standards, the average poor person in the United States is rich! The material possessions of America's poor would be considered lavish in another time and in another place. For example, based on data from 2005 to 2009, 42% of poor households in the United States owned their own homes, nearly 75% owned a car, and 64% have cable or satellite TV. Over 80% of poor households had air conditioning. Forty years ago, only 36% of the entire population in the United States had air conditioning. The average poor person in the United States has more living space than the average *person* in London, Paris, Vienna, or Athens.[8]

We often think of poverty as meaning that poor people are unable to purchase adequate food. Yet, according to Department of Agriculture surveys, 83% of poor people report that they have adequate food and 96% of poor parents report that their children are never hungry because they cannot afford food. In short, poor people in the United States enjoy a standard of living that would be considered quite comfortable in many parts of the developed world—and lavish in the less developed world.[9]

But people judge their incomes relative to incomes of people around them, not relative to people everywhere on the planet or to people in years past. You may feel poor when you compare yourself to some of your classmates who may have fancier cars or better clothes. And a family of four in a Los Angeles slum with an annual income of $13,000 surely does not feel rich because its income is many times higher than the average family income in Ethiopia or of Americans of several decades ago. While the material possessions of poor Americans are vast by Ethiopian standards, they are low in comparison to how the average American lives. What we think of as poverty clearly depends more on what people around us are earning than on some absolute measure of income.

Both the absolute and relative income approaches are used in discussions of the poverty problem. When we speak of the number of poor people, we are typically using an absolute income test of poverty. When we speak of the problems of those at the bottom of the income distribution, we are speaking in terms of a relative income test. In the European Union, for example, the poverty line is set at 60% of the median income of each member nation in a particular year. That is an example of a relative measure of poverty. In the rest of this section, we focus on the absolute income test of poverty used in the United States.

2.2   The Demographics of Poverty

There is no iron law of poverty that dictates that a household with certain characteristics will be poor. Nonetheless, poverty is much more highly concentrated among some groups than among others. The six characteristics of families that are important for describing who in the United States constitute the poor are whether or not the family is headed by a female, age, the level of education, whether or not the head of the family is working, the race of the household, and geography.

Figure 10.4 shows poverty rates for various groups and for the population as a whole in 2010. What does it tell us?

1. A family headed by a female is more than five times as likely to live in poverty as compared to a family with a husband present. This fact contributes to child poverty.

2. Children under 18 are about two times more likely to be poor than "middle-aged" (45–64) persons.

3. The less education the adults in the family have, the more likely the family is to be poor. A college education is an almost sure ticket out of poverty; the poverty rate for college graduates is just 4.7%.

4. The poverty rate is higher among those who do not work than among those who do. The poverty rate for people who did not work was about nine times the poverty rate of those who worked full time.

5. The prevalence of poverty varies by race and ethnicity. Specifically, the poverty rate in 2010 for whites (non-Hispanic origin) was less than half that for Hispanics or of blacks.

6. The poverty rate in cities is higher than in other areas of residence.

The incidence of poverty soars when several of these demographic factors associated with poverty are combined. For example, the poverty rate for families with children that are headed by women who lack a high school education is higher than 50%.

The new, more broad-based Supplemental Poverty Measure shows an increase of only 0.1 compared to the official poverty rate measure, but bigger differences for different segments of the population. For example, a smaller percentage of people under the age of 18 are poor according to the supplemental poverty measure (18.2% versus 22.5%), while a larger percentage of those over 64 years of age are considered poor (15.9% versus 9.0%). The new measure also shows lower poverty rates among blacks, renters, people living outside metropolitan areas, and those covered by only public health insurance. Other groups show the same or higher poverty rates.[10]

FIGURE 10.4 The Demographics of Poverty in the United States, 2010

Poverty rates in the United States vary significantly according to a variety of demographic factors. Panels (a) through (f) compare poverty rates among different groups of the U.S. population. The data are for 2010.

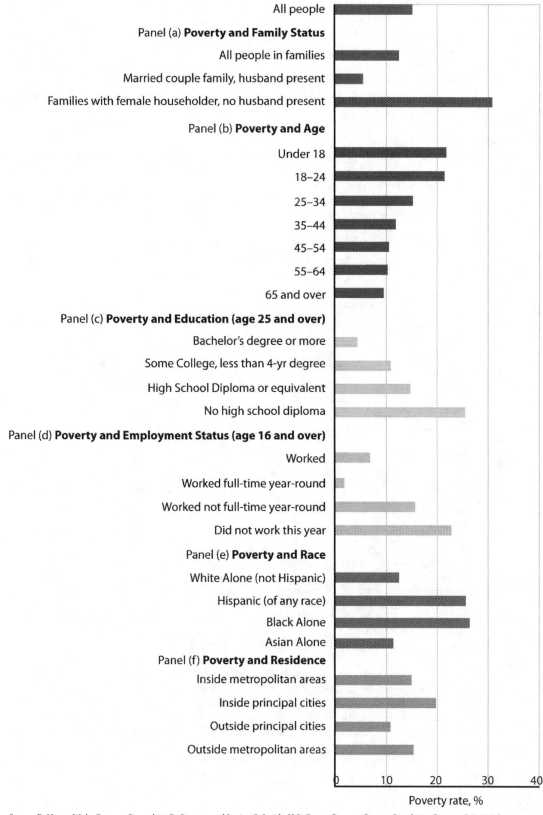

Source: DeNavas-Walt, Carmen, Bernadette D. Proctor, and Jessica C. Smith, U.S. Census Bureau, Current Population Reports, P60-239, Income, Poverty, and Health Insurance Coverage: 2010, U.S. Government Printing Office, Washington DC, 2011. Data for educational attainment, employment status, and residence from the Annual Social and Economic Supplement 2010, poverty tables at http://www.census.gov/hhes/www/cpstables/032011/pov/toc.htm.

2.3 Government Policy and Poverty

Consider a young single parent with three small children. The parent is not employed and has no support from other relatives. What does the government provide for the family?

The primary form of cash assistance is likely to come from a program called Temporary Assistance for Needy Families (TANF). This program began with the passage of the Personal Responsibility and Work Opportunity Reconciliation Act of 1996. It replaced Aid to Families with Dependent Children (AFDC). TANF is funded by the federal government but administered through the states. Eligibility is limited to two years of continuous payments and to five years in a person's lifetime, although 20% of a state's caseload may be exempted from this requirement.

In addition to this assistance, the family is likely to qualify for food stamps, which are vouchers that can be exchanged for food at the grocery store. The family may also receive rent vouchers, which can be used as payment for private housing. The family may qualify for Medicaid, a program that pays for physician and hospital care as well as for prescription drugs.

A host of other programs provide help ranging from counseling in nutrition to job placement services. The parent may qualify for federal assistance in attending college. The children may participate in the Head Start program, a program of preschool education designed primarily for low-income children. If the poverty rate in the area is unusually high, local public schools the children attend may receive extra federal aid. **Welfare programs** are the array of programs that government provides to alleviate poverty.

In addition to public sector support, a wide range of help is available from private sector charities. These may provide scholarships for education, employment assistance, and other aid.

Figure 10.5 shows participation rates in the major federal programs to help the poor.

welfare programs

The array of programs that government provides to alleviate poverty.

FIGURE 10.5 Welfare Programs and the Poor

Many people who fall below the poverty line have not received aid from particular programs.

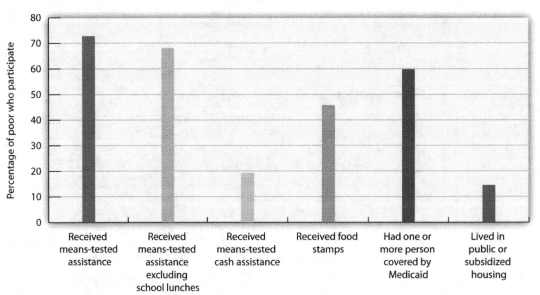

Source: U.S. Census Bureau, Current Population Survey, 2010 Annual Social and Economic Supplement.

Not all people whose incomes fall below the poverty line received aid. In 2010, a substantial majority of those counted as poor received some form of aid. However, as shown in Figure 10.5, the percentages who were helped by individual programs were much lower. Less than 20% of people below the poverty line received some form of cash assistance in 2010. About 45% received food stamps and nearly 60% lived in a household in which one or more people received medical services through Medicaid. Only about one-seventh of the people living in poverty received some form of housing aid.

Although for the most part poverty programs are federally funded, individual states set eligibility standards and administer the programs. Allowing states to establish their own programs was a hallmark feature of the 1996 welfare reform. As state budgets have come under greater pressure, many states have tightened standards.

Cash Versus Noncash Assistance

Aid provided to people falls into two broad categories: cash and noncash assistance. **Cash assistance** is a money payment that a recipient can spend as he or she wishes. **Noncash assistance** is the provision of specific goods and services, such as food or medical services, job training, or subsidized child care rather than cash.

Noncash assistance is the most important form of aid to the poor. The large share of noncash relative to cash assistance raises two issues. First, since the poor would be better off (that is, reach a higher level of satisfaction) with cash rather than noncash assistance, why is noncash aid such a large percentage of total aid to the poor? Second, the importance of noncash assistance raises an important issue concerning the methodology by which the poverty rate is measured in the United States. We examine these issues in turn.

1. Why Noncash Aid?

    Suppose you had a choice between receiving $515 or a television set worth $515. Neither gift is taxable. Which would you take?

    Given a choice between cash and an equivalent value in merchandise, you would probably take the cash. Unless the television set happened to be exactly what you would purchase with the $515, you could find some other set of goods and services that you would prefer to the TV set. The same is true of funds that you can spend on anything versus funds whose spending is restricted. Given a choice of $515 that you could spend on anything and $515 that you could spend only on food, which would you choose? A given pool of funds allows consumers a greater degree of satisfaction than does a specific set of goods and services.

    We can conclude that poor people who receive government aid would be better off from their own perspectives with cash grants than with noncash aid. Why, then, is most government aid given as noncash benefits?

    Economists have suggested two explanations. The first is based on the preferences of donors. Recipients might prefer cash, but the preferences of donors matter also. The donors, in this case, are taxpayers. Suppose they want poor people to have specific things—perhaps food, housing, and medical care.

    Given such donor preferences, it is not surprising to find aid targeted at providing these basic goods and services. A second explanation has to do with the political clout of the poor. The poor are not likely to be successful competitors in the contest to be at the receiving end of public sector income redistribution efforts; most redistribution goes to people who are not poor. But firms that provide services such as housing or medical care might be highly effective lobbyists for programs that increase the demand for their products. They could be expected to seek more help for the poor in the form of noncash aid that increases their own demand and profits.[11]

2. Poverty Management and Noncash Aid

    Only cash income is counted in determining the official poverty rate. The value of food, medical care, or housing provided through various noncash assistance programs is not included in household income. That is an important omission, because most government aid is noncash aid. Data for the official poverty rate thus do not reflect the full extent to which government programs act to reduce poverty.

    The Census Bureau estimates the impact of noncash assistance on poverty. If a typical household would prefer, say, $515 in cash to $515 in food stamps, then $515 worth of food stamps is not valued at $515 in cash. Economists at the Census Bureau adjust the value of noncash aid downward to reflect an estimate of its lesser value to households. Suppose, for example, that given the choice between $515 in food stamps and $475 in cash, a household reports that it is indifferent between the two—either would be equally satisfactory. That implies that $515 in food stamps generates satisfaction equal to $475 in cash; the food stamps are thus "worth" $475 to the household.

2.4 Welfare Reform

The welfare system in the United States came under increasing attack in the 1980s and early 1990s. It was perceived to be expensive, and it had clearly failed to eliminate poverty. Many observers worried that welfare was becoming a way of life for people who had withdrawn from the labor force, and that existing welfare programs did not provide an incentive for people to work. President Clinton made welfare reform one of the key issues in the 1992 presidential campaign.

The Personal Responsibility and Work Opportunity Reconciliation Act of 1996 was designed to move people from welfare to work. It eliminated the entitlement aspect of welfare by defining a maximum period of eligibility. It gave states considerable scope in designing their own programs. In the first

cash assistance

A money payment that an aid recipient can spend as he or she wishes.

noncash assistance

The provision of specific goods and services, such as food or medical services, job training, or subsidized child care rather than cash.

years following welfare reform, the number of people on welfare dropped by several million. Much research on the impact of reform showed that caseloads declined and employment increased and that the law did not have an adverse effect on poverty or the well-being of children. This positive outcome seemed to have resulted from an expansion of the earned income tax credit that also occurred, the overall low unemployment rate until the most recent few years, and larger behavioral responses than had been expected.[12]

Advocates of welfare reform proclaimed victory, while critics pointed to the booming economy, the tight labor market, and the general increase in the number of jobs over the same period. The recession that began at the end of 2007 and the ensuing slow recovery in the unemployment rate provided a real-time test of the effects of the reform. Economists Marianne Bitler and Hilary Hoynes analyzed the impact of welfare reform during the Great Recession on nonelderly families with children. They found that participation in cash assistance programs seemed less responsive to the downturn but that participation in noncash safety net programs, particularly the food stamp program, had become more responsive. They did find some evidence that the increase in poverty or near-poverty status might have been greater than it would have been without the reform.[13]

2.5 Explaining Poverty

Just as the increase in income inequality begs for explanation, so does the question of why poverty seems so persistent. Should not the long periods of economic growth in the 1980s and 1990s and from 2003 to late 2007 have substantially reduced poverty? Have the various government programs been ineffective?

Clearly, some of the same factors that have contributed to rising income inequality have also contributed to the persistence of poverty. In particular, the increases in households headed by females and the growing gaps in wages between skilled and unskilled workers have been major contributors.

Tax policy changes have reduced the extent of poverty. In addition to general reductions in tax rates, the Earned Income Tax Credit, which began in 1975 and was expanded in the 1990s, provides people below a certain income level with a supplement for each dollar of income earned. This supplement, roughly 30 cents for every dollar earned, is received as a tax refund at the end of the year.

FIGURE 10.6 Percentages of Population in Eight Countries with Disposable Incomes Less Than 1/2 the National Median

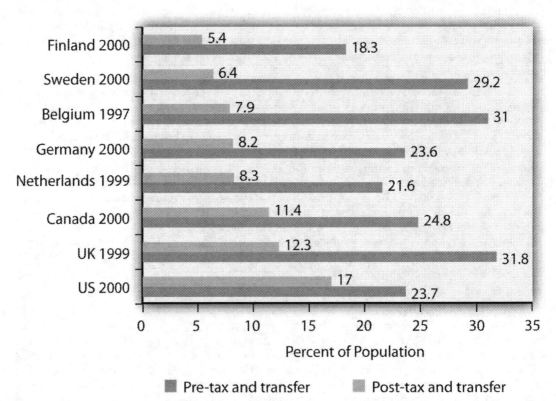

Source: Timothy M. Smeeding, "Public Policy, Economic Inequality, and Poverty: The United States in Comparative Perspectives," Social Science Quarterly, 86 (December 2005): 955–983.

Taken together, though, transfer payment and tax programs in the United States are less effective in reducing poverty than are the programs of other developed countries. Figure 10.6 shows the percentage of the population in eight developed countries with a disposable income (income after taxes) less than one-half the national median. The figure shows this percentage both before and after tax and transfer payment programs are considered. Clearly, the United States is the least aggressive in seeking to eliminate poverty among the eight countries shown.

Poverty and Work

How does poverty relate to work? Look back at Figure 10.4. Many of the poor are children or adults over age 65 and some are already working full time. Taken together, these three groups represent more than half of those in poverty. Also included amongst the poor are people who are ill or disabled, people who do not work due to family or home reasons, and people who are in school. The Census Bureau found in 2010 that of the nation's 46.2 million poor people, nearly 3 million reported they were not working or worked only part of the year or part time because they could not find full-time work.[14] So, while more employment opportunities would partly alleviate poverty, reducing unemployment is clearly only part of the answer.

Poverty and Welfare Programs

How effective have government programs been in alleviating poverty? The Census Bureau's supplemental poverty measure begins to answer that question. For example, those calculations show a reduction of two percentage points in the poverty rate, from 18% to 16%, when the earned income tax credit is included, ceteris paribus. Inclusion of the Supplemental Nutritional Assistance Program reduced the poverty rate by 1.7%, and housing subsidies reduced it by 0.9%. Other programs each had smaller effects on poverty reduction. But it is also important to distinguish between the poverty rate and the degree of poverty. Cash programs might reduce the degree of poverty but might not affect a family's income enough to actually move that family above the poverty line. Thus, even though the gap between the family's income and the poverty line is lessened, the family is still classified as poor and would thus still be included in the poverty-rate figures.

KEY TAKEAWAYS

- Poverty may be defined according to a relative or an absolute definition.
- Official estimates of the number of people who are "poor" are typically based on an absolute definition of poverty, one that many view as inadequate and dated.
- Several demographic factors appear to be associated with poverty. Families headed by single women are three times as likely to be poor as are other families. Poverty is also associated with low levels of education and with minority status.
- There is a wide range of welfare programs; the majority of welfare spending is for noncash assistance. Those receiving this aid do not have it counted as income in the official calculations of poverty.
- Welfare reform has focused on requiring recipients to enter the labor force. Many poor people, however, are not candidates for the labor force.

TRY IT!

The Smiths, a family of four, have an income of $20,500 in 2006. Using the absolute income test approach and the data given in the chapter, determine if this family is poor. Use the relative income test to determine if this family is poor.

Case in Point

Welfare Reform in Britain and in the United States

© 2010 Jupiterimages Corporation

The governments of the United States and of Great Britain have taken sharply different courses in their welfare reform efforts. In the United States, the primary reform effort was undertaken in 1996, with the declaration to eliminate welfare as an entitlement and the beginning of programs that required recipients to enter the labor force within two years. President Clinton promised to "end welfare as we know it."

In Britain, the government of Tony Blair took a radically different approach. Prime Minister Blair promised to "make welfare popular again." His government undertook to establish what he called a "third way" to welfare reform, one that emphasized returning recipients to the workforce but that also sought explicitly to end child poverty.

The British program required recipients to get counseling aimed at encouraging them to return to the labor force. It did not, however, require that they obtain jobs. It also included a program of "making work pay," the primary feature of which was the creation of a National Minimum Wage, one that was set higher than the minimum wage in the United States. In the United States, the minimum wage equaled 34% of median private sector wages in 2002; the British minimum wage was set at 45% of the median private sector wage in 2002.

The British program, which was called the New Deal, featured tax benefits for poor families with children, whether they worked or not. It also included a Sure Start program of child care for poor people with children under three years old. In short, the Blair program was a more extensive social welfare program than the 1996 act in the United States.

The table below compares results of the two programs in terms of their impact on child poverty, using an "absolute" poverty line and also using a relative poverty line.

Child Poverty Rates, Pre- and Post- Reform		
United Kingdom	**Absolute (percent)**	**Relative (percent)**
1997–1998	24	25
2002–2003	12	21
Change	−12	−4
United States	**Absolute (percent)**	**Relative (percent)**
1992	19	38
2001	13	35
Change	−6	−3

Child Poverty Rates in Single-Mother Families, Pre- and Post- Reform		
United Kingdom	**Absolute (percent)**	**Relative (percent)**
1997–1998	40	41
2002–2003	15	33
Change	−25	−8
United States	**Absolute (percent)**	**Relative (percent)**
1992	44	67
2001	28	59
Change	−16	−8

The relative measure of child poverty is the method of measuring poverty adopted by the European Union. It draws the poverty line at 60% of median income. The poverty line is thus a moving target against which it is more difficult to make progress.

Hills and Waldfogel compared the British results to those in the United States in terms of the relative impact on welfare caseloads, employment of women having families, and reduction in child poverty. They note that reduction in welfare caseloads was much greater in the United States, with caseloads falling from 5.5 million to 2.3 million. In Britain, the reduction in caseloads was much smaller. In terms of impact on employment among women, the United States again experienced a much more significant increase. In terms of reduction of child poverty, however, the British approach clearly achieved a greater reduction. The British approach also increased incomes of families in the bottom 10% of the income distribution (i.e., the bottom decile) by more than that achieved in the United States. In Britain, incomes of families in the bottom decile rose 22%, and for families with children they rose 24%. In the United States, those in the bottom decile had more modest gains.

Would the United States ever adopt a New Deal program such as the Blair program in Great Britain? That, according to Hills and Waldfogel, would require a change in attitudes in the United States that they regard as unlikely.

Source: John Hills and Jane Waldfogel, "A 'Third Way' in Welfare Reform? Evidence from the United Kingdom," Journal of Policy Analysis and Management, 23(4) (2004): 765–88.

ANSWER TO TRY IT! PROBLEM

According to the absolute income test, the Smiths are poor because their income of $20,500 falls below the 2006 poverty threshold of $20,614. According to the relative income test, they are not poor because their $20,500 income is above the upper limit of the lowest quintile, $20,035.

3.   THE ECONOMICS OF DISCRIMINATION

LEARNING OBJECTIVES

1. Define discrimination, identify some sources of it, and illustrate Becker's model of discrimination using demand and supply in a hypothetical labor market.
2. Assess the effectiveness of government efforts to reduce discrimination in the United States.

We have seen that being a female head of household or being a member of a racial minority increases the likelihood of being at the low end of the income distribution and of being poor. In the real world, we know that on average women and members of racial minorities receive different wages from white male workers, even though they may have similar qualifications and backgrounds. They might be charged different prices or denied employment opportunities. This section examines the economic forces that create such discrimination, as well as the measures that can be used to address it.

3.1   Discrimination in the Marketplace: A Model

discrimination

When people with similar economic characteristics experience different economic outcomes because of their race, sex, or other noneconomic characteristics.

Discrimination occurs when people with similar economic characteristics experience different economic outcomes because of their race, sex, or other noneconomic characteristics. A black worker whose skills and experience are identical to those of a white worker but who receives a lower wage is a victim of discrimination. A woman denied a job opportunity solely on the basis of her gender is the victim of discrimination. To the extent that discrimination exists, a country will not be allocating resources efficiently; the economy will be operating inside its production possibilities curve.

Pioneering work on the economics of discrimination was done by Gary S. Becker, an economist at the University of Chicago, who won the Nobel Prize in economics in 1992. He suggested that discrimination occurs because of people's preferences or attitudes. If enough people have prejudices against certain racial groups, or against women, or against people with any particular characteristic, the market will respond to those preferences.

In Becker's model, discriminatory preferences drive a wedge between the outcomes experienced by different groups. Discriminatory preferences can make salespeople less willing to sell to one group than to another or make consumers less willing to buy from the members of one group than from another or to make workers of one race or sex or ethnic group less willing to work with those of another race, sex, or ethnic group.

Let us explore Becker's model by examining labor-market discrimination against black workers. We begin by assuming that no discriminatory preferences or attitudes exist. For simplicity, suppose that the supply curves of black and white workers are identical; they are shown as a single curve in Figure 10.7. Suppose further that all workers have identical marginal products; they are equally productive. In the absence of racial preferences, the demand for workers of both races would be D. Black and white workers would each receive a wage W per unit of labor. A total of L black workers and L white workers would be employed.

Now suppose that employers have discriminatory attitudes that cause them to assume that a black worker is less productive than an otherwise similar white worker. Now employers have a lower demand, D_B, for black than for white workers. Employers pay black workers a lower wage, W_B, and employ fewer of them, L_B instead of L, than they would in the absence of discrimination.

3.2 Sources of Discrimination

As illustrated in Figure 10.7, racial prejudices on the part of employers produce discrimination against black workers, who receive lower wages and have fewer employment opportunities than white workers. Discrimination can result from prejudices among other groups in the economy as well.

One source of discriminatory prejudices is other workers. Suppose, for example, that white workers prefer not to work with black workers and require a wage premium for doing so. Such preferences would, in effect, raise the cost to the firm of hiring black workers. Firms would respond by demanding fewer of them, and wages for black workers would fall.

Another source of discrimination against black workers could come from customers. If the buyers of a firm's product prefer not to deal with black employees, the firm might respond by demanding fewer of them. In effect, prejudice on the part of consumers would lower the revenue that firms can generate from the output of black workers.

Whether discriminatory preferences exist among employers, employees, or consumers, the impact on the group discriminated against will be the same. Fewer members of that group will be employed, and their wages will be lower than the wages of other workers whose skills and experience are otherwise similar.

Race and sex are not the only characteristics that affect hiring and wages. Some studies have found that people who are short, overweight, or physically unattractive also suffer from discrimination, and charges of discrimination have been voiced by disabled people and by homosexuals. Whenever discrimination occurs, it implies that employers, workers, or customers have discriminatory preferences. For the effects of such preferences to be felt in the marketplace, they must be widely shared.

There are, however, market pressures that can serve to lessen discrimination. For example, if some employers hold discriminatory preferences but others do not, it will be profit enhancing for those who do not to hire workers from the group being discriminated against. Because workers from this group are less expensive to hire, costs for non-discriminating firms will be lower. If the market is at least somewhat competitive, firms who continue to discriminate may be driven out of business.

3.3 Discrimination in the United States Today

Reacting to demands for social change brought on most notably by the civil rights and women's movements, the federal government took action against discrimination. In 1954, the U.S. Supreme Court rendered its decision that so-called separate but equal schools for black and white children were inherently unequal, and the Court ordered that racially segregated schools be integrated. The Equal Pay Act of 1963 requires employers to pay the same wages to men and women who do substantially the same work. Federal legislation was passed in 1965 to ensure that minorities were not denied the right to vote.

Congress passed the most important federal legislation against discrimination in 1964. The Civil Rights Act barred discrimination on the basis of race, sex, or ethnicity in pay, promotion, hiring, firing, and training. An Executive Order issued by President Lyndon Johnson in 1967 required federal contractors to implement affirmative action programs to ensure that members of minority groups and women were given equal opportunities in employment. The practical effect of the order was to require that these employers increase the percentage of women and minorities in their work forces. Affirmative action programs for minorities followed at most colleges and universities.

What has been the outcome of these efforts to reduce discrimination? A starting point is to look at wage differences among different groups. Gaps in wages between males and females and between blacks and whites have fallen over time. In 1955, the wages of black men were about 60% of those of white men; in 2010, they were 74% of those of white men. For black men, the reduction in the wage gap occurred primarily between 1965 and 1973. In contrast, the gap between the wages of black women and white men closed more substantially, and progress in closing the gap continued after 1973, albeit at a slower rate. Specifically, the wages of black women were about 35% of those of white men in 1955, 58% in 1975, and 70% in 2010. For white women, the pattern of gain is still different. The wages of white women were about 65% of those of white men in 1955 and fell to about 60% from the mid-1960s to the late 1970s. The wages of white females relative to white males have improved, however, over the last 40

FIGURE 10.7 Prejudice and Discrimination

If employers, customers, or employees have discriminatory preferences, and those preferences are widespread, then the marketplace will result in discrimination. Here, black workers receive a lower wage and fewer of them are employed than would be the case in the absence of discriminatory preferences.

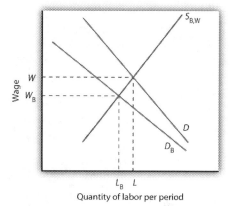

years. In 2010, white female wages were 80% of white male wages. While there has been improvement in wage gaps between black men, black women, and white women vis-à-vis white men, a substantial gap still remains. Figure 10.8 shows the wage differences for the period 1969–2010.

FIGURE 10.8 The Wage Gap

The exhibit shows the wages of white women, black women, and black men as a percentage of the wages of white men from 1969–2010. As you can see, the gap has closed considerably, but there remains a substantial gap between the wages of white men and those of other groups in the economy. Part of the difference is a result of discrimination.

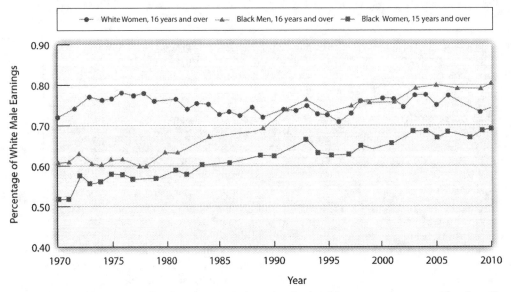

Source: Table 37. Median weekly earnings of full-time wage and salary workers, by selected characteristics. For recent years, http://www.bls.gov/cps/tables.htm.

One question that economists try to answer is the extent to which the gaps are due to discrimination per se and the extent to which they reflect other factors, such as differences in education, job experience, or choices that individuals in particular groups make about labor-force participation. Once these factors are accounted for, the amount of the remaining wage differential due to discrimination is less than the raw differentials presented in Figure 10.8 would seem to indicate.

There is evidence as well that the wage differential due to discrimination against women and blacks, as measured by empirical studies, has declined over time. For example, a number of studies have concluded that black men in the 1980s and 1990s experienced a 12 to 15% loss in earnings due to labor-market discrimination.[15] University of Chicago economist James Heckman denies that the entire 12% to 15% differential is due to racial discrimination, pointing to problems inherent in measuring and comparing human capital among individuals. Nevertheless, he reports that the earnings loss due to discrimination similarly measured would have been between 30 and 40% in 1940 and still over 20% in 1970.[16]

Can civil rights legislation take credit for the reductions in labor-market discrimination over time? To some extent, yes. A study by Heckman and John J. Donohue III, a law professor at Northwestern University, concluded that the landmark 1964 Civil Rights Act, as well as other civil rights activity leading up to the act, had the greatest positive impact on blacks in the South during the decade following its passage. Evidence of wage gains by black men in other regions of the country was, however, minimal. Most federal activity was directed toward the South, and the civil rights effort shattered an entire way of life that had subjugated black Americans and had separated them from mainstream life.[17]

In recent years, affirmative action programs have been under attack. Proposition 209, passed in California in 1996, and Initiative 200, passed in Washington State in 1998, bar preferential treatment due to race in admission to public colleges and universities in those states. The 1996 Hopwood case against the University of Texas, decided by the United States Court of Appeals for the Fifth Circuit, eliminated the use of race in university admissions, both public and private, in Texas, Louisiana, and Mississippi. Then Supreme Court decisions in 2003 concerning the use of affirmative action at the University of Michigan upheld race conscious admissions, so long as applicants are still considered individually and decisions are based of multiple criteria.

Controversial research by two former Ivy League university presidents, political scientist Derek Bok of Harvard University and economist William G. Bowen of Princeton University, concluded that affirmative action policies have created the backbone of the black middle class and taught white students the value of integration. The study focused on affirmative action at 28 elite colleges and universities. It found that while blacks enter those institutions with lower test scores and grades than those of whites, receive lower grades, and graduate at a lower rate, after graduation blacks earn advanced degrees at rates identical to those of their former white classmates and are more active in civic affairs.[18]

While stricter enforcement of civil rights laws or new programs designed to reduce labor-market discrimination may serve to further improve earnings of groups that have been historically discriminated against, wage gaps between groups also reflect differences in choices and in "premarket" conditions, such as family environment and early education. Some of these premarket conditions may themselves be the result of discrimination.

The narrowing in wage differentials may reflect the dynamics of the Becker model at work. As people's preferences change, or are forced to change due to competitive forces and changes in the legal environment, discrimination against various groups will decrease. However, it may be a long time before discrimination disappears from the labor market, not only due to remaining discriminatory preferences but also because the human capital and work characteristics that people bring to the labor market are decades in the making. The election of Barack Obama as president of the United States in 2008 is certainly a hallmark in the long and continued struggle against discrimination.

KEY TAKEAWAYS

- Discrimination means that people of similar economic characteristics experience unequal economic outcomes as a result of noneconomic factors such as race or sex.
- Discrimination occurs in the marketplace only if employers, employees, or customers have discriminatory preferences and if such preferences are widely shared.
- Competitive markets will tend to reduce discrimination if enough individuals lack such prejudices and take advantage of discrimination practiced by others.
- Government intervention in the form of antidiscrimination laws may have reduced the degree of discrimination in the economy. There is considerable disagreement on this question but wage gaps have declined over time in the United States.

TRY IT!

Use a production possibilities curve to illustrate the impact of discrimination on the production of goods and services in the economy. Label the horizontal axis as consumer goods per year. Label the vertical axis as capital goods per year. Label a point A that shows an illustrative bundle of the two which can be produced given the existence of discrimination. Label another point B that lies on the production possibilities curve above and to the right of point A. Use these two points to describe the outcome that might be expected if discrimination were eliminated.

Case in Point

Early Intervention Programs

Many authors have pointed out that differences in "pre-market" conditions may drive observed differences in market outcomes for people in different groups. Significant inroads to the reduction of poverty may lie in improving the educational opportunities available to minority children and others living in poverty-level households, but at what point in their lives is the pay-off to intervention the largest? Professor James Heckman, in an op-ed essay in *The Wall Street Journal*, argues that the key to improving student performance and adult competency lies in early intervention in education.

Professor Heckman notes that spending on children after they are already in school has little impact on their later success. Reducing class sizes, for example, does not appear to promote gains in factors such as attending college or earning higher incomes. What does seem to matter is earlier intervention. By the age of eight , differences in learning abilities are essentially fixed. But, early intervention to improve cognitive and especially non-cognitive abilities (the latter include qualities such as perseverance, motivation, and self-restraint) has been shown to produce significant benefits. In an experiment begun several decades ago known as the Perry intervention, four-year-old children from disadvantaged homes were given programs designed to improve their chances for success in school. Evaluations of the program 40 years later found that it had a 15 to 17% rate of return in terms of the higher wages earned by men and women who had participated in the program compared to those from similar backgrounds who did not—the program's benefit-cost ratio was 8 to 1. Professor Heckman argues that even earlier intervention among disadvantaged groups would be desirable—perhaps as early as six months of age.

Economists Rob Grunewald and Art Rolnick of the Federal Reserve Bank of Minneapolis have gone so far as to argue that, because of the high returns to early childhood development programs, which they estimate at 12% per year to the public, state and local governments, can promote more economic development in their areas by supporting early childhood programs than they currently do by offering public subsidies to attract new businesses to their locales or to build new sports stadiums, none of which offers the prospects of such a high rate of return.

Sources: James Heckman, "Catch 'em Young," The Wall Street Journal, January 10, 2006, p. A-14; Rob Grunewald and Art Rolnick, "Early Childhood Development on a Large Scale," Federal Reserve Bank of Minneapolis The Region, June 2005.

ANSWER TO TRY IT! PROBLEM

Discrimination leads to an inefficient allocation of resources and results in production levels that lie inside the production possibilities curve (*PPC*) (point A). If discrimination were eliminated, the economy could increase production to a point on the *PPC*, such as B.

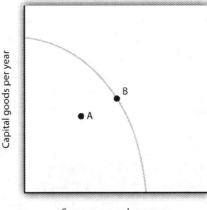

---

4. REVIEW AND PRACTICE

Summary

In this chapter, we looked at three issues related to the question of fairness: income inequality, poverty, and discrimination.

The distribution of income in the United States has become more unequal in the last four decades. Among the factors contributing to increased inequality have been changes in family structure, technological change, and tax policy. While rising inequality can be a concern, there is a good deal of movement of families up and down the distribution of income, though recently mobility may have decreased somewhat.

Poverty can be measured using an absolute or a relative income standard. The official measure of poverty in the United States relies on an absolute standard. This measure tends to overstate the poverty rate because it does not count noncash welfare aid as income. The new supplemental poverty measures have begun to take these programs into account. Poverty is concentrated among female-headed households, minorities, people with relatively little education, and people who are not in the labor force. Children have a particularly high poverty rate.

Welfare reform in 1996 focused on moving people off welfare and into work. It limits the number of years that individuals can receive welfare payments and allows states to design the specific parameters of their own welfare programs. Following the reform, the number of people on welfare fell dramatically. The long-term impact on poverty is still under investigation.

Federal legislation bans discrimination. Affirmative action programs, though controversial, are designed to enhance opportunities for minorities and women. Wage gaps between women and white males and between blacks and white males have declined since the 1950s. For black males, however, most of the reduction occurred between 1965 and 1973. Much of the decrease in wage gaps is due to acquisition of human capital by women and blacks, but some of the decrease also reflects a reduction in discrimination.

CONCEPT PROBLEMS

1. Explain how rising demand for college-educated workers and falling demand for high-school-educated workers contributes to increased inequality of the distribution of income.

2. Discuss the advantages and disadvantages of the following three alternatives for dealing with the rising inequality of wages.

   a. Increase the minimum wage each year so that wages for unskilled workers rise as fast as wages for skilled workers.

   b. Subsidize the wages of unskilled workers.

   c. Do nothing.

3. How would you define poverty? How would you determine whether a particular family is poor? Is the test you have proposed an absolute or a relative test?

4. Why does the failure to adjust the poverty line for regional differences in living costs lead to an understatement of poverty in some states and an overstatement of poverty in others?

5. The text argues that welfare recipients could achieve higher levels of satisfaction if they received cash rather than in-kind aid. Use the same argument to make a case that gifts given at Christmas should be in cash rather than specific items. Why do you suppose they usually are not?

6. Suppose a welfare program provides a basic grant of $10,000 per year to poor families but reduces the grant by $1 for every $1 of income earned. How would such a program affect a household's incentive to work?

7. Welfare reform calls for a two-year limit on welfare payments, after which recipients must go to work. Suppose a recipient with children declines work offers. Should aid be cut? What about the children?

8. How would you tackle the welfare problem? State the goals you would seek, and explain how the measures you propose would work to meet those goals.

9. Suppose a common but unfounded belief held that people with blue eyes were not as smart as people with brown eyes. What would we expect to happen to the relative wages of the two groups? Suppose you were an entrepreneur who knew that the common belief was wrong. What could you do to enhance your profits? Suppose other entrepreneurs acted in the same way. How would the wages of people with blue eyes be affected?

10. The Case in Point on Income Inequality in the United States versus continental Western Europe argues that people get, in effect, what they expect. People in the United States attribute success to hard work and skill, while people in Continental Western Europe attribute success to connections, luck, and corruption. With what set of views do you agree? Explain.

11. The Case in Point on welfare reform in Britain versus that in the United States argues that the British system, before it could be adopted in the United States, would require a change in attitudes in the United States. What sort of change would it require? Do you prefer the British approach? Why or why not?

12. James Heckman of the University of Chicago advocates a program of early intervention targeted at low income families. What are the advantages of such an approach? The disadvantages?

13. Give five reasons that the income distribution in the United States has become more unequal in the last several decades. Do you regard this as a problem for society? Why or why not?

14. Suppose that all welfare aid were converted to programs of cash assistance. Total spending on welfare would remain unchanged. How would this affect the poverty rate? Why?

NUMERICAL PROBLEMS

1. Here are income distribution data for three countries, from the *Human Development Report 2005*, table 15. Note that here we report only four data points rather than the five associated with each quintile. These emphasize the distribution at the extremes of the distribution.

	Poorest 10%	Poorest 20%	Richest 20%	Richest 10%
Panama	0.7	2.4	60.3	43.3
Sweden	3.6	9.1	36.6	22.2
Singapore	1.9	5.0	49.0	32.8

   a. Plot the Lorenz curves for each in a single graph.

   b. Compare the degree of inequality for the three countries. (Do not forget to convert the data to cumulative shares; e.g., the lowest 80% of the population in Panama receives 39.7% of total income.)

   c. Compare your results to the Lorenz curve given in the text for the United States. Which country in your chart appears closest to the United States in terms of its income distribution?

2. Looking at Figure 10.7 suppose the wage that black workers are receiving in a discriminatory environment, W_B, is $25 per hour, while the wage that white workers receive, W, is $30 per hour. Now suppose a regulation is imposed that requires that black workers be paid $30 per hour also.

   a. How does this affect the employment of black workers?

   b. How does this affect the wages of black workers?

   c. How does this affect their total income? Explain.

3. Suppose the poverty line in the United States was set according to the test required in the European Union: a household is poor if its income is less than 60% of the median household income. Here are annual data for median household income in the United States for the period 1994–2004. The data also give the percentage of the households that fall below 60% of the median household income.

	Median Household Income in the U.S.	Percent of households with income below 60% of median
1994	40,677	30.1
1995	41,943	30.4
1996	42,544	29.9
1997	43,430	29.1
1998	45,003	27.8
1999	46,129	27.1
2000	46,058	26.4
2001	45,062	27.4
2002	44,546	27.8
2003	44,482	28.3
2004	44,389	28.3

Source: U.S Census Bureau, Current Population Reports, P60-229; Income in 2004 CPI-U-RS adjusted dollars; column 3 estimated by authors using Table A-1, p. 31.

   a. Plot the data on a graph.

   b. Is this a relative or an absolute definition of poverty?

   c. Why do you think the percent of households with incomes below 60% of the median fell from 1994 to 2000 and has risen since?

   d. Discuss the measurement issues involved in the data you have presented.

   e. Discuss the elements of the system of counting the incomes of low income people in the United States and explain how it relates to your answer in (d).

4. Consider the following model of the labor market in the United States. Suppose that the labor market consists of two parts, a market for skilled workers and the market for unskilled workers, with different demand and supply curves for each as given below. The initial wage for skilled workers is $20 per hour; the initial wage for unskilled workers is $7 per hour.

   a. Draw the demand and supply curves for the two markets so that they intersect at the wages given above.

b. How does increased demand for skilled workers and a reduced demand for unskilled workers affect the initial solution?

c. How is the Lorenz curve for the United States economy affected by this development? Illustrate the old and the new Lorenz curves.

d. Suppose there is an increase in immigration from Mexico. How will this affect the two markets for labor?

e. Suppose Professor Heckman's recommendation for early intervention for low income children is followed and that it has the impact he predicts. How will this affect the two markets today? In 20 years? Illustrate and explain how the demand and/or supply curves in each market will be affected.

f. What would the impact of the change in (d) be on the Lorenz curve for the United States 20 years from now?

ENDNOTES

1. "Not Quite Together," *Economist*, October 22, 2011; Douglas Schoen, "Polling the Occupy Wall Street Crowd," *Wall Street Journal Online*, October 18, 2011; "Public Divided Over Occupy Wall Street Movement," Pew Charitable Trust Pew Research Center for the People & the Press, http://www.people-press.org/2011/10/24/public-divided-over-occupy-wall-street-movement/.

2. Congressional Budget Office, "Trends in the Distribution of Household Income Between 1979 and 2007," October 2011, http://www.cbo.gov/ftpdocs/124xx/doc12485/10-25-HouseholdIncome.pdf.

3. Anthony P. Carnevale, Stephen J. Rose, and Ban Cheah, *The College Payoff: Education, Occupation, and Lifetime Earnings*, Georgetown University Center on Education and the Workforce: 2011, http://cew.georgetown.edu/collegepayoff.

4. Carmen DeNavas-Walt, Bernadette D. Proctor, and Jessica C. Smith, U.S. Census Bureau, Current Population Reports, P60-239, *Income, Poverty, and Health Insurance Coverage in the United States: 2010*, U.S. Government Printing Office, Washington, DC, 2011.

5. Katharine Bradbury, "Trends in U.S. Family Income Mobility, 1969–2006," Federal Reserve Bank of Boston Working Paper no. 11-10, October 20, 2011.

6. Rea S. Hederman, Jr., "Census Report Adds New Twist to Income Inequality Data," Heritage Foundation, Policy Research and Analysis, No. 1592, August 29, 2007.

7. Kathleen Short, U.S. Census Bureau, Current Population Reports P60-241, *Supplemental Poverty Measure: 2010*, U.S. Government Printing Office, Washington, DC, November 2011.

8. Robert Rector and Rachel Sheffield, "Understanding Poverty in the United States: Surprising Facts about America's Poor," Heritage Foundation, Policy Research & Analysis, No. 2607, September 13, 2011.

9. Ibid.

10. Kathleen Short, U.S. Census Bureau, Current Population Reports P60-241, *Supplemental Poverty Measure: 2010*, U.S. Government Printing Office, Washington, DC, November 2011.

11. Students who have studied rent seeking behavior will recognize this argument. It falls within the public choice perspective of public finance theory.

12. Marianne P. Bitler and Hilary W. Hoynes, "The State of the Social Safety Net in the Post-Welfare Reform Era," *Brookings Papers on Economic Activity* (Fall 2010): 71–127.

13. Marianne P. Bitler and Hilary W. Hoynes, "The State of the Social Safety Net in the Post-Welfare Reform Era," *Brookings Papers on Economic Activity* (Fall 2010): 71–127.

14. Current Population Survey, Annual Social and Economic Supplement 2010, Table POV24.

15. William A. Darity and Patrick L. Mason, "Evidence on Discrimination in Employment," *Journal of Economic Perspectives* 12:2 (Spring 1998): 63–90.

16. James J. Heckman, "Detecting Discrimination," *Journal of Economic Perspectives* 12:2 (Spring 1998): 101–16.

17. John J. Donohue III and James Heckman, "Continuous Versus Episodic Change: The Impact of Civil Rights Policy on the Economic Status of Blacks," *Journal of Economic Literature* 29 (December 1991): 1603–43.

18. Derek Bok and William G. Bowen, *The Shape of the River: Long-Term Consequences of Considering Race in College and University Admissions* (Princeton, N. J.: Princeton University Press, 1998).

CHAPTER 11

Macroeconomics: The Big Picture

START UP: ECONOMY LIMPS ALONG

The U.S. economy seemed to be doing well overall after the recession of 2001. Growth had been normal, unemployment had stayed low, and inflation seemed to be under control. The economy began to unravel at the end of 2007—total output fell in the fourth quarter and again in the first quarter of 2008. It recovered—barely—in the second quarter. Then things went sour…very sour. The economies of the United States and those of much of the world were rocked by the worst financial crisis in nearly 80 years.

A good deal of the U.S. economy's momentum when things were going well had been fueled by rising house prices. Between 1995 and 2007, housing prices in the United States more than doubled. As house prices rose, consumers who owned houses felt wealthier and increased their consumption purchases. That helped fuel economic growth. The boom in housing prices had been encouraged by policies of the nation's monetary authority, the Federal Reserve, which had shifted to an expansionary monetary policy that held short-term interest rates below the inflation rate. Another development, subprime mortgages—mortgage loans to buyers whose credit or income would not ordinarily qualify for mortgage loans—helped bring on the ultimate collapse. When they were first developed, subprime mortgage loans seemed a hugely profitable investment for banks and a good deal for home buyers. Financial institutions developed a wide range of instruments based on "mortgage-backed securities." As long as house prices kept rising, the system worked and was profitable for virtually all players in the mortgage market. Many firms undertook investments in mortgage-backed securities that assumed house prices would keep rising. Large investment banks bet heavily that house prices would continue rising. Powerful members of Congress pressured two government-sponsored enterprises, Fannie Mae (the Federal National Mortgage Association) and Freddie Mac (the Federal Home Loan Mortgage Corporation), to be even more aggressive in encouraging banks to make mortgage loans to low-income families. The pressure came from the executive branch of government as well—under both Democratic and Republican administrations. In 1996, the Department of Housing and Urban Development (under Bill Clinton, a Democrat) required that 12% of mortgages purchased by Fannie Mae and Freddie Mac be for households with incomes less than 60% of the median income in their region. That target was increased to 20% in 2000, 22% in 2005 (then under George W. Bush, a Republican), and was to have increased to 28% in 2008.[1] But that final target would not be reached, as both Fannie Mae and Freddie Mac were seized by the government in 2008. To top things off, a loosening in bank and investment bank regulations gave financial institutions greater leeway in going overboard with purchases of mortgage-backed securities. As house prices began falling in 2007, a system based on the assumption they would continue rising began to unravel very fast. The investment bank Bear Stearns and insurance company American International Group (AIG) required massive infusions of federal money to keep them afloat. In September of 2008, firm after firm with assets tied to mortgage-backed securities began to fail. In some cases, the government rescued them; in other cases, such as Lehman Brothers, they were allowed to fail.

The financial crisis had dramatic and immediate effects on the economy. The economy's total output fell at an annual rate of 3.7% in the third quarter of 2008 and 8.9% in the fourth quarter of 2008. Consumers, having weathered higher gasoline prices and higher food prices for most of the year, reduced their consumption expenditures as the value of their houses and the stocks they held plunged—consumption fell at an annual rate of 3.8% in the third quarter and 5.1% in the fourth quarter. As cold fear gripped financial markets and expectations of further slowdown ensued, firms cut down on investment spending, which includes spending on plant and equipment used in production. While this nonresidential investment component of output fell at an annual rate of 0.8%, the residential component fell even faster as housing investment sank at an annual rate of 23.9%. Government purchases and net exports rose, but not enough to offset reductions in consumption and private investment. As output shrank, unemployment rose sharply. Through the first nine months of 2008 there was concern that price levels in the United States and in most of the world economies were rising rapidly, but toward the end of the year the concern shifted to whether or not the price level might fall.

This recession, which officially began in December 2007 and ended in June 2009, was brutal: At 18 months in length, it was the longest U.S. recession since World War II. The nation's output fell by more than 5%. The unemployment rate rose dramatically, hitting 10% in October 2009 and remaining above 9% throughout 2010. To many people in 2010 and 2011, it certainly did not feel as if the "Great Recession," as many had begun to refer to it, had really ended. The unemployment rate had come down some but still remained elevated. Housing prices still seemed to be falling or, at best, crawling along a floor. There was, though, a little good news at the end of 2011: real GDP had increased at an annual rate of 3.0% in the fourth quarter, the largest quarterly increase that year. For the entire year, however, real GDP had risen by just 1.7%.

Even the relatively good news in the fourth quarter came with a sour note: most of the increase in GDP had come as firms had increased their inventories, and economists warned that growth was likely to slow in 2012 as firms began cutting back on those expanded inventories. Sure enough, real GDP increased at an annual rate of just 1.9% in the first quarter of 2012, according to the Commerce Department.

An important question, of course, is why the recovery has been so slow. Since the recovery began in June 2009, this has been the slowest recovery since World War II. Several factors have contributed to the slow pace of expansion.

First, the financial crisis that developed in 2008, as mentioned, was particularly severe. Financial crises shake confidence and limit investment. Uncertainty was also created by increased government regulation of economic activity and by the possibility of increased taxes.

Furthermore, the impact of massive government debts—propelled by government deficits going into the recession, the fall in revenue due to the recession, and massive government stimulus programs in response to the recession—added to a general uncertainty about what future policies might be required. Domestic political battles may have contributed to this uncertainty as well. External factors, such as economic crises in Europe and the rising price of oil, also threatened the economy.

Output, employment, and the price level are the key variables in the study of macroeconomics, which is the analysis of aggregate values of economic variables. What determines a country's output, and why does output in some economies expand while in others it contracts? Why do some economies grow faster than others? What causes prices throughout an economy to fluctuate, and how do such fluctuations affect people? What causes employment and unemployment? Why does a country's unemployment rate fluctuate? Why do different countries have different unemployment rates?

We would pronounce an economy "healthy" if its annual output of goods and services were growing at a rate it can sustain, its price level stable, and its unemployment rate low. What would constitute "good" numbers for each of these variables depends on time and place, but those are the outcomes that most people would agree are desirable for the aggregate economy. When the economy deviates from what is considered good performance, there are often calls for the government to "do something" to improve performance. How government policies affect economic performance is a major topic of macroeconomics. When the financial and economic crises struck throughout the world in 2008, there was massive intervention from world central banks and from governments throughout the world in an effort to stimulate their economies.

This chapter provides a preliminary sketch of the most important macroeconomic issues: growth of total output and the business cycle, changes in the price level, and unemployment. Grappling with these issues will be important to you not only in your exploration of macroeconomics but throughout your life.

1.   GROWTH OF REAL GDP AND BUSINESS CYCLES

LEARNING OBJECTIVES

1. **Define real gross domestic product and explain how its calculation avoids both double-counting and the effects of changes in the price level.**
2. **Identify the phases of a business cycle.**
3. **Relate business cycles to the overall long-run trend in real GDP in the United States.**

To determine whether the economy of a nation is growing or shrinking in size, economists use a measure of total output called real GDP. **Real GDP**, short for real gross domestic product, is the total value of all final goods and services produced during a particular year or period, adjusted to eliminate the effects of changes in prices. Let us break that definition up into parts.

Notice that only "final" goods and services are included in GDP. Many goods and services are purchased for use as inputs in producing something else. For example, a pizza parlor buys flour to make pizzas. If we counted the value of the flour and the value of the pizza, we would end up counting the flour twice and thus overstating the value of total production. Including only final goods avoids double-counting. If the flour is produced during a particular period but has not been sold, then it is a "final good" for that period and is counted.

We want to determine whether the economy's output is growing or shrinking. If each final good or service produced, from hammers to haircuts, were valued at its current market price, and then we were to add the values of all such items produced, we would not know if the total had changed because output changed or because prices changed or both. The market value of all final goods and services produced can rise even if total output falls. To isolate the behavior of total output only, we must hold prices constant at some level. For example, if we measure the value of basketball output over time using a fixed price for valuing the basketballs, then only an increase in the number of basketballs produced could increase the value of the contribution made by basketballs to total output. By making such an adjustment for basketballs and all other goods and services, we obtain a value for real GDP. In contrast, **nominal GDP**, usually just referred to as gross domestic product (GDP), is the total value of final goods and services for a particular period valued in terms of prices for that period. For example, real GDP fell in the third quarter of 2008. But, because the price level in the United States was rising, nominal GDP rose 3.6%.

real GDP

The total value of all final goods and services produced during a particular year or period, adjusted to eliminate the effects of changes in prices.

nominal GDP

The total value of final goods and services for a particular period valued in terms of prices for that period.

business cycle

The economy's pattern of expansion, then contraction, then expansion again.

expansion

A sustained period in which real GDP is rising.

recession

A sustained period in which real GDP is falling.

We will save a detailed discussion of the computation of GDP for another chapter. In this section, our goal is to use the concept of real GDP to look at the **business cycle**—the economy's pattern of expansion, then contraction, then expansion again—and at growth of real GDP.

1.1 Phases of the Business Cycle

Figure 11.1 shows a stylized picture of a typical business cycle. It shows that economies go through periods of increasing and decreasing real GDP, but that over time they generally move in the direction of increasing levels of real GDP. A sustained period in which real GDP is rising is an **expansion**; a sustained period in which real GDP is falling is a **recession**. Typically, an economy is said to be in a recession when real GDP drops for two consecutive quarters, but in the United States, the responsibility of defining precisely when the economy is in recession is left to the Business Cycle Dating Committee of the National Bureau of Economic Research (NBER). The committee defines a recession as a "significant decline in economic activity spread across the economy, lasting more than a few months, normally visible in real GDP, real income, employment, industrial production, and wholesale-retail sales."[2]

FIGURE 11.1 Phases of the Business Cycle

The business cycle is a series of expansions and contractions in real GDP. The cycle begins at a peak and continues through a recession, a trough, and an expansion. A new cycle begins at the next peak. Here, the first peak occurs at time t_1, the trough at time t_2, and the next peak at time t_3. Notice that there is a tendency for real GDP to rise over time.

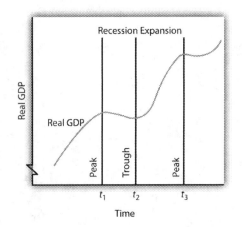

At time t_1 in Figure 11.1, an expansion ends and real GDP turns downward. The point at which an expansion ends and a recession begins is called the **peak** of the business cycle. Real GDP then falls during a period of recession. Eventually it starts upward again (at time t_2). The point at which a recession ends and an expansion begins is called the **trough** of the business cycle. The expansion continues until another peak is reached at time t_3.[3] A complete business cycle is defined by the passage from one peak to the next.

Because the Business Cycle Dating Committee dates peaks and troughs by specific months, and because real GDP is estimated only on a quarterly basis by the Bureau of Economic Analysis, the committee relies on a variety of other indicators that are published monthly, including real personal income, employment, industrial production, and real wholesale and retail sales. The committee typically determines that a recession has happened long after it has actually begun and sometimes ended! In large part, that avoids problems when data released about the economy are revised, and the committee avoids having to reverse itself on its determination of when a recession begins or ends, something it has never done. In December 2008, the committee announced that a recession in the United States had begun in December 2007. In September 2010, the committee announced that this recession had ended in June 2009.

1.2 Business Cycles and the Growth of Real GDP in the United States

Figure 11.2 shows movements in real GDP in the United States from 1960 to 2013. Over those years, the economy experienced eight recessions, shown by the shaded areas in the chart. Although periods of expansion have been more prolonged than periods of recession, we see the cycle of economic activity that characterizes economic life.

Real GDP clearly grew between 1960 and 2013. While the economy experienced expansions and recessions, its general trend during the period was one of rising real GDP. The average annual rate of growth of real GDP was about 3.1%.

During the post–World War II period, the average expansion has lasted 58 months, and the average recession has lasted about 11 months. The 2001 recession, which lasted eight months, was thus slightly shorter than the average. The 2007–2009 recession lasted 18 months; it was the longest of the post–World War II period.

Economists have sought for centuries to explain the forces at work in a business cycle. Not only are the currents that move the economy up or down intellectually fascinating but also an understanding of them is of tremendous practical importance. A business cycle is not just a movement along a curve in a textbook. It is new jobs for people, or the loss of them. It is new income, or the loss of it. It is the funds to build new schools or to provide better health care—or the lack of funds to do all those things. The story of the business cycle is the story of progress and plenty, of failure and sacrifice.

peak

The point of the business cycle at which an expansion ends and a recession begins.

trough

The point of the business cycle at which a recession ends and an expansion begins.

FIGURE 11.2 Expansions and Recessions, 1960–2013

The chart shows movements in real GDP since 1960. Recessions—periods of falling real GDP—are shown as shaded areas. On average, the annual rate of growth of real GDP over the period was 3.1% per year.

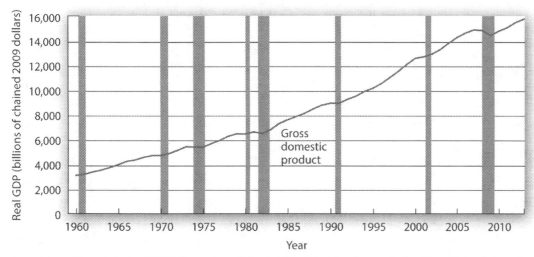

Source: Bureau of Economic Analysis, NIPA Table 1.1.6 (revised February 28, 2014). Real Gross Domestic Product, Chained Dollars [Billions of chained (2005) dollars]. Seasonally adjusted at annual rates.

During the most recent recession, the job outlook for college graduates deteriorated. According to a National Association of Colleges and Employers study, 20% of college graduates seeking jobs were able to obtain one after graduation in 2009. In 2010, that percentage rose to 24%, but the average salary had slipped 1.7% from the previous year. The unemployment rate for college graduates under age 25 rose from 3.7% in April 2007 to 8% in April 2010. Over the same two-year period, the unemployment rate for high school graduates who had never enrolled in college rose from 11.4% to 24.5%.[4]

The effects of recessions extend beyond the purely economic realm and influence the social fabric of society as well. Suicide rates and property crimes—burglary, larceny, and motor vehicle theft tend to rise during recessions. Even popular music appears to be affected. Terry F. Pettijohn II, a psychologist at Coastal Carolina University, has studied Billboard No. 1 songs from 1955 to 2003. He finds that during recessions, popular songs tend to be longer and slower, and to have more serious lyrics. "It's 'Bridge over Troubled Water' or 'That's What Friends Are For'," he says. During expansions, songs tend to be faster, shorter, and somewhat sillier, such as "At the Hop" or "My Sharona."[5]

In our study of macroeconomics, we will gain an understanding of the forces at work in the business cycle. We will also explore policies through which the public sector might act to make recessions less severe and, perhaps, to prolong expansions. We turn next to an examination of price-level changes and unemployment.

KEY TAKEAWAYS

- Real gross domestic product (real GDP) is a measure of the value of all final goods and services produced during a particular year or period, adjusted to eliminate the effects of price changes.
- The economy follows a path of expansion, then contraction, then expansion again. These fluctuations make up the business cycle.
- The point at which an expansion becomes a recession is called the peak of a business cycle; the point at which a recession becomes an expansion is called the trough.
- Over time, the general trend for most economies is one of rising real GDP. On average, real GDP in the United States has grown at a rate of over 3% per year since 1960.

TRY IT!

The data below show the behavior of real GDP in Turkey from the first quarter of 2001 through the third quarter of 2002. Use the data to plot real GDP in Turkey and indicate the phases of the business cycle.

Period	Real GDP (billions of New Turkish lira, 1987 prices)
First quarter, 2001	24.1
Second quarter, 2001	26.0
Third quarter, 2001	33.1
Fourth quarter, 2001	27.1
First quarter, 2002	24.6
Second quarter, 2002	28.3
Third quarter, 2002	35.7

Case in Point

The Art of Predicting Recessions

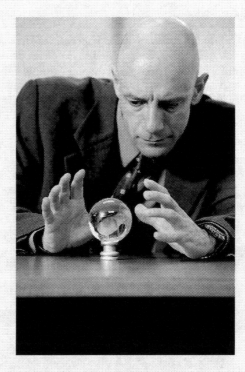

People who make a living tracking the economy and trying to predict its future do not do a very good job at predicting turning points in economic activity. The 52 economists surveyed by the *Wall Street Journal* each month did predict that the economy would slip into a recession in the third quarter of 2008. They made that prediction, however, in October—after the third quarter had ended. In September, the last month of the third quarter, the average forecast among the 52 economists had the economy continuing to grow through the third and fourth quarters of 2008. That September survey was taken before the financial crisis hit, a crisis that took virtually everyone by surprise. Of course, as we have already noted, the third-quarter downturn had not been identified as a recession by the NBER's Business Cycle Dating Committee as of November of 2008.

Predicting business cycle turning points has always been a tricky business. The experience of the recession of 2001 illustrates this. As the accompanying table shows, even as late as September 10, 2001, only 13 out of the 100 Blue Chip forecasters had answered in the affirmative to the question, "Has the United States slipped into a recession?" even though we now know the recession had begun the previous March. Comparing the data that were originally released by the U.S. Bureau of Economic Analysis shortly after the end of each quarter with the revised data that were released after July 2002 provides an important insight into explaining why the forecasters seem to have done so badly. As the graph on pre-revision and post-revision estimates of real GDP growth shows, the data released shortly after the end of each quarter showed an economy expanding through the second quarter of 2001, whereas the revised data show the economy contracting modestly in the first quarter of 2001 and then more forcefully in the second quarter. Only after the attacks on the World Trade Center in New York City and the Pentagon in Washington, D.C., on September 11, 2001, did most of the Blue Chip forecasters realize the economy was in recession.

The National Bureau of Economic Research (NBER) Business Cycle Dating Committee in November 2001 released a press announcement dating the onset of the recession as March 2001. The committee argued that "before the attacks of September 11, it is possible that the decline in the economy would have been too mild to qualify as a recession. The attacks clearly deepened the contraction and may have been an important factor in turning the episode into a recession." While surprising at the time, the revised data suggest that the committee made a good call.

This episode in economic history also points out the difference between the common definition of a recession as two consecutive quarters of declining real GDP and the NBER Dating Committee's continued insistence that it does not define a recession in this way. Rather the committee looks not only at real GDP but also at employment, income, and other factors. The behavior of employment during 2001 seems to have been an important factor in the November 2001 decision to proclaim March 2001 as the peak despite the misleading information on real GDP coming out of the Bureau of Economic Analysis at the time. The slow pickup in employment may also, though, have made it hesitate to call November 2001 the trough until July 2003.

Question posed: "Has the United States slipped into a recession?"		
Date	Percent of Blue Chip responders answering "Yes"	Percent of Blue Chip responders answering "No"
February 2001	5	95
June 2001	7	93
July 2001	13	87
August 2001	5	85
September 10, 2001	13	87
September 19, 2001	82	18

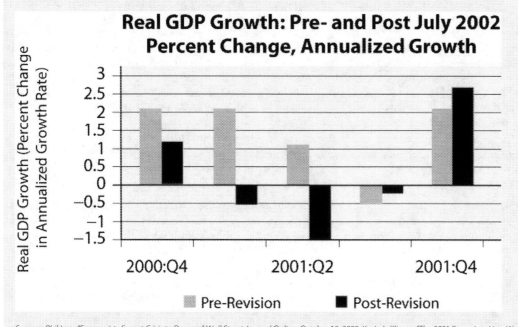

Real GDP Growth: Pre- and Post July 2002 Percent Change, Annualized Growth

Sources: Phil Izzo, "Economists Expect Crisis to Deepen," Wall Street Journal Online, October 10, 2008; Kevin L. Kliesen, "The 2001 Recession: How Was It Different and What Developments May Have Caused It?" Federal Reserve Bank of St. Louis Review, September/October 2003: 23–37; http://www.nber.org/cycles/; "Press Release," Business Cycle Dating Committee, National Bureau of Economic Research, press release, Cambridge, Massachusetts, July 17, 2002.

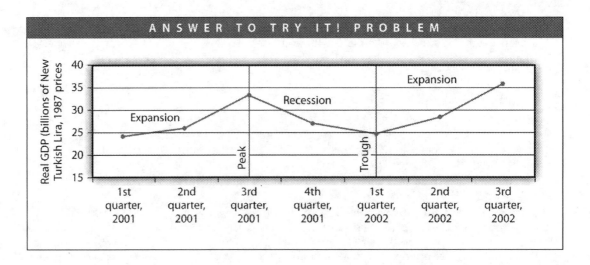

ANSWER TO TRY IT! PROBLEM

2. PRICE-LEVEL CHANGES

LEARNING OBJECTIVES

1. Define inflation and deflation, explain how their rates are determined, and articulate why price-level changes matter.
2. Explain what a price index is and outline the general steps in computing a price index.
3. Describe and compare different price indexes.
4. Explain how to convert nominal values to real values and explain why it is useful to make this calculation.
5. Discuss the biases that may arise from price indexes that employ fixed market baskets of goods and services.

Concern about changes in the price level has always dominated economic discussion. With inflation in the United States generally averaging only between 2% and 3% each year since 1990, it may seem surprising how much attention the behavior of the price level still commands. Yet inflation was a concern in 2004 when there was fear that the rising price of oil could trigger higher prices in other areas. Just the year before, when inflation fell below 2%, there was talk about the risk of deflation. That did not happen; prices continued rising. Inflation rose substantially in the first half of 2008, renewing fears about subsequent further increases. And 2010 brought renewed concern of possible deflation. Just what are inflation and deflation? How are they measured? And most important, why do we care? These are some of the questions we will explore in this section.

Inflation is an increase in the average level of prices, and **deflation** is a decrease in the average level of prices. In an economy experiencing inflation, most prices are likely to be rising, whereas in an economy experiencing deflation, most prices are likely to be falling.

There are two key points in these definitions:

1. Inflation and deflation refer to changes in the average level of prices, not to changes in particular prices. An increase in medical costs is not inflation. A decrease in gasoline prices is not deflation. Inflation means the average level of prices is rising, and deflation means the average level of prices is falling.

2. Inflation and deflation refer to *rising* prices and *falling* prices, respectively; therefore, they do not have anything to do with the *level* of prices at any one time. "High" prices do not imply the presence of inflation, nor do "low" prices imply deflation. Inflation means a positive *rate of change* in average prices, and deflation means a negative *rate of change* in average prices.

2.1 Why Do We Care?

What difference does it make if the average level of prices changes? First, consider the impact of inflation.

Inflation is measured as the annual rate of increase in the average level of prices. Figure 11.3 shows how volatile inflation has been in the United States over the past four decades. In the 1960s the

inflation

An increase in the average level of prices.

deflation

A decrease in the average level of prices.

inflation rate rose, and it became dramatically worse in the 1970s. The inflation rate plunged in the 1980s and continued to ease downward in the 1990s. It remained low in the early 2000s, began to accelerate in 2007, and has remained low since then.

FIGURE 11.3 Inflation, 1960–2013

The U.S. inflation rate, measured as the annual rate of change in the average level of prices paid by consumers, varied considerably over the 1960–2013 period.

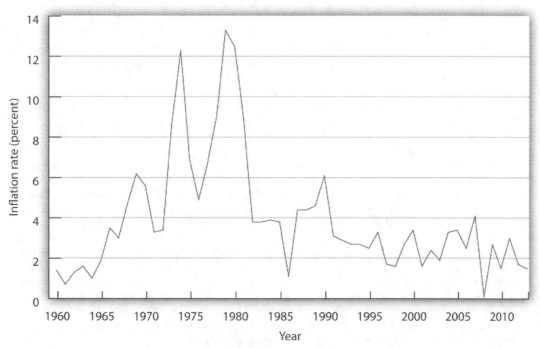

Source: Bureau of Labor Statistics, All Urban Consumers CPI-U, 1982–84 = 100, Dec.–Dec. inflation rate.

Whether one regards inflation as a "good" thing or a "bad" thing depends very much on one's economic situation. If you are a borrower, unexpected inflation is a good thing—it reduces the value of money that you must repay. If you are a lender, it is a bad thing because it reduces the value of future payments you will receive. Whatever any particular person's situation may be, inflation always produces the following effects on the economy: it reduces the value of money and it reduces the value of future monetary obligations. It can also create uncertainty about the future.

Suppose that you have just found a $10 bill you stashed away in 1990. Prices have increased by about 50% since then; your money will buy less than what it would have purchased when you put it away. Your money has thus lost value.

Money loses value when its purchasing power falls. Since inflation is a rise in the level of prices, the amount of goods and services a given amount of money can buy falls with inflation.

Just as inflation reduces the value of money, it reduces the value of future claims on money. Suppose you have borrowed $100 from a friend and have agreed to pay it back in one year. During the year, however, prices double. That means that when you pay the money back, it will buy only half as much as it could have bought when you borrowed it. That is good for you but tough on the person who lent you the money. Of course, if you and your friend had anticipated such rapid inflation, you might have agreed to pay back a larger sum to adjust for it. When people anticipate inflation, they can adjust for its consequences in determining future obligations. But *unanticipated* inflation helps borrowers and hurts lenders.

Inflation's impact on future claims can be particularly hard on people who must live on a fixed income, that is, on an income that is predetermined through some contractual arrangement and does not change with economic conditions. An annuity, for example, typically provides a fixed stream of money payments. Retirement pensions sometimes generate fixed income. Inflation erodes the value of such payments.

Given the danger posed by inflation for people on fixed incomes, many retirement plans provide for indexed payments. An indexed payment is one whose dollar amount changes with the rate of change in the price level. If a payment changes at the same rate as the rate of change in the price level, the purchasing power of the payment remains constant. Social Security payments, for example, are indexed to maintain their purchasing power.

Because inflation reduces the purchasing power of money, the threat of future inflation can make people reluctant to lend for long periods. From a lender's point of view, the danger of a long-term commitment of funds is that future inflation will wipe out the value of the amount that will eventually be paid back. Lenders are reluctant to make such commitments.

Uncertainty can be particularly pronounced in countries where extremely high inflation is a threat. **Hyperinflation** is generally defined as an inflation rate in excess of 200% per year. It is always caused by the rapid printing of money. Several countries have endured episodes of hyperinflation. The worst case was in Hungary immediately after World War II, when Hungary's price level was tripling *every day*. The second-worst case of hyperinflation belongs to Zimbabwe, which is the first country to have experienced hyperinflation in the 21st century. Zimbabwe's price index was doubling daily: a loaf of bread that cost 200,000 Zimbabwe dollars in February 2008 cost 1.6 trillion Zimbabwe dollars by August.[6] The annual inflation rate reached 89.7 sextillion percent in November of that year.[7] (On the off chance you haven't been counting in the sextillions a lot lately, 89.7 sextillion equates to 897 followed by 20 zeroes.) Two months later, Zimbabwe finally gave up on printing money and took the Zimbabwe dollar out of circulation. Exchange is now carried out using U.S. dollars or South African rand—and Zimbabwe's period of hyperinflation has come to an end.

Do the problems associated with inflation imply that deflation would be a good thing? The answer is simple: no. Like inflation, deflation changes the value of money and the value of future obligations. It also creates uncertainty about the future.

If there is deflation, the real value of a given amount of money rises. In other words, if there had been deflation since 2000, a $10 bill you had stashed away in 2000 would buy more goods and services today. That sounds good, but should you buy $10 worth of goods and services now when you would be able to buy even more for your $10 in the future if the deflation continues? When Japan experienced deflation in the late 1990s and early 2000s, Japanese consumers seemed to be doing just that—waiting to see if prices would fall further. They were spending less per person and, as we will see throughout our study of macroeconomics, less consumption often meant less output, fewer jobs, and the prospect of a recurring recession.

And, if you had to use the $10 to pay back a debt you owed, the purchasing power of your money would be higher than when you borrowed the money. The lender would feel good about being able to buy more with the $10 than you were able to, but you would feel like you had gotten a raw deal.

Unanticipated deflation hurts borrowers and helps lenders. If the parties anticipate the deflation, a loan agreement can be written to reflect expected changes in the price level.

The threat of deflation can make people reluctant to borrow for long periods. Borrowers become reluctant to enter into long-term contracts because they fear that deflation will raise the value of the money they must pay back in the future. In such an environment, firms may be reluctant to borrow to build new factories, for example. This is because they fear that the prices at which they can sell their output will drop, making it difficult for them to repay their loans.

Deflation was common in the United States in the latter third of the 19th century. In the 20th century, there was a period of deflation after World War I and again during the Great Depression in the 1930s.

2.2 Price Indexes

How do we actually measure inflation and deflation (that is, changes in the price level)? Price-level change is measured as the percentage rate of change in the level of prices. But how do we find a price level?

Economists measure the price level with a price index. A **price index** is a number whose movement reflects movement in the average level of prices. If a price index rises 10%, it means the average level of prices has risen 10%.

There are four steps one must take in computing a price index:

1. Select the kinds and quantities of goods and services to be included in the index. A list of these goods and services, and the quantities of each, is the "market basket" for the index.
2. Determine what it would cost to buy the goods and services in the market basket in some period that is the base period for the index. A **base period** is a time period against which costs of the market basket in other periods will be compared in computing a price index. Most often, the base period for an index is a single year. If, for example, a price index had a base period of 1990, costs of the basket in other periods would be compared to the cost of the basket in 1990. We will encounter one index, however, whose base period stretches over three years.
3. Compute the cost of the market basket in the current period.
4. Compute the price index. It equals the current cost divided by the base-period cost of the market basket.

hyperinflation

An inflation rate in excess of 200% per year.

price index

A number whose movement reflects movement in the average level of prices.

base period

A time period against which costs of the market basket in other periods will be compared in computing a price index.

EQUATION 11.1

Price index = current cost of basket / base-period cost of basket

(While published price indexes are typically reported with this number multiplied by 100, our work with indexes will be simplified by omitting this step.)

Suppose that we want to compute a price index for movie fans, and a survey of movie watchers tells us that a typical fan rents 4 movies on DVD and sees 3 movies in theaters each month. At the theater, this viewer consumes a medium-sized soft drink and a medium-sized box of popcorn. Our market basket thus might include 4 DVD rentals, 3 movie admissions, 3 medium soft drinks, and 3 medium servings of popcorn.

Our next step in computing the movie price index is to determine the cost of the market basket. Suppose we surveyed movie theaters and DVD-rental stores in 2011 to determine the average prices of these items, finding the values given in Table 11.1. At those prices, the total monthly cost of our movie market basket in 2011 was $48. Now suppose that in 2012 the prices of movie admissions and DVD rentals rise, soft-drink prices at movies fall, and popcorn prices remain unchanged. The combined effect of these changes pushes the 2012 cost of the basket to $50.88.

TABLE 11.1 Pricing a Market Basket

To compute a price index, we need to define a market basket and determine its price. The table gives the composition of the movie market basket and prices for 2011 and 2012. The cost of the entire basket rises from $48 in 2011 to $50.88 in 2012.

Item	Quantity in Basket	2011 Price	Cost in 2011 Basket	2012 Price	Cost in 2012 Basket
DVD rental	4	$2.25	$9.00	$2.97	$11.88
Movie admission	3	7.75	23.25	8.00	24.00
Popcorn	3	2.25	6.75	2.25	6.75
Soft drink	3	3.00	9.00	2.75	8.25
Total cost of basket		**2011**	$48.00	**2012**	$50.88

Using the data in Table 11.1, we could compute price indexes for each year. Recall that a price index is the ratio of the current cost of the basket to the base-period cost. We can select any year we wish as the base year; take 2011. The 2012 movie price index (MPI) is thus

$$MPI_{2012} = \$50.88 / \$48 = 1.06$$

The value of any price index in the base period is always 1. In the case of our movie price index, the 2011 index would be the current (2011) cost of the basket, $48, divided by the base-period cost, which is the same thing: $48/$48 = 1.

The Consumer Price Index (CPI)

One widely used price index in the United States is the **consumer price index (CPI)**, a price index whose movement reflects changes in the prices of goods and services typically purchased by consumers. When the media report the U.S. inflation rate, the number cited is usually a rate computed using the CPI. The CPI is also used to determine whether people's incomes are keeping up with the costs of the things they buy. The CPI is often used to measure changes in the cost of living, though as we shall see, there are problems in using it for this purpose.

The market basket for the CPI contains thousands of goods and services. The composition of the basket is determined by the Bureau of Labor Statistics (BLS), an agency of the Department of Labor, based on Census Bureau surveys of household buying behavior. Surveyors tally the prices of the goods and services in the basket each month in cities all over the United States to determine the current cost of the basket. The major categories of items in the CPI are food and beverages, housing, apparel, transportation, medical care, recreation, education and communication, and other goods and services.

The current cost of the basket of consumer goods and services is then compared to the base-period cost of that same basket. The base period for the CPI is 1982–1984; the base-period cost of the basket is its average cost over this period. Each month's CPI thus reflects the ratio of the current cost of the basket divided by its base-period cost.

consumer price index (CPI)

A price index whose movement reflects changes in the prices of goods and services typically purchased by consumers.

EQUATION 11.2

CPI = current cost of basket / 1982–1984 cost of basket

Like many other price indexes, the CPI is computed with a fixed market basket. The composition of the basket generally remains unchanged from one period to the next. Because buying patterns change, however, the basket is revised accordingly on a periodic basis. The base period, though, was still 1982–1984.

The Implicit Price Deflator

implicit price deflator

A price index for all final goods and services produced; it is the ratio of nominal GDP to real GDP.

Values for nominal and real GDP, described earlier in this chapter, provide us with the information to calculate the most broad-based price index available. The **implicit price deflator**, a price index for all final goods and services produced, is the ratio of nominal GDP to real GDP.

In computing the implicit price deflator for a particular period, economists define the market basket quite simply: it includes all the final goods and services produced during that period. The nominal GDP gives the current cost of that basket; the real GDP adjusts the nominal GDP for changes in prices. The implicit price deflator is thus given by

EQUATION 11.3

$$\text{Implicit price deflator} = \text{nominal GDP} / \text{real GDP}$$

For example, in 2011, nominal GDP in the United States was $15,094.5 billion, and real GDP was $13,315.3 billion. Thus, the implicit price deflator was 1.134. Following the convention of multiplying price indexes by 100, the published number for the implicit price deflator was 113.4.

In our analysis of the determination of output and the price level in subsequent chapters, we will use the implicit price deflator as the measure of the price level in the economy.

The PCE Price Index

personal consumption expenditures price index

A price index that includes durable goods, nondurable goods, and services and is provided along with estimates for prices of each component of consumption spending.

The Bureau of Economic Analysis also produces price index information for each of the components of GDP (that is, a separate price index for consumer prices, prices for different components of gross private domestic investment, and government spending). The **personal consumption expenditures price index**, or PCE price index, includes durable goods, nondurable goods, and services and is provided along with estimates for prices of each component of consumption spending. Because prices for food and energy can be volatile, the price measure that excludes food and energy is often used as a measure of underlying, or "core," inflation. Note that the PCE price index differs substantially from the consumer price index, primarily because it is not a "fixed basket" index.[8] The PCE price index has become a politically important measure of inflation since the Federal Reserve (discussed in detail in later chapters) uses it as its primary measure of price levels in the United States.

2.3   Computing the Rate of Inflation or Deflation

The rate of inflation or deflation is the percentage rate of change in a price index between two periods. Given price-index values for two periods, we can calculate the rate of inflation or deflation as the change in the index divided by the initial value of the index, stated as a percentage:

EQUATION 11.4

$$\text{Rate of inflation or deflation} = \text{percentage change in index} / \text{initial value of index}$$

To calculate inflation in movie prices over the 2011–2012 period, for example, we could apply Equation 11.4 to the price indexes we computed for those two years as follows:

$$\text{Movie inflation rate in 2012} = (1.06 - 1.00) / 1.00 = 0.06 = 6\%$$

The CPI is often used for calculating price-level change for the economy. For example, the rate of inflation in 2011 can be computed from the December 2010 price level (2.186) and the December 2011 level (2.263):

$$\text{Inflation rate} = (2.263 - 2.186) / 2.186 = 0.035 = 3.5\%$$

2.4   Computing Real Values Using Price Indexes

Suppose your uncle started college in 2001 and had a job busing dishes that paid $5 per hour. In 2011 you had the same job; it paid $6 per hour. Which job paid more?

At first glance, the answer is straightforward: $6 is a higher wage than $5. But $1 had greater purchasing power in 2001 than in 2011 because prices were lower in 2001 than in 2011. To obtain a valid comparison of the two wages, we must use dollars of equivalent purchasing power. A value expressed in units of constant purchasing power is a **real value**. A value expressed in dollars of the current period is called a **nominal value**. The $5 wage in 2001 and the $6 wage in 2011 are nominal wages.

To convert nominal values to real values, we divide by a price index. The real value for a given period is the nominal value for that period divided by the price index for that period. This procedure gives us a value in dollars that have the purchasing power of the base period for the price index used. Using the CPI, for example, yields values expressed in dollars of 1982–1984 purchasing power, the base period for the CPI. The real value of a nominal amount X at time t, X_t, is found using the price index for time t:

EQUATION 11.5

$$\text{Real value of } X_t = X_t \,/\, \text{price index at time } t$$

Let us compute the real value of the $6 wage for busing dishes in 2011 versus the $5 wage paid to your uncle in 2001. The CPI in 2001 was 177.1; in 2011 it was 224.9. Real wages for the two years were thus

$$\text{Real wage in 2001} = \$5 \,/\, 1.771 = \$2.82$$

$$\text{Real wage in 2011} = \$6 \,/\, 2.249 = \$2.67$$

Given the nominal wages in our example, you earned about 5% less in real terms in 2011 than your uncle did in 2001.

Price indexes are useful. They allow us to see how the general level of prices has changed. They allow us to estimate the rate of change in prices, which we report as the rate of inflation or deflation. And they give us a tool for converting nominal values to real values so we can make better comparisons of economic performance across time.

Are Price Indexes Accurate Measures of Price-Level Changes?

Price indexes that employ fixed market baskets are likely to overstate inflation (and understate deflation) for four reasons:

1. Because the components of the market basket are fixed, the index does not incorporate consumer responses to changing relative prices.
2. A fixed basket excludes new goods and services.
3. Quality changes may not be completely accounted for in computing price-level changes.
4. The type of store in which consumers choose to shop can affect the prices they pay, and the price indexes do not reflect changes consumers have made in where they shop.

To see how these factors can lead to inaccurate measures of price-level changes, suppose the price of chicken rises and the price of beef falls. The law of demand tells us that people will respond by consuming less chicken and more beef. But if we use a fixed market basket of goods and services in computing a price index, we will not be able to make these adjustments. The market basket holds constant the quantities of chicken and beef consumed. The importance in consumer budgets of the higher chicken price is thus overstated, while the importance of the lower beef price is understated. More generally, a fixed market basket will overstate the importance of items that rise in price and understate the importance of items that fall in price. This source of bias is referred to as the substitution bias.

The new-product bias, a second source of bias in price indexes, occurs because it takes time for new products to be incorporated into the market basket that makes up the CPI. A good introduced to the market after the basket has been defined will not, of course, be included in it. But a new good, once successfully introduced, is likely to fall in price. When VCRs were first introduced, for example, they generally cost more than $1,000. Within a few years, an equivalent machine cost less than $200. But when VCRs were introduced, the CPI was based on a market basket that had been defined in the early 1970s. There was no VCR in the basket, so the impact of this falling price was not reflected in the index. The DVD player was introduced into the CPI within a year of its availability.

A third price index bias, the quality-change bias, comes from improvements in the quality of goods and services. Suppose, for example, that Ford introduces a new car with better safety features and a smoother ride than its previous model. Suppose the old model cost $20,000 and the new model costs $24,000, a 20% increase in price. Should economists at the Bureau of Labor Statistics (BLS) simply record the new model as being 20% more expensive than the old one? Clearly, the new model is not the same product as the old model. BLS economists faced with such changes try to adjust for quality. To the extent that such adjustments understate quality change, they overstate any increase in the price level.

The fourth source of bias is called the outlet bias. Households can reduce some of the impact of rising prices by shopping at superstores or outlet stores (such as T.J. Maxx, Wal-Mart, or factory outlet stores), though this often means they get less customer service than at traditional department stores or at smaller retail stores. However, since such shopping has increased in recent years, it must be that for their customers, the reduction in prices has been more valuable to them than loss of service. Prior to 1998, the CPI did not account for a change in the number of households shopping at these newer kinds of stores in a timely manner, but the BLS now does quarterly surveys and updates its sample of stores much more frequently. Another form of this bias arises because the government data collectors do not collect price data on weekends and holidays, when many stores run sales.

Economists differ on the degree to which these biases result in inaccuracies in recording price-level changes. In late 1996, Michael Boskin, an economist at Stanford University, chaired a panel of economists appointed by the Senate Finance Committee to determine the magnitude of the problem in the United States. The panel reported that the CPI was overstating inflation in the United States by 0.8 to 1.6 percentage points per year. Their best estimate was 1.1 percentage points, as shown in Table 11.2. Since then, the Bureau of Labor Statistics has made a number of changes to correct for these sources of bias and since August 2002 has reported a new consumer price index called the Chained Consumer Price Index for all Urban Consumers (C-CPU-U) that attempts to provide a closer approximation to a "cost-of-living" index by utilizing expenditure data that reflect the substitutions that consumers make across item categories in response to changes in relative prices.[9] However, a 2006 study by Robert Gordon, a professor at Northwestern University and a member of the original 1996 Boskin Commission, estimates that the total bias is still about 0.8 percentage points per year, as also shown in Table 11.2.

TABLE 11.2 Estimates of Bias in the Consumer Price Index

The Boskin Commission reported that the CPI overstates the rate of inflation by 0.8 to 1.6 percentage points due to the biases shown, with a best-guess estimate of 1.1. A 2006 study by Robert Gordon estimates that the bias fell but is still about 0.8 percentage points.

Sources of Bias	1997 Estimate	2006 Estimate
Substitution	0.4	0.4
New products and quality change	0.6	0.3
Switching to new outlets	0.1	0.1
Total	1.1	0.8
Plausible range	0.8–1.6	—

Source: Robert J. Gordon, "The Boskin Commission Report: A Retrospective One Decade Later" (National Bureau of Economic Research Working Paper 12311, June 2006), available at http://www.nber.org/papers/w12311.

These findings of upward bias have enormous practical significance. With annual inflation running below 2% in three out of the last 10 years and averaging 2.7% over the 10 years, it means that the United States has come close to achieving price stability for almost a decade.

To the extent that the computation of price indexes overstates the rate of inflation, then the use of price indexes to correct nominal values results in an understatement of gains in real incomes. For example, average nominal hourly earnings of U.S. production workers were $13.01 in 1998 and $17.42 in 2007. Adjusting for CPI-measured inflation, the average real hourly earnings was $7.98 in 1998 and $8.40 in 2007, suggesting that real wages rose about 5.3% over the period. If inflation was overstated by 0.8% per year over that entire period, as suggested by Gordon's updating of the Boskin Commission's best estimate, then, adjusting for this overstatement, real wages should have been reported as $7.98 for 1998 and $9.01 for 2007, a gain of nearly 13%.

Also, because the CPI is used as the basis for calculating U.S. government payments for programs such as Social Security and for adjusting tax brackets, this price index affects the government's budget balance, the difference between government revenues and government expenditures. The Congressional Budget Office has estimated that correcting the biases in the index would have increased revenue by $2 billion and reduced outlays by $4 billion in 1997. By 2007, the U.S. government's budget would have had an additional $140 billion if the bias were removed.

KEY TAKEAWAYS

- Inflation is an increase in the average level of prices, and deflation is a decrease in the average level of prices. The rate of inflation or deflation is the percentage rate of change in a price index.
- The consumer price index (CPI) is the most widely used price index in the United States.
- Nominal values can be converted to real values by dividing by a price index.
- Inflation and deflation affect the real value of money, of future obligations measured in money, and of fixed incomes. Unanticipated inflation and deflation create uncertainty about the future.
- Economists generally agree that the CPI and other price indexes that employ fixed market baskets of goods and services do not accurately measure price-level changes. Biases include the substitution bias, the new-product bias, the quality-change bias, and the outlet bias.

TRY IT!

Suppose that nominal GDP is $10 trillion in 2003 and $11 trillion in 2004, and that the implicit price deflator has gone from 1.063 in 2003 to 1.091 in 2004. Compute real GDP in 2003 and 2004. Using the percentage change in the implicit price deflator as the gauge, what was the inflation rate over the period?

Case in Point

Take Me Out to the Ball Game …

The cost of a trip to the old ball game rose 2% in 2011, according to *Team Marketing Report*, a Chicago-based newsletter. The report bases its estimate on its fan price index, whose market basket includes four adult average-priced tickets, two small draft beers, four small soft drinks, four regular-sized hot dogs, parking for one car, two game programs, and two least expensive, adult-sized adjustable baseball caps. The average price of the market basket was $197.35 in 2011.

Team Marketing compiles the cost of the basket for each of major league baseball's 30 teams. According to this compilation, the Boston Red Sox was the most expensive team to watch in 2011; the Arizona Diamondbacks was the cheapest. The table shows the cost of the fan price index market basket for 2011.

Team	Basket Cost	Team	Basket Cost
Boston Red Sox	$339.01	Baltimore Orioles	$174.10
New York Yankees	$338.32	Cleveland Indians	$170.96
Chicago Cubs	$305.60	Florida Marlins	$170.24
Chicago White Sox	$258.68	Atlanta Braves	$169.02
New York Mets	$241.74	Cincinnati Reds	$162.24
Philadelphia Phillies	$240.66	Colorado Rockies	$161.00
Los Angeles Dodgers	$226.36	Milwaukee Brewers	$160.40
St. Louis Cardinals	$223.18	Kansas City Royals	$159.80
Houston Astros	$221.36	Texas Rangers	$159.40
Minnesota Twins	$213.16	Tampa Bay Rays	$139.68
Toronto Blue Jays	$212.68	Los Angeles Angels	$129.50
San Francisco Giants	$208.15	Pittsburgh Pirates	$127.71
Detroit Tigers	$207.28	San Diego Padres	$125.81
Washington Nationals	$196.34	Arizona Diamondbacks	$120.96
Seattle Mariners	$183.59		
Oakland Athletics	$178.09	**MLB Average**	**$197.35**

Source: Team Marketing Report, "TMR's Fan Cost Index Major League Baseball 2011," available at http://www.teammarketing.com.

ANSWER TO TRY IT! PROBLEM

Rearranging Equation 11.3, real GDP = nominal GDP/implicit price deflator. Therefore,

$$\text{Real GDP in 2003} = \$10 \text{ trillion}/1.063 = \$9.4 \text{ trillion.}$$

$$\text{Real GDP in 2004} = \$11 \text{ trillion}/1.091 = \$10.1 \text{ trillion.}$$

Thus, in this economy in real terms, GDP has grown by $0.7 trillion.

To find the rate of inflation, we refer to Equation 11.4, and we calculate:

$$\text{Inflation rate in 2004} = (1.091 - 1.063)/1.063 = 0.026 = 2.6\%$$

Thus, the price level rose 2.6% between 2003 and 2004.

3. UNEMPLOYMENT

LEARNING OBJECTIVES

1. **Explain how unemployment is measured in the United States.**
2. **Define three different types of unemployment.**
3. **Define and illustrate graphically what is meant by the natural level of employment. Relate the natural level of employment to the natural rate of unemployment.**

For an economy to produce all it can and achieve a solution on its production possibilities curve, the factors of production in the economy must be fully employed. Failure to fully employ these factors leads to a solution inside the production possibilities curve in which society is not achieving the output it is capable of producing.

In thinking about the employment of society's factors of production, we place special emphasis on labor. The loss of a job can wipe out a household's entire income; it is a more compelling human problem than, say, unemployed capital, such as a vacant apartment. In measuring unemployment, we thus focus on labor rather than on capital and natural resources.

3.1   Measuring Unemployment

The Bureau of Labor Statistics defines a person as unemployed if he or she is not working but is looking for and available for work. The **labor force** is the total number of people working or unemployed. The **unemployment rate** is the percentage of the labor force that is unemployed.

To estimate the unemployment rate, government surveyors fan out across the country each month to visit roughly 60,000 households. At each of these randomly selected households, the surveyor asks about the employment status of each adult (everyone age 16 or over) who lives there. Many households include more than one adult; the survey gathers information on about roughly 100,000 adults. The surveyor asks if each adult is working. If the answer is yes, the person is counted as employed. If the answer is no, the surveyor asks if that person has looked for work at some time during the previous four weeks and is available for work at the time of the survey. If the answer to that question is yes, the person is counted as unemployed. If the answer is no, that person is not counted as a member of the labor force. Figure 11.4 shows the survey's results for the civilian (nonmilitary) population for February 2014. The unemployment rate is then computed as the number of people unemployed divided by the labor force—the sum of the number of people not working but available and looking for work plus the number of people working. In February 2014, the unemployment rate was 6.7%.

FIGURE 11.4   Computing the Unemployment Rate

A monthly survey of households divides the civilian adult population into three groups. Those who have jobs are counted as employed; those who do not have jobs but are looking for them and are available for work are counted as unemployed; and those who are not working and are not looking for work are not counted as members of the labor force. The unemployment rate equals the number of people looking for work divided by the sum of the number of people looking for work and the number of people employed. Values are for February 2014. All numbers are in thousands.

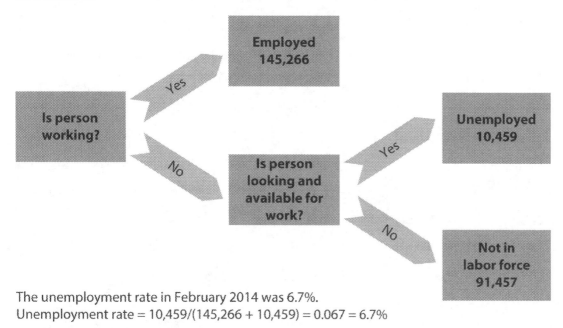

The unemployment rate in February 2014 was 6.7%.
Unemployment rate = 10,459/(145,266 + 10,459) = 0.067 = 6.7%

There are several difficulties with the survey. The old survey, designed during the 1930s, put the "Are you working?" question differently depending on whether the respondent was a man or woman. A man was asked, "Last week, did you do any work for pay or profit?" A woman was asked, "What were you doing for work last week, keeping house or something else?" Consequently, many women who were looking for paid work stated that they were "keeping house"; those women were not counted as unemployed. The BLS did not get around to fixing the survey—asking women the same question it asked men—until 1994. The first time the new survey question was used, the unemployment rate among women rose by 0.5 percentage point. More than 50 million women are in the labor force; the change added more than a quarter of a million workers to the official count of the unemployed.[10]

The problem of understating unemployment among women has been fixed, but others remain. A worker who has been cut back to part-time work still counts as employed, even if that worker would prefer to work full time. A person who is out of work, would like to work, has looked for work in the past year, and is available for work, but who has given up looking, is considered a discouraged worker. Discouraged workers are not counted as unemployed, but a tally is kept each month of the number of discouraged workers.

The official measures of employment and unemployment can yield unexpected results. For example, when firms expand output, they may be reluctant to hire additional workers until they can be sure the demand for increased output will be sustained. They may respond first by extending the hours of employees previously reduced to part-time work or by asking full-time personnel to work overtime. None of that will increase employment, because people are simply counted as "employed" if they are working, regardless of how much or how little they are working. In addition, an economic expansion may make discouraged workers more optimistic about job prospects, and they may resume their job searches. Engaging in a search makes them unemployed again—and increases unemployment. Thus, an economic expansion may have little effect initially on employment and may even increase unemployment.

3.2 Types of Unemployment

Workers may find themselves unemployed for different reasons. Each source of unemployment has quite different implications, not only for the workers it affects but also for public policy.

Figure 11.5 applies the demand and supply model to the labor market. The price of labor is taken as the real wage, which is the nominal wage divided by the price level; the symbol used to represent the real wage is the Greek letter omega, ω. The supply curve is drawn as upward sloping, though steep, to reflect studies showing that the quantity of labor supplied at any one time is nearly fixed. Thus, an increase in the real wage induces a relatively small increase in the quantity of labor supplied. The demand curve shows the quantity of labor demanded at each real wage. The lower the real wage, the greater the quantity of labor firms will demand. In the case shown here, the real wage, ω_e, equals the equilibrium solution defined by the intersection of the demand curve D_1 and the supply curve S_1. The quantity of labor demanded, L_e, equals the quantity supplied. The employment level at which the quantity of labor demanded equals the quantity supplied is called the **natural level of employment**. It is sometimes referred to as full employment.

natural level of employment

The employment level at which the quantity of labor demanded equals the quantity supplied.

FIGURE 11.5 The Natural Level of Employment

The employment level at which the quantity of labor demanded equals the quantity supplied is called the natural level of employment. Here, the natural level of employment is L_e, which is achieved at a real wage ω_e.

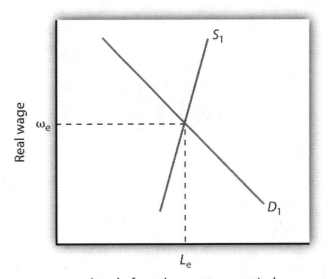

Even if the economy is operating at its natural level of employment, there will still be some unemployment. The rate of unemployment consistent with the natural level of employment is called the **natural rate of unemployment**. Business cycles may generate additional unemployment. We discuss these various sources of unemployment below.

natural rate of unemployment

The rate of unemployment consistent with the natural level of employment.

Frictional Unemployment

Even when the quantity of labor demanded equals the quantity of labor supplied, not all employers and potential workers have found each other. Some workers are looking for jobs, and some employers are looking for workers. During the time it takes to match them up, the workers are unemployed. Unemployment that occurs because it takes time for employers and workers to find each other is called **frictional unemployment**.

The case of college graduates engaged in job searches is a good example of frictional unemployment. Those who did not land a job while still in school will seek work. Most of them will find jobs, but it will take time. During that time, these new graduates will be unemployed. If information about the labor market were costless, firms and potential workers would instantly know everything they needed to know about each other and there would be no need for searches on the part of workers and firms. There would be no frictional unemployment. But information is costly. Job searches are needed to produce this information, and frictional unemployment exists while the searches continue.

The government may attempt to reduce frictional unemployment by focusing on its source: information costs. Many state agencies, for example, serve as clearinghouses for job market information. They encourage firms seeking workers and workers seeking jobs to register with them. To the extent that such efforts make labor-market information more readily available, they reduce frictional unemployment.

Structural Unemployment

Another reason there can be unemployment even if employment equals its natural level stems from potential mismatches between the skills employers seek and the skills potential workers offer. Every worker is different; every job has its special characteristics and requirements. The qualifications of job seekers may not match those that firms require. Even if the number of employees firms demand equals the number of workers available, people whose qualifications do not satisfy what firms are seeking will find themselves without work. Unemployment that results from a mismatch between worker qualifications and the characteristics employers require is called **structural unemployment**.

Structural unemployment emerges for several reasons. Technological change may make some skills obsolete or require new ones. The widespread introduction of personal computers since the 1980s, for example, has lowered demand for typists who lacked computer skills.

Structural unemployment can occur if too many or too few workers seek training or education that matches job requirements. Students cannot predict precisely how many jobs there will be in a particular category when they graduate, and they are not likely to know how many of their fellow students are training for these jobs. Structural unemployment can easily occur if students guess wrong about how many workers will be needed or how many will be supplied.

Structural unemployment can also result from geographical mismatches. Economic activity may be booming in one region and slumping in another. It will take time for unemployed workers to relocate and find new jobs. And poor or costly transportation may block some urban residents from obtaining jobs only a few miles away.

Public policy responses to structural unemployment generally focus on job training and education to equip workers with the skills firms demand. The government publishes regional labor-market information, helping to inform unemployed workers of where jobs can be found. The North American Free Trade Agreement (NAFTA), which created a free trade region encompassing Mexico, the United States, and Canada, has created some structural unemployment in the three countries. In the United States, the legislation authorizing the pact also provided for job training programs for displaced U.S. workers.

Although government programs may reduce frictional and structural unemployment, they cannot eliminate it. Information in the labor market will always have a cost, and that cost creates frictional unemployment. An economy with changing demands for goods and services, changing technology, and changing production costs will always have some sectors expanding and others contracting—structural unemployment is inevitable. An economy at its natural level of employment will therefore have frictional and structural unemployment.

Cyclical Unemployment

Of course, the economy may not be operating at its natural level of employment, so unemployment may be above or below its natural level. In a later chapter we will explore what happens when the economy generates employment greater or less than the natural level. **Cyclical unemployment** is unemployment in excess of the unemployment that exists at the natural level of employment.

Figure 11.6 shows the unemployment rate in the United States for the period from 1960 through 2013. We see that it has fluctuated considerably. How much of it corresponds to the natural rate of unemployment varies over time with changing circumstances. For example, in a country with a demographic "bulge" of new entrants into the labor force, frictional unemployment is likely to be high,

frictional unemployment

Unemployment that occurs because it takes time for employers and workers to find each other.

structural unemployment

Unemployment that results from a mismatch between worker qualifications and the characteristics employers require.

cyclical unemployment

Unemployment in excess of the unemployment that exists at the natural level of employment.

because it takes the new entrants some time to find their first jobs. This factor alone would raise the natural rate of unemployment. A demographic shift toward more mature workers would lower the natural rate. During recessions, highlighted in Figure 11.6, the part of unemployment that is cyclical unemployment grows. The analysis of fluctuations in the unemployment rate, and the government's responses to them, will occupy center stage in much of the remainder of this book.

FIGURE 11.6 Unemployment Rate, 1960–2013

The chart shows the unemployment rate for each year from 1960 to 2011. Recessions are shown as shaded areas.

Source: Economic Report of the President, 2014, Table B-42.

KEY TAKEAWAYS

- People who are not working but are looking and available for work at any one time are considered unemployed. The unemployment rate is the percentage of the labor force that is unemployed.
- When the labor market is in equilibrium, employment is at the natural level and the unemployment rate equals the natural rate of unemployment.
- Even if employment is at the natural level, the economy will experience frictional and structural unemployment. Cyclical unemployment is unemployment in excess of that associated with the natural level of employment.

TRY IT!

Given the data in the table, compute the unemployment rate in Year 1 and in Year 2. Explain why, in this example, both the number of people employed and the unemployment rate increased.

Year	Number employed (in millions)	Number unemployed (in millions)
1	20	2
2	21	2.4

Case in Point

Might Increased Structural Unemployment Explain the "Jobless Recovery" Following the 2001 Recession?

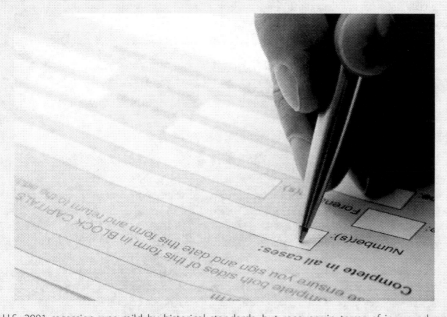

The U.S. 2001 recession was mild by historical standards, but recovery in terms of increased employment seemed painfully slow in coming. Economists Erica Goshen and Simon Potter at the Federal Reserve Bank of New York think the reason for the slow recovery in jobs may have actually reflected structural changes in the U.S. economy. They argue that during the recession permanent rather than temporary layoffs predominated and that it takes longer for firms to hire workers into new positions than to hire them back into former jobs.

What is their evidence? When the layoff is temporary, the employer "suspends" the job, due to slack demand, and the employee expects to be recalled once demand picks up. With a permanent layoff, the employer eliminates the job. So, they looked at the contribution of temporary layoffs to the unemployment rate during the recent recession compared to the situation in the four recessions before 1990. In the earlier recessions, unemployment from temporary layoffs rose when the economy was shrinking and fell after the economy began to recover. In both the 1991 and 2001 recessions, temporary layoffs were minor. Then, the authors examined job flows in 70 industries. They classified layoffs in an industry as being cyclical in nature if the job losses during the recession were reversed during the recovery but structural if job losses for the industry continued during the recovery. Their analysis revealed that during the recession of the early 1980s, job losses were about evenly split between cyclical and structural changes. In the 1991 recession and then more strongly in the 2001 recession, structural changes dominated. "Most of the industries that lost jobs during the [2001] recession—for example, communications, electronic equipment, and securities and commodities brokers—[were] still losing jobs" in 2003. "The trend revealed . . . is one in which jobs are relocated from some industries to others, not reclaimed by the same industries that lost them earlier."

The authors suggest three possible reasons for the recent increased role of structural change: (1) The structural decline in some industries could be the result of overexpansion in those industries during the 1990s. The high tech and telecommunications industries in particular could be examples of industries that were overbuilt before the 2001 recession. (2) Improved government policies may have reduced cyclical unemployment. Examination of macroeconomic policy in future chapters will return to this issue. (3) New management strategies to reduce costs may be promoting leaner staffing. For firms adopting such strategies, a recession may provide an opportunity to reorganize the production process permanently and reduce payrolls in the process.

Goshen and Potter point out that, for workers, finding new jobs is harder than simply returning to old ones. For firms, making decisions about the nature of new jobs is time consuming at best. The uncertainty created by the war in Iraq and the imposition of new accounting standards following the "Enron"-like scandals may have further prolonged the creation of new jobs.

Source: Erica L. Goshen and Simon Potter, "Has Structural Change Contributed to a Jobless Recovery?" Federal Reserve Bank of New York Current Issues in Economics and Finance 9, no. 8 (August 2003): 1–7.

In Year 1 the total labor force includes 22 million workers, and so the unemployment rate is 2/22 = 9.1%. In Year 2 the total labor force numbers 23.4 million workers; therefore the unemployment rate is 2.4/23.4 = 10.3%. In this example, both the number of people employed and the unemployment rate rose, because more people (23.4 − 22 = 1.4 million) entered the labor force, of whom 1 million found jobs and 0.4 million were still looking for jobs.

4. REVIEW AND PRACTICE

Summary

In this chapter we examined growth in real GDP and business cycles, price-level changes, and unemployment. We saw how these phenomena are defined and looked at their consequences.

Examining real GDP, rather than nominal GDP, over time tells us whether the economy is expanding or contracting. Real GDP in the United States shows a long upward trend, but with the economy going through phases of expansion and recession around that trend. These phases make up the business cycle. An expansion reaches a peak, and the economy falls into a recession. The recession reaches a trough and begins an expansion again.

Inflation is an increase in the price level and deflation is a decrease in the price level. The rate of inflation or deflation is the percentage rate of change in a price index. We looked at the calculation of the consumer price index (CPI) and the implicit price deflator. The CPI is widely used in the calculation of price-level changes. There are, however, biases in its calculation: the substitution bias, the new-product bias, the quality-change bias, and the outlet bias.

Inflation and deflation affect economic activity in several ways. They change the value of money and of claims on money. Unexpected inflation benefits borrowers and hurts lenders. Unexpected deflation benefits lenders and hurts borrowers. Both inflation and deflation create uncertainty and make it difficult for individuals and firms to enter into long-term financial commitments.

The unemployment rate is measured as the percentage of the labor force not working but seeking work. Frictional unemployment occurs because information about the labor market is costly; it takes time for firms seeking workers and workers seeking firms to find each other. Structural unemployment occurs when there is a mismatch between the skills offered by potential workers and the skills sought by firms. Both frictional and structural unemployment occur even if employment and the unemployment rate are at their natural levels. Cyclical unemployment is unemployment that is in excess of that associated with the natural level of employment.

CONCEPT PROBLEMS

1. Describe the phases of a business cycle.

2. On the basis of recent news reports, what phase of the business cycle do you think the economy is in now? What is the inflation or deflation rate? The unemployment rate?

3. Suppose you compare your income this year and last year and find that your nominal income fell but your real income rose. How could this have happened?

4. Suppose you calculate a grocery price inflation rate. Using the arguments presented in the chapter, explain possible sources of upward bias in the rate you calculate, relative to the actual trend of food prices.

5. Name three items you have purchased during the past year that have increased in quality during the year. What kind of adjustment would you make in assessing their prices for the CPI?

6. Why do some people gain and other people lose from inflation and deflation?

7. Suppose unemployed people leave a state to obtain jobs in other states. What do you predict will happen to the unemployment rate in the state experiencing the out-migration? What might happen to the unemployment rates in the states experiencing in-migration?

8. Minority teenagers have the highest unemployment rates of any group. One reason for this phenomenon is high transportation costs for many minority teens. What form of unemployment (cyclical, frictional, or structural) do high transportation costs suggest?

9. Welfare reforms enacted in 1996 put more pressure on welfare recipients to look for work. The new law mandated cutting off benefits after a certain length of time. How do you think this provision might affect the unemployment rate?

10. American workers work more hours than their European counterparts. Should Congress legislate a shorter workweek?

NUMERICAL PROBLEMS

1. Plot the quarterly data for real GDP for the last two years. (You can find the data online at http://www.whitehouse.gov/administration/eop/cea/economic-indicators. Relate recent changes in real GDP to the concept of the phases of the business cycle.)

2. Suppose that in 2013, the items in the market basket for our movie price index cost $53.40. Use the information in the chapter to compute the price index for that year. How does the rate of movie price inflation from 2012 to 2013 compare with the rate from 2011 to 2012?

3. Recompute the movie price indexes for 2011 and 2012 using 2012 as the base year. Now compute the rate of inflation for the 2011–2012 period. Compare your result to the inflation rate calculated for that same period using 2011 as the base year.

4. Here are some statistics for August 2006. Compute the unemployment rate for that month (all figures are in thousands).

Population (Civilian, noninstitutional)	229,167
Civilian Labor Force	151,698
Participation Rate	66.2%
Not in Labor Force	77,469
Employed	144,579
Unemployed	7,119

5. Suppose an economy has 10,000 people who are not working but looking and available for work and 90,000 people who are working. What is its unemployment rate? Now suppose 4,000 of the people looking for work get discouraged and give up their searches. What happens to the unemployment rate? Would you interpret this as good news for the economy or bad news? Explain.

6. The average price of going to a baseball game in 2011, based on the observations in the Case in Point, was $197.35. Using this average as the equivalent of a base year, compute fan price indexes for:

    a. The New York Yankees.

    b. The Chicago Cubs.

    c. The Boston Red Sox.

    d. The Tampa Bay Rays.

    e. The team of your choice.

7. Suppose you are given the following data for a small economy:

    Number of unemployed workers: 1,000,000.

    Labor force: 10,000,000.

    Based on this data, answer the following:

    a. What is the unemployment rate?

    b. Can you determine whether the economy is operating at its full employment level?

    c. Now suppose people who had been seeking jobs become discouraged, and give up their job searches. The labor force shrinks to 900,500 workers, and unemployment falls to 500,000 workers. What is the unemployment rate now? Has the economy improved?

8. Nominal GDP for an economy is $10 trillion. Real GDP is $9 trillion. What is the value of the implicit price deflator?

9. Suppose you are given the following data for an economy:

Month	Real GDP	Employment
1	$10.0 trillion	100 million
2	$10.4 trillion	104 million
3	$10.5 trillion	105 million
4	$10.3 trillion	103 million
5	$10.2 trillion	102 million
6	$10.3 trillion	103 million
7	$10.6 trillion	106 million
8	$10.7 trillion	107 million
9	$10.6 trillion	106 million

a. Plot the data for real GDP, with the time period on the horizontal axis and real GDP on the vertical axis.

b. There are two peaks. When do they occur?

c. When does the trough occur?

10. The Consumer Price Index in Period 1 is 107.5. It is 103.8 in Period 2. Is this a situation of inflation or deflation? What is the rate?

ENDNOTES

1. Russell Roberts, "How Government Stoked the Mania," *Wall Street Journal*, October 3, 2008, p. A21.

2. "The NBER's Recession Dating Procedure," National Bureau of Economic Research, January 7, 2008.

3. Some economists prefer to break the expansion phase into two parts. The recovery phase is said to be the period between the previous trough and the time when the economy achieves its previous peak level of real GDP. The "expansion" phase is from that point until the following peak.

4. Steven Greenhouse, "Job Market Gets Better for U.S. Graduates, but Only Slightly: Offers Will Increase 5% Over Last Year; Average Starting Salaries Are Down," *The International Herald Tribune*, May 26, 2010, Finance 16.

5. Tamar Lewin, "A Hemline Index, Updated," *New York Times*, October 19, 2008, Section WK, 1.

6. "Zimbabwe Inflation Hits 11,200,000%," CNN.com, August 19, 2008, available at http://edition.cnn.com/2008/BUSINESS/08/19/zimbabwe.inflation/index.html.

7. Steve H. Hanke, "R.I.P. Zimbabwe Dollar," Cato Institute, May 3, 2010, available at http://www.cato.org/zimbabwe.

8. For a comparison of price measures, including a comparison of the PCE price index and the Consumer Price Index, see Brian C. Moyer, "Comparing Price Measures—The CPI and PCE Price Index" (lecture, National Association for Business Economics, 2006 Washington Economic Policy Conference, March 13–14, 2006), available at http://www.bea.gov/papers/pdf/Moyer_NABE.pdf.

9. Robert Cage, John Greenlees, and Patrick Jackman, "Introducing the Chained Consumer Price Index" (paper, Seventh Meeting of the International Working Group on Price Indices, Paris, France, May 2003), available at http://stats.bls.gov/cpi/superlink.htm.

10. For a description of the new survey and other changes introduced in the method of counting unemployment, see Janet L. Norwood and Judith M. Tanur, "Unemployment Measures for the Nineties," *Public Opinion Quarterly* 58, no. 2 (Summer 1994): 277–94.

CHAPTER 12

Measuring Total Output and Income

START UP: THE LOCKUP

It is early morning when a half-dozen senior officials enter the room at the Commerce Department in Washington. Once inside, they will have no communication with the outside world until they have completed their work later that day. They will have no telephone, no computer links. They will be able to slip out to an adjoining restroom, but only in pairs. It is no wonder the room is called "the Lockup." The Lockup produces one of the most important indicators of economic activity we have: the official estimate of the value of the economy's total output, known as its gross domestic product (GDP).

When the team has finished its computations, the results will be placed in a sealed envelope. A government messenger will hand carry the envelope to the Executive Office Building and deliver it to a senior adviser to the president of the United States. The adviser will examine its contents, then carry it across the street to the White House and give it to the president.

The senior officials who meet in secret to compute GDP are not spies; they are economists. The adviser who delivers the estimate to the president is the chairman of the Council of Economic Advisers.

The elaborate precautions for secrecy do not end there. At 7:30 the next morning, journalists from all over the world will gather in an electronically sealed auditorium at the Commerce Department. There they will be given the GDP figure and related economic indicators, along with an explanation. The reporters will have an hour to prepare their reports, but they will not be able to communicate with anyone else until an official throws the switch at 8:30. At that instant their computers will connect to their news services, and they will be able to file their reports. These will be major stories on the Internet and in the next editions of the nation's newspapers; the estimate of the previous quarter's GDP will be one of the lead items on television and radio news broadcasts that day.

The clandestine preparations for the release of quarterly GDP figures reflect the importance of this indicator. The estimate of GDP provides the best available reading of macroeconomic performance. It will affect government policy, and it will influence millions of decisions in the private sector. Prior knowledge of the GDP estimate could be used to anticipate the response in the stock and bond markets, so great care is taken that only a handful of trusted officials have access to the information until it is officially released.

The GDP estimate took on huge significance in the fall of 2008 as the United States and much of the rest of the world went through the wrenching experience of the worst financial crisis since the Great Depression of the 1930s. The expectation that the financial crisis would lead to an economic collapse was widespread, and the quarterly announcements of GDP figures were more anxiously awaited than ever.

The primary measure of the ups and downs of economic activity—the business cycle—is real GDP. When an economy's output is rising, the economy creates more jobs, more income, and more opportunities for people. In the long run, an economy's output and income, relative to its population, determine the material standard of living of its people.

Clearly GDP is an important indicator of macroeconomic performance. It is the topic we will consider in this chapter. We will learn that GDP can be measured either in terms of the total value of output produced or as the total value of income generated in producing that output. We will begin with an examination of measures of GDP in terms of output. Our initial focus will be on nominal GDP: the value of total output measured in current prices. We will turn to real GDP—a measure of output that has been adjusted for price level changes—later in the chapter. We will refer to nominal GDP simply as GDP. When we discuss the real value of the measure, we will call it real GDP.

1. MEASURING TOTAL OUTPUT

LEARNING OBJECTIVES

1. **Define gross domestic product and its four major spending components and illustrate the various flows using the circular flow model.**
2. **Distinguish between measuring GDP as the sum of the values of final goods and services and as the sum of values added at each stage of production.**
3. **Distinguish between gross domestic product and gross national product.**

An economy produces a mind-boggling array of goods and services every year. For example, Domino's Pizza produces hundreds of millions of pizzas. The United States Steel Corporation, the nation's largest steel company, produces tens of millions of tons of steel. A small logging company in Colorado produces a couple million board feet of lumber. A university football team draws more than half a million fans to its home games. A pediatric nurse in Los Angeles delivers hundreds of babies and takes care of several hundred additional patients. A list of all the goods and services an economy produces in any year would be virtually endless.

So—what kind of year is the year we are looking at? We would not get very far trying to wade through a list of all the goods and services produced that year. It is helpful to have instead a single number that measures total output in the economy; that number is GDP.

1.1 The Components of GDP

We can divide the goods and services produced during any period into four broad components, based on who buys them. These components of GDP are personal consumption (C), gross private domestic investment (I), government purchases (G), and net exports (X_n). Thus

EQUATION 12.1

$$\text{GDP} = \text{consumption } (C) + \text{private investment } (I) + \text{government purchases } (G) + \text{net exports } (X_n),$$

or

$$\text{GDP} = C + I + G + X_n$$

flow variable

A variable that is measured over a specific period of time.

stock variable

A variable that is independent of time.

We will examine each of these components, and we will see how each fits into the pattern of macroeconomic activity. Before we begin, it will be helpful to distinguish between two types of variables: stocks and flows. A **flow variable** is a variable that is measured over a specific period of time. A **stock variable** is a variable that is independent of time. Income is an example of a flow variable. To say one's income is, for example, $1,000 is meaningless without a time dimension. Is it $1,000 per hour? Per day? Per week? Per month? Until we know the time period, we have no idea what the income figure means. The balance in a checking account is an example of a stock variable. When we learn that the balance in a checking account is $1,000, we know precisely what that means; we do not need a time dimension. We will see that stock and flow variables play very different roles in macroeconomic analysis.

The components of GDP are flow variables. We use the **circular flow model**, which shows flows of spending and income through the economy, to examine each in turn.

Personal Consumption

Personal consumption is a flow variable that measures the value of goods and services purchased by households during a time period. Purchases by households of groceries, health-care services, clothing, and automobiles—all are counted as consumption.

The production of consumer goods and services accounts for about 70% of total output. Because consumption is such a large part of GDP, economists seeking to understand the determinants of GDP must pay special attention to the determinants of consumption.

Personal consumption represents a demand for goods and services placed on firms by households. Figure 12.1 presents a circular flow model for an economy that produces only personal consumption goods and services. (We will add the other components of GDP to the circular flow as we discuss them.) Spending for these goods flows from households to firms; it is the arrow labeled "Personal consumption." Firms produce these goods and services using factors of production: labor, capital, and natural resources. These factors are ultimately owned by households. The production of goods and services thus generates income to households; we see this income as the flow from firms to households, labeled "Factor incomes" in the exhibit.

In exchange for payments that flow from households to firms, there is a flow of consumer goods and services from firms to households. This flow is shown in Figure 12.1 as an arrow going from firms to households. When you buy a soda, for example, your payment to the store is part of the flow of personal consumption; the soda is part of the flow of consumer goods and services that goes from the store to a household—yours.

Similarly, the lower arrow in Figure 12.1 shows the flow of factors of production—labor, capital, and natural resources—from households to firms. If you work for a firm, your labor is part of this flow. The wages you receive are part of the factor incomes that flow from firms to households.

FIGURE 12.1 Personal Consumption in the Circular Flow

Personal consumption spending flows from households to firms. In return, consumer goods and services flow from firms to households. To produce the goods and services households demand, firms employ factors of production owned by households. There is thus a flow of factor services from households to firms, and a flow of payments of factor incomes from firms to households.

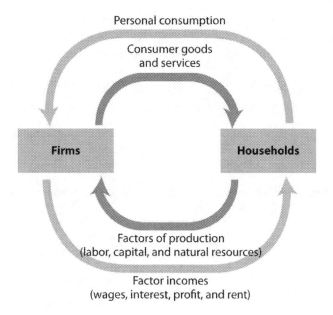

Private Investment

Gross private domestic investment is the value of all goods produced during a period for use in the production of other goods and services. Like personal consumption, gross private domestic investment is a flow variable. It is often simply referred to as "private investment." A hammer produced for a carpenter is private investment. A printing press produced for a magazine publisher is private investment, as is a conveyor-belt system produced for a manufacturing firm. Capital includes all the goods that have been produced for use in producing other goods; it is a stock variable. Private investment is a flow variable that adds to the stock of capital during a period.

circular flow model

Model that shows the flows of spending and income through the economy.

personal consumption

A flow variable that measures the value of goods and services purchased by households during a time period.

gross private domestic investment

The value of all goods produced during a period for use in the production of other goods and services.

Heads Up!

The term *"investment"* can generate confusion. In everyday conversation, we use the term *"investment"* to refer to uses of money to earn income. We say we have invested in a stock or invested in a bond. Economists, however, restrict *"investment"* to activities that increase the economy's stock of capital. The purchase of a share of stock does not add to the capital stock; it is not investment in the economic meaning of the word. We refer to the exchange of financial assets, such as stocks or bonds, as financial investment to distinguish it from the creation of capital that occurs as the result of investment. Only when new capital is produced does investment occur. Confusing the economic concept of private investment with the concept of financial investment can cause misunderstanding of the way in which key components of the economy relate to one another.

Gross private domestic investment includes three flows that add to or maintain the nation's capital stock: expenditures by business firms on new buildings, plants, tools, equipment, and software that will be used in the production of goods and services; expenditures on new residential housing; and changes in business inventories. Any addition to a firm's inventories represents an addition to investment; a reduction subtracts from investment. For example, if a clothing store stocks 1,000 pairs of jeans, the jeans represent an addition to inventory and are part of gross private domestic investment. As the jeans are sold, they are subtracted from inventory and thus subtracted from investment.

By recording additions to inventories as investment and reductions from inventories as subtractions from investment, the accounting for GDP records production in the period in which it occurs. Suppose, for example, that Levi Strauss manufactures 1 million pairs of jeans late in 2011 and distributes them to stores at the end of December. The jeans will be added to inventory; they thus count as investment in 2011 and enter GDP for that year. Suppose they are sold in January 2012. They will be counted as consumption in GDP for 2012 but subtracted from inventory, and from investment. Thus, the production of the jeans will add to GDP in 2011, when they were produced. They will not count in 2012, save for any increase in the value of the jeans resulting from the services provided by the retail stores that sold them.

Private investment accounts for about 15% of GDP—but, at times, even less. Despite its relatively small share of total economic activity, private investment plays a crucial role in the macroeconomy for two reasons:

1. Private investment represents a choice to forgo current consumption in order to add to the capital stock of the economy. Private investment therefore adds to the economy's capacity to produce and shifts its production possibilities curve outward. Investment is thus one determinant of economic growth, which is explored in another chapter.

2. Private investment is a relatively volatile component of GDP; it can change dramatically from one year to the next. Fluctuations in GDP are often driven by fluctuations in private investment. We will examine the determinants of private investment in a chapter devoted to the study of investment.

Private investment represents a demand placed on firms for the production of capital goods. While it is a demand placed on firms, it flows from firms. In the circular flow model in Figure 12.2, we see a flow of investment going from firms to firms. The production of goods and services for consumption generates factor incomes to households; the production of capital goods for investment generates income to households as well.

Figure 12.2 shows only spending flows and omits the physical flows represented by the arrows in Figure 12.1. This simplification will make our analysis of the circular flow model easier. It will also focus our attention on spending flows, which are the flows we will be studying in this section.

Government Purchases

Government agencies at all levels purchase goods and services from firms. They purchase office equipment, vehicles, buildings, janitorial services, and so on. Many government agencies also produce goods and services. Police departments produce police protection. Public schools produce education. The National Aeronautics and Space Administration (NASA) produces space exploration.

Government purchases are the sum of purchases of goods and services from firms by government agencies plus the total value of output produced by government agencies themselves during a time period. Government purchases make up about 20% of GDP.

Government purchases are not the same thing as government spending. Much government spending takes the form of **transfer payments**, which are payments that do not require the recipient to produce a good or service in order to receive them. Transfer payments include Social Security and other types of assistance to retired people, welfare payments to poor people, and unemployment compensation to people who have lost their jobs. Transfer payments are certainly significant—they account for roughly half of all federal government spending in the United States. They do not count in a nation's GDP, because they do not reflect the production of a good or service.

Government purchases represent a demand placed on firms, represented by the flow shown in Figure 12.3. Like all the components of GDP, the production of goods and services for government agencies creates factor incomes for households.

FIGURE 12.3 Government Purchases in the Circular Flow

Purchases of goods and services by government agencies create demands on firms. As firms produce these goods and services, they create factor incomes for households.

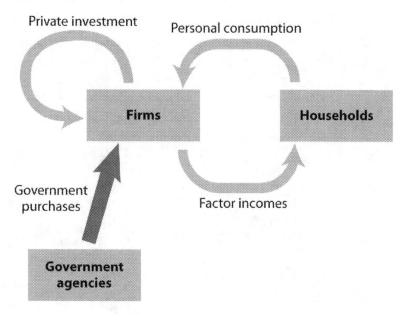

Net Exports

Sales of a country's goods and services to buyers in the rest of the world during a particular time period represent its **exports**. A purchase by a Japanese buyer of a Ford Taurus produced in the United States is a U.S. export. Exports also include such transactions as the purchase of accounting services from a New York accounting firm by a shipping line based in Hong Kong or the purchase of a ticket to Disney World by a tourist from Argentina. **Imports** are purchases of foreign-produced goods and services by a country's residents during a period. United States imports include such transactions as the purchase by Americans of cars produced in Japan or tomatoes grown in Mexico or a stay in a French hotel by a tourist from the United States. Subtracting imports from exports yields **net exports**.

EQUATION 12.2

$$\text{Exports } (X) - \text{imports } (M) = \text{net exports } (X_n)$$

FIGURE 12.2 Private Investment in the Circular Flow

Private investment constitutes a demand placed on firms by other firms. It also generates factor incomes for households. To simplify the diagram, only the spending flows are shown—the corresponding flows of goods and services have been omitted.

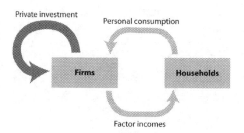

government purchases

The sum of purchases of goods and services from firms by government agencies plus the total value of output produced by government agencies themselves during a time period.

transfer payments

Payments that do not require the recipient to produce a good or service in order to receive them.

exports

Sales of a country's goods and services to buyers in the rest of the world during a particular time period.

imports

Purchases of foreign-produced goods and services by a country's residents during a period.

net exports

Exports minus imports.

trade deficit

Negative net exports.

trade surplus

Positive net exports.

In 2013, foreign buyers purchased $2,757.0 billion worth of goods and services from the United States. In the same year, U.S. residents, firms, and government agencies purchased $2,259.8 billion worth of goods and services from foreign countries. The difference between these two figures, -$497.3 billion, represented the net exports of the U.S. economy in 2013. Net exports were negative because imports exceeded exports. Negative net exports constitute a **trade deficit**. The amount of the deficit is the amount by which imports exceed exports. When exports exceed imports there is a **trade surplus**. The magnitude of the surplus is the amount by which exports exceed imports.

The United States has recorded more deficits than surpluses since World War II, but the amounts have typically been relatively small, only a few billion dollars. The trade deficit began to soar, however, in the 1980s and again in the 2000s. We will examine the reasons for persistent trade deficits in another chapter. The rest of the world plays a key role in the domestic economy and, as we will see later in the book, there is nothing particularly good or bad about trade surpluses or deficits. Goods and services produced for export represent roughly 14% of GDP, and the goods and services the United States imports add significantly to our standard of living.

In the circular flow diagram in Figure 12.4, net exports are shown with an arrow connecting firms to the rest of the world. The balance between the flows of exports and imports is net exports. When there is a trade surplus, net exports are positive and add spending to the circular flow. A trade deficit implies negative net exports; spending flows from firms to the rest of the world.

The production of goods and services for personal consumption, private investment, government purchases, and net exports makes up a nation's GDP. Firms produce these goods and services in response to demands from households (personal consumption), from other firms (private investment), from government agencies (government purchases), and from the rest of the world (net exports). All of this production creates factor income for households. Figure 12.5 shows the circular flow model for all the spending flows we have discussed. Each flow is numbered for use in the exercise at the end of this section.

FIGURE 12.4 Net Exports in the Circular Flow

Net exports represent the balance between exports and imports. Net exports can be positive or negative. If they are positive, net export spending flows from the rest of the world to firms. If they are negative, spending flows from firms to the rest of the world.

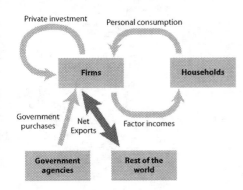

FIGURE 12.5 Spending in the Circular Flow Model

GDP equals the sum of production by firms of goods and services for personal consumption (1), private investment (2), government purchases (3), and net exports (4). The circular flow model shows these flows and shows that the production of goods and services generates factor incomes (5) to households.

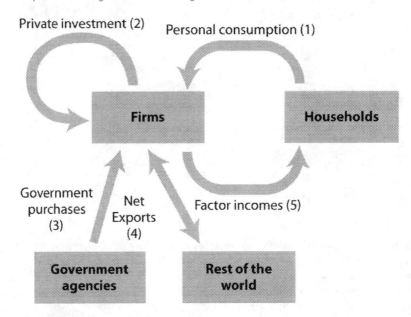

The circular flow model identifies some of the forces at work in the economy, forces that we will be studying in later chapters. For example, an increase in any of the flows that place demands on firms (personal consumption, private investment, government purchases, and exports) will induce firms to expand their production. This effect is characteristic of the expansion phase of the business cycle. An increase in production will require firms to employ more factors of production, which will create more income for households. Households are likely to respond with more consumption, which will induce still more production, more income, and still more consumption. Similarly, a reduction in any of the demands placed on firms will lead to a reduction in output, a reduction in firms' use of factors of production, a reduction in household incomes, a reduction in income, and so on. This sequence of events is characteristic of the contraction phase of the business cycle. Much of our work in macroeconomics will involve an analysis of the forces that prompt such changes in demand and an examination of the economy's response to them.

Figure 12.6 shows the size of the components of GDP in 2013. We see that the production of goods and services for personal consumption accounted for about 70% of GDP. Imports exceeded exports, so net exports were negative.

FIGURE 12.6   Components of GDP, 2013 in Billions of Dollars

Consumption makes up the largest share of GDP. Net exports were negative in 2011. Total GDP—the sum of personal consumption, private investment, government purchases, and net exports—equaled $16,797.5 billion in 2011.

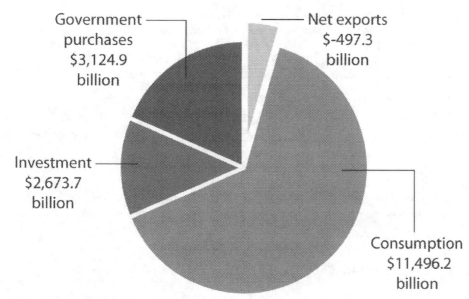

Source: Bureau of Economic Analysis, National Income and Product Accounts, Table 1.1.5 (revised February 28, 2014)

1.2   Final Goods and Value Added

GDP is the total value of all *final* goods and services produced during a particular period valued at prices in that period. That is not the same as the total value of all goods and services produced during a period. This distinction gives us another method of estimating GDP in terms of output.

Suppose, for example, that a logger cuts some trees and sells the logs to a sawmill. The mill makes lumber and sells it to a construction firm, which builds a house. The market price for the lumber includes the value of the logs; the price of the house includes the value of the lumber. If we try to estimate GDP by adding the value of the logs, the lumber, and the house, we would be counting the lumber twice and the logs three times. This problem is called "double counting," and the economists who compute GDP seek to avoid it.

In the case of logs used for lumber and lumber produced for a house, GDP would include the value of the house. The lumber and the logs would not be counted as additional production because they are intermediate goods that were produced for use in building the house.

Another approach to estimating the value of final production is to estimate for each stage of production the **value added**, the amount by which the value of a firm's output exceeds the value of the goods and services the firm purchases from other firms. Table 12.1 illustrates the use of value added in the production of a house.

value added

The amount by which the value of a firm's output exceeds the value of the goods and services the firm purchases from other firms.

TABLE 12.1 Final Value and Value Added

If we sum the value added at each stage of the production of a good or service, we get the final value of the item. The example shown here involves the construction of a house, which is produced from lumber that is, in turn, produced from logs.

Good	Produced by	Purchased by	Price	Value Added
Logs	Logger	Sawmill	$12,000	$12,000
Lumber	Sawmill	Construction firm	$25,000	$13,000
House	Construction firm	Household	$125,000	$100,000
		Final Value	**$125,000**	
		Sum of Values Added		**$125,000**

Suppose the logs produced by the logger are sold for $12,000 to a mill, and that the mill sells the lumber it produces from these logs for $25,000 to a construction firm. The construction firm uses the lumber to build a house, which it sells to a household for $125,000. (To simplify the example, we will ignore inputs other than lumber that are used to build the house.) The value of the final product, the house, is $125,000. The value added at each stage of production is estimated as follows:

a. The logger adds $12,000 by cutting the logs.

b. The mill adds $13,000 ($25,000 − $12,000) by cutting the logs into lumber.

c. The construction firm adds $100,000 ($125,000 − $25,000) by using the lumber to build a house.

The sum of values added at each stage ($12,000 + $13,000 + $100,000) equals the final value of the house, $125,000.

The value of an economy's output in any period can thus be estimated in either of two ways. The values of final goods and services produced can be added directly, or the values added at each stage in the production process can be added. The Commerce Department uses both approaches in its estimate of the nation's GDP.

1.3   GNP: An Alternative Measure of Output

gross national product (GNP)

The total value of final goods and services produced during a particular period with factors of production owned by the residents of a particular country.

While GDP represents the most commonly used measure of an economy's output, economists sometimes use an alternative measure. **Gross national product (GNP)** is the total value of final goods and services produced during a particular period with factors of production owned by the residents of a particular country.

The difference between GDP and GNP is a subtle one. The GDP of a country equals the value of final output produced within the borders of that country; the GNP of a country equals the value of final output produced using factors owned by residents of the country. Most production in a country employs factors of production owned by residents of that country, so the two measures overlap. Differences between the two measures emerge when production in one country employs factors of production *owned* by residents of other countries.

Suppose, for example, that a resident of Bellingham, Washington, owns and operates a watch repair shop across the Canadian–U.S. border in Victoria, British Columbia. The value of watch repair services produced at the shop would be counted as part of Canada's GDP because they are produced in Canada. That value would not, however, be part of U.S. GDP. But, because the watch repair services were produced using capital and labor provided by a resident of the United States, they would be counted as part of GNP in the United States and not as part of GNP in Canada.

Because most production fits in both a country's GDP as well as its GNP, there is seldom much difference between the two measures. The relationship between GDP and GNP is given by

EQUATION 12.3

GDP+net income received from abroad by residents of a nation = GNP

In 2013, for example, GDP equaled $16,912.9 billion. We add income receipts of $822.0 billion earned by residents of the United States from the rest of the world and then subtract income payments of $559.1 billion that went from the United States to the rest of the world to get GNP of $17,175.9 billion for the third quarter of 2013. GNP is often used in international comparisons of income; we shall examine those later in this chapter.

KEY TAKEAWAYS

- GDP is the sum of final goods and services produced for consumption (C), private investment (I), government purchases (G), and net exports (X_n). Thus GDP = $C + I + G + X_n$.
- GDP can be viewed in the context of the circular flow model. Consumption goods and services are produced in response to demands from households; investment goods are produced in response to demands for new capital by firms; government purchases include goods and services purchased by government agencies; and net exports equal exports less imports.
- Total output can be measured two ways: as the sum of the values of final goods and services produced and as the sum of values added at each stage of production.
- GDP plus net income received from other countries equals GNP. GNP is the measure of output typically used to compare incomes generated by different economies.

TRY IT!

Here is a two-part exercise.

1. Suppose you are given the following data for an economy:

Personal consumption	$1,000
Home construction	100
Increase in inventories	40
Equipment purchases by firms	60
Government purchases	100
Social Security payments to households	40
Government welfare payments	100
Exports	50
Imports	150

   Identify the number of the flow in Figure 12.5 to which each of these items corresponds. What is the economy's GDP?

2. Suppose a dairy farm produces raw milk, which it sells for $1,000 to a dairy. The dairy produces cream, which it sells for $3,000 to an ice cream manufacturer. The ice cream manufacturer uses the cream to make ice cream, which it sells for $7,000 to a grocery store. The grocery store sells the ice cream to consumers for $10,000. Compute the value added at each stage of production, and compare this figure to the final value of the product produced. Report your results in a table similar to that given in Table 12.1.

Case in Point

The Spread of the Value Added Tax

Outside the United States, the value added tax (VAT) has become commonplace. Governments of more than 120 countries use it as their primary means of raising revenue. While the concept of the VAT originated in France in the 1920s, no country adopted it until after World War II. In 1948, France became the first country in the world to use the VAT. In 1967, Brazil became the first country in the Western Hemisphere to do so. The VAT spread to other western European and Latin American countries in the 1970s and 1980s and then to countries in the Asia/Pacific region, central European and former Soviet Union area, and Africa in the 1990s and early 2000s.

What is the VAT? It is equivalent to a sales tax on final goods and services but is collected at each stage of production.

Take the example given in Table 12.1, which is a simplified illustration of a house built in three stages. If there were a sales tax of 10% on the house, the household buying it would pay $137,500, of which the construction firm would keep $125,000 of the total and turn $12,500 over to the government.

With a 10% VAT, the sawmill would pay the logger $13,200, of which the logger would keep $12,000 and turn $1,200 over to the government. The sawmill would sell the lumber to the construction firm for $27,500—keeping $26,200, which is the $25,000 for the lumber itself and $1,200 it already paid in tax. The government at this stage would get $1,300, the difference between the $2,500 the construction firm collected as tax and the $1,200 the sawmill already paid in tax to the logger at the previous stage. The household would pay the construction firm $137,500. Of that total, the construction firm would turn over to the government $10,000, which is the difference between the $12,500 it collected for the government in tax from the household and the $2,500 in tax that it already paid when it bought the lumber from the sawmill. The table below shows that in the end, the tax revenue generated by a 10% VAT is the same as that generated by a 10% tax on final sales.

Why bother to tax in stages instead of just on final sales? One reason is simply record keeping, since it may be difficult to determine in practice if any particular sale is the final one. In the example, the construction firm does not need to know if it is selling the house to a household or to some intermediary business.

Also, the VAT may lead to higher revenue collected. For example, even if somehow the household buying the house avoided paying the tax, the government would still have collected some tax revenue at earlier stages of production. With a tax on retail sales, it would have collected nothing. The VAT has another advantage from the point of view of government agencies. It has the appearance at each stage of taking a smaller share. The individual amounts collected are not as obvious to taxpayers as a sales tax might be.

Good	Price	Value Added	Tax Collected	− Tax Already Paid	= Value Added Tax
Logs	$12,000	$12,000	$1,200	− $0	= $1,200
Lumber	$25,000	$13,000	$2,500	− $1,200	= $1,300
House	$125,000	$100,000	$12,500	− $2,500	= $10,000
Total			**$16,200**	**−$3,700**	**= $12,500**

ANSWERS TO TRY IT! PROBLEMS

1. GDP equals $1,200 and is computed as follows (the numbers in parentheses correspond to the flows in Figure 12.5):

Personal consumption (1)	$1,000
Private investment (2)	200
Housing	100
Equipment and software	60
Inventory change	40
Government purchases (3)	100
Net exports (4)	−100
GDP	$1,200

Notice that neither welfare payments nor Social Security payments to households are included. These are transfer payments, which are not part of the government purchases component of GDP.

2. Here is the table of value added.

Good	Produced by	Purchased by	Price	Value Added
Raw milk	Dairy farm	Dairy	$1,000	$1,000
Cream	Dairy	Ice cream maker	3,000	2,000
Ice cream	Ice cream manufacturer	Grocery store	7,000	4,000
Retail ice cream	Grocery store	Consumer	10,000	3,000
		Final Value	**$10,000**	
		Sum of Values Added		**$10,000**

2. MEASURING TOTAL INCOME

LEARNING OBJECTIVES

1. **Define gross domestic income and explain its relationship to gross domestic product.**
2. **Discuss the components of gross domestic income.**
3. **Define disposable personal income and explain how to calculate it from GDP.**

We saw in the last section that the production of goods and services generates factor incomes to households. The production of a given value of goods and services generates an equal value of total income. **Gross domestic income (GDI)** equals the total income generated in an economy by the production of final goods and services during a particular period. It is a flow variable. Because an economy's total output equals the total income generated in producing that output, GDP = GDI. We can estimate GDP either by measuring total output or by measuring total income.

Consider a $4 box of Cheerios. It is part of total output and thus is part of GDP. Who gets the $4? Part of the answer to that question can be found by looking at the cereal box. Cheerios are made from oat flour, wheat starch, sugar, salt, and a variety of vitamins and minerals. Therefore, part of the $4 goes to the farmers who grew the oats, the wheat, and the beets or cane from which the sugar was extracted. Workers and machines at General Mills combined the ingredients, crafted all those little O's, toasted them, and put them in a box. The workers were paid part of the $4 as wages. The owners of General Mills and the capital it used received part of the $4 as profit. The box containing the Cheerios was made from a tree, so a lumber company somewhere received part of the $4. The truck driver who brought the box of cereal to the grocery store got part of the $4, as did the owner of the truck itself and the owner of the oil that fueled the truck. The clerk who rang up the sale at the grocery store was paid part of the $4. And so on.

How much of the $4 was income generated in the production of the Cheerios? The answer is simple: all of it. Some of the money went to workers as wages. Some went to owners of the capital and natural resources used to produce it. Profits generated along the way went to the owners of the firms

gross domestic income (GDI)

The total income generated in an economy by the production of final goods and services during a particular period.

involved. All these items represent costs of producing the Cheerios and also represent income to households.

Part of the $4 cost of the Cheerios, while it makes up a portion of GDI, does not represent ordinary income actually earned by households. That part results from two other production costs: depreciation and taxes related to the production of the Cheerios. Nevertheless, they are treated as a kind of income; we will examine their role in GDI below.

As it is with Cheerios, so it is with everything else. The value of output equals the income generated as the output is produced.

2.1   The Components of GDI

Employee compensation is the largest among the components of factor income. Factor income also includes profit, rent, and interest. In addition, GDI includes charges for depreciation and taxes associated with production. Depreciation and production-related taxes, such as sales taxes, make up part of the cost of producing goods and services and must be accounted for in estimating GDI. We will discuss each of these components of GDI next.

Employee Compensation

Compensation of employees in the form of wages, salaries, and benefits makes up the largest single component of income generated in the production of GDP. In 2013, employee compensation represented over 50% of GDI.

The structure of employee compensation has changed dramatically in the last several decades. In 1950, virtually all employee compensation—95% of it—came in the form of wages and salaries. The remainder, about 5%, came in the form of additional benefits such as employer contributions to retirement programs and health insurance. In 2013, the share of benefits was about 30% of total employee compensation.

Profits

The profit component of income earned by households equals total revenues of firms less costs as measured by conventional accounting. Profits amounted to about 18% of GDI in 2013, down sharply from five decades earlier, when profits represented about 25% of the income generated in GDI.[1]

Profits are the reward the owners of firms receive for being in business. The opportunity to earn profits is the driving force behind production in a market economy.

Rental Income

Rental income, such as the income earned by owners of rental housing or payments for the rent of natural resources, is the smallest component of GDI (about 3%); it is the smallest of the income flows to households. The meaning of rent in the computation of GDI is the same as its meaning in conventional usage; it is a charge for the temporary use of some capital asset or natural resource.[2]

Net Interest

Businesses both receive and pay interest. GDI includes net interest, which equals interest paid less interest received by domestic businesses, plus interest received from foreigners less interest paid to foreigners. Interest payments on mortgage and home improvement loans are counted as interest paid by businesses, because homeowners are treated as businesses in the income accounts. In 2013, net interest accounted for about 4% of GDI.

Depreciation

depreciation

A measure of the amount of capital that wears out or becomes obsolete during a period.

Over time the machinery and buildings that are used to produce goods and services wear out or become obsolete. A farmer's tractor, for example, wears out as it is used. A technological change may make some equipment obsolete. The introduction of personal computers, for example, made the electric typewriters used by many firms obsolete. **Depreciation** is a measure of the amount of capital that wears out or becomes obsolete during a period. Depreciation is referred to in official reports as the consumption of fixed capital.

Depreciation is a cost of production, so it represents part of the price charged for goods and services. It is therefore counted as part of the income generated in the production of those goods and services. Depreciation represented about 15.5% of GDI in 2013.

Indirect Taxes

The final component of the income measure of GDI is indirect business taxes.[3] **Indirect taxes** are taxes imposed on the production or sale of goods and services or on other business activity. (By contrast, a **direct tax** is a tax imposed directly on income; the personal income and corporate income taxes are direct taxes.) Indirect taxes, which include sales and excise taxes and property taxes, make up part of the cost to firms of producing goods and services. Like depreciation, they are part of the price of those goods and services and are therefore treated as part of the income generated in their production. Indirect business taxes amounted to nearly 7% of GDI in 2013.

Table 12.2 shows the components of GDI in 2013. Employee compensation represented the largest share of GDI. The exhibit also shows the components of GDP for the same year.

In principle, GDP and GDI should be equal, but their estimated values never are, because the data come from different sources. Output data from a sample of firms are used to estimate GDP, while income data from a sample of households are used to estimate GDI. The difference is the statistical discrepancy shown in the right-hand column of Table 12.2. Some of the difficulties with these data are examined in the Case in Point feature on discrepancies between GDP and GDI.

TABLE 12.2 GDP and GDI, 2013

The table shows the composition of GDP and GDI in the third quarter of 2013 (in billions of dollars at an annual rate). Notice the rough equality of the two measures. (They are not quite equal because of measurement errors; the difference is due to a statistical discrepancy and is reduced significantly over time as the data are revised.)

Gross domestic product	$16,912.9	Gross domestic income	$17,004.6
Personal consumption expenditures	$11,537.7	Compensation of employees	8,896.8
Gross private domestic investment	$2,738.0	Profits[4]	3,067.5
Government consumption expenditures and gross investment	$3,137.5	Rental income of persons	596.3
Net exports of goods and services	−$500.2	Net interest	615.5
		Taxes on production and imports[5]	1,168.6
		Consumption of fixed capital (depreciation)	2,659.6
		Statistical discrepancy	−91.7

Source: Bureau of Economic Analysis, National Income and Product Accounts, Tables 1.10 and 1.1.5 (revised February 28, 2014).

2.2 Tracing Income from the Economy to Households

We have seen that the production of goods and services generates income for households. Thus, the value of total output equals the value of total income in an economy. But we have also seen that our measure of total income, GDI, includes such things as depreciation and indirect business taxes that are not actually received by households. Households also receive some income, such as transfer payments, that does not count as part of GDP or GDI. Because the income households actually receive plays an important role in determining their consumption, it is useful to examine the relationship between a nation's total output and the income households actually receive.

Table 12.3 traces the path we take in going from GDP to **disposable personal income**, which equals the income households have available to spend on goods and services. We first convert GDP to GNP and then subtract elements of GNP that do not represent income received by households and add payments such as transfer payments that households receive but do not earn in the production of GNP. Disposable personal income is either spent for personal consumption or saved by households.

Indirect taxes

Taxes imposed on the production or sale of goods and services or on other business activity.

direct tax

Taxes imposed directly on income.

disposable personal income

The income households have available to spend on goods and services.

TABLE 12.3 From GDP to Disposable Personal Income

GDP, a measure of total output, equals GDI, the total income generated in the production of goods and services in an economy. The chart traces the path from GDP to disposable personal income, which equals the income households actually receive. We first convert GDP to GNP. Then, we subtract depreciation to obtain net national product and subtract the statistical discrepancy to arrive at national income (i.e., gross national income [GNI] net of depreciation and the statistical discrepancy). Next, we subtract components of GNP and GNI that do not represent income actually received by households, such as taxes on production and imports, corporate profit and payroll taxes (contributions to social insurance), and corporate retained earnings. We add items such as transfer payments that are income to households but are not part of GNP and GNI. The adjustments shown are the most important adjustments in going from GNP and GNI to disposable personal income; several smaller adjustments (e.g., subsidies, business current transfer payments [net], and current surplus of government enterprises) have been omitted.

GDP + net factor earnings from abroad	=	gross national product (GNP)
GNP − depreciation (consumption of fixed capital)	=	net national product (NNP)
NNP − statistical discrepancy	=	national income (NI)
NI − income earned but not received [e.g., taxes on production and imports, social security payroll taxes, corporate profit taxes, and retained earnings] + transfer payments and other income received but not earned in the production of GNP	=	personal income (PI)
PI − personal income taxes	=	disposable personal income (DPI)

KEY TAKEAWAYS

- Gross domestic product, GDP, equals gross domestic income, GDI, which includes compensation, profits, rental income, indirect taxes, and depreciation.
- We can use GDP, a measure of total output, to compute disposable personal income, a measure of income received by households and available for them to spend.

TRY IT!

The following income data refer to the same economy for which you had output data in the first part of the previous Try It! Compute GDI from the data below and confirm that your result equals the GDP figure you computed in the previous Try It! Assume that GDP = GNP for this problem (that is, assume all factor incomes are earned and paid in the domestic economy).

Employee compensation	$700
Social Security payments to households	40
Welfare payments	100
Profits	200
Rental income	50
Net interest	25
Depreciation	50
Indirect taxes	175

Case in Point

The GDP–GDI Gap

GDP equals GDI; at least, that is the way it is supposed to work. But in an enormously complex economy, the measurement of these two variables inevitably goes awry. Estimates of the two are never quite equal. In recent years, the absolute value of the gap has been quite sizable, while in other years, it has been quite small. For example, for the years 2006 through 2010, GDI has differed from GDP by −242.3, −12.0, −2.4, 77.4, and 0.8 billion per year, respectively.

Although the gap seems large at times, it represents a remarkably small fraction of measured activity—around 1% or less. Of course, 1% of a big number is still a big number. But it is important to remember that, relative to the size of the economy, the gap between GDI and GDP is not large. The gap is listed as a "statistical discrepancy" in the Department of Commerce reporting of the two numbers.

Why does the gap exist? From an accounting point of view, it should not. The total value of final goods and services produced must be equal to the total value of income generated in that production. But output is measured from sales and inventory figures collected from just 10% of commercial establishments. Preliminary income figures are obtained from household surveys, but these represent a tiny fraction of households. More complete income data are provided by income tax returns, but these are available to the economists who estimate GDI only after a two- to four-year delay.

The Department of Commerce issues revisions of its GDP and GDI estimates as more complete data become available. With each revision, the gap between GDP and GDI estimates is significantly reduced.

While GDP and GDI figures cannot provide precise measures of economic activity, they come remarkably close. Indeed, given that the numbers come from entirely different sources, the fact that they come as close as they do provides an impressive check of the accuracy of the department's estimates of GDP and GDI.

ANSWER TO TRY IT! PROBLEM

GDI equals $1,200. Note that this value equals the value for GDP obtained from the estimate of output in the first part of the previous Try It! Here is the computation:

Employee compensation	$700
Profits	200
Rental income	50
Net interest	25
Depreciation	50
Indirect taxes	175
GDI	$1,200

Once again, note that Social Security and welfare payments to households are transfer payments. They do not represent payments to household factors of production for current output of goods and services, and therefore are not included in GDI.

3. GDP AND ECONOMIC WELL-BEING

LEARNING OBJECTIVES

1. Discuss and give examples of measurement and conceptual problems in using real GDP as a measure of economic performance and of economic well-being.
2. Explain the use of per capita real GNP or GDP to compare economic performance across countries and discuss its limitations.

GDP is the measure most often used to assess the economic well-being of a country. Besides measuring the pulse of a country, it is the figure used to compare living standards in different countries.

Of course, to use GDP as an indicator of overall economic performance, we must convert nominal GDP to real GDP, since nominal values can rise or fall simply as a result of changes in the price level. For example, the movie *Avatar*, released in 2009, brought in $761 million—the highest amount to date in gross box office receipts, while *Gone with the Wind*, released in 1939, earned only $199 million and ranks 117th in terms of nominal receipts. But does that mean that *Avatar* actually did better than *Gone with the Wind*? After all, the average price of a movie ticket in 1939 was about 25 cents. At the time of *Avatar*, the average ticket price was about $7.50. A better way to compare these two movies in terms of popularity is to control for the price of movie tickets—the same strategy that economists use with real GDP in order to determine whether output is rising or falling. Adjusting the nominal box-office receipts using 2012 movie prices to obtain real revenue reveals that in real terms *Gone with the Wind* continues to be the top real grosser of all time with real box-office receipts of about $1.6 billion. *Avatar*'s real box-office receipts amounted to a mere $776 million.[6] As illustrated by this example on revenues from popular movies, we might draw erroneous conclusions about performance if we base them on nominal values instead of on real values. In contrast, real GDP, despite the problems with price indexes that were explained in another chapter, provides a reasonable measure of the total output of an economy, and changes in real GDP provide an indication of the direction of movement in total output.

We begin this section by noting some of the drawbacks of using real GDP as a measure of the economic welfare of a country. Despite these shortcomings, we will see that it probably remains our best single indicator of macroeconomic performance.

3.1 Measurement Problems in Real GDP

There are two measurement problems, other than those associated with adjusting for price level changes, in using real GDP to assess domestic economic performance.

Revisions

The first estimate of real GDP for a calendar quarter is called the advance estimate. It is issued about a month after the quarter ends. To produce a measure so quickly, officials at the Department of Commerce must rely on information from relatively few firms and households. One month later, it issues a revised estimate, and a month after that it issues its final estimate. Often the advance estimate of GDP and the final estimate do not correspond. The recession of 2001, for example, began in March of that year. But the first estimates of real GDP for the second and third quarters of 2001 showed output continuing to rise. It was not until later revisions that it became clear that a recession had been under way.

But the revision story does not end there. Every summer, the Commerce Department issues revised figures for the previous two or three years. Once every five years, the department conducts an extensive analysis that traces flows of inputs and outputs throughout the economy. It focuses on the outputs of some firms that are inputs to other firms. In the process of conducting this analysis, the department revises real GDP estimates for the previous five years. Sometimes the revisions can paint a picture of economic activity that is quite different from the one given even by the revised estimates of GDP. For example, revisions of the data for the 1990–1991 recession issued several years later showed that the recession had been much more serious than had previously been apparent, and the recovery was more pronounced. Concerning the most recent recession, the first estimates of fourth quarter 2008 GDP showed that the U.S. economy shrank by 3.8%. The first revision, however, showed a drop of 6.8%, and the second revision showed a drop of 8.9%!

The Service Sector

Another problem lies in estimating production in the service sector. The output of goods in an economy is relatively easy to compute. There are so many bushels of corn, so many pounds of beef. But what is the output of a bank? Of a hospital? It is easy to record the dollar value of output to enter in nominal GDP, but estimating the quantity of output to use in real GDP is quite another matter. In some cases, the Department of Commerce estimates service sector output based on the quantity of labor used. For example, if this technique were used in the banking industry and banking used 10% more labor, the department would report that production has risen 10%. If the number of employees remains unchanged, reported output remains unchanged. In effect, this approach assumes that output per worker—productivity—in those sectors remains constant when studies have indicated that productivity has increased greatly in the service sector. Since 1990 progress has been made in measurement in this area, which allows in particular for better estimation of productivity changes and price indexes for different service sector industries, but more remains to be done in this large sector of the U.S. economy.[7]

3.2   Conceptual Problems with Real GDP

A second set of limitations of real GDP stems from problems inherent in the indicator itself. Real GDP measures market activity. Goods and services that are produced and exchanged in a market are counted; goods and services that are produced but that are not exchanged in markets are not.[8]

Household Production

Suppose you are considering whether to eat at home for dinner tonight or to eat out. You could cook dinner for yourself at a cost of $5 for the ingredients plus an hour or so of your time. Alternatively, you could buy an equivalent meal at a restaurant for perhaps $15. Your decision to eat out rather than cook would add $10 to the GDP.

But that $10 addition would be misleading. After all, if you had stayed home you might have produced an equivalent meal. The only difference is that the value of your time would not have been counted. But surely your time is not worthless; it is just not counted. Similarly, GDP does not count the value of your efforts to clean your own house, to wash your own car, or to grow your own vegetables. In general, GDP omits the entire value added by members of a household who do household work themselves.

There is reason to believe this omission is serious. Economists J. Steven Landefeld and Stephanie H. McCulla of the U.S. Bureau of Economic Analysis estimated in a 2000 paper the value of household output from 1946 to 1997. Their estimate of household output in 1946 was 50% of reported GDP. Since then, that percentage has fallen, because more women have entered the workforce, so that more production that once took place in households now occurs in the market. Households now eat out more, purchase more prepared foods at the grocery store, hire out child-care services they once performed themselves, and so on. Their estimate for 1997, for example, suggests that household production amounted to 36% of reported GDP.[9]

This problem is especially significant when GDP is used to make comparisons across countries. In low-income countries, a much greater share of goods and services is not exchanged in a market. Estimates of GDP in such countries are adjusted to reflect nonmarket production, but these adjustments are inevitably imprecise.

Underground and Illegal Production

Some production goes unreported in order to evade taxes or the law. It is not likely to be counted in GDP. Legal production for which income is unreported in order to evade taxes generally takes place in what is known as the "underground economy." For example, a carpenter might build a small addition to a dentist's house in exchange for orthodontic work for the carpenter's children. Although income has been earned and output generated in this example of bartering, the transaction is unlikely to be reported for income tax or other purposes and thus is not counted in GDP. Illegal activities are not reported for income taxes for obvious reasons and are thus difficult to include in GDP.

Leisure

Leisure is an economic good. All other things being equal, more leisure is better than less leisure.

But all other things are not likely to be equal when it comes to consuming leisure. Consuming more leisure means supplying less work effort. And that means producing less GDP. If everyone decided to work 10% fewer hours, GDP would fall. But that would not mean that people were worse off. In fact, their choice of more leisure would suggest they prefer the extra leisure to the goods and services they give up by consuming it. Consequently, a reduction in GDP would be accompanied by an increase in satisfaction, not a reduction.

The GDP Accounts Ignore "Bads"

Suppose a wave of burglaries were to break out across the United States. One would expect people to respond by buying more and louder burglar alarms, better locks, fiercer German shepherds, and more guard services than they had before. To the extent that they pay for these by dipping into savings rather than replacing other consumption, GDP increases. An epidemic might have much the same effect on GDP by driving up health-care spending. But that does not mean that crime and disease are good things; it means only that crime and disease may force an increase in the production of goods and services counted in the GDP.

Similarly, the GDP accounts ignore the impact of pollution on the environment. We might produce an additional $200 billion in goods and services but create pollution that makes us feel worse off by, say, $300 billion. The GDP accounts simply report the $200 billion in increased production. Indeed, some of the environmental degradation might itself boost GDP. Dirtier air may force us to wash clothes more often, to paint buildings more often, and to see the doctor more often, all of which will tend to increase GDP!

Conclusion: GDP and Human Happiness

More GDP cannot necessarily be equated with more human happiness. But more GDP does mean more of the goods and services we measure. It means more jobs. It means more income. And most people seem to place a high value on these things. For all its faults, GDP does measure the production of most goods and services. And goods and services get produced, for the most part, because we want them. We might thus be safe in giving two cheers for GDP—and holding back the third in recognition of the conceptual difficulties that are inherent in using a single number to summarize the output of an entire economy.

3.3 International Comparisons of Real GDP and GNP

Real GDP or GNP estimates are often used in comparing economic performance among countries. In making such comparisons, it is important to keep in mind the general limitations to these measures of economic performance that we noted earlier. Further, countries use different methodologies for collecting and compiling data.

Three other issues are important in comparing real GDP or GNP for different countries: the adjustment of these figures for population, adjusting to a common currency, and the incorporation of nonmarket production.

In international comparisons of real GNP or real GDP, economists generally make comparisons not of real GNP or GDP but of **per capita real GNP or GDP**, which equals a country's real GNP or GDP divided by its population. For example, suppose Country A has a real GDP of about $4,000 billion and Country B has a real GDP of about $40 billion. We can conclude that Country A produced 100 times more goods and services than did Country B. But if Country A has 200 times as many people as Country B (for example, 200 million people in Country A and 1 million in Country B), then Country A's per capita output will be half that of Country B ($20,000 versus $40,000 in this example).

Figure 12.7 compares per capita real GNP for 11 countries in 2010. It is based on data that uses a measure called "international dollars" in order to correct for differences in the purchasing power of $1 across countries. The data also attempt to adjust for nonmarket production (such as that of rural families that grow their own food, make their own clothing, and produce other household goods and services themselves).

per capita real GNP or GDP

A country's real GNP or GDP divided by its population.

FIGURE 12.7 Comparing Per Capita Real GNP, 2010

There is a huge gap between per capita income in one of the poorest countries in the world, the Democratic Republic of Congo, and wealthier nations such as the United States and Luxembourg.

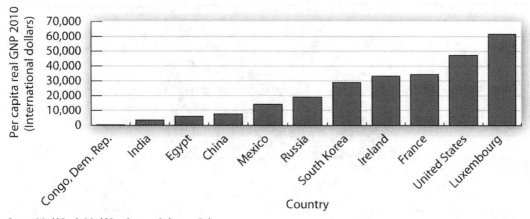

Source: World Bank, World Development Indicators Online

The disparities in income are striking; Luxembourg, the country with the highest per capita real GNP, had an income level nearly 200 times greater than the Democratic Republic of Congo, the country with the lowest per capita real GNP.

What can we conclude about international comparisons in levels of GDP and GNP? Certainly we must be cautious. There are enormous difficulties in estimating any country's total output. Comparing one country's output to another presents additional challenges. But the fact that a task is difficult does not mean it is impossible. When the data suggest huge disparities in levels of GNP per capita, for example, we observe real differences in living standards.

KEY TAKEAWAYS

- Real GDP or real GNP is often used as an indicator of the economic well-being of a country.
- Problems in the measurement of real GDP, in addition to problems encountered in converting from nominal to real GDP, stem from revisions in the data and the difficulty of measuring output in some sectors, particularly the service sector.
- Conceptual problems in the use of real GDP as a measure of economic well-being include the facts that it does not include nonmarket production and that it does not properly adjust for "bads" produced in the economy.
- Per capita real GDP or GNP can be used to compare economic performance in different countries.

TRY IT!

What impact would each of the following have on real GDP? Would economic well-being increase or decrease as a result?

1. On average, people in a country decide to increase the number of hours they work by 5%.
2. Spending on homeland security increases in response to a terrorist attack.
3. The price level and nominal GDP increase by 10%.

Case in Point

Per Capita Real GDP and Olympic Medal Counts

In the popular lore, the Olympics provide an opportunity for the finest athletes in the world to compete with each other head-to-head on the basis of raw talent and hard work. And yet, contenders from Laos tend to finish last or close to it in almost any event in which they compete. One Laotian athlete garnered the unenviable record of having been the slowest entrant in the nearly half-century long history of the 20-kilometer walk. In contrast, U.S. athletes won 103 medals at the 2004 Athens Olympics and 110 medals at the 2008 Beijing Olympics. Why do Laotians fare so poorly and Americans so well, with athletes from other countries falling in between?

Economists Daniel K. N. Johnson and Ayfer Ali have been able to predict with astonishing accuracy the number of medals different countries will win on the basis of a handful of factors, including population, climate, political structure, and real per capita GDP. For example, they predicted that the United States would win 103 medals in Athens and that is precisely how many the United States won. They predicted 103 medals for the United States in Beijing; 110 were won. They did not expect the Laotians to win any medals in either Athens or Beijing, and that was indeed the outcome.

Johnson and Ali estimated that summer game participant nations average one more medal per additional $1,000 of per capita real GDP. With per capita real GDP in Laos less than the equivalent of $500 compared to per capita real GDP in the United States of about $38,000, the results for these two nations could be considered a foregone conclusion. According to Johnson and Ali, "High productive capacity or income per person displays an ability to pay the costs necessary to send athletes to the Games, and may also be associated with a higher quality of training and better equipment." For example, a Laotian swimmer at Athens, Vilayphone Vongphachanh, had never practiced in an Olympic-size pool, and a runner, Sirivanh Ketavong, had worn the same running shoes for four years.

The good news is that as the per capita real GDP in some relatively poor countries has risen, the improved living standards have led to increased Olympic medal counts. China, for instance, won 28 medals in 1988 and 63 in 2004. As the host for the 2008 games, it won an impressive total of 100 medals.

While not a perfect measure of the well-being of people in a country, per capita real GDP does tell us about the opportunities available to the average citizen in a country. Americans would surely find it hard to imagine living at the level of consumption of the average Laotian. In *The Progress Paradox: How Life Gets Better While People Feel Worse*, essayist Gregg Easterbrook notes that a higher material standard of living is not associated with higher reported happiness. But, he concludes, the problems of prosperity seem less serious than those of poverty, and prosperity gives people and nations the means to address problems. The Olympic medal count for each nation strongly reflects its average standard of living and hence the opportunities available to its citizens.

Sources: Gregg Easterbrook, The Progress Paradox: How Life Gets Better While People Feel Worse (New York: Random House, 2003); Daniel K. N. Johnson and Ayfer Ali, "A Tale of Two Seasons: Participation and Medal Counts at the Summer and Winter Olympic Games," Social Science Quarterly 84, no. 4 (December 2004): 974–93; David Wallechinsky, "Why I'll Cheer for Laos," Parade Magazine, August 8, 2004, p. 8.

4.   REVIEW AND PRACTICE

Summary

This chapter focused on the measurement of GDP. The total value of output (GDP) equals the total value of income generated in producing that output (GDI). We can illustrate the flows of spending and income through the economy with the circular flow model. Firms produce goods and services in response to demands from households (personal consumption), other firms (private investment), government agencies (government purchases), and the rest of the world (net exports). This production, in turn, creates a flow of factor incomes to households. Thus, GDP can be estimated using two types of data: (1) data that show the total value of output and (2) data that show the total value of income generated by that output.

In looking at GDP as a measure of output, we divide it into four components: consumption, investment, government purchases, and net exports. GDP equals the sum of final values produced in each of these areas. It can also be measured as the sum of values added at each stage of production. The components of GDP measured in terms of income (GDI) are employee compensation, profits, rental income, net interest, depreciation, and indirect taxes.

We also explained other measures of income such as GNP and disposable personal income. Disposable personal income is an important economic indicator, because it is closely related to personal consumption, the largest component of GDP.

GDP is often used as an indicator of how well off a country is. Of course, to use it for this purpose, we must be careful to use real GDP rather than nominal GDP. Still, there are problems with our estimate of real GDP. Problems encountered in converting nominal GDP to real GDP were discussed in the previous chapter. In this chapter we looked at additional measurement problems and conceptual problems.

Frequent revisions in the data sometimes change our picture of the economy considerably. Accounting for the service sector is quite difficult. Conceptual problems include the omission of nonmarket production and of underground and illegal production. GDP ignores the value of leisure and includes certain "bads."

We cannot assert with confidence that more GDP is a good thing and that less is bad. However, real GDP remains our best single indicator of economic performance. It is used not only to indicate how any one economy is performing over time but also to compare the economic performance of different countries.

CONCEPT PROBLEMS

1. GDP is used as a measure of macroeconomic performance. What, precisely, does it measure?

2. Many economists have attempted to create a set of social accounts that would come closer to measuring the economic well-being of the society than does GDP. What modifications of the current approach would you recommend to them?

3. Every good produced creates income for the owners of the factors of production that created the product or service. For a recent purchase you made, try to list all the types of factors of production involved in making the product available, and try to determine who received income as a result of your purchase.

4. Explain how the sale of used textbooks in your campus bookstore affects the GDP calculation.

5. Look again at the circular flow diagram in Figure 12.5 and assume it is drawn for the United States. State the flows in which each of the following transactions would be entered.

    a. A consumer purchases fresh fish at a local fish market.

    b. A grocery store acquires 1,000 rolls of paper towels for later resale.

    c. NASA purchases a new Saturn rocket.

    d. People in France flock to see the latest Brad Pitt movie.

    e. A construction firm builds a new house.

    f. A couple from Seattle visits Guadalajara and stays in a hotel there.

    g. The city of Dallas purchases computer paper from a local firm.

6. Suggest an argument for and an argument against counting in GDP all household-produced goods and services that are not sold, such as the value of child care or home-cooked meals.

7. Suppose a nation's firms make heavy use of factors of production owned by residents of foreign countries, while foreign firms make relatively little use of factors owned by residents of that nation. How does the nation's GDP compare to its GNP?

8. Suppose Country A has the same GDP as Country B, and that neither nation's residents own factors of production used by foreign firms, nor do either nation's firms use factors of production owned by foreign residents. Suppose that, relative to Country B, depreciation, indirect business taxes, and personal income taxes in Country A are high, while welfare and Social Security payments to households in Country A are relatively low. Which country has the higher disposable personal income? Why?

9. Suppose that virtually everyone in the United States decides to take life a little easier, and the length of the average workweek falls by 25%. How will that affect GDP? Per capita GDP? How will it affect economic welfare?

10. Comment on the following statement: "It does not matter that the value of the labor people devote to producing things for themselves is not counted in GDP; because we make the same 'mistake' every year, relative values are unaffected."

11. Name some of the services, if any, you produced at home that do get counted in GDP. Are there any goods you produce that are not counted?

12. Marijuana is sometimes estimated to be California's largest cash crop. It is not included in estimates of GDP. Should it be?

NUMERICAL PROBLEMS

1. Given the following nominal data, compute GDP. Assume net factor incomes from abroad = 0 (that is, GDP = GNP).

Nominal Data for GDP and NNP	$ Billions
Consumption	2,799.8
Depreciation	481.6
Exports	376.2
Gross private domestic investment	671.0
Indirect taxes	331.4
Government purchases	869.7
Government transfer payments	947.8
Imports	481.7

2. Find data for each of the following countries on real GDP and population. Use the data to calculate the GDP per capita for each of the following countries:

   a. Mozambique
   b. India
   c. Pakistan
   d. United States
   e. Canada
   f. Russia
   g. Brazil
   h. Iran
   i. Colombia

3. Now construct a bar graph showing your results in the previous problem, organizing the countries from the highest to the lowest GNP per capita, with countries on the horizontal axis and GNP per capita on the vertical axis.

4. Suppose Country A has a GDP of $4 trillion. Residents of this country earn $500 million from assets they own in foreign countries. Residents of foreign countries earn $300 million from assets they own in Country A. Compute:

   a. Country A's net foreign income.
   b. Country A's GNP.

5. Suppose a country's GDP equals $500 billion for a particular year. Economists in the country estimate that household production equals 40% of GDP.

   a. What is the value of the country's household production for that year?
   b. Counting both GDP and household production, what is the country's total output for the year?

6. A miner extracts iron from the earth. A steel mill converts the iron to steel beams for use in construction. A construction company uses the steel beams to make a building. Assume that the total product of these firms represents the only components of the building and that they will have no other uses. Complete the following table:

Company	Product	Total Sales	Value Added
Acme Mining	iron ore	$100,000	?
Fuller Mill	steel beams	$175,000	?
Crane Construction	building	$1,100,000	?
Total Value Added			?

7. You are given the data below for 2008 for the imaginary country of Amagre, whose currency is the G.

Consumption	350 billion G
Transfer payments	100 billion G
Investment	100 billion G
Government purchases	200 billion G
Exports	50 billion G
Imports	150 billion G
Bond purchases	200 billion G
Earnings on foreign investments	75 billion G
Foreign earnings on Amagre investment	25 billion G

    a. Compute net foreign investment.

    b. Compute net exports.

    c. Compute GDP.

    d. Compute GNP.

ENDNOTES

1. Although reported separately by the Department of Commerce, we have combined proprietors' income (typically independent business owners and farmers) with corporate profits to simplify the discussion.

2. If you have studied microeconomics, you know that the term "*rent*" in economics has a quite different meaning. The national income and product accounts use the accounting, not the economic, meaning of "*rent*."

3. The adjustment for indirect business taxes includes two other minor elements: transfer payments made by business firms and surpluses or deficits of government enterprises.

4. Profit is corporate profit ($1,706.8) plus proprietors' income ($1,360.7), both with inventory valuation and capital consumption adjustment.

5. Indirect taxes include taxes on production and imports of $1,149.0 plus business transfer payments ($120.1) less subsidies ($59.1) and current surplus of government enterprise (−$41.4). Prior to the 2003 National Income and Product Accounts (NIPA) revisions, the category "taxes on production and imports" was, with some technical and other minor adjustments, referred to as "indirect business taxes." See Brent R. Moulton and Eugene P. Seskin, "Preview of the 2003 Comprehensive Revision of the National Income and Product Accounts," Bureau of Economic Analysis, *Survey of Current Business*, June 2003, pp. 17–34.

6. Based on estimates at "Domestic Grosses Adjusted for Ticket Price Inflation," Box Office Mojo, accessed April 10, 2012, http://boxofficemojo.com/alltime/adjusted.htm.

7. Jack E. Triplett and Barry P. Bosworth, "The State of Data for Services Productivity Measurement in the United States," *International Productivity Monitor* 16 (Spring 2008): 53–70.

8. There are two exceptions to this rule. The value of food produced and consumed by farm households is counted in GDP. More important, an estimate of the rental values of owner-occupied homes is included. If a family rents a house, the rental payments are included in GDP. If a family lives in a house it owns, the Department of Commerce estimates what the house would rent for and then includes that rent in the GDP estimate, even though the house's services were not exchanged in the marketplace.

9. J. Steven Landefeld and Stephanie H. McCulla, "Accounting for Nonmarket Household Production within a National Accounts Framework," *Review of Income & Wealth* 46, no. 3 (September 2000): 289–307.

CHAPTER 13

Aggregate Demand and Aggregate Supply

START UP: THE GREAT WARNING

The first warning came from the Harvard Economic Society, an association of Harvard economics professors, early in 1929. The society predicted in its weekly newsletter that the seven-year-old expansion was coming to an end. Recession was ahead. Almost no one took the warning seriously. The economy, fueled by soaring investment, had experienced stunning growth. The 1920s had seen the emergence of many entirely new industries—automobiles, public power, home appliances, synthetic fabrics, radio, and motion pictures. The decade seemed to have acquired a momentum all its own. Prosperity was not about to end, no matter what a few economists might say.

Summer came, and no recession was apparent. The Harvard economists withdrew their forecast. As it turned out, they lost their nerve too soon. Indeed, industrial production had already begun to fall. The worst downturn in our history, the Great Depression, had begun.

The collapse was swift. The stock market crashed in October 1929. Real GDP plunged nearly 10% by 1930. By the time the economy hit bottom in 1933, real GDP had fallen 30%, unemployment had increased from 3.2% in 1929 to 25% in 1933, and prices, measured by the implicit price deflator, had plunged 23% from their 1929 level. The depression held the economy in its cruel grip for more than a decade; it was not until World War II that full employment was restored.

In this chapter we go beyond explanations of the main macroeconomic variables to introduce a model of macroeconomic activity that we can use to analyze problems such as fluctuations in gross domestic product (real GDP), the price level, and employment: the model of aggregate demand and aggregate supply. We will use this model throughout our exploration of macroeconomics. In this chapter we will present the broad outlines of the model; greater detail, more examples, and more thorough explanations will follow in subsequent chapters.

We will examine the concepts of the aggregate demand curve and the short- and long-run aggregate supply curves. We will identify conditions under which an economy achieves an equilibrium level of real GDP that is consistent with full employment of labor. **Potential output** is the level of output an economy can achieve when labor is employed at its natural level. Potential output is also called the natural level of real GDP. When an economy fails to produce at its potential, there may be actions that the government or the central bank can take to push the economy toward it, and in this chapter we will begin to consider the pros and cons of doing so.

potential output

The level of output an economy can achieve when labor is employed at its natural level.

1.   AGGREGATE DEMAND

LEARNING OBJECTIVES

1. **Define potential output, also called the natural level of GDP.**
2. **Define aggregate demand, represent it using a hypothetical aggregate demand curve, and identify and explain the three effects that cause this curve to slope downward.**
3. **Distinguish between a change in the aggregate quantity of goods and services demanded and a change in aggregate demand.**
4. **Use examples to explain how each component of aggregate demand can be a possible aggregate demand shifter.**
5. **Explain what a multiplier is and tell how to calculate it.**

aggregate demand

The relationship between the total quantity of goods and services demanded (from all the four sources of demand) and the price level, all other determinants of spending unchanged.

aggregate demand curve

A graphical representation of aggregate demand.

Firms face four sources of demand: households (personal consumption), other firms (investment), government agencies (government purchases), and foreign markets (net exports). **Aggregate demand** is the relationship between the total quantity of goods and services demanded (from all the four sources of demand) and the price level, all other determinants of spending unchanged. The **aggregate demand curve** is a graphical representation of aggregate demand.

1.1   The Slope of the Aggregate Demand Curve

We will use the implicit price deflator as our measure of the price level; the aggregate quantity of goods and services demanded is measured as real GDP. The table in Figure 13.1 gives values for each component of aggregate demand at each price level for a hypothetical economy. Various points on the aggregate demand curve are found by adding the values of these components at different price levels. The aggregate demand curve for the data given in the table is plotted on the graph in Figure 13.1. At point A, at a price level of 1.18, $11,800 billion worth of goods and services will be demanded; at point C, a reduction in the price level to 1.14 increases the quantity of goods and services demanded to $12,000 billion; and at point E, at a price level of 1.10, $12,200 billion will be demanded.

FIGURE 13.1 Aggregate Demand

An aggregate demand curve (*AD*) shows the relationship between the total quantity of output demanded (measured as real GDP) and the price level (measured as the implicit price deflator). At each price level, the total quantity of goods and services demanded is the sum of the components of real GDP, as shown in the table. There is a negative relationship between the price level and the total quantity of goods and services demanded, all other things unchanged.

Point on aggregate demand curve	Price level	$C+$	$I+$	$G+$	$X_n=$	Aggregate demand
A	1.18	8,400	1,820	2,150	−570	11,800
B	1.16	8,450	1,860	2,150	−560	11,900
C	1.14	8,500	1,900	2,150	−550	12,000
D	1.12	8,550	1,940	2,150	−540	12,100
E	1.10	8,600	1,980	2,150	−530	12,200

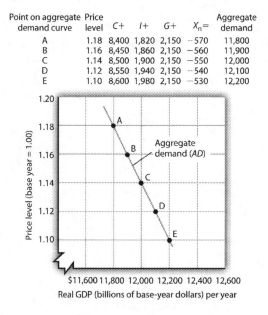

The negative slope of the aggregate demand curve suggests that it behaves in the same manner as an ordinary demand curve. But we *cannot* apply the reasoning we use to explain downward-sloping demand curves in individual markets to explain the downward-sloping aggregate demand curve. There are two reasons for a negative relationship between price and quantity demanded in individual markets. First, a lower price induces people to substitute more of the good whose price has fallen for other goods, increasing the quantity demanded. Second, the lower price creates a higher real income. This normally increases quantity demanded further.

Neither of these effects is relevant to a change in prices in the aggregate. When we are dealing with the average of all prices—the price level—we can no longer say that a fall in prices will induce a change in relative prices that will lead consumers to buy more of the goods and services whose prices have fallen and less of the goods and services whose prices have not fallen. The price of corn may have fallen, but the prices of wheat, sugar, tractors, steel, and most other goods or services produced in the economy are likely to have fallen as well.

Furthermore, a reduction in the price level means that it is not just the prices consumers pay that are falling. It means the prices people receive—their wages, the rents they may charge as landlords, the interest rates they earn—are likely to be falling as well. A falling price level means that goods and services are cheaper, but incomes are lower, too. There is no reason to expect that a change in real income will boost the quantity of goods and services demanded—indeed, no change in real income would occur. If nominal incomes and prices all fall by 10%, for example, real incomes do not change.

Why, then, does the aggregate demand curve slope downward? One reason for the downward slope of the aggregate demand curve lies in the relationship between real wealth (the stocks, bonds, and other assets that people have accumulated) and consumption (one of the four components of aggregate demand). When the price level falls, the real value of wealth increases—it packs more purchasing power. For example, if the price level falls by 25%, then $10,000 of wealth could purchase more goods and services than it would have if the price level had not fallen. An increase in wealth will induce people to increase their consumption. The consumption component of aggregate demand will thus be greater at lower price levels than at higher price levels. The tendency for a change in the price level to affect real wealth and thus alter consumption is called the **wealth effect**; it suggests a negative relationship between the price level and the real value of consumption spending.

A second reason the aggregate demand curve slopes downward lies in the relationship between interest rates and investment. A lower price level lowers the demand for money, because less money is required to buy a given quantity of goods. What economists mean by money demand will be explained in more detail in a later chapter. But, as we learned in studying demand and supply, a reduction in the demand for something, all other things unchanged, lowers its price. In this case, the "something" is money and its price is the interest rate. A lower price level thus reduces interest rates. Lower interest rates make borrowing by firms to build factories or buy equipment and other capital more attractive. A lower interest rate means lower mortgage payments, which tends to increase investment in residential houses. Investment thus rises when the price level falls. The tendency for a change in the price level to affect the interest rate and thus to affect the quantity of investment demanded is called the **interest rate effect**. John Maynard Keynes, a British economist whose analysis of the Great Depression and what to do about it led to the birth of modern macroeconomics, emphasized this effect. For this reason, the interest rate effect is sometimes called the Keynes effect.

A third reason for the rise in the total quantity of goods and services demanded as the price level falls can be found in changes in the net export component of aggregate demand. All other things unchanged, a lower price level in an economy reduces the prices of its goods and services relative to foreign-produced goods and services. A lower price level makes that economy's goods more attractive to foreign buyers, increasing exports. It will also make foreign-produced goods and services less attractive to the economy's buyers, reducing imports. The result is an increase in net exports. The **international trade effect** is the tendency for a change in the price level to affect net exports.

Taken together, then, a fall in the price level means that the quantities of consumption, investment, and net export components of aggregate demand may all rise. Since government purchases are determined through a political process, we assume there is no causal link between the price level and the real volume of government purchases. Therefore, this component of GDP does not contribute to the downward slope of the curve.

In general, a change in the price level, with all other determinants of aggregate demand unchanged, causes a movement along the aggregate demand curve. A movement along an aggregate demand curve is a **change in the aggregate quantity of goods and services demanded**. A movement from point A to point B on the aggregate demand curve in Figure 13.1 is an example. Such a change is a response to a change in the price level.

Notice that the axes of the aggregate demand curve graph are drawn with a break near the origin to remind us that the plotted values reflect a relatively narrow range of changes in real GDP and the price level. We do not know what might happen if the price level or output for an entire economy approached zero. Such a phenomenon has never been observed.

wealth effect

The tendency for a change in the price level to affect real wealth and thus alter consumption.

interest rate effect

The tendency for a change in the price level to affect the interest rate and thus to affect the quantity of investment demanded.

international trade effect

The tendency for a change in the price level to affect net exports.

change in the aggregate quantity of goods and services demanded

Movement along an aggregate demand curve.

1.2 Changes in Aggregate Demand

Aggregate demand changes in response to a change in any of its components. An increase in the total quantity of consumer goods and services demanded at every price level, for example, would shift the aggregate demand curve to the right. A change in the aggregate quantity of goods and services demanded at every price level is a **change in aggregate demand**, which shifts the aggregate demand curve. Increases and decreases in aggregate demand are shown in Figure 13.2.

FIGURE 13.2 Changes in Aggregate Demand

An increase in consumption, investment, government purchases, or net exports shifts the aggregate demand curve AD_1 to the right as shown in Panel (a). A reduction in one of the components of aggregate demand shifts the curve to the left, as shown in Panel (b).

What factors might cause the aggregate demand curve to shift? Each of the components of aggregate demand is a possible aggregate demand shifter. We shall look at some of the events that can trigger changes in the components of aggregate demand and thus shift the aggregate demand curve.

Changes in Consumption

Several events could change the quantity of consumption at each price level and thus shift aggregate demand. One determinant of consumption is consumer confidence. If consumers expect good economic conditions and are optimistic about their economic prospects, they are more likely to buy major items such as cars or furniture. The result would be an increase in the real value of consumption at each price level and an increase in aggregate demand. In the second half of the 1990s, sustained economic growth and low unemployment fueled high expectations and consumer optimism. Surveys revealed consumer confidence to be very high. That consumer confidence translated into increased consumption and increased aggregate demand. In contrast, a decrease in consumption would accompany diminished consumer expectations and a decrease in consumer confidence, as happened after the stock market crash of 1929. The same problem has plagued the economies of most Western nations in 2008 as declining consumer confidence has tended to reduce consumption. A survey by the Conference Board in September of 2008 showed that just 13.5% of consumers surveyed expected economic conditions in the United States to improve in the next six months. Similarly pessimistic views prevailed in the previous two months. That contributed to the decline in consumption that occurred in the third quarter of the year.

Another factor that can change consumption and shift aggregate demand is tax policy. A cut in personal income taxes leaves people with more after-tax income, which may induce them to increase their consumption. The federal government in the United States cut taxes in 1964, 1981, 1986, 1997, and 2003; each of those tax cuts tended to increase consumption and aggregate demand at each price level.

In the United States, another government policy aimed at increasing consumption and thus aggregate demand has been the use of rebates in which taxpayers are simply sent checks in hopes that those checks will be used for consumption. Rebates have been used in 1975, 2001, and 2008. In each case the rebate was a one-time payment. Careful studies by economists of the 1975 and 2001 rebates showed little impact on consumption. Final evidence on the impact of the 2008 rebates is not yet in, but early results suggest a similar outcome. In a subsequent chapter, we will investigate arguments about whether temporary increases in income produced by rebates are likely to have a significant impact on consumption.

Transfer payments such as welfare and Social Security also affect the income people have available to spend. At any given price level, an increase in transfer payments raises consumption and aggregate demand, and a reduction lowers consumption and aggregate demand.

Changes in Investment

Investment is the production of new capital that will be used for future production of goods and services. Firms make investment choices based on what they think they will be producing in the future. The expectations of firms thus play a critical role in determining investment. If firms expect their sales to go up, they are likely to increase their investment so that they can increase production and meet consumer demand. Such an increase in investment raises the aggregate quantity of goods and services demanded at each price level; it increases aggregate demand.

Changes in interest rates also affect investment and thus affect aggregate demand. We must be careful to distinguish such changes from the interest rate effect, which causes a movement along the aggregate demand curve. A change in interest rates that results from a change in the price level affects investment in a way that is already captured in the downward slope of the aggregate demand curve; it causes a movement along the curve. A change in interest rates for some other reason shifts the curve. We examine reasons interest rates might change in another chapter.

Investment can also be affected by tax policy. One provision of the Job and Growth Tax Relief Reconciliation Act of 2003 was a reduction in the tax rate on certain capital gains. Capital gains result when the owner of an asset, such as a house or a factory, sells the asset for more than its purchase price (less any depreciation claimed in earlier years). The lower capital gains tax could stimulate investment, because the owners of such assets know that they will lose less to taxes when they sell those assets, thus making assets subject to the tax more attractive.

Changes in Government Purchases

Any change in government purchases, all other things unchanged, will affect aggregate demand. An increase in government purchases increases aggregate demand; a decrease in government purchases decreases aggregate demand.

Many economists argued that reductions in defense spending in the wake of the collapse of the Soviet Union in 1991 tended to reduce aggregate demand. Similarly, increased defense spending for the wars in Afghanistan and Iraq increased aggregate demand. Dramatic increases in defense spending to fight World War II accounted in large part for the rapid recovery from the Great Depression.

Changes in Net Exports

A change in the value of net exports at each price level shifts the aggregate demand curve. A major determinant of net exports is foreign demand for a country's goods and services; that demand will vary with foreign incomes. An increase in foreign incomes increases a country's net exports and aggregate demand; a slump in foreign incomes reduces net exports and aggregate demand. For example, several major U.S. trading partners in Asia suffered recessions in 1997 and 1998. Lower real incomes in those countries reduced U.S. exports and tended to reduce aggregate demand.

Exchange rates also influence net exports, all other things unchanged. A country's **exchange rate** is the price of its currency in terms of another currency or currencies. A rise in the U.S. exchange rate means that it takes more Japanese yen, for example, to purchase one dollar. That also means that U.S. traders get more yen per dollar. Since prices of goods produced in Japan are given in yen and prices of goods produced in the United States are given in dollars, a rise in the U.S. exchange rate increases the price to foreigners for goods and services produced in the United States, thus reducing U.S. exports; it reduces the price of foreign-produced goods and services for U.S. consumers, thus increasing imports to the United States. A higher exchange rate tends to reduce net exports, reducing aggregate demand. A lower exchange rate tends to increase net exports, increasing aggregate demand.

Foreign price levels can affect aggregate demand in the same way as exchange rates. For example, when foreign price levels fall relative to the price level in the United States, U.S. goods and services become relatively more expensive, reducing exports and boosting imports in the United States. Such a reduction in net exports reduces aggregate demand. An increase in foreign prices relative to U.S. prices has the opposite effect.

The trade policies of various countries can also affect net exports. A policy by Japan to increase its imports of goods and services from India, for example, would increase net exports in India.

exchange rate

The price of a currency in terms of another currency or currencies.

The Multiplier

A change in any component of aggregate demand shifts the aggregate demand curve. Generally, the aggregate demand curve shifts by more than the amount by which the component initially causing it to shift changes.

Suppose that net exports increase due to an increase in foreign incomes. As foreign demand for domestically made products rises, a country's firms will hire additional workers or perhaps increase the average number of hours that their employees work. In either case, incomes will rise, and higher incomes will lead to an increase in consumption. Taking into account these other increases in the components of aggregate demand, the aggregate demand curve will shift by more than the initial shift caused by the initial increase in net exports.

The **multiplier** is the ratio of the change in the quantity of real GDP demanded at each price level to the initial change in one or more components of aggregate demand that produced it:

EQUATION 13.1

$$\text{Multiplier} = \frac{\Delta \text{ (real GDP demanded at each price level)}}{\text{initial } \Delta \text{ (component of } AD)}$$

We use the capital Greek letter delta (Δ) to mean "change in." In the aggregate demand–aggregate supply model presented in this chapter, it is the number by which we multiply an initial change in aggregate demand to obtain the amount by which the aggregate demand curve shifts as a result of the initial change. In other words, we can use Equation 13.1 to solve for the change in real GDP demanded at each price level:

EQUATION 13.2

$$\Delta \text{ (real GDP demanded at each price level)} = \text{multiplier} \times \text{initial } \Delta \text{ (component of } AD)$$

Suppose that the initial increase in net exports is $100 billion and that the initial $100-billion increase generates additional consumption of $100 billion at each price level. In Panel (a) of Figure 13.3, the aggregate demand curve shifts to the right by $200 billion—the amount of the initial increase in net exports times the multiplier of 2. We obtained the value for the multiplier in this example by plugging $200 billion (the initial $100-billion increase in net exports plus the $100-billion increase that it generated in consumption) into the numerator of Equation 13.1 and $100 billion into the denominator. Similarly, a decrease in net exports of $100 billion leads to a decrease in aggregate demand of $200 billion at each price level, as shown in Panel (b).

FIGURE 13.3 The Multiplier

A change in one component of aggregate demand shifts the aggregate demand curve by more than the initial change. In Panel (a), an initial increase of $100 billion of net exports shifts the aggregate demand curve to the right by $200 billion at each price level. In Panel (b), a decrease of net exports of $100 billion shifts the aggregate demand curve to the left by $200 billion. In this example, the multiplier is 2.

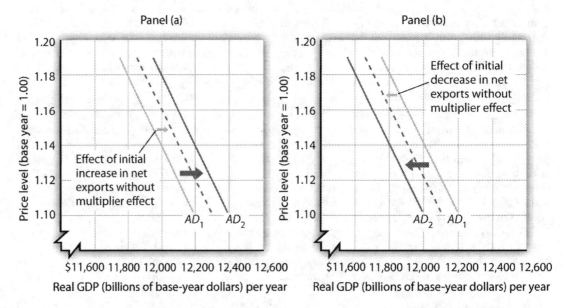

multiplier

The ratio of the change in the quantity of real GDP demanded at each price level to the initial change in one or more components of aggregate demand that produced it.

KEY TAKEAWAYS

- Potential output is the level of output an economy can achieve when labor is employed at its natural level. When an economy fails to produce at its potential, the government or the central bank may try to push the economy toward its potential.

- The aggregate demand curve represents the total of consumption, investment, government purchases, and net exports at each price level in any period. It slopes downward because of the wealth effect on consumption, the interest rate effect on investment, and the international trade effect on net exports.

- The aggregate demand curve shifts when the quantity of real GDP demanded at each price level changes.

- The multiplier is the number by which we multiply an initial change in aggregate demand to obtain the amount by which the aggregate demand curve shifts at each price level as a result of the initial change.

TRY IT!

Explain the effect of each of the following on the aggregate demand curve for the United States:

1. A decrease in consumer optimism
2. An increase in real GDP in the countries that buy U.S. exports
3. An increase in the price level
4. An increase in government spending on highways

Case in Point

The Multiplied Economic Impact of SARS on China's Economy

Severe Acute Respiratory Syndrome (SARS), an atypical pneumonia-like disease, broke onto the world scene in late 2002. In March 2003, the World Health Organization (WHO) issued its first worldwide alert and a month later its first travel advisory, which recommended that travelers avoid Hong Kong and the southern province of China, Guangdong. Over the next few months, additional travel advisories were issued for other parts of China, Taiwan, and briefly for Toronto, Canada. By the end of June, all WHO travel advisories had been removed.

To estimate the overall impact of SARS on the Chinese economy in 2003, economists Wen Hai, Zhong Zhao, and Jian Want of Peking University's China Center for Economic Research conducted a survey of Beijing's tourism industry in April 2003. Based on findings from the Beijing area, they projected the tourism sector of China as a whole would lose $16.8 billion—of which $10.8 billion came from an approximate 50% reduction in foreign tourist revenue and $6 billion from curtailed domestic tourism, as holiday celebrations were cancelled and domestic travel restrictions imposed.

To figure out the total impact of SARS on China's economy, they argued that the multiplier for tourism revenue in China is between 2 and 3. Since the SARS outbreak only began to have a major economic impact after March, they assumed a smaller multiplier of 1.5 for all of 2003. They thus predicted that the Chinese economy would be $25.3 billion smaller in 2003 as a result of SARS.

Source: Wen Hai, Zhong Zhao, and Jian Wan, "The Short-Term Impact of SARS on the Chinese Economy," Asian Economic Papers 3, no. 1 (Winter 2004): 57–61.

2. AGGREGATE DEMAND AND AGGREGATE SUPPLY: THE LONG RUN AND THE SHORT RUN

LEARNING OBJECTIVES

1. **Distinguish between the short run and the long run, as these terms are used in macroeconomics.**

2. **Draw a hypothetical long-run aggregate supply curve and explain what it shows about the natural levels of employment and output at various price levels, given changes in aggregate demand.**

3. **Draw a hypothetical short-run aggregate supply curve, explain why it slopes upward, and explain why it may shift; that is, distinguish between a change in the aggregate quantity of goods and services supplied and a change in short-run aggregate supply.**

4. **Discuss various explanations for wage and price stickiness.**

5. **Explain and illustrate what is meant by equilibrium in the short run and relate the equilibrium to potential output.**

short run

In macroeconomic analysis, a period in which wages and some other prices are sticky and do not respond to changes in economic conditions.

sticky price

A price that is slow to adjust to its equilibrium level, creating sustained periods of shortage or surplus.

long run

In macroeconomic analysis, a period in which wages and prices are flexible.

In macroeconomics, we seek to understand two types of equilibria, one corresponding to the short run and the other corresponding to the long run. The **short run** in macroeconomic analysis is a period in which wages and some other prices do not respond to changes in economic conditions. In certain markets, as economic conditions change, prices (including wages) may not adjust quickly enough to maintain equilibrium in these markets. A **sticky price** is a price that is slow to adjust to its equilibrium level, creating sustained periods of shortage or surplus. Wage and price stickiness prevent the economy from achieving its natural level of employment and its potential output. In contrast, the **long run** in macroeconomic analysis is a period in which wages and prices are flexible. In the long run, employment will move to its natural level and real GDP to potential.

We begin with a discussion of long-run macroeconomic equilibrium, because this type of equilibrium allows us to see the macroeconomy after full market adjustment has been achieved. In contrast, in the short run, price or wage stickiness is an obstacle to full adjustment. Why these deviations from the potential level of output occur and what the implications are for the macroeconomy will be discussed in the section on short-run macroeconomic equilibrium.

2.1 The Long Run

As we saw in a previous chapter, the natural level of employment occurs where the real wage adjusts so that the quantity of labor demanded equals the quantity of labor supplied. When the economy achieves its natural level of employment, it achieves its potential level of output. We will see that real GDP eventually moves to potential, because all wages and prices are assumed to be flexible in the long run.

Long-Run Aggregate Supply

The **long-run aggregate supply (LRAS) curve** relates the level of output produced by firms to the price level in the long run. In Panel (b) of Figure 13.4, the long-run aggregate supply curve is a vertical line at the economy's potential level of output. There is a single real wage at which employment reaches its natural level. In Panel (a) of Figure 13.4, only a real wage of ω_e generates natural employment L_e. The economy could, however, achieve this real wage with any of an infinitely large set of nominal wage and price-level combinations. Suppose, for example, that the equilibrium real wage (the ratio of wages to the price level) is 1.5. We could have that with a nominal wage level of 1.5 and a price level of 1.0, a nominal wage level of 1.65 and a price level of 1.1, a nominal wage level of 3.0 and a price level of 2.0, and so on.

> **long-run aggregate supply (LRAS) curve**
>
> A graphical representation that relates the level of output produced by firms to the price level in the long run.

FIGURE 13.4 Natural Employment and Long-Run Aggregate Supply

When the economy achieves its natural level of employment, as shown in Panel (a) at the intersection of the demand and supply curves for labor, it achieves its potential output, as shown in Panel (b) by the vertical long-run aggregate supply curve LRAS at Y_P.

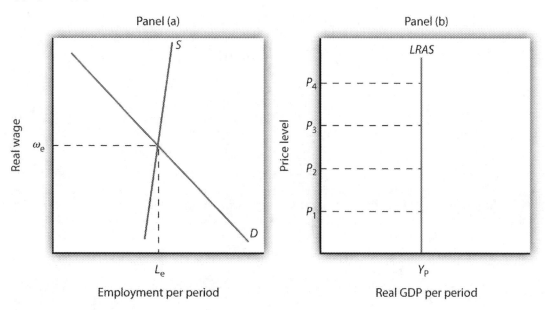

In Panel (b) we see price levels ranging from P_1 to P_4. Higher price levels would require higher nominal wages to create a real wage of ω_e, and flexible nominal wages would achieve that in the long run.

In the long run, then, the economy can achieve its natural level of employment and potential output at any price level. This conclusion gives us our long-run aggregate supply curve. With only one level of output at any price level, the long-run aggregate supply curve is a vertical line at the economy's potential level of output of Y_P.

Equilibrium Levels of Price and Output in the Long Run

The intersection of the economy's aggregate demand curve and the long-run aggregate supply curve determines its equilibrium real GDP and price level in the long run. Figure 13.5 depicts an economy in long-run equilibrium. With aggregate demand at AD_1 and the long-run aggregate supply curve as shown, real GDP is $12,000 billion per year and the price level is 1.14. If aggregate demand increases to AD_2, long-run equilibrium will be reestablished at real GDP of $12,000 billion per year, but at a higher price level of 1.18. If aggregate demand decreases to AD_3, long-run equilibrium will still be at real GDP of $12,000 billion per year, but with the now lower price level of 1.10.

FIGURE 13.5 Long-Run Equilibrium

Long-run equilibrium occurs at the intersection of the aggregate demand curve and the long-run aggregate supply curve. For the three aggregate demand curves shown, long-run equilibrium occurs at three different price levels, but always at an output level of $12,000 billion per year, which corresponds to potential output.

2.2 The Short Run

Analysis of the macroeconomy in the short run—a period in which stickiness of wages and prices may prevent the economy from operating at potential output—helps explain how deviations of real GDP from potential output can and do occur. We will explore the effects of changes in aggregate demand and in short-run aggregate supply in this section.

Short-Run Aggregate Supply

The model of aggregate demand and long-run aggregate supply predicts that the economy will eventually move toward its potential output. To see how nominal wage and price stickiness can cause real GDP to be either above or below potential in the short run, consider the response of the economy to a change in aggregate demand. Figure 13.6 shows an economy that has been operating at potential output of $12,000 billion and a price level of 1.14. This occurs at the intersection of AD_1 with the long-run aggregate supply curve at point B. Now suppose that the aggregate demand curve shifts to the right (to AD_2). This could occur as a result of an increase in exports. (The shift from AD_1 to AD_2 includes the multiplied effect of the increase in exports.) At the price level of 1.14, there is now excess demand and pressure on prices to rise. If all prices in the economy adjusted quickly, the economy would quickly settle at potential output of $12,000 billion, but at a higher price level (1.18 in this case).

Is it possible to expand output above potential? Yes. It may be the case, for example, that some people who were in the labor force but were frictionally or structurally unemployed find work because of the ease of getting jobs at the going nominal wage in such an environment. The result is an economy operating at point A in Figure 13.6 at a higher price level and with output temporarily above potential.

Consider next the effect of a reduction in aggregate demand (to AD_3), possibly due to a reduction in investment. As the price level starts to fall, output also falls. The economy finds itself at a price level–output combination at which real GDP is below potential, at point C. Again, price stickiness is to blame. The prices firms receive are falling with the reduction in demand. Without corresponding reductions in nominal wages, there will be an increase in the real wage. Firms will employ less labor and produce less output.

By examining what happens as aggregate demand shifts over a period when price adjustment is incomplete, we can trace out the short-run aggregate supply curve by drawing a line through points A, B, and C. The **short-run aggregate supply (SRAS) curve** is a graphical representation of the relationship between production and the price level in the short run. Among the factors held constant in drawing a short-run aggregate supply curve are the capital stock, the stock of natural resources, the level of technology, and the prices of factors of production.

short-run aggregate supply (SRAS) curve

A graphical representation of the relationship between production and the price level in the short run.

FIGURE 13.6 Deriving the Short-Run Aggregate Supply Curve

The economy shown here is in long-run equilibrium at the intersection of AD_1 with the long-run aggregate supply curve. If aggregate demand increases to AD_2, in the short run, both real GDP and the price level rise. If aggregate demand decreases to AD_3, in the short run, both real GDP and the price level fall. A line drawn through points A, B, and C traces out the short-run aggregate supply curve $SRAS$.

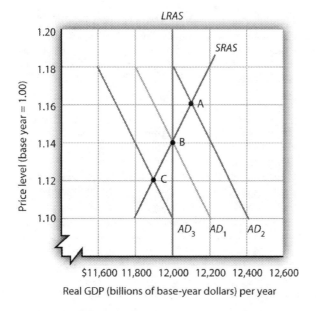

FIGURE 13.7 Changes in Short-Run Aggregate Supply

A reduction in short-run aggregate supply shifts the curve from $SRAS_1$ to $SRAS_2$ in Panel (a). An increase shifts it to the right to $SRAS_3$, as shown in Panel (b).

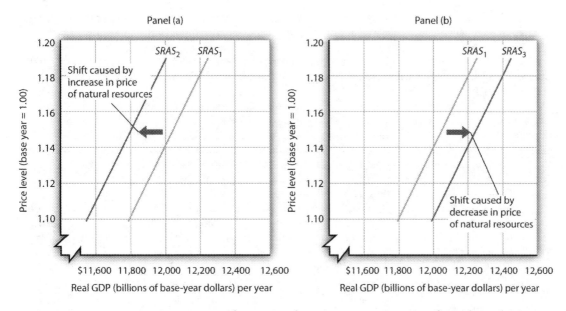

A change in the price level produces a **change in the aggregate quantity of goods and services supplied** and is illustrated by the movement along the short-run aggregate supply curve. This occurs between points A, B, and C in Figure 13.6.

change in the aggregate quantity of goods and services supplied

Movement along the short-run aggregate supply curve.

change in short-run aggregate supply

A change in the aggregate quantity of goods and services supplied at every price level in the short run.

A change in the quantity of goods and services supplied at every price level in the short run is a **change in short-run aggregate supply**. Changes in the factors held constant in drawing the short-run aggregate supply curve shift the curve. (These factors may also shift the long-run aggregate supply curve; we will discuss them along with other determinants of long-run aggregate supply in the next chapter.)

One type of event that would shift the short-run aggregate supply curve is an increase in the price of a natural resource such as oil. An increase in the price of natural resources or any other factor of production, all other things unchanged, raises the cost of production and leads to a reduction in short-run aggregate supply. In Panel (a) of Figure 13.7, $SRAS_1$ shifts leftward to $SRAS_2$. A decrease in the price of a natural resource would lower the cost of production and, other things unchanged, would allow greater production from the economy's stock of resources and would shift the short-run aggregate supply curve to the right; such a shift is shown in Panel (b) by a shift from $SRAS_1$ to $SRAS_3$.

Reasons for Wage and Price Stickiness

Wage or price stickiness means that the economy may not always be operating at potential. Rather, the economy may operate either above or below potential output in the short run. Correspondingly, the overall unemployment rate will be below or above the natural level.

Many prices observed throughout the economy do adjust quickly to changes in market conditions so that equilibrium, once lost, is quickly regained. Prices for fresh food and shares of common stock are two such examples.

Other prices, though, adjust more slowly. Nominal wages, the price of labor, adjust very slowly. We will first look at why nominal wages are sticky, due to their association with the unemployment rate, a variable of great interest in macroeconomics, and then at other prices that may be sticky.

Wage Stickiness

Wage contracts fix nominal wages for the life of the contract. The length of wage contracts varies from one week or one month for temporary employees, to one year (teachers and professors often have such contracts), to three years (for most union workers employed under major collective bargaining agreements). The existence of such explicit contracts means that both workers and firms accept some wage at the time of negotiating, even though economic conditions could change while the agreement is still in force.

Think about your own job or a job you once had. Chances are you go to work each day knowing what your wage will be. Your wage does not fluctuate from one day to the next with changes in demand or supply. You may have a formal contract with your employer that specifies what your wage will be over some period. Or you may have an informal understanding that sets your wage. Whatever the nature of your agreement, your wage is "stuck" over the period of the agreement. Your wage is an example of a sticky price.

One reason workers and firms may be willing to accept long-term nominal wage contracts is that negotiating a contract is a costly process. Both parties must keep themselves adequately informed about market conditions. Where unions are involved, wage negotiations raise the possibility of a labor strike, an eventuality that firms may prepare for by accumulating additional inventories, also a costly process. Even when unions are not involved, time and energy spent discussing wages takes away from time and energy spent producing goods and services. In addition, workers may simply prefer knowing that their nominal wage will be fixed for some period of time.

Some contracts do attempt to take into account changing economic conditions, such as inflation, through cost-of-living adjustments, but even these relatively simple contingencies are not as widespread as one might think. One reason might be that a firm is concerned that while the aggregate price level is rising, the prices for the goods and services it sells might not be moving at the same rate. Also, cost-of-living or other contingencies add complexity to contracts that both sides may want to avoid.

Even markets where workers are not employed under explicit contracts seem to behave as if such contracts existed. In these cases, wage stickiness may stem from a desire to avoid the same uncertainty and adjustment costs that explicit contracts avert.

Finally, minimum wage laws prevent wages from falling below a legal minimum, even if unemployment is rising. Unskilled workers are particularly vulnerable to shifts in aggregate demand.

Price Stickiness

Rigidity of other prices becomes easier to explain in light of the arguments about nominal wage stickiness. Since wages are a major component of the overall cost of doing business, wage stickiness may lead to output price stickiness. With nominal wages stable, at least some firms can adopt a "wait and see" attitude before adjusting their prices. During this time, they can evaluate information about why sales are rising or falling (Is the change in demand temporary or permanent?) and try to assess likely reactions by consumers or competing firms in the industry to any price changes they might make (Will consumers be angered by a price increase, for example? Will competing firms match price changes?).

In the meantime, firms may prefer to adjust output and employment in response to changing market conditions, leaving product price alone. Quantity adjustments have costs, but firms may assume that the associated risks are smaller than those associated with price adjustments.

Another possible explanation for price stickiness is the notion that there are adjustment costs associated with changing prices. In some cases, firms must print new price lists and catalogs, and notify customers of price changes. Doing this too often could jeopardize customer relations.

Yet another explanation of price stickiness is that firms may have explicit long-term contracts to sell their products to other firms at specified prices. For example, electric utilities often buy their inputs of coal or oil under long-term contracts.

Taken together, these reasons for wage and price stickiness explain why aggregate price adjustment may be incomplete in the sense that the change in the price level is insufficient to maintain real GDP at its potential level. These reasons do not lead to the conclusion that no price adjustments occur. But the adjustments require some time. During this time, the economy may remain above or below its potential level of output.

Equilibrium Levels of Price and Output in the Short Run

To illustrate how we will use the model of aggregate demand and aggregate supply, let us examine the impact of two events: an increase in the cost of health care and an increase in government purchases. The first reduces short-run aggregate supply; the second increases aggregate demand. Both events change equilibrium real GDP and the price level in the short run.

A Change in the Cost of Health Care

In the United States, most people receive health insurance for themselves and their families through their employers. In fact, it is quite common for employers to pay a large percentage of employees' health insurance premiums, and this benefit is often written into labor contracts. As the cost of health care has gone up over time, firms have had to pay higher and higher health insurance premiums. With nominal wages fixed in the short run, an increase in health insurance premiums paid by firms raises the cost of employing each worker. It affects the cost of production in the same way that higher wages would. The result of higher health insurance premiums is that firms will choose to employ fewer workers.

FIGURE 13.8   An Increase in Health Insurance Premiums Paid by Firms

An increase in health insurance premiums paid by firms increases labor costs, reducing short-run aggregate supply from $SRAS_1$ to $SRAS_2$. The price level rises from P_1 to P_2 and output falls from Y_1 to Y_2.

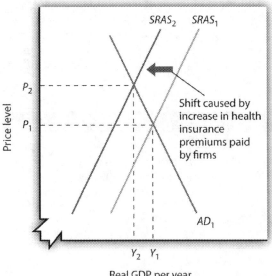

Suppose the economy is operating initially at the short-run equilibrium at the intersection of AD_1 and $SRAS_1$, with a real GDP of Y_1 and a price level of P_1, as shown in Figure 13.8. This is the initial equilibrium price and output in the short run. The increase in labor cost shifts the short-run aggregate supply curve to $SRAS_2$. The price level rises to P_2 and real GDP falls to Y_2.

A reduction in health insurance premiums would have the opposite effect. There would be a shift to the right in the short-run aggregate supply curve with pressure on the price level to fall and real GDP to rise.

A Change in Government Purchases

Suppose the federal government increases its spending for highway construction. This circumstance leads to an increase in U.S. government purchases and an increase in aggregate demand.

Assuming no other changes affect aggregate demand, the increase in government purchases shifts the aggregate demand curve by a multiplied amount of the initial increase in government purchases to AD_2 in Figure 13.9. Real GDP rises from Y_1 to Y_2, while the price level rises from P_1 to P_2. Notice that the increase in real GDP is less than it would have been if the price level had not risen.

FIGURE 13.9 An Increase in Government Purchases

An increase in government purchases boosts aggregate demand from AD_1 to AD_2. Short-run equilibrium is at the intersection of AD_2 and the short-run aggregate supply curve $SRAS_1$. The price level rises to P_2 and real GDP rises to Y_2.

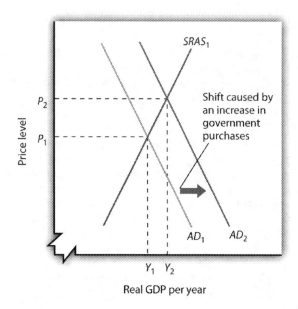

In contrast, a reduction in government purchases would reduce aggregate demand. The aggregate demand curve shifts to the left, putting pressure on both the price level and real GDP to fall.

In the short run, real GDP and the price level are determined by the intersection of the aggregate demand and short-run aggregate supply curves. Recall, however, that the short run is a period in which sticky prices may prevent the economy from reaching its natural level of employment and potential output. In the next section, we will see how the model adjusts to move the economy to long-run equilibrium and what, if anything, can be done to steer the economy toward the natural level of employment and potential output.

KEY TAKEAWAYS

- The short run in macroeconomics is a period in which wages and some other prices are sticky. The long run is a period in which full wage and price flexibility, and market adjustment, has been achieved, so that the economy is at the natural level of employment and potential output.

- The long-run aggregate supply curve is a vertical line at the potential level of output. The intersection of the economy's aggregate demand and long-run aggregate supply curves determines its equilibrium real GDP and price level in the long run.

- The short-run aggregate supply curve is an upward-sloping curve that shows the quantity of total output that will be produced at each price level in the short run. Wage and price stickiness account for the short-run aggregate supply curve's upward slope.

- Changes in prices of factors of production shift the short-run aggregate supply curve. In addition, changes in the capital stock, the stock of natural resources, and the level of technology can also cause the short-run aggregate supply curve to shift.

- In the short run, the equilibrium price level and the equilibrium level of total output are determined by the intersection of the aggregate demand and the short-run aggregate supply curves. In the short run, output can be either below or above potential output.

The tools we have covered in this section can be used to understand the Great Depression of the 1930s. We know that investment and consumption began falling in late 1929. The reductions were reinforced by plunges in net exports and government purchases over the next four years. In addition, nominal wages plunged 26% between 1929 and 1933. We also know that real GDP in 1933 was 30% below real GDP in 1929. Use the tools of aggregate demand and short-run aggregate supply to graph and explain what happened to the economy between 1929 and 1933.

Case in Point

The U.S. Recession of 2001

What were the causes of the U.S. recession of 2001? Economist Kevin Kliesen of the Federal Reserve Bank of St. Louis points to four factors that, taken together, shifted the aggregate demand curve to the left and kept it there for a long enough period to keep real GDP falling for about nine months. They were the fall in stock market prices, the decrease in business investment both for computers and software and in structures, the decline in the real value of exports, and the aftermath of 9/11. Notable exceptions to this list of culprits were the behavior of consumer spending during the period and new residential housing, which falls into the investment category.

During the expansion in the late 1990s, a surging stock market probably made it easier for firms to raise funding for investment in both structures and information technology. Even though the stock market bubble burst well before the actual recession, the continuation of projects already underway delayed the decline in the investment component of GDP. Also, spending for information technology was probably prolonged as firms dealt with Y2K computing issues, that is, computer problems associated with the change in the date from 1999 to 2000. Most computers used only two digits to indicate the year, and when the year changed from '99 to '00, computers did not know how to interpret the change, and extensive reprogramming of computers was required.

Real exports fell during the recession because (1) the dollar was strong during the period and (2) real GDP growth in the rest of the world fell almost 5% from 2000 to 2001.

Then, the terrorist attacks of 9/11, which literally shut down transportation and financial markets for several days, may have prolonged these negative tendencies just long enough to turn what might otherwise have been a mild decline into enough of a downtown to qualify the period as a recession.

During this period the measured price level was essentially stable—with the implicit price deflator rising by less than 1%. Thus, while the aggregate demand curve shifted left as a result of all the reasons given above, there was also a leftward shift in the short-run aggregate supply curve.

Source: Kevin L. Kliesen, "The 2001 Recession: How Was It Different and What Developments May Have Caused It?," The Federal Reserve Bank of St. Louis Review, September/October 2003, 23–37.

All components of aggregate demand (consumption, investment, government purchases, and net exports) declined between 1929 and 1933. Thus the aggregate demand curve shifted markedly to the left, moving from AD_{1929} to AD_{1933}. The reduction in nominal wages corresponds to an increase in short-run aggregate supply from $SRAS_{1929}$ to $SRAS_{1933}$. Since real GDP in 1933 was less than real GDP in 1929, we know that the movement in the aggregate demand curve was greater than that of the short-run aggregate supply curve.

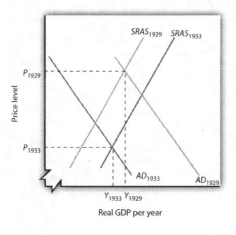

3. RECESSIONARY AND INFLATIONARY GAPS AND LONG-RUN MACROECONOMIC EQUILIBRIUM

LEARNING OBJECTIVES

1. **Explain and illustrate graphically recessionary and inflationary gaps and relate these gaps to what is happening in the labor market.**
2. **Identify the various policy choices available when an economy experiences an inflationary or recessionary gap and discuss some of the pros and cons that make these choices controversial.**

The intersection of the economy's aggregate demand and short-run aggregate supply curves determines equilibrium real GDP and price level in the short run. The intersection of aggregate demand and long-run aggregate supply determines its long-run equilibrium. In this section we will examine the process through which an economy moves from equilibrium in the short run to equilibrium in the long run.

The long run puts a nation's macroeconomic house in order: only frictional and structural unemployment remain, and the price level is stabilized. In the short run, stickiness of nominal wages and other prices can prevent the economy from achieving its potential output. Actual output may exceed or fall short of potential output. In such a situation the economy operates with a gap. When output is above potential, employment is above the natural level of employment. When output is below potential, employment is below the natural level.

3.1 Recessionary and Inflationary Gaps

At any time, real GDP and the price level are determined by the intersection of the aggregate demand and short-run aggregate supply curves. If employment is below the natural level of employment, real GDP will be below potential. The aggregate demand and short-run aggregate supply curves will intersect to the left of the long-run aggregate supply curve.

FIGURE 13.10   A Recessionary Gap

If employment is below the natural level, as shown in Panel (a), then output must be below potential. Panel (b) shows the recessionary gap $Y_P - Y_1$, which occurs when the aggregate demand curve AD and the short-run aggregate supply curve SRAS intersect to the left of the long-run aggregate supply curve LRAS.

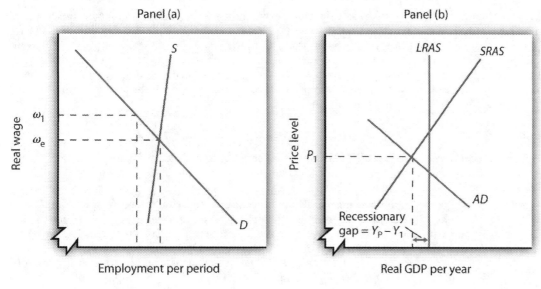

FIGURE 13.11   An Inflationary Gap

Panel (a) shows that if employment is above the natural level, then output must be above potential. The inflationary gap, shown in Panel (b), equals $Y_1 - Y_P$. The aggregate demand curve AD and the short-run aggregate supply curve SRAS intersect to the right of the long-run aggregate supply curve LRAS.

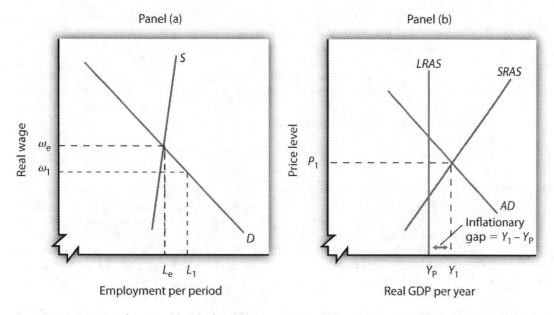

Suppose an economy's natural level of employment is L_e, shown in Panel (a) of Figure 13.10. This level of employment is achieved at a real wage of ω_e. Suppose, however, that the initial real wage ω_1 exceeds this equilibrium value. Employment at L_1 falls short of the natural level. A lower level of employment produces a lower level of output; the aggregate demand and short-run aggregate supply curves, AD and SRAS, intersect to the left of the long-run aggregate supply curve LRAS in Panel (b). The gap between the level of real GDP and potential output, when real GDP is less than potential, is called a **recessionary gap**.

Just as employment can fall short of its natural level, it can also exceed it. If employment is greater than its natural level, real GDP will also be greater than its potential level. Figure 13.11 shows an economy with a natural level of employment of L_e in Panel (a) and potential output of Y_P in Panel (b). If the real wage ω_1 is less than the equilibrium real wage ω_e, then employment L_1 will exceed the natural level. As a result, real GDP, Y_1, exceeds potential. The gap between the level of real GDP and potential

recessionary gap

The gap between the level of real GDP and potential output, when real GDP is less than potential.

inflationary gap

The gap between the level of real GDP and potential output, when real GDP is greater than potential.

output, when real GDP is greater than potential, is called an **inflationary gap**. In Panel (b), the inflationary gap equals $Y_1 - Y_P$.

3.2 Restoring Long-Run Macroeconomic Equilibrium

We have already seen that the aggregate demand curve shifts in response to a change in consumption, investment, government purchases, or net exports. The short-run aggregate supply curve shifts in response to changes in the prices of factors of production, the quantities of factors of production available, or technology. Now we will see how the economy responds to a shift in aggregate demand or short-run aggregate supply using two examples presented earlier: a change in government purchases and a change in health-care costs. By returning to these examples, we will be able to distinguish the long-run response from the short-run response.

A Shift in Aggregate Demand: An Increase in Government Purchases

Suppose an economy is initially in equilibrium at potential output YP as in Figure 13.12. Because the economy is operating at its potential, the labor market must be in equilibrium; the quantities of labor demanded and supplied are equal.

FIGURE 13.12 Long-Run Adjustment to an Inflationary Gap

An increase in aggregate demand to AD_2 boosts real GDP to Y_2 and the price level to P_2, creating an inflationary gap of $Y_2 - Y_P$. In the long run, as price and nominal wages increase, the short-run aggregate supply curve moves to $SRAS_2$. Real GDP returns to potential.

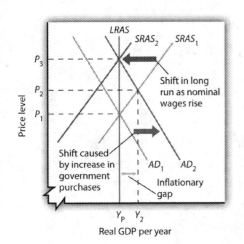

Now suppose aggregate demand increases because one or more of its components (consumption, investment, government purchases, and net exports) has increased at each price level. For example, suppose government purchases increase. The aggregate demand curve shifts from AD_1 to AD_2 in Figure 13.12. That will increase real GDP to Y_2 and force the price level up to P_2 in the short run. The higher price level, combined with a fixed nominal wage, results in a lower real wage. Firms employ more workers to supply the increased output.

The economy's new production level Y_2 exceeds potential output. Employment exceeds its natural level. The economy with output of Y_2 and price level of P_2 is only in short-run equilibrium; there is an inflationary gap equal to the difference between Y_2 and Y_P. Because real GDP is above potential, there will be pressure on prices to rise further.

Ultimately, the nominal wage will rise as workers seek to restore their lost purchasing power. As the nominal wage rises, the short-run aggregate supply curve will begin shifting to the left. It will continue to shift as long as the nominal wage rises, and the nominal wage will rise as long as there is an inflationary gap. These shifts in short-run aggregate supply, however, will reduce real GDP and thus begin to close this gap. When the short-run aggregate supply curve reaches $SRAS_2$, the economy will have returned to its potential output, and employment will have returned to its natural level. These adjustments will close the inflationary gap.

A Shift in Short-Run Aggregate Supply: An Increase in the Cost of Health Care

Again suppose, with an aggregate demand curve at AD_1 and a short-run aggregate supply at $SRAS_1$, an economy is initially in equilibrium at its potential output Y_P, at a price level of P_1, as shown in Figure 13.13. Now suppose that the short-run aggregate supply curve shifts owing to a rise in the cost of health care. As we explained earlier, because health insurance premiums are paid primarily by firms for their workers, an increase in premiums raises the cost of production and causes a reduction in the short-run aggregate supply curve from $SRAS_1$ to $SRAS_2$.

As a result, the price level rises to P_2 and real GDP falls to Y_2. The economy now has a recessionary gap equal to the difference between Y_P and Y_2. Notice that this situation is particularly disagreeable, because both unemployment and the price level rose.

With real GDP below potential, though, there will eventually be pressure on the price level to fall. Increased unemployment also puts pressure on nominal wages to fall. In the long run, the short-run aggregate supply curve shifts back to $SRAS_1$. In this case, real GDP returns to potential at Y_P, the price level falls back to P_1, and employment returns to its natural level. These adjustments will close the recessionary gap.

How sticky prices and nominal wages are will determine the time it takes for the economy to return to potential. People often expect the government or the central bank to respond in some way to try to close gaps. This issue is addressed next.

3.3 Gaps and Public Policy

If the economy faces a gap, how do we get from that situation to potential output?

Gaps present us with two alternatives. First, we can do nothing. In the long run, real wages will adjust to the equilibrium level, employment will move to its natural level, and real GDP will move to its potential. Second, we can do something. Faced with a recessionary or an inflationary gap, policy makers can undertake policies aimed at shifting the aggregate demand or short-run aggregate supply curves in a way that moves the economy to its potential. A policy choice to take no action to try to close a recessionary or an inflationary gap, but to allow the economy to adjust on its own to its potential output, is a **nonintervention policy**. A policy in which the government or central bank acts to move the economy to its potential output is called a **stabilization policy**.

Nonintervention or Expansionary Policy?

Figure 13.14 illustrates the alternatives for closing a recessionary gap. In both panels, the economy starts with a real GDP of Y_1 and a price level of P_1. There is a recessionary gap equal to Y_P − Y_1. In Panel (a), the economy closes the gap through a process of self-correction. Real and nominal wages will fall as long as employment remains below the natural level. Lower nominal wages shift the short-run aggregate supply curve. The process is a gradual one, however, given the stickiness of nominal wages, but after a series of shifts in the short-run aggregate supply curve, the economy moves toward equilibrium at a price level of P_2 and its potential output of Y_P.

FIGURE 13.14 Alternatives in Closing a Recessionary Gap

Panel (a) illustrates a gradual closing of a recessionary gap. Under a nonintervention policy, short-run aggregate supply shifts from $SRAS_1$ to $SRAS_2$. Panel (b) shows the effects of expansionary policy acting on aggregate demand to close the gap.

Panel (a)

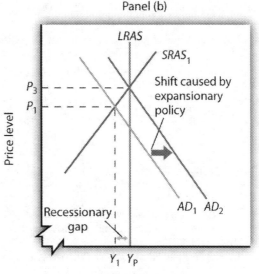

Panel (b)

FIGURE 13.13 Long-Run Adjustment to a Recessionary Gap

A decrease in aggregate supply from $SRAS_1$ to $SRAS_2$ reduces real GDP to Y_2 and raises the price level to P_2, creating a recessionary gap of Y_P − Y_2. In the long run, as prices and nominal wages decrease, the short-run aggregate supply curve moves back to $SRAS_1$ and real GDP returns to potential.

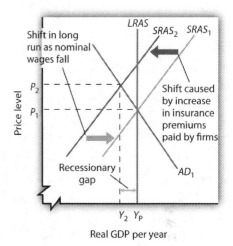

nonintervention policy

A policy choice to take no action to try to close a recessionary or an inflationary gap, but to allow the economy to adjust on its own to its potential output.

stabilization policy

A policy in which the government or central bank acts to move the economy to its potential output.

Panel (b) illustrates the stabilization alternative. Faced with an economy operating below its potential, public officials act to stimulate aggregate demand. For example, the government can increase government purchases of goods and services or cut taxes. Tax cuts leave people with more after-tax income to spend, boost their consumption, and increase aggregate demand. As AD_1 shifts to AD_2 in Panel (b) of Figure 13.14, the economy achieves output of Y_P, but at a higher price level, P_3. A stabilization policy designed to increase real GDP is known as an **expansionary policy**.

Nonintervention or Contractionary Policy?

Figure 13.15 illustrates the alternatives for closing an inflationary gap. Employment in an economy with an inflationary gap exceeds its natural level—the quantity of labor demanded exceeds the long-run supply of labor. A nonintervention policy would rely on nominal wages to rise in response to the shortage of labor. As nominal wages rise, the short-run aggregate supply curve begins to shift, as shown in Panel (a), bringing the economy to its potential output when it reaches $SRAS_2$ and P_2.

FIGURE 13.15 Alternatives in Closing an Inflationary Gap

Panel (a) illustrates a gradual closing of an inflationary gap. Under a nonintervention policy, short-run aggregate supply shifts from $SRAS_1$ to $SRAS_2$. Panel (b) shows the effects of contractionary policy to reduce aggregate demand from AD_1 to AD_2 in order to close the gap.

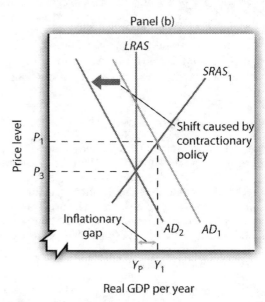

A stabilization policy that reduces the level of GDP is a **contractionary policy**. Such a policy would aim at shifting the aggregate demand curve from AD_1 to AD_2 to close the gap, as shown in Panel (b). A policy to shift the aggregate demand curve to the left would return real GDP to its potential at a price level of P_3.

For both kinds of gaps, a combination of letting market forces in the economy close part of the gap and of using stabilization policy to close the rest of the gap is also an option. Later chapters will explain stabilization policies in more detail, but there are essentially two types of stabilization policy: fiscal policy and monetary policy. **Fiscal policy** is the use of government purchases, transfer payments, and taxes to influence the level of economic activity. **Monetary policy** is the use of central bank policies to influence the level of economic activity.

To Intervene or Not to Intervene: An Introduction to the Controversy

How large are inflationary and recessionary gaps? Panel (a) of Figure 13.16 shows potential output versus the actual level of real GDP in the United States since 1960. Real GDP appears to follow potential output quite closely, although you see some periods where there have been inflationary or recessionary gaps. Panel (b) shows the sizes of these gaps expressed as percentages of potential output. The percentage gap is positive during periods of inflationary gaps and negative during periods of recessionary gaps. Over the last 50 years, the economy has seldom departed by more than 5% from its potential output. So the size and duration of the recessionary gap from 2009 to 2011 certainly stand out.

FIGURE 13.16   Real GDP and Potential Output

Panel (a) shows potential output (the blue line) and actual real GDP (the purple line) since 1960. Panel (b) shows the gap between potential and actual real GDP expressed as a percentage of potential output. Inflationary gaps are shown in green and recessionary gaps are shown in yellow.

Source: Bureau of Economic Analysis, NIPA Table 1.1.6 (revised February 28, 2014). Real Gross Domestic Product, Chained Dollars [Billions of chained (2009) dollars]. Seasonally adjusted at annual rates; Congressional Budget Office, The Budget and Economic Outlook: An Update, February 2014.

Panel (a) gives a long-run perspective on the economy. It suggests that the economy generally operates at about potential output. In Panel (a), the gaps seem minor. Panel (b) gives a short-run perspective; the view it gives emphasizes the gaps. Both of these perspectives are important. While it is reassuring to see that the economy is often close to potential, the years in which there are substantial gaps have real effects: Inflation or unemployment can harm people.

Some economists argue that stabilization policy can and should be used when recessionary or inflationary gaps exist. Others urge reliance on the economy's own ability to correct itself. They sometimes argue that the tools available to the public sector to influence aggregate demand are not likely to shift the curve, or they argue that the tools would shift the curve in a way that could do more harm than good.

Economists who advocate stabilization policies argue that prices are sufficiently sticky that the economy's own adjustment to its potential will be a slow process—and a painful one. For an economy with a recessionary gap, unacceptably high levels of unemployment will persist for too long a time. For an economy with an inflationary gap, the increased prices that occur as the short-run aggregate supply curve shifts upward impose too high an inflation rate in the short run. These economists believe it is far preferable to use stabilization policy to shift the aggregate demand curve in an effort to shorten the time the economy is subject to a gap.

Economists who favor a nonintervention approach accept the notion that stabilization policy can shift the aggregate demand curve. They argue, however, that such efforts are not nearly as simple in the real world as they may appear on paper. For example, policies to change real GDP may not affect the economy for months or even years. By the time the impact of the stabilization policy occurs, the state of the economy might have changed. Policy makers might choose an expansionary policy when a contractionary one is needed or vice versa. Other economists who favor nonintervention also question how sticky prices really are and if gaps even exist.

The debate over how policy makers should respond to recessionary and inflationary gaps is an ongoing one. These issues of nonintervention versus stabilization policies lie at the heart of the macroeconomic policy debate. We will return to them as we continue our analysis of the determination of output and the price level.

KEY TAKEAWAYS

- When the aggregate demand and short-run aggregate supply curves intersect below potential output, the economy has a recessionary gap. When they intersect above potential output, the economy has an inflationary gap.
- Inflationary and recessionary gaps are closed as the real wage returns to equilibrium, where the quantity of labor demanded equals the quantity supplied. Because of nominal wage and price stickiness, however, such an adjustment takes time.
- When the economy has a gap, policy makers can choose to do nothing and let the economy return to potential output and the natural level of employment on its own. A policy to take no action to try to close a gap is a nonintervention policy.
- Alternatively, policy makers can choose to try to close a gap by using stabilization policy. Stabilization policy designed to increase real GDP is called expansionary policy. Stabilization policy designed to decrease real GDP is called contractionary policy.

TRY IT!

Using the scenario of the Great Depression of the 1930s, as analyzed in the previous Try It!, tell what kind of gap the U.S. economy faced in 1933, assuming the economy had been at potential output in 1929. Do you think the unemployment rate was above or below the natural rate of unemployment? How could the economy have been brought back to its potential output?

Case in Point

This Time Is Different, Or Is It?

In an analysis that spans 66 countries over nearly eight centuries, economists Carmen Reinhart and Kenneth Rogoff investigate hundreds of financial crises and the economic busts each leaves in its wake. With a database that includes crisis episodes that go back as far as 12th-century China and medieval Europe and continue until the financial crisis of 2007–2008, the authors look at the patterns of economic behavior that characterize the periods leading up to financial crises and the patterns that characterize the recoveries.

They argue that looking over a long period of history is necessary because financial crises are "rare" events. Financial crises occur at varying intervals, and researchers studying a period of 25 years or so may not encounter the equivalent of a 100-year, category 5 hurricane that hits a major, low-lying city with a faulty levee system.

In general, such crises follow periods of relative economic calm. For example, the period in the United States from the mid-1980s until 2007 was often referred to as the Great Moderation. During such periods, inflationary and recessionary gaps may occur, but they are relatively small and short-lived. Societies begin to feel that they have tamed the business cycle, that policy makers have gotten smarter, and that moderation will continue.

But then it happens. The accumulation of too much debt by governments, businesses, or consumers leads to a financial meltdown. As housing prices are run up, for example, people tend to find ways to justify their heavy borrowing and to rationalize the ascent in prices: Demographics have changed; mortgage terms have improved; the regulation we have put in place is better this time; it's better to buy now, before prices go up even more; housing prices won't fall. Memories of the last crisis fade. "This time is different," they argue.

But Reinhart and Rogoff provide convincing evidence that "this time" is usually not different. Large-scale debt buildups lead to crises of confidence, and a financial crisis ensues. The aftermath is typically a severe and prolonged recessionary gap. On average, they find the following to be true:

1. The collapse in asset market prices is large and long-lasting. Housing prices decline an average of 35% over 6 years, and stock prices decline an average of 56% over 3.5 years.

2. Peak-to-trough GDP falls 9% on average, and the recession averages 2 years in length.

3. The unemployment rate rises 7 percentage points over a 4-year period.

4. Government debt swells due to bailout costs and, more importantly, because tax revenues fall off due to lower GDP.

5. V-shaped recoveries in stock prices are more common than V-shaped recoveries in housing prices or employment.

To what extent is the financial crisis of the late 2000s likely to follow this typical pattern? The authors argue that experience with expansionary fiscal policy in such circumstances is actually quite limited. Most often, governments are shut out of borrowing markets when crises hit. Japan's government explicitly tried to implement fiscal stimulus, but the authors warn against drawing conclusions from one such example. The authors caution that governments should weigh any potential benefit of fiscal stimulus against the problem of higher public debt. They also note that central banks in 2007–2008 acted quickly and aggressively with expansionary monetary policies. But, they caution against "push[ing] too far the conceit that we are smarter than our predecessors" (p. 238). The global nature of the current situation only adds to the difficulty of recovering fully.

There was a company failure around 15 years ago that looked like a big deal at the time, but now seems like little more than a blip. The authors quote a trader who, during this event, presciently remarked, "More money has been lost because of four words than at the point of a gun. Those words are 'This time is different.'"

Source: Carmen M. Reinhart and Kenneth S. Rogoff, This Time Is Different: Eight Centuries of Financial Folly (Princeton: Princeton University Press, 2009).

A N S W E R   T O   T R Y   I T !   P R O B L E M

To the graph in the previous Try It! problem we add the long-run aggregate supply curve to show that, with output below potential, the U.S. economy in 1933 was in a recessionary gap. The unemployment rate was above the natural rate of unemployment. Indeed, real GDP in 1933 was about 30% below what it had been in 1929, and the unemployment rate had increased from 3% to 25%. Note that during the period of the Great Depression, wages did fall. The notion of nominal wage and other price stickiness discussed in this section should not be construed to mean complete wage and price inflexibility. Rather, during this period, nominal wages and other prices were not flexible enough to restore the economy to the potential level of output. There are two basic choices on how to close recessionary gaps. Nonintervention would mean waiting for wages to fall further. As wages fall, the short-run aggregate supply curve would continue to shift to the right. The alternative would be to use some type of expansionary policy. This would shift the aggregate demand curve to the right. These two options were illustrated in Figure 13.15.

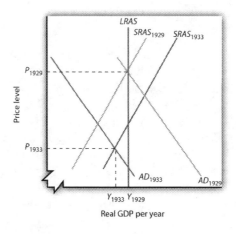

4. REVIEW AND PRACTICE

Summary

In this chapter, we outlined the model of aggregate demand and aggregate supply. We saw that the aggregate demand curve slopes downward, reflecting the tendency for the aggregate quantity of goods and services demanded to rise as the price level falls and to fall as the price level rises. The negative relationship between the price level and the quantity of goods and services demanded results from the wealth effect for consumption, the interest rate effect for investment, and the international trade effect for net exports. We examined the factors that can shift the aggregate demand curve as well. Generally, the aggregate demand curve shifts by a multiple of the initial amount by which the component causing it to shift changes.

We distinguished between two types of equilibria in macroeconomics—one corresponding to the short run, a period of analysis in which nominal wages and some prices are sticky, and the other corresponding to the long run, a period in which full wage and price flexibility, and hence market adjustment, have been achieved. Long-run equilibrium occurs at the intersection of the aggregate demand curve with the long-run aggregate supply curve. The long-run aggregate supply curve is a vertical line at the economy's potential level of output. Short-run equilibrium occurs at the intersection of the aggregate demand curve with the short-run aggregate supply curve. The short-run aggregate supply curve relates the quantity of total output produced to the price level in the short run. It is upward sloping because of wage and price stickiness. In short-run equilibrium, output can be below or above potential.

If an economy is initially operating at its potential output, then a change in aggregate demand or short-run aggregate supply will induce a recessionary or inflationary gap. Such a gap will be closed in the long run by changes in the nominal wage, which will shift the short-run aggregate supply curve to the left (to close an inflationary gap) or to the right (to close a recessionary gap). Policy makers might respond to a recessionary or inflationary gap with a nonintervention policy, or they could use stabilization policy.

CONCEPT PROBLEMS

1. Explain how the following changes in aggregate demand or short-run aggregate supply, other things held unchanged, are likely to affect the level of total output and the price level in the short run.

    a. An increase in aggregate demand

    b. A decrease in aggregate demand

    c. An increase in short-run aggregate supply

    d. A reduction in short-run aggregate supply

2. Explain why a change in one component of aggregate demand will cause the aggregate demand curve to shift by a multiple of the initial change.

3. Use the model of aggregate demand and short-run aggregate supply to explain how each of the following would affect real GDP and the price level in the short run.

    a. An increase in government purchases

    b. A reduction in nominal wages

    c. A major improvement in technology

    d. A reduction in net exports

4. How would an increase in the supply of labor affect the natural level of employment and potential output? How would it affect the real wage, the level of real GDP, and the price level in the short run? How would it affect long-run aggregate supply? What kind of gaps would be created?

5. Give three reasons for the downward slope of the aggregate demand curve.

6. "When the price level falls, people's wealth increases. When wealth increases, the real volume of consumption increases. Therefore, a decrease in the price level will cause the aggregate demand curve to shift to the right." Do you agree? Explain.

7. Suppose the economy has a recessionary gap. We know that if we do nothing, the economy will close the gap on its own. Alternatively, we could arrange for an increase in aggregate demand (say, by increasing government spending) to close the gap. How would your views about the degree of price stickiness in the economy influence your views on whether such a policy would be desirable?

8. The cost of hiring workers includes not only payments made directly to workers, that is, wages, but payments made on behalf of workers as well, such as contributions by employers to pension plans and to health-care insurance for employees. How would a decrease in the cost of employer-provided health insurance affect the economy? Using Figure 13.8 as a guide, draw a graph to illustrate your answer.

9. Suppose nominal wages never changed. What would be the significance of such a characteristic?

10. Suppose the minimum wage were increased sharply. How would this affect the equilibrium price level and output level in the model of aggregate demand and aggregate supply in the short run? In the long run?

11. Explain the short-run impact of each of the following.

    a. A discovery that makes cold fusion a reality, greatly reducing the cost of producing energy

    b. An increase in the payroll tax

NUMERICAL PROBLEMS

1. Suppose the aggregate demand and short-run aggregate supply schedules for an economy whose potential output equals $2,700 are given by the table.

	Aggregate Quantity of Goods and Services	
Price Level	Demanded	Supplied
0.50	$3,500	$1,000
0.75	3,000	2,000
1.00	2,500	2,500
1.25	2,000	2,700
1.50	1,500	2,800

   a. Draw the aggregate demand, short-run aggregate supply, and long-run aggregate supply curves.
   b. State the short-run equilibrium level of real GDP and the price level.
   c. Characterize the current economic situation. Is there an inflationary or a recessionary gap? If so, how large is it?
   d. Now suppose aggregate demand increases by $700 at each price level; for example, the aggregate quantity of goods and services demanded at a price level of 0.50 now equals $4,200. Show the new aggregate demand curve, state the new short-run equilibrium price level and real GDP, and state whether there is an inflationary or a recessionary gap and give its size.

2. An economy is characterized by the values in the table for aggregate demand and short-run aggregate supply. Its potential output is $1,500.

	Aggregate Quantity of Goods and Services	
Price Level	Demanded	Supplied
0.50	$2,500	$1,500
0.75	2,000	2,000
1.00	1,500	2,300
1.25	1,000	2,500
1.50	500	2,600

   a. Draw the aggregate demand, short-run aggregate supply, and long-run aggregate supply curves.
   b. State the equilibrium level of real GDP and the price level.
   c. Characterize the current economic situation. Is there an inflationary or a recessionary gap? If so, how large is it?
   d. Now suppose that nominal wages rise and that the price level required to induce a particular level of total output rises by 0.50. For example, a price level of 1.00 is now required to induce producers to produce a real GDP of $1,500. Show the new short-run aggregate supply curve, state the new equilibrium price level and real GDP, and state whether there is an inflationary or a recessionary gap and give its size. Why might such a change occur?

3. Suppose the price level in a particular economy equals 1.3 and that the quantity of real GDP demanded at that price level is $1,200. An increase of 0.1 point in the price level reduces the quantity of real GDP demanded by $220, and a reduction of 0.1 point would produce an increase in the quantity of real GDP demanded of $220. Draw the aggregate demand curve and show the price level and quantity of real GDP demanded at three points.

4. Suppose an economy is described by the following aggregate demand and short-run aggregate supply curves. The potential level of output is $10 trillion.

	Aggregate Quantity of Goods and Services	
Price Level	Demanded	Supplied
3.0	$11.0 trillion	$9.0 trillion
3.4	$10.8 trillion	$9.2 trillion
3.8	$10.6 trillion	$9.4 trillion
4.2	$10.4 trillion	$9.6 trillion
4.6	$10.2 trillion	$9.8 trillion
5.0	$10.0 trillion	$10.0 trillion
5.4	$9.8 trillion	$10.2 trillion
5.8	$9.6 trillion	$10.4 trillion
6.2	$9.4 trillion	$10.6 trillion
6.6	$9.2 trillion	$10.8 trillion
7.0	$9.0 trillion	$11.0 trillion

   a. Draw the aggregate demand and short-run aggregate supply curves.

   b. What is the initial real GDP?

   c. What is the initial price level?

   d. What kind of gap, if any, exists?

   e. After the increase in health-care costs, each level of real GDP requires an increase in the price level of 0.8. For example, producing $9.0 trillion worth of goods and services now requires a price level of 3.8. What is the short-run equilibrium level of real GDP?

   f. After the health-care cost increase, what is the new equilibrium price level in the short run?

   g. What sort of gap, if any, now exists?

5. According to Alaskan state economist Mark Edwards, the multiplier effect of Alaska's trade with Japan is such that for every $1 billion exported from Alaska to Japan another $600 million is added to the state's economy.[1] Calculate the size of the export multiplier.

6. The Nottinghamshire Research Observatory in England calculated that students who attend Nottingham Technical University spend about £2,760 each in the local economy for a total of £50.45 million. In total, the impact of their spending on the local economy is £63 million.[2] Calculate the size of the student spending multiplier.

7. In Goa, India, the multiplier effect of iron ore exports is calculated to be 1.62.[3] Calculate the impact of an additional 1,000 rupees of iron ore exports on the economy of Goa.

ENDNOTES

1. Matt Volz, "Trade Officials Hopeful for Japanese Recovery," *Associated Press and Local Wire*, June 22, 2004, BC cycle.

2. "University Brings in £250m to Economy," *Nottingham Evening Post*, November 4, 2004, p. 37.

3. Vidyut Kumar Ta, "Iron Ore Mining Gives Impetus to Goa's Economy," *Times of India*, April 30, 2003.

CHAPTER 14
Economic Growth

START UP: HOW IMPORTANT IS ECONOMIC GROWTH?

How important is economic growth? The best way to answer that question is to imagine life without growth—to imagine that we did not have the gains growth brings.

For starters, divide your family's current income by six and imagine what your life would be like. Think about the kind of housing your family could afford, the size of your entertainment budget, whether you could still attend school. That will give you an idea of life a century ago in the United States, when average household incomes, adjusted for inflation, were about one-sixth what they are today. People had far smaller homes, they rarely had electricity in their homes, and only a tiny percentage of the population could even consider a college education.

To get a more recent perspective, consider how growth has changed living standards over the past half century or so. In 1950, the United States was the world's richest nation. But if households were rich then, subsequent economic growth has made them far richer. Average per capita real income has tripled since then. Indeed, the average household income in 1950, which must have seemed lofty then, was below what we now define as the poverty line for a household of four, even after adjusting for inflation. Economic growth during the last 60-plus years has dramatically boosted our standard of living—and our standard of what it takes to get by.

One gauge of rising living standards is housing. A half century ago, most families did not own homes. Today, about two-thirds do. Those homes have gotten a lot bigger: new homes built today are more than twice the size of new homes built 50 years ago. Some household appliances, such as telephones or washing machines, that we now consider basic, were luxuries a half century ago. In 1950, less than two-thirds of housing units had complete plumbing facilities. Today, over 99% do.

Economic growth has brought gains in other areas as well. For one thing, we are able to afford more schooling. In 1950, the median number of years of school completed by adults age 25 or over was 6.8. Today, about 87% have completed 12 years of schooling and about 30% have completed 4 years of college. We also live longer. A baby born in 1950 had a life expectancy of 68 years. A baby born in 2008 had an expected life of nearly 10 years longer.

Of course, while economic growth can improve our material well-being, it is no panacea. Americans today worry about the level of violence in society, environmental degradation, and what seems to be a loss of basic values. But while it is easy to be dismayed about many challenges of modern life, we can surely be grateful for our material wealth. Our affluence gives us the opportunity to grapple with some of our most difficult problems and to enjoy a range of choices that people only a few decades ago could not have imagined.

We learned a great deal about economic growth in the context of the production possibilities curve. Our purpose in this chapter is to relate the concept of economic growth to the model of aggregate demand and aggregate supply that we developed in the previous chapter and will use throughout our exploration of macroeconomics.

We will review the forces that determine a nation's economic growth rate and examine the prospects for growth in the future. We begin by looking at the significance of growth to the overall well-being of society.

1. THE SIGNIFICANCE OF ECONOMIC GROWTH

LEARNING OBJECTIVES

1. **Define economic growth and explain it using the production possibilities model and the concept of potential output.**
2. **State the rule of 72 and use it to show how even small differences in growth rates can have major effects on a country's potential output over time.**
3. **Calculate the percentage rate of growth of output per capita.**

To demonstrate the impact of economic growth on living standards of a nation, we must start with a clear definition of economic growth and then study its impact over time. We will also see how population growth affects the relationship between economic growth and the standard of living an economy is able to achieve.

1.1   Defining Economic Growth

Economic growth is a long-run process that occurs as an economy's potential output increases. Changes in real GDP from quarter to quarter or even from year to year are short-run fluctuations that occur as aggregate demand and short-run aggregate supply change. Regardless of media reports stating that the economy grew at a certain rate in the last quarter or that it is expected to grow at a particular rate during the next year, short-run changes in real GDP say little about economic growth. In the long run, economic activity moves toward its level of potential output. Increases in potential constitute economic growth.

Earlier we defined economic growth as the process through which an economy achieves an outward shift in its production possibilities curve. How does a shift in the production possibilities curve relate to a change in potential output? To produce its potential level of output, an economy must operate on its production possibilities curve. An increase in potential output thus implies an outward shift in the production possibilities curve. In the framework of the macroeconomic model of aggregate demand and aggregate supply, we show economic growth as a shift to the right in the long-run aggregate supply curve.

There are three key points about economic growth to keep in mind:

1. Growth is a process. It is not a single event; rather, it is an unfolding series of events.
2. We define growth in terms of the economy's ability to produce goods and services, as indicated by its level of potential output.
3. Growth suggests that the economy's ability to produce goods and services is rising. A discussion of economic growth is thus a discussion of the series of events that increase the economy's ability to produce goods and services.

Figure 14.1 shows the record of economic growth for the U.S. economy over the past century. The graph shows annual levels of actual real GDP and of potential output. We see that the economy has experienced dramatic growth over the past century; potential output has soared nearly 20-fold. The figure also reminds us of a central theme of our analysis of macroeconomics: real GDP fluctuates about potential output. Real GDP sagged well below its potential (initially more than 40% below and then remaining at about 20% below for most of the decade) during the Great Depression of the 1930s and rose well above its potential (about 30% above) as the nation mobilized its resources to fight World War II. With the exception of these two periods, real GDP has remained fairly close to the economy's potential output. In the recession of 1981, real GDP was almost 7% below its potential, and during the recession that began at the end of 2007, real GDP fell more than 7% below its potential. In 2013, the economy was still about 4.5% below its potential. Nonetheless, since 1950, the actual level of real GDP has deviated from potential output by an average of less than 1%.

FIGURE 14.1 A Century of Economic Growth

At the start of the 21st century, the level of potential output reached a level nearly 20 times its level a century earlier. Over the years, actual real GDP fluctuated about a rising level of potential output.

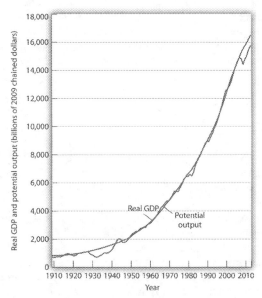

Sources: 1910–1949 data from Christina D. Romer, "World War I and the Postwar Depression: A Reinterpretation Based on Alternative Estimates of GNP," Journal of Monetary Economics 22 (1988): 91–115; data for 1950–2013 from Congressional Budget Office, The Budget and Economic Outlook: An Update, February 2014.

We urge you to take some time with Figure 14.1. Over the course of the last century, it is economic growth that has taken center stage. Certainly, the fluctuations about potential output have been important. The recessionary gaps—periods when real GDP slipped below its potential—were often wrenching experiences in which millions of people endured great hardship. The inflationary gaps—periods when real GDP rose above its potential level—often produced dramatic increases in price levels. Those fluctuations mattered. It was the unemployment and/or the inflation that came with them that made headlines. But it was the quiet process of economic growth that pushed living standards ever higher. We must understand growth if we are to understand how we got where we are, and where we are likely to be going during the 21st century.

Figure 14.2 tells us why we use changes in potential output, rather than actual real GDP, as our measure of economic growth. Actual values of real GDP are affected not just by changes in the potential level of output, but also by the cyclical fluctuations about that level of output.

Given our definition of economic growth, we would say that the hypothetical economy depicted in Figure 14.2 grew at a 2.5% annual rate throughout the period. If we used actual values of real GDP, however, we would obtain quite different interpretations. Consider, for example, the first decade of this period: it began with a real GDP of $900 billion and a recessionary gap, and it ended in year 10 with a real GDP of $1,408 billion and an inflationary gap. If we record growth as the annual rate of change between these levels, we find an annual rate of growth of 4.6%—a rather impressive performance.

Now consider the second decade shown in Figure 14.2. It began in year 10, and it ended in year 20 with a recessionary gap. If we measure the growth rate over that period by looking at beginning and ending values of actual real GDP, we compute an annual growth rate of 0.5%. Viewed in this way, performance in the first decade is spectacular while performance in the second is rather lackluster. But these figures depend on the starting and ending points we select; the growth rate of potential output was 2.5% throughout the period.

FIGURE 14.2 *Cyclical Change Versus Growth*

The use of actual values of real GDP to measure growth can give misleading results. Here, an economy's potential output (shown in green) grows at a steady rate of 2.5% per year, with actual values of real GDP fluctuating about that trend. If we measure growth in the first 10 years as the annual rate of change between beginning and ending values of real GDP, we get a growth rate of 4.6%. The rate for the second decade is 0.5%. Growth estimates based on changes in real GDP are affected by cyclical changes that do not represent economic growth.

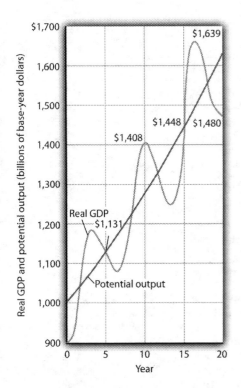

exponential growth

When a quantity grows at a given percentage rate.

rule of 72

A variable's approximate doubling time equals 72 divided by the growth rate, stated as a whole number.

By measuring economic growth as the rate of increase in potential output, we avoid such problems. One way to do this is to select years in which the economy was operating at the natural level of employment and then to compute the annual rate of change between those years. The result is an estimate of the rate at which potential output increased over the period in question. For the economy shown in Figure 14.2, for example, we see that real GDP equaled its potential in years 5 and 15. Real GDP in year 5 was $1,131, and real GDP in year 15 was $1,448. The annual rate of change between these two years was 2.5%. If we have estimates of potential output, of course, we can simply compute annual rates of change between any two years.

1.2   The Rule of 72 and Differences in Growth Rates

The Case in Point on presidents and growth at the end of this section suggests a startling fact: the U.S. growth rate began slowing in the 1970s, did not recover until the mid-1990s, only to slow down again in the 2000s. The question we address here is: does it matter? Does a percentage point drop in the growth rate make much difference? It does. To see why, let us investigate what happens when a variable grows at a particular percentage rate.

Suppose two economies with equal populations start out at the same level of real GDP but grow at different rates. Economy A grows at a rate of 3.5%, and Economy B grows at a rate of 2.4%. After a year, the difference in real GDP will hardly be noticeable. After a decade, however, real GDP in Economy A will be 11% greater than in Economy B. Over longer periods, the difference will be more dramatic. After 100 years, for example, income in Economy A will be nearly three times as great as in Economy B. If population growth in the two countries has been the same, the people of Economy A will have a far higher standard of living than those in Economy B. The difference in real GDP per person will be roughly equivalent to the difference that exists today between Great Britain and Mexico.

Over time, small differences in growth rates create large differences in incomes. An economy growing at a 3.5% rate increases by 3.5% of its initial value in the first year. In the second year, the economy increases by 3.5% of that new, higher value. In the third year, it increases by 3.5% of a still higher value. When a quantity grows at a given percentage rate, it experiences **exponential growth**. A variable that grows exponentially follows a path such as those shown for potential output in Figure 14.1 and Figure 14.2. These curves become steeper over time because the growth rate is applied to an ever-larger base.

A variable growing at some exponential rate doubles over fixed intervals of time. The doubling time is given by the **rule of 72**, which states that a variable's approximate doubling time equals 72 divided by the growth rate, stated as a whole number. If the level of income were increasing at a 9% rate, for example, its doubling time would be roughly 72/9, or 8 years.[1]

Let us apply this concept of a doubling time to the reduction in the U.S. growth rate. Had the U.S. economy continued to grow at a 3.5% rate after 1970, then its potential output would have doubled roughly every 20 years (72/3.5 = 20). That means potential output would have doubled by 1990, would double again by 2010, and would double again by 2030. Real GDP in 2030 would thus be eight times as great as its 1970 level. Growing at a 2.4% rate, however, potential output doubles only every 30 years (72/2.4 = 30). It would take until 2000 to double once from its 1970 level, and it would double once more by 2030. Potential output in 2030 would thus be four times its 1970 level if the economy grew at a 2.4% rate (versus eight times its 1970 level if it grew at a 3.5% rate). The 1.1% difference in growth rates produces a 100% difference in potential output by 2030. The different growth paths implied by these growth rates are illustrated in Figure 14.3.

FIGURE 14.3 Differences in Growth Rates

The chart suggests the significance in the long run of a small difference in the growth rate of real GDP. We begin in 1970, when real GDP equaled $2,873.9 billion. If real GDP grew at an annual rate of 3.5% from that year, it would double roughly every 20 years: in 1990, 2010, and 2030. Growth at a 2.4% rate, however, implies doubling every 30 years: in 2000 and 2030. By 2030, the 3.5% growth rate leaves real GDP at twice the level that would be achieved by 2.4% growth.

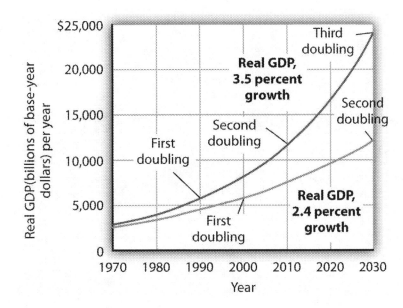

1.3 Growth in Output per Capita

Of course, it is not just how fast potential output grows that determines how fast the average person's material standard of living rises. For that purpose, we examine economic growth on a per capita basis. An economy's **output per capita** equals real GDP per person. If we let *N* equal population, then

output per capita
Real GDP per person.

EQUATION 14.1

$$\text{Output per capita} = \frac{\text{real GDP}}{N}$$

In the United States in 2013, for example, real GDP was $15,759 billion (annual rate). The U.S. population was 315 million. Real U.S. output per capita thus equaled $50,000.

We use output per capita as a gauge of an economy's material standard of living. If the economy's population is growing, then output must rise as rapidly as the population if output per capita is to remain unchanged. If, for example, population increases by 2%, then real GDP would have to rise by 2% to maintain the current level of output per capita. If real GDP rises by less than 2%, output per capita will fall. If real GDP rises by more than 2%, output per capita will rise. More generally, we can write:

EQUATION 14.2

% rate of growth of output per capita $\cong$ % rate of growth of output − % rate of growth of population

For economic growth to translate into a higher standard of living on average, economic growth must exceed population growth. From 1970 to 2004, for example, Sierra Leone's population grew at an annual rate of 2.1% per year, while its real GDP grew at an annual rate of 1.4%; its output per capita thus fell at a rate of 0.7% per year. Over the same period, Singapore's population grew at an annual rate of 2.1% per year, while its real GDP grew 7.4% per year. The resultant 5.3% annual growth in output per capita transformed Singapore from a relatively poor country to a country with the one of the highest per capita incomes in the world.

KEY TAKEAWAYS

- Economic growth is the process through which an economy's production possibilities curve shifts outward. We measure it as the rate at which the economy's potential level of output increases.
- Measuring economic growth as the rate of increase of the actual level of real GDP can lead to misleading results due to the business cycle.
- Growth of a quantity at a particular percentage rate implies exponential growth. When something grows exponentially, it doubles over fixed intervals of time; these intervals may be computed using the rule of 72.
- Small differences in rates of economic growth can lead to large differences in levels of potential output over long periods of time.
- To assess changes in average standards of living, we subtract the percentage rate of growth of population from the percentage rate of growth of output to get the percentage rate of growth of output per capita.

TRY IT!

Suppose an economy's potential output and real GDP is $5 million in 2000 and its rate of economic growth is 3% per year. Also suppose that its population is 5,000 in 2000, and that its population grows at a rate of 1% per year. Compute GDP per capita in 2000. Now estimate GDP and GDP per capita in 2072, using the rule of 72. At what rate does GDP per capita grow? What is its doubling time? Is this result consistent with your findings for GDP per capita in 2000 and in 2072?

Case in Point

Presidents and Economic Growth

President	Annual Increase in Real GDP (%)	Growth Rate (%)
Truman 1949–1952	5.4	4.4
Eisenhower 1953–1960	2.5	3.3
Kennedy-Johnson 1961–1968	5.1	4.4
Nixon-Ford 1969–1976	2.8	3.4
Carter 1977–1980	3.2	3.1
Reagan 1981–1988	3.5	3.1
G. H. W. Bush 1989–1992	2.1	2.9
Clinton 1993–2000	3.8	3.3
G. W. Bush 2001–2008	1.6	2.6

Presidents are often judged by the rate at which the economy grew while they were in office. This test is unfair on two counts. First, a president has little to do with the forces that determine growth. And second, such tests simply compute the annual rate of growth in real GDP over the course of a presidential term, which we know can be affected by cyclical factors. A president who takes office when the economy is down and goes out with the economy up will look like an economic star; a president with the bad luck to have reverse circumstances will seem like a dud. Here are annual rates of change in real GDP for each of the postwar presidents, together with rates of economic growth, measured as the annual rate of change in potential output.

The presidents' economic records are clearly affected by luck. Presidents Truman, Kennedy, Reagan, and Clinton, for example, began their terms when the economy had a recessionary gap and ended them with an inflationary gap or at about potential output. Real GDP thus rose faster than potential output during their presidencies. The Eisenhower, Nixon-Ford, G. H. W. Bush, and G. W. Bush administrations each started with an inflationary gap or at about potential and ended with a recessionary gap, thus recording rates of real GDP increase below the rate of gain in potential. Only Jimmy Carter, who came to office and left it with recessionary gaps, presided over a relatively equivalent rate of increase in actual GDP versus potential output.

How did Barack Obama fare? Only time will tell.

ANSWER TO TRY IT! PROBLEM

GDP per capita in 2000 equals $1,000 ($5,000,000/5,000). If GDP rises 3% per year, it doubles every 24 years (= 72/3). Thus, GDP will be $10,000,000 in 2024, $20,000,000 in 2048, and $40,000,000 in 2072. Growing at a rate of 1% per year, population will have doubled once by 2072 to 10,000. GDP per capita will thus be $4,000 (= $40,000,000/10,000). Notice that GDP rises by eight times its original level, while the increase in GDP per capita is fourfold. The latter value represents a growth rate in output per capita of 2% per year, which implies a doubling time of 36 years. That gives two doublings in GDP per capita between 2000 and 2072 and confirms a fourfold increase.

2. GROWTH AND THE LONG-RUN AGGREGATE SUPPLY CURVE

LEARNING OBJECTIVES

1. Explain and illustrate graphically the concept of the aggregate production function. Explain how its shape relates to the concept of diminishing marginal returns.
2. Derive the long-run aggregate supply curve from the model of the labor market and the aggregate production function.
3. Explain how the long-run aggregate supply curve shifts in responses to shifts in the aggregate production function or to shifts in the demand for or supply of labor.

Economic growth means the economy's potential output is rising. Because the long-run aggregate supply curve is a vertical line at the economy's potential, we can depict the process of economic growth as one in which the long-run aggregate supply curve shifts to the right.

FIGURE 14.4 Economic Growth and the Long-Run Aggregate Supply Curve

Because economic growth is the process through which the economy's potential output is increased, we can depict it as a series of rightward shifts in the long-run aggregate supply curve. Notice that with exponential growth, each successive shift in *LRAS* is larger and larger.

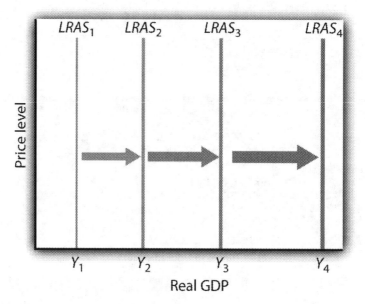

Figure 14.4 illustrates the process of economic growth. If the economy begins at potential output of Y_1, growth increases this potential. The figure shows a succession of increases in potential to Y_2, then Y_3, and Y_4. If the economy is growing at a particular percentage rate, and if the levels shown represent successive years, then the size of the increases will become larger and larger, as indicated in the figure.

Because economic growth can be considered as a process in which the long-run aggregate supply curve shifts to the right, and because output tends to remain close to this curve, it is important to gain a deeper understanding of what determines long-run aggregate supply (*LRAS*). We shall examine the derivation of *LRAS* and then see what factors shift the curve. We shall begin our work by defining an aggregate production function.

2.1   The Aggregate Production Function

aggregate production function

Function that relates the total output of an economy to the total amount of labor employed in the economy, all other determinants of production (capital, natural resources, and technology) being unchanged.

An **aggregate production function** relates the total output of an economy to the total amount of labor employed in the economy, all other determinants of production (that is, capital, natural resources, and technology) being unchanged. An economy operating on its aggregate production function is producing its potential level of output.

Figure 14.5 shows an aggregate production function (*PF*). It shows output levels for a range of employment between 120 million and 140 million workers. When the level of employment is 120 million, the economy produces a real GDP of $11,500 billion (point A). A level of employment of 130 million produces a real GDP of $12,000 billion (point B), and when 140 million workers are employed, a real GDP of $12,300 billion is produced (point C). In drawing the aggregate production function, the amount of labor varies, but everything else that could affect output, specifically the quantities of other factors of production and technology, is fixed.

diminishing marginal returns

Situation that occurs when additional units of a variable factor add less and less to total output, given constant quantities of other factors.

The shape of the aggregate production function shows that as employment increases, output increases, but at a decreasing rate. Increasing employment from 120 million to 130 million, for example, increases output by $500 billion to $12,000 billion at point B. The next 10 million workers increase production by $300 billion to $12,300 billion at point C. This example illustrates diminishing marginal returns. **Diminishing marginal returns** occur when additional units of a variable factor add less and less to total output, given constant quantities of other factors.

FIGURE 14.5 The Aggregate Production Function

An aggregate production function (*PF*) relates total output to total employment, assuming all other factors of production and technology are fixed. It shows that increases in employment lead to increases in output but at a decreasing rate.

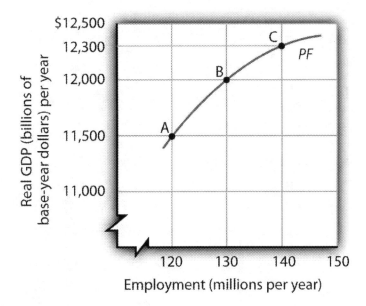

It is easy to picture the problem of diminishing marginal returns in the context of a single firm. The firm is able to increase output by adding workers. But because the firm's plant size and stock of equipment are fixed, the firm's capital per worker falls as it takes on more workers. Each additional worker adds less to output than the worker before. The firm, like the economy, experiences diminishing marginal returns.

2.2 The Aggregate Production Function, the Market for Labor, and Long-Run Aggregate Supply

To derive the long-run aggregate supply curve, we bring together the model of the labor market, introduced in the first macro chapter and the aggregate production function.

As we learned, the labor market is in equilibrium at the natural level of employment. The demand and supply curves for labor intersect at the real wage at which the economy achieves its natural level of employment. We see in Panel (a) of Figure 14.6 that the equilibrium real wage is ω_1 and the natural level of employment is L_1. Panel (b) shows that with employment of L_1, the economy can produce a real GDP of Y_P. That output equals the economy's potential output. It is that level of potential output that determines the position of the long-run aggregate supply curve in Panel (c).

FIGURE 14.6 Deriving the Long-Run Aggregate Supply Curve

Panel (a) shows that the equilibrium real wage is ω_1, and the natural level of employment is L_1. Panel (b) shows that with employment of L_1, the economy can produce a real GDP of Y_P. That output equals the economy's potential output. It is at that level of potential output that we draw the long-run aggregate supply curve in Panel (c).

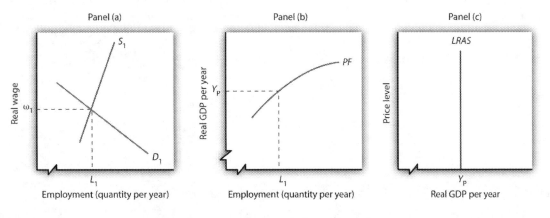

Changes in Long-Run Aggregate Supply

The position of the long-run aggregate supply curve is determined by the aggregate production function and the demand and supply curves for labor. A change in any of these will shift the long-run aggregate supply curve.

Figure 14.7 shows one possible shifter of long-run aggregate supply: a change in the production function. Suppose, for example, that an improvement in technology shifts the aggregate production function in Panel (b) from PF_1 to PF_2. Other developments that could produce an upward shift in the curve include an increase in the capital stock or in the availability of natural resources.

FIGURE 14.7 Shift in the Aggregate Production Function and the Long-Run Aggregate Supply Curve

An improvement in technology shifts the aggregate production function upward in Panel (b). Because labor is more productive, the demand for labor shifts to the right in Panel (a), and the natural level of employment increases to L_2. In Panel (c) the long-run aggregate supply curve shifts to the right to Y_2.

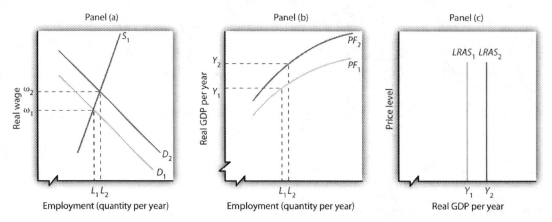

productivity

The amount of output per worker.

The shift in the production function to PF_2 means that labor is now more productive than before. This will affect the demand for labor in Panel (a). Before the technological change, firms employed L_1 workers at a real wage ω_1. If workers are more productive, firms will find it profitable to hire more of them at ω_1. The demand curve for labor thus shifts to D_2 in Panel (a). The real wage rises to ω_2, and the natural level of employment rises to L_2. The increase in the real wage reflects labor's enhanced **productivity**, the amount of output per worker. To see how potential output changes, we see in Panel (b) how much output can be produced given the new natural level of employment and the new aggregate production function. The real GDP that the economy is capable of producing rises from Y_1 to Y_2. The higher output is a reflection of a higher natural level of employment, along with the fact that labor has become more productive as a result of the technological advance. In Panel (c) the long-run aggregate supply curve shifts to the right to the vertical line at Y_2.

This analysis dispels a common misconception about the impact of improvements in technology or increases in the capital stock on employment. Some people believe that technological gains or increases in the stock of capital reduce the demand for labor, reduce employment, and reduce real wages. Certainly the experience of the United States and most other countries belies that notion. Between 1990 and 2007, for example, the U.S. capital stock and the level of technology increased dramatically. During the same period, employment and real wages rose, suggesting that the demand for labor increased by more than the supply of labor. As some firms add capital or incorporate new technologies, some workers at those firms may lose their jobs. But for the economy as a whole, new jobs become available *and* they generally offer higher wages. The demand for labor rises.

Another event that can shift the long-run aggregate supply curve is an increase in the supply of labor, as shown in Figure 14.8. An increased supply of labor could result from immigration, an increase in the population, or increased participation in the labor force by the adult population. Increased participation by women in the labor force, for example, has tended to increase the supply curve for labor during the past several decades.

FIGURE 14.8 Increase in the Supply of Labor and the Long-Run Aggregate Supply Curve

An increase in the supply of labor shifts the supply curve in Panel (a) to S_2, and the natural level of employment rises to L_2. The real wage falls to ω_2. With increased labor, the aggregate production function in Panel (b) shows that the economy is now capable of producing real GDP at Y_2. The long-run aggregate supply curve in Panel (c) shifts to $LRAS_2$.

In Panel (a), an increase in the labor supply shifts the supply curve to S_2. The increase in the supply of labor does not change the stock of capital or natural resources, nor does it change technology—it therefore does not shift the aggregate production function. Because there is no change in the production function, there is no shift in the demand for labor. The real wage falls from ω_1 to ω_2 in Panel (a), and the natural level of employment rises from L_1 to L_2. To see the impact on potential output, Panel (b) shows that employment of L_2 can produce real GDP of Y_2. The long-run aggregate supply curve in Panel (c) thus shifts to $LRAS_2$. Notice, however, that this shift in the long-run aggregate supply curve to the right is associated with a reduction in the real wage to ω_2.

Of course, the aggregate production function and the supply curve of labor can shift together, producing higher real wages at the same time population rises. That has been the experience of most industrialized nations. The increase in real wages in the United States between 1990 and 2007, for example, came during a period in which an increasing population increased the supply of labor. The demand for labor increased by more than the supply, pushing the real wage up. The accompanying Case in Point looks at gains in real wages in the face of technological change, an increase in the stock of capital, and rapid population growth in the United States during the 19th century.

Our model of long-run aggregate supply tells us that in the long run, real GDP, the natural level of employment, and the real wage are determined by the economy's production function and by the demand and supply curves for labor. Unless an event shifts the aggregate production function, the demand curve for labor, or the supply curve for labor, it affects neither the natural level of employment nor potential output. Economic growth occurs only if an event shifts the economy's production function or if there is an increase in the demand for or the supply of labor.

KEY TAKEAWAYS

- The aggregate production function relates the level of employment to the level of real GDP produced per period.
- The real wage and the natural level of employment are determined by the intersection of the demand and supply curves for labor. Potential output is given by the point on the aggregate production function corresponding to the natural level of employment. This output level is the same as that shown by the long-run aggregate supply curve.
- Economic growth can be shown as a series of shifts to the right in *LRAS*. Such shifts require either upward shifts in the production function or increases in demand for or supply of labor.

TRY IT!

Suppose that the quantity of labor supplied is 50 million workers when the real wage is $20,000 per year and that potential output is $2,000 billion per year. Draw a three-panel graph similar to the one presented in Figure 14.8 to show the economy's long-run equilibrium. Panel (a) of your graph should show the demand and supply curves for labor, Panel (b) should show the aggregate production function, and Panel (c) should show the long-run aggregate supply curve. Now suppose a technological change increases the economy's output with the same quantity of labor as before to $2,200 billion, and the real wage rises to $21,500. In response, the quantity of labor supplied increases to 51 million workers. In the same three panels you have already drawn, sketch the new curves that result from this change. Explain what happens to the level of employment, the level of potential output, and the long-run aggregate supply curve. (Hint: you have information for only one point on each of the curves you draw—two for the supply of labor; simply draw curves of the appropriate shape. Do not worry about getting the scale correct.)

Case in Point

Technological Change, Employment, and Real Wages During the Industrial Revolution

Technological change and the capital investment that typically comes with it are often criticized because they replace labor with machines, reducing employment. Such changes, critics argue, hurt workers. Using the model of aggregate demand and aggregate supply, however, we arrive at a quite different conclusion. The model predicts that improved technology will increase the demand for labor and boost real wages.

The period of industrialization, generally taken to be the time between the Civil War and World War I, was a good test of these competing ideas. Technological changes were dramatic as firms shifted toward mass production and automation. Capital investment soared. Immigration increased the supply of labor. What happened to workers?

Employment more than doubled during this period, consistent with the prediction of our model. It is harder to predict, from a theoretical point of view, the consequences for real wages. The latter third of the 19th century was a period of massive immigration to the United States. Between 1865 and 1880, more than 5 million people came to the United States from abroad; most were of working age. The pace accelerated between 1880 and 1923, when more than 23 million people moved to the United States from other countries. Immigration increased the supply of labor, which should reduce the real wage. There were thus two competing forces at work: Technological change and capital investment tended to increase real wages, while immigration tended to reduce them by increasing the supply of labor.

The evidence suggests that the forces of technological change and capital investment proved far more powerful than increases in labor supply. Real wages soared 60% between 1860 and 1890. They continued to increase after that. Real wages in manufacturing, for example, rose 37% from 1890 to 1914.

Technological change and capital investment displace workers in some industries. But for the economy as a whole, they increase worker productivity, increase the demand for labor, and increase real wages.

Sources: Wage data taken from Clarence D. Long, Wages and Earnings in the United States, 1860–1990 (Princeton, NJ: Princeton University Press, 1960), p. 109, and from Albert Rees, Wages in Manufacturing, 1890–1914 (Princeton, NJ: Princeton University Press, 1961), pp. 3–5. Immigration figures taken from Gary M. Walton and Hugh Rockoff, History of the American Economy, 6th ed. (New York: Harcourt Brace Jovanovich, 1990), p. 371.

ANSWER TO TRY IT! PROBLEM

The production function in Panel (b) shifts up to PF_2. Because it reflects greater productivity of labor, firms will increase their demand for labor, and the demand curve for labor shifts to D_2 in Panel (a). $LRAS_1$ shifts to $LRAS_2$ in Panel (c). Employment and potential output rise. Potential output will be greater than $2,200 billion.

Panel (a)

Panel (b)

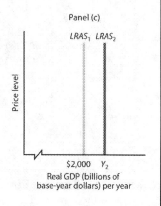

Panel (c)

3. DETERMINANTS OF ECONOMIC GROWTH

L E A R N I N G   O B J E C T I V E S

1. **Discuss the sources of economic growth.**
2. **Discuss possible reasons why countries grow at different rates.**

In this section, we review the main determinants of economic growth. We also examine the reasons for the widening disparities in economic growth rates among countries in recent years.

3.1 The Sources of Economic Growth

As we have learned, there are two ways to model economic growth: (1) as an outward shift in an economy's production possibilities curve, and (2) as a shift to the right in its long-run aggregate supply curve. In drawing either one at a point in time, we assume that the economy's factors of production and its technology are unchanged. Changing these will shift both curves. Therefore, anything that increases the quantity or quality of factors of production or that improves the technology available to the economy contributes to economic growth.

The sources of growth for the U.S. economy in the 20th century were presented in the chapter on choices in production. There we learned that the main sources of growth for the United States from 1960 to 2007 were divided between increases in the quantities of labor and of physical capital (about 65%) and in improvements in the qualities of the factors of production and technology (about 35%). Since 2000, however, the contributions from improvements in factor quality and technology have accounted for about half the economic growth in the United States.

In order to devote resources to increasing physical and human capital and to improving technology—activities that will enhance future production—society must forgo using them now to produce consumer goods. Even though the people in the economy would enjoy a higher standard of living today without this sacrifice, they are willing to reduce present consumption in order to have more goods and services available for the future.

As a college student, you personally made such a choice. You decided to devote time to study that you could have spent earning income. With the higher income, you could enjoy greater consumption today. You made this choice because you expect to earn higher income in the future and thus to enjoy greater consumption in the future. Because many other people in the society also choose to acquire more education, society allocates resources to produce education. The education produced today will enhance the society's human capital and thus its economic growth.

All other things equal, higher saving allows more resources to be devoted to increases in physical and human capital and technological improvement. In other words, saving, which is income not spent on consumption, promotes economic growth by making available resources that can be channeled into growth-enhancing uses.

3.2 Explaining Recent Disparities in Growth Rates

Toward the end of the 20th century, it appeared that some of the world's more affluent countries were growing robustly while others were growing more slowly or even stagnating. This observation was confirmed in a major study by the Organisation for Economic Co-operation and Development (OECD),[2] whose members are listed in Table 14.1. The table shows that for the OECD countries as a whole, economic growth per capita fell from an average of 2.2% per year in the 1980s to an average of 1.9% per year in the 1990s. The higher standard deviation in the latter period confirms an increased disparity of growth rates in the more recent period. Moreover, the data on individual countries show that per capita growth in some countries (specifically, the United States, Canada, Ireland, Netherlands, Norway, and Spain) picked up, especially in the latter half of the 1990s, while it decelerated in most of the countries of continental Europe and Japan.

TABLE 14.1 Growing Disparities in Rates of Economic Growth

Variation in the growth in real GDP per capita has widened among the world's leading industrialized economies.

Trend Growth of GDP per Capita			
Country	1980–1990	1990–2000	1996–2000
United States	2.1	2.3	2.8
Japan	3.3	1.4	0.9
Germany	1.9	1.2	1.7
France	1.6	1.5	1.9
Italy	2.3	1.5	1.7
United Kingdom	2.2	2.1	2.3
Canada	1.4	1.7	2.6
Austria	2.1	1.9	2.3
Belgium	2.0	1.9	2.3
Denmark	1.9	1.9	2.3
Finland	2.2	2.1	3.9
Greece	0.5	1.8	2.7
Iceland	1.7	1.5	2.6
Ireland	3.0	6.4	7.9
Luxembourg	4.0	4.5	4.6
Netherlands	1.6	2.4	2.7
Portugal	3.1	2.8	2.7
Spain	2.3	2.7	3.2
Sweden	1.7	1.5	2.6
Switzerland	1.4	0.4	1.1
Turkey	2.1	2.1	1.9
Australia	1.6	2.4	2.8
New Zealand	1.4	1.2	1.8
Mexico	0.0	1.6	2.7
Korea	7.2	5.1	4.2
Hungary	—	2.3	3.5
Poland	—	4.2	4.8
Czech Republic	—	1.7	1.4
OECD24*	2.2	1.9	2.2
Standard Deviation of OECD24	0.74	1.17	1.37
*Excludes Czech Republic, Hungary, Korea, Mexico, Poland, and Slovak Republic			

Source: Excerpted from Table 1.1 Organisation for Economic Co-operation and Development, Sources of Economic Growth in OECD Countries, 2003: p. 32–33.

The study goes on to try to explain the reasons for the divergent growth trends. The main findings were:

- In general, countries with accelerating per capita growth rates also experienced significant increases in employment, while those with stagnant or declining employment generally experienced reductions in per capita growth rates.

- Enhancements in human capital contributed to labor productivity and economic growth, but in slower growing countries such improvements were not enough to offset the impact of reduced or stagnant labor utilization.

- Information and communication technology has contributed to economic growth both through rapid technological progress within the information and communication technology industry itself as well as, more recently, through the use of information and communication technology equipment in other industries. This has made an important contribution to growth in several of the faster growing countries.

- Other factors associated with more growth include: investments in physical and human capital, sound macroeconomic policies (especially low inflation), private sector research and development, trade exposure, and better developed financial markets. Results concerning the impact of the size of the government and of public sector research and development on growth were more difficult to interpret.

- With qualifications, the study found that strict regulation of product markets (for example, regulations that reduce competition) and strict employment protection legislation (for example, laws that make hiring and firing of workers more difficult) had negative effects on growth.

- All countries show a large number of firms entering and exiting markets. But, a key difference between the United States and Europe is that new firms in the United States start out smaller and less productive than those of Europe but grow faster when they are successful. The report hypothesizes that lower start-up costs and less strict labor market regulations may encourage U.S. entrepreneurs to enter a market and then to expand, if warranted. European entrepreneurs may be less willing to experiment in a market in the first place.

The general concern in the second half of the 1970s and the 1980s was that economic growth was slowing down and that it might not be possible to reverse this pattern. The 1990s and early 2000s, in which growth picked up in some countries but not in others, suggested that the problem was not universal and led to a search for the reasons for the disparities in growth rates that emerged. The OECD study described above gives some possible explanations. The findings of that study practically beg countries to examine closely their economic policies at a variety of levels and to consider changes that may add flexibility to their economies.

To spur this process, in 2005, the OECD started a new annual publication called *Going for Growth*. The inaugural edition identified five priority structural policy areas specific to each OECD country. The policies were categorized as either improving labor utilization or improving productivity. Suggestions for improved labor utilization ranged from changing tax policies to improving incentives for females to enter, and for older people to remain in, the workforce. Suggestions for improved productivity ranged from education reform to privatization of state-owned industries. As an example, the priorities proposed for the United States in 2005 included (1) limiting increases in labor costs by reforming Medicare to restrain health care costs, (2) encouraging private saving by shifting the burden of taxation toward consumption, (3) improving primary and secondary education, (4) reducing trade-distorting agricultural price supports, and (5) promoting transparency and accountability of corporate governance.[3]

The 2010 edition of *Going for Growth*[4] took stock of the progress made over the five-year period leading up to 2010. While two-thirds of the OECD countries took some legislative action in at least one priority area, the scope and depth of this progress varied immensely across countries.

Figure 14.9 summarizes this progress using two alternative measures. Panel (a) shows a responsiveness rate, which measures significant actions taken, and Panel (b) shows a follow-through rate, which measures whether priorities could be dropped due to reform implementation.

As we can see, the responsiveness and follow-through rates vary widely. Turkey and the Czech Republic stand out as the countries having undertaken substantial reform. The United States stands out as the country having shown neither responsiveness nor follow-through. While the relatively strong performance of the United States at the end of the 20th century, as shown in Table 14.1, could indicate relatively less need for growth-enhancing reforms, the comparative lack of progress since 2005 raises doubt concerning the ability to maintain strong economic growth going forward.

In closing, it is worth reiterating that economic freedom and higher incomes tend to go together. Countries could not have attained high levels of income if they had not maintained the economic freedom that contributed to high incomes in the first place. Thus, it is also likely that rates of economic growth in the future will be related to the amount of economic freedom countries choose. We shall see in later chapters that monetary and fiscal policies that are used to stabilize the economy in the short run can also have an impact on long-run economic growth.

FIGURE 14.9 Responsiveness to and Follow-Through of *Going for Growth* Recommendations across Countries since 2005

Panel (a) measures the 2005 to 2009 rate of responsiveness to the reform priorities given to each country in 2005. Panel (b) shows the reform follow-through rates. Growth-enhancing policy reforms across countries varied widely during this period.

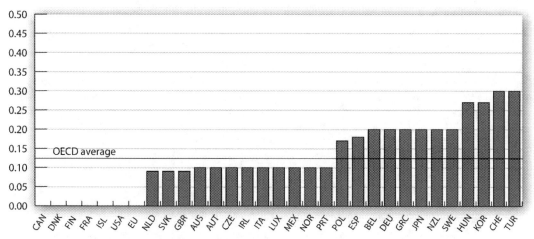

Source: Organisation for Economic Co-operation and Development, Going for Growth 2010, Figure 2.6, p. 75.

KEY TAKEAWAYS

- The main sources of growth for the United States from 1948 to 2007 were divided between increases in the quantities of labor and of physical capital (about 65%) and in improvements in the qualities of the factors of production and technology (about 35%). Since 2000, however, improvements in factor quality and technology have contributed to about half the economic growth in the United States.

- There has been a growing disparity in the rates of economic growth in industrialized countries in recent decades, which may reflect various differences in economic structures and policies.

TRY IT!

All other things unchanged, compare the position of a country's expected production possibility curve and the expected position of its long-run aggregate supply curve if:

1. Its labor force increases in size by 3% per year compared to 2% per year.

2. Its saving rate falls from 15% to 10%.

3. It passes a law making it more difficult to fire workers.

4. Its level of education rises more quickly than it has in the past.

Case in Point

Economic Growth in Poor Countries ... or Lack Thereof

Economist William Easterly in his aptly named book *The Elusive Quest for Growth: Economists' Adventures and Misadventures in the Tropics* admits that after 50 years of searching for the magic formula for turning poor countries into rich ones, the quest remains elusive.

Poor countries just need more physical capital, you say? Easterly points out that between 1960 and 1985, the capital stock per worker in both Gambia and Japan rose by over 500%. The result? In Gambia, output per worker over the 25-year period rose 2%; in Japan, output per worker rose 260%.

So, it must be that poor countries need more human capital? Again, he finds startling comparisons. For example, human capital expanded faster in Zambia than in Korea, but Zambia's annual growth rate is 7 percentage points below Korea's.

Too much population growth? Too little? More foreign aid? Too much? As Easterly proceeds, writing a prescription for growth seems ever more difficult: "None has delivered as promised," he concludes (p. xi).

While Easterly does not offer his own new panacea for how to move countries to a higher level of per capita GDP, where the model presented in this chapter does seem to provide some explanations of why a country's growth rate may vary over time or differ from another country's, he does argue that creating incentives for growth in poor countries is crucial. Acknowledging a role for plain luck, Easterly argues that good government policies—ones that keep low such negatives as inflation, corruption, and red tape—and quality institutions and laws—ones that, for example, honor contracts and reward merit—will help.

How to actually improve such incentives might constitute the next great quest:

> "We have learned once and for all that there are no magical elixirs to bring a happy ending to our quest for growth. Prosperity happens when all the players in the development game have the right incentives. It happens when government incentives induce technological adaptation, high-quality investment in machines, and high-quality schooling. It happens when donors face incentives that induce them to give aid to countries with good policies where aid will have high payoffs, not to countries with poor policies where aid is wasted. It happens when the poor get good opportunities and incentives, which requires government welfare programs that reward rather than penalize earning income. It happens when politics is not polarized between antagonistic interest groups.... The solutions are a lot more difficult to describe than the problems. The way forward must be to create incentives for growth for the trinity of governments, donors, and individuals." (p. 289–90)

Source: William Easterly, The Elusive Quest for Growth: Economists' Adventures and Misadventures in the Tropics (Cambridge: MIT Press, 2002).

ANSWER TO TRY IT! PROBLEM

Situations 1 and 4 should lead to a shift further outward in the country's production possibility curve and further to the right in its long-run aggregate supply curve. Situations 2 and 3 should lead to smaller outward shifts in the country's production possibility curve and smaller rightward shifts in its long-run aggregate supply curve.

4.   REVIEW AND PRACTICE

Summary

We saw that economic growth can be measured by the rate of increase in potential output. Measuring the rate of increase in actual real GDP can confuse growth statistics by introducing elements of cyclical variation.

Growth is an exponential process. A variable increasing at a fixed percentage rate doubles over fixed intervals. The doubling time is approximated by the rule of 72. The exponential nature of growth means that small differences in growth rates have large effects over long periods of time. Per capita rates of increase in real GDP are found by subtracting the growth rate of the population from the growth rate of GDP.

Growth can be shown in the model of aggregate demand and aggregate supply as a series of rightward shifts in the long-run aggregate supply curve. The position of the *LRAS* is determined by the aggregate production function and by the demand and supply curves for labor. A rightward shift in *LRAS* results either from an upward shift in the production function, due to increases in factors of production other than labor or to improvements in technology, or from an increase in the demand for or the supply of labor.

Saving plays an important role in economic growth, because it allows for more capital to be available for future production, so the rate of economic growth can rise. Saving thus promotes growth.

In recent years, rates of growth among the world's industrialized countries have grown more disparate. Recent research suggests this may be related to differing labor and product market conditions, differences in the diffusion of information and communications technologies, as well as differences in macroeconomic and trade policies. Evidence on the role that government plays in economic growth was less conclusive.

CONCEPT PROBLEMS

1. Suppose the people in a certain economy decide to stop saving and instead use all their income for consumption. They do nothing to add to their stock of human or physical capital. Discuss the prospects for growth of such an economy.

2. Singapore has a saving rate that is roughly three times greater than that of the United States. Its greater saving rate has been one reason why the Singapore economy has grown faster than the U.S. economy. Suppose that if the United States increased its saving rate to, say, twice the Singapore level, U.S. growth would surpass the Singapore rate. Would that be a good idea?

3. Suppose an increase in air pollution causes capital to wear out more rapidly, doubling the rate of depreciation. How would this affect economic growth?

4. Some people worry that increases in the capital stock will bring about an economy in which everything is done by machines, with no jobs left for people. What does the model of economic growth presented in this chapter predict?

5. China's annual rate of population growth was 1.2% from 1975 to 2003 and is expected to be 0.6% from 2003 through 2015. How do you think this will affect the rate of increase in real GDP? How will this affect the rate of increase in per capita real GDP?

6. Suppose technology stops changing. Explain the impact on economic growth.

7. Suppose a series of terrorist attacks destroys half the capital in the United States but does not affect the population. What will happen to potential output and to the real wage?

8. "Given the rate at which scientists are making new discoveries, we will soon reach the point that no further discoveries can be made. Economic growth will come to a stop." Discuss.

9. Suppose real GDP increases during President Obama's term in office at a 5% rate. Would that imply that his policies were successful in "growing the economy"?

10. Suppose that for some country it was found that its economic growth was based almost entirely on increases in quantities of factors of production. Why might such growth be difficult to sustain?

NUMERICAL PROBLEMS

1. The population of the world in 2003 was 6.314 billion. It grew between 1975 and 2003 at an annual rate of 1.6%. Assume that it continues to grow at this rate.

    a. Compute the doubling time.

    b. Estimate the world population in 2048 and 2093 (assuming all other things remain unchanged).

2. With a world population in 2003 of 6.314 billion and a projected population growth rate of 1.1% instead (which is the United Nations' projection for the period 2003 to 2015).

    a. Compute the doubling time.

    b. State the year in which the world's population would be 12.628 billion.

3. Suppose a country's population grows at the rate of 2% per year and its output grows at the rate of 3% per year.

    a. Calculate its rate of growth of per capita output.

    b. If instead its population grows at 3% per year and its output grows at 2% per year, calculate its rate of growth of per capita output.

4. The rate of economic growth per capita in France from 1996 to 2000 was 1.9% per year, while in Korea over the same period it was 4.2%. Per capita real GDP was $28,900 in France in 2003, and $12,700 in Korea. Assume the growth rates for each country remain the same.

    a. Compute the doubling time for France's per capita real GDP.

    b. Compute the doubling time for Korea's per capita real GDP.

    c. What will France's per capita real GDP be in 2045?

    d. What will Korea's per capita real GDP be in 2045?

5. Suppose real GDPs in country A and country B are identical at $10 trillion dollars in 2005. Suppose country A's economic growth rate is 2% and country B's is 4% and both growth rates remain constant over time.

    a. On a graph, show country A's potential output until 2025.

    b. On the same graph, show country B's potential output.

    c. Calculate the percentage difference in their levels of potential output in 2025.

    Suppose country A's population grows 1% per year and country B's population grows 3% per year.

    d. On a graph, show country A's potential output per capita in 2025.

    e. On the same graph, show country B's potential output per capita in 2025.

    f. Calculate the percentage difference in their levels of potential output per capita in 2025.

6. Two countries, A and B, have identical levels of real GDP per capita. In Country A, an increase in the capital stock increases the potential output by 10%. Country B also experiences a 10% increase in its potential output, but this increase is the result of an increase in its labor force. Using aggregate production functions and labor-market analyses for the two countries, illustrate and explain how these events are likely to affect living standards in the two economies.

7. Suppose the information below characterizes an economy:

Employment (in millions)	Real GDP (in billions)
1	200
2	700
3	1,100
4	1,400
5	1,650
6	1,850
7	2,000
8	2,100
9	2,170
10	2,200

    a. Construct the aggregate production function for this economy.

    b. What kind of returns does this economy experience? How do you know?

    c. Assuming that total available employment is 7 million, draw the economy's long-run aggregate supply curve.

Suppose that improvement in technology means that real GDP at each level of employment rises by $200 billion.

    d. Construct the new aggregate production function for this economy.

    e. Construct the new long-run aggregate supply curve for the economy.

8. In Table 14.1, we can see that Japan's growth rate of per capita real GDP fell from 3.3% per year in the 1980s to 1.4% per year in the 1990s.

    a. Compare the percent increase in its per capita real GDP over the 20-year period to what it would have been if it had maintained the 3.3% per capita growth rate of the 1980s.

    b. Japan's per capita GDP in 1980 was about $24,000 (in U.S. 2000 dollars) in 1980. Calculate what it would have been if the growth rate of the 1980s had been maintained Calculate about how much it is, given the actual growth rates over the two decades.

    c. In Table 14.1, we can see that Ireland's growth rate of per capita real GDP grew from 3.0% per year in the 1980s to 6.4% per year in the 1990s.

    d. Compare the percent increase in its per capita real GDP over the 20-year period to what it would have been if it had maintained the 3.0% per capita growth rate of the 1980s.

    e. Ireland's per capita GDP in 1980 was about $10,000 (in U.S. 2000 dollars). Calculate what it would have been if the growth rate of the 1980s had been maintained. Calculate about how much it is, given the actual growth rates over the two decades.

ENDNOTES

1. Notice the use of the words *roughly* and *approximately*. The actual value of an income of \$1,000 growing at rate r for a period of n years is $\$1,000 \times (1 + r)^n$. After 8 years of growth at a 9% rate, income would thus be $\$1,000 (1 + 0.09)^8 = \$1,992.56$. The rule of 72 predicts that its value will be \$2,000. The rule of 72 gives an approximation, not an exact measure, of the impact of exponential growth.

2. The material in this section is based on Organisation for Economic Co-operation and Development, *The Sources of Economic Growth in OECD Countries*, 2003.

3. Organisation for Economic Co-operation and Development, *Economic Policy Reforms: Going for Growth 2005*, available at http://www.OECD.org/economics/goingforgrowth.

4. Organisation for Economic Co-operation and Development, *Economic Policy Reforms: Going for Growth 2010*, available at http://www.OECD.org/economics/goingforgrowth.

CHAPTER 15
The Nature and Creation of Money

START UP: HOW MANY MACKS DOES IT COST?

Larry Levine helped a client prepare divorce papers a few years ago. He was paid in mackerel.

"It's the coin of the realm," his client, Mark Bailey told the *Wall Street Journal*. The two men were prisoners at the time at the federal penitentiary at Lompoc, California.

By the time his work on the case was completed, he had accumulated "a stack of macks," Mr. Levine said. He used his fishy hoard to buy items such as haircuts at the prison barber shop, to have his laundry pressed, or to have his cell cleaned.

The somewhat unpleasant fish emerged as the currency of choice in many federal prisons in 1994 when cigarettes, the previous commodity used as currency, were banned. Plastic bags of mackerel sold for about $1 in prison commissaries. Almost no one likes them, so the prison money supply did not get eaten. Prisoners knew other prisoners would readily accept macks, so they were accepted in exchange for goods and services. Their $1 price made them convenient as a unit of account. And, as Mr. Levine's experience suggests, they acted as a store of value. As we shall see, macks served all three functions of money—they were a medium of exchange, a unit of account, and a store of value.[1]

In this chapter and the next we examine money and the way it affects the level of real GDP and the price level. In this chapter, we will focus on the nature of money and the process through which it is created.

As the experience of the prisoners in Lompoc suggests, virtually anything can serve as money. Historically, salt, horses, tobacco, cigarettes, gold, and silver have all served as money. We shall examine the characteristics that define a good as money.

We will also introduce the largest financial institution in the world, the Federal Reserve System of the United States. The Fed, as it is commonly called, plays a key role in determining the quantity of money in the United States. We will see how the Fed operates and how it attempts to control the supply of money.

1. WHAT IS MONEY?

LEARNING OBJECTIVES

1. Define money and discuss its three basic functions.
2. Distinguish between commodity money and fiat money, giving examples of each.
3. Define what is meant by the money supply and tell what is included in the Federal Reserve System's two definitions of it (M1 and M2).

If cigarettes and mackerel can be used as money, then just what is money? **Money** is anything that serves as a medium of exchange. A **medium of exchange** is anything that is widely accepted as a means of payment. In Romania under Communist Party rule in the 1980s, for example, Kent cigarettes served as a medium of exchange; the fact that they could be exchanged for other goods and services made them money.

Money, ultimately, is defined by people and what they do. When people use something as a medium of exchange, it becomes money. If people were to begin accepting basketballs as payment for most goods and services, basketballs would be money. We will learn in this chapter that changes in the way people use money have created new types of money and changed the way money is measured in recent decades.

1.1 The Functions of Money

Money serves three basic functions. By definition, it is a medium of exchange. It also serves as a unit of account and as a store of value—as the "mack" did in Lompoc.

A Medium of Exchange

The exchange of goods and services in markets is among the most universal activities of human life. To facilitate these exchanges, people settle on something that will serve as a medium of exchange—they select something to be money.

We can understand the significance of a medium of exchange by considering its absence. **Barter** occurs when goods are exchanged directly for other goods. Because no one item serves as a medium of exchange in a barter economy, potential buyers must find things that individual sellers will accept. A buyer might find a seller who will trade a pair of shoes for two chickens. Another seller might be willing to provide a haircut in exchange for a garden hose. Suppose you were visiting a grocery store in a barter economy. You would need to load up a truckful of items the grocer might accept in exchange for groceries. That would be an uncertain affair; you could not know when you headed for the store which items the grocer might agree to trade. Indeed, the complexity—and cost—of a visit to a grocery store in a barter economy would be so great that there probably would not be any grocery stores! A moment's contemplation of the difficulty of life in a barter economy will demonstrate why human societies invariably select something—sometimes more than one thing—to serve as a medium of exchange, just as prisoners in federal penitentiaries accepted mackerel.

A Unit of Account

Ask someone in the United States what he or she paid for something, and that person will respond by quoting a price stated in dollars: "I paid $75 for this radio," or "I paid $15 for this pizza." People do not say, "I paid five pizzas for this radio." That statement might, of course, be literally true in the sense of the opportunity cost of the transaction, but we do not report prices that way for two reasons. One is that people do not arrive at places like Radio Shack with five pizzas and expect to purchase a radio. The other is that the information would not be very useful. Other people may not think of values in pizza terms, so they might not know what we meant. Instead, we report the value of things in terms of money.

Money serves as a **unit of account**, which is a consistent means of measuring the value of things. We use money in this fashion because it is also a medium of exchange. When we report the value of a good or service in units of money, we are reporting what another person is likely to have to pay to obtain that good or service.

---

money

Anything that serves as a medium of exchange.

medium of exchange

Anything that is widely accepted as a means of payment.

barter

When goods are exchanged directly for other goods.

unit of account

A consistent means of measuring the value of things.

A Store of Value

The third function of money is to serve as a **store of value**, that is, an item that holds value over time. Consider a $20 bill that you accidentally left in a coat pocket a year ago. When you find it, you will be pleased. That is because you know the bill still has value. Value has, in effect, been "stored" in that little piece of paper.

Money, of course, is not the only thing that stores value. Houses, office buildings, land, works of art, and many other commodities serve as a means of storing wealth and value. Money differs from these other stores of value by being readily exchangeable for other commodities. Its role as a medium of exchange makes it a convenient store of value.

Because money acts as a store of value, it can be used as a standard for future payments. When you borrow money, for example, you typically sign a contract pledging to make a series of future payments to settle the debt. These payments will be made using money, because money acts as a store of value.

Money is not a risk-free store of value, however. We saw in the chapter that introduced the concept of inflation that inflation reduces the value of money. In periods of rapid inflation, people may not want to rely on money as a store of value, and they may turn to commodities such as land or gold instead.

1.2   Types of Money

Although money can take an extraordinary variety of forms, there are really only two types of money: money that has intrinsic value and money that does not have intrinsic value.

Commodity money is money that has value apart from its use as money. Mackerel in federal prisons is an example of commodity money. Mackerel could be used to buy services from other prisoners; they could also be eaten.

Gold and silver are the most widely used forms of commodity money. Gold and silver can be used as jewelry and for some industrial and medicinal purposes, so they have value apart from their use as money. The first known use of gold and silver coins was in the Greek city-state of Lydia in the beginning of the seventh century B.C. The coins were fashioned from electrum, a natural mixture of gold and silver.

One disadvantage of commodity money is that its quantity can fluctuate erratically. Gold, for example, was one form of money in the United States in the 19th century. Gold discoveries in California and later in Alaska sent the quantity of money soaring. Some of this nation's worst bouts of inflation were set off by increases in the quantity of gold in circulation during the 19th century. A much greater problem exists with commodity money that can be produced. In the southern part of colonial America, for example, tobacco served as money. There was a continuing problem of farmers increasing the quantity of money by growing more tobacco. The problem was sufficiently serious that vigilante squads were organized. They roamed the countryside burning tobacco fields in an effort to keep the quantity of tobacco, hence money, under control. (Remarkably, these squads sought to control the money supply by burning tobacco grown by other farmers.)

Another problem is that commodity money may vary in quality. Given that variability, there is a tendency for lower-quality commodities to drive higher-quality commodities out of circulation. Horses, for example, served as money in colonial New England. It was common for loan obligations to be stated in terms of a quantity of horses to be paid back. Given such obligations, there was a tendency to use lower-quality horses to pay back debts; higher-quality horses were kept out of circulation for other uses. Laws were passed forbidding the use of lame horses in the payment of debts. This is an example of Gresham's law: the tendency for a lower-quality commodity (bad money) to drive a higher-quality commodity (good money) out of circulation. Unless a means can be found to control the quality of commodity money, the tendency for that quality to decline can threaten its acceptability as a medium of exchange.

But something need not have intrinsic value to serve as money. **Fiat money** is money that some authority, generally a government, has ordered to be accepted as a medium of exchange. The **currency**—paper money and coins—used in the United States today is fiat money; it has no value other than its use as money. You will notice that statement printed on each bill: "This note is legal tender for all debts, public and private."

store of value
An item that holds value over time.

commodity money
Money that has value apart from its use as money.

fiat money
Money that some authority, generally a government, has ordered to be accepted as a medium of exchange.

currency
Paper money and coins.

checkable deposits

Balances in checking accounts.

check

A written order to a bank to transfer ownership of a checkable deposit.

Checkable deposits, which are balances in checking accounts, and traveler's checks are other forms of money that have no intrinsic value. They can be converted to currency, but generally they are not; they simply serve as a medium of exchange. If you want to buy something, you can often pay with a check or a debit card. A **check** is a written order to a bank to transfer ownership of a checkable deposit. A debit card is the electronic equivalent of a check. Suppose, for example, that you have $100 in your checking account and you write a check to your campus bookstore for $30 or instruct the clerk to swipe your debit card and "charge" it $30. In either case, $30 will be transferred from your checking account to the bookstore's checking account. *Notice that it is the checkable deposit, not the check or debit card, that is money.* The check or debit card just tells a bank to transfer money, in this case checkable deposits, from one account to another.

What makes something money is really found in its acceptability, not in whether or not it has intrinsic value or whether or not a government has declared it as such. For example, fiat money tends to be accepted so long as too much of it is not printed too quickly. When that happens, as it did in Russia in the 1990s, people tend to look for other items to serve as money. In the case of Russia, the U.S. dollar became a popular form of money, even though the Russian government still declared the ruble to be its fiat money.

Heads Up!

The term *money*, as used by economists and throughout this book, has the very specific definition given in the text. People can hold assets in a variety of forms, from works of art to stock certificates to currency or checking account balances. Even though individuals may be very wealthy, only when they are holding their assets in a form that serves as a medium of exchange do they, according to the precise meaning of the term, have "money." To qualify as "money," something must be widely accepted as a medium of exchange.

1.3 Measuring Money

money supply

The total quantity of money in the economy at any one time.

The total quantity of money in the economy at any one time is called the **money supply**. Economists measure the money supply because it affects economic activity. What should be included in the money supply? We want to include as part of the money supply those things that serve as media of exchange. However, the items that provide this function have varied over time.

Before 1980, the basic money supply was measured as the sum of currency in circulation, traveler's checks, and checkable deposits. Currency serves the medium-of-exchange function very nicely but denies people any interest earnings. (Checking accounts did not earn interest before 1980.)

Over the last few decades, especially as a result of high interest rates and high inflation in the late 1970s, people sought and found ways of holding their financial assets in ways that earn interest and that can easily be converted to money. For example, it is now possible to transfer money from your savings account to your checking account using an automated teller machine (ATM), and then to withdraw cash from your checking account. Thus, many types of savings accounts are easily converted into currency.

liquidity

The ease with which an asset can be converted into currency.

Economists refer to the ease with which an asset can be converted into currency as the asset's **liquidity**. Currency itself is perfectly liquid; you can always change two $5 bills for a $10 bill. Checkable deposits are almost perfectly liquid; you can easily cash a check or visit an ATM. An office building, however, is highly illiquid. It can be converted to money only by selling it, a time-consuming and costly process.

As financial assets other than checkable deposits have become more liquid, economists have had to develop broader measures of money that would correspond to economic activity. In the United States, the final arbiter of what is and what is not measured as money is the Federal Reserve System. Because it is difficult to determine what (and what not) to measure as money, the Fed reports several different measures of money, including M1 and M2.

M1 is the narrowest of the Fed's money supply definitions. It includes currency in circulation, checkable deposits, and traveler's checks. **M2** is a broader measure of the money supply than M1. It includes M1 and other deposits such as small savings accounts (less than $100,000), as well as accounts such as money market mutual funds (MMMFs) that place limits on the number or the amounts of the checks that can be written in a certain period.

M2 is sometimes called the broadly defined money supply, while M1 is the narrowly defined money supply. The assets in M1 may be regarded as perfectly liquid; the assets in M2 are highly liquid, but somewhat less liquid than the assets in M1. Even broader measures of the money supply include large time-deposits, money market mutual funds held by institutions, and other assets that are somewhat less liquid than those in M2. Figure 15.1 shows the composition of M1 and M2 in December 2013.

FIGURE 15.1 The Two Ms: December 2013

M1, the narrowest definition of the money supply, includes assets that are perfectly liquid. M2 provides a broader measure of the money supply and includes somewhat less liquid assets. Amounts represent money supply data in billions of dollars for December 2013, seasonally adjusted.

M1 = $2,648.3   M2 = $10,958.8

Checkable deposits, $1,485.0

Currency in circulation, $1,159.8

Traveler's checks, $3.5

Small denomination time deposits, $544.9

Money market mutual funds (by individuals), $632.4

M1, $2,648.3

Savings deposits (including money market deposit accounts), $7,133.2

Source: Federal Reserve Statistical Release H.6, Tables 3 and 4 (February 27, 2014). Amounts are in billions of dollars for December 2013, seasonally adjusted.

Heads Up!

Credit cards are not money. A credit card identifies you as a person who has a special arrangement with the card issuer in which the issuer will lend you money and transfer the proceeds to another party whenever you want. Thus, if you present a MasterCard to a jeweler as payment for a $500 ring, the firm that issued you the card will lend you the $500 and send that money, less a service charge, to the jeweler. You, of course, will be required to repay the loan later. But a card that says you have such a relationship is not money, just as your debit card is not money.

With all the operational definitions of money available, which one should we use? Economists generally answer that question by asking another: Which measure of money is most closely related to real GDP and the price level? As that changes, so must the definition of money.

In 1980, the Fed decided that changes in the ways people were managing their money made M1 useless for policy choices. Indeed, the Fed now pays little attention to M2 either. It has largely given up tracking a particular measure of the money supply. The choice of what to measure as money remains the subject of continuing research and considerable debate.

M1

The narrowest of the Fed's money supply definitions that includes currency in circulation, checkable deposits, and traveler's checks.

M2

A broader measure of the money supply than M1 that includes M1 and other deposits.

KEY TAKEAWAYS

- Money is anything that serves as a medium of exchange. Other functions of money are to serve as a unit of account and as a store of value.
- Money may or may not have intrinsic value. Commodity money has intrinsic value because it has other uses besides being a medium of exchange. Fiat money serves only as a medium of exchange, because its use as such is authorized by the government; it has no intrinsic value.
- The Fed reports several different measures of money, including M1 and M2.

TRY IT!

Which of the following are money in the United States today and which are not? Explain your reasoning in terms of the functions of money.

1. Gold
2. A Van Gogh painting
3. A dime

Case in Point

Fiat-less Money

"We don't have a currency of our own," proclaimed Nerchivan Barzani, the Kurdish regional government's prime minister in a news interview in 2003. But, even without official recognition by the government, the so-called "Swiss" dinar certainly seemed to function as a fiat money. Here is how the Kurdish area of northern Iraq, during the period between the Gulf War in 1991 and the fall of Saddam Hussein in 2003, came to have its own currency, despite the pronouncement of its prime minister to the contrary.

After the Gulf War, the northern, mostly Kurdish area of Iraq was separated from the rest of Iraq though the enforcement of the no-fly-zone. Because of United Nations sanctions that barred the Saddam Hussein regime in the south from continuing to import currency from Switzerland, the central bank of Iraq announced it would replace the "Swiss" dinars, so named because they had been printed in Switzerland, with locally printed currency, which became known as "Saddam" dinars. Iraqi citizens in southern Iraq were given three weeks to exchange their old dinars for the new ones. In the northern part of Iraq, citizens could not exchange their notes and so they simply continued to use the old ones.

And so it was that the "Swiss" dinar for a period of about 10 years, even without government backing or any law establishing it as legal tender, served as northern Iraq's fiat money. Economists use the word "*fiat*," which in Latin means "let it be done," to describe money that has no intrinsic value. Such forms of money *usually* get their value because a government or authority has declared them to be legal tender, but, as this story shows, it does not really require much "fiat" for a convenient, in-and-of-itself worthless, medium of exchange to evolve.

What happened to both the "Swiss" and "Saddam" dinars? After the Coalition Provisional Authority (CPA) assumed control of all of Iraq, Paul Bremer, then head of the CPA, announced that a new Iraqi dinar would be exchanged for both of the existing currencies over a three-month period ending in January 2004 at a rate that implied that one "Swiss" dinar was valued at 150 "Saddam" dinars. Because Saddam Hussein's regime had printed many more "Saddam" dinars over the 10-year period, while no "Swiss" dinars had been printed, and because the cheap printing of the "Saddam" dinars made them easy to counterfeit, over the decade the "Swiss" dinars became relatively more valuable and the exchange rate that Bremer offered about equalized the purchasing power of the two currencies. For example, it took about 133 times as many "Saddam" dinars as "Swiss" dinars to buy a man's suit in Iraq at the time. The new notes, sometimes called "Bremer" dinars, were printed in Britain and elsewhere and flown into Iraq on 22 flights using Boeing 747s and other large aircraft. In both the northern and southern parts of Iraq, citizens turned in their old dinars for the new ones, suggesting at least more confidence at that moment in the "Bremer" dinar than in either the "Saddam" or "Swiss" dinars.

Sources: Mervyn A. King, "The Institutions of Monetary Policy" (lecture, American Economics Association Annual Meeting, San Diego, January 4, 2004), available at http://www.bis.org/review/r040202b.pdf; Hal R. Varian, "Paper Currency Can Have Value without Government Backing, but Such Backing Adds Substantially to Its Value," New York Times, January 15, 2004, p. C2.

ANSWERS TO TRY IT! PROBLEMS

1. Gold is not money because it is not used as a medium of exchange. In addition, it does not serve as a unit of account. It may, however, serve as a store of value.
2. A Van Gogh painting is not money. It serves as a store of value. It is highly illiquid but could eventually be converted to money. It is neither a medium of exchange nor a unit of account.
3. A dime is money and serves all three functions of money. It is, of course, perfectly liquid.

---

2.   THE BANKING SYSTEM AND MONEY CREATION

LEARNING OBJECTIVES

1. **Explain what banks are, what their balance sheets look like, and what is meant by a fractional reserve banking system.**
2. **Describe the process of money creation (destruction), using the concept of the deposit multiplier.**
3. **Describe how and why banks are regulated and insured.**

Where does money come from? How is its quantity increased or decreased? The answer to these questions suggests that money has an almost magical quality: *money is created by banks when they issue loans.* In effect, money is created by the stroke of a pen or the click of a computer key.

We will begin by examining the operation of banks and the banking system. We will find that, like money itself, the nature of banking is experiencing rapid change.

2.1   Banks and Other Financial Intermediaries

An institution that amasses funds from one group and makes them available to another is called a **financial intermediary**. A pension fund is an example of a financial intermediary. Workers and firms place earnings in the fund for their retirement; the fund earns income by lending money to firms or by purchasing their stock. The fund thus makes retirement saving available for other spending. Insurance companies are also financial intermediaries, because they lend some of the premiums paid by their customers to firms for investment. Mutual funds make money available to firms and other institutions by purchasing their initial offerings of stocks or bonds.

Banks play a particularly important role as financial intermediaries. Banks accept depositors' money and lend it to borrowers. With the interest they earn on their loans, banks are able to pay interest to their depositors, cover their own operating costs, and earn a profit, all the while maintaining the ability of the original depositors to spend the funds when they desire to do so. One key characteristic of banks is that they offer their customers the opportunity to open checking accounts, thus creating checkable deposits. These functions define a **bank**, which is a financial intermediary that accepts deposits, makes loans, and offers checking accounts.

financial intermediary

An institution that amasses funds from one group and makes them available to another.

bank

A financial intermediary that accepts deposits, makes loans, and offers checking accounts.

Over time, some nonbank financial intermediaries have become more and more like banks. For example, brokerage firms usually offer customers interest-earning accounts and make loans. They now allow their customers to write checks on their accounts.

The fact that banks account for a declining share of U.S. financial assets alarms some observers. We will see that banks are more tightly regulated than are other financial institutions; one reason for that regulation is to maintain control over the money supply. Other financial intermediaries do not face the same regulatory restrictions as banks. Indeed, their relative freedom from regulation is one reason they have grown so rapidly. As other financial intermediaries become more important, central authorities begin to lose control over the money supply.

The declining share of financial assets controlled by "banks" began to change in 2008. Many of the nation's largest investment banks—financial institutions that provided services to firms but were not regulated as commercial banks—began having serious financial difficulties as a result of their investments tied to home mortgage loans. As home prices in the United States began falling, many of those mortgage loans went into default. Investment banks that had made substantial purchases of securities whose value was ultimately based on those mortgage loans themselves began failing. Bear Stearns, one of the largest investment banks in the United States, required federal funds to remain solvent. Another large investment bank, Lehman Brothers, failed. In an effort to avoid a similar fate, several other investment banks applied for status as ordinary commercial banks subject to the stringent regulation those institutions face. One result of the terrible financial crisis that crippled the U.S. and other economies in 2008 may be greater control of the money supply by the Fed.

2.2 Bank Finance and a Fractional Reserve System

Bank finance lies at the heart of the process through which money is created. To understand money creation, we need to understand some of the basics of bank finance.

Banks accept deposits and issue checks to the owners of those deposits. Banks use the money collected from depositors to make loans. The bank's financial picture at a given time can be depicted using a simplified **balance sheet**, which is a financial statement showing assets, liabilities, and net worth. **Assets** are anything of value. **Liabilities** are obligations to other parties. **Net worth** equals assets less liabilities. All these are given dollar values in a firm's balance sheet. The sum of liabilities plus net worth therefore must equal the sum of all assets. On a balance sheet, assets are listed on the left, liabilities and net worth on the right.

The main way that banks earn profits is through issuing loans. Because their depositors do not typically all ask for the entire amount of their deposits back at the same time, banks lend out most of the deposits they have collected—to companies seeking to expand their operations, to people buying cars or homes, and so on. Banks keep only a fraction of their deposits as cash in their vaults and in deposits with the Fed. These assets are called **reserves**. Banks lend out the rest of their deposits. A system in which banks hold reserves whose value is less than the sum of claims outstanding on those reserves is called a **fractional reserve banking system**.

Table 15.1 shows a consolidated balance sheet for commercial banks in the United States for January 2012. Banks hold reserves against the liabilities represented by their checkable deposits. Notice that these reserves were a small fraction of total deposit liabilities of that month. Most bank assets are in the form of loans.

balance sheet

A financial statement showing assets, liabilities, and net worth.

assets

Anything of value.

liabilities

Obligations to other parties.

net worth

Assets less liabilities.

reserves

Bank assets held as cash in vaults and in deposits with the Federal Reserve.

fractional reserve banking system

System in which banks hold reserves whose value is less than the sum of claims outstanding on those reserves.

TABLE 15.1 The Consolidated Balance Sheet for U.S. Commercial Banks, January 2012

This balance sheet for all commercial banks in the United States shows their financial situation in billions of dollars, seasonally adjusted, in January 2012.

Assets		Liabilities and Net Worth	
Reserves	$1,592.9	Checkable deposits	$8,517.9
Other assets	$1,316.2	Borrowings	1,588.1
Loans	$7,042.0	Other liabilities	1,049.4
Securities	$2,546.1		
Total assets	$12,497.2	Total liabilities	$11,155.4
		Net worth	$1,341.8

Source: Federal Reserve Statistical Release H.8 (February 17, 2012).

In the next section, we will learn that money is created when banks issue loans.

2.3 Money Creation

To understand the process of money creation today, let us create a hypothetical system of banks. We will focus on three banks in this system: Acme Bank, Bellville Bank, and Clarkston Bank. Assume that all banks are required to hold reserves equal to 10% of their checkable deposits. The quantity of reserves banks are required to hold is called **required reserves**. The reserve requirement is expressed as a **required reserve ratio**; it specifies the ratio of reserves to checkable deposits a bank must maintain. Banks may hold reserves in excess of the required level; such reserves are called **excess reserves**. Excess reserves plus required reserves equal total reserves.

Because banks earn relatively little interest on their reserves held on deposit with the Federal Reserve, we shall assume that they seek to hold no excess reserves. When a bank's excess reserves equal zero, it is **loaned up**. Finally, we shall ignore assets other than reserves and loans and deposits other than checkable deposits. To simplify the analysis further, we shall suppose that banks have no net worth; their assets are equal to their liabilities.

Let us suppose that every bank in our imaginary system begins with $1,000 in reserves, $9,000 in loans outstanding, and $10,000 in checkable deposit balances held by customers. The balance sheet for one of these banks, Acme Bank, is shown in Table 15.2. The required reserve ratio is 0.1: Each bank must have reserves equal to 10% of its checkable deposits. Because reserves equal required reserves, excess reserves equal zero. Each bank is loaned up.

TABLE 15.2 A Balance Sheet for Acme Bank

We assume that all banks in a hypothetical system of banks have $1,000 in reserves, $10,000 in checkable deposits, and $9,000 in loans. With a 10% reserve requirement, each bank is loaned up; it has zero excess reserves.

Acme Bank			
Assets		**Liabilities**	
Reserves	$1,000	Deposits	$10,000
Loans	$9,000		

Acme Bank, like every other bank in our hypothetical system, initially holds reserves equal to the level of required reserves. Now suppose one of Acme Bank's customers deposits $1,000 in cash in a checking account. The money goes into the bank's vault and thus adds to reserves. The customer now has an additional $1,000 in his or her account. Two versions of Acme's balance sheet are given here. The first shows the changes brought by the customer's deposit: reserves and checkable deposits rise by $1,000. The second shows how these changes affect Acme's balances. Reserves now equal $2,000 and checkable deposits equal $11,000. With checkable deposits of $11,000 and a 10% reserve requirement, Acme is required to hold reserves of $1,100. With reserves equaling $2,000, Acme has $900 in excess reserves.

At this stage, there has been no change in the money supply. When the customer brought in the $1,000 and Acme put the money in the vault, currency in circulation fell by $1,000. At the same time, the $1,000 was added to the customer's checking account balance, so the money supply did not change.

FIGURE 15.2

Acme Bank, Changes in Balance Sheet		Acme Bank, Balance Sheet	
Assets	**Liabilities**	**Assets**	**Liabilities**
Reserves +$1,000	Deposits +$1,000	Reserves $2,000	Deposits $11,000
		Loans $9,000	
		(Excess reserves = $900)	

Because Acme earns only a low interest rate on its excess reserves, we assume it will try to loan them out. Suppose Acme lends the $900 to one of its customers. It will make the loan by crediting the customer's checking account with $900. Acme's outstanding loans and checkable deposits rise by $900. The $900 in checkable deposits is new money; Acme created it when it issued the $900 loan. Now you know where money comes from—it is created when a bank issues a loan.

FIGURE 15.3

Acme Bank, Changes in Balance Sheet		Acme Bank, Balance Sheet	
Assets	Liabilities	Assets	Liabilities
Loans + $900	Deposits + $900	Reserves $2,000 Loans $9,900	Deposits $11,900

Presumably, the customer who borrowed the $900 did so in order to spend it. That customer will write a check to someone else, who is likely to bank at some other bank. Suppose that Acme's borrower writes a check to a firm with an account at Bellville Bank. In this set of transactions, Acme's checkable deposits fall by $900. The firm that receives the check deposits it in its account at Bellville Bank, increasing that bank's checkable deposits by $900. Bellville Bank now has a check written on an Acme account. Bellville will submit the check to the Fed, which will reduce Acme's deposits with the Fed—its reserves—by $900 and increase Bellville's reserves by $900.

FIGURE 15.4

Acme Bank, Changes in Balance Sheet		Acme Bank, Balance Sheet	
Assets	Liabilities	Assets	Liabilities
Reserves − $900	Deposits − $900	Reserves $1,100 Loans $9,900	Deposits $11,000

Bellville Bank, Changes in Balance Sheet		Bellville Bank, Balance Sheet	
Assets	Liabilities	Assets	Liabilities
Reserves + $900	Deposits + $900	Reserves $1,900 Loans $9,000	Deposits $10,900
		(Excess reserves = $810)	

Notice that Acme Bank emerges from this round of transactions with $11,000 in checkable deposits and $1,100 in reserves. It has eliminated its excess reserves by issuing the loan for $900; Acme is now loaned up. Notice also that from Acme's point of view, it has not created any money! It merely took in a $1,000 deposit and emerged from the process with $1,000 in additional checkable deposits.

The $900 in new money Acme created when it issued a loan has not vanished—it is now in an account in Bellville Bank. Like the magician who shows the audience that the hat from which the rabbit appeared was empty, Acme can report that it has not created any money. There is a wonderful irony in the magic of money creation: banks create money when they issue loans, but no one bank ever seems to keep the money it creates. That is because money is created within the banking system, not by a single bank.

The process of money creation will not end there. Let us go back to Bellville Bank. Its deposits and reserves rose by $900 when the Acme check was deposited in a Bellville account. The $900 deposit required an increase in required reserves of $90. Because Bellville's reserves rose by $900, it now has $810 in excess reserves. Just as Acme lent the amount of its excess reserves, we can expect Bellville to lend this $810. The next set of balance sheets shows this transaction. Bellville's loans and checkable deposits rise by $810.

FIGURE 15.5

Bellville Bank, Changes in Balance Sheet		Bellville Bank, Balance Sheet	
Assets	Liabilities	Assets	Liabilities
Loans +$810	Deposits +$810	Reserves $1,900 Loans $9,810	Deposits $11,710

The $810 that Bellville lent will be spent. Let us suppose it ends up with a customer who banks at Clarkston Bank. Bellville's checkable deposits fall by $810; Clarkston's rise by the same amount. Clarkston submits the check to the Fed, which transfers the money from Bellville's reserve account to Clarkston's. Notice that Clarkston's deposits rise by $810; Clarkston must increase its reserves by $81. But its reserves have risen by $810, so it has excess reserves of $729.

FIGURE 15.6

Bellville Bank, Changes in Balance Sheet		Bellville Bank, Balance Sheet	
Assets	Liabilities	Assets	Liabilities
Reserves −$810	Deposits −$810	Reserves $1,090 Loans $9,810	Deposits $10,900

Clarkston Bank, Changes in Balance Sheet		Clarkston Bank, Balance Sheet	
Assets	Liabilities	Assets	Liabilities
Reserves +$810	Deposits +$810	Reserves $1,810 Loans $9,000	Deposits $10,810
		(Excess reserves = $729)	

Notice that Bellville is now loaned up. And notice that it can report that it has not created any money either! It took in a $900 deposit, and its checkable deposits have risen by that same $900. The $810 it created when it issued a loan is now at Clarkston Bank.

The process will not end there. Clarkston will lend the $729 it now has in excess reserves, and the money that has been created will end up at some other bank, which will then have excess reserves—and create still more money. And that process will just keep going as long as there are excess reserves to pass through the banking system in the form of loans. How much will ultimately be created by the system as a whole? With a 10% reserve requirement, each dollar in reserves backs up $10 in checkable deposits. The $1,000 in cash that Acme's customer brought in adds $1,000 in reserves to the banking system. It can therefore back up an additional $10,000! In just the three banks we have shown, checkable deposits have risen by $2,710 ($1,000 at Acme, $900 at Bellville, and $810 at Clarkston). Additional banks in the system will continue to create money, up to a maximum of $7,290 among them. Subtracting the original $1,000 that had been a part of currency in circulation, we see that the money supply could rise by as much as $9,000.

Heads Up!

Notice that when the banks received new deposits, they could make new loans only up to the amount of their excess reserves, not up to the amount of their deposits and total reserve increases. For example, with the new deposit of $1,000, Acme Bank was able to make additional loans of $900. If instead it made new loans equal to its increase in total reserves, then after the customers who received new loans wrote checks to others, its reserves would be less than the required amount. In the case of Acme, had it lent out an additional $1,000, after checks were written against the new loans, it would have been left with only $1,000 in reserves against $11,000 in deposits, for a reserve ratio of only 0.09, which is less than the required reserve ratio of 0.1 in the example.

2.4　The Deposit Multiplier

deposit multiplier

The ratio of the maximum possible change in checkable deposits (ΔD) to the change in reserves (ΔR).

We can relate the potential increase in the money supply to the change in reserves that created it using the **deposit multiplier** (m_d), which equals the ratio of the maximum possible change in checkable deposits (ΔD) to the change in reserves (ΔR). In our example, the deposit multiplier was 10:

EQUATION 15.1

$$m_d = \frac{\Delta D}{\Delta R} = \frac{\$10,000}{\$1,000} = 10$$

To see how the deposit multiplier m_d is related to the required reserve ratio, we use the fact that if banks in the economy are loaned up, then reserves, R, equal the required reserve ratio (rrr) times checkable deposits, D:

EQUATION 15.2

$$R = rrrD$$

A change in reserves produces a change in loans and a change in checkable deposits. Once banks are fully loaned up, the change in reserves, ΔR, will equal the required reserve ratio times the change in deposits, ΔD:

EQUATION 15.3

$$\Delta R = rrr\Delta D$$

Solving for ΔD, we have

EQUATION 15.4

$$\frac{1}{rrr}\Delta R = \Delta D$$

Dividing both sides by ΔR, we see that the deposit multiplier, m_d, is $1/rrr$:

EQUATION 15.5

$$\frac{1}{rrr} = \frac{\Delta D}{\Delta R} = m_d$$

The deposit multiplier is thus given by the reciprocal of the required reserve ratio. With a required reserve ratio of 0.1, the deposit multiplier is 10. A required reserve ratio of 0.2 would produce a deposit multiplier of 5. The higher the required reserve ratio, the lower the deposit multiplier.

Actual increases in checkable deposits will not be nearly as great as suggested by the deposit multiplier. That is because the artificial conditions of our example are not met in the real world. Some banks hold excess reserves, customers withdraw cash, and some loan proceeds are not spent. Each of these factors reduces the degree to which checkable deposits are affected by an increase in reserves. The basic mechanism, however, is the one described in our example, and it remains the case that checkable deposits increase by a multiple of an increase in reserves.

The entire process of money creation can work in reverse. When you withdraw cash from your bank, you reduce the bank's reserves. Just as a deposit at Acme Bank increases the money supply by a multiple of the original deposit, your withdrawal reduces the money supply by a multiple of the amount you withdraw. And just as money is created when banks issue loans, it is destroyed as the loans are repaid. A loan payment reduces checkable deposits; it thus reduces the money supply.

Suppose, for example, that the Acme Bank customer who borrowed the $900 makes a $100 payment on the loan. Only part of the payment will reduce the loan balance; part will be interest. Suppose $30 of the payment is for interest, while the remaining $70 reduces the loan balance. The effect of the payment on Acme's balance sheet is shown below. Checkable deposits fall by $100, loans fall by $70, and net worth rises by the amount of the interest payment, $30.

Similar to the process of money creation, the money reduction process decreases checkable deposits by, at most, the amount of the reduction in deposits times the deposit multiplier.

2.5   The Regulation of Banks

FIGURE 15.7

Banks are among the most heavily regulated of financial institutions. They are regulated in part to protect individual depositors against corrupt business practices. Banks are also susceptible to crises of confidence. Because their reserves equal only a fraction of their deposit liabilities, an effort by customers to get all their cash out of a bank could force it to fail. A few poorly managed banks could create such a crisis, leading people to try to withdraw their funds from well-managed banks. Another reason for the high degree of regulation is that variations in the quantity of money have important effects on the economy as a whole, and banks are the institutions through which money is created.

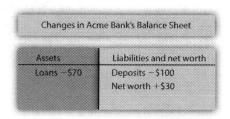

Deposit Insurance

From a customer's point of view, the most important form of regulation comes in the form of deposit insurance. For commercial banks, this insurance is provided by the Federal Deposit Insurance Corporation (FDIC). Insurance funds are maintained through a premium assessed on banks for every $100 of bank deposits.

If a commercial bank fails, the FDIC guarantees to reimburse depositors up to $250,000 (raised from $100,000 during the financial crisis of 2008) per insured bank, for each account ownership category. From a depositor's point of view, therefore, it is not necessary to worry about a bank's safety.

One difficulty this insurance creates, however, is that it may induce the officers of a bank to take more risks. With a federal agency on hand to bail them out if they fail, the costs of failure are reduced. Bank officers can thus be expected to take more risks than they would otherwise, which, in turn, makes failure more likely. In addition, depositors, knowing that their deposits are insured, may not scrutinize the banks' lending activities as carefully as they would if they felt that unwise loans could result in the loss of their deposits.

Thus, banks present us with a fundamental dilemma. A fractional reserve system means that banks can operate only if their customers maintain their confidence in them. If bank customers lose confidence, they are likely to try to withdraw their funds. But with a fractional reserve system, a bank actually holds funds in reserve equal to only a small fraction of its deposit liabilities. If its customers think a bank will fail and try to withdraw their cash, the bank is likely to fail. Bank panics, in which frightened customers rush to withdraw their deposits, contributed to the failure of one-third of the nation's banks between 1929 and 1933. Deposit insurance was introduced in large part to give people confidence in their banks and to prevent failure. But the deposit insurance that seeks to prevent bank failures may lead to less careful management—and thus encourage bank failure.

Regulation to Prevent Bank Failure

To reduce the number of bank failures, banks are limited in what they can do. Banks are required to maintain a minimum level of net worth as a fraction of total assets. Regulators from the FDIC regularly perform audits and other checks of individual banks to ensure they are operating safely.

The FDIC has the power to close a bank whose net worth has fallen below the required level. In practice, it typically acts to close a bank when it becomes insolvent, that is, when its net worth becomes negative. Negative net worth implies that the bank's liabilities exceed its assets.

When the FDIC closes a bank, it arranges for depositors to receive their funds. When the bank's funds are insufficient to return customers' deposits, the FDIC uses money from the insurance fund for this purpose. Alternatively, the FDIC may arrange for another bank to purchase the failed bank. The FDIC, however, continues to guarantee that depositors will not lose any money.

Regulation in Response to Financial Crises

In the aftermath of the Great Depression and the banking crisis that accompanied it, laws were passed to try to make the banking system safer. The Glass-Steagall Act of that period created the FDIC and the separation between commercial banks and investment banks. Over time, the financial system in the United States and in other countries began to change, and in 1999, a law was passed in the United

States that essentially repealed the part of the Glass-Steagall Act that had created the separation between commercial and investment banking. Proponents of eliminating the separation between the two types of banks argued that banks could better diversify their portfolios if allowed to participate in other parts of the financial markets and that banks in other countries operated without such a separation.

Similar to the reaction to the banking crisis of the 1930s, the financial crisis of 2008 and the Great Recession led to calls for financial market reform. The result was the Dodd-Frank Wall Street Reform and Consumer Protection Act, usually referred to as the Dodd-Frank Act, which was passed in July 2010. More than 2,000 pages in length, the regulations to implement most provisions of this act were set to take place over a nearly two-year period, with some provisions expected to take even longer to implement. This act created the Consumer Financial Protection Agency to oversee and regulate various aspects of consumer credit markets, such as credit card and bank fees and mortgage contracts. It also created the Financial Stability Oversight Council (FSOC) to assess risks for the entire financial industry. The FSOC can recommend that a nonbank financial firm, such as a hedge fund that is perhaps threatening the stability of the financial system (i.e., getting "too big to fail"), become regulated by the Federal Reserve. If such firms do become insolvent, a process of liquidation similar to what occurs when the FDIC takes over a bank can be applied. The Dodd-Frank Act also calls for implementation of the Volcker rule, which was named after the former chair of the Fed who argued the case. The Volcker rule is meant to ban banks from using depositors' funds to engage in certain types of speculative investments to try to enhance the profits of the bank, at least partly reinstating the separation between commercial and investment banking that the Glass-Steagall Act had created. There are many other provisions in this wide-sweeping legislation that are designed to improve oversight of nonbank financial institutions, increase transparency in the operation of various forms of financial instruments, regulate credit rating agencies such as Moody's and Standard & Poor's, and so on. Given the lag time associated with fully implementing the legislation, it will probably be many years before its impact can be fully assessed.

KEY TAKEAWAYS

- Banks are financial intermediaries that accept deposits, make loans, and provide checking accounts for their customers.
- Money is created within the banking system when banks issue loans; it is destroyed when the loans are repaid.
- An increase (decrease) in reserves in the banking system can increase (decrease) the money supply. The maximum amount of the increase (decrease) is equal to the deposit multiplier times the change in reserves; the deposit multiplier equals the reciprocal of the required reserve ratio.
- Bank deposits are insured and banks are heavily regulated.
- Similar to the passage of the Glass-Steagall Act during the Great Depression, the Dodd-Frank Act was the comprehensive financial reform legislation that responded to the financial crisis in 2008 and the Great Recession.

TRY IT!

1. Suppose Acme Bank initially has $10,000 in deposits, reserves of $2,000, and loans of $8,000. At a required reserve ratio of 0.2, is Acme loaned up? Show the balance sheet of Acme Bank at present.

2. Now suppose that an Acme Bank customer, planning to take cash on an extended college graduation trip to India, withdraws $1,000 from her account. Show the changes to Acme Bank's balance sheet and Acme's balance sheet after the withdrawal. By how much are its reserves now deficient?

3. Acme would probably replenish its reserves by reducing loans. This action would cause a multiplied contraction of checkable deposits as other banks lose deposits because their customers would be paying off loans to Acme. How large would the contraction be?

Case in Point

A Big Bank Goes Under

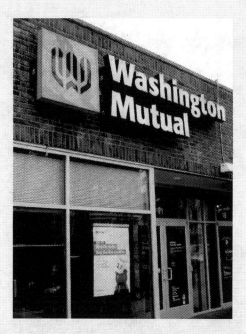

It was the darling of Wall Street—it showed rapid growth and made big profits. Washington Mutual, a savings and loan based in the state of Washington, was a relatively small institution whose CEO, Kerry K. Killinger, had big plans. He wanted to transform his little Seattle S&L into the Wal-Mart of banks.

Mr. Killinger began pursuing a relatively straightforward strategy. He acquired banks in large cities such as Chicago and Los Angeles. He acquired banks up and down the east and west coasts. He aggressively extended credit to low-income individuals and families—credit cards, car loans, and mortgages. In making mortgage loans to low-income families, WaMu, as the bank was known, quickly became very profitable. But it was exposing itself to greater and greater risk, according to the *New York Times*.

Housing prices in the United States more than doubled between 1997 and 2007. During that time, loans to even low-income households were profitable. But, as housing prices began falling in 2007, banks such as WaMu began to experience losses as homeowners began to walk away from houses whose values suddenly fell below their outstanding mortgages. WaMu began losing money in 2007 as housing prices began falling. The company had earned $3.6 billion in 2006, and swung to a loss of $67 million in 2007, according to the *Puget Sound Business Journal*. Mr. Killinger was ousted by the board early in September of 2008. The bank failed later that month. It was the biggest bank failure in the history of the United States.

The Federal Deposit Insurance Corporation (FDIC) had just rescued another bank, IndyMac, which was only a tenth the size of WaMu, and would have done the same for WaMu if it had not been able to find a company to purchase it. But in this case, JPMorgan Chase agreed to take it over—its deposits, bank branches, and its troubled asset portfolio. The government and the Fed even negotiated the deal behind WaMu's back! The then chief executive officer of the company, Alan H. Fishman, was reportedly flying from New York to Seattle when the deal was finalized.

The government was anxious to broker a deal that did not require use of the FDIC's depleted funds following IndyMac's collapse. But it would have done so if a buyer had not been found. As the FDIC reports on its Web site: "Since the FDIC's creation in 1933, no depositor has ever lost even one penny of FDIC-insured funds."

Sources: Eric Dash and Andrew Ross Sorkin, "Government Seizes WaMu and Sells Some Assets," New York Times, September 25, 2008, p. A1; Kirsten Grind, "Insiders Detail Reasons for WaMu's Failure," Puget Sound Business Journal, January 23, 2009; and FDIC Web site at https://www.fdic.gov/edie/fdic_info.html.

ANSWERS TO TRY IT! PROBLEMS

1. Acme Bank is loaned up, since $2,000/$10,000 = 0.2, which is the required reserve ratio. Acme's balance sheet is:

Assets	Liabilities plus net worth
Reserves $2,000	Deposits $10,000
Loans $8,000	

2. Acme Bank's balance sheet after losing $1,000 in deposits:

Acme Bank, Changes in Balance Sheet		Acme Bank, Balance Sheet	
Assets	Liabilities	Assets	Liabilities
Reserves −$1,000	Deposits −$1,000	Reserves $1,000	Deposits $9,000
		Loans $8,000	

Required reserves are deficient by $800. Acme must hold 20% of its deposits, in this case $1,800 (0.2 × $9,000 = $1,800), as reserves, but it has only $1,000 in reserves at the moment.

3. The contraction in checkable deposits would be

$$\Delta D = (1/0.2) \times (-\$1,000) = -\$5,000$$

3. THE FEDERAL RESERVE SYSTEM

LEARNING OBJECTIVES

1. **Explain the primary functions of central banks.**
2. **Describe how the Federal Reserve System is structured and governed.**
3. **Identify and explain the tools of monetary policy.**
4. **Describe how the Fed creates and destroys money when it buys and sells federal government bonds.**

central bank

A bank that acts as a banker to the central government, acts as a banker to banks, acts as a regulator of banks, conducts monetary policy, and supports the stability of the financial system.

The Federal Reserve System of the United States, or Fed, is the U.S. central bank. Japan's central bank is the Bank of Japan; the European Union has established the European Central Bank. Most countries have a central bank. A **central bank** performs five primary functions: (1) it acts as a banker to the central government, (2) it acts as a banker to banks, (3) it acts as a regulator of banks, (4) it conducts monetary policy, and (5) it supports the stability of the financial system.

For the first 137 years of its history, the United States did not have a true central bank. While a central bank was often proposed, there was resistance to creating an institution with such enormous power. A series of bank panics slowly increased support for the creation of a central bank. The bank panic of 1907 proved to be the final straw. Bank failures were so widespread, and depositor losses so heavy, that concerns about centralization of power gave way to a desire for an institution that would provide a stabilizing force in the banking industry. Congress passed the Federal Reserve Act in 1913, creating the Fed and giving it all the powers of a central bank.

3.1   Structure of the Fed

In creating the Fed, Congress determined that a central bank should be as independent of the government as possible. It also sought to avoid too much centralization of power in a single institution. These potentially contradictory goals of independence and decentralized power are evident in the Fed's structure and in the continuing struggles between Congress and the Fed over possible changes in that structure.

In an effort to decentralize power, Congress designed the Fed as a system of 12 regional banks, as shown in Figure 15.8. Each of these banks operates as a kind of bankers' cooperative; the regional banks are owned by the commercial banks in their districts that have chosen to be members of the Fed. The owners of each Federal Reserve bank select the board of directors of that bank; the board selects the bank's president.

FIGURE 15.8   The 12 Federal Reserve Districts and the Cities Where Each Bank Is Located

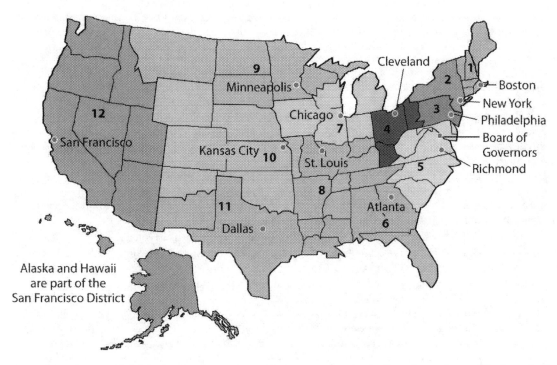

Several provisions of the Federal Reserve Act seek to maintain the Fed's independence. The board of directors for the entire Federal Reserve System is called the Board of Governors. The seven members of the board are appointed by the president of the United States and confirmed by the Senate. To ensure a large measure of independence from any one president, the members of the Board of Governors have 14-year terms. One member of the board is selected by the president of the United States to serve as chairman for a four-year term.

As a further means of ensuring the independence of the Fed, Congress authorized it to buy and sell federal government bonds. This activity is a profitable one that allows the Fed to pay its own bills. The Fed is thus not dependent on a Congress that might otherwise be tempted to force a particular set of policies on it. The Fed is limited in the profits it is allowed to earn; its "excess" profits are returned to the Treasury.

It is important to recognize that the Fed is technically not part of the federal government. Members of the Board of Governors do not legally have to answer to Congress, the president, or anyone else. The president and members of Congress can certainly try to influence the Fed, but they cannot order it to do anything. Congress, however, created the Fed. It could, by passing another law, abolish the Fed's independence. The Fed can maintain its independence only by keeping the support of Congress—and that sometimes requires being responsive to the wishes of Congress.

In recent years, Congress has sought to increase its oversight of the Fed. The chairman of the Federal Reserve Board is required to report to Congress twice each year on its monetary policy, the set of policies that the central bank can use to influence economic activity.

3.2 Powers of the Fed

The Fed's principal powers stem from its authority to conduct monetary policy. It has three main policy tools: setting reserve requirements, operating the discount window and other credit facilities, and conducting open-market operations.

Reserve Requirements

The Fed sets the required ratio of reserves that banks must hold relative to their deposit liabilities. In theory, the Fed could use this power as an instrument of monetary policy. It could lower reserve requirements when it wanted to increase the money supply and raise them when it wanted to reduce the money supply. In practice, however, the Fed does not use its power to set reserve requirements in this way. The reason is that frequent manipulation of reserve requirements would make life difficult for bankers, who would have to adjust their lending policies to changing requirements.

The Fed's power to set reserve requirements was expanded by the Monetary Control Act of 1980. Before that, the Fed set reserve requirements only for commercial banks that were members of the Federal Reserve System. Most banks are not members of the Fed; the Fed's control of reserve requirements thus extended to only a minority of banks. The 1980 act required virtually all banks to satisfy the Fed's reserve requirements.

The Discount Window and Other Credit Facilities

discount rate

The interest rate charged by the Fed when it lends reserves to banks.

A major responsibility of the Fed is to act as a lender of last resort to banks. When banks fall short on reserves, they can borrow reserves from the Fed through its discount window. The **discount rate** is the interest rate charged by the Fed when it lends reserves to banks. The Board of Governors sets the discount rate.

Lowering the discount rate makes funds cheaper to banks. A lower discount rate could place downward pressure on interest rates in the economy. However, when financial markets are operating normally, banks rarely borrow from the Fed, reserving use of the discount window for emergencies. A typical bank borrows from the Fed only about once or twice per year.

federal funds market

A market in which banks lend reserves to one another.

federal funds rate

The interest rate charged when one bank lends reserves to another.

Instead of borrowing from the Fed when they need reserves, banks typically rely on the federal funds market to obtain reserves. The **federal funds market** is a market in which banks lend reserves to one another. The **federal funds rate** is the interest rate charged for such loans; it is determined by banks' demand for and supply of these reserves. The ability to set the discount rate is no longer an important tool of Federal Reserve policy.

To deal with the recent financial and economic conditions, the Fed greatly expanded its lending beyond its traditional discount window lending. As falling house prices led to foreclosures, private investment banks and other financial institutions came under increasing pressure. The Fed made credit available to a wide range of institutions in an effort to stem the crisis. In 2008, the Fed bailed out two major housing finance firms that had been established by the government to prop up the housing industry—Fannie Mae (the Federal National Mortgage Association) and Freddie Mac (the Federal Home Mortgage Corporation). Together, the two institutions backed the mortgages of half of the nation's mortgage loans.[2] It also agreed to provide $85 billion to AIG, the huge insurance firm. AIG had a subsidiary that was heavily exposed to mortgage loan losses, and that crippled the firm. The Fed determined that AIG was simply too big to be allowed to fail. Many banks had ties to the giant institution, and its failure would have been a blow to those banks. As the United States faced the worst financial crisis since the Great Depression, the Fed took center stage. Whatever its role in the financial crisis of 2007–2008, the Fed remains an important backstop for banks and other financial institutions needing liquidity. And for that, it uses the traditional discount window, supplemented with a wide range of other credit facilities. The Case in Point in this section discusses these new credit facilities.

Open-Market Operations

bond

A promise by the issuer of the bond to pay the owner of the bond a payment or a series of payments on a specific date or dates.

open-market operations

The buying and selling of federal government bonds by the Fed.

The Fed's ability to buy and sell federal government bonds has proved to be its most potent policy tool. A **bond** is a promise by the issuer of the bond (in this case the federal government) to pay the owner of the bond a payment or a series of payments on a specific date or dates. The buying and selling of federal government bonds by the Fed are called **open-market operations**. When the Fed buys or sells government bonds, it adds or subtracts reserves from the banking system. Such changes affect the money supply.

Suppose the Fed buys a government bond in the open market. It writes a check on its own account to the seller of the bond. When the seller deposits the check at a bank, the bank submits the check to the Fed for payment. The Fed "pays" the check by crediting the bank's account at the Fed, so the bank has more reserves.

The Fed's purchase of a bond can be illustrated using a balance sheet. Suppose the Fed buys a bond for $1,000 from one of Acme Bank's customers. When that customer deposits the check at Acme, checkable deposits will rise by $1,000. The check is written on the Federal Reserve System; the Fed will credit Acme's account. Acme's reserves thus rise by $1,000. With a 10% reserve requirement, that will create $900 in excess reserves and set off the same process of money expansion as did the cash deposit we have already examined. The difference is that the Fed's purchase of a bond created new reserves with the stroke of a pen, where the cash deposit created them by removing $1,000 from currency in circulation. The purchase of the $1,000 bond by the Fed could thus increase the money supply by as much as $10,000, the maximum expansion suggested by the deposit multiplier.

FIGURE 15.9

Changes in Acme Bank's Balance Sheet	
Assets	**Liabilities plus net worth**
Reserves +$1,000	Deposits +$1,000

Where does the Fed get $1,000 to purchase the bond? It simply creates the money when it writes the check to purchase the bond. On the Fed's balance sheet, assets increase by $1,000 because the Fed now has the bond; bank deposits with the Fed, which represent a liability to the Fed, rise by $1,000 as well.

When the Fed sells a bond, it gives the buyer a federal government bond that it had previously purchased and accepts a check in exchange. The bank on which the check was written will find its deposit with the Fed reduced by the amount of the check. That bank's reserves and checkable deposits will fall by equal amounts; the reserves, in effect, disappear. The result is a reduction in the money supply. The Fed thus increases the money supply by buying bonds; it reduces the money supply by selling them.

Figure 15.10 shows how the Fed influences the flow of money in the economy. Funds flow from the public—individuals and firms—to banks as deposits. Banks use those funds to make loans to the public—to individuals and firms. The Fed can influence the volume of bank lending by buying bonds and thus injecting reserves into the system. With new reserves, banks will increase their lending, which creates still more deposits and still more lending as the deposit multiplier goes to work. Alternatively, the Fed can sell bonds. When it does, reserves flow out of the system, reducing bank lending and reducing deposits.

The Fed's purchase or sale of bonds is conducted by the Open Market Desk at the Federal Reserve Bank of New York, one of the 12 district banks. Traders at the Open Market Desk are guided by policy directives issued by the Federal Open Market Committee (FOMC). The FOMC consists of the seven members of the Board of Governors plus five regional bank presidents. The president of the New York Federal Reserve Bank serves as a member of the FOMC; the other 11 bank presidents take turns filling the remaining four seats.

The FOMC meets eight times per year to chart the Fed's monetary policies. In the past, FOMC meetings were closed, with no report of the committee's action until the release of the minutes six weeks after the meeting. Faced with pressure to open its proceedings, the Fed began in 1994 issuing a report of the decisions of the FOMC immediately after each meeting.

In practice, the Fed sets targets for the federal funds rate. To achieve a lower federal funds rate, the Fed goes into the open market buying securities and thus increasing the money supply. When the Fed raises its target rate for the federal funds rate, it sells securities and thus reduces the money supply.

FIGURE 15.10 The Fed and the Flow of Money in the Economy

Individuals and firms (the public) make deposits in banks; banks make loans to individuals and firms. The Fed can buy bonds to inject new reserves into the system, thus increasing bank lending, which creates new deposits, creating still more lending as the deposit multiplier goes to work. Alternatively, the Fed can sell bonds, withdrawing reserves from the system, thus reducing bank lending and reducing total deposits.

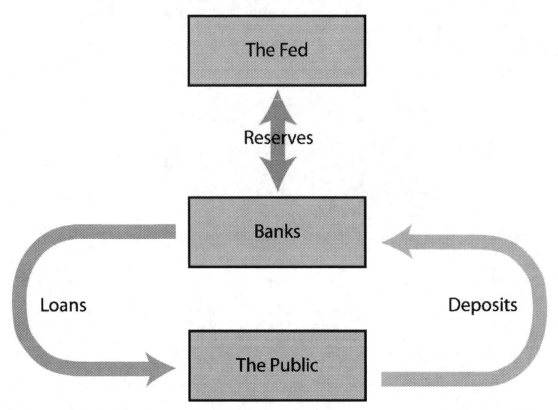

Traditionally, the Fed has bought and sold short-term government securities; however, in dealing with the condition of the economy in 2009, wherein the Fed has already set the target for the federal funds rate at near zero, the Fed has announced that it will also be buying longer term government securities. In so doing, it hopes to influence longer term interest rates, such as those related to mortgages.

KEY TAKEAWAYS

- The Fed, the central bank of the United States, acts as a bank for other banks and for the federal government. It also regulates banks, sets monetary policy, and maintains the stability of the financial system.
- The Fed sets reserve requirements and the discount rate and conducts open-market operations. Of these tools of monetary policy, open-market operations are the most important.
- Starting in 2007, the Fed began creating additional credit facilities to help stabilize the financial system.
- The Fed creates new reserves and new money when it purchases bonds. It destroys reserves and thus reduces the money supply when it sells bonds.

TRY IT!

Suppose the Fed sells $8 million worth of bonds.

1. How do bank reserves change?
2. Will the money supply increase or decrease?
3. What is the maximum possible change in the money supply if the required reserve ratio is 0.2?

Case in Point

Fed Supports the Financial System by Creating New Credit Facilities

Well before most of the public became aware of the precarious state of the U.S. financial system, the Fed began to see signs of growing financial strains and to act on reducing them. In particular, the Fed saw that short-term interest rates that are often quite close to the federal funds rate began to rise markedly above it. The widening spread was alarming, because it suggested that lender confidence was declining, even for what are generally considered low-risk loans. Commercial paper, in which large companies borrow funds for a period of about a month to manage their cash flow, is an example. Even companies with high credit ratings were having to pay unusually high interest rate premiums in order to get funding, or in some cases could not get funding at all.

To deal with the drying up of credit markets, in late 2007 the Fed began to create an alphabet soup of new credit facilities. Some of these were offered in conjunction with the Department of the Treasury, which had more latitude in terms of accepting some credit risk. The facilities differed in terms of collateral used, the duration of the loan, which institutions were eligible to borrow, and the cost to the borrower. For example, the Primary Dealer Credit Facility (PDCF) allowed primary dealers (i.e., those financial institutions that normally handle the Fed's open market operations) to obtain overnight loans. The Term Asset-Backed Securities Loan Facility (TALF) allowed a wide range of companies to borrow, using the primary dealers as conduits, based on qualified asset-backed securities related to student, auto, credit card, and small business debt, for a three-year period. Most of these new facilities were designed to be temporary. Starting in 2009 and 2010, the Fed began closing a number of them or at least preventing them from issuing new loans.

The common goal of all of these various credit facilities was to increase liquidity in order to stimulate private spending. For example, these credit facilities encouraged banks to pare down their excess reserves (which grew enormously as the financial crisis unfolded and the economy deteriorated) and to make more loans. In the words of then Fed Chairman Ben Bernanke:

> "Liquidity provision by the central bank reduces systemic risk by assuring market participants that, should short-term investors begin to lose confidence, financial institutions will be able to meet the resulting demands for cash without resorting to potentially destabilizing fire sales of assets. Moreover, backstopping the liquidity needs of financial institutions reduces funding stresses and, all else equal, should increase the willingness of those institutions to lend and make markets."

The legal authority for most of these new credit facilities came from a particular section of the Federal Reserve Act that allows the Board of Governors "in unusual and exigent circumstances" to extend credit to a wide range of market players.

Sources: Ben S. Bernanke, "The Crisis and the Policy Response" (Stemp Lecture, London School of Economics, London, England, January 13, 2009); Richard DiCecio and Charles S. Gascon, "New Monetary Policy Tools?" Federal Reserve Bank of St. Louis Monetary Trends, May 2008; Federal Reserve Board of Governors Web site at http://www.federalreserve.gov/monetarypolicy/default.htm.

4. REVIEW AND PRACTICE

Summary

In this chapter we investigated the money supply and looked at how it is determined. Money is anything that serves as a medium of exchange. Whatever serves as money also functions as a unit of account and as a store of value. Money may or may not have intrinsic value. In the United States, the total of currency in circulation, traveler's checks, and checkable deposits equals M1. A broader measure of the money supply is M2, which includes M1 plus assets that are highly liquid, but less liquid than those in M1.

Banks create money when they issue loans. The ability of banks to issue loans is controlled by their reserves. Reserves consist of cash in bank vaults and bank deposits with the Fed. Banks operate in a fractional reserve system; that is, they maintain reserves equal to only a small fraction of their deposit liabilities. Banks are heavily regulated to protect individual depositors and to prevent crises of confidence. Deposit insurance protects individual depositors. Financial reform legislation was enacted in response to the banking crisis during the Great Depression and again in response to the financial crisis in 2008 and the Great Recession.

A central bank serves as a bank for banks, a regulator of banks, a manager of the money supply, a bank for a nation's government, and a supporter of financial markets generally. In the financial crisis that rocked the United States and much of the world in 2008, the Fed played a central role in keeping bank and nonbank institutions afloat and in keeping credit available. The Federal Reserve System (Fed) is the central bank for the United States. The Fed is governed by a Board of Governors whose members are appointed by the president of the United States, subject to confirmation by the Senate.

The Fed can lend to banks and other institutions through the discount window and other credit facilities, change reserve requirements, and engage in purchases and sales of federal government bonds in the open market. Decisions to buy or sell bonds are made by the Federal Open Market Committee (FOMC); the Fed's open-market operations represent its primary tool for influencing the money supply. Purchases of bonds by the Fed initially increase the reserves of banks. With excess reserves on hand, banks will attempt to increase their loans, and in the process the money supply will change by an amount less than or equal to the deposit multiplier times the change in reserves. Similarly, the Fed can reduce the money supply by selling bonds.

CONCEPT PROBLEMS

1. Airlines have "frequent flier" clubs in which customers accumulate miles according to the number of miles they have flown with the airline. Frequent flier miles can then be used to purchase other flights, to rent cars, or to stay in some hotels. Are frequent flier miles money?

2. Debit cards allow an individual to transfer funds directly in a checkable account to a merchant without writing a check. How is this different from the way credit cards work? Are either credit cards or debit cards money? Explain.

3. Many colleges sell special cards that students can use to purchase everything from textbooks or meals in the cafeteria to use of washing machines in the dorm. Students deposit money in their cards; as they use their cards for purchases, electronic scanners remove money from the cards. To replenish a card's money, a student makes a cash deposit that is credited to the card. Would these cards count as part of the money supply?

4. A smart card, also known as an electronic purse, is a plastic card that can be loaded with a monetary value. Its developers argue that, once widely accepted, it could replace the use of currency in vending machines, parking meters, and elsewhere. Suppose smart cards came into widespread use. Present your views on the following issues:

    a. Would you count balances in the purses as part of the money supply? If so, would they be part of M1? M2?

    b. Should any institution be permitted to issue them, or should they be restricted to banks?

    c. Should the issuers be subject to reserve requirements?

    d. Suppose they were issued by banks. How do you think the use of such purses would affect the money supply? Explain your answer carefully.

5. Which of the following items is part of M1? M2?

    a. $0.27 cents that has accumulated under a couch cushion.

    b. Your $2,000 line of credit with your Visa account.

    c. The $210 balance in your checking account.

    d. $417 in your savings account.

    e. 10 shares of stock your uncle gave you on your 18th birthday, which are now worth $520.

    f. $200 in traveler's checks you have purchased for your spring-break trip.

6. In the Middle Ages, goldsmiths took in customers' deposits (gold coins) and issued receipts that functioned much like checks do today. People used the receipts as a medium of exchange. Goldsmiths also issued loans by writing additional receipts against which they were holding no gold to borrowers. Were goldsmiths engaging in fractional reserve banking? Why do you think that customers turned their gold over to goldsmiths? Who benefited from the goldsmiths' action? Why did such a system generally work? When would it have been likely to fail?

7. A $1,000 deposit in Acme Bank has increased reserves by $1,000. A loan officer at Acme reasons as follows: "The reserve requirement is 10%. That means that the $1,000 in new reserves can back $10,000 in checkable deposits. Therefore I'll loan an additional $10,000." Is there any problem with the loan officer's reasoning? Explain.

8. When the Fed buys and sells bonds through open-market operations, the money supply changes, but there is no effect on the money supply when individuals buy and sell bonds. Explain.

NUMERICAL PROBLEMS

1. Consider the following example of bartering:

   1 10-ounce T-bone steak can be traded for 5 soft drinks.
   1 soft drink can be traded for 10 apples.
   100 apples can be traded for a T-shirt.
   5 T-shirts can be exchanged for 1 textbook.
   It takes 4 textbooks to get 1 VCR.

   a. How many 10-ounce T-bone steaks could you exchange for 1 textbook? How many soft drinks? How many apples?

   b. State the price of T-shirts in terms of apples, textbooks, and soft drinks.

   c. Why do you think we use money as a unit of account?

2. Assume that the banking system is loaned up and that any open-market purchase by the Fed directly increases reserves in the banks. If the required reserve ratio is 0.2, by how much could the money supply expand if the Fed purchased $2 billion worth of bonds?

3. Suppose the Fed sells $5 million worth of bonds to Econobank.

   a. What happens to the reserves of the bank?

   b. What happens to the money supply in the economy as a whole if the reserve requirement is 10%, all payments are made by check, and there is no net drain into currency?

   c. How would your answer in part b be affected if you knew that some people involved in the money creation process kept some of their funds as cash?

4. If half the banks in the nation borrow additional reserves totaling $10 million at the Fed discount window, and at the same time the other half of the banks reduce their excess reserves by a total of $10 million, what is likely to happen to the money supply? Explain.

5. Suppose a bank with a 10% reserve requirement has $10 million in reserves and $100 million in checkable deposits, and a major corporation makes a deposit of $1 million.

   a. Explain how the deposit affects the bank's reserves and checkable deposits.

   b. By how much can the bank increase its lending?

6. Suppose a bank with a 25% reserve requirement has $50 million in reserves and $200 million in checkable deposits, and one of the bank's depositors, a major corporation, writes a check to another corporation for $5 million. The check is deposited in another bank.

   a. Explain how the withdrawal affects the bank's reserves and checkable deposits.

   b. By how much will the bank have to reduce its lending?

7. Suppose the bank in problem 6 faces a 20% reserve requirement. The customer writes the same check. How will this affect your answers?

8. Now consider an economy in which the central bank has just purchased $8 billion worth of government bonds from banks in the economy. What would be the effect of this purchase on the money supply in the country, assuming reserve requirements of:

   a. 10%.

   b. 15%.

   c. 20%.

   d. 25%.

9. Now consider the same economy, and the central bank sells $8 billion worth of government bonds to local banks. State the likely effects on the money supply under reserve requirements of:

   a. 10%.

   b. 15%.

   c. 20%.

   d. 25%.

10. How would the purchase of $8 billion of bonds by the central bank from local banks be likely to affect interest rates? How about the effect on interest rates of the sale of $8 billion worth of bonds? Explain your answers carefully.

ENDNOTES

1. Justin Scheck, "Mackerel Economics in Prison Leads to Appreciation for Oily Fish,"
    Wall Street Journal, October 2, 2008, p. A1.

2. Sam Zuckerman, "Feds Take Control of Fannie Mae, Freddie Mac," *The San Francisco Chronicle*, September 8, 2008, p. A-1.

CHAPTER 16

Financial Markets, the Fed, and Monetary Policy

START UP: THE FED'S EXTRAORDINARY CHALLENGES IN 2008

"The Federal Reserve will employ all available tools to promote the resumption of sustainable economic growth and to preserve price stability. In particular, the Committee anticipates that weak economic conditions are likely to warrant exceptionally low levels of the federal funds rate for some time." So went the statement issued by the Federal Open Market Committee on December 16, 2008, that went on to say that the new target range for the federal funds rate would be between 0% and 0.25%. For the first time in its history, the Fed was targeting a rate below 1%. It was also acknowledging the difficulty of hitting a specific rate target when the target is so low. And, finally, it was experimenting with extraordinary measures based on a section of the Federal Reserve Act that allows it to take such measures when conditions in financial markets are deemed "unusual and exigent."

The Fed was responding to the broad-based weakness of the U.S. economy, the strains in **financial markets**, and the tightness of credit. Unlike some other moments in U.S. economic history, it did not have to worry about inflation, at least not in the short term. On the same day, consumer prices were reported to have fallen by 1.7% for the month of November. Indeed, commentators were beginning to fret over the possibility of deflation and how the Fed could continue to support the economy when it had already used all of its federal funds rate ammunition.

Anticipating this concern, the Fed's statement went on to discuss other ways it was planning to support the economy over the months to come. These included buying mortgage-backed securities to support the mortgage and housing markets, buying long-term Treasury bills, and creating other new credit facilities to make credit more easily available to households and small businesses. These options recalled a speech that Ben Bernanke had made six years earlier, when he was a member of the Federal Reserve Board of Governors but still nearly four years away from being named its chair, titled "Deflation: Making Sure 'It' Doesn't Happen Here." In the 2002 speech, he laid out how these tools, along with tax cuts, were the equivalent of what Nobel Prize–winning economist Milton Friedman meant by a "helicopter drop" of money. The speech earned Bernanke the nickname of Helicopter Ben.

The Fed's decisions of mid-December put it in uncharted territory. In the 1990s, when faced with a situation similar to that of the United States in 2008, Japan had tried a similar strategy, though somewhat less comprehensively and more belatedly, and with only limited success. In his 2002 speech, Bernanke suggested that Japanese authorities had not gone far enough. Only history will tell us whether the Fed will be more successful and how well these new strategies will work.

This chapter provides the building blocks for understanding financial markets. Beginning with an overview of bond and foreign exchange markets, we will examine how they are related to the level of real GDP and the price level. The second section completes the model of the money market. We have learned that the Fed can change the amount of reserves in the banking system, and when it does, the money supply changes. Here we explain money demand—the quantity of money people and firms want to hold—which, together with money supply, leads to an equilibrium rate of interest.

The model of aggregate demand and supply shows how changes in the components of aggregate demand affect GDP and the price level. In this chapter, we will learn that changes in the financial markets can affect aggregate demand—and in turn can lead to changes in real GDP and the price level. Showing how the financial markets fit into the model of aggregate demand and aggregate supply we developed earlier provides a more complete picture of how the macroeconomy works.

This chapter then examines in greater detail monetary policy and the roles of central banks in carrying out that policy. Our primary focus will be on the U.S. Federal Reserve System. The basic tools used by central banks in many countries are similar, but their institutional structure and their roles in their respective countries can differ.

1.   THE BOND AND FOREIGN EXCHANGE MARKETS

LEARNING OBJECTIVES

1. **Explain and illustrate how the bond market works and discuss the relationship between the price of a bond and that bond's interest rate.**
2. **Explain and illustrate the relationship between a change in demand for or supply of bonds and macroeconomic activity.**
3. **Explain and illustrate how the foreign exchange market works and how a change in demand for a country's currency or a change in its supply affects macroeconomic activity.**

In this section, we will look at the bond market and at the market for foreign exchange. Events in these markets can affect the price level and output for the entire economy.

1.1   The Bond Market

In their daily operations and in pursuit of new projects, institutions such as firms and governments often borrow. They may seek funds from a bank. Many institutions, however, obtain credit by selling bonds. The federal government is one institution that issues bonds. A local school district might sell bonds to finance the construction of a new school. Your college or university has probably sold bonds to finance new buildings on campus. Firms often sell bonds to finance expansion. The market for bonds is an enormously important one.

When an institution sells a bond, it obtains the price paid for the bond as a kind of loan. The institution that issues the bond is obligated to make payments on the bond in the future. The interest rate is determined by the price of the bond. To understand these relationships, let us look more closely at bond prices and interest rates.

Bond Prices and Interest Rates

Suppose the manager of a manufacturing company needs to borrow some money to expand the factory. The manager could do so in the following way: he or she prints, say, 500 pieces of paper, each bearing the company's promise to pay the bearer $1,000 in a year. These pieces of paper are bonds, and the company, as the issuer, promises to make a single payment. The manager then offers these bonds for sale, announcing that they will be sold to the buyers who offer the highest prices. Suppose the highest price offered is $950, and all the bonds are sold at that price. Each bond is, in effect, an obligation to repay buyers $1,000. The buyers of the bonds are being paid $50 for the service of lending $950 for a year.

The $1,000 printed on each bond is the **face value of the bond**; it is the amount the issuer will have to pay on the **maturity date** of the bond—the date when the loan matures, or comes due. The $950 at which they were sold is their price. The difference between the face value and the price is the amount paid for the use of the money obtained from selling the bond.

An **interest rate** is the payment made for the use of money, expressed as a percentage of the amount borrowed. Bonds you sold command an interest rate equal to the difference between the face value and the bond price, divided by the bond price, and then multiplied by 100 to form a percentage:

EQUATION 16.1

$$\frac{\text{Face value} - \text{bond price}}{\text{Bond price}} \times 100 = \text{interest rate}$$

At a price of $950, the interest rate is 5.3%

$$\frac{\$1,000 - \$950}{\$950} \times 100 = 5.3 \%$$

The interest rate on any bond is determined by its price. As the price falls, the interest rate rises. Suppose, for example, that the best price the manager can get for the bonds is $900. Now the interest rate is 11.1%. A price of $800 would mean an interest rate of 25%; $750 would mean an interest rate of 33.3%; a price of $500 translates into an interest rate of 100%. The lower the price of a bond relative to its face value, the higher the interest rate.

Bonds in the real world are more complicated than the piece of paper in our example, but their structure is basically the same. They have a face value (usually an amount between $1,000 and $100,000) and a maturity date. The maturity date might be three months from the date of issue; it might be 30 years.

Whatever the period until it matures, and whatever the face value of the bond may be, its issuer will attempt to sell the bond at the highest possible price. Buyers of bonds will seek the lowest prices they can obtain. Newly issued bonds are generally sold in auctions. Potential buyers bid for the bonds, which are sold to the highest bidders. The lower the price of the bond relative to its face value, the higher the interest rate.

Both private firms and government entities issue bonds as a way of raising funds. The original buyer need not hold the bond until maturity. Bonds can be resold at any time, but the price the bond will fetch at the time of resale will vary depending on conditions in the economy and the financial markets.

Figure 16.1 illustrates the market for bonds. Their price is determined by demand and supply. Buyers of newly issued bonds are, in effect, lenders. Sellers of newly issued bonds are borrowers—recall that corporations, the federal government, and other institutions sell bonds when they want to borrow money. Once a newly issued bond has been sold, its owner can resell it; a bond may change hands several times before it matures.

Bonds are not exactly the same sort of product as, say, broccoli or some other good or service. Can we expect bonds to have the same kind of downward-sloping demand curves and upward-sloping supply curves we encounter for ordinary goods and services? Yes. Consider demand. At lower prices, bonds pay higher interest. That makes them more attractive to buyers of bonds and thus increases the quantity demanded. On the other hand, lower prices mean higher costs to borrowers—suppliers of bonds—and should reduce the quantity supplied. Thus, the negative relationship between price and quantity demanded and the positive relationship between price and quantity supplied suggested by conventional demand and supply curves holds true in the market for bonds.

If the quantity of bonds demanded is not equal to the quantity of bonds supplied, the price will adjust almost instantaneously to balance the two. Bond prices are perfectly flexible in that they change immediately to balance demand and supply. Suppose, for example, that the initial price of bonds is $950, as shown by the intersection of the demand and supply curves in Figure 16.1. We will assume that all bonds have equal risk and a face value of $1,000 and that they mature in one year. Now suppose that borrowers increase their borrowing by offering to sell more bonds at every interest rate. This increases the supply of bonds: the supply curve shifts to the right from S_1 to S_2. That, in turn, lowers the equilibrium price of bonds—to $900 in Figure 16.1. The lower price for bonds means a higher interest rate.

face value of a bond

The amount the issuer of a bond will have to pay on the maturity date.

maturity date

The date when a bond matures, or comes due.

interest rate

Payment made for the use of money, expressed as a percentage of the amount borrowed.

FIGURE 16.1 The Bond Market

The equilibrium price for bonds is determined where the demand and supply curves intersect. The initial solution here is a price of $950, implying an interest rate of 5.3%. An increase in borrowing, all other things equal, increases the supply of bonds to S_2 and forces the price of bonds down to $900. The interest rate rises to 11.1%.

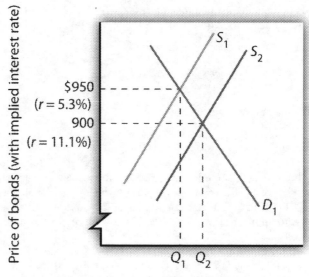

The Bond Market and Macroeconomic Performance

The connection between the bond market and the economy derives from the way interest rates affect aggregate demand. For example, investment is one component of aggregate demand, and interest rates affect investment. Firms are less likely to acquire new capital (that is, plant and equipment) if interest rates are high; they're more likely to add capital if interest rates are low.[1]

If bond prices fall, interest rates go up. Higher interest rates tend to discourage investment, so aggregate demand will fall. A fall in aggregate demand, other things unchanged, will mean fewer jobs and less total output than would have been the case with lower rates of interest. In contrast, an increase in the price of bonds lowers interest rates and makes investment in new capital more attractive. That change may boost investment and thus boost aggregate demand.

Figure 16.2 shows how an event in the bond market can stimulate changes in the economy's output and price level. In Panel (a), an increase in demand for bonds raises bond prices. Interest rates thus fall. Lower interest rates increase the quantity of investment demanded, shifting the aggregate demand curve to the right, from AD_1 to AD_2 in Panel (b). Real GDP rises from Y_1 to Y_2; the price level rises from P_1 to P_2. In Panel (c), an increase in the supply of bonds pushes bond prices down. Interest rates rise. The quantity of investment is likely to fall, shifting aggregate demand to the left, from AD_1 to AD_2 in Panel (d). Output and the price level fall from Y_1 to Y_2 and from P_1 to P_2, respectively. Assuming other determinants of aggregate demand remain unchanged, higher interest rates will tend to reduce aggregate demand and lower interest rates will tend to increase aggregate demand.

In thinking about the impact of changes in interest rates on aggregate demand, we must remember that some events that change aggregate demand can affect interest rates. We will examine those events in subsequent chapters. Our focus in this chapter is on the way in which events that originate in financial markets affect aggregate demand.

FIGURE 16.2 Bond Prices and Macroeconomic Activity

An increase in the demand for bonds to D_2 in Panel (a) raises the price of bonds to P^b_2, which lowers interest rates and boosts investment. That increases aggregate demand to AD_2 in Panel (b); real GDP rises to Y_2 and the price level rises to P_2. An increase in the supply of bonds to S_2 lowers bond prices to P^b_2 in Panel (c) and raises interest rates. The higher interest rate, taken by itself, is likely to cause a reduction in investment and aggregate demand. AD_1 falls to AD_2, real GDP falls to Y_2, and the price level falls to P_2 in Panel (d).

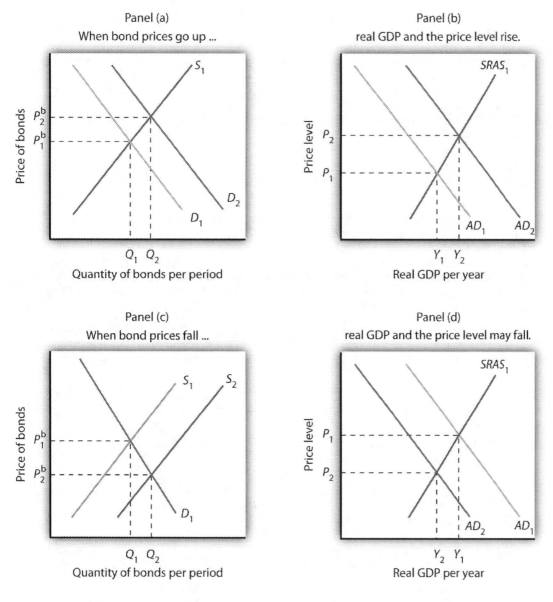

1.2   Foreign Exchange Markets

Another financial market that influences macroeconomic variables is the **foreign exchange market**, a market in which currencies of different countries are traded for one another. Since changes in exports and imports affect aggregate demand and thus real GDP and the price level, the market in which currencies are traded has tremendous importance in the economy.

Foreigners who want to purchase goods and services or assets in the United States must typically pay for them with dollars. United States purchasers of foreign goods must generally make the purchase in a foreign currency. An Egyptian family, for example, exchanges Egyptian pounds for dollars in order to pay for admission to Disney World. A German financial investor purchases dollars to buy U.S. government bonds. A family from the United States visiting India, on the other hand, needs to obtain Indian rupees in order to make purchases there. A U.S. bank wanting to purchase assets in Mexico City first purchases pesos. These transactions are accomplished in the foreign exchange market.

The foreign exchange market is not a single location in which currencies are traded. The term refers instead to the entire array of institutions through which people buy and sell currencies. It

foreign exchange market

A market in which currencies of different countries are traded for one another.

includes a hotel desk clerk who provides currency exchange as a service to hotel guests, brokers who arrange currency exchanges worth billions of dollars, and governments and central banks that exchange currencies. Major currency dealers are linked by computers so that they can track currency exchanges all over the world.

The Exchange Rate

A country's exchange rate is the price of its currency in terms of another currency or currencies. On December 12, 2008, for example, the dollar traded for 91.13 Japanese yen, 0.75 euros, 10.11 South African rands, and 13.51 Mexican pesos. There are as many exchange rates for the dollar as there are countries whose currencies exchange for the dollar—roughly 200 of them.

trade-weighted exchange rate

An index of exchange rates.

Economists summarize the movement of exchange rates with a **trade-weighted exchange rate**, which is an index of exchange rates. To calculate a trade-weighted exchange rate index for the U.S. dollar, we select a group of countries, weight the price of the dollar in each country's currency by the amount of trade between that country and the United States, and then report the price of the dollar based on that trade-weighted average. Because trade-weighted exchange rates are so widely used in reporting currency values, they are often referred to as exchange rates themselves. We will follow that convention in this text.

Determining Exchange Rates

The rates at which most currencies exchange for one another are determined by demand and supply. How does the model of demand and supply operate in the foreign exchange market?

The demand curve for dollars relates the number of dollars buyers want to buy in any period to the exchange rate. An increase in the exchange rate means it takes more foreign currency to buy a dollar. A higher exchange rate, in turn, makes U.S. goods and services more expensive for foreign buyers and reduces the quantity they will demand. That is likely to reduce the quantity of dollars they demand. Foreigners thus will demand fewer dollars as the price of the dollar—the exchange rate—rises. Consequently, the demand curve for dollars is downward sloping, as in Figure 16.3.

FIGURE 16.3 Determining an Exchange Rate

The equilibrium exchange rate is the rate at which the quantity of dollars demanded equals the quantity supplied. Here, equilibrium occurs at exchange rate *E*, at which *Q* dollars are exchanged per period.

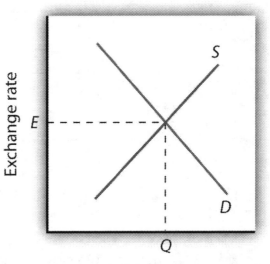

The supply curve for dollars emerges from a similar process. When people and firms in the United States purchase goods, services, or assets in foreign countries, they must purchase the currency of those countries first. They supply dollars in exchange for foreign currency. The supply of dollars on the foreign exchange market thus reflects the degree to which people in the United States are buying foreign money at various exchange rates. A higher exchange rate means that a dollar trades for more foreign currency. In effect, the higher rate makes foreign goods and services cheaper to U.S. buyers, so U.S. consumers will purchase more foreign goods and services. People will thus supply more dollars at a higher exchange rate; we expect the supply curve for dollars to be upward sloping, as suggested in Figure 16.3.

In addition to private individuals and firms that participate in the foreign exchange market, most governments participate as well. A government might seek to lower its exchange rate by selling its currency; it might seek to raise the rate by buying its currency. Although governments often participate in foreign exchange markets, they generally represent a very small share of these markets. The most important traders are private buyers and sellers of currencies.

Exchange Rates and Macroeconomic Performance

People purchase a country's currency for two quite different reasons: to purchase goods or services in that country, or to purchase the assets of that country—its money, its capital, its stocks, its bonds, or its real estate. Both of these motives must be considered to understand why demand and supply in the foreign exchange market may change.

One thing that can cause the price of the dollar to rise, for example, is a reduction in bond prices in American markets. Figure 16.4 illustrates the effect of this change. Suppose the supply of bonds in the U.S. bond market increases from S_1 to S_2 in Panel (a). Bond prices will drop. Lower bond prices mean higher interest rates. Foreign financial investors, attracted by the opportunity to earn higher returns in the United States, will increase their demand for dollars on the foreign exchange market in order to purchase U.S. bonds. Panel (b) shows that the demand curve for dollars shifts from D_1 to D_2. Simultaneously, U.S. financial investors, attracted by the higher interest rates at home, become less likely to make financial investments abroad and thus supply fewer dollars to exchange markets. The fall in the price of U.S. bonds shifts the supply curve for dollars on the foreign exchange market from S_1 to S_2, and the exchange rate rises from E_1 to E_2.

FIGURE 16.4 Shifts in Demand and Supply for Dollars on the Foreign Exchange Market

In Panel (a), an increase in the supply of bonds lowers bond prices to P^b_2 (and thus raises interest rates). Higher interest rates boost the demand and reduce the supply for dollars, increasing the exchange rate in Panel (b) to E_2. These developments in the bond and foreign exchange markets are likely to lead to a reduction in net exports and in investment, reducing aggregate demand from AD_1 to AD_2 in Panel (c). The price level in the economy falls to P_2, and real GDP falls from Y_1 to Y_2.

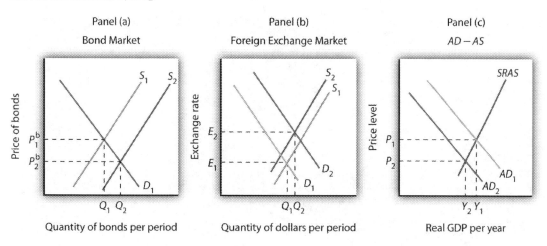

The higher exchange rate makes U.S. goods and services more expensive to foreigners, so it reduces exports. It makes foreign goods cheaper for U.S. buyers, so it increases imports. Net exports thus fall, reducing aggregate demand. Panel (c) shows that output falls from Y_1 to Y_2; the price level falls from P_1 to P_2. This development in the foreign exchange market reinforces the impact of higher interest rates we observed in Figure 16.2, Panels (c) and (d). They not only reduce investment—they reduce net exports as well.

KEY TAKEAWAYS

- A bond represents a borrower's debt; bond prices are determined by demand and supply.
- The interest rate on a bond is negatively related to the price of the bond. As the price of a bond increases, the interest rate falls.
- An increase in the interest rate tends to decrease the quantity of investment demanded and, hence, to decrease aggregate demand. A decrease in the interest rate increases the quantity of investment demanded and aggregate demand.
- The demand for dollars on foreign exchange markets represents foreign demand for U.S. goods, services, and assets. The supply of dollars on foreign exchange markets represents U.S. demand for foreign goods, services, and assets. The demand for and the supply of dollars determine the exchange rate.
- A rise in U.S. interest rates will increase the demand for dollars and decrease the supply of dollars on foreign exchange markets. As a result, the exchange rate will increase and aggregate demand will decrease. A fall in U.S. interest rates will have the opposite effect.

TRY IT!

Suppose the supply of bonds in the U.S. market decreases. Show and explain the effects on the bond and foreign exchange markets. Use the aggregate demand/aggregate supply framework to show and explain the effects on investment, net exports, real GDP, and the price level.

Case in Point

Bill Gross's *Mea Culpa*

In October 2011, bond fund manager Bill Gross sent out an extraordinary open letter titled "Mea Culpa." He was taking the blame for the poor performance of Pimco Total Return Bond Fund, the huge fund he manages. After years of stellar performance, what had gone wrong?

Earlier in 2011, Mr. Gross announced that he would avoid U.S. Treasury bonds. He assumed that as the U.S. and other countries' economies recovered, interest rates would begin to rise and, hence, U.S. bond prices would fall. When Mr. Gross pulled out of U.S. Treasuries, he used some of the cash to buy other types of debt, such as that of emerging markets. He also held onto some cash. He warned others to shun Treasuries as well.

However, as the financial situation in Europe weakened over worries about government debt in various European countries—starting with Greece and then spilling over to Portugal, Spain, Italy, and others—investors around the world flocked toward Treasuries, pushing Treasury bond prices up. It was a rally that Mr. Gross's customers missed.

From where did the financial investors get the funds to buy Treasuries? In part, these funds were obtained from some of the same types of bonds that were then in the Pimco fund portfolio. As a result, the prices of bonds in the Pimco fund fell.

In the letter, Mr. Gross wrote, "The simple fact is that the portfolio at midyear was positioned for what we call a 'New Normal' developed world economy—2% real growth and 2% inflation. When growth estimates quickly changed it was obvious that I had misjudged the fly ball: E-CF or for nonbaseball aficionados—error center-field." In the fall of 2011, he shifted gears and began buying U.S. Treasuries, assuming that a weak global economy would keep interest rates low. He was foiled again, as interest rates started to rise a bit.

In the end, 2011 turned out to be a bad year for the fund, ranking poorly compared to its peers. But after many successful years, it retained its five-star rating by Morningstar in 2012. We must wait to see whether Mr. Gross will get his groove back. In the letter, he concluded, 'There is no 'quit' in me or anyone else on the Pimco premises. The early morning and even midnight hours have gone up, not down, to match the increasing complexity of the global financial markets. The competitive fire burns even hotter. I/we respect our competition but we want to squash them each and every day…"

Source: "Bill Gross Apologizes to Pimco Fund Owners for 'Bad Year,'" Los Angeles Times, October 14, 2011, online version.

ANSWER TO TRY IT! PROBLEM

If the supply of bonds decreases from S_1 to S_2, bond prices will rise from P^b_1 to P^b_2, as shown in Panel (a). Higher bond prices mean lower interest rates. Lower interest rates in the United States will make financial investments in the United States less attractive to foreigners. As a result, their demand for dollars will decrease from D_1 to D_2, as shown in Panel (b). Similarly, U.S. financial investors will look abroad for higher returns and thus supply more dollars to foreign exchange markets, shifting the supply curve from S_1 to S_2. Thus, the exchange rate will decrease. The quantity of investment rises due to the lower interest rates. Net exports rise because the lower exchange rate makes U.S. goods and services more attractive to foreigners, thus increasing exports, and makes foreign goods less attractive to U.S. buyers, thus reducing imports. Increases in investment and net exports imply a rightward shift in the aggregate demand curve from AD_1 to AD_2. Real GDP and the price level increase.

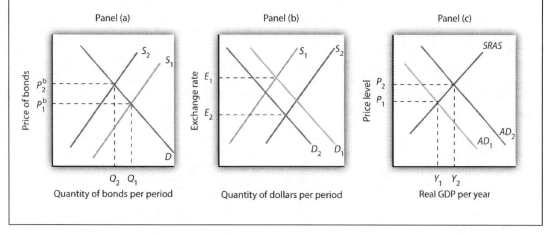

2. DEMAND, SUPPLY, AND EQUILIBRIUM IN THE MONEY MARKET

LEARNING OBJECTIVES

1. **Explain the motives for holding money and relate them to the interest rate that could be earned from holding alternative assets, such as bonds.**
2. **Draw a money demand curve and explain how changes in other variables may lead to shifts in the money demand curve.**
3. **Illustrate and explain the notion of equilibrium in the money market.**
4. **Use graphs to explain how changes in money demand or money supply are related to changes in the bond market, in interest rates, in aggregate demand, and in real GDP and the price level.**

In this section we will explore the link between money markets, bond markets, and interest rates. We first look at the demand for money. The demand curve for money is derived like any other demand curve, by examining the relationship between the "price" of money (which, we will see, is the interest rate) and the quantity demanded, holding all other determinants unchanged. We then link the demand for money to the concept of money supply developed in the last chapter, to determine the equilibrium rate of interest. In turn, we show how changes in interest rates affect the macroeconomy.

2.1 The Demand for Money

In deciding how much money to hold, people make a choice about how to hold their wealth. How much wealth shall be held as money and how much as other assets? For a given amount of wealth, the answer to this question will depend on the relative costs and benefits of holding money versus other assets. The **demand for money** is the relationship between the quantity of money people want to hold and the factors that determine that quantity.

To simplify our analysis, we will assume there are only two ways to hold wealth: as money in a checking account, or as funds in a bond market mutual fund that purchases long-term bonds on behalf of its subscribers. A bond fund is not money. Some money deposits earn interest, but the return on these accounts is generally lower than what could be obtained in a bond fund. The advantage of checking accounts is that they are highly liquid and can thus be spent easily. We will think of the demand for money as a curve that represents the outcomes of choices between the greater liquidity of money deposits and the higher interest rates that can be earned by holding a bond fund. The difference between the interest rates paid on money deposits and the interest return available from bonds is the cost of holding money.

Motives for Holding Money

One reason people hold their assets as money is so that they can purchase goods and services. The money held for the purchase of goods and services may be for everyday transactions such as buying groceries or paying the rent, or it may be kept on hand for contingencies such as having the funds available to pay to have the car fixed or to pay for a trip to the doctor.

The **transactions demand for money** is money people hold to pay for goods and services they anticipate buying. When you carry money in your purse or wallet to buy a movie ticket or maintain a checking account balance so you can purchase groceries later in the month, you are holding the money as part of your transactions demand for money.

The money people hold for contingencies represents their **precautionary demand for money**. Money held for precautionary purposes may include checking account balances kept for possible home repairs or health-care needs. People do not know precisely when the need for such expenditures will occur, but they can prepare for them by holding money so that they'll have it available when the need arises.

People also hold money for speculative purposes. Bond prices fluctuate constantly. As a result, holders of bonds not only earn interest but experience gains or losses in the value of their assets. Bondholders enjoy gains when bond prices rise and suffer losses when bond prices fall. Because of this, expectations play an important role as a determinant of the demand for bonds. Holding bonds is one alternative to holding money, so these same expectations can affect the demand for money.

John Maynard Keynes, who was an enormously successful speculator in bond markets himself, suggested that bondholders who anticipate a drop in bond prices will try to sell their bonds ahead of the price drop in order to avoid this loss in asset value. Selling a bond means converting it to money. Keynes referred to the **speculative demand for money** as the money held in response to concern that bond prices and the prices of other financial assets might change.

Of course, money is money. One cannot sort through someone's checking account and locate which funds are held for transactions and which funds are there because the owner of the account is worried about a drop in bond prices or is taking a precaution. We distinguish money held for different motives in order to understand how the quantity of money demanded will be affected by a key determinant of the demand for money: the interest rate.

Interest Rates and the Demand for Money

The quantity of money people hold to pay for transactions and to satisfy precautionary and speculative demand is likely to vary with the interest rates they can earn from alternative assets such as bonds. When interest rates rise relative to the rates that can be earned on money deposits, people hold less money. When interest rates fall, people hold more money. The logic of these conclusions about the money people hold and interest rates depends on the people's motives for holding money.

The quantity of money households want to hold varies according to their income and the interest rate; different average quantities of money held can satisfy their transactions and precautionary demands for money. To see why, suppose a household earns and spends $3,000 per month. It spends an equal amount of money each day. For a month with 30 days, that is $100 per day. One way the household could manage this spending would be to leave the money in a checking account, which we will assume pays zero interest. The household would thus have $3,000 in the checking account when the month begins, $2,900 at the end of the first day, $1,500 halfway through the month, and zero at the end of the last day of the month. Averaging the daily balances, we find that the quantity of money the household demands equals $1,500. This approach to money management, which we will call the "cash approach," has the virtue of simplicity, but the household will earn no interest on its funds.

Consider an alternative money management approach that permits the same pattern of spending. At the beginning of the month, the household deposits $1,000 in its checking account and the other $2,000 in a bond fund. Assume the bond fund pays 1% interest per month, or an annual interest rate of 12.7%. After 10 days, the money in the checking account is exhausted, and the household withdraws another $1,000 from the bond fund for the next 10 days. On the 20th day, the final $1,000 from the bond fund goes into the checking account. With this strategy, the household has an average daily balance of $500, which is the quantity of money it demands. Let us call this money management strategy the "bond fund approach."

Remember that both approaches allow the household to spend $3,000 per month, $100 per day. The cash approach requires a quantity of money demanded of $1,500, while the bond fund approach lowers this quantity to $500.

The bond fund approach generates some interest income. The household has $1,000 in the fund for 10 days (1/3 of a month) and $1,000 for 20 days (2/3 of a month). With an interest rate of 1% per month, the household earns $10 in interest each month ([$1,000 × 0.01 × 1/3] + [$1,000 × 0.01 × 2/3]). The disadvantage of the bond fund, of course, is that it requires more attention—$1,000 must be transferred from the fund twice each month. There may also be fees associated with the transfers.

Of course, the bond fund strategy we have examined here is just one of many. The household could begin each month with $1,500 in the checking account and $1,500 in the bond fund, transferring $1,500 to the checking account midway through the month. This strategy requires one less transfer, but it also generates less interest—$7.50 (= $1,500 × 0.01 × 1/2). With this strategy, the household demands a quantity of money of $750. The household could also maintain a much smaller average quantity of money in its checking account and keep more in its bond fund. For simplicity, we can think of any strategy that involves transferring money in and out of a bond fund or another interest-earning asset as a bond fund strategy.

Which approach should the household use? That is a choice each household must make—it is a question of weighing the interest a bond fund strategy creates against the hassle and possible fees associated with the transfers it requires. Our example does not yield a clear-cut choice for any one household, but we can make some generalizations about its implications.

First, a household is more likely to adopt a bond fund strategy when the interest rate is higher. At low interest rates, a household does not sacrifice much income by pursuing the simpler cash strategy. As the interest rate rises, a bond fund strategy becomes more attractive. That means that the higher the interest rate, the lower the quantity of money demanded.

Second, people are more likely to use a bond fund strategy when the cost of transferring funds is lower. The creation of savings plans, which began in the 1970s and 1980s, that allowed easy transfer of funds between interest-earning assets and checkable deposits tended to reduce the demand for money.

Some money deposits, such as savings accounts and money market deposit accounts, pay interest. In evaluating the choice between holding assets as some form of money or in other forms such as bonds, households will look at the differential between what those funds pay and what they could earn in the bond market. A higher interest rate in the bond market is likely to increase this differential; a lower interest rate will reduce it. An increase in the spread between rates on money deposits and the interest rate in the bond market reduces the quantity of money demanded; a reduction in the spread increases the quantity of money demanded.

Firms, too, must determine how to manage their earnings and expenditures. However, instead of worrying about $3,000 per month, even a relatively small firm may be concerned about $3,000,000 per month. Rather than facing the difference of $10 versus $7.50 in interest earnings used in our household example, this small firm would face a difference of $2,500 per month ($10,000 versus $7,500). For very large firms such as Toyota or AT&T, interest rate differentials among various forms of holding their financial assets translate into millions of dollars per day.

How is the speculative demand for money related to interest rates? When financial investors believe that the prices of bonds and other assets will fall, their speculative demand for money goes up. The speculative demand for money thus depends on expectations about future changes in asset prices. Will this demand also be affected by present interest rates?

If interest rates are low, bond prices are high. It seems likely that if bond prices are high, financial investors will become concerned that bond prices might fall. That suggests that high bond prices—low interest rates—would increase the quantity of money held for speculative purposes. Conversely, if bond prices are already relatively low, it is likely that fewer financial investors will expect them to fall still further. They will hold smaller speculative balances. Economists thus expect that the quantity of money demanded for speculative reasons will vary negatively with the interest rate.

The Demand Curve for Money

We have seen that the transactions, precautionary, and speculative demands for money vary negatively with the interest rate. Putting those three sources of demand together, we can draw a demand curve for money to show how the interest rate affects the total quantity of money people hold. The **demand curve for money** shows the quantity of money demanded at each interest rate, all other things unchanged. Such a curve is shown in Figure 16.5. An increase in the interest rate reduces the quantity of money demanded. A reduction in the interest rate increases the quantity of money demanded.

FIGURE 16.5 The Demand Curve for Money

The demand curve for money shows the quantity of money demanded at each interest rate. Its downward slope expresses the negative relationship between the quantity of money demanded and the interest rate.

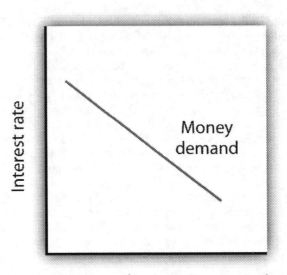

The relationship between interest rates and the quantity of money demanded is an application of the law of demand. If we think of the alternative to holding money as holding bonds, then the interest rate—or the differential between the interest rate in the bond market and the interest paid on money deposits—represents the price of holding money. As is the case with all goods and services, an increase in price reduces the quantity demanded.

Other Determinants of the Demand for Money

We draw the demand curve for money to show the quantity of money people will hold at each interest rate, all other determinants of money demand unchanged. A change in those "other determinants" will shift the demand for money. Among the most important variables that can shift the demand for money are the level of income and real GDP, the price level, expectations, transfer costs, and preferences.

Real GDP

A household with an income of $10,000 per month is likely to demand a larger quantity of money than a household with an income of $1,000 per month. That relationship suggests that money is a normal good: as income increases, people demand more money at each interest rate, and as income falls, they demand less.

An increase in real GDP increases incomes throughout the economy. The demand for money in the economy is therefore likely to be greater when real GDP is greater.

The Price Level

The higher the price level, the more money is required to purchase a given quantity of goods and services. All other things unchanged, the higher the price level, the greater the demand for money.

Expectations

The speculative demand for money is based on expectations about bond prices. All other things unchanged, if people expect bond prices to fall, they will increase their demand for money. If they expect bond prices to rise, they will reduce their demand for money.

The expectation that bond prices are about to change actually causes bond prices to change. If people expect bond prices to fall, for example, they will sell their bonds, exchanging them for money. That will shift the supply curve for bonds to the right, thus lowering their price. The importance of expectations in moving markets can lead to a self-fulfilling prophecy.

Expectations about future price levels also affect the demand for money. The expectation of a higher price level means that people expect the money they are holding to fall in value. Given that expectation, they are likely to hold less of it in anticipation of a jump in prices.

Expectations about future price levels play a particularly important role during periods of hyperinflation. If prices rise very rapidly and people expect them to continue rising, people are likely to try to reduce the amount of money they hold, knowing that it will fall in value as it sits in their wallets or their bank accounts. Toward the end of the great German hyperinflation of the early 1920s, prices were doubling as often as three times a day. Under those circumstances, people tried not to hold money even for a few minutes—within the space of eight hours money would lose half its value!

Transfer Costs

For a given level of expenditures, reducing the quantity of money demanded requires more frequent transfers between nonmoney and money deposits. As the cost of such transfers rises, some consumers will choose to make fewer of them. They will therefore increase the quantity of money they demand. In general, the demand for money will increase as it becomes more expensive to transfer between money and nonmoney accounts. The demand for money will fall if transfer costs decline. In recent years, transfer costs have fallen, leading to a decrease in money demand.

Preferences

Preferences also play a role in determining the demand for money. Some people place a high value on having a considerable amount of money on hand. For others, this may not be important.

Household attitudes toward risk are another aspect of preferences that affect money demand. As we have seen, bonds pay higher interest rates than money deposits, but holding bonds entails a risk that bond prices might fall. There is also a chance that the issuer of a bond will default, that is, will not pay the amount specified on the bond to bondholders; indeed, bond issuers may end up paying nothing at all. A money deposit, such as a savings deposit, might earn a lower yield, but it is a safe yield. People's attitudes about the trade-off between risk and yields affect the degree to which they hold their wealth as money. Heightened concerns about risk in the last half of 2008 led many households to increase their demand for money.

Figure 16.6 shows an increase in the demand for money. Such an increase could result from a higher real GDP, a higher price level, a change in expectations, an increase in transfer costs, or a change in preferences.

FIGURE 16.6   An Increase in Money Demand

An increase in real GDP, the price level, or transfer costs, for example, will increase the quantity of money demanded at any interest rate r, increasing the demand for money from D_1 to D_2. The quantity of money demanded at interest rate r rises from M to M'. The reverse of any such events would reduce the quantity of money demanded at every interest rate, shifting the demand curve to the left.

Quantity of money per period

2.2   The Supply of Money

The **supply curve of money** shows the relationship between the quantity of money supplied and the market interest rate, all other determinants of supply unchanged. We have learned that the Fed, through its open-market operations, determines the total quantity of reserves in the banking system. We shall assume that banks increase the money supply in fixed proportion to their reserves. Because the quantity of reserves is determined by Federal Reserve policy, we draw the supply curve of money in Figure 16.7 as a vertical line, determined by the Fed's monetary policies. In drawing the supply curve of money as a vertical line, we are assuming the money supply does not depend on the interest rate. Changing the quantity of reserves and hence the money supply is an example of monetary policy.

FIGURE 16.7   The Supply Curve of Money

We assume that the quantity of money supplied in the economy is determined as a fixed multiple of the quantity of bank reserves, which is determined by the Fed. The supply curve of money is a vertical line at that quantity.

2.3   Equilibrium in the Market for Money

The **money market** is the interaction among institutions through which money is supplied to individuals, firms, and other institutions that demand money. **Money market equilibrium** occurs at the interest rate at which the quantity of money demanded is equal to the quantity of money supplied. Figure 16.8 combines demand and supply curves for money to illustrate equilibrium in the market for money. With a stock of money (M), the equilibrium interest rate is r.

FIGURE 16.8   Money Market Equilibrium

The market for money is in equilibrium if the quantity of money demanded is equal to the quantity of money supplied. Here, equilibrium occurs at interest rate r.

2.4   Effects of Changes in the Money Market

A shift in money demand or supply will lead to a change in the equilibrium interest rate. Let's look at the effects of such changes on the economy.

Changes in Money Demand

Suppose that the money market is initially in equilibrium at r_1 with supply curve S and a demand curve D_1 as shown in Panel (a) of Figure 16.9. Now suppose that there is a decrease in money demand, all other things unchanged. A decrease in money demand could result from a decrease in the cost of transferring between money and nonmoney deposits, from a change in expectations, or from a change in preferences.[2] Panel (a) shows that the money demand curve shifts to the left to D_2. We can see that the interest rate will fall to r_2. To see why the interest rate falls, we recall that if people want to hold less money, then they will want to hold more bonds. Thus, Panel (b) shows that the demand for bonds increases. The higher price of bonds means lower interest rates; lower interest rates restore equilibrium in the money market.

FIGURE 16.9   A Decrease in the Demand for Money

A decrease in the demand for money due to a change in transactions costs, preferences, or expectations, as shown in Panel (a), will be accompanied by an increase in the demand for bonds as shown in Panel (b), and a fall in the interest rate. The fall in the interest rate will cause a rightward shift in the aggregate demand curve from AD_1 to AD_2, as shown in Panel (c). As a result, real GDP and the price level rise.

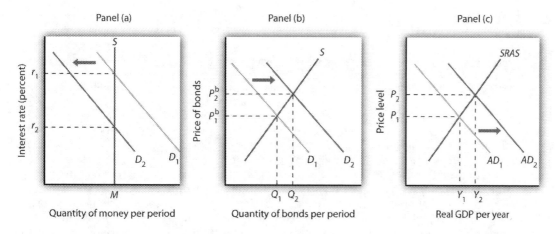

Lower interest rates in turn increase the quantity of investment. They also stimulate net exports, as lower interest rates lead to a lower exchange rate. The aggregate demand curve shifts to the right as shown in Panel (c) from AD_1 to AD_2. Given the short-run aggregate supply curve SRAS, the economy moves to a higher real GDP and a higher price level.

An increase in money demand due to a change in expectations, preferences, or transactions costs that make people want to hold more money at each interest rate will have the opposite effect. The money demand curve will shift to the right and the demand for bonds will shift to the left. The resulting higher interest rate will lead to a lower quantity of investment. Also, higher interest rates will lead to a higher exchange rate and depress net exports. Thus, the aggregate demand curve will shift to the left. All other things unchanged, real GDP and the price level will fall.

Changes in the Money Supply

Now suppose the market for money is in equilibrium and the Fed changes the money supply. All other things unchanged, how will this change in the money supply affect the equilibrium interest rate and aggregate demand, real GDP, and the price level?

Suppose the Fed conducts open-market operations in which it buys bonds. This is an example of expansionary monetary policy. The impact of Fed bond purchases is illustrated in Panel (a) of Figure 16.10. The Fed's purchase of bonds shifts the demand curve for bonds to the right, raising bond prices to P^b_2. As we learned, when the Fed buys bonds, the supply of money increases. Panel (b) of Figure 16.10 shows an economy with a money supply of M, which is in equilibrium at an interest rate of r_1. Now suppose the bond purchases by the Fed as shown in Panel (a) result in an increase in the money supply to M'; that policy change shifts the supply curve for money to the right to S_2. At the original interest rate r_1, people do not wish to hold the newly supplied money; they would prefer to hold nonmoney assets. To reestablish equilibrium in the money market, the interest rate must fall to increase the quantity of money demanded. In the economy shown, the interest rate must fall to r_2 to increase the quantity of money demanded to M'.

FIGURE 16.10 An Increase in the Money Supply

The Fed increases the money supply by buying bonds, increasing the demand for bonds in Panel (a) from D_1 to D_2 and the price of bonds to P^b_2. This corresponds to an increase in the money supply to M' in Panel (b). The interest rate must fall to r_2 to achieve equilibrium. The lower interest rate leads to an increase in investment and net exports, which shifts the aggregate demand curve from AD_1 to AD_2 in Panel (c). Real GDP and the price level rise.

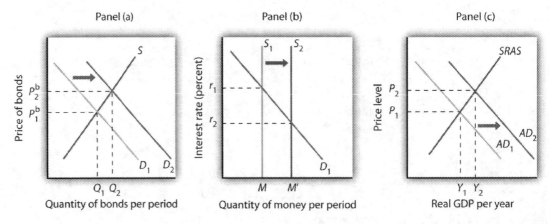

The reduction in interest rates required to restore equilibrium to the market for money after an increase in the money supply is achieved in the bond market. The increase in bond prices lowers interest rates, which will increase the quantity of money people demand. Lower interest rates will stimulate investment and net exports, via changes in the foreign exchange market, and cause the aggregate demand curve to shift to the right, as shown in Panel (c), from AD_1 to AD_2. Given the short-run aggregate supply curve $SRAS$, the economy moves to a higher real GDP and a higher price level.

Open-market operations in which the Fed sells bonds—that is, a contractionary monetary policy—will have the opposite effect. When the Fed sells bonds, the supply curve of bonds shifts to the right and the price of bonds falls. The bond sales lead to a reduction in the money supply, causing the money supply curve to shift to the left and raising the equilibrium interest rate. Higher interest rates lead to a shift in the aggregate demand curve to the left.

As we have seen in looking at both changes in demand for and in supply of money, the process of achieving equilibrium in the money market works in tandem with the achievement of equilibrium in the bond market. The interest rate determined by money market equilibrium is consistent with the interest rate achieved in the bond market.

KEY TAKEAWAYS

- People hold money in order to buy goods and services (transactions demand), to have it available for contingencies (precautionary demand), and in order to avoid possible drops in the value of other assets such as bonds (speculative demand).
- The higher the interest rate, the lower the quantities of money demanded for transactions, for precautionary, and for speculative purposes. The lower the interest rate, the higher the quantities of money demanded for these purposes.
- The demand for money will change as a result of a change in real GDP, the price level, transfer costs, expectations, or preferences.
- We assume that the supply of money is determined by the Fed. The supply curve for money is thus a vertical line. Money market equilibrium occurs at the interest rate at which the quantity of money demanded equals the quantity of money supplied.
- All other things unchanged, a shift in money demand or supply will lead to a change in the equilibrium interest rate and therefore to changes in the level of real GDP and the price level.

In 2005 the Fed was concerned about the possibility that the United States was moving into an inflationary gap, and it adopted a contractionary monetary policy as a result. Draw a four-panel graph showing this policy and its expected results. In Panel (a), use the model of aggregate demand and aggregate supply to illustrate an economy with an inflationary gap. In Panel (b), show how the Fed's policy will affect the market for bonds. In Panel (c), show how it will affect the demand for and supply of money. In Panel (d), show how it will affect the exchange rate. Finally, return to Panel (a) and incorporate these developments into your analysis of aggregate demand and aggregate supply, and show how the Fed's policy will affect real GDP and the price level in the short run.

Case in Point

Money in Today's World

The models of the money and bond markets presented in this chapter suggest that the Fed can control the interest rate by deciding on a money supply that would lead to the desired equilibrium interest rate in the money market. Yet, Fed policy announcements typically focus on what it wants the federal funds rate to be with scant attention to the money supply. Whereas throughout the 1990s, the Fed would announce a target federal funds rate and also indicate an expected change in the money supply, in 2000, when legislation requiring it to do so expired, it abandoned the practice of setting money supply targets.

Why the shift? The factors that have made focusing on the money supply as a policy target difficult for the past 25 years are first banking deregulation in the 1980s followed by financial innovations associated with technological changes—in particular the maturation of electronic payment and transfer mechanisms—thereafter.

Before the 1980s, M1 was a fairly reliable measure of the money people held, primarily for transactions. To buy things, one used cash, checks written on demand deposits, or traveler's checks. The Fed could thus use reliable estimates of the money demand curve to predict what the money supply would need to be in order to bring about a certain interest rate in the money market.

Legislation in the early 1980s allowed for money market deposit accounts (MMDAs), which are essentially interest-bearing savings accounts on which checks can be written. MMDAs are part of M2. Shortly after, other forms of payments for transactions developed or became more common. For example, credit and debit card use has mushroomed (from $10.8 billion in 1990 to $30 billion in 2000), and people can pay their credit card bills, electronically or with paper checks, from accounts that are part of either M1 or M2. Another innovation of the last 20 years is the automatic transfer service (ATS) that allows consumers to move money between checking and savings accounts at an ATM machine, or online, or through prearranged agreements with their financial institutions. While we take these methods of payment for granted today, they did not exist before 1980 because of restrictive banking legislation and the lack of technological know-how. Indeed, before 1980, being able to pay bills from accounts that earned interest was unheard of.

Further blurring the lines between M1 and M2 has been the development and growing popularity of what are called retail sweep programs. Since 1994, banks have been using retail-sweeping software to dynamically reclassify balances as either checking account balances (part of M1) or MMDAs (part of M2). They do this to avoid reserve requirements on checking accounts. The software not only moves the funds but also ensures that the bank does not exceed the legal limit of six reclassifications in any month. In the last 10 years these retail sweeps rose from zero to nearly the size of M1 itself!

Such changes in the ways people pay for transactions and banks do their business have led economists to think about new definitions of money that would better track what is actually used for the purposes behind the money demand curve. One notion is called MZM, which stands for "money zero maturity." The idea behind MZM is that people can easily use any deposits that do not have specified maturity terms to pay for transactions, as these accounts are quite liquid, regardless of what classification of money they fall into. Some research shows that using MZM allows for a stable picture of the money market. Until more agreement has been reached, though, we should expect the Fed to continue to downplay the role of the money supply in its policy deliberations and to continue to announce its intentions in terms of the federal funds rate.

Source: Pedre Teles and Ruilin Zhou, "A Stable Money Demand: Looking for the Right Monetary Aggregate," Federal Reserve Bank of Chicago Economic Perspectives 29 (First Quarter, 2005): 50–59.

In Panel (a), with the aggregate demand curve AD_1, short-run aggregate supply curve $SRAS$, and long-run aggregate supply curve $LRAS$, the economy has an inflationary gap of $Y_1 - Y_P$. The contractionary monetary policy means that the Fed sells bonds—a rightward shift of the bond supply curve in Panel (b), which decreases the money supply—as shown by a leftward shift in the money supply curve in Panel (c). In Panel (b), we see that the price of bonds falls, and in Panel (c) that the interest rate rises. A higher interest rate will reduce the quantity of investment demanded. The higher interest rate also leads to a higher exchange rate, as shown in Panel (d), as the demand for dollars increases and the supply decreases. The higher exchange rate will lead to a decrease in net exports. As a result of these changes in financial markets, the aggregate demand curve shifts to the left to AD_2 in Panel (a). If all goes according to plan (and we will learn in the next chapter that it may not!), the new aggregate demand curve will intersect $SRAS$ and $LRAS$ at Y_P.

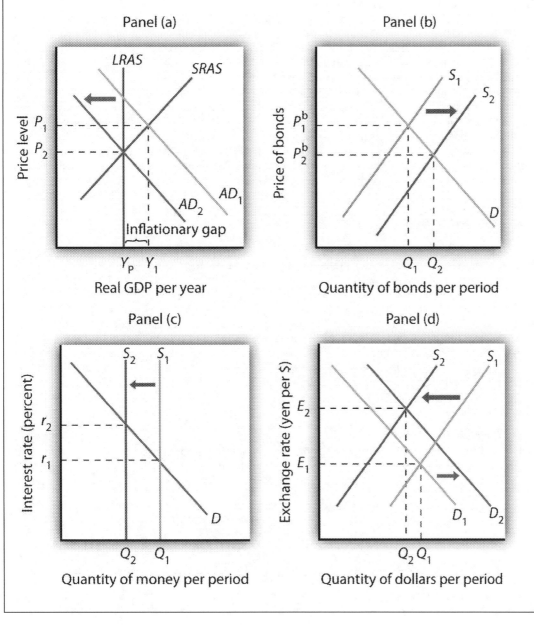

3. MONETARY POLICY IN THE UNITED STATES

In many respects, the Fed is the most powerful maker of economic policy in the United States. Congress can pass laws, but the president must execute them; the president can propose laws, but only Congress can pass them. The Fed, however, both sets and carries out monetary policy. Deliberations about fiscal policy can drag on for months, even years, but the Federal Open Market Committee (FOMC) can, behind closed doors, set monetary policy in a day—and see that policy implemented within hours. The Board of Governors can change the discount rate or reserve requirements at any time. The impact of the Fed's policies on the economy can be quite dramatic. The Fed can push interest rates up or down. It can promote a recession or an expansion. It can cause the inflation rate to rise or fall. The Fed wields enormous power.

But to what ends should all this power be directed? With what tools are the Fed's policies carried out? And what problems exist in trying to achieve the Fed's goals? This section reviews the goals of monetary policy, the tools available to the Fed in pursuing those goals, and the way in which monetary policy affects macroeconomic variables.

3.1 Goals of Monetary Policy

When we think of the goals of monetary policy, we naturally think of standards of macroeconomic performance that seem desirable—a low unemployment rate, a stable price level, and economic growth. It thus seems reasonable to conclude that the goals of monetary policy should include the maintenance of full employment, the avoidance of inflation or deflation, and the promotion of economic growth.

But these goals, each of which is desirable in itself, may conflict with one another. A monetary policy that helps to close a recessionary gap and thus promotes full employment may accelerate inflation. A monetary policy that seeks to reduce inflation may increase unemployment and weaken economic growth. You might expect that in such cases, monetary authorities would receive guidance from legislation spelling out goals for the Fed to pursue and specifying what to do when achieving one goal means not achieving another. But as we shall see, that kind of guidance does not exist.

The Federal Reserve Act

When Congress established the Federal Reserve System in 1913, it said little about the policy goals the Fed should seek. The closest it came to spelling out the goals of monetary policy was in the first paragraph of the Federal Reserve Act, the legislation that created the Fed:

> *"An Act to provide for the establishment of Federal reserve banks, to furnish an elastic currency, [to make loans to banks], to establish a more effective supervision of banking in the United States, and for other purposes."*

In short, nothing in the legislation creating the Fed anticipates that the institution will act to close recessionary or inflationary gaps, that it will seek to spur economic growth, or that it will strive to keep the price level steady. There is no guidance as to what the Fed should do when these goals conflict with one another.

The Employment Act of 1946

The first U.S. effort to specify macroeconomic goals came after World War II. The Great Depression of the 1930s had instilled in people a deep desire to prevent similar calamities in the future. That desire, coupled with the 1936 publication of John Maynard Keynes's prescription for avoiding such problems through government policy (*The General Theory of Employment, Interest and Money*), led to the passage of the Employment Act of 1946, which declared that the federal government should "use all practical means . . . to promote maximum employment, production and purchasing power." The act also created the Council of Economic Advisers (CEA) to advise the president on economic matters.

The Fed might be expected to be influenced by this specification of federal goals, but because it is an independent agency, it is not required to follow any particular path. Furthermore, the legislation does not suggest what should be done if the goals of achieving full employment and maximum purchasing power conflict.

The Full Employment and Balanced Growth Act of 1978

The clearest, and most specific, statement of federal economic goals came in the Full Employment and Balanced Growth Act of 1978. This act, generally known as the Humphrey–Hawkins Act, specified that by 1983 the federal government should achieve an unemployment rate among adults of 3% or less, a civilian unemployment rate of 4% or less, and an inflation rate of 3% or less. Although these goals have the virtue of specificity, they offer little in terms of practical policy guidance. The last time the civilian unemployment rate in the United States fell below 4% was 1969, and the inflation rate that year was 6.2%. In 2000, the unemployment rate touched 4%, and the inflation rate that year was 3.4%, so the goals were close to being met. Except for 2007 when inflation hit 4.1%, inflation has hovered between 1.6% and 3.4% in all the other years between 1991 and 2011, so the inflation goal was met or nearly met, but unemployment fluctuated between 4.0% and 9.6% during those years.

The Humphrey-Hawkins Act requires that the chairman of the Fed's Board of Governors report twice each year to Congress about the Fed's monetary policy. These sessions provide an opportunity for members of the House and Senate to express their views on monetary policy.

Federal Reserve Policy and Goals

Perhaps the clearest way to see the Fed's goals is to observe the policy choices it makes. Since 1979, following a bout of double-digit inflation, its actions have suggested that the Fed's primary goal is to keep inflation under control. Provided that the inflation rate falls within acceptable limits, however, the Fed will also use stimulative measures to attempt to close recessionary gaps.

In 1979, the Fed, then led by Paul Volcker, launched a deliberate program of reducing the inflation rate. It stuck to that effort through the early 1980s, even in the face of a major recession. That effort achieved its goal: the annual inflation rate fell from 13.3% in 1979 to 3.8% in 1982. The cost, however, was great. Unemployment soared past 9% during the recession. With the inflation rate below 4%, the Fed shifted to a stimulative policy early in 1983. This episode may have made the jobs of Mr. Volcker's successors somewhat easier, though, in the sense that it gave credibility to the Fed as a serious inflation fighter when necessary.

In 1990, when the economy slipped into a recession, the Fed, with Alan Greenspan at the helm, engaged in aggressive open-market operations to stimulate the economy, despite the fact that the inflation rate had jumped to 6.1%. Much of that increase in the inflation rate, however, resulted from an oil-price boost that came in the wake of Iraq's invasion of Kuwait that year. A jump in prices that occurs at the same time as real GDP is slumping suggests a leftward shift in short-run aggregate supply, a shift that creates a recessionary gap. Fed officials concluded that the upturn in inflation in 1990 was a temporary phenomenon and that an expansionary policy was an appropriate response to a weak economy. Once the recovery was clearly under way, the Fed shifted to a neutral policy, seeking neither to boost nor to reduce aggregate demand. Early in 1994, the Fed shifted to a contractionary policy, selling bonds to reduce the money supply and raise interest rates. Then Fed Chairman Greenspan indicated that the move was intended to head off any possible increase in inflation from its 1993 rate of 2.7%. Although the economy was still in a recessionary gap when the Fed acted, Greenspan indicated that any acceleration of the inflation rate would be unacceptable.

By March 1997 the inflation rate had fallen to 2.4%. The Fed became concerned that inflationary pressures were increasing and tightened monetary policy, raising the goal for the federal funds interest rate to 5.5%. Inflation remained well below 2.0% throughout the rest of 1997 and 1998. In the fall of 1998, with inflation low, the Fed was concerned that the economic recession in much of Asia and slow growth in Europe would reduce growth in the United States. In quarter-point steps it reduced the goal for the federal funds rate to 4.75%. With real GDP growing briskly in the first half of 1999, the Fed became concerned that inflation would increase, even though the inflation rate at the time was about 2%, and in June 1999, it raised its goal for the federal funds rate to 5% and continued raising the rate until it reached 6.5% in May 2000.

With inflation under control, it then began lowering the federal funds rate to stimulate the economy. It continued lowering through the brief recession of 2001 and beyond. There were 11 rate cuts in 2001, with the rate at the end of that year at 1.75%; in late 2002 the rate was cut to 1.25%, and in mid-2003 it was cut to 1.0%.

Then, with growth picking up and inflation again a concern, the Fed began again in the middle of 2004 to increase rates. By the end of 2006, the rate stood at 5.25% as a result of 17 quarter-point rate increases.

Starting in September 2007, the Fed, since 2006 led by Ben Bernanke, shifted gears and began lowering the federal funds rate, mostly in larger steps or 0.5 to 0.75 percentage points. Though initially somewhat concerned with inflation, it sensed that the economy was beginning to slow down. It moved aggressively to lower rates over the course of the next 15 months, and by the end of 2008, the rate was targeted at between 0% and 0.25%. In late 2008 through 2013, beginning with the threat of deflation and then progressing into a period during which inflation ran fairly low, the Fed seemed quite willing to use all of its options to try to keep financial markets running smoothly. The Fed attempted, in the initial period, to moderate the recession, and then it tried to support the rather lackluster growth that followed. In January 2014 the Fed went on record to say that it intended to keep the federal funds rate at extremely low levels so long as the unemployment rate stayed above 6.5% and possibly even if it went below that, assuming that inflation remained in check.

What can we infer from these episodes in the 1980s, 1990s, and the first decade of this century? It seems clear that the Fed is determined not to allow the high inflation rates of the 1970s to occur again. When the inflation rate is within acceptable limits, the Fed will undertake stimulative measures in response to a recessionary gap or even in response to the possibility of a growth slowdown. Those limits seem to have tightened over time. In the late 1990s and early 2000s, it appeared that an inflation rate above 3%—or any indication that inflation might rise above 3%—would lead the Fed to adopt a contractionary policy. While on the Federal Reserve Board in the early 2000s, Ben Bernanke had been an advocate of inflation targeting. Under that system, the central bank announces its inflation target and then adjusts the federal funds rate if the inflation rate moves above or below the central bank's target. Mr. Bernanke indicated his preferred target to be an expected increase in the price level, as measured by the price index for consumer goods and services excluding food and energy, of between 1% and 2%. Thus, the inflation goal appears to have tightened even more—to a rate of 2% or less. If inflation were expected to remain below 2%, however, the Fed would undertake stimulative measures to close a recessionary gap. Whether the Fed will hold to that goal will not really be tested until further macroeconomic experiences unfold.

3.2   Monetary Policy and Macroeconomic Variables

We saw in an earlier chapter that the Fed has three tools at its command to try to change aggregate demand and thus to influence the level of economic activity. It can buy or sell federal government bonds through open-market operations, it can change the discount rate, or it can change reserve requirements. It can also use these tools in combination. In the next section of this chapter, where we discuss the notion of a liquidity trap, we will also introduce more extraordinary measures that the Fed has at its disposal.

Most economists agree that these tools of monetary policy affect the economy, but they sometimes disagree on the precise mechanisms through which this occurs, on the strength of those mechanisms, and on the ways in which monetary policy should be used. Before we address some of these issues, we shall review the ways in which monetary policy affects the economy in the context of the model of aggregate demand and aggregate supply. Our focus will be on open-market operations, the purchase or sale by the Fed of federal bonds.

Expansionary Monetary Policy

The Fed might pursue an expansionary monetary policy in response to the initial situation shown in Panel (a) of Figure 16.11. An economy with a potential output of Y_P is operating at Y_1; there is a recessionary gap. One possible policy response is to allow the economy to correct this gap on its own, waiting for reductions in nominal wages and other prices to shift the short-run aggregate supply curve $SRAS_1$ to the right until it intersects the aggregate demand curve AD_1 at Y_P. An alternative is a stabilization policy that seeks to increase aggregate demand to AD_2 to close the gap. An expansionary monetary policy is one way to achieve such a shift.

To carry out an expansionary monetary policy, the Fed will buy bonds, thereby increasing the money supply. That shifts the demand curve for bonds to D_2, as illustrated in Panel (b). Bond prices rise to P^b_2. The higher price for bonds reduces the interest rate. These changes in the bond market are consistent with the changes in the money market, shown in Panel (c), in which the greater money supply leads to a fall in the interest rate to r_2. The lower interest rate stimulates investment. In addition, the lower interest rate reduces the demand for and increases the supply of dollars in the currency market, reducing the exchange rate to E_2 in Panel (d). The lower exchange rate will stimulate net exports. The combined impact of greater investment and net exports will shift the aggregate demand curve to the right. The curve shifts by an amount equal to the multiplier times the sum of the initial changes in investment and net exports. In Panel (a), this is shown as a shift to AD_2, and the recessionary gap is closed.

FIGURE 16.11 Expansionary Monetary Policy to Close a Recessionary Gap

In Panel (a), the economy has a recessionary gap $Y_P - Y_1$. An expansionary monetary policy could seek to close this gap by shifting the aggregate demand curve to AD_2. In Panel (b), the Fed buys bonds, shifting the demand curve for bonds to D_2 and increasing the price of bonds to P^b_2. By buying bonds, the Fed increases the money supply to M' in Panel (c). The Fed's action lowers interest rates to r_2. The lower interest rate also reduces the demand for and increases the supply of dollars, reducing the exchange rate to E_2 in Panel (d). The resulting increases in investment and net exports shift the aggregate demand curve in Panel (a).

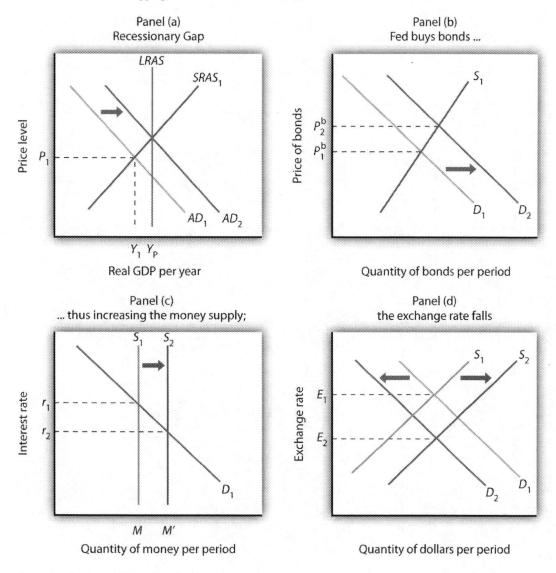

Contractionary Monetary Policy

The Fed will generally pursue a contractionary monetary policy when it considers inflation a threat. Suppose, for example, that the economy faces an inflationary gap; the aggregate demand and short-run aggregate supply curves intersect to the right of the long-run aggregate supply curve, as shown in Panel (a) of Figure 16.12.

FIGURE 16.12 A Contractionary Monetary Policy to Close an Inflationary Gap

In Panel (a), the economy has an inflationary gap $Y_1 - Y_P$. A contractionary monetary policy could seek to close this gap by shifting the aggregate demand curve to AD_2. In Panel (b), the Fed sells bonds, shifting the supply curve for bonds to S_2 and lowering the price of bonds to $P^b{}_2$. The lower price of bonds means a higher interest rate, r_2, as shown in Panel (c). The higher interest rate also increases the demand for and decreases the supply of dollars, raising the exchange rate to E_2 in Panel (d), which will increase net exports. The decreases in investment and net exports are responsible for decreasing aggregate demand in Panel (a).

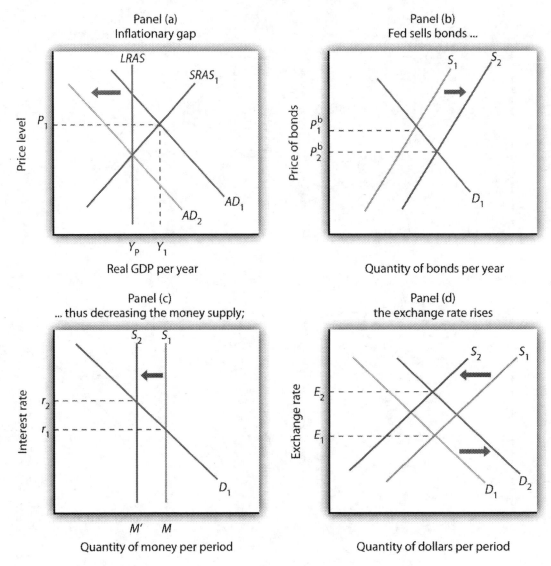

To carry out a contractionary policy, the Fed sells bonds. In the bond market, shown in Panel (b) of Figure 16.12, the supply curve shifts to the right, lowering the price of bonds and increasing the interest rate. In the money market, shown in Panel (c), the Fed's bond sales reduce the money supply and raise the interest rate. The higher interest rate reduces investment. The higher interest rate also induces a greater demand for dollars as foreigners seek to take advantage of higher interest rates in the United States. The supply of dollars falls; people in the United States are less likely to purchase foreign interest-earning assets now that U.S. assets are paying a higher rate. These changes boost the exchange rate, as shown in Panel (d), which reduces exports and increases imports and thus causes net exports to fall. The contractionary monetary policy thus shifts aggregate demand to the left, by an amount equal to the multiplier times the combined initial changes in investment and net exports, as shown in Panel (a).

KEY TAKEAWAYS

- The Federal Reserve Board and the Federal Open Market Committee are among the most powerful institutions in the United States.
- The Fed's primary goal appears to be the control of inflation. Providing that inflation is under control, the Fed will act to close recessionary gaps.
- Expansionary policy, such as a purchase of government securities by the Fed, tends to push bond prices up and interest rates down, increasing investment and aggregate demand. Contractionary policy, such as a sale of government securities by the Fed, pushes bond prices down, interest rates up, investment down, and aggregate demand shifts to the left.

TRY IT!

The figure shows an economy operating at a real GDP of Y_1 and a price level of P_1, at the intersection of AD_1 and $SRAS_1$.

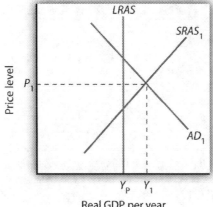

1. What kind of gap is the economy experiencing?
2. What type of monetary policy (expansionary or contractionary) would be appropriate for closing the gap?
3. If the Fed decided to pursue this policy, what type of open-market operations would it conduct?
4. How would bond prices, interest rates, and the exchange rate change?
5. How would investment and net exports change?
6. How would the aggregate demand curve shift?

Case in Point

A Brief History of the Greenspan Fed

With the passage of time and the fact that the fallout on the economy turned out to be relatively minor, it is hard in retrospect to realize how scary a situation Alan Greenspan and the Fed faced just two months after his appointment as Chairman of the Federal Reserve Board. On October 12, 1987, the stock market had its worst day ever. The Dow Jones Industrial Average plunged 508 points, wiping out more than $500 billion in a few hours of feverish trading on Wall Street. That drop represented a loss in value of over 22%. In comparison, the largest daily drop in 2008 of 778 points on September 29, 2008, represented a loss in value of about 7%.

When the Fed faced another huge plunge in stock prices in 1929—also in October—members of the Board of Governors met and decided that no action was necessary. Determined not to repeat the terrible mistake of 1929, one that helped to usher in the Great Depression, Alan Greenspan immediately reassured the country, saying that the Fed would provide adequate liquidity, by buying federal securities, to assure that economic activity would not fall. As it turned out, the damage to the economy was minor and the stock market quickly regained value.

In the fall of 1990, the economy began to slip into recession. The Fed responded with expansionary monetary policy—cutting reserve requirements, lowering the discount rate, and buying Treasury bonds.

Interest rates fell quite quickly in response to the Fed's actions, but, as is often the case, changes to the components of aggregate demand were slower in coming. Consumption and investment began to rise in 1991, but their growth was weak, and unemployment continued to rise because growth in output was too slow to keep up with growth in the labor force. It was not until the fall of 1992 that the economy started to pick up steam. This episode demonstrates an important difficulty with stabilization policy: attempts to manipulate aggregate demand achieve shifts in the curve, but with a lag.

Throughout the rest of the 1990s, with some tightening when the economy seemed to be moving into an inflationary gap and some loosening when the economy seemed to be possibly moving toward a recessionary gap—especially in 1998 and 1999 when parts of Asia experienced financial turmoil and recession and European growth had slowed down—the Fed helped steer what is now referred to as the Goldilocks (not too hot, not too cold, just right) economy.

The U.S. economy again experienced a mild recession in 2001 under Greenspan. At that time, the Fed systematically conducted expansionary policy. Similar to its response to the 1987 stock market crash, the Fed has been credited with maintaining liquidity following the dot-com stock market crash in early 2001 and the attacks on the World Trade Center and the Pentagon in September 2001.

When Greenspan retired in January 2006, many hailed him as the greatest central banker ever. As the economy faltered in 2008 and as the financial crisis unfolded throughout the year, however, the question of how the policies of Greenspan's Fed played into the current difficulties took center stage. Testifying before Congress in October 2008, he said that the country faces a "once-in-a-century credit tsunami," and he admitted, "I made a mistake in presuming that the self-interests of organizations, specifically banks and others, were such as that they were best capable of protecting their own shareholders and their equity in their firms." The criticisms he has faced are twofold: that the very low interest rates used to fight the 2001 recession and maintained for too long fueled the real estate bubble and that he did not promote appropriate regulations to deal with the new financial instruments that were created in the early 2000s. While supporting some additional regulations when he testified before Congress, he also warned that overreacting could be dangerous: "We have to recognize that this is almost surely a once-in-a-century phenomenon, and, in that regard, to realize the types of regulation that would prevent this from happening in the future are so onerous as to basically suppress the growth rate in the economy and . . . the standards of living of the American people."

ANSWERS TO TRY IT! PROBLEMS

1. Inflationary gap
2. Contractionary
3. Open-market sales of bonds
4. The price of bonds would fall. The interest rate and the exchange rate would rise.
5. Investment and net exports would fall.
6. The aggregate demand curve would shift to the left.

4. PROBLEMS AND CONTROVERSIES OF MONETARY POLICY

LEARNING OBJECTIVES

1. **Explain the three kinds of lags that can influence the effectiveness of monetary policy.**
2. **Identify the macroeconomic targets at which the Fed can aim in managing the economy, and discuss the difficulties inherent in using each of them as a target.**
3. **Discuss how each of the following influences a central bank's ability to achieve its desired macroeconomic outcomes: political pressures, the degree of impact on the economy (including the situation of a liquidity trap), and the rational expectations hypothesis.**

The Fed has some obvious advantages in its conduct of monetary policy. The two policy-making bodies, the Board of Governors and the Federal Open Market Committee (FOMC), are small and largely independent from other political institutions. These bodies can thus reach decisions quickly and implement them immediately. Their relative independence from the political process, together with the fact that they meet in secret, allows them to operate outside the glare of publicity that might otherwise be focused on bodies that wield such enormous power.

Despite the apparent ease with which the Fed can conduct monetary policy, it still faces difficulties in its efforts to stabilize the economy. We examine some of the problems and uncertainties associated with monetary policy in this section.

4.1 Lags

Perhaps the greatest obstacle facing the Fed, or any other central bank, is the problem of lags. It is easy enough to show a recessionary gap on a graph and then to show how monetary policy can shift aggregate demand and close the gap. In the real world, however, it may take several months before anyone even realizes that a particular macroeconomic problem is occurring. When monetary authorities become aware of a problem, they can act quickly to inject reserves into the system or to withdraw reserves from it. Once that is done, however, it may be a year or more before the action affects aggregate demand.

The delay between the time a macroeconomic problem arises and the time at which policy makers become aware of it is called a **recognition lag**. The 1990–1991 recession, for example, began in July 1990. It was not until late October that members of the FOMC noticed a slowing in economic activity, which prompted a stimulative monetary policy. In contrast, the most recent recession began in December 2007, and Fed easing began in September 2007.

Recognition lags stem largely from problems in collecting economic data. First, data are available only after the conclusion of a particular period. Preliminary estimates of real GDP, for example, are released about a month after the end of a quarter. Thus, a change that occurs early in a quarter will not be reflected in the data until several months later. Second, estimates of economic indicators are subject to

recognition lag

The delay between the time a macroeconomic problem arises and the time at which policy makers become aware of it.

revision. The first estimates of real GDP in the third quarter of 1990, for example, showed it increasing. Not until several months had passed did revised estimates show that a recession had begun. And finally, different indicators can lead to different interpretations. Data on employment and retail sales might be pointing in one direction while data on housing starts and industrial production might be pointing in another. It is one thing to look back after a few years have elapsed and determine whether the economy was expanding or contracting. It is quite another to decipher changes in real GDP when one is right in the middle of events. Even in a world brimming with computer-generated data on the economy, recognition lags can be substantial.

Only after policy makers recognize there is a problem can they take action to deal with it. The delay between the time at which a problem is recognized and the time at which a policy to deal with it is enacted is called the **implementation lag**. For monetary policy changes, the implementation lag is quite short. The FOMC meets eight times per year, and its members may confer between meetings through conference calls. Once the FOMC determines that a policy change is in order, the required open-market operations to buy or sell federal bonds can be put into effect immediately.

Policy makers at the Fed still have to contend with the **impact lag**, the delay between the time a policy is enacted and the time that policy has its impact on the economy.

The impact lag for monetary policy occurs for several reasons. First, it takes some time for the deposit multiplier process to work itself out. The Fed can inject new reserves into the economy immediately, but the deposit expansion process of bank lending will need time to have its full effect on the money supply. Interest rates are affected immediately, but the money supply grows more slowly. Second, firms need some time to respond to the monetary policy with new investment spending—if they respond at all. Third, a monetary change is likely to affect the exchange rate, but that translates into a change in net exports only after some delay. Thus, the shift in the aggregate demand curve due to initial changes in investment and in net exports occurs after some delay. Finally, the multiplier process of an expenditure change takes time to unfold. It is only as incomes start to rise that consumption spending picks up.

The problem of lags suggests that monetary policy should respond not to statistical reports of economic conditions in the recent past but to conditions *expected* to exist in the future. In justifying the imposition of a contractionary monetary policy early in 1994, when the economy still had a recessionary gap, Greenspan indicated that the Fed expected a one-year impact lag. The policy initiated in 1994 was a response not to the economic conditions thought to exist at the time but to conditions expected to exist in 1995. When the Fed used contractionary policy in the middle of 1999, it argued that it was doing so to forestall a possible increase in inflation. When the Fed began easing in September 2007, it argued that it was doing so to forestall adverse effects to the economy of falling housing prices. In these examples, the Fed appeared to be looking forward. It must do so with information and forecasts that are far from perfect.

Estimates of the length of time required for the impact lag to work itself out range from six months to two years. Worse, the length of the lag can vary—when they take action, policy makers cannot know whether their choices will affect the economy within a few months or within a few years. Because of the uncertain length of the impact lag, efforts to stabilize the economy through monetary policy could be destabilizing. Suppose, for example, that the Fed responds to a recessionary gap with an expansionary policy but that by the time the policy begins to affect aggregate demand, the economy has already returned to potential GDP. The policy designed to correct a recessionary gap could create an inflationary gap. Similarly, a shift to a contractionary policy in response to an inflationary gap might not affect aggregate demand until after a self-correction process had already closed the gap. In that case, the policy could plunge the economy into a recession.

4.2   Choosing Targets

In attempting to manage the economy, on what macroeconomic variables should the Fed base its policies? It must have some target, or set of targets, that it wants to achieve. The failure of the economy to achieve one of the Fed's targets would then trigger a shift in monetary policy. The choice of a target, or set of targets, is a crucial one for monetary policy. Possible targets include interest rates, money growth rates, and the price level or expected changes in the price level.

Interest Rates

Interest rates, particularly the federal funds rate, played a key role in recent Fed policy. The FOMC does not decide to increase or decrease the money supply. Rather, it engages in operations to nudge the federal funds rate up or down.

Up until August 1997, it had instructed the trading desk at the New York Federal Reserve Bank to conduct open-market operations in a way that would either maintain, increase, or ease the current "degree of pressure" on the reserve positions of banks. That degree of pressure was reflected by the

---

implementation lag

The delay between the time at which a problem is recognized and the time at which a policy to deal with it is enacted.

impact lag

The delay between the time a policy is enacted and the time that policy has its impact on the economy.

federal funds rate; if existing reserves were less than the amount banks wanted to hold, then the bidding for the available supply would send the federal funds rate up. If reserves were plentiful, then the federal funds rate would tend to decline. When the Fed increased the degree of pressure on reserves, it sold bonds, thus reducing the supply of reserves and increasing the federal funds rate. The Fed decreased the degree of pressure on reserves by buying bonds, thus injecting new reserves into the system and reducing the federal funds rate.

The current operating procedures of the Fed focus explicitly on interest rates. At each of its eight meetings during the year, the FOMC sets a specific target or target range for the federal funds rate. When the Fed lowers the target for the federal funds rate, it buys bonds. When it raises the target for the federal funds rate, it sells bonds.

Money Growth Rates

Until 2000, the Fed was required to announce to Congress at the beginning of each year its target for money growth that year and each report dutifully did so. At the same time, the Fed report would mention that its money growth targets were benchmarks based on historical relationships rather than guides for policy. As soon as the legal requirement to report targets for money growth ended, the Fed stopped doing so. Since in recent years the Fed has placed more importance on the federal funds rate, it must adjust the money supply in order to move the federal funds rate to the level it desires. As a result, the money growth targets tended to fall by the wayside, even over the last decade in which they were being reported. Instead, as data on economic conditions unfolded, the Fed made, and continues to make, adjustments in order to affect the federal funds interest rate.

Price Level or Expected Changes in the Price Level

Some economists argue that the Fed's primary goal should be price stability. If so, an obvious possible target is the price level itself. The Fed could target a particular price level or a particular rate of change in the price level and adjust its policies accordingly. If, for example, the Fed sought an inflation rate of 2%, then it could shift to a contractionary policy whenever the rate rose above 2%. One difficulty with such a policy, of course, is that the Fed would be responding to past economic conditions with policies that are not likely to affect the economy for a year or more. Another difficulty is that inflation could be rising when the economy is experiencing a recessionary gap. An example of this, mentioned earlier, occurred in 1990 when inflation increased due to the seemingly temporary increase in oil prices following Iraq's invasion of Kuwait. The Fed faced a similar situation in the first half of 2008 when oil prices were again rising. If the Fed undertakes contractionary monetary policy at such times, then its efforts to reduce the inflation rate could worsen the recessionary gap.

One solution to this problem is to focus not on the past rate of inflation or even the current rate of inflation, but on the expected rate of inflation, as revealed by various indicators, over a period of say six months or a year.

By 2010, the central banks of about 30 developed or developing countries had adopted specific inflation targeting. Inflation targeters include Australia, Brazil, Canada, Great Britain, New Zealand, South Korea, and, most recently, Turkey and Indonesia. A study by economist Carl Walsh found that inflationary experiences among developed countries have been similar, regardless of whether their central banks had explicit or more flexible inflation targets. For developing countries, however, he found that inflation targeting enhanced macroeconomic performance, in terms of both lower inflation and greater overall stability.[3]

4.3 Political Pressures

The institutional relationship between the leaders of the Fed and the executive and legislative branches of the federal government is structured to provide for the Fed's independence. Members of the Board of Governors are appointed by the president, with confirmation by the Senate, but the 14-year terms of office provide a considerable degree of insulation from political pressure. A president exercises greater influence in the choice of the chairman of the Board of Governors; that appointment carries a four-year term. Neither the president nor Congress has any direct say over the selection of the presidents of Federal Reserve district banks. They are chosen by their individual boards of directors with the approval of the Board of Governors.

The degree of independence that central banks around the world have varies. A central bank is considered to be more independent if it is insulated from the government by such factors as longer term appointments of its governors and fewer requirements to finance government budget deficits. Studies in the 1980s and early 1990s showed that, in general, greater central bank independence was associated with lower average inflation and that there was no systematic relationship between central bank independence and other indicators of economic performance, such as real GDP growth or unemployment.[4] By the rankings used in those studies, the Fed was considered quite independent, second only to Switzerland and the German *Bundesbank* at the time. Perhaps as a result of such findings, a number of countries have granted greater independence to their central banks in the last decade. The charter for the European Central Bank, which began operations in 1998, was modeled on that of the German *Bundesbank*. Its charter states explicitly that its primary objective is to maintain price stability. Also, since 1998, central bank independence has increased in the United Kingdom, Canada, Japan, and New Zealand.

While the Fed is formally insulated from the political process, the men and women who serve on the Board of Governors and the FOMC are human beings. They are not immune to the pressures that can be placed on them by members of Congress and by the president. The chairman of the Board of Governors meets regularly with the president and the executive staff and also reports to and meets with congressional committees that deal with economic matters.

The Fed was created by the Congress; its charter could be altered—or even revoked—by that same body. The Fed is in the somewhat paradoxical situation of having to cooperate with the legislative and executive branches in order to preserve its independence.

4.4   The Degree of Impact on the Economy

The problem of lags suggests that the Fed does not know with certainty *when* its policies will work their way through the financial system to have an impact on macroeconomic performance. The Fed also does not know with certainty *to what extent* its policy decisions will affect the macroeconomy.

For example, investment can be particularly volatile. An effort by the Fed to reduce aggregate demand in the face of an inflationary gap could be partially offset by rising investment demand. But, generally, contractionary policies do tend to slow down the economy as if the Fed were "pulling on a rope." That may not be the case with expansionary policies. Since investment depends crucially on expectations about the future, business leaders must be optimistic about economic conditions in order to expand production facilities and buy new equipment. That optimism might not exist in a recession. Instead, the pessimism that might prevail during an economic slump could prevent lower interest rates from stimulating investment. An effort to stimulate the economy through monetary policy could be like "pushing on a string." The central bank could push with great force by buying bonds and engaging in quantitative easing, but little might happen to the economy at the other end of the string.

liquidity trap

Situation that exists when a change in monetary policy has no effect on interest rates.

What if the Fed cannot bring about a change in interest rates? A **liquidity trap** is said to exist when a change in monetary policy has no effect on interest rates. This would be the case if the money demand curve were horizontal at some interest rate, as shown in Figure 16.13. If a change in the money supply from M to M' cannot change interest rates, then, unless there is some other change in the economy, there is no reason for investment or any other component of aggregate demand to change. Hence, traditional monetary policy is rendered totally ineffective; its degree of impact on the economy is nil. At an interest rate of zero, since bonds cease to be an attractive alternative to money, which is at least useful for transactions purposes, there would be a liquidity trap.

With the federal funds rate in the United States close to zero at the end of 2008, the possibility that the country was in or nearly in a liquidity trap could not be dismissed. As discussed in the introduction to the chapter, at the same time the Fed lowered the federal funds rate to close to zero, it mentioned that it intended to pursue additional, nontraditional measures. What the Fed seeks to do is to make firms and consumers want to spend now by using a tool not aimed at reducing the interest rate, since it cannot reduce the interest rate below zero. It thus shifts its focus to the price level and to avoiding expected deflation. For example, if the public expects the price level to fall by 2% and the interest rate is zero, by holding money, the money is actually earning a positive *real* interest rate of 2%—the difference between the *nominal* interest rate and the expected deflation rate. Since the nominal rate of interest cannot fall below zero (Who would, for example, want to lend at an interest rate below zero when lending is risky whereas cash is not? In short, it does not make sense to lend $10 and get less than $10 back.), expected deflation makes holding cash very attractive and discourages spending since people will put off purchases because goods and services are expected to get cheaper.

FIGURE 16.13 A Liquidity Trap

When a change in the money supply has no effect on the interest rate, the economy is said to be in a liquidity trap.

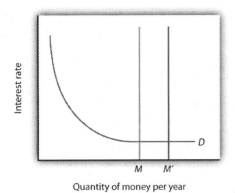

To combat this "wait-and-see" mentality, the Fed or another central bank, using a strategy referred to as **quantitative easing**, must convince the public that it will keep interest rates very low by providing substantial reserves for as long as is necessary to avoid deflation. In other words, it is aimed at creating expected inflation. For example, at the Fed's October 2003 meeting, it announced that it would keep the federal funds rate at 1% for "a considerable period." When the Fed lowered the rate to between 0% and 0.25% in December 2008, it added that "the committee anticipates that weak economic conditions are likely to warrant exceptionally low levels of the federal funds rate for some time." After working so hard to convince economic players that it will not tolerate inflation above 2%, the Fed, when in such a situation, must convince the public that it will tolerate inflation, but of course not too much! If it is successful, this extraordinary form of expansionary monetary policy will lead to increased purchases of goods and services, compared to what they would have been with expected deflation. Also, by providing banks with lots of liquidity, the Fed is hoping to encourage them to lend.

The Japanese economy provides an interesting modern example of a country that attempted quantitative easing. With a recessionary gap starting in the early 1990s and deflation in most years from 1995 on, Japan's central bank, the Bank of Japan, began to lower the call money rate (equivalent to the federal funds rate in the United States), reaching near zero by the late 1990s. With growth still languishing, Japan appeared to be in a traditional liquidity trap. In late 1999, the Bank of Japan announced that it would maintain a zero interest rate policy for the foreseeable future, and in March 2001 it officially began a policy of quantitative easing. In 2006, with the price level rising modestly, Japan ended quantitative easing and began increasing the call rate again. It should be noted that the government simultaneously engaged in expansionary fiscal policy.

How well did these policies work in Japan? The economy began to grow modestly in 2003, though deflation between 1% and 2% remained. Some researchers feel that the Bank of Japan ended quantitative easing too early. Also, delays in implementing the policy, as well as delays in restructuring the banking sector, exacerbated Japan's problems.[5]

During the recession of 2008 and 2009 and the recovery period that followed, the Fed argued that it also engaged in credit easing.[6] **Credit easing** is a strategy that involves the extension of central bank lending to influence more broadly the proper functioning of credit markets and to improve liquidity. The specific new credit facilities that the Fed created were discussed in the Case in Point in the chapter on the nature and creation of money. In general, the Fed is hoping that these new credit facilities will improve liquidity in a variety of credit markets, ranging from those used by money market mutual funds to those involved in student and car loans.

4.5   Rational Expectations

One hypothesis suggests that monetary policy may affect the price level but not real GDP. The **rational expectations hypothesis** states that people use all available information to make forecasts about future economic activity and the price level, and they adjust their behavior to these forecasts.

Figure 16.14 uses the model of aggregate demand and aggregate supply to show the implications of the rational expectations argument for monetary policy. Suppose the economy is operating at Y_P, as illustrated by point A. An increase in the money supply boosts aggregate demand to AD_2. In the analysis we have explored thus far, the shift in aggregate demand would move the economy to a higher level of real GDP and create an inflationary gap. That, in turn, would put upward pressure on wages and other prices, shifting the short-run aggregate supply curve to $SRAS_2$ and moving the economy to point B, closing the inflationary gap in the long run. The rational expectations hypothesis, however, suggests a quite different interpretation.

Suppose people observe the initial monetary policy change undertaken when the economy is at point A and calculate that the increase in the money supply will ultimately drive the price level up to point B. Anticipating this change in prices, people adjust their behavior. For example, if the increase in the price level from P_1 to P_2 is a 10% change, workers will anticipate that the prices they pay will rise 10%, and they will demand 10% higher wages. Their employers, anticipating that the prices they will receive will also rise, will agree to pay those higher wages. As nominal wages increase, the short-run aggregate supply curve *immediately* shifts to $SRAS_2$. The result is an upward movement along the long-run aggregate supply curve, $LRAS$. There is no change in real GDP. The monetary policy has no effect, other than its impact on the price level. This rational expectations argument relies on wages and prices being sufficiently flexible—not sticky, as described in an earlier chapter—so that the change in expectations will allow the short-run aggregate supply curve to shift quickly to $SRAS_2$.

quantitative easing

Policy in which a bank convinces the public that it will keep interest rates very low by providing substantial reserves for as long as is necessary to avoid deflation.

credit easing

A strategy that involves the extension of central bank lending to influence more broadly the proper functioning of credit markets and to improve liquidity.

rational expectations hypothesis

Individuals form expectations about the future based on the information available to them, and they act on those expectations.

FIGURE 16.14 Monetary Policy and
Rational Expectations

Suppose the economy is operating at point A
and that individuals have rational expectations.
They calculate that an expansionary monetary
policy undertaken at price level P_1 will raise
prices to P_2. They adjust their
expectations—and wage
demands—accordingly, quickly shifting the
short-run aggregate supply curve to $SRAS_2$.
The result is a movement along the long-run
aggregate supply curve $LRAS$ to point B, with
no change in real GDP.

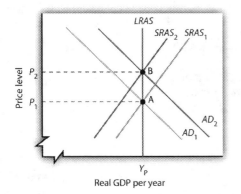

One important implication of the rational expectations argument is that a contractionary monetary policy could be painless. Suppose the economy is at point B in Figure 16.14, and the Fed reduces the money supply in order to shift the aggregate demand curve back to AD_1. In the model of aggregate demand and aggregate supply, the result would be a recession. But in a rational expectations world, people's expectations change, the short-run aggregate supply immediately shifts to the right, and the economy moves painlessly down its long-run aggregate supply curve $LRAS$ to point A. Those who support the rational expectations hypothesis, however, also tend to argue that monetary policy should not be used as a tool of stabilization policy.

For some, the events of the early 1980s weakened support for the rational expectations hypothesis; for others, those same events strengthened support for this hypothesis. As we saw in the introduction to an earlier chapter, in 1979 President Jimmy Carter appointed Paul Volcker as Chairman of the Federal Reserve and pledged his full support for whatever the Fed might do to contain inflation. Mr. Volcker made it clear that the Fed was going to slow money growth and boost interest rates. He acknowledged that this policy would have costs but said that the Fed would stick to it as long as necessary to control inflation. Here was a monetary policy that was clearly announced and carried out as advertised. But the policy brought on the most severe recession since the Great Depression—a result that seems inconsistent with the rational expectations argument that changing expectations would prevent such a policy from having a substantial effect on real GDP.

Others, however, argue that people were aware of the Fed's pronouncements but were skeptical about whether the anti-inflation effort would persist, since the Fed had not vigorously fought inflation in the late 1960s and the 1970s. Against this history, people adjusted their estimates of inflation downward slowly. In essence, the recession occurred because people were surprised that the Fed was serious about fighting inflation.

Regardless of where one stands on this debate, one message does seem clear: once the Fed has proved it is serious about maintaining price stability, doing so in the future gets easier. To put this in concrete terms, Volcker's fight made Greenspan's work easier, and Greenspan's legacy of low inflation made Bernanke's and, starting in February 2014, Janet Yellen's easier.

KEY TAKEAWAYS

- Macroeconomic policy makers must contend with recognition, implementation, and impact lags.
- Potential targets for macroeconomic policy include interest rates, money growth rates, and the price level or expected rates of change in the price level.
- Even if a central bank is structured to be independent of political pressure, its officers are likely to be affected by such pressure.
- To counteract liquidity traps or the possibility thereof, central banks have used quantitative-easing and credit-easing strategies.
- No central bank can know in advance how its policies will affect the economy; the rational expectations hypothesis predicts that central bank actions will affect the money supply and the price level but not the real level of economic activity.

TRY IT!

The scenarios below describe the U.S. recession and recovery in the early 1990s. Identify the lag that may have contributed to the difficulty in using monetary policy as a tool of economic stabilization.

1. The U.S. economy entered into a recession in July 1990. The Fed countered with expansionary monetary policy in October 1990, ultimately lowering the federal funds rate from 8% to 3% in 1992.

2. Investment began to increase, although slowly, in early 1992, and surged in 1993.

Case in Point

The Fed and the ECB: A Tale of Divergent Monetary Policies

In the spring of 2013, the European Central Bank (ECB) began to raise interest rates, while the Federal Reserve Bank held fast to its low rate policy. With the economies of both Europe and the United States weak, why the split in direction?

For one thing, at the time, the U.S. economy looked weaker than did Europe's economy as a whole. Moreover, the recession in the United States had been deeper. For example, the unemployment rate in the United States more than doubled during the Great Recession and its aftermath, while in the eurozone, it had risen only 40%.

But the divergence also reflected the different legal environments in which the two central banks operate. The ECB has a clear mandate to fight inflation, while the Fed has more leeway in pursuing both price stability and full employment. The ECB has a specific inflation target, and the inflation measure it uses covers all prices. The Fed, with its more flexible inflation target, has tended to focus on "core" inflation, which excludes gasoline and food prices, both of which are apt to be volatile. Using each central bank's preferred inflation measure, European inflation was, at the time of the ECB rate hike, running at 2.6%, while in the United States, it was at 1.6%.

Europe also differs from the United States in its degree of unionization. Because of Europe's higher level of unionization and collective bargaining, there is a sense that any price increases in Europe will translate into sustained inflation more rapidly there than they will in the United States.

Recall, however, that the eurozone is made up of 17 diverse countries. As made evident by the headline news from most of 2011 and into 2012, a number of countries in the eurozone were experiencing sovereign debt crises (meaning that there was fear that their governments could not meet their debt obligations) as well as more severe economic conditions. Higher interest rates make their circumstances that much more difficult. While it is true that various states in the United States can experience very different economic circumstances when the Fed sets what is essentially a "national" monetary policy, having a single monetary policy for different countries presents additional problems. One reason for this this difference is that labor mobility is higher in the United States than it is across the countries of Europe. Also, the United States can use its "national" fiscal policy to help weaker states.

In the fall of 2011, the ECB reversed course. At its first meeting under its new president, Mario Draghi, in November 2011, it lowered rates, citing slower growth and growing concerns about the sovereign debt crisis. A further rate cut followed in December. Interestingly, the inflation rate at the time of the cuts was running at about 3%, which was above the ECB's stated goal of 2%. The ECB argued that it was forecasting lower inflation for the future. So even the ECB has some flexibility and room for discretion.

Sources: Emily Kaiser and Mark Felsenthal, "Seven Reasons Why the Fed Won't Follow the ECB," Reuters Business and Financial News, April 7, 2011, available http://www.reuters.com/article/2011/04/07/us-usa-fed-ecb-idUSTRE73663420110407; David Mchugh, "ECB Cuts Key Rate a Quarter Point to Help Economy," USA Today, December 8, 2011, available http://www.usatoday.com/money/economy/story/2011-12-08/ecb-rate-cut/51733442/1; Fernanda Nechio, "Monetary Policy When One Size Does Not Fit All," Federal Reserve Bank of San Francisco Economic Letter, June 13, 2011.

ANSWERS TO TRY IT! PROBLEMS

1. The recognition lag: the Fed did not seem to "recognize" that the economy was in a recession until several months after the recession began.
2. The impact lag: investment did not pick up quickly after interest rates were reduced. Alternatively, it could be attributed to the expansionary monetary policy's not having its desired effect, at least initially, on investment.

5. REVIEW AND PRACTICE

Summary

We began this chapter by looking at bond and foreign exchange markets and showing how each is related to the level of real GDP and the price level. Bonds represent the obligation of the seller to repay the buyer the face value by the maturity date; their interest rate is determined by the demand and supply for bonds. An increase in bond prices means a drop in interest rates. A reduction in bond prices means interest rates have risen. The price of the dollar is determined in foreign exchange markets by the demand and supply for dollars.

We then saw how the money market works. The quantity of money demanded varies negatively with the interest rate. Factors that cause the demand curve for money to shift include changes in real GDP, the price level, expectations, the cost of transferring funds between money and nonmoney accounts, and preferences, especially preferences concerning risk. Equilibrium in the market for money is achieved at the interest rate at which the quantity of money demanded equals the quantity of money supplied. We assume that the supply of money is determined by the Fed. An increase in money demand raises the equilibrium interest rate, and a decrease in money demand lowers the equilibrium interest rate. An increase in the money supply lowers the equilibrium interest rate; a reduction in the money supply raises the equilibrium interest rate.

We then examined in more detail how monetary policy is carried out. Part of the Fed's power stems from the fact that it has no legislative mandate to seek particular goals. That leaves the Fed free to set its own goals. In recent years, its primary goal has seemed to be the maintenance of an inflation rate below 2% to 3%. Given success in meeting that goal, the Fed has used its tools to stimulate the economy to close recessionary gaps. Once the Fed has made a choice to undertake an expansionary or contractionary policy, we can trace the impact of that policy on the economy.

There are a number of problems in the use of monetary policy. These include various types of lags, the issue of the choice of targets in conducting monetary policy, political pressures placed on the process of policy setting, and uncertainty as to how great an impact the Fed's policy decisions have on macroeconomic variables. We highlighted the difficulties for monetary policy if the economy is in or near a liquidity trap and discussed the use of quantitative easing and credit easing in such situations. If people have rational expectations and respond to those expectations in their wage and price choices, then changes in monetary policy may have no effect on real GDP.

CONCEPT PROBLEMS

1. What factors might increase the demand for bonds? The supply?

2. What would happen to the market for bonds if a law were passed that set a minimum price on bonds that was above the equilibrium price?

3. When the price of bonds decreases, the interest rate rises. Explain.

4. One journalist writing about the complex interactions between various markets in the economy stated, "When the government spends more than it takes in taxes it must sell bonds to finance its excess expenditures. But selling bonds drives interest rates down and thus stimulates the economy by encouraging more investment and decreasing the foreign exchange rate, which helps our export industries." Carefully analyze the statement. Do you agree? Why or why not?

5. What do you predict will happen to the foreign exchange rate if interest rates in the United States increase dramatically over the next year? Explain, using a graph of the foreign exchange market. How would such a change affect real GDP and the price level?

6. Suppose the government were to increase its purchases, issuing bonds to finance these purchases. Use your knowledge of the bond and foreign exchange markets to explain how this would affect investment and net exports.

7. How would each of the following affect the demand for money?

    a. A tax on bonds held by individuals

    b. A forecast by the Fed that interest rates will rise sharply in the next quarter

    c. A wave of muggings

    d. An announcement of an agreement between Congress and the president that, beginning in the next fiscal year, government spending will be reduced by an amount sufficient to eliminate all future borrowing

8. Some low-income countries do not have a bond market. In such countries, what substitutes for money do you think people would hold?

9. Explain what is meant by the statement that people are holding more money than they want to hold.

10. Explain how the Fed's sale of government bonds shifts the supply curve for money.

11. Trace the impact of a sale of government bonds by the Fed on bond prices, interest rates, investment, net exports, aggregate demand, real GDP, and the price level.

12. Suppose the Fed were required to conduct monetary policy so as to hold the unemployment rate below 4%, the goal specified in the Humphrey–Hawkins Act. What implications would this have for the economy?

13. The statutes of the recently established European Central Bank (ECB) state that its primary objective is to maintain price stability. How does this charter differ from that of the Fed? What significance does it have for monetary policy?

14. Do you think the Fed should be given a clearer legislative mandate concerning macroeconomic goals? If so, what should it be?

15. Referring to the Case in Point on targeting, what difference does it make whether the target is the inflation rate of the past year or the expected inflation rate over the next year?

16. In a speech in January 1995,[7] Federal Reserve Chairman Alan Greenspan used a transportation metaphor to describe some of the difficulties of implementing monetary policy. He referred to the criticism levied against the Fed for shifting in 1994 to an anti-inflation, contractionary policy when the inflation rate was still quite low:

> *To successfully navigate a bend in the river, the barge must begin the turn well before the bend is reached. Even so, currents are always changing and even an experienced crew cannot foresee all the events that might occur as the river is being navigated. A year ago, the Fed began its turn (a shift toward an expansionary monetary policy), and it was successful.*

Mr. Greenspan was referring, of course, to the problem of lags. What kind of lag do you think he had in mind? What do you suppose the reference to changing currents means?

17. In a speech in August 1999,[8] Mr. Greenspan said,

> *We no longer have the luxury to look primarily to the flow of goods and services, as conventionally estimated, when evaluating the macroeconomic environment in which monetary policy must function. There are important—but extremely difficult—questions surrounding the behavior of asset prices and the implications of this behavior for the decisions of households and businesses.*

The asset price that Mr. Greenspan was referring to was the U.S. stock market, which had been rising sharply in the weeks and months preceding this speech. Inflation and unemployment were both low at that time. What issues concerning the conduct of monetary policy was Mr. Greenspan raising?

18. The text notes that prior to August 1997 (when it began specifying a target value for the federal funds rate), the FOMC adopted directives calling for the trading desk at the New York Federal Reserve Bank to increase, decrease, or maintain the existing degree of pressure on reserve positions. On the meeting dates given in the first column, the FOMC voted to decrease pressure on reserve positions (that is, adopt a more expansionary policy). On the meeting dates given in the second column, it voted to increase reserve pressure:

July 5–6, 1995	February 3–4, 1994
December 19, 1995	January 31–February 1, 1995
January 30–31, 1996	March 25, 1997

Recent minutes of the FOMC can be found at the Federal Reserve Board of Governors website. Pick one of these dates on which a decrease in reserve pressure was ordered and one on which an increase was ordered and find out why that particular policy was chosen.

19. Since August 1997, the Fed has simply set a specific target for the federal funds rate. The following four dates show the first four times after August 1997 that the Fed voted to set a new target for the federal funds rate:

September 29, 1998	November 17, 1998
June 29, 1999	August 24, 1999

Pick one of these dates and find out why it chose to change its target for the federal funds rate on that date.

20. Four meetings in 2008 at which the Fed changed the target for the federal funds rate occurred on the following dates:

January 30, 2008	March 18, 2008
October 8, 2008	October 29, 2008

Pick one of these dates and find out why it chose to change its target for the federal funds rate on that date.

21. Trace the impact of an expansionary monetary policy on bond prices, interest rates, investment, the exchange rate, net exports, real GDP, and the price level. Illustrate your analysis graphically.

22. Trace the impact of a contractionary monetary policy on bond prices, interest rates, investment, the exchange rate, net exports, real GDP, and the price level. Illustrate your analysis graphically.

NUMERICAL PROBLEMS

1. Compute the rate of interest associated with each of these bonds that matures in one year:

	Face Value	Selling Price
a.	$100	$80
b.	$100	$90
c.	$100	$95
d.	$200	$180
e.	$200	$190
f.	$200	$195

    g. Describe the relationship between the selling price of a bond and the interest rate.

2. Suppose that the demand and supply schedules for bonds that have a face value of $100 and a maturity date one year hence are as follows:

Price ($)	Quantity Demanded	Quantity Supplied
100	0	600
95	100	500
90	200	400
85	300	300
80	400	200
75	500	100
70	600	0

    a. Draw the demand and supply curves for these bonds, find the equilibrium price, and determine the interest rate.

    b. Now suppose the quantity demanded increases by 200 bonds at each price. Draw the new demand curve and find the new equilibrium price. What has happened to the interest rate?

3. Compute the dollar price of a German car that sells for 40,000 euros at each of the following exchange rates:

    a. $1 = 1 euro

    b. $1 = 0.8 euro

    c. $1 = 0.75 euro

4. Consider the euro-zone of the European Union and Japan. The demand and supply curves for euros are given by the following table (prices for the euro are given in Japanese yen; quantities of euros are in millions):

Price (in Euros)	Euros Demanded	Euros Supplied
75	0	600
70	100	500
65	200	400
60	300	300
55	400	200
50	500	100
45	600	0

    a. Draw the demand and supply curves for euros and state the equilibrium exchange rate (in yen) for the euro. How many euros are required to purchase one yen?

    b. Suppose an increase in interest rates in the European Union increases the demand for euros by 100 million at each price. At the same time, it reduces the supply by 100 million at each price. Draw the new demand and supply curves and state the new equilibrium exchange rate for the euro. How many euros are now required to purchase one yen?

    c. How will the event in (b) affect net exports in the European Union?

    d. How will the event in (b) affect aggregate demand in the European Union?

    e. How will the event in (b) affect net exports in Japan?

    f. How will the event in (b) affect aggregate demand in Japan?

5. Suppose you earn $6,000 per month and spend $200 in each of the month's 30 days. Compute your average quantity of money demanded if:

    a. You deposit your entire earnings in your checking account at the beginning of the month.

    b. You deposit $2,000 into your checking account on the 1st, 11th, and 21st days of the month.

    c. You deposit $1,000 into your checking account on the 1st, 6th, 11th, 16th, 21st, and 26th days of the month.

    d. How would you expect the interest rate to affect your decision to opt for strategy (a), (b), or (c)?

6. Suppose the quantity demanded of money at an interest rate of 5% is $2 billion per day, at an interest rate of 3% is $3 billion per day, and at an interest rate of 1% is $4 billion per day. Suppose the money supply is $3 billion per day.

    a. Draw a graph of the money market and find the equilibrium interest rate.

    b. Suppose the quantity of money demanded decreases by $1 billion per day at each interest rate. Graph this situation and find the new equilibrium interest rate. Explain the process of achieving the new equilibrium in the money market.

    c. Suppose instead that the money supply decreases by $1 billion per day. Explain the process of achieving the new equilibrium in the money market.

7. We know that the U.S. economy faced a recessionary gap in 2008 and that the Fed responded with an expansionary monetary policy. Present the results of the Fed's action in a four-panel graph. In Panel (a), show the initial situation, using the model of aggregate demand and aggregate supply. In Panel (b), show how the Fed's policy affects the bond market and bond prices. In Panel (c), show how the market for U.S. dollars and the exchange rate will be affected. In Panel (d), incorporate these developments into your analysis of aggregate demand and aggregate supply, and show how the Fed's policy will affect real GDP and the price level in the short run.

ENDNOTES

1. Consumption may also be affected by changes in interest rates. For example, if interest rates fall, consumers can more easily obtain credit and thus are more likely to purchase cars and other durable goods. To simplify, we ignore this effect.

2. In this chapter we are looking only at changes that originate in financial markets to see their impact on aggregate demand and aggregate supply. Changes in the price level and in real GDP also shift the money demand curve, but these changes are the result of changes in aggregate demand or aggregate supply and are considered in more advanced courses in macroeconomics.

3. Carl E. Walsh, "Inflation Targeting: What Have We Learned?," *International Finance* 12, no. 2 (2009): 195–233.

4. See, for example, Alberto Alesina and Lawrence H. Summers, "Central Bank Independence and Macroeconomic Performance: Some Comparative Evidence," *Journal of Money, Credit, and Banking* 25, no. 2 (May 1993): 151–62.

5. "Bringing an End to Deflation under the New Monetary Policy Framework," *OECD Economic Surveys: Japan 2008* 4 (April 2008): 49–61 and Mark M. Spiegel, "Did Quantitative Easing by the Bank of Japan Work?" *FRBSF Economic Letter* 2006, no. 28 (October 20, 2006): 1–3.

6. Ben S. Bernanke, "The Crisis and the Policy Response" (Stamp Lecture, London School of Economics, London, England, January 13, 2009) and Janet L. Yellen, "U.S. Monetary Policy Objectives in the Short Run and the Long Run" (speech, Allied Social Sciences Association annual meeting, San Francisco, California, January 4, 2009).

7. Speech by Alan Greenspan before the Board of Directors of the National Association of Home Builders, January 28, 1995.

8. Alan Greenspan, "New challenges for monetary policy," speech delivered before a symposium sponsored by the Federal Reserve Bank of Kansas City in Jackson Hole, Wyoming, on August 27, 1999. Mr. Greenspan was famous for his convoluted speech, which listeners often found difficult to understand. CBS correspondent Andrea Mitchell, to whom Mr. Greenspan is married, once joked that he had proposed to her three times and that she had not understood what he was talking about on his first two efforts.

CHAPTER 17

Government and Fiscal Policy

START UP: A MASSIVE STIMULUS

Shaken by the severity of both the recession that began in December 2007 and the financial crisis that occurred in the fall of 2008, Congress passed a huge $784 billion stimulus package in February 2009. President Obama described the measure as only "the beginning" of what the federal government ultimately would do to right the economy.

Over a quarter of the American Recovery and Reinvestment Act (ARRA) was for a variety of temporary tax rebates and credits for individuals and firms. For example, each worker making less than $75,000 a year received $400 ($800 for a working couple earning up to $150,000) as a kind of rebate for payroll taxes. That works out to $8 a week. Qualifying college students became eligible for $2,500 tax credits for educational expenses. During a certain period, a first-time homebuyer was eligible for a tax credit. The other roughly three-quarters of the ARRA were for a variety of government spending programs, including temporary transfers to state and local governments, extended unemployment insurance and other transfers to people (such as food stamps), and increased infrastructure spending. The president said that the measure would "ignite spending by businesses and consumers ... and make the investment necessary for lasting growth and economic prosperity."[1] Shortly after the passage of the ARRA, Congress passed the Cash for Clunkers program, which for a limited period of time allowed car buyers to trade in less-fuel-efficient cars for rebates of up to $4,500 toward buying new cars that met certain higher fuel-efficiency standards.

The ARRA illustrates an important difficulty of using fiscal policy in an effort to stabilize economic activity. It was passed over a year after the recession began. Only about 20% of the spending called for by the legislation took place in 2009, rising to about two-thirds through the middle of 2010. It was a guess what state the economy would be in then. As it turned out, the recession had officially ended, but there was still a large recessionary gap, and unemployment was still a major concern. There was a great deal of media controversy about how effective the policy had been and whether the resulting increase in national debt was worth it. Concern over the expanded size of the federal government created by the stimulus measures became a rallying cry for the Tea Party movement. A fiscal stimulus package of over $150 billion had already been tried earlier in February 2008 under President George W. Bush. It included $100 billion in temporary tax rebates to households—up to $600 for individuals and $1,200 for couples—and over $50 billion in tax breaks for businesses. The boost to aggregate demand seemed slight—consumers saved much of their rebate money. In November 2008, unemployment insurance benefits were extended for seven additional weeks, in recognition of the growing unemployment problem.

President Obama argued that his proposals for dealing with the economy in the short term would, coincidentally, also promote long-term economic health. Some critics argued for a greater focus on actual tax cuts while others were concerned about whether the spending would focus on getting the greatest employment increase or be driven by political considerations.

How do government tax and expenditure policies affect real GDP and the price level? Why do economists differ so sharply in assessing the likely impact of such policies? Can fiscal policy be used to stabilize the economy in the short run? What are the long-run effects of government spending and taxing?

We begin with a look at the government's budget to see how it spends the tax revenue it collects. Clearly, the government's budget is not always in balance, so we will also look at government deficits and debt. We will then look at how fiscal policy works to stabilize the economy, distinguishing between built-in stabilization methods and discretionary measures. We will end the chapter with a discussion of why fiscal policy is so controversial.

As in the previous chapter on monetary policy, our primary focus will be U.S. policy. However, the tools available to governments around the world are quite similar, as are the issues surrounding the use of fiscal policy.

1. GOVERNMENT AND THE ECONOMY

LEARNING OBJECTIVES

1. **Understand the major components of U.S. government spending and sources of government revenues.**
2. **Define the terms *budget surplus, budget deficit, balanced budget*, and *national debt*, and discuss their trends over time in the United States.**

We begin our analysis of fiscal policy with an examination of government purchases, transfer payments, and taxes in the U.S. economy.

1.1 Government Purchases

The government-purchases component of aggregate demand includes all purchases by government agencies of goods and services produced by firms, as well as direct production by government agencies themselves. When the federal government buys staples and staplers, the transaction is part of government purchases. The production of educational and research services by public colleges and universities is also counted in the government-purchases component of GDP.

While government spending has grown over time, government purchases as a share of GDP declined from over 20% until the early 1990s to under 18% in 2001. Since then, though, the percentage of government purchases in GDP began to increase back toward 20% and then beyond. This first occurred as military spending picked up, and then, more recently, it rose even further during the 2007–2009 recession. In the last two years, the percentage has again fallen below 20%.

Figure 17.1 shows federal as well as state and local government purchases as a percentage of GDP from 1960 to 2013. Notice the changes that have occurred over this period. In 1960, the federal government accounted for the majority share of total purchases. Since then, however, federal purchases have fallen by almost half relative to GDP, while state and local purchases relative to GDP have risen.

FIGURE 17.1 Federal, State, and Local Purchases Relative to GDP, 1960–2013

Government purchases were generally above 20% of GDP from 1960 until the early 1990s and then below 20% of GDP except during the 2007–2009 recession.

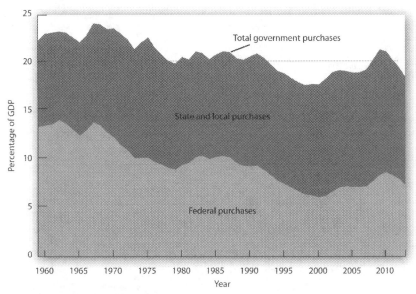

Source: Bureau of Economic Analysis, NIPA Table 1.1 and 3.1 (revised February 28, 2014).

1.2 Transfer Payments

A **transfer payment** is the provision of aid or money to an individual who is not required to provide anything in exchange for the payment. Social Security and welfare benefits are examples of transfer payments. During the 2007-2009 recession, transfers rose.

A number of changes have influenced transfer payments over the past several decades. First, they increased rapidly during the late 1960s and early 1970s. This was the period in which federal programs such as Medicare (health insurance for the elderly) and Medicaid (health insurance for the poor) were created and other programs were expanded.

Figure 17.2 shows that transfer payment spending by the federal government and by state and local governments has risen as a percentage of GDP. In 1960, such spending totaled about 6% of GDP; in recent years, it has been above 16%. The federal government accounts for the bulk of transfer payment spending in the United States.

Transfer payment spending relative to GDP tends to fluctuate with the business cycle. Transfer payments fell during the late 1970s, a period of expansion, then rose as the economy slipped into a recessionary gap during the 1979–1982 period. Transfer payments fell during the expansion that began late in 1982, then began rising in 1989 as the expansion began to slow. Transfer payments continued to rise relative to GDP during the recessions of 1990–1991 and 2001–2002 and then fell as the economy entered expansionary phases after each of those recessions. During the 2007—2009 recession, transfer payments rose again.

When economic activity falls, incomes fall, people lose jobs, and more people qualify for aid. People qualify to receive welfare benefits, such as cash, food stamps, or Medicaid, only if their income falls below a certain level. They qualify for unemployment compensation by losing their jobs. More people qualify for transfer payments during recessions. When the economy expands, incomes and employment rise, and fewer people qualify for welfare or unemployment benefits. Spending for those programs therefore tends to fall during an expansion.

transfer payment

The provision of aid or money to an individual who is not required to provide anything in exchange.

FIGURE 17.2 Federal, State, and Local Transfer Payments as a Percentage of GDP, 1960–2013

The chart shows transfer payment spending as a percentage of GDP from 1960 through 2013. This spending rose dramatically relative to GDP during the late 1960s and the 1970s as federal programs expanded. More recently, sharp increases in health-care costs have driven upward the spending for transfer payment programs such as Medicare and Medicaid. Transfer payments fluctuate with the business cycle, rising in times of recession and falling during times of expansion. As such, they rose sharply during the deep 2007-2009 recession.

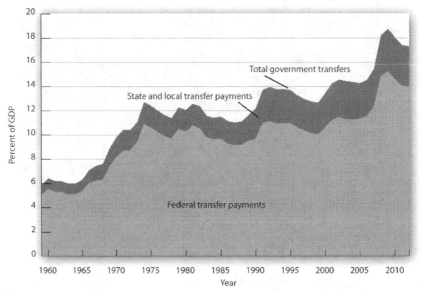

Source: Bureau of Economic Analysis, NIPA Table 1.1, 3.2, and 3.3 (revised February 28, 2014).

Figure 17.3 summarizes trends in government spending since 1960. It shows three categories of government spending relative to GDP: government purchases, transfer payments, and net interest. Net interest includes payments of interest by governments at all levels on money borrowed, less interest earned on saving.

FIGURE 17.3 Government Spending as a Percentage of GDP, 1960–2013

This chart shows three major categories of government spending as percentages of GDP: government purchases, transfer payments, and net interest.

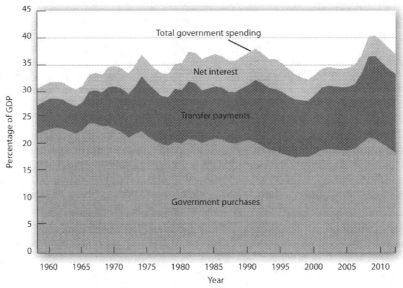

Source: Bureau of Economic Analysis, NIPA Table 1.1 and 3.1 (revised February 28, 2014).

1.3 Taxes

Taxes affect the relationship between real GDP and personal disposable income; they therefore affect consumption. They also influence investment decisions. Taxes imposed on firms affect the profitability of investment decisions and therefore affect the levels of investment firms will choose. Payroll taxes imposed on firms affect the costs of hiring workers; they therefore have an impact on employment and on the real wages earned by workers.

The bulk of federal receipts come from the personal income tax and from payroll taxes. State and local tax receipts are dominated by property taxes and sales taxes. The federal government, as well as state and local governments, also collects taxes imposed on business firms, such as taxes on corporate profits. Figure 17.4 shows the composition of federal, state, and local receipts in a recent year.

FIGURE 17.4 The Composition of Federal, State, and Local Revenues

Federal receipts come primarily from payroll taxes and from personal taxes such as the personal income tax. State and local tax receipts come from a variety of sources; the most important are property taxes, sales taxes, income taxes, and grants from the federal government. Data are for third-quarter 2013, in billions of dollars, seasonally adjusted at annual rates.

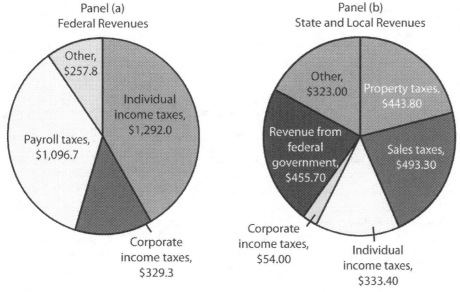

Source: Bureau of Economic Analysis, NIPA Table 3.2 and 3.3 (revised February 28, 2014).

1.4 The Government Budget Balance

The government's budget balance is the difference between the government's revenues and its expenditures. A **budget surplus** occurs if government revenues exceed expenditures. A **budget deficit** occurs if government expenditures exceed revenues. The minus sign is often omitted when reporting a deficit. If the budget surplus equals zero, we say the government has a **balanced budget**.

Figure 17.5 compares federal, state, and local government revenues to expenditures relative to GDP since 1960. The government's budget was generally in surplus in the 1960s, then mostly in deficit since, except for a brief period between 1998 and 2001. Bear in mind that these data are for all levels of government.

budget surplus

Situation that occurs if government revenues exceed expenditures.

budget deficit

Situation that occurs if government expenditures exceed revenues.

balanced budget

Situation that occurs if the budget surplus equals zero.

FIGURE 17.5 Government Revenue and Expenditure as a Percentage of GDP, 1960–2013

The government's budget was generally in surplus in the 1960s, then mostly in deficit since, except for a brief period between 1998 and 2001.

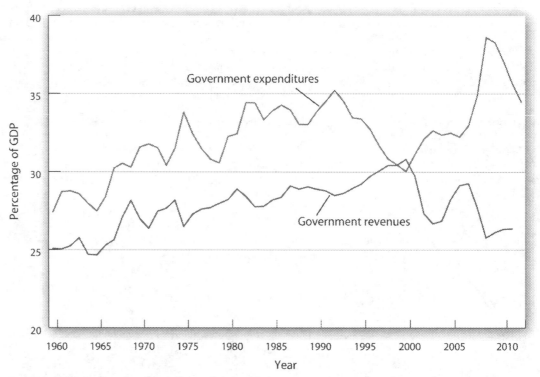

Source: Bureau of Economic Analysis, NIPA Table 1.1 and 3.1 (revised February 28, 2014).

The administration of George W. Bush saw a large increase in the federal deficit. In part, this was the result of the government's response to the terrorist attacks in 2001. It also results, however, from large increases in federal spending at all levels together with tax cuts in 2001, 2002, and 2003. The federal deficit grew even larger during the administration of Barack Obama. The increase stemmed from both reduced revenues and increased spending resulting from the recession that began in 2007 and the stimulus.

1.5   The National Debt

national debt

The sum of all past federal deficits, minus any surpluses.

The **national debt** is the sum of all past federal deficits, minus any surpluses. Figure 17.6 shows the national debt as a percentage of GDP. It suggests that, relative to the level of economic activity, the debt is well below the levels reached during World War II. The ratio of debt to GDP rose from 1981 to 1996 and fell in the last years of the 20th century; it began rising again in 2002 and has risen substantially since the recession that began in 2007.

FIGURE 17.6 The National Debt and the Economy, 1929–2013

The national debt relative to GDP was at its peak during World War II and then fell dramatically over the next few decades. The ratio of debt to GDP rose from 1981 to 1996 and fell in the last years of the 20th century; it began rising again in 2002, markedly so since 2009.

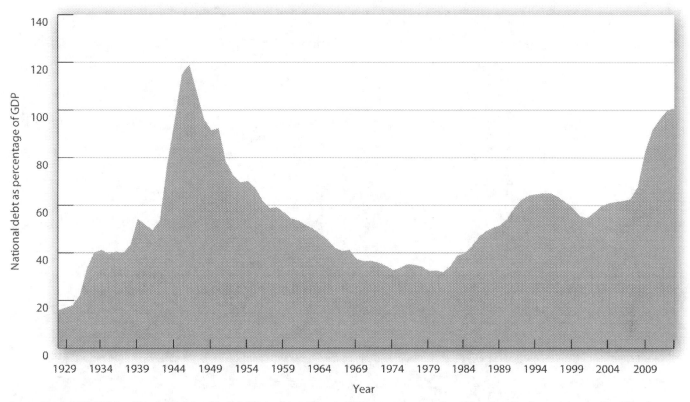

Sources: Data for 1929–1938 from Historical Statistics of the United States, Colonial Times to 1957—not strictly comparable with later data. Data for remaining years from Office of Management and Budget, Budget of the United States Government, Fiscal Year 2014, Historical Tables.

Judged by international standards, the U.S. national debt relative to its GDP is above average. Figure 17.7 shows national debt as a percentage of GDP for 32 countries in 2012. It also shows deficits or surpluses as a percentage of GDP.

In the United States, Congress authorizes the maximum amount of federal government borrowing. In an intense struggle between the Republican-majority U.S. House of Representatives and the Obama administration and the Democratic-majority U.S. Senate in the summer of 2011 that almost resulted in a government shutdown as the then debt ceiling had been reached, the Budget Control Act of 2011 raised the borrowing limit and resulted in a $1 trillion deficit reduction over ten years with additional reductions scheduled to follow. The Act provided for across-the board (with only a few exceptions) spending cuts, called sequestration, if Congress failed to agree on those further deficit-reducing measures. In the fall of 2013 with another debt ceiling breach looming, a 16-day government shutdown did occur when the House of Representatives would only agree to pass a general budget resolution even at the sequestration level if it included provisions to defund the Patient Protection and Affordable Care Act (often referred to as Obamacare), which the Senate refused to go along with. The shutdown ended with legislation, opposed by most Republicans in the House, to raise the debt ceiling and to allow government spending to resume temporarily while an actual spending bill was worked out. In late 2013, Congress finally agreed on a bipartisan two-year budget that reduced sequestration, and in early 2014 it agreed to raise the debt ceiling. These deals put these issues aside until after the U.S. congressional elections in November 2014.

FIGURE 17.7 Debts and Deficits for 32 Nations, 2012

The chart shows national debt as a percentage of GDP and deficits or surpluses as a percentage of GDP in 2012. The national debt of the United States relative to its GDP was above average among these nations.

Country	National Debt as percentage of GDP	Deficit (-) or surplus as percentage of GDP
Japan	218.8	-9.5
Greece	167.3	-9.0
Italy	142.2	-2.9
Portugal	134.5	-6.5
Iceland	129.6	-3.8
Ireland	127.5	-8.1
France	109.3	-4.8
Belgium	104.0	-4.1
United Kingdom	102.4	-6.2
United States	102.1	-9.3
Canada	96.1	-3.4
Spain	92.8	-10.6
Hungary	90.1	-2.1
Germany	88.3	0.1
Austria	85.6	-2.5
Netherlands	82.7	-4.0
Israel	68.2	-4.9
Finland	64.0	-2.2
Poland	62.4	-3.9
Slovenia	61.6	-3.8
Denmark	59.3	-3.9
Slovak Republic	56.9	-4.5
Czech Republic	55.7	-4.4
Sweden	48.8	-0.4
New Zealand	42.6	-3.9
Switzerland	42.4	-0.2
Korea	35.5	1.7
Norway	34.4	13.8
Australia	32.4	-3.5
Luxembourg	30.2	-0.6
Estonia	13.6	-0.2
Average	83.3	-3.5

Source: Organisation for Economic Co-operation and Development (OECD). Key Tables from OECD. (November 19, 2013).

KEY TAKEAWAYS

- Over the last 50 years, government purchases fell from about 20% of U.S. GDP to below 20%, but have been rising over the last decade.
- Transfer payment spending has risen sharply, both in absolute terms and as a percentage of real GDP since 1960.
- The bulk of federal revenues comes from income and payroll taxes. State and local revenues consist primarily of sales and property taxes.
- The government budget balance is the difference between government revenues and government expenditures.
- The national debt is the sum of all past federal deficits minus any surpluses.

TRY IT!

What happens to the national debt when there is a budget surplus? What happens to it when there is a budget deficit? What happens to the national debt if there is a decrease in a surplus? What happens to it if the deficit falls?

Case in Point

Generational Accounting

One method of assessing the degree to which current fiscal policies affect future generations is through a device introduced in the early 1990s called generational accounting. It measures the impact of current fiscal policies on different generations in the economy, including future generations. Generational accounting is now practiced by governments in many countries, including the United States and the European Union.

As populations age, the burden of current fiscal policy is increasingly borne by younger people in the population. In most countries, economists computing generational accounts have found that people age 40 or below will pay more in taxes than they receive in transfer payments, while those age 60 or above will receive more in transfers than they pay in taxes. The differences are huge. According to a recent study by Jagadeesh Gokhale, summarized in the table below, in 2004 in the United States, a male age 30 could expect to pay $201,300 more than he receives in government transfers during his lifetime, while another male age 75 could expect to receive $171,100 more in transfers than he paid in taxes during his lifetime. That is a difference of $372,400! For future generations, those born after the year 2004, the difference is even more staggering. A male born after the year 2005 can expect to pay $332,200 more in taxes than he will receive in transfer payments. For a woman, the differences are also large but not as great. A woman age 30 in 2004 could expect to pay $30,200 more in taxes than she will receive in transfers during her lifetime, while a woman age 75 could expect to receive transfers of $184,100 in excess of her lifetime tax burden.

The table below gives generational accounting estimates for the United States for the year 2004 for males and females. Figures shown are in thousands of 2004 dollars. Notice that the net burden on females is much lower than for males. That is because women live longer than men and thus receive Social Security and Medicare benefits over a longer period of time. Women also have lower labor force participation rates and earn less than men, and pay lower taxes as a result.

Year of birth	Age in 2004	Male	Female
2005 (future born)	−1	333.2	26.0
2004 (newborn)	0	104.3	8.1
1989	15	185.7	42.0
1974	30	201.3	30.2
1959	45	67.8	−54.1
1944	60	−162.6	−189.4
1929	75	−171.1	−184.1
1914	90	−65.0	−69.2

Generational accounting has its critics—for example, the table above only measures direct taxes and transfers but omits benefits from government spending on public goods and services. In addition, government spending programs can be modified, which would alter the impact on future generations. Nonetheless, it does help to focus attention on the sustainability of current fiscal policies. Can future generations pay for Social Security, Medicare, and other retirement and health care spending as currently configured? Should they be asked to do so?

Source: Jagadeesh Gokhale, "Generational Accounting," The New Palgrave Dictionary of Economics Online, 2nd ed., 2008.

ANSWER TO TRY IT! PROBLEM

A budget surplus leads to a decline in national debt; a budget deficit causes the national debt to grow. If there is a decrease in a budget surplus, national debt still declines but by less than it would have had the surplus not gotten smaller. If there is a decrease in the budget deficit, the national debt still grows, but by less than it would have if the deficit had not gotten smaller.

2. THE USE OF FISCAL POLICY TO STABILIZE THE ECONOMY

LEARNING OBJECTIVES

1. **Define automatic stabilizers and explain how they work.**
2. **Explain and illustrate graphically how discretionary fiscal policy works and compare the changes in aggregate demand that result from changes in government purchases, income taxes, and transfer payments.**

Fiscal policy—the use of government expenditures and taxes to influence the level of economic activity—is the government counterpart to monetary policy. Like monetary policy, it can be used in an effort to close a recessionary or an inflationary gap.

Some tax and expenditure programs change automatically with the level of economic activity. We will examine these first. Then we will look at how discretionary fiscal policies work. Four examples of discretionary fiscal policy choices were the tax cuts introduced by the Kennedy, Reagan, and George W. Bush administrations and the increase in government purchases proposed by President Clinton in 1993. The 2009 fiscal stimulus bill passed in the first months of the administration of Barack Obama included both tax rebates and spending increases. All were designed to stimulate aggregate demand and close recessionary gaps.

2.1 Automatic Stabilizers

Certain government expenditure and taxation policies tend to insulate individuals from the impact of shocks to the economy. Transfer payments have this effect. Because more people become eligible for income supplements when income is falling, transfer payments reduce the effect of a change in real

GDP on disposable personal income and thus help to insulate households from the impact of the change. Income taxes also have this effect. As incomes fall, people pay less in income taxes.

Any government program that tends to reduce fluctuations in GDP automatically is called an **automatic stabilizer**. Automatic stabilizers tend to increase GDP when it is falling and reduce GDP when it is rising.

automatic stabilizer

Any government program that tends to reduce fluctuations in GDP automatically.

To see how automatic stabilizers work, consider the decline in real GDP that occurred during the recession of 1990–1991. Real GDP fell 1.6% from the peak to the trough of that recession. The reduction in economic activity automatically reduced tax payments, reducing the impact of the downturn on disposable personal income. Furthermore, the reduction in incomes increased transfer payment spending, boosting disposable personal income further. Real disposable personal income thus fell by only 0.9% during the 1990—1991 recession, a much smaller percentage than the reduction in real GDP. Rising transfer payments and falling tax collections helped cushion households from the impact of the recession and kept real GDP from falling as much as it would have otherwise.

Automatic stabilizers have emerged as key elements of fiscal policy. Increases in income tax rates and unemployment benefits have enhanced their importance as automatic stabilizers. The introduction in the 1960s and 1970s of means-tested federal transfer payments, in which individuals qualify depending on their income, added to the nation's arsenal of automatic stabilizers. The advantage of automatic stabilizers is suggested by their name. As soon as income starts to change, they go to work. Because they affect disposable personal income directly, and because changes in disposable personal income are closely linked to changes in consumption, automatic stabilizers act swiftly to reduce the degree of changes in real GDP.

It is important to note that changes in expenditures and taxes that occur through automatic stabilizers do not shift the aggregate demand curve. Because they are automatic, their operation is already incorporated in the curve itself.

2.2 Discretionary Fiscal Policy Tools

As we begin to look at deliberate government efforts to stabilize the economy through fiscal policy choices, we note that most of the government's taxing and spending is for purposes other than economic stabilization. For example, the increase in defense spending in the early 1980s under President Ronald Reagan and in the administration of George W. Bush were undertaken primarily to promote national security. That the increased spending affected real GDP and employment was a by-product. The effect of such changes on real GDP and the price level is secondary, but it cannot be ignored. Our focus here, however, is on discretionary fiscal policy that is undertaken with the intention of stabilizing the economy. As we have seen, the tax cuts introduced by the Bush administration were justified as expansionary measures.

Discretionary government spending and tax policies can be used to shift aggregate demand. Expansionary fiscal policy might consist of an increase in government purchases or transfer payments, a reduction in taxes, or a combination of these tools to shift the aggregate demand curve to the right. A contractionary fiscal policy might involve a reduction in government purchases or transfer payments, an increase in taxes, or a mix of all three to shift the aggregate demand curve to the left.

Figure 17.8 illustrates the use of fiscal policy to shift aggregate demand in response to a recessionary gap and an inflationary gap. In Panel (a), the economy produces a real GDP of Y_1, which is below its potential level of Y_p. An expansionary fiscal policy seeks to shift aggregate demand to AD_2 in order to close the gap. In Panel (b), the economy initially has an inflationary gap at Y_1. A contractionary fiscal policy seeks to reduce aggregate demand to AD_2 and close the gap. Now we shall look at how specific fiscal policy options work. In our preliminary analysis of the effects of fiscal policy on the economy, we will assume that at a given price level these policies do not affect interest rates or exchange rates. We will relax that assumption later in the chapter.

FIGURE 17.8 Expansionary and Contractionary Fiscal Policies to Shift Aggregate Demand

In Panel (a), the economy faces a recessionary gap ($Y_P - Y_1$). An expansionary fiscal policy seeks to shift aggregate demand to AD_2 to close the gap. In Panel (b), the economy faces an inflationary gap ($Y_1 - Y_P$). A contractionary fiscal policy seeks to reduce aggregate demand to AD_2 to close the gap.

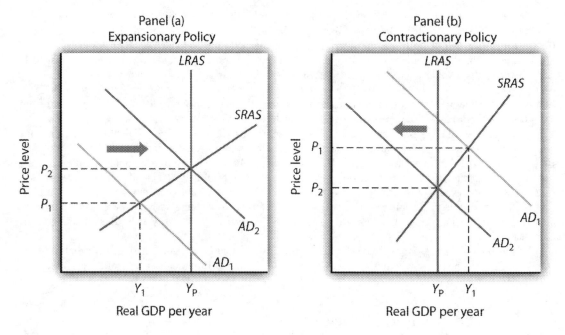

2.3   Changes in Government Purchases

One policy through which the government could seek to shift the aggregate demand curve is a change in government purchases. We learned that the aggregate demand curve shifts to the right by an amount equal to the initial change in government purchases times the multiplier. This multiplied effect of a change in government purchases occurs because the increase in government purchases increases income, which in turn increases consumption. Then, part of the impact of the increase in aggregate demand is absorbed by higher prices, preventing the full increase in real GDP that would have occurred if the price level did not rise.

FIGURE 17.9 An Increase in Government Purchases

The economy shown here is initially in equilibrium at a real GDP of $12,000 billion and a price level of P_1. An increase of $200 billion in the level of government purchases (ΔG) shifts the aggregate demand curve to the right by $400 billion to AD_2. The equilibrium level of real GDP rises to $12,300 billion, while the price level rises to P_2.

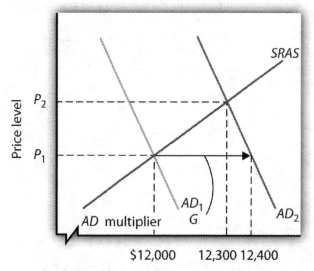

Figure 17.9 shows the effect of an increase in government purchases of $200 billion. The initial price level is P_1 and the initial equilibrium real GDP is $12,000 billion. Suppose the multiplier is 2. The $200 billion increase in government purchases increases the total quantity of goods and services demanded, at a price level of P_1, by $400 billion (the $200 billion increase in government purchases times the multiplier) to $12,400 billion. The aggregate demand thus shifts to the right by that amount to AD_2. The equilibrium level of real GDP rises to $12,300 billion, and the price level rises to P_2.

A reduction in government purchases would have the opposite effect. The aggregate demand curve would shift to the left by an amount equal to the initial change in government purchases times the multiplier. Real GDP and the price level would fall.

2.4   Changes in Business Taxes

One of the first fiscal policy measures undertaken by the Kennedy administration in the 1960s was an investment tax credit. An investment tax credit allows a firm to reduce its tax liability by a percentage of the investment it undertakes during a particular period. With an investment tax credit of 10%, for example, a firm that engaged in $1 million worth of investment during a year could reduce its tax liability for that year by $100,000. The investment tax credit introduced by the Kennedy administration was later repealed. It was reintroduced during the Reagan administration in 1981, then abolished by the Tax Reform Act of 1986. President Clinton called for a new investment tax credit in 1993 as part of his job stimulus proposal, but that proposal was rejected by Congress. The Bush administration reinstated the investment tax credit as part of its tax cut package.

An investment tax credit is intended, of course, to stimulate additional private sector investment. A reduction in the tax rate on corporate profits would be likely to have a similar effect. Conversely, an increase in the corporate income tax rate or a reduction in an investment tax credit could be expected to reduce investment.

A change in investment affects the aggregate demand curve in precisely the same manner as a change in government purchases. It shifts the aggregate demand curve by an amount equal to the initial change in investment times the multiplier.

An increase in the investment tax credit, or a reduction in corporate income tax rates, will increase investment and shift the aggregate demand curve to the right. Real GDP and the price level will rise. A reduction in the investment tax credit, or an increase in corporate income tax rates, will reduce investment and shift the aggregate demand curve to the left. Real GDP and the price level will fall.[2]

2.5   Changes in Income Taxes

Income taxes affect the consumption component of aggregate demand. An increase in income taxes reduces disposable personal income and thus reduces consumption (but by less than the change in disposable personal income). That shifts the aggregate demand curve leftward by an amount equal to the initial change in consumption that the change in income taxes produces times the multiplier.[3] A reduction in income taxes increases disposable personal income, increases consumption (but by less than the change in disposable personal income), and increases aggregate demand.

Suppose, for example, that income taxes are reduced by $200 billion. Only some of the increase in disposable personal income will be used for consumption and the rest will be saved. Suppose the initial increase in consumption is $180 billion. Then the shift in the aggregate demand curve will be a multiple of $180 billion; if the multiplier is 2, aggregate demand will shift to the right by $360 billion. Thus, as compared to the $200-billion increase in government purchases that we saw in Figure 17.9, the shift in the aggregate demand curve due to an income tax cut is somewhat less, as is the effect on real GDP and the price level.

2.6   Changes in Transfer Payments

Changes in transfer payments, like changes in income taxes, alter the disposable personal income of households and thus affect their consumption, which is a component of aggregate demand. A change in transfer payments will thus shift the aggregate demand curve because it will affect consumption. Because consumption will change by less than the change in disposable personal income, a change in transfer payments of some amount will result in a smaller change in real GDP than would a change in government purchases of the same amount. As with income taxes, a $200-billion increase in transfer payments will shift the aggregate demand curve to the right by less than the $200-billion increase in government purchases that we saw in Figure 17.9.

Table 17.1 summarizes U.S. fiscal policies undertaken to shift aggregate demand since the 1964 tax cuts. We see that expansionary policies have been chosen in response to recessionary gaps and that contractionary policies have been chosen in response to inflationary gaps. Changes in government purchases and in taxes have been the primary tools of fiscal policy in the United States.

TABLE 17.1 Fiscal Policy in the United States Since 1964

The table lists the major proposed uses of discretionary policy over a period of more than four decades.

Year	Situation	Policy response
1968	Inflationary gap	A temporary tax increase, first recommended by President Johnson's Council of Economic Advisers in 1965, goes into effect. This one-time surcharge of 10% is added to individual income tax liabilities.
1969	Inflationary gap	President Nixon, facing a continued inflationary gap, orders cuts in government purchases.
1975	Recessionary gap	President Ford, facing a recession induced by an OPEC oil-price increase, proposes a temporary 10% tax cut. It is passed almost immediately and goes into effect within two months.
1981	Recessionary gap	President Reagan had campaigned on a platform of increased defense spending and a sharp cut in income taxes. The tax cuts are approved in 1981 and are implemented over a period of three years. The increased defense spending begins in 1981. While the Reagan administration rejects the use of fiscal policy as a stabilization tool, its policies tend to increase aggregate demand early in the 1980s.
1992	Recessionary gap	President Bush had rejected the use of expansionary fiscal policy during the recession of 1990–1991. Indeed, he agreed late in 1990 to a cut in government purchases and a tax increase. In a campaign year, however, he orders a cut in withholding rates designed to increase disposable personal income in 1992 and to boost consumption.
1993	Recessionary gap	President Clinton calls for a $16-billion jobs package consisting of increased government purchases and tax cuts aimed at stimulating investment. The president says the plan will create 500,000 new jobs. The measure is rejected by Congress.
2001	Recessionary gap	President Bush campaigned to reduce taxes in order to reduce the size of government and encourage long-term growth. When he took office in 2001, the economy was weak and the $1.35-billion tax cut was aimed at both long-term tax relief and at stimulating the economy in the short term. It included, for example, a personal income tax rebate of $300 to $600 per household. With unemployment still high a couple of years into the expansion, another tax cut was passed in 2003.
2008	Recessionary gap	Fiscal stimulus package of $150 billion to spur economy. It included $100 billion in tax rebates and $50 billion in tax cuts for businesses.
2009	Recessionary gap	Fiscal stimulus package of $784 billion included tax rebates and increased government spending passed in early days of President Obama's administration.
2010–2012	Recessionary gap	Extensions of the payroll tax reduction and unemployment insurance benefits continued.

KEY TAKEAWAYS

- Discretionary fiscal policy may be either expansionary or contractionary.
- A change in government purchases shifts the aggregate demand curve at a given price level by an amount equal to the initial change in government purchases times the multiplier. The change in real GDP, however, will be reduced by the fact that the price level will change.
- A change in income taxes or government transfer payments shifts the aggregate demand curve by a multiple of the initial change in consumption (which is less than the change in personal disposable income) that the change in income taxes or transfer payments causes. Then, the change in real GDP will be reduced by the fact that the price level will change.
- A change in government purchases has a larger impact on the aggregate demand curve than does an equal change in income taxes or transfers.
- Changes in business tax rates, including an investment tax credit, can be used to influence the level of investment and thus the level of aggregate demand.

TRY IT!

Suppose the economy has an inflationary gap. What fiscal policies might be used to close the gap? Using the model of aggregate demand and aggregate supply, illustrate the effect of these policies.

Case in Point

How Large *Is* the Fiscal Multiplier?

There is a wide range of opinions among economists regarding the size of the fiscal multiplier. In 2011, the American Economic Association's *Journal of Economic Literature* published three papers on this topic in a special section titled "Forum: The Multiplier." The papers provide at least two-and-a-half different answers!

In her paper titled "Can Government Purchases Stimulate the Economy?," Valerie Ramey concludes that the size of the government purchases multiplier depends on many factors but that, when the increase in government purchases is temporary and financed by government borrowing, the multiplier "is probably between 0.8 and 1.5. Reasonable people can argue, however, that the data do not reject 0.5 to 2." This is quite a wide range.

In "An Empirical Analysis of the Revival of Fiscal Activism in the 2000s," John Taylor argues that the various components of the recent fiscal packages (tax cuts, aid to states, and increased government purchases) had little effect on the economy—implying a multiplier of zero or nearly so. Using aggregate quarterly data simulations for the 2000s, he argues that transfers and tax cuts were used by households to increase saving, that the increase in government purchases were too small to have made much of a difference, and that state and local governments used their stimulus dollars for transfers or to reduce their borrowing.

In "On Measuring the Effects of Fiscal Policy in Recessions," Jonathan Parker essentially argues that the statistical models built to date are ultimately inadequate and that we will only be able to get at the answer as better and more refined studies are conducted. Noting that the multiplier effect of fiscal policy is likely to depend on the state of the economy, he concludes that "an important difficulty with further investigation is the limited macroeconomic data available on the effects of policy in recessions (or deep recessions)." Perhaps we need a few more Great Recessions in order to figure this out.

In another American Economic Association publication, the *Journal of Economic Perspectives*, Alan Auerbach, William Gale, and Benjamin Harris provide an extensive review of the variety in multiplier estimates, which they acknowledge is "embarrassingly large" after so many years of trying to measure it. Concerning the 2009 American Recovery and Reinvestment Act, though, they write, "If a fiscal stimulus were ever to be considered appropriate, the beginning of 2009 was such a time....In these circumstances, our judgment is that a fiscal expansion carried much smaller risks than the lack of one would have."

Sources: Alan J. Auerbach, William G. Gale, and Benjamin H. Harris, "Activist Fiscal Policy," Journal of Economic Perspectives 24, no. 4 (Fall 2010): 141–64; Jonathan A. Parker, "On Measuring the Effects of Fiscal Policy in Recessions," Journal of Economic Literature 49, no. 3 (September 2011): 703–18; Valerie A. Ramey, "Can Government Purchases Stimulate the Economy?," Journal of Economic Literature 49, no. 3 (September 2011): 673–85; John B. Taylor, "An Empirical Analysis of the Revival of Fiscal Activism in the 2000s," Journal of Economic Literature 49, no. 3 (September 2011): 686–702.

ANSWER TO TRY IT! PROBLEM

Fiscal policies that could be used to close an inflationary gap include reductions in government purchases and transfer payments and increases in taxes. As shown in Panel (b) of Figure 17.8, the goal would be to shift the aggregate demand curve to the left so that it will intersect the short-run aggregate supply curve at Y_P.

3. ISSUES IN FISCAL POLICY

The discussion in the previous section about the use of fiscal policy to close gaps suggests that economies can be easily stabilized by government actions to shift the aggregate demand curve. However, as we discovered with monetary policy in the previous chapter, government attempts at stabilization are fraught with difficulties.

3.1 Lags

Discretionary fiscal policy is subject to the same lags that we discussed for monetary policy. It takes some time for policy makers to realize that a recessionary or an inflationary gap exists—the *recognition lag*. Recognition lags stem largely from the difficulty of collecting economic data in a timely and accurate fashion. The current recession was not identified until October 2008, when the Business Cycle Dating Committee of the National Bureau of Economic Research announced that it had begun in December 2007. Then, more time elapses before a fiscal policy, such as a change in government purchases or a change in taxes, is agreed to and put into effect—the *implementation lag*. Finally, still more time goes by before the policy has its full effect on aggregate demand—the *impact lag*.

Changes in fiscal policy are likely to involve a particularly long implementation lag. A tax cut was proposed to presidential candidate John F. Kennedy in 1960 as a means of ending the recession that year. He recommended it to Congress in 1962. It was not passed until 1964, three years after the recession had ended. Some economists have concluded that the long implementation lag for discretionary fiscal policy makes this stabilization tool ineffective. Fortunately, automatic stabilizers respond automatically to changes in the economy. They thus avoid not only the implementation lag but also the recognition lag.

The implementation lag results partly from the nature of bureaucracy itself. The CBO estimate that only a portion of the spending for the stimulus plan passed in 2009 will be spent in the next two years is an example of the implementation lag. Government spending requires bureaucratic approval of that spending. For example, a portion of the stimulus plan must go through the Department of Energy. One division of the department focuses on approving loan guarantees for energy-saving industrial projects. It was created early in 2007 as part of another effort to stimulate economic activity. A Minnesota company, Sage Electrochromics, has developed a process for producing windows that can be darkened or lightened on demand to reduce energy use in buildings. Sage applied two years ago for a guarantee on a loan of $66 million to build a plant that would employ 250 workers. Its application has not been approved. In fact, the loan approval division, which will be crucial for projects in the stimulus plan, has never approved any application made to it in its two years in existence!

Energy Secretary Steven Chu, a Nobel Prize-winning physicist, recognizes the urgency of the problem. In an interview with the *Wall Street Journal*, Dr. Chu said that his agency would have to do better. "Otherwise, it's just going to be a bust," he said.[4]

3.2 Crowding Out

Because an expansionary fiscal policy either increases government spending or reduces revenues, it increases the government budget deficit or reduces the surplus. A contractionary policy is likely to reduce a deficit or increase a surplus. In either case, fiscal policy thus affects the bond market. Our analysis of monetary policy showed that developments in the bond market can affect investment and net exports. We shall find in this section that the same is true for fiscal policy.

crowding out

The tendency for an expansionary fiscal policy to reduce other components of aggregate demand.

Figure 17.10 shows the impact of an expansionary fiscal policy: an increase in government purchases. The increase in government purchases increases the deficit or reduces the surplus. In either case, the Treasury will sell more bonds than it would have otherwise, shifting the supply curve for bonds to the right in Panel (a). That reduces the price of bonds, raising the interest rate. The increase in the interest rate reduces the quantity of private investment demanded. The higher interest rate increases the demand for and reduces the supply of dollars in the foreign exchange market, raising the exchange rate in Panel (b). A higher exchange rate reduces net exports. Panel (c) shows the effects of all these changes on the aggregate demand curve. Before the change in government purchases, the economy is in equilibrium at a real GDP of Y_1, determined by the intersection of AD_1 and the short-run aggregate supply curve. The increase in government expenditures would shift the curve outward to AD_2 if there were no adverse impact on investment and net exports. But the reduction in investment and net exports partially offsets this increase. Taking the reduction in investment and net exports into account means that the aggregate demand curve shifts only to AD_3. The tendency for an expansionary fiscal policy to reduce other components of aggregate demand is called **crowding out**. In the short run, this policy leads to an increase in real GDP to Y_2 and a higher price level, P_2.

FIGURE 17.10   An Expansionary Fiscal Policy and Crowding Out

In Panel (a), increased government purchases are financed through the sale of bonds, lowering their price to $P^b{}_2$. In Panel (b), the higher interest rate causes the exchange rate to rise, reducing net exports. Increased government purchases would shift the aggregate demand curve to AD_2 in Panel (c) if there were no crowding out. Crowding out of investment and net exports, however, causes the aggregate demand curve to shift only to AD_3. Then a higher price level means that GDP rises only to Y_2.

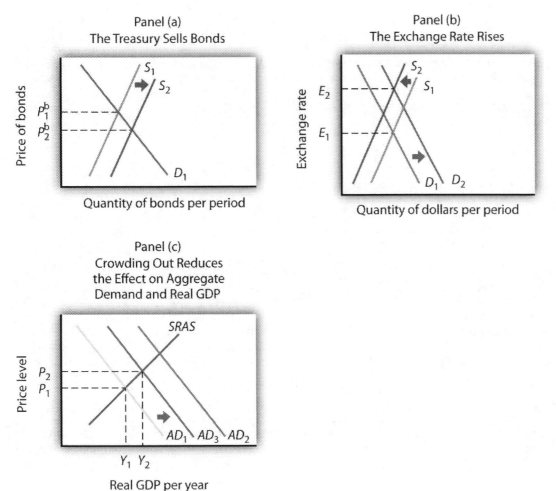

Crowding out reduces the effectiveness of any expansionary fiscal policy, whether it be an increase in government purchases, an increase in transfer payments, or a reduction in income taxes. Each of these policies increases the deficit and thus increases government borrowing. The supply of bonds increases, interest rates rise, investment falls, the exchange rate rises, and net exports fall.

Note, however, that it is private investment that is crowded out. The expansionary fiscal policy could take the form of an increase in the investment component of government purchases. As we have

KEY TAKEAWAYS

- Discretionary fiscal policy involves the same kind of lags as monetary policy. However, the implementation lag in fiscal policy is likely to be more pronounced, while the impact lag is likely to be less pronounced.
- Expansionary fiscal policy may result in the crowding out of private investment and net exports, reducing the impact of the policy. Similarly, contractionary policy may "crowd in" additional investment and net exports, reducing the contractionary impact of the policy.
- Supply-side economics stresses the use of fiscal policy to stimulate economic growth. Advocates of supply-side economics generally favor tax cuts to stimulate economic growth.

TRY IT!

Do the following hypothetical situations tend to enhance or make more difficult the use of fiscal policy as a stabilization tool?

1. Better and more speedily available data on the state of the economy
2. A finding that private sector investment spending is not much affected by interest rate changes
3. A finding that the supply-side effects of a tax cut are substantial

Case in Point

Crowding Out in Canada

In an intriguing study, economist Baotai Wang examined the degree of crowding out of Canadian private investment as a result of government expenditures from 1961–2000. What made Professor Wang's analysis unusual was that he divided Canadian government expenditures into five categories: expenditures for health and education, expenditures for capital and infrastructure, expenditures for the protection of persons and property (which included defense spending), expenditures for debt services, and expenditures for government and social services.

Mr. Wang found that only government expenditures for capital and infrastructure crowded out private investment. While these expenditures reduced private investment, they represented increased public sector investment for things such as highways and ports.

Expenditures for health and education actually "crowded in" private sector investment. These expenditures, Mr. Wang argued, represented increases in human capital. Such increases complement returns on private sector investment and therefore increase it.

Mr. Wang found that Canadian government expenditures for debt service, the protection of persons and property, and for government and social services had no effect on private sector investment. He argued that expenditures for protection of persons and property may involve some crowding out, but that they also stimulated private investment by firms winning government contracts for defense purchases. The same explanation could be applied to government expenditures for government and social services. These also include an element of investment in human capital.

His results suggest that crowding out depends on the nature of spending done by the government. Some kinds of spending clearly did not crowd out private sector investment in Canada.

Source: Baotai Wang, "Effects of Government Expenditure on Private Investment: Canadian Empirical Evidence," Empirical Economics 30, no. 2 (September 2005): 493–504.

A N S W E R S   T O   T R Y   I T !   P R O B L E M S

1. Data on the economy that are more accurate and more speedily available should enhance the use of fiscal policy by reducing the length of the recognition lag.

2. If private sector investment does not respond much to interest rate changes, then there will be less crowding out when expansionary policies are undertaken. That is, the rising interest rates that accompany expansionary fiscal policy will not reduce investment spending much, making the shift in the aggregate demand curve to the right greater than it would be otherwise. Also, the use of contractionary fiscal policy would be more effective, since the fall in interest rates would "invite in" less investment spending, making the shift in the aggregate demand curve to the left greater than it would otherwise be.

3. Large supply-side effects enhance the impact of tax cuts. For a given expansionary policy, without the supply-side effects, GDP would advance only to the point where the aggregate demand curve intersects the short-run aggregate supply curve. With the supply-side effects, both the short-run and long-run aggregate supply curves shift to the right. The intersection of the *AD* curve with the now increased short-run aggregate supply curve will be farther to the right than it would have been in the absence of the supply-side effects. The potential level of real GDP will also increase.

4. REVIEW AND PRACTICE

Summary

The government sector plays a major role in the economy. The spending, tax, and transfer policies of local, state, and federal agencies affect aggregate demand and aggregate supply and thus affect the level of real GDP and the price level. An expansionary policy tends to increase real GDP. Such a policy could be used to close a recessionary gap. A contractionary fiscal policy tends to reduce real GDP. A contractionary policy could be used to close an inflationary gap.

Government purchases of goods and services have a direct impact on aggregate demand. An increase in government purchases shifts the aggregate demand curve by the amount of the initial change in government purchases times the multiplier. Changes in personal income taxes or in the level of transfer payments affect disposable personal income. They change consumption, though initially by less than the amount of the change in taxes or transfers. They thus cause somewhat smaller shifts in the aggregate demand curve than do equal changes in government purchases.

There are several issues in the use of fiscal policies for stabilization purposes. They include lags associated with fiscal policy, crowding out, the choice of which fiscal policy tool to use, and the possible burdens of accumulating national debt.

CONCEPT PROBLEMS

1. What is the difference between government expenditures and government purchases? How do the two variables differ in terms of their effect on GDP?

2. Federally funded student aid programs generally reduce benefits by $1 for every $1 that recipients earn. Do such programs represent government purchases or transfer payments? Are they automatic stabilizers?

3. Crowding out reduces the degree to which a change in government purchases influences the level of economic activity. Is it a form of automatic stabilizer?

4. Why is it important to try to determine the size of the fiscal policy multiplier?

5. Suppose an economy has an inflationary gap. How does the government's actual budget deficit or surplus compare to the deficit or surplus it would have at potential output?

6. Suppose the president was given the authority to increase or decrease federal spending by as much as $100 billion in order to stabilize economic activity. Do you think this would tend to make the economy more or less stable?

7. Suppose the government increases purchases in an economy with a recessionary gap. How would this policy affect bond prices, interest rates, investment, net exports, real GDP, and the price level? Show your results graphically.

8. Suppose the government cuts transfer payments in an economy with an inflationary gap. How would this policy affect bond prices, interest rates, investment, the exchange rate, net exports, real GDP, and the price level? Show your results graphically.

9. Suppose that at the same time the government undertakes expansionary fiscal policy, such as a cut in taxes, the Fed undertakes contractionary monetary policy. How would this policy affect bond prices, interest rates, investment, net exports, real GDP, and the price level? Show your results graphically.

10. Given the nature of the implementation lag discussed in the text, discuss possible measures that might reduce the lag.

NUMERICAL PROBLEMS

1. Look up the table on Federal Receipts and Outlays, by Major Category, in the most recent *Economic Report of the President* available in your library or on the Internet.

   a. Complete the following table:

Category	Total outlays	Percentage of total outlays
National defense		
International affairs		
Health		
Medicare		
Income security		
Social Security		
Net interest		
Other		

   b. Construct a pie chart showing the percentages of spending for each category in the total.

2. Look up the table on ownership of U.S. Treasury securities in the most recent *Economic Report of the President* available on the Internet.

   a. Make a pie chart showing the percentage owned by various groups in the earliest year shown in the table.

   b. Make a pie chart showing the percentage owned by various groups in the most recent year shown in the table.

   c. What are some of the major changes in ownership of U.S. government debt over the period?

3. Suppose a country has a national debt of $5,000 billion, a GDP of $10,000 billion, and a budget deficit of $100 billion.

   a. How much will its new national debt be?

   b. Compute its debt-GDP ratio.

   c. Suppose its GDP grows by 1% in the next year and the budget deficit is again $100 billion. Compute its new level of national debt and its new debt-GDP ratio.

4. Suppose a country's debt rises by 10% and its GDP rises by 12%.

   a. What happens to the debt-GDP ratio?

   b. Does the relative level of the initial values affect your answer?

5. The data below show a country's national debt and its prime lending rate.

Year	National debt (billions of $)	Lending rate (%)
1992	4,064	6.0
1993	4,411	6.0
1994	4,692	8.5
1995	4,973	8.7
1996	5,224	8.3
1997	5,413	8.5

   a. Plot the relationship between national debt and the lending rate.

   b. Based on your graph, does crowding out appear to be a problem?

6. Suppose a country increases government purchases by $100 billion. Suppose the multiplier is 1.5 and the economy's real GDP is $5,000 billion.

   a. In which direction will the aggregate demand curve shift and by how much?

   b. Explain using a graph why the change in real GDP is likely to be smaller than the shift in the aggregate demand curve.

7. Suppose a country decreases government purchases by $100 billion. Suppose the multiplier is 1.5 and the economy's real GDP is $5,000 billion.

   a. In which direction will the aggregate demand curve shift and by how much?
   b. Explain using a graph why the change in real GDP is likely to be smaller than the shift in the aggregate demand curve.

8. Suppose a country decreases income taxes by $100 billion, and this leads to an increase in consumption spending of $90 billion. Suppose the multiplier is 1.5 and the economy's real GDP is $5,000 billion.

   a. In which direction will the aggregate demand curve shift and by how much?
   b. Explain using a graph why the change in real GDP is likely to be smaller than the shift in the aggregate demand curve.

9. Suppose a country increases income taxes by $100 billion, and this leads to a decrease in consumption spending of $90 billion. Suppose the multiplier is 1.5 and the economy's real GDP is $5,000 billion.

   a. In which direction will the aggregate demand curve shift and by how much?
   b. Explain using a graph why the change in real GDP is likely to be smaller than the shift in the aggregate demand curve.

10. Suppose a country institutes an investment tax credit, and this leads to an increase in investment spending of $100 billion. Suppose the multiplier is 1.5 and the economy's real GDP is $5,000 billion.

   a. In which direction will the aggregate demand curve shift and by how much?
   b. Explain using a graph why the change in real GDP is likely to be smaller than the shift in the aggregate demand curve.

11. Suppose a country repeals an investment tax credit, and this leads to a decrease in investment spending of $100 billion. Suppose the multiplier is 1.5 and the economy's real GDP is $5,000 billion.

   a. In which direction will the aggregate demand curve shift and by how much?
   b. Explain using a graph why the change in real GDP is likely to be smaller than the shift in the aggregate demand curve.

12. Explain why the shifts in the aggregate demand curves in questions 7 through 11 above are the same or different in absolute value.

ENDNOTES

1. Barack Obama, Weekly Address of the President to the Nation, February 14, 2009, available at http://www.whitehouse.gov/blog/09/02/14/A-major-milestone/.

2. Investment also affects the long-run aggregate supply curve, since a change in the capital stock changes the potential level of real GDP. We examined this earlier in the chapter on economic growth.

3. A change in tax rates will change the value of the multiplier. The reason is explained in another chapter.

4. Stephen Power and Neil King, Jr., "Next Challenge on Stimulus: Spending All That Money," *Wall Street Journal*, February 13, 2009, p. A1.

CHAPTER 18

A Brief History of Macroeconomic Thought and Policy

START UP: THREE REVOLUTIONS IN MACROECONOMIC THOUGHT

It is the 1930s. Many people have begun to wonder if the United States will ever escape the Great Depression's cruel grip. Forecasts that prosperity lies just around the corner take on a hollow ring.

The collapse seems to defy the logic of the dominant economic view—that economies should be able to reach full employment through a process of self-correction. The old ideas of macroeconomics do not seem to work, and it is not clear what new ideas should replace them.

In Britain, Cambridge University economist John Maynard Keynes is struggling with ideas that he thinks will stand the conventional wisdom on its head. He is confident that he has found the key not only to understanding the Great Depression but also to correcting it.

It is the 1960s. Most economists believe that Keynes's ideas best explain fluctuations in economic activity. The tools Keynes suggested have won widespread acceptance among governments all over the world; the application of expansionary fiscal policy in the United States appears to have been a spectacular success. But economist Milton Friedman of the University of Chicago continues to fight a lonely battle against what has become the Keynesian orthodoxy. He argues that money, not fiscal policy, is what affects aggregate demand. He insists not only that fiscal policy cannot work, but that monetary policy should not be used to move the economy back to its potential output. He counsels a policy of steady money growth, leaving the economy to adjust to long-run equilibrium on its own.

It is 1970. The economy has just taken a startling turn: Real GDP has fallen, but inflation has remained high. A young economist at Carnegie–Mellon University, Robert E. Lucas, Jr., finds this a paradox, one that he thinks cannot be explained by Keynes's theory. Along with several other economists, he begins work on a radically new approach to macroeconomic thought, one that will challenge Keynes's view head-on. Lucas and his colleagues suggest a world in which self-correction is swift, rational choices by individuals generally cancel the impact of fiscal and monetary policies, and stabilization efforts are likely to slow economic growth.

John Maynard Keynes, Milton Friedman, and Robert E. Lucas, Jr., each helped to establish a major school of macroeconomic thought. Although their ideas clashed sharply, and although there remains considerable disagreement among economists about a variety of issues, a broad consensus among economists concerning macroeconomic policy seemed to emerge in the 1980s, 1990s, and early 2000s. The Great Recession and the financial crisis in the late 2000s, though, set off another round of controversy.

In this chapter we will examine the macroeconomic developments of six decades: the 1930s, 1960s, 1970s, 1980s, 1990s, and 2000s. We will use the aggregate demand–aggregate supply model to explain macroeconomic changes during these periods, and we will see how the three major economic schools were affected by these events. We will also see how these schools of thought affected macroeconomic policy. Finally, we will see how the evolution of macroeconomic thought and policy influenced how economists design policy prescriptions for dealing with the recession that began in late 2007, which turned out to be the largest since the Great Depression.

In examining the ideas of these schools, we will incorporate concepts such as the potential output and the natural level of employment. While such terms had not been introduced when some of the major schools of thought first emerged, we will use them when they capture the ideas economists were presenting.

1.   THE GREAT DEPRESSION AND KEYNESIAN ECONOMICS

LEARNING OBJECTIVES

1. **Explain the basic assumptions of the classical school of thought that dominated macroeconomic thinking before the Great Depression, and tell why the severity of the Depression struck a major blow to this view.**
2. **Compare Keynesian and classical macroeconomic thought, discussing the Keynesian explanation of prolonged recessionary and inflationary gaps as well as the Keynesian approach to correcting these problems.**

It is hard to imagine that anyone who lived during the Great Depression was not profoundly affected by it. From the beginning of the Depression in 1929 to the time the economy hit bottom in 1933, real GDP plunged nearly 30%. Real per capita disposable income sank nearly 40%. More than 12 million people were thrown out of work; the unemployment rate soared from 3% in 1929 to 25% in 1933. Some 85,000 businesses failed. Hundreds of thousands of families lost their homes. By 1933, about half of all mortgages on all urban, owner-occupied houses were delinquent.[1]

The economy began to recover after 1933, but a huge recessionary gap persisted. Another downturn began in 1937, pushing the unemployment rate back up to 19% the following year.

The contraction in output that began in 1929 was not, of course, the first time the economy had slumped. But never had the U.S. economy fallen so far and for so long a period. Economic historians estimate that in the 75 years before the Depression there had been 19 recessions. But those contractions had lasted an average of less than two years. The Great Depression lasted for more than a decade. The severity and duration of the Great Depression distinguish it from other contractions; it is for that reason that we give it a much stronger name than "recession."

Figure 18.1 shows the course of real GDP compared to potential output during the Great Depression. The economy did not approach potential output until 1941, when the pressures of world war forced sharp increases in aggregate demand.

FIGURE 18.1 The Depression and the Recessionary Gap

The dark-shaded area shows real GDP from 1929 to 1942, the upper line shows potential output, and the light-shaded area shows the difference between the two—the recessionary gap. The gap nearly closed in 1941; an inflationary gap had opened by 1942. The chart suggests that the recessionary gap remained very large throughout the 1930s.

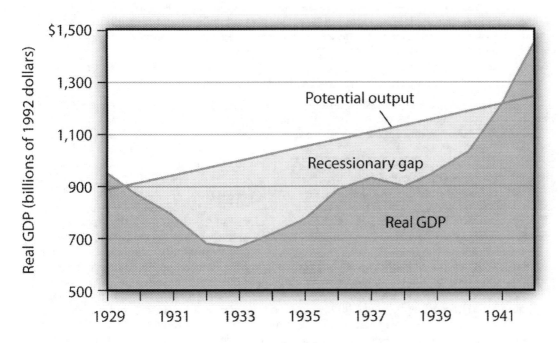

1.1   The Classical School and the Great Depression

The Great Depression came as a shock to what was then the conventional wisdom of economics. To see why, we must go back to the classical tradition of macroeconomics that dominated the economics profession when the Depression began.

Classical economics is the body of macroeconomic thought associated primarily with 19th-century British economist David Ricardo. His *Principles of Political Economy and Taxation*, published in 1817, established a tradition that dominated macroeconomic thought for over a century. Ricardo focused on the long run and on the forces that determine and produce growth in an economy's potential output. He emphasized the ability of flexible wages and prices to keep the economy at or near its natural level of employment.

According to the classical school, achieving what we now call the natural level of employment and potential output is not a problem; the economy can do that on its own. Classical economists recognized, however, that the process would take time. Ricardo admitted that there could be *temporary* periods in which employment would fall below the natural level. But his emphasis was on the long run, and in the long run all would be set right by the smooth functioning of the price system.

Economists of the classical school saw the massive slump that occurred in much of the world in the late 1920s and early 1930s as a short-run aberration. The economy would right itself in the long run, returning to its potential output and to the natural level of employment.

> **classical economics**
>
> The body of macroeconomic thought, associated primarily with 19th-century British economist David Ricardo, that focused on the long run and on the forces that determine and produce growth in an economy's potential output.

1.2   Keynesian Economics

In Britain, which had been plunged into a depression of its own, John Maynard Keynes had begun to develop a new framework of macroeconomic analysis, one that suggested that what for Ricardo were "temporary effects" could persist for a long time, and at terrible cost. Keynes's 1936 book, *The General Theory of Employment, Interest and Money*, was to transform the way many economists thought about macroeconomic problems.

Keynes versus the Classical Tradition

In a nutshell, we can say that Keynes's book shifted the thrust of macroeconomic thought from the concept of aggregate supply to the concept of aggregate demand. Ricardo's focus on the tendency of an economy to reach potential output inevitably stressed the supply side—an economy tends to operate at a level of output given by the long-run aggregate supply curve. Keynes, in arguing that what we now call recessionary or inflationary gaps could be created by shifts in aggregate demand, moved the focus of macroeconomic analysis to the demand side. He argued that prices in the short run are quite sticky and suggested that this stickiness would block adjustments to full employment.

Keynes dismissed the notion that the economy would achieve full employment in the long run as irrelevant. "In the long run," he wrote acidly, "we are all dead."

Keynes's work spawned a new school of macroeconomic thought, the Keynesian school. **Keynesian economics** asserts that changes in aggregate demand can create gaps between the actual and potential levels of output, and that such gaps can be prolonged. Keynesian economists stress the use of fiscal and of monetary policy to close such gaps.

Keynesian Economics and the Great Depression

The experience of the Great Depression certainly seemed consistent with Keynes's argument. A reduction in aggregate demand took the economy from above its potential output to below its potential output, and, as we saw in Figure 18.1, the resulting recessionary gap lasted for more than a decade. While the Great Depression affected many countries, we shall focus on the U.S. experience.

The plunge in aggregate demand began with a collapse in investment. The investment boom of the 1920s had left firms with an expanded stock of capital. As the capital stock approached its desired level, firms did not need as much new capital, and they cut back investment. The stock market crash of 1929 shook business confidence, further reducing investment. Real gross private domestic investment plunged nearly 80% between 1929 and 1932. We have learned of the volatility of the investment component of aggregate demand; it was very much in evidence in the first years of the Great Depression.

Other factors contributed to the sharp reduction in aggregate demand. The stock market crash reduced the wealth of a small fraction of the population (just 5% of Americans owned stock at that time), but it certainly reduced the consumption of the general population. The stock market crash also reduced consumer confidence throughout the economy. The reduction in wealth and the reduction in confidence reduced consumption spending and shifted the aggregate demand curve to the left.

Fiscal policy also acted to reduce aggregate demand. As consumption and income fell, governments at all levels found their tax revenues falling. They responded by raising tax rates in an effort to balance their budgets. The federal government, for example, doubled income tax rates in 1932. Total government tax revenues as a percentage of GDP shot up from 10.8% in 1929 to 16.6% in 1933. Higher tax rates tended to reduce consumption and aggregate demand.

Other countries were suffering declining incomes as well. Their demand for U.S. goods and services fell, reducing the real level of exports by 46% between 1929 and 1933. The Smoot–Hawley Tariff Act of 1930 dramatically raised tariffs on products imported into the United States and led to retaliatory trade-restricting legislation around the world. This act, which more than 1,000 economists opposed in a formal petition, contributed to the collapse of world trade and to the recession.

As if all this were not enough, the Fed, in effect, conducted a sharply contractionary monetary policy in the early years of the Depression. The Fed took no action to prevent a wave of bank failures that swept the country at the outset of the Depression. Between 1929 and 1933, one-third of all banks in the United States failed. As a result, the money supply plunged 31% during the period.

The Fed could have prevented many of the failures by engaging in open-market operations to inject new reserves into the system and by lending reserves to troubled banks through the discount window. But it generally refused to do so; Fed officials sometimes even applauded bank failures as a desirable way to weed out bad management!

Figure 18.2 shows the shift in aggregate demand between 1929, when the economy was operating just above its potential output, and 1933. The plunge in aggregate demand produced a recessionary gap. Our model tells us that such a gap should produce falling wages, shifting the short-run aggregate supply curve to the right. That happened; nominal wages plunged roughly 20% between 1929 and 1933. But we see that the shift in short-run aggregate supply was insufficient to bring the economy back to its potential output.

The failure of shifts in short-run aggregate supply to bring the economy back to its potential output in the early 1930s was partly the result of the magnitude of the reductions in aggregate demand, which plunged the economy into the deepest recessionary gap ever recorded in the United States. We know that the short-run aggregate supply curve began shifting to the right in 1930 as nominal wages fell, but these shifts, which would ordinarily increase real GDP, were overwhelmed by continued reductions in aggregate demand.

Keynesian economics

The body of macroeconomic thought that asserts that changes in aggregate demand can create gaps between the actual and potential levels of output, and that such gaps can be prolonged. It stresses the use of fiscal and monetary policy to close such gaps.

FIGURE 18.2 Aggregate Demand and Short-Run Aggregate Supply: 1929–1933

Slumping aggregate demand brought the economy well below the full-employment level of output by 1933. The short-run aggregate supply curve increased as nominal wages fell. In this analysis, and in subsequent applications in this chapter of the model of aggregate demand and aggregate supply to macroeconomic events, we are ignoring shifts in the long-run aggregate supply curve in order to simplify the diagram.

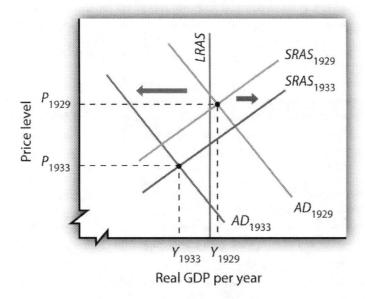

A further factor blocking the economy's return to its potential output was federal policy. President Franklin Roosevelt thought that falling wages and prices were in large part to blame for the Depression; programs initiated by his administration in 1933 sought to block further reductions in wages and prices. That stopped further reductions in nominal wages in 1933, thus stopping further shifts in aggregate supply. With recovery blocked from the supply side, and with no policy in place to boost aggregate demand, it is easy to see now why the economy remained locked in a recessionary gap so long.

FIGURE 18.3 World War II Ends the Great Depression

Increased U.S. government purchases, prompted by the beginning of World War II, ended the Great Depression. By 1942, increasing aggregate demand had pushed real GDP beyond potential output.

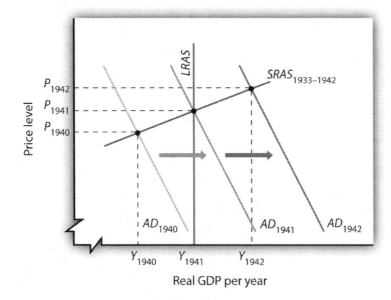

Keynes argued that expansionary fiscal policy represented the surest tool for bringing the economy back to full employment. The United States did not carry out such a policy until world war prompted increased federal spending for defense. New Deal policies did seek to stimulate employment through a variety of federal programs. But, with state and local governments continuing to cut purchases and raise taxes, the net effect of government at all levels on the economy did not increase aggregate demand during the Roosevelt administration until the onset of world war.[2] As Figure 18.3 shows, expansionary fiscal policies forced by the war had brought output back to potential by 1941. The U.S. entry into World War II after Japan's attack on American forces in Pearl Harbor in December of 1941 led to much sharper increases in government purchases, and the economy pushed quickly into an inflationary gap.

For Keynesian economists, the Great Depression provided impressive confirmation of Keynes's ideas. A sharp reduction in aggregate demand had gotten the trouble started. The recessionary gap created by the change in aggregate demand had persisted for more than a decade. And expansionary fiscal policy had put a swift end to the worst macroeconomic nightmare in U.S. history—even if that policy had been forced on the country by a war that would prove to be one of the worst episodes of world history.

KEY TAKEAWAYS

- Classical economic thought stressed the ability of the economy to achieve what we now call its potential output in the long run. It thus stressed the forces that determine the position of the long-run aggregate supply curve as the determinants of income.

- Keynesian economics focuses on changes in aggregate demand and their ability to create recessionary or inflationary gaps. Keynesian economists argue that sticky prices and wages would make it difficult for the economy to adjust to its potential output.

- Because Keynesian economists believe that recessionary and inflationary gaps can persist for long periods, they urge the use of fiscal and monetary policy to shift the aggregate demand curve and to close these gaps.

- Aggregate demand fell sharply in the first four years of the Great Depression. As the recessionary gap widened, nominal wages began to fall, and the short-run aggregate supply curve began shifting to the right. These shifts, however, were not sufficient to close the recessionary gap. World War II forced the U.S. government to shift to a sharply expansionary fiscal policy, and the Depression ended.

TRY IT!

Imagine that it is 1933. President Franklin Roosevelt has just been inaugurated and has named you as his senior economic adviser. Devise a program to bring the economy back to its potential output. Using the model of aggregate demand and aggregate supply, demonstrate graphically how your proposal could work.

Case in Point

Early Views on Stickiness

Although David Ricardo's focus on the long run emerged as the dominant approach to macroeconomic thought, not all of his contemporaries agreed with his perspective. Many 18th- and 19th-century economists developed theoretical arguments suggesting that changes in aggregate demand could affect the real level of economic activity in the short run. Like the new Keynesians, they based their arguments on the concept of price stickiness.

Henry Thornton's 1802 book, *An Enquiry into the Nature and Effects of the Paper Credit of Great Britain*, argued that a reduction in the money supply could, because of wage stickiness, produce a short-run slump in output:

> "The tendency, however, of a very great and sudden reduction of the accustomed number of
> bank notes, is to create an unusual and temporary distress, and a fall of price arising from
> that distress. But a fall arising from temporary distress, will be attended probably with no
> correspondent fall in the rate of wages; for the fall of price, and the distress, will be understood
> to be temporary, and the rate of wages, we know, is not so variable as the price of goods.
> There is reason, therefore, to fear that the unnatural and extraordinary low price arising from
> the sort of distress of which we now speak, would occasion much discouragement of the
> fabrication of manufactures."

A half-century earlier, David Hume had noted that an increase in the quantity of money would boost output in the short run, again because of the stickiness of prices. In an essay titled "Of Money," published in 1752, Hume described the process through which an increased money supply could boost output:

> "At first, no alteration is perceived; by degrees the price rises, first of one commodity, then of
> another, till the whole at least reaches a just proportion with the new quantity of (money)
> which is in the kingdom. In my opinion, it is only in this interval or intermediate situation …
> that the encreasing quantity of gold and silver is favourable to industry."

Hume's argument implies sticky prices; some prices are slower to respond to the increase in the money supply than others.

Economists of the 18th and 19th century are generally lumped together as adherents to the classical school, but their views were anything but uniform. Many developed an analytical framework that was quite similar to the essential elements of new Keynesian economists today. Economist Thomas Humphrey, at the Federal Reserve Bank of Richmond, marvels at the insights shown by early economists: "When you read these old guys, you find out first that they didn't speak with one voice. There was no single body of thought to which everyone subscribed. And second, you find out how much they *knew*. You could take Henry Thornton's 1802 book as a textbook in any money course today."

Source: Thomas M. Humphrey, "Nonneutrality of Money in Classical Monetary Thought," Federal Reserve Bank of Richmond Economic Review 77, no. 2 (March/April 1991): 3–15, and personal interview.

ANSWER TO TRY IT! PROBLEM

An expansionary fiscal or monetary policy, or a combination of the two, would shift aggregate demand to the right as shown in Panel (a), ideally returning the economy to potential output. One piece of evidence suggesting that fiscal policy would work is the swiftness with which the economy recovered from the Great Depression once World War II forced the government to carry out such a policy. An alternative approach would be to do nothing. Ultimately, that should force nominal wages down further, producing increases in short-run aggregate supply, as in Panel (b). We do not know if such an approach might have worked; federal policies enacted in 1933 prevented wages and prices from falling further than they already had.

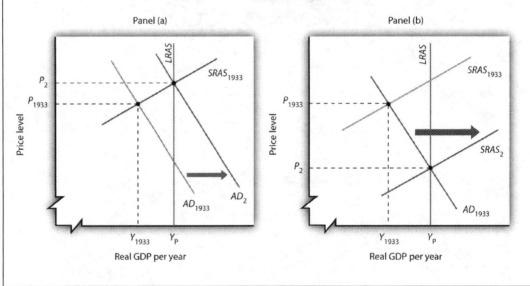

2. KEYNESIAN ECONOMICS IN THE 1960S AND 1970S

LEARNING OBJECTIVES

1. **Briefly summarize the monetarist school of thought that emerged in the 1960s, and discuss how the experiences of the 1960s and 1970s seemed to be broadly consistent with it.**
2. **Briefly summarize the new classical school of thought that emerged in the 1970s, and discuss how the experiences of the 1970s seemed to be broadly consistent with it.**
3. **Summarize the lessons that economists learned from the decade of the 1970s.**

The experience of the Great Depression led to the widespread acceptance of Keynesian ideas among economists, but its acceptance as a basis for economic policy was slower. The administrations of Presidents Roosevelt, Truman, and Eisenhower rejected the notion that fiscal policy could or should be used to manipulate real GDP. Truman vetoed a 1948 Republican-sponsored tax cut aimed at stimulating the economy after World War II (Congress, however, overrode the veto), and Eisenhower resisted stimulative measures to deal with the recessions of 1953, 1957, and 1960.

It was the administration of President John F. Kennedy that first used fiscal policy with the intent of manipulating aggregate demand to move the economy toward its potential output. Kennedy's willingness to embrace Keynes's ideas changed the nation's approach to fiscal policy for the next two decades.

2.1   Expansionary Policy in the 1960s

We can think of the macroeconomic history of the 1960s as encompassing two distinct phases. The first showed the power of Keynesian policies to correct economic difficulties. The second showed the power of these same policies to create them.

Correcting a Recessionary Gap

President Kennedy took office in 1961 with the economy in a recessionary gap. He had appointed a team of economic advisers who believed in Keynesian economics, and they advocated an activist approach to fiscal policy. The new president was quick to act on their advice.

Expansionary policy served the administration's foreign-policy purposes. Kennedy argued that the United States had fallen behind the Soviet Union, its avowed enemy, in military preparedness. He won approval from Congress for sharp increases in defense spending in 1961.

The Kennedy administration also added accelerated depreciation to the tax code. Under the measure, firms could deduct depreciation expenses more quickly, reducing their taxable profits—and thus their taxes—early in the life of a capital asset. The measure encouraged investment. The administration also introduced an investment tax credit, which allowed corporations to reduce their income taxes by 10% of their investment in any one year. The combination of increased defense spending and tax measures to stimulate investment provided a quick boost to aggregate demand.

The Fed followed the administration's lead. It, too, shifted to an expansionary policy in 1961. The Fed purchased government bonds to increase the money supply and reduce interest rates.

As shown in Panel (a) of Figure 18.4, the expansionary fiscal and monetary policies of the early 1960s had pushed real GDP to its potential by 1963. But the concept of potential output had not been developed in 1963; Kennedy administration economists had defined full employment to be an unemployment rate of 4%. The actual unemployment rate in 1963 was 5.7%; the perception of the time was that the economy needed further stimulus.

FIGURE 18.4   The Two Faces of Expansionary Policy in the 1960s

Expansionary fiscal and monetary policy early in the 1960s (Panel [a]) closed a recessionary gap, but continued expansionary policy created an inflationary gap by the end of the decade (Panel [b]). The short-run aggregate supply curve began shifting to the left, but expansionary policy continued to shift aggregate demand to the right and kept the economy in an inflationary gap.

Expansionary Policy and an Inflationary Gap

Kennedy proposed a tax cut in 1963, which Congress would approve the following year, after the president had been assassinated. In retrospect, we may regard the tax cut as representing a kind of a recognition lag— policy makers did not realize the economy had already reached what we now recognize was its potential output. Instead of closing a recessionary gap, the tax cut helped push the economy into an inflationary gap, as illustrated in Panel (b) of Figure 18.4.

The expansionary policies, however, did not stop with the tax cut. Continued increases in federal spending for the newly expanded war in Vietnam and for President Lyndon Johnson's agenda of domestic programs, together with continued high rates of money growth, sent the aggregate demand curve further to the right. While President Johnson's Council of Economic Advisers recommended contractionary policy as early as 1965, macroeconomic policy remained generally expansionary through 1969. Wage increases began shifting the short-run aggregate supply curve to the left, but expansionary policy continued to increase aggregate demand and kept the economy in an inflationary gap for the last six years of the 1960s. Panel (b) of Figure 18.4 shows expansionary policies pushing the economy beyond its potential output after 1963.

The 1960s had demonstrated two important lessons about Keynesian macroeconomic policy. First, stimulative fiscal and monetary policy could be used to close a recessionary gap. Second, fiscal policies could have a long implementation lag. The tax cut recommended by President Kennedy's economic advisers in 1961 was not enacted until 1964—after the recessionary gap it was designed to fight had been closed. The tax increase recommended by President Johnson's economic advisers in 1965 was not passed until 1968—after the inflationary gap it was designed to close had widened.

Macroeconomic policy after 1963 pushed the economy into an inflationary gap. The push into an inflationary gap did produce rising employment and a rising real GDP. But the inflation that came with it, together with other problems, would create real difficulties for the economy and for macroeconomic policy in the 1970s.

2.2 The 1970s: Troubles from the Supply Side

For many observers, the use of Keynesian fiscal and monetary policies in the 1960s had been a triumph. That triumph turned into a series of macroeconomic disasters in the 1970s as inflation and unemployment spiraled to ever-higher levels. The fiscal and monetary medicine that had seemed to work so well in the 1960s seemed capable of producing only instability in the 1970s. The experience of the period shook the faith of many economists in Keynesian remedies and made them receptive to alternative approaches.

This section describes the major macroeconomic events of the 1970s. It then examines the emergence of two schools of economic thought as major challengers to the Keynesian orthodoxy that had seemed so dominant a decade earlier.

Macroeconomic Policy: Coping with the Supply Side

When Richard Nixon became president in 1969, he faced a very different economic situation than the one that had confronted John Kennedy eight years earlier. The economy had clearly pushed beyond full employment; the unemployment rate had plunged to 3.6% in 1968. Inflation, measured using the implicit price deflator, had soared to 4.3%, the highest rate that had been recorded since 1951. The economy needed a cooling off. Nixon, the Fed, and the economy's own process of self-correction delivered it.

FIGURE 18.5 The Economy Closes an Inflationary Gap

The Nixon administration and the Fed joined to end the expansionary policies that had prevailed in the 1960s, so that aggregate demand did not rise in 1970, but the short-run aggregate supply curve shifted to the left as the economy responded to an inflationary gap.

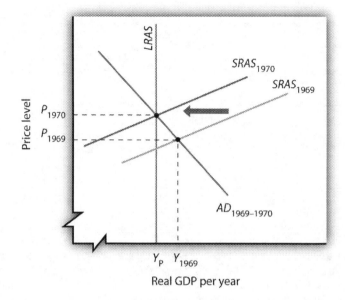

Figure 18.5 tells the story—it is a simple one. The economy in 1969 was in an inflationary gap. It had been in such a gap for years, but this time policy makers were no longer forcing increases in aggregate demand to keep it there. The adjustment in short-run aggregate supply brought the economy back to its potential output.

But what we can see now as a simple adjustment seemed anything but simple in 1970. Economists did not think in terms of shifts in short-run aggregate supply. Keynesian economics focused on shifts in aggregate demand, not supply.

For the Nixon administration, the slump in real GDP in 1970 was a recession, albeit an odd one. The price level had risen sharply. That was not, according to the Keynesian story, supposed to happen; there was simply no reason to expect the price level to soar when real GDP and employment were falling.

The administration dealt with the recession by shifting to an expansionary fiscal policy. By 1973, the economy was again in an inflationary gap. The economy's 1974 adjustment to the gap came with another jolt. The Organization of Petroleum Exporting Countries (OPEC) tripled the price of oil. The resulting shift to the left in short-run aggregate supply gave the economy another recession and another jump in the price level.

The second half of the decade was, in some respects, a repeat of the first. The administrations of Gerald Ford and then Jimmy Carter, along with the Fed, pursued expansionary policies to stimulate the economy. Those helped boost output, but they also pushed up prices. As we saw in the chapter on inflation and unemployment, inflation and unemployment followed a cycle to higher and higher levels.

The 1970s presented a challenge not just to policy makers, but to economists as well. The sharp changes in real GDP and in the price level could not be explained by a Keynesian analysis that focused on aggregate demand. Something else was happening. As economists grappled to explain it, their efforts would produce the model with which we have been dealing and around which a broad consensus of economists has emerged. But, before that consensus was to come, two additional elements of the puzzle had to be added. The first was the recognition of the importance of monetary policy. The second was the recognition of the role of aggregate supply, both in the long and in the short run.

The Monetarist Challenge

The idea that changes in the money supply are the principal determinant of the nominal value of total output is one of the oldest in economic thought. It is implied by the equation of exchange:

EQUATION 18.1

$$MV = \text{nominal GDP}$$

equation of exchange

The money supply (*M*) times its velocity (*V*) equals nominal GDP.

velocity

The number of times the money supply is spent to obtain the goods and services that make up GDP during a particular time period.

The **equation of exchange** shows that the money supply M times its velocity V equals nominal GDP. **Velocity** is the number of times the money supply is spent to obtain the goods and services that make up GDP during a particular time period.

To see that nominal GDP is the price level multiplied by real GDP, recall from an earlier chapter that the implicit price deflator P equals nominal GDP divided by real GDP:

EQUATION 18.2

$$P = \frac{\text{Nominal GDP}}{\text{Real GDP}}$$

Multiplying both sides by real GDP, we have

EQUATION 18.3

$$\text{Nominal GDP} = P \times \text{real GDP}$$

Letting Y equal real GDP, we can rewrite the equation of exchange as

EQUATION 18.4

$$MV = PY$$

We shall use the equation of exchange to see how it represents spending in a hypothetical economy that consists of 50 people, each of whom has a car. Each person has $10 in cash and no other money. The money supply of this economy is thus $500. Now suppose that the sole economic activity in this economy is car washing. Each person in the economy washes one other person's car once a month, and the price of a car wash is $10. In one month, then, a total of 50 car washes are produced at a price of $10 each. During that month, the money supply is spent once.

Applying the equation of exchange to this economy, we have a money supply M of $500 and a velocity V of 1. Because the only good or service produced is car washing, we can measure real GDP as the number of car washes. Thus Y equals 50 car washes. The price level P is the price of a car wash: $10. The equation of exchange for a period of 1 month is

$$\$500 \times 1 = \$10 \times 50$$

Now suppose that in the second month everyone washes someone else's car again. Over the full two-month period, the money supply has been spent twice—the velocity over a period of two months is 2. The total output in the economy is $1,000—100 car washes have been produced over a two-month period at a price of $10 each. Inserting these values into the equation of exchange, we have

$$\$500 \times 2 = \$10 \times 100$$

Suppose this process continues for one more month. For the three-month period, the money supply of $500 has been spent three times, for a velocity of 3. We have

$$\$500 \times 3 = \$10 \times 150$$

The essential thing to note about the equation of exchange is that it always holds. That should come as no surprise. The left side, MV, gives the money supply times the number of times that money is spent on goods and services during a period. It thus measures total spending. The right side is nominal GDP. But that is a measure of total spending on goods and services as well. Nominal GDP is the value of all final goods and services produced during a particular period. Those goods and services are either sold or added to inventory. If they are sold, then they must be part of total spending. If they are added to inventory, then some firm must have either purchased them or paid for their production; they thus represent a portion of total spending. In effect, the equation of exchange says simply that total spending on goods and services, measured as MV, equals total spending on goods and services, measured as PY (or nominal GDP). The equation of exchange is thus an identity, a mathematical expression that is true by definition.

To apply the equation of exchange to a real economy, we need measures of each of the variables in it. Three of these variables are readily available. The Department of Commerce reports the price level (that is, the implicit price deflator) and real GDP. The Federal Reserve Board reports M2, a measure of the money supply. For the second quarter of 2008, the values of these variables at an annual rate were

$M = \$7,635.4$ billion
$P = 1.22$
$Y = 11,727.4$ billion

To solve for the velocity of money, V, we divide both sides of Equation 18.4 by M:

EQUATION 18.5

$$V = \frac{PY}{M}$$

Using the data for the second quarter of 2008 to compute velocity, we find that V then was equal to 1.87. A velocity of 1.87 means that the money supply was spent 1.87 times in the purchase of goods and services in the second quarter of 2008.

Assume for the moment that velocity is constant, expressed as $\overline{V}$. Our equation of exchange is now written as

EQUATION 18.6

$$M\overline{V} = PY$$

A constant value for velocity would have two important implications:

1. Nominal GDP could change *only* if there were a change in the money supply. Other kinds of changes, such as a change in government purchases or a change in investment, could have no effect on nominal GDP.

2. A change in the money supply would always change nominal GDP, and by an equal percentage.

In short, if velocity were constant, a course in macroeconomics would be quite simple. The quantity of money would determine nominal GDP; nothing else would matter.

Indeed, when we look at the behavior of economies over long periods of time, the prediction that the quantity of money determines nominal output holds rather well. Figure 18.6 compares long-term averages in the growth rates of M2 and nominal GNP for 11 countries (Canada, Denmark, France, Italy, Japan, the Netherlands, Norway, Sweden, Switzerland, the United Kingdom, and the United States) for more than a century. These are the only countries that have consistent data for such a long period. The lines representing inflation, M2 growth, and nominal GDP growth do seem to move together most of the time, suggesting that velocity is constant when viewed over the long run.

FIGURE 18.6   Inflation, M2 Growth, and GDP Growth

The chart shows the behavior of price-level changes, the growth of M2, and the growth of nominal GDP for 11 countries using the average value of each variable. Viewed in this light, the relationship between money growth and nominal GDP seems quite strong.

Source: Alfred A. Haug and William G. Dewald, "Longer-Term Effects of Monetary Growth on Real and Nominal Variables, Major Industrial Countries, 1880–2001" (European Central Bank Working Paper Series No. 382, August 2004).

Moreover, price-level changes also follow the same pattern that changes in M2 and nominal GNP do. Why is this?

We can rewrite the equation of exchange, $M\overline{V} = PY$, in terms of percentage rates of change. When two products, such as $M\overline{V}$ and PY, are equal, and the variables themselves are changing, then the sums of the percentage rates of change are approximately equal:

EQUATION 18.7

$$\%\Delta M + \%\Delta V \cong \%\Delta P + \%\Delta Y$$

The Greek letter Δ (delta) means "change in." Assume that velocity is constant in the long run, so that $\%\Delta V = 0$. We also assume that real GDP moves to its potential level, Y_P, in the long run. With these assumptions, we can rewrite Equation 18.7 as follows:

EQUATION 18.8

$$\%\Delta M \cong \%\Delta P + \%\Delta Y_P$$

Subtracting $\%\Delta Y_P$ from both sides of Equation 18.8, we have the following:

EQUATION 18.9

$$\%\Delta M - \%\Delta Y_P \cong \%\Delta P$$

Equation 18.9 has enormously important implications for monetary policy. It tells us that, in the long run, the rate of inflation, $\%\Delta P$, equals the difference between the rate of money growth and the rate of increase in potential output, $\%\Delta Y_P$, given our assumption of constant velocity. Because potential output is likely to rise by, at most, a few percentage points per year, the rate of money growth will be close to the rate of inflation in the long run.

Classical economists stressed the long run and thus the determination of the economy's potential output. This meant that changes in the price level were, in the long run, the result of changes in the money supply, assuming the stability of velocity.

At roughly the same time Keynesian economics was emerging as the dominant school of macroeconomic thought, some economists focused on changes in the money supply as the primary determinant of changes in the nominal value of output. Led by Milton Friedman, they stressed the role of changes in the money supply as the principal determinant of changes in nominal output in the short run as well as in the long run. They argued that fiscal policy had no effect on the economy. Their "money rules" doctrine led to the name *monetarists*. The **monetarist school** holds that changes in the money supply are the primary cause of changes in nominal GDP.

monetarist school

The body of macroeconomic thought that holds that changes in the money supply are the primary cause of changes in nominal GDP.

Monetarists generally argue that the impact lags of monetary policy—the lags from the time monetary policy is undertaken to the time the policy affects nominal GDP—are so long and variable that trying to stabilize the economy using monetary policy can be destabilizing. Monetarists thus are critical of activist stabilization policies. They argue that, because of crowding-out effects, fiscal policy has no effect on GDP. Monetary policy does, but it should not be used. Instead, most monetarists urge the Fed to increase the money supply at a fixed annual rate, preferably the rate at which potential output rises. With stable velocity, that would eliminate inflation in the long run. Recessionary or inflationary gaps could occur in the short run, but monetarists generally argue that self-correction will take care of them more effectively than would activist monetary policy.

While monetarists differ from Keynesians in their assessment of the impact of fiscal policy, the primary difference between the two schools lies in their degree of optimism about whether stabilization policy can, in fact, be counted on to bring the economy back to its potential output. For monetarists, the complexity of economic life and the uncertain nature of lags mean that efforts to use monetary policy to stabilize the economy can be destabilizing. Monetarists argued that the difficulties encountered by policy makers as they tried to respond to the dramatic events of the 1970s demonstrated the superiority of a policy that simply increased the money supply at a slow, steady rate.

Monetarists could also cite the apparent validity of an adjustment mechanism proposed by Milton Friedman in 1968. As the economy continued to expand in the 1960s, and as unemployment continued to fall, Friedman said that unemployment had fallen below its natural rate, the rate consistent with equilibrium in the labor market. Any divergence of unemployment from its natural rate, he insisted, would necessarily be temporary. He suggested that the low unemployment of 1968 (the rate was 3.6% that year) meant that workers had been surprised by rising prices. Higher prices had produced a real wage below what workers and firms had expected. Friedman predicted that as workers demanded and got higher nominal wages, the price level would shoot up and unemployment would rise. That, of course, is precisely what happened in 1970 and 1971. Friedman's notion of the natural rate of unemployment buttressed the monetarist argument that the economy moves to its potential output on its own.

Perhaps the most potent argument from the monetarist camp was the behavior of the economy itself. During the 1960s, monetarist and Keynesian economists alike could argue that economic performance was consistent with their respective views of the world. Keynesians could point to expansions in economic activity that they could ascribe to expansionary fiscal policy, but economic activity also moved closely with changes in the money supply, just as monetarists predicted. During the 1970s, however, it was difficult for Keynesians to argue that policies that affected aggregate demand were having the predicted impact on the economy. Changes in aggregate supply had repeatedly pushed the economy off a Keynesian course. But monetarists, once again, could point to a consistent relationship between changes in the money supply and changes in economic activity.

Figure 18.7 shows the movement of nominal GDP and M2 during the 1960s and 1970s. In the figure, annual percentage changes in M2 are plotted against percentage changes in nominal GDP a year later to account for the lagged effects of changes in the money supply. We see that there was a close relationship between changes in the quantity of money and subsequent changes in nominal GDP.

Monetarist doctrine emerged as a potent challenge to Keynesian economics in the 1970s, largely because of the close correspondence between nominal GDP and the money supply. The next section examines another school of thought that came to prominence in the 1970s.

FIGURE 18.7 M2 and Nominal GDP, 1960–1980

The chart shows annual rates of change in M2 and in nominal GDP, lagged one year. The observation for 1961, for example, shows that nominal GDP increased 3.5% and that M2 increased 4.9% in the previous year, 1960. The two variables showed a close relationship in the 1960s and 1970s.

New Classical Economics: A Focus on Aggregate Supply

Much of the difficulty policy makers encountered during the decade of the 1970s resulted from shifts in aggregate supply. Keynesian economics and, to a lesser degree, monetarism had focused on aggregate demand. As it became clear that an analysis incorporating the supply side was an essential part of the macroeconomic puzzle, some economists turned to an entirely new way of looking at macroeconomic issues.

These economists started with what we identified at the beginning of this text as a distinguishing characteristic of economic thought: a focus on individuals and their decisions. Keynesian economics employed aggregate analysis and paid little attention to individual choices. Monetarist doctrine was based on the analysis of individuals' maximizing behavior with respect to money demand, but it did not extend that analysis to decisions that affect aggregate supply. The new approach aimed at an analysis of how individual choices would affect the entire spectrum of economic activity.

new classical economics

The approach to macroeconomic analysis built from an analysis of individual maximizing choices and emphasizing wage and price flexibility.

These economists rejected the entire framework of conventional macroeconomic analysis. Indeed, they rejected the very term. For them there is no macroeconomics, nor is there something called microeconomics. For them, there is only economics, which they regard as the analysis of behavior based on individual maximization. The analysis of the determination of the price level and real GDP becomes an application of basic economic theory, not a separate body of thought. The approach to macroeconomic analysis built from an analysis of individual maximizing choices is called **new classical economics**.

Like classical economic thought, new classical economics focuses on the determination of long-run aggregate supply and the economy's ability to reach this level of output quickly. But the similarity ends there. Classical economics emerged in large part before economists had developed sophisticated mathematical models of maximizing behavior. The new classical economics puts mathematics to work in an extremely complex way to generalize from individual behavior to aggregate results.

Because the new classical approach suggests that the economy will remain at or near its potential output, it follows that the changes we observe in economic activity result not from changes in aggregate demand but from changes in long-run aggregate supply. New classical economics suggests that economic changes don't necessarily imply economic problems.

New classical economists pointed to the supply-side shocks of the 1970s, both from changes in oil prices and changes in expectations, as evidence that their emphasis on aggregate supply was on the mark. They argued that the large observed swings in real GDP reflected underlying changes in the economy's potential output. The recessionary and inflationary gaps that so perplexed policy makers during the 1970s were not gaps at all, the new classical economists insisted. Instead, they reflected changes in the economy's own potential output.

rational expectations hypothesis

Individuals form expectations about the future based on the information available to them, and they act on those expectations.

Two particularly controversial propositions of new classical theory relate to the impacts of monetary and of fiscal policy. Both are implications of the **rational expectations hypothesis**, which assumes that individuals form expectations about the future based on the information available to them, and that they act on those expectations.

FIGURE 18.8 Contractionary Monetary Policy: With and Without Rational Expectations

Panels (a) and (b) show an economy operating at potential output (1); a contractionary monetary policy shifts aggregate demand to AD_2. Panel (a) shows the kind of response we have studied up to this point; real GDP falls to Y_2 in period (2); the recessionary gap is closed in the long run by falling nominal wages that cause an increase in short-run aggregate supply in period (3). Panel (b) shows the rational expectations argument. People anticipate the impact of the contractionary policy when it is undertaken, so that the short-run aggregate supply curve shifts to the right at the same time the aggregate demand curve shifts to the left. The result is a reduction in the price level but no change in real GDP; the solution moves from (1) to (2).

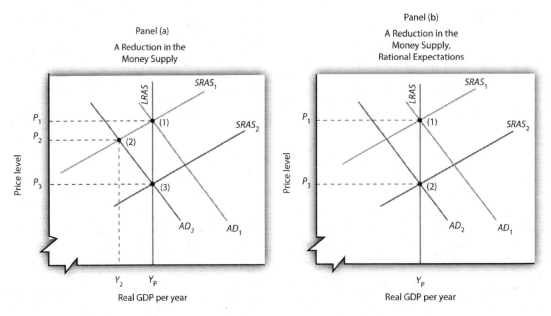

The rational expectations hypothesis suggests that monetary policy, even though it will affect the aggregate demand curve, might have no effect on real GDP. This possibility, which was suggested by Robert Lucas, is illustrated in Figure 18.8. Suppose the economy is initially in equilibrium at point 1 in Panel (a). Real GDP equals its potential output, Y_P. Now suppose a reduction in the money supply causes aggregate demand to fall to AD_2. In our model, the solution moves to point 2; the price level falls to P_2, and real GDP falls to Y_2. There is a recessionary gap. In the long run, the short-run aggregate supply curve shifts to $SRAS_2$, the price level falls to P_3, and the economy returns to its potential output at point 3.

The new classical story is quite different. Consumers and firms observe that the money supply has fallen and anticipate the eventual reduction in the price level to P_3. They adjust their expectations accordingly. Workers agree to lower nominal wages, and the short-run aggregate supply curve shifts to $SRAS_2$. This occurs as aggregate demand falls. As suggested in Panel (b), the price level falls to P_3, and output remains at potential. The solution moves from (1) to (2) with no loss in real GDP.

In this new classical world, there is only one way for a change in the money supply to affect output, and that is for the change to take people by surprise. An unexpected change cannot affect expectations, so the short-run aggregate supply curve does not shift in the short run, and events play out as in Panel (a). Monetary policy can affect output, but only if it takes people by surprise.

The new classical school offers an even stronger case against the operation of fiscal policy. It argues that fiscal policy does not shift the aggregate demand curve at all! Consider, for example, an expansionary fiscal policy. Such a policy involves an increase in government purchases or transfer payments or a cut in taxes. Any of these policies will increase the deficit or reduce the surplus. New classical economists argue that households, when they observe the government carrying out a policy that increases the debt, will anticipate that they, or their children, or their children's children, will end up paying more in taxes. And, according to the new classical story, these households will reduce their consumption as a result. This will, the new classical economists argue, cancel any tendency for the expansionary policy to affect aggregate demand.

Lessons from the 1970s

The 1970s put Keynesian economics and its prescription for activist policies on the defensive. The period lent considerable support to the monetarist argument that changes in the money supply were the primary determinant of changes in the nominal level of GDP. A series of dramatic shifts in aggregate supply gave credence to the new classical emphasis on long-run aggregate supply as the primary determinant of real GDP. Events did not create the new ideas, but they produced an environment in which those ideas could win greater support.

For economists, the period offered some important lessons. These lessons, as we will see in the next section, forced a rethinking of some of the ideas that had dominated Keynesian thought. The experience of the 1970s suggested the following:

1. The short-run aggregate supply curve could not be viewed as something that provided a passive path over which aggregate demand could roam. The short-run aggregate supply curve could shift in ways that clearly affected real GDP, unemployment, and the price level.

2. Money mattered more than Keynesians had previously suspected. Keynes had expressed doubts about the effectiveness of monetary policy, particularly in the face of a recessionary gap. Work by monetarists suggested a close correspondence between changes in M2 and subsequent changes in nominal GDP, convincing many Keynesian economists that money was more important than they had thought.

3. Stabilization was a more difficult task than many economists had anticipated. Shifts in aggregate supply could frustrate the efforts of policy makers to achieve certain macroeconomic goals.

KEY TAKEAWAYS

- Beginning in 1961, expansionary fiscal and monetary policies were used to close a recessionary gap; this was the first major U.S. application of Keynesian macroeconomic policy.

- The experience of the 1960s and 1970s appeared to be broadly consistent with the monetarist argument that changes in the money supply are the primary determinant of changes in nominal GDP.

- The new classical school's argument that the economy operates at its potential output implies that real GDP is determined by long-run aggregate supply. The experience of the 1970s, in which changes in aggregate supply forced changes in real GDP and in the price level, seemed consistent with the new classical economists' arguments that focused on aggregate supply.

- The experience of the 1970s suggested that changes in the money supply and in aggregate supply were more important determinants of economic activity than many Keynesians had previously thought.

Draw the aggregate demand and the short-run and long-run aggregate supply curves for an economy operating with an inflationary gap. Show how expansionary fiscal and/or monetary policies would affect such an economy. Now show how this economy could experience a recession and an increase in the price level at the same time.

Case in Point

Tough Medicine Is Hard to Stomach: Macroeconomic Policy in the 1960s

The Keynesian prescription for an inflationary gap seems simple enough. The federal government applies contractionary fiscal policy, or the Fed applies contractionary monetary policy, or both. But what seems simple in a graph can be maddeningly difficult in the real world. The medicine for an inflationary gap is tough, and it is tough to take.

President Johnson's new chairman of the Council of Economic Advisers, Gardner Ackley, urged the president in 1965 to adopt fiscal policies aimed at nudging the aggregate demand curve back to the left. The president reluctantly agreed and called in the chairman of the House Ways and Means Committee, the committee that must initiate all revenue measures, to see what he thought of the idea. Wilbur Mills flatly told Johnson that he wouldn't even hold hearings to consider a tax increase. For the time being, the tax boost was dead.

The Federal Reserve System did slow the rate of money growth in 1966. But fiscal policy remained sharply expansionary. Mr. Ackley continued to press his case, and in 1967 President Johnson proposed a temporary 10% increase in personal income taxes. Mr. Mills now endorsed the measure. The temporary tax boost went into effect the following year. The Fed, concerned that the tax hike would be *too* contractionary, countered the administration's shift in fiscal policy with a policy of vigorous money growth in 1967 and 1968.

The late 1960s suggested a sobering reality about the new Keynesian orthodoxy. Stimulating the economy was politically more palatable than contracting it. President Kennedy, while he was not able to win approval of his tax cut during his lifetime, did manage to put the other expansionary aspects of his program into place early in his administration. The Fed reinforced his policies. Dealing with an inflationary gap proved to be quite another matter. President Johnson, a master of the legislative process, took three years to get even a mildly contractionary tax increase put into place, and the Fed acted to counter the impact of this measure by shifting to an expansionary policy.

The second half of the 1960s was marked, in short, by persistent efforts to boost aggregate demand, efforts that kept the economy in an inflationary gap through most of the decade. It was a gap that would usher in a series of supply-side troubles in the next decade.

Even with an inflationary gap, it is possible to pursue expansionary fiscal and monetary policies, shifting the aggregate demand curve to the right, as shown. The inflationary gap will, however, produce an increase in nominal wages, reducing short-run aggregate supply over time. In the case shown here, real GDP rises at first, then falls back to potential output with the reduction in short-run aggregate supply.

3.   MACROECONOMICS FOR THE 21ST CENTURY

LEARNING OBJECTIVES

1. **Discuss how the Fed incorporated a strong inflation constraint and lags into its policies from the 1980s onwards.**
2. **Describe the fiscal policies that were undertaken from the 1980s onwards and their rationales.**
3. **Discuss the challenges that events from the 1980s onwards raised for the monetarist and new classical schools of thought.**
4. **Summarize the views and policy approaches of the new Keynesian school of economic thought.**

Following the recession that ended in 1982, the last two decades of the 20th century and the early years of the 21st century have sometimes been referred to as the Great Moderation. Yes, there were recessions, but they were fairly mild and short-lived. Prematurely, economists began to pat themselves on the backs for having tamed the business cycle. There was a sense that macroeconomic theory and policy had helped with this improved performance. The ideas associated with macroeconomic theory and policy incorporated elements of Keynesian economics, monetarism, and new classical economics. All three schools of macroeconomic thought contributed to the development of a new school of macroeconomic thought: the new Keynesian school.

new Keynesian economics

A body of macroeconomic thought that stresses the stickiness of prices and the need for activist stabilization policies through the manipulation of aggregate demand to keep the economy operating close to its potential output. It incorporates monetarist ideas about the importance of monetary policy and new classical ideas about the importance of aggregate supply, both in the long run and in the short run.

New Keynesian economics is a body of macroeconomic thought that stresses the stickiness of prices and the need for activist stabilization policies through the manipulation of aggregate demand to keep the economy operating close to its potential output. It incorporates monetarist ideas about the importance of monetary policy and new classical ideas about the importance of aggregate supply, both in the long run and in the short run.

Another "new" element in new Keynesian economic thought is the greater use of microeconomic analysis to explain macroeconomic phenomena, particularly the analysis of price and wage stickiness. We saw in the chapter that introduced the model of aggregate demand and aggregate supply, for example, that sticky prices and wages may be a response to the preferences of consumers and of firms. That idea emerged from research by economists of the new Keynesian school.

New Keynesian ideas guide macroeconomic policy; they are the basis for the model of aggregate demand and aggregate supply with which we have been working. To see how the new Keynesian school has come to dominate macroeconomic policy, we shall review the major macroeconomic events and policies of the 1980s, 1990s, and early 2000s.

3.1   The 1980s and Beyond: Advances in Macroeconomic Policy

The exercise of monetary and of fiscal policy has changed dramatically in the last few decades.

The Revolution in Monetary Policy

It is fair to say that the monetary policy revolution of the last two decades began on July 25, 1979. On that day, President Jimmy Carter appointed Paul Volcker to be chairman of the Fed's Board of Governors. Mr. Volcker, with President Carter's support, charted a new direction for the Fed. The new direction damaged Mr. Carter politically but ultimately produced dramatic gains for the economy.

Oil prices rose sharply in 1979 as war broke out between Iran and Iraq. Such an increase would, by itself, shift the short-run aggregate supply curve to the left, causing the price level to rise and real GDP to fall. But expansionary fiscal and monetary policies had pushed aggregate demand up at the same time. As a result, real GDP stayed at potential output, while the price level soared. The implicit price deflator jumped 8.1%; the CPI rose 13.5%, the highest inflation rate recorded in the 20th century. Public opinion polls in 1979 consistently showed that most people regarded inflation as the leading problem facing the nation.

FIGURE 18.9   The Fed's Fight Against Inflation

By 1979, expansionary fiscal and monetary policies had brought the economy to its potential output. Then war between Iran and Iraq caused oil prices to increase, shifting the short-run aggregate supply curve to the left. In the second half of 1979, the Fed launched an aggressive contractionary policy aimed at reducing inflation. The Fed's action shifted the aggregate demand curve to the left. The result in 1980 was a recession with continued inflation.

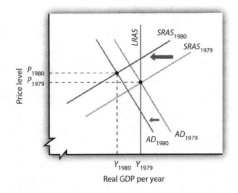

Chairman Volcker charted a monetarist course of fixing the growth rate of the money supply at a rate that would bring inflation down. After the high rates of money growth of the past, the policy was sharply contractionary. Its first effects were to shift the aggregate demand curve to the left. Continued oil price increases produced more leftward shifts in the short-run aggregate supply curve, and the economy suffered a recession in 1980. Inflation remained high. Figure 18.9 shows how the combined shifts in aggregate demand and short-run aggregate supply produced a reduction in real GDP and an increase in the price level.

The Fed stuck to its contractionary guns, and the inflation rate finally began to fall in 1981. But the recession worsened. Unemployment soared, shooting above 10% late in the year. It was, up to that point, the worst recession since the Great Depression. The inflation rate, though, fell sharply in 1982, and the Fed began to shift to a modestly expansionary policy in 1983. But inflation had been licked. Inflation, measured by the implicit price deflator, dropped to a 4.1% rate that year, the lowest since 1967.

The Fed's actions represented a sharp departure from those of the previous two decades. Faced with soaring unemployment, the Fed did not shift to an expansionary policy until inflation was well under control. Inflation continued to edge downward through most of the remaining years of the 20th century and into the new century. The Fed has clearly shifted to a stabilization policy with a strong inflation constraint. It shifts to expansionary policy when the economy has a recessionary gap, but only if it regards inflation as being under control.

This concern about inflation was evident again when the U.S. economy began to weaken in 2008, and there was initially discussion among the members of the Federal Open Market Committee about whether or not easing would contribute to inflation. At that time, it looked like inflation was becoming a more serious problem, largely due to increases in oil and other commodity prices. Some members of the Fed, including then Chairman Bernanke, argued that these price increases were likely to be temporary and the Fed began using expansionary monetary policy early on. By late summer and early fall, inflationary pressures had subsided, and all the members of the FOMC were behind continued expansionary policy. Indeed, at that point, the Fed let it be known that it was willing to do anything in its power to fight the current recession.

The next major advance in monetary policy came in the 1990s, under Federal Reserve Chairman Alan Greenspan. The Fed had shifted to an expansionary policy as the economy slipped into a recession when Iraq's invasion of Kuwait in 1990 began the Persian Gulf War and sent oil prices soaring. By early 1994, real GDP was rising, but the economy remained in a recessionary gap. Nevertheless, the Fed announced on February 4, 1994, that it had shifted to a contractionary policy, selling bonds to boost interest rates and to reduce the money supply. While the economy had not reached its potential output, Chairman Greenspan explained that the Fed was concerned that it might push past its potential output within a year. The Fed, for the first time, had explicitly taken the impact lag of monetary policy into account. The issue of lags was also a part of Fed discussions in the 2000s.

Fiscal Policy: A Resurgence of Interest

President Ronald Reagan, whose 1980 election victory was aided by a recession that year, introduced a tax cut, combined with increased defense spending, in 1981. While this expansionary fiscal policy was virtually identical to the policy President Kennedy had introduced 20 years earlier, President Reagan rejected Keynesian economics, embracing supply-side arguments instead. He argued that the cut in tax rates, particularly in high marginal rates, would encourage work effort. He reintroduced an investment tax credit, which stimulated investment. With people working harder and firms investing more, he expected long-run aggregate supply to increase more rapidly. His policy, he said, would stimulate economic growth.

The tax cut and increased defense spending increased the federal deficit. Increased spending for welfare programs and unemployment compensation, both of which were induced by the plunge in real GDP in the early 1980s, contributed to the deficit as well. As deficits continued to rise, they began to dominate discussions of fiscal policy. In 1990, with the economy slipping into a recession, President George H. W. Bush agreed to a tax increase despite an earlier promise not to do so. President Bill Clinton, whose 1992 election resulted largely from the recession of 1990–1991, introduced another tax increase in 1994, with the economy still in a recessionary gap. Both tax increases were designed to curb the rising deficit.

Congress in the first years of the 1990s rejected the idea of using an expansionary fiscal policy to close a recessionary gap on grounds it would increase the deficit. President Clinton, for example, introduced a stimulus package of increased government investment and tax cuts designed to stimulate private investment in 1993; a Democratic Congress rejected the proposal. The deficit acted like a straitjacket for fiscal policy. The Bush and Clinton tax increases, coupled with spending restraint and increased revenues from economic growth, brought an end to the deficit in 1998.

Initially, it was expected that the budget surplus would continue well into the new century. But, this picture changed rapidly. President George W. Bush campaigned on a platform of large tax cuts, arguing that less government intervention in the economy would be good for long-term economic growth. His administration saw the enactment of two major pieces of tax-cutting legislation in 2001 and 2003. Coupled with increases in government spending, in part for defense but also for domestic purposes including a Medicare prescription drug benefit, the government budget surpluses gave way to budget deficits. To deal with times of economic weakness during President Bush's administration, temporary tax cuts were enacted, both in 2001 and again in 2008.

As the economy continued to weaken in 2008, there was a resurgence of interest in using discretionary increases in government spending, as discussed in the Case in Point, to respond to the recession. Three factors were paramount: (1) the temporary tax cuts had provided only a minor amount of stimulus to the economy, as sizable portions had been used for saving rather than spending, (2) expansionary monetary policy, while useful, had not seemed adequate, and (3) the recession threatening the global economy was larger than those in recent economic history.

3.2   The Rise of New Keynesian Economics

New Keynesian economics emerged in the last three decades as the dominant school of macroeconomic thought for two reasons. First, it successfully incorporated important monetarist and new classical ideas into Keynesian economics. Second, developments in the 1980s and 1990s shook economists' confidence in the ability of the monetarist or the new classical school alone to explain macroeconomic change.

Monetary Change and Monetarism

Look again at Figure 18.7. The close relationship between M2 and nominal GDP in the 1960s and 1970s helped win over many economists to the monetarist camp. Now look at Figure 18.10. It shows the same two variables, M2 and nominal GDP, from the 1980s through 2013. The tidy relationship between the two seems to have vanished. What happened?

FIGURE 18.10 M2 and Nominal GDP, 1980–2013

The close relationship between M2 and nominal GDP a year later that had prevailed in the 1960s and 1970s seemed to vanish from the 1980s onward.

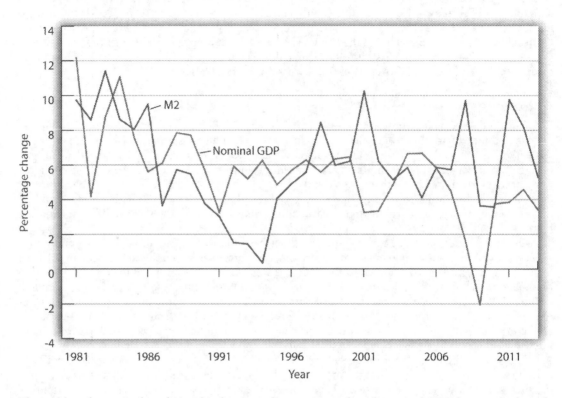

The sudden change in the relationship between the money stock and nominal GDP has resulted partly from public policy. Deregulation of the banking industry in the early 1980s produced sharp changes in the ways individuals dealt with money, thus changing the relationship of money to economic activity. Banks have been freed to offer a wide range of financial alternatives to their customers. One of the most important developments has been the introduction of bond funds offered by banks. These funds allowed customers to earn the higher interest rates paid by long-term bonds while at the same time being able to transfer funds easily into checking accounts as needed. Balances in these bond funds are not counted as part of M2. As people shifted assets out of M2 accounts and into bond funds, velocity rose. That changed the once-close relationship between changes in the quantity of money and changes in nominal GDP.

Many monetarists have argued that the experience of the 1980s, 1990s, and 2000s reinforces their view that the instability of velocity in the short run makes monetary policy an inappropriate tool for short-run stabilization. They continue to insist, however, that the velocity of M2 remains stable in the long run. But tFF appears to have diverged in recent years from its long-run path. Although it may return to its long-run level, the stability of velocity remains very much in doubt. Because of this instability, in 2000, when the Fed was no longer required by law to report money target ranges, it discontinued the practice.

The New Classical School and Responses to Policy

New classical economics suggests that people should have responded to the fiscal and monetary policies of the 1980s in predictable ways. They did not, and that has created new doubts among economists about the validity of the new classical argument.

The rational expectations hypothesis predicts that if a shift in monetary policy by the Fed is anticipated, it will have no effect on real GDP. The slowing in the rate of growth of the money supply over the period from 1979 to 1982 was surely well known. The Fed announced at the outset what it was going to do, and then did it. It had the full support first of President Carter and then of President Reagan. But the policy plunged the economy into what was then its worst recession since the Great Depression. The experience hardly seemed consistent with new classical logic. New classical economists argued that people may have doubted the Fed would keep its word, but the episode still cast doubt on the rational expectations argument.

The public's response to the huge deficits of the Reagan era also seemed to belie new classical ideas. One new classical argument predicts that people will increase their saving rate in response to an increase in public sector borrowing. The resultant reduction in consumption will cancel the impact of the increase in deficit-financed government expenditures. But the private saving rate in the United States *fell* during the 1980s. New classical economists contend that standard measures of saving do not fully represent the actual saving rate, but the experience of the 1980s did not seem to support the new classical argument.

The events of the 1980s do not suggest that either monetarist or new classical ideas should be abandoned, but those events certainly raised doubts about relying solely on these approaches. Similarly, doubts about Keynesian economics raised by the events of the 1970s led Keynesians to modify and strengthen their approach.

A Macroeconomic Consensus?

While there is less consensus on macroeconomic policy issues than on some other economic issues (particularly those in the microeconomic and international areas), surveys of economists generally show that the new Keynesian approach has emerged as the preferred approach to macroeconomic analysis. The finding that about 80% of economists agree that expansionary fiscal measures can deal with recessionary gaps certainly suggests that most economists can be counted in the new Keynesian camp. Neither monetarist nor new classical analysis would support such measures. At the same time, there is considerable discomfort about actually using discretionary fiscal policy, as the same survey shows that about 70% of economists feel that discretionary fiscal policy should be avoided and that the business cycle should be managed by the Fed.[3] Just as the new Keynesian approach appears to have won support among most economists, it has become dominant in terms of macroeconomic policy. In the United States, the Great Recession was fought using traditional monetary and fiscal policies, while other policies were used concurrently to deal with the financial crisis that occurred at the same time.

Did the experience of the 2007–2009 recession affect economists' views concerning macroeconomic policy? One source for gauging possible changes in the opinions of economists is the twice-yearly survey of economic policy among the National Association for Business Economics (NABE).[4] According to the August 2010 survey of 242 members of NABE, almost 60% were supportive of monetary policy at that time, which was expansionary and continued to be so into 2014. Concerning fiscal policy, there was less agreement. Still, according to the survey taken at the time the 2009 fiscal stimulus was being debated, 22% characterized it as "about right," another third found it too restrictive, and only one third found it too stimulative. In the August 2010 survey, 39% thought fiscal policy "about right," 24% found it too restrictive, and 37% found it too stimulative. Also, nearly 75% ranked promotion of economic growth as more important than deficit reduction, roughly two thirds supported the extension of unemployment benefits, and 60% agreed that awarding states with federal assistance funds from the 2009 stimulus package was appropriate. Taken together, the new Keynesian approach still seems to reflect the dominant opinion.

Is the Great Moderation Over?

As did the Great Depression of the 1930s, the Great Recession of the late 2000s generated great fear. Even though it officially ended in the middle of 2009, the state of the economy was the major issue over which the 2012 U.S. presidential election was fought, as the two major political parties offered their competing visions. Unemployment was still high, the housing sector had still not recovered, and the European debt situation loomed in the background. Another lurking question was whether the experience of the recent deep recession, the related financial crisis, and the slow recovery from them would become the new "normal" or whether macroeconomic performance would return to being less volatile.

Economist Todd Clark at the Federal Reserve Bank of Kansas attempted to answer this question.[5] He first looked at the various explanations for the lower volatility of the U.S. economy during the 25-year period that preceded the Great Recession. Three broad reasons were given: structural changes, improved monetary policy, and good luck. While there is disagreement in the literature as to the relative importance of each of these, Clark argues that there is no reason to assume that the first two explanations for moderation will not continue to have moderating influences. For example, one positive structural change has been better inventory management, and he sees no reason why firms should become less able in the future to manage their inventories using the newly developed techniques. Similarly, in the future, monetary authorities should be able to continue to make the better decisions that they made during the Great Moderation. The element that can vary is luck. During the Great Moderation, the economy experienced fewer serious shocks. For example, oil prices were fairly stable. In contrast, during the recent recession, the price of oil rose from $54 per barrel in January 2007 to $134 per barrel in June 2008. The bursting of the housing price bubble and the ensuing crisis in financial markets was another major shock contributing to the depth and length of the recent recession. Clark says, "Accordingly, once the crisis subsides and the period of very bad luck passes, macroeconomic volatility will likely decline. In the future, the permanence of structural change and improved monetary policy that occurred in years past should ensure that low volatility is the norm."[6] Let's hope that he is correct.

- The actions of the Fed starting in late 1979 reflected a strong inflation constraint and a growing recognition of the impact lag for monetary policy.
- Reducing the deficit dominated much of fiscal policy discussion during the 1980s and 1990s.
- The events of the 1980s and early 1990s do not appear to have been consistent with the hypotheses of either the monetarist or new classical schools.
- New Keynesian economists have incorporated major elements of the ideas of the monetarist and new classical schools into their formulation of macroeconomic theory.

TRY IT!

Show the effect of an expansionary monetary policy on real GDP

1. according to new Keynesian economics
2. according to the rational expectations hypothesis

In both cases, consider both the short-run and the long-run effects.

Case in Point

Steering on a Difficult Course

Imagine that you are driving a test car on a special course. You get to steer, accelerate, and brake, but you cannot be sure whether the car will respond to your commands within a few feet or within a few miles. The windshield and side windows are blackened, so you cannot see where you are going or even where you are. You can only see where you have been with the rear-view mirror. The course is designed so that you will face difficulties you have never experienced. Your job is to get through the course unscathed. Oh, and by the way, you have to observe the speed limit, but you do not know what it is. Have a nice trip.

Now imagine that the welfare of people all over the world will be affected by how well you drive the course. They are watching you. They are giving you a great deal of often-conflicting advice about what you should do. Thinking about the problems you would face driving such a car will give you some idea of the obstacle course fiscal and monetary authorities must negotiate. They cannot know where the economy is going or where it is—economic indicators such as GDP and the CPI only suggest where the economy has been. And the perils through which it must steer can be awesome indeed.

One policy response that most acknowledge as having been successful was how the Fed dealt with the financial crises in Southeast Asia and elsewhere that shook the world economy in 1997 and 1998. There were serious concerns at the time that economic difficulties around the world would bring the high-flying U.S. economy to its knees and worsen an already difficult economic situation in other countries. The Fed had to steer through the pitfalls that global economic crises threw in front of it.

In the fall of 1998, the Fed chose to accelerate to avoid a possible downturn. The Federal Open Market Committee (FOMC) engaged in expansionary monetary policy by lowering its target for the federal funds rate. Some critics argued at the time that the Fed's action was too weak to counter the impact of world economic crisis. Others, though, criticized the Fed for undertaking an expansionary policy when the U.S. economy seemed already to be in an inflationary gap.

In the summer of 1999, the Fed put on the brakes, shifting back to a slightly contractionary policy. It raised the target for the federal funds rate, first to 5.0% and then to 5.25%. These actions reflected concern about speeding when in an inflationary gap.

But was the economy speeding? Was it in an inflationary gap? Certainly, the U.S. unemployment rate of 4.2% in the fall of 1999 stood well below standard estimates of the natural rate of unemployment. There were few, if any, indications that inflation was a problem, but the Fed had to recognize that inflation might not appear for a very long time after the Fed had taken a particular course. As noted in the text, this was also during a time when the once-close relationship between money growth and nominal GDP seemed to break down. The shifts in demand for money created unexplained and unexpected changes in velocity.

The outcome of the Fed's actions has been judged a success. While with 20/20 hindsight the Fed's decisions might seem obvious, in fact it was steering a car whose performance seemed less and less predictable over a course that was becoming more and more treacherous.

Since 2008, both the Fed and the government have been again trying to get the economy back on track. In this case, the car was already in the ditch. The Fed decided on a "no holds barred" approach. It moved aggressively to lower the federal funds rate target and engaged in a variety of other measures to improve liquidity to the banking system, to lower other interest rates by purchasing longer-term securities (such as 10-year treasuries and those of Fannie Mae and Freddie Mac), and, working with the Treasury Department, to provide loans related to consumer and business debt.

Continuing on smaller expansionary fiscal policy begun under President George W. Bush, the Obama administration for its part advocated and Congress passed a massive spending and tax relief package of more than $800 billion. Besides the members of his economic team, many economists seem to be on board in using discretionary fiscal policy in this instance. Federal Reserve Bank of San Francisco President Janet Yellen put it this way: "The new enthusiasm for fiscal stimulus, and particularly government spending, represents a huge evolution in mainstream thinking." A notable convert to using fiscal policy to deal with this recession was Harvard economist and former adviser to President Ronald Reagan, Martin Feldstein. His spending proposal encouraged increased military spending and he stated, "While good tax policy can contribute to ending the recession, the heavy lifting will have to be done by increased government spending."

Predictably, not all economists jumped onto the fiscal policy bandwagon. Concerns included whether so-called shovel-ready projects could really be implemented in time, whether government spending would crowd out private spending, whether monetary policy alone was providing enough stimulus, and whether the spending would flow efficiently to truly worthwhile projects. As discussed elsewhere in this text, the controversy persists. But the fact that a variety of expansionary policies were used to ease the recession and spur the recovery is not in doubt.

Sources: Ben S. Bernanke, "The Crisis and the Policy Response" (speech, London School of Economics, January 13, 2009); Louis Uchitelle, "Economists Warm to Government Spending but Debate Its Form," New York Times, January 7, 2009, p. B1.

Panel (a) shows an expansionary monetary policy according to new Keynesian economics. Aggregate demand increases, with no immediate reduction in short-run aggregate supply. Real GDP rises to Y_2. In the long run, nominal wages rise, reducing short-run aggregate supply and returning real GDP to potential. Panel (b) shows what happens with rational expectations. When the Fed increases the money supply, people anticipate the rise in prices. Workers and firms agree to an increase in nominal wages, so that there is a reduction in short-run aggregate supply at the same time there is an increase in aggregate demand. The result is no change in real GDP; it remains at potential. There is, however, an increase in the price level.

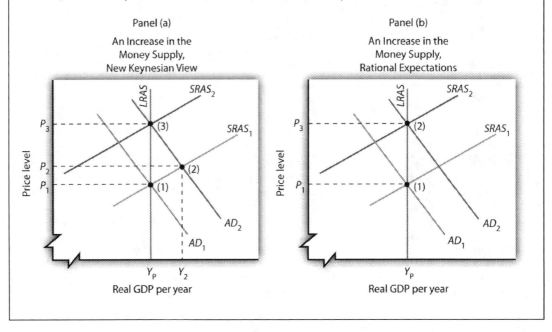

4.   REVIEW AND PRACTICE

Summary

We have surveyed the experience of the United States in light of the economic theories that prevailed or emerged during five decades. We have seen that events in the past century have had significant effects on the ways in which economists look at and interpret macroeconomic ideas.

Before the Great Depression, macroeconomic thought was dominated by the classical school. That body of theory stressed the economy's ability to reach full employment equilibrium on its own. The severity and duration of the Depression caused many economists to rethink their acceptance of natural equilibrating forces in the economy.

John Maynard Keynes issued the most telling challenge. He argued that wage rigidities and other factors could prevent the economy from closing a recessionary gap on its own. Further, he showed that expansionary fiscal and monetary policies could be used to increase aggregate demand and move the economy to its potential output. Although these ideas did not immediately affect U.S. policy, the increases in aggregate demand brought by the onset of World War II did bring the economy to full employment. Many economists became convinced of the validity of Keynes's analysis and his prescriptions for macroeconomic policy.

Keynesian economics dominated economic policy in the United States in the 1960s. Fiscal and monetary policies increased aggregate demand and produced what was then the longest expansion in U.S. history. But the economy pushed well beyond full employment in the latter part of the decade, and inflation increased. While Keynesians were dominant, monetarist economists argued that it was monetary policy that accounted for the expansion of the 1960s and that fiscal policy could not affect aggregate demand.

Efforts by the Nixon administration in 1969 and 1970 to cool the economy ran afoul of shifts in the short-run aggregate supply curve. The ensuing decade saw a series of shifts in aggregate supply that contributed to three more recessions by 1982. As economists studied these shifts, they developed further the basic notions we now express in the aggregate demand–aggregate supply model: that changes in aggregate demand and aggregate supply affect income and the price level; that changes in fiscal and monetary policy can affect aggregate demand; and that in the long run, the economy moves to its potential level of output.

The events of the 1980s and beyond raised serious challenges for the monetarist and new classical schools. New Keynesian economists formulated revisions in their theories, incorporating many of the ideas suggested by monetarist and new classical economists. The new, more powerful theory of macroeconomic events has won considerable support among economists today.

CONCEPT PROBLEMS

1. "For many years, the hands-off fiscal policies advocated by the classical economists held sway with American government. When times were hard, the prevailing response was to tough it out, awaiting the 'inevitable' turnaround. The lessons of the Great Depression and a booming wartime economy have since taught us, however, that government intervention is sometimes necessary and desirable—and that to an extent, we can take charge of our own economic lives." Evaluate the foregoing quotation based upon the discussion in this chapter. How would you classify the speaker in terms of a school of economic thought?

2. In his 1982 *Economic Report of the President*, Ronald Reagan said, "We simply cannot blame crop failures and oil price increases for our basic inflation problem. The continuous, underlying cause was poor government policy." What policies might he have been referring to?

3. Many journalists blamed economic policies of the Reagan administration for the extremely high levels of unemployment in 1982 and 1983. Given the record of the rest of the decade, do you agree that President Reagan's economic policies were a failure? Why or why not?

4. The day after the U.S. stock market crash of October 19, 1987, Federal Reserve Board Chairman Alan Greenspan issued the following statement: "The Federal Reserve, consistent with its responsibilities as the nation's central bank, affirmed today its readiness to serve as a source of liquidity to support the economic and financial system." Evaluate why the Fed chairman might have been prompted to make such a statement.

5. Compare the rationale of the Reagan administration for the 1981 tax reductions with the rationale behind the Kennedy–Johnson tax cut of 1964, the Bush tax cut of 2001, and the Bush tax cut of 2003.

6. Suppose we observed an economy in which changes in the money supply produce no changes whatever in nominal GDP. What could we conclude about velocity?

7. Suppose price levels were falling 10% per day. How would this affect the demand for money? How would it affect velocity? What can you conclude about the role of velocity during periods of rapid price change?

8. Suppose investment increases and the money supply does not change. Use the model of aggregate demand and aggregate supply to predict the impact of such an increase on nominal GDP. Now what happens in terms of the variables in the equation of exchange?

9. The text notes that a 10% increase in the money supply may not increase the price level by 10% in the short run. Explain why.

10. If the economy is operating below its potential output, what kind of gap exists? What kinds of fiscal or monetary policies might you use to close this gap? Can you think of any objection to the use of such policies?

11. If the economy is operating above its potential output, what kind of gap exists? What kinds of fiscal or monetary policies might you use to close this gap? Can you think of any objection to the use of such policies?

12. In *General Theory*, Keynes wrote of the importance of ideas. The world, he said, is ruled by little else. How important do you think his ideas have been for economic policy today?

13. State whether each of the following events appears to be the result of a shift in short-run aggregate supply or aggregate demand, and state the direction of the shift involved.

    a. The price level rises sharply while real GDP falls.

    b. The price level and real GDP rise.

    c. The price level falls while real GDP rises.

    d. The price level and real GDP fall.

14. Explain whether each of the following events and policies will affect the aggregate demand curve or the short-run aggregate supply curve, and state what will happen to the price level and real GDP.

    a. Oil prices rise.

    b. The Fed sells bonds.

    c. Government purchases increase.

    d. Federal taxes increase.

    e. The government slashes transfer payment spending.

    f. Oil prices fall.

15. Using the model of aggregate demand and aggregate supply, illustrate an economy with a recessionary gap. Show how a policy of nonintervention would ultimately close the gap. Show the alternative of closing the gap through stabilization policy.

16. Using the model of aggregate demand and aggregate supply, illustrate an economy with an inflationary gap. Show how a policy of nonintervention would ultimately close the gap. Show the alternative of closing the gap through stabilization policy.

NUMERICAL PROBLEMS

1. Here are annual values for M2 and for nominal GDP (all figures are in billions of dollars) for the mid-1990s.

Year	M2	Nominal GDP
1993	3,482.0	$6,657.4
1994	3,498.1	7,072.2
1995	3,642.1	7,397.7
1996	3,820.5	7,816.9
1997	4,034.1	8,304.3

    a. Compute the velocity for each year.

    b. Compute the fraction of nominal GDP that was being held as money.

    c. What is your conclusion about the stability of velocity in this five-year period?

2. Here are annual values for M2 and for nominal GDP (all figures are in billions of dollars) for the mid-2000s.

Year	M2	Nominal GDP
2003	6,055.5	$10,960.8
2004	6,400.7	11,685.9
2005	6,659.7	12,421.9
2006	7,012.3	13,178.4
2007	7,404.3	13,807.5

    a. Compute the velocity for each year.

    b. Compute the fraction of nominal GDP that was being held as money.

    c. What is your conclusion about the stability of velocity in this five-year period?

3. The following data show M1 for the years 1993 to 1997, respectively (all figures are in billions of dollars): 1,129.6; 1,150.7; 1,127.4; 1,081.3; 1,072.5.

    a. Compute the M1 velocity for these years. (Nominal GDP for these years is shown in problem 1.)

    b. If you were going to use a money target, would M1 or M2 have been preferable during the 1990s? Explain your reasoning.

4. The following data show M1 for the years 2003 to 2007, respectively (all figures are in billions of dollars): 1,306.1; 1,376.3; 1,374.5; 1,366.5; 1,366.5

    a. Compute the M1 velocity for these years. (Nominal GDP for these years is shown in problem 2.)

    b. If you were going to use a money target, would M1 or M2 have been preferable during the 2000s? Explain your reasoning.

5. Assume a hypothetical economy in which the velocity is constant at 2 and real GDP is always at a constant potential of $4,000. Suppose the money supply is $1,000 in the first year, $1,100 in the second year, $1,200 in the third year, and $1,300 in the fourth year.

    a. Using the equation of exchange, compute the price level in each year.

    b. Compute the inflation rate for each year.

    c. Explain why inflation varies, even though the money supply rises by $100 each year.

    d. If the central bank wanted to keep inflation at zero, what should it have done to the money supply each year?

    e. If the central bank wanted to keep inflation at 10% each year, what money supply should it have targeted in each year?

6. Suppose the velocity of money is constant and potential output grows by 3% per year. By what percentage should the money supply grow in order to achieve the following inflation rate targets?

    a. 0%

    b. 1%

    c. 2%

7. Suppose the velocity of money is constant and potential output grows by 5% per year. For each of the following money supply growth rates, what will the inflation rate be?

    a. 4%

b. 5%

c. 6%

8. Suppose that a country whose money supply grew by about 20% a year over the long run had an annual inflation rate of about 20% and that a country whose money supply grew by about 50% a year had an annual inflation rate of about 50%. Explain this finding in terms of the equation of exchange.

ENDNOTES

1. David C. Wheelock, "The Federal Response to Home Mortgage Distress: Lessons from the Great Depression," *Federal Reserve Bank of St. Louis Review* 90, no. 3 (Part 1) (May/June 2008): 133–48.

2. For a discussion of fiscal policy during the Great Depression, see E. Cary Brown, "Fiscal Policy in the 'Thirties: A Reappraisal," *American Economic Review* 46, no. 5 (December 1956): 857–79.

3. Dan Fuller and Doris Geide-Stevenson, "Consensus among Economists: Revisited," *Journal of Economic Education* 34, no. 4 (Fall 2003): 369–87.

4. National Association for Business Economics, Economic Policy Surveys, March 2009 and August 2010, available at http://www.nabe.com.

5. Todd E. Clark, "Is the Great Moderation Over? An Empirical Analysis," *Federal Reserve Bank of Kansas City Economic Review* 94, no. 4 (Fourth Quarter 2009): 5–42.

6. Ibid., 27.

CHAPTER 19

Appendix A: Graphs in Economics

A glance through the pages of this book should convince you that there are a lot of graphs in economics. The language of graphs is one means of presenting economic ideas. If you are already familiar with graphs, you will have no difficulty with this aspect of your study. If you have never used graphs or have not used them in some time, this appendix will help you feel comfortable with the graphs you will encounter in this text.

1. HOW TO CONSTRUCT AND INTERPRET GRAPHS

LEARNING OBJECTIVES

1. **Understand how graphs show the relationship between two or more variables and explain how a graph elucidates the nature of the relationship.**
2. **Define the slope of a curve.**
3. **Distinguish between a movement along a curve, a shift in a curve, and a rotation in a curve.**

Much of the analysis in economics deals with relationships between variables. A variable is simply a quantity whose value can change. A **graph** is a pictorial representation of the relationship between two or more variables. The key to understanding graphs is knowing the rules that apply to their construction and interpretation. This section defines those rules and explains how to draw a graph.

graph

A pictorial representation of the relationship between two or more variables.

1.1 Drawing a Graph

To see how a graph is constructed from numerical data, we will consider a hypothetical example. Suppose a college campus has a ski club that organizes day-long bus trips to a ski area about 100 miles from the campus. The club leases the bus and charges $10 per passenger for a round trip to the ski area. In addition to the revenue the club collects from passengers, it also receives a grant of $200 from the school's student government for each day the bus trip is available. The club thus would receive $200 even if no passengers wanted to ride on a particular day.

The table in Figure 19.1 shows the relationship between two variables: the number of students who ride the bus on a particular day and the revenue the club receives from a trip. In the table, each combination is assigned a letter (A, B, etc.); we will use these letters when we transfer the information from the table to a graph.

FIGURE 19.1 Ski Club Revenues

The ski club receives $10 from each passenger riding its bus for a trip to and from the ski area plus a payment of $200 from the student government for each day the bus is available for these trips. The club's revenues from any single day thus equal $200 plus $10 times the number of passengers. The table relates various combinations of the number of passengers and club revenues.

Combination	Number of passengers	Club revenue
A	0	$200
B	10	300
C	20	400
D	30	500
E	40	600

We can illustrate the relationship shown in the table with a graph. The procedure for showing the relationship between two variables, like the ones in Figure 19.1, on a graph is illustrated in Figure 19.2. Let us look at the steps involved.

FIGURE 19.2 Plotting a Graph

Here we see how to show the information given in Figure 19.1 in a graph.

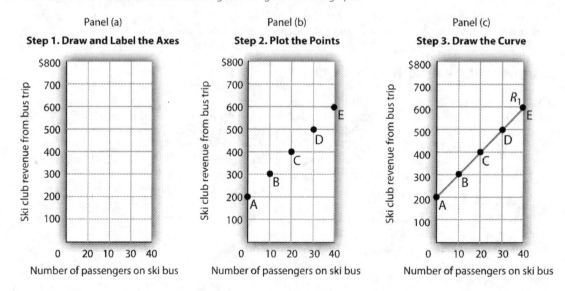

Step 1. Draw and Label the Axes

The two variables shown in the table are the number of passengers taking the bus on a particular day and the club's revenue from that trip. We begin our graph in Panel (a) of Figure 19.2 by drawing two axes to form a right angle. Each axis will represent a variable. The axes should be carefully labeled to reflect what is being measured on each axis.

It is customary to place the independent variable on the horizontal axis and the dependent variable on the vertical axis. Recall that, when two variables are related, the dependent variable is the one that changes in response to changes in the independent variable. Passengers generate revenue, so we can consider the number of passengers as the independent variable and the club's revenue as the dependent variable. The number of passengers thus goes on the horizontal axis; the club's revenue from a trip goes on the vertical axis. In some cases, the variables in a graph cannot be considered independent or dependent. In those cases, the variables may be placed on either axis; we will encounter such a case in the chapter that introduces the production possibilities model. In other cases, economists simply ignore the rule; we will encounter that case in the chapter that introduces the model of demand and supply. The rule that the independent variable goes on the horizontal axis and the dependent variable goes on the vertical usually holds, but not always.

The point at which the axes intersect is called the **origin** of the graph. Notice that in Figure 19.2 the origin has a value of zero for each variable.

In drawing a graph showing numeric values, we also need to put numbers on the axes. For the axes in Panel (a), we have chosen numbers that correspond to the values in the table. The number of passengers ranges up to 40 for a trip; club revenues from a trip range from $200 (the payment the club receives from student government) to $600. We have extended the vertical axis to $800 to allow some changes we will consider below. We have chosen intervals of 10 passengers on the horizontal axis and $100 on the vertical axis. The choice of particular intervals is mainly a matter of convenience in drawing and reading the graph; we have chosen the ones here because they correspond to the intervals given in the table.

We have drawn vertical lines from each of the values on the horizontal axis and horizontal lines from each of the values on the vertical axis. These lines, called gridlines, will help us in Step 2.

Step 2. Plot the Points

Each of the rows in the table in Figure 19.1 gives a combination of the number of passengers on the bus and club revenue from a particular trip. We can plot these values in our graph.

We begin with the first row, A, corresponding to zero passengers and club revenue of $200, the payment from student government. We read up from zero passengers on the horizontal axis to $200 on the vertical axis and mark point A. This point shows that zero passengers result in club revenues of $200.

The second combination, B, tells us that if 10 passengers ride the bus, the club receives $300 in revenue from the trip—$100 from the $10-per-passenger charge plus the $200 from student government. We start at 10 passengers on the horizontal axis and follow the gridline up. When we travel up in a graph, we are traveling with respect to values on the vertical axis. We travel up by $300 and mark point B.

Points in a graph have a special significance. They relate the values of the variables on the two axes to each other. Reading to the left from point B, we see that it shows $300 in club revenue. Reading down from point B, we see that it shows 10 passengers. Those values are, of course, the values given for combination B in the table.

We repeat this process to obtain points C, D, and E. Check to be sure that you see that each point corresponds to the values of the two variables given in the corresponding row of the table.

The graph in Panel (b) is called a scatter diagram. A **scatter diagram** shows individual points relating values of the variable on one axis to values of the variable on the other.

Step 3. Draw the Curve

The final step is to draw the curve that shows the relationship between the number of passengers who ride the bus and the club's revenues from the trip. The term "curve" is used for any line in a graph that shows a relationship between two variables.

We draw a line that passes through points A through E. Our curve shows club revenues; we shall call it R_1. Notice that R_1 is an upward-sloping straight line. Notice also that R_1 intersects the vertical axis at $200 (point A). The point at which a curve intersects an axis is called the **intercept** of the curve. We often refer to the vertical or horizontal intercept of a curve; such intercepts can play a special role in economic analysis. The vertical intercept in this case shows the revenue the club would receive on a day it offered the trip and no one rode the bus.

To check your understanding of these steps, we recommend that you try plotting the points and drawing R_1 for yourself in Panel (a). Better yet, draw the axes for yourself on a sheet of graph paper and plot the curve.

1.2   The Slope of a Curve

In this section, we will see how to compute the slope of a curve. The slopes of curves tell an important story: they show the rate at which one variable changes with respect to another.

origin

The point at which the axes of a graph intersect.

scatter diagram

A graph that shows individual points relating values of the variable on one axis to values of the variable on the other.

intercept

The point at which a curve intersects an axis.

The **slope** of a curve equals the ratio of the change in the value of the variable on the vertical axis to the change in the value of the variable on the horizontal axis, measured between two points on the curve. You may have heard this called "the rise over the run." In equation form, we can write the definition of the slope as

EQUATION 19.1

$$\text{Slope} = \frac{\text{vertical change}}{\text{horizontal change}}$$

Equation 19.1 is the first equation in this text. Figure 19.3 provides a short review of working with equations. The material in this text relies much more heavily on graphs than on equations, but we will use equations from time to time. It is important that you understand how to use them.

FIGURE 19.3 Reading and Using Equations

Many equations in economics begin in the form of Equation 19.1, with the statement that one thing (in this case the slope) equals another (the vertical change divided by the horizontal change). In this example, the equation is written in words. Sometimes we use symbols in place of words. The basic idea though, is always the same: the term represented on the left side of the equals sign equals the term on the right side. In Equation 19.1 there are three variables: the slope, the vertical change, and the horizontal change. If we know the values of two of the three, we can compute the third. In the computation of slopes that follow, for example, we will use values for the two variables on the right side of the equation to compute the slope.

$$\text{Slope} = \frac{\text{vertical change}}{\text{horizontal change}}$$

Figure 19.4 shows R_1 and the computation of its slope between points B and D. Point B corresponds to 10 passengers on the bus; point D corresponds to 30. The change in the horizontal axis when we go from B to D thus equals 20 passengers. Point B corresponds to club revenues of $300; point D corresponds to club revenues of $500. The change in the vertical axis equals $200. The slope thus equals $200/20 passengers, or $10/passenger.

We have applied the definition of the slope of a curve to compute the slope of R_1 between points B and D. That same definition is given in Equation 19.1. Applying the equation, we have:

$$\text{Slope} = \frac{\text{vertical change}}{\text{horizontal change}} = \frac{\$200}{20 \text{ passengers}} = \$10 \,/\, \text{passenger}$$

The slope of this curve tells us the amount by which revenues rise with an increase in the number of passengers. It should come as no surprise that this amount equals the price per passenger. Adding a passenger adds $10 to the club's revenues.

Notice that we can compute the slope of R_1 between any two points on the curve and get the same value; the slope is constant. Consider, for example, points A and E. The vertical change between these points is $400 (we go from revenues of $200 at A to revenues of $600 at E). The horizontal change is 40 passengers (from zero passengers at A to 40 at E). The slope between A and E thus equals $400/(40 passengers) = $10/passenger. We get the same slope regardless of which pair of points we pick on R_1 to compute the slope. The slope of R_1 can be considered a constant, which suggests that it is a straight line. When the curve showing the relationship between two variables has a constant slope, we say there is a **linear relationship** between the variables. A **linear curve** is a curve with constant slope.

FIGURE 19.4 Computing the Slope of a Curve

1. Select two points; we have selected points B and D.
2. The slope equals the vertical change divided by the horizontal change between the two points.
3. Between points B and D, the slope equals **$200/20 passengers = $10/passenger.**
4. The slope of this curve is the price per passenger. The fact that it is positive suggests a positive relationship between revenue per trip and the number of passengers riding the bus. Because the slope of this curve is $10/passenger between any two points on the curve, the relationship between club revenue per trip and the number of passengers is linear.

$$\text{Slope} = \frac{\text{vertical change}}{\text{horizontal change}} = \frac{\$200}{20 \text{ passengers}} = \$10/\text{passenger}$$

The fact that the slope of our curve equals $10/passenger tells us something else about the curve—$10/passenger is a positive, not a negative, value. A curve whose slope is positive is upward sloping. As we travel up and to the right along R_1, we travel in the direction of increasing values for both variables. A **positive relationship** between two variables is one in which both variables move in the same direction. Positive relationships are sometimes called direct relationships. There is a positive relationship between club revenues and passengers on the bus. We will look at a graph showing a negative relationship between two variables in the next section.

1.3   A Graph Showing a Negative Relationship

A **negative relationship** is one in which two variables move in opposite directions. A negative relationship is sometimes called an inverse relationship. The slope of a curve describing a negative relationship is always negative. A curve with a negative slope is always downward sloping.

As an example of a graph of a negative relationship, let us look at the impact of the cancellation of games by the National Basketball Association during the 1998–1999 labor dispute on the earnings of one player: Shaquille O'Neal. During the 1998–1999 season, O'Neal was the center for the Los Angeles Lakers.

O'Neal's salary with the Lakers in 1998–1999 would have been about $17,220,000 had the 82 scheduled games of the regular season been played. But a contract dispute between owners and players resulted in the cancellation of 32 games. Mr. O'Neal's salary worked out to roughly $210,000 per game, so the labor dispute cost him well over $6 million. Presumably, he was able to eke out a living on his lower income, but the cancellation of games cost him a great deal.

We show the relationship between the number of games canceled and O'Neal's 1998–1999 basketball earnings graphically in Figure 19.5. Canceling games reduced his earnings, so the number of games canceled is the independent variable and goes on the horizontal axis. O'Neal's earnings are the dependent variable and go on the vertical axis. The graph assumes that his earnings would have been $17,220,000 had no games been canceled (point A, the vertical intercept). Assuming that his earnings fell by $210,000 per game canceled, his earnings for the season were reduced to $10,500,000 by the cancellation of 32 games (point B). We can draw a line between these two points to show the relationship between games canceled and O'Neal's 1998–1999 earnings from basketball. In this graph, we have inserted a break in the vertical axis near the origin. This allows us to expand the scale of the axis over the range from $10,000,000 to $18,000,000. It also prevents a large blank space between the origin and an income of $10,500,000—there are no values below this amount.

positive relationship

Relationship that exists between two variables when both variables move in the same direction.

negative relationship

Relationship that exists between two variables when the variables move in opposite directions.

FIGURE 19.5 Canceling Games and Reducing Shaquille O'Neal's Earnings

If no games had been canceled during the 1998–1999 basketball season, Shaquille O'Neal would have earned $17,220,000 (point A). Assuming that his salary for the season fell by $210,000 for each game canceled, the cancellation of 32 games during the dispute between NBA players and owners reduced O'Neal's earnings to $10,500,000 (point B).

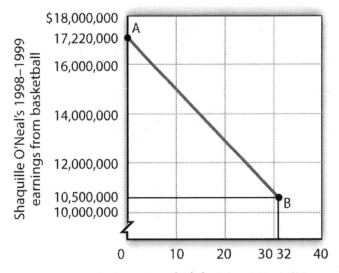

What is the slope of the curve in Figure 19.5? We have data for two points, A and B. At A, O'Neal's basketball salary would have been $17,220,000. At B, it is $10,500,000. The vertical change between points A and B equals -$6,720,000. The change in the horizontal axis is from zero games canceled at A to 32 games canceled at B. The slope is thus

$$\text{Slope} = \frac{\text{vertical change}}{\text{horizontal change}} = \frac{-\$6,720,000}{32 \text{ games}} = -\$210,000 \Big/ \text{game}$$

Notice that this time the slope is negative, hence the downward-sloping curve. As we travel down and to the right along the curve, the number of games canceled rises and O'Neal's salary falls. In this case, the slope tells us the rate at which O'Neal lost income as games were canceled.

The slope of O'Neal's salary curve is also constant. That means there was a linear relationship between games canceled and his 1998–1999 basketball earnings.

1.4 Shifting a Curve

When we draw a graph showing the relationship between two variables, we make an important assumption. We assume that all other variables that might affect the relationship between the variables in our graph are unchanged. When one of those other variables changes, the relationship changes, and the curve showing that relationship shifts.

shift in a curve

Change in the graph of a relationship between two variables that implies new values of one variable at each value of the other variable.

Consider, for example, the ski club that sponsors bus trips to the ski area. The graph we drew in Figure 19.2 shows the relationship between club revenues from a particular trip and the number of passengers on that trip, assuming that all other variables that might affect club revenues are unchanged. Let us change one. Suppose the school's student government increases the payment it makes to the club to $400 for each day the trip is available. The payment was $200 when we drew the original graph. Panel (a) of Figure 19.6 shows how the increase in the payment affects the table we had in Figure 19.1; Panel (b) shows how the curve shifts. Each of the new observations in the table has been labeled with a prime: A′, B′, etc. The curve R_1 shifts upward by $200 as a result of the increased payment. A **shift in a curve** implies new values of one variable at each value of the other variable. The new curve is labeled R_2. With 10 passengers, for example, the club's revenue was $300 at point B on R_1. With the increased payment from the student government, its revenue with 10 passengers rises to $500 at point B′ on R_2. We have a shift in the curve.

FIGURE 19.6 Shifting a Curve: An Increase in Revenues

The table in Panel (a) shows the new level of revenues the ski club receives with varying numbers of passengers as a result of the increased payment from student government. The new curve is shown in dark purple in Panel (b). The old curve is shown in light purple.

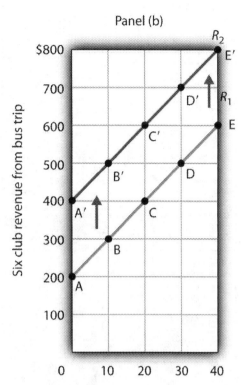

Panel (b)

Panel (a)

Combination	Number of passengers	Club revenue (with $400 payment from student government)
A′	0	$400
B′	10	500
C′	20	600
D′	30	700
E′	40	800

It is important to distinguish between shifts in curves and movements along curves. A **movement along a curve** is a change from one point on the curve to another that occurs when the dependent variable changes in response to a change in the independent variable. If, for example, the student government is paying the club $400 each day it makes the ski bus available and 20 passengers ride the bus, the club is operating at point C′ on R_2. If the number of passengers increases to 30, the club will be at point D′ on the curve. This is a movement along a curve; the curve itself does not shift.

Now suppose that, instead of increasing its payment, the student government eliminates its payments to the ski club for bus trips. The club's only revenue from a trip now comes from its $10/passenger charge. We have again changed one of the variables we were holding unchanged, so we get another shift in our revenue curve. The table in Panel (a) of Figure 19.7 shows how the reduction in the student government's payment affects club revenues. The new values are shown as combinations A″ through E″ on the new curve, R_3, in Panel (b). Once again we have a shift in a curve, this time from R_1 to R_3.

movement along a curve
Change from one point on the curve to another that occurs when the dependent variable changes in response to a change in the independent variable.

FIGURE 19.7 Shifting a Curve: A Reduction in Revenues

The table in Panel (a) shows the impact on ski club revenues of an elimination of support from the student government for ski bus trips. The club's only revenue now comes from the $10 it charges to each passenger. The new combinations are shown as A″ – E″. In Panel (b) we see that the original curve relating club revenue to the number of passengers has shifted down.

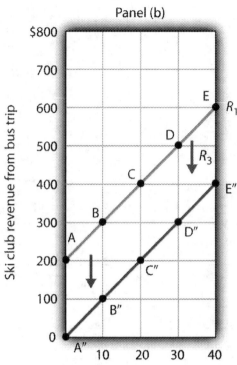

Panel (a)

Combination	Number of passengers	Club revenue (with no payment from student government)
A″	0	0
B″	10	100
C″	20	200
D″	30	300
E″	40	400

The shifts in Figure 19.6 and Figure 19.7 left the slopes of the revenue curves unchanged. That is because the slope in all these cases equals the price per ticket, and the ticket price remains unchanged. Next, we shall see how the slope of a curve changes when we rotate it about a single point.

1.5 Rotating a Curve

rotation of a curve

Change in a curve that occurs when its slope changes with one point on the curve fixed.

A **rotation of a curve** occurs when we change its slope, with one point on the curve fixed. Suppose, for example, the ski club changes the price of its bus rides to the ski area to $30 per trip, and the payment from the student government remains $200 for each day the trip is available. This means the club's revenues will remain $200 if it has no passengers on a particular trip. Revenue will, however, be different when the club has passengers. Because the slope of our revenue curve equals the price per ticket, the slope of the revenue curve changes.

Panel (a) of Figure 19.8 shows what happens to the original revenue curve, R_1, when the price per ticket is raised. Point A does not change; the club's revenue with zero passengers is unchanged. But with 10 passengers, the club's revenue would rise from $300 (point B on R_1) to $500 (point B′ on R_4). With 20 passengers, the club's revenue will now equal $800 (point C′ on R_4).

FIGURE 19.8 Rotating a Curve

A curve is said to rotate when a single point remains fixed while other points on the curve move; a rotation always changes the slope of a curve. Here an increase in the price per passenger to $30 would rotate the revenue curve from R_1 to R_4 in Panel (a). The slope of R_4 is $30 per passenger.

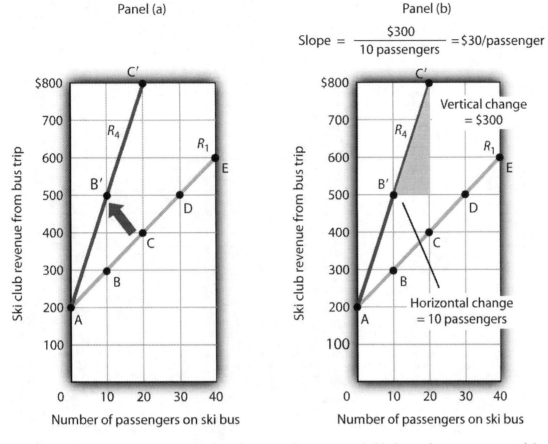

The new revenue curve R_4 is steeper than the original curve. Panel (b) shows the computation of the slope of the new curve between points B′ and C′. The slope increases to $30 per passenger—the new price of a ticket. The greater the slope of a positively sloped curve, the steeper it will be.

We have now seen how to draw a graph of a curve, how to compute its slope, and how to shift and rotate a curve. We have examined both positive and negative relationships. Our work so far has been with linear relationships. Next we will turn to nonlinear ones.

KEY TAKEAWAYS

- A graph shows a relationship between two or more variables.
- An upward-sloping curve suggests a positive relationship between two variables. A downward-sloping curve suggests a negative relationship between two variables.
- The slope of a curve is the ratio of the vertical change to the horizontal change between two points on the curve. A curve whose slope is constant suggests a linear relationship between two variables.
- A change from one point on the curve to another produces a movement along the curve in the graph. A shift in the curve implies new values of one variable at each value of the other variable. A rotation in the curve implies that one point remains fixed while the slope of the curve changes.

T R Y   I T !

The following table shows the relationship between the number of gallons of gasoline people in a community are willing and able to buy per week and the price per gallon. Plot these points in the grid provided and label each point with the letter associated with the combination. Notice that there are breaks in both the vertical and horizontal axes of the grid. Draw a line through the points you have plotted. Does your graph suggest a positive or a negative relationship? What is the slope between A and B? Between B and C? Between A and C? Is the relationship linear?

Combination	Price per gallon	Number of gallons (per week)
A	$1.00	1.000
B	1.20	900
C	1.40	800

Now suppose you are given the following information about the relationship between price per gallon and the number of gallons per week gas stations in the community are willing to sell.

Combination	Price per gallon	Number of gallons (per week)
D	$1.00	800
E	1.20	900
F	1.40	1,000

Plot these points in the grid provided and draw a curve through the points you have drawn. Does your graph suggest a positive or a negative relationship? What is the slope between D and E? Between E and F? Between D and F? Is this relationship linear?

Here is the first graph. The curve's downward slope tells us there is a negative relationship between price and the quantity of gasoline people are willing and able to buy. This curve, by the way, is a demand curve (the next one is a supply curve). We will study demand and supply soon; you will be using these curves a great deal. The slope between A and B is −0.002 (slope = vertical change/horizontal change = −0.20/100). The slope between B and C and between A and C is the same. That tells us the curve is linear, which, of course, we can see—it is a straight line.

Here is the supply curve. Its upward slope tells us there is a positive relationship between price per gallon and the number of gallons per week gas stations are willing to sell. The slope between D and E is 0.002 (slope equals vertical change/horizontal change = 0.20/100). Because the curve is linear, the slope is the same between any two points, for example, between E and F and between D and F.

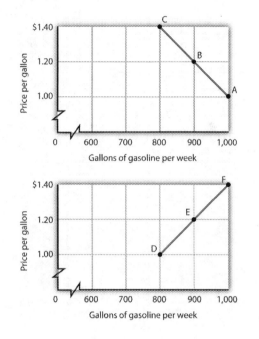

2. NONLINEAR RELATIONSHIPS AND GRAPHS WITHOUT NUMBERS

L E A R N I N G   O B J E C T I V E S

1. **Understand nonlinear relationships and how they are illustrated with nonlinear curves.**
2. **Explain how to estimate the slope at any point on a nonlinear curve.**
3. **Explain how graphs without numbers can be used to understand the nature of relationships between two variables.**

In this section we will extend our analysis of graphs in two ways: first, we will explore the nature of nonlinear relationships; then we will have a look at graphs drawn without numbers.

2.1 Graphs of Nonlinear Relationships

In the graphs we have examined so far, adding a unit to the independent variable on the horizontal axis always has the same effect on the dependent variable on the vertical axis. When we add a passenger riding the ski bus, the ski club's revenues always rise by the price of a ticket. The cancellation of one more game in the 1998–1999 basketball season would always reduce Shaquille O'Neal's earnings by $210,000. The slopes of the curves describing the relationships we have been discussing were constant; the relationships were linear.

FIGURE 19.9 A Nonlinear Curve

The table in Panel (a) shows the relationship between the number of bakers Felicia Alvarez employs per day and the number of loaves of bread produced per day. This information is plotted in Panel (b). This is a nonlinear relationship; the curve connecting these points in Panel (c) (Loaves of bread produced) has a changing slope.

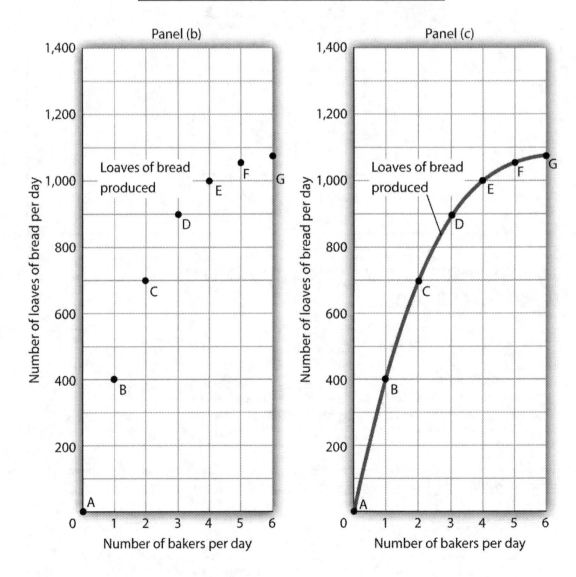

Panel (a)

Combination	Bakers per day	Loaves of bread produced per day
A	0	0
B	1	400
C	2	700
D	3	900
E	4	1,000
F	5	1,050
G	6	1,075

Many relationships in economics are nonlinear. A **nonlinear relationship** between two variables is one for which the slope of the curve showing the relationship changes as the value of one of the variables changes. A **nonlinear curve** is a curve whose slope changes as the value of one of the variables changes.

Consider an example. Suppose Felicia Alvarez, the owner of a bakery, has recorded the relationship between her firm's daily output of bread and the number of bakers she employs. The relationship she has recorded is given in the table in Panel (a) of Figure 19.9. The corresponding points are plotted in Panel (b). Clearly, we cannot draw a straight line through these points. Instead, we shall have to draw a nonlinear curve like the one shown in Panel (c).

Inspecting the curve for loaves of bread produced, we see that it is upward sloping, suggesting a positive relationship between the number of bakers and the output of bread. But we also see that the curve becomes flatter as we travel up and to the right along it; it is nonlinear and describes a nonlinear relationship.

How can we estimate the slope of a nonlinear curve? After all, the slope of such a curve changes as we travel along it. We can deal with this problem in two ways. One is to consider two points on the curve and to compute the slope between those two points. Another is to compute the slope of the curve at a single point.

When we compute the slope of a curve between two points, we are really computing the slope of a straight line drawn between those two points. In Figure 19.10, we have computed slopes between pairs of points A and B, C and D, and E and F on our curve for loaves of bread produced. These slopes equal 400 loaves/baker, 200 loaves/baker, and 50 loaves/baker, respectively. They are the slopes of the dashed-line segments shown. These dashed segments lie close to the curve, but they clearly are not on the curve. After all, the dashed segments are straight lines. Our curve relating the number of bakers to daily bread production is not a straight line; the relationship between the bakery's daily output of bread and the number of bakers is nonlinear.

FIGURE 19.10 Estimating Slopes for a Nonlinear Curve

We can estimate the slope of a nonlinear curve between two points. Here, slopes are computed between points A and B, C and D, and E and F. When we compute the slope of a nonlinear curve between two points, we are computing the slope of a straight line between those two points. Here the lines whose slopes are computed are the dashed lines between the pairs of points.

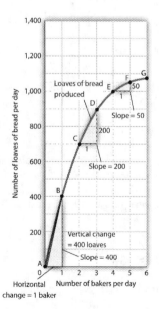

Every point on a nonlinear curve has a different slope. To get a precise measure of the slope of such a curve, we need to consider its slope at a single point. To do that, we draw a line tangent to the curve at that point. A **tangent line** is a straight line that touches, but does not intersect, a nonlinear curve at only one point. The slope of a tangent line equals the slope of the curve at the point at which the tangent line touches the curve.

Consider point D in Panel (a) of Figure 19.11. We have drawn a tangent line that just touches the curve showing bread production at this point. It passes through points labeled M and N. The vertical change between these points equals 300 loaves of bread; the horizontal change equals two bakers. The slope of the tangent line equals 150 loaves of bread/baker (300 loaves/2 bakers). The slope of our bread production curve at point D equals the slope of the line tangent to the curve at this point. In Panel (b),

nonlinear relationship

Relationship between two variables in which the slope of the curve showing the relationship changes as the value of one of the variables changes.

nonlinear curve

A curve whose slope changes as the value of one of the variables changes.

tangent line

A straight line that touches, but does not intersect, a nonlinear curve at only one point.

we have sketched lines tangent to the curve for loaves of bread produced at points B, D, and F. Notice that these tangent lines get successively flatter, suggesting again that the slope of the curve is falling as we travel up and to the right along it.

Notice that we have not been given the information we need to compute the slopes of the tangent lines that touch the curve for loaves of bread produced at points B and F. In this text, we will not have occasion to compute the slopes of tangent lines. Either they will be given or we will use them as we did here—to see what is happening to the slopes of nonlinear curves.

In the case of our curve for loaves of bread produced, the fact that the slope of the curve falls as we increase the number of bakers suggests a phenomenon that plays a central role in both microeconomic and macroeconomic analysis. As we add workers (in this case bakers), output (in this case loaves of bread) rises, but by smaller and smaller amounts. Another way to describe the relationship between the number of workers and the quantity of bread produced is to say that as the number of workers increases, the output increases at a decreasing rate. In Panel (b) of Figure 19.11 we express this idea with a graph, and we can gain this understanding by looking at the tangent lines, even though we do not have specific numbers. Indeed, much of our work with graphs will not require numbers at all.

FIGURE 19.11 Tangent Lines and the Slopes of Nonlinear Curves

Because the slope of a nonlinear curve is different at every point on the curve, the precise way to compute slope is to draw a tangent line; the slope of the tangent line equals the slope of the curve at the point the tangent line touches the curve. In Panel (a), the slope of the tangent line is computed for us: it equals 150 loaves/baker. Generally, we will not have the information to compute slopes of tangent lines. We will use them as in Panel (b), to observe what happens to the slope of a nonlinear curve as we travel along it. We see here that the slope falls (the tangent lines become flatter) as the number of bakers rises.

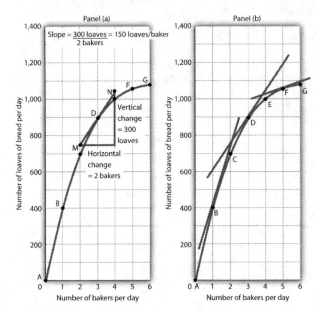

We turn next to look at how we can use graphs to express ideas even when we do not have specific numbers.

2.2 Graphs Without Numbers

We know that a positive relationship between two variables can be shown with an upward-sloping curve in a graph. A negative or inverse relationship can be shown with a downward-sloping curve. Some relationships are linear and some are nonlinear. We illustrate a linear relationship with a curve whose slope is constant; a nonlinear relationship is illustrated with a curve whose slope changes. Using these basic ideas, we can illustrate hypotheses graphically even in cases in which we do not have numbers with which to locate specific points.

Consider first a hypothesis suggested by recent medical research: eating more fruits and vegetables each day increases life expectancy. We can show this idea graphically. Daily fruit and vegetable consumption (measured, say, in grams per day) is the independent variable; life expectancy (measured in years) is the dependent variable. Panel (a) of Figure 19.12 shows the hypothesis, which suggests a positive relationship between the two variables. Notice the vertical intercept on the curve we have drawn; it implies that even people who eat no fruit or vegetables can expect to live at least a while!

Panel (b) illustrates another hypothesis we hear often: smoking cigarettes reduces life expectancy. Here the number of cigarettes smoked per day is the independent variable; life expectancy is the dependent variable. The hypothesis suggests a negative relationship. Hence, we have a downward-sloping curve.

FIGURE 19.12 Graphs Without Numbers

We often use graphs without numbers to suggest the nature of relationships between variables. The graphs in the four panels correspond to the relationships described in the text.

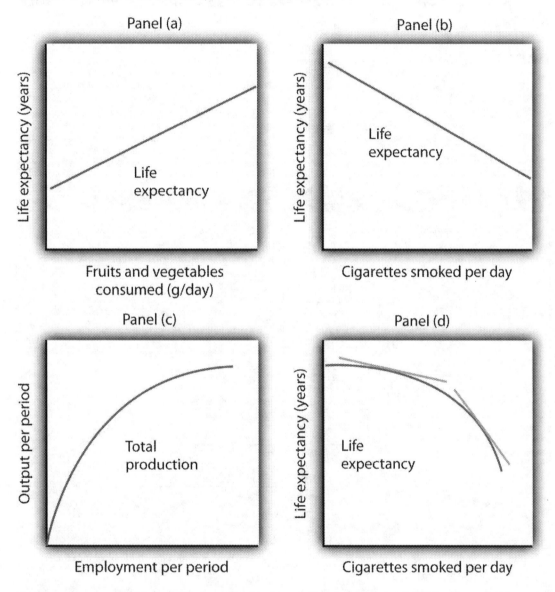

Now consider a general form of the hypothesis suggested by the example of Felicia Alvarez's bakery: increasing employment each period increases output each period, but by smaller and smaller amounts. As we saw in Figure 19.9, this hypothesis suggests a positive, nonlinear relationship. We have drawn a curve in Panel (c) of Figure 19.12 that looks very much like the curve for bread production in Figure 19.11. It is upward sloping, and its slope diminishes as employment rises.

Finally, consider a refined version of our smoking hypothesis. Suppose we assert that smoking cigarettes does reduce life expectancy and that increasing the number of cigarettes smoked per day reduces life expectancy by a larger and larger amount. Panel (d) shows this case. Again, our life expectancy curve slopes downward. But now it suggests that smoking only a few cigarettes per day reduces life expectancy only a little but that life expectancy falls by more and more as the number of cigarettes smoked per day increases.

We have sketched lines tangent to the curve in Panel (d). The slopes of these tangent lines are negative, suggesting the negative relationship between smoking and life expectancy. They also get steeper as the number of cigarettes smoked per day rises. Whether a curve is linear or nonlinear, a steeper curve is one for which the absolute value of the slope rises as the value of the variable on the horizontal axis rises. When we speak of the absolute value of a negative number such as −4, we ignore the minus sign and simply say that the absolute value is 4. The absolute value of −8, for example, is greater than the absolute value of −4, and a curve with a slope of −8 is steeper than a curve whose slope is −4.

Thus far our work has focused on graphs that show a relationship between variables. We turn finally to an examination of graphs and charts that show values of one or more variables, either over a period of time or at a single point in time.

KEY TAKEAWAYS

- The slope of a nonlinear curve changes as the value of one of the variables in the relationship shown by the curve changes.
- A nonlinear curve may show a positive or a negative relationship.
- The slope of a curve showing a nonlinear relationship may be estimated by computing the slope between two points on the curve. The slope at any point on such a curve equals the slope of a line drawn tangent to the curve at that point.
- We can illustrate hypotheses about the relationship between two variables graphically, even if we are not given numbers for the relationships. We need only draw and label the axes and then draw a curve consistent with the hypothesis.

TRY IT!

Consider the following curve drawn to show the relationship between two variables, A and B (we will be using a curve like this one in the next chapter). Explain whether the relationship between the two variables is positive or negative, linear or nonlinear. Sketch two lines tangent to the curve at different points on the curve, and explain what is happening to the slope of the curve.

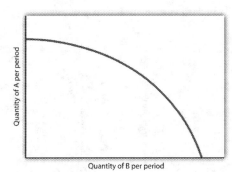

The relationship between variable A shown on the vertical axis and variable B shown on the horizontal axis is negative. This is sometimes referred to as an inverse relationship. Variables that give a straight line with a constant slope are said to have a linear relationship. In this case, however, the relationship is nonlinear. The slope changes all along the curve. In this case the slope becomes steeper as we move downward to the right along the curve, as shown by the two tangent lines that have been drawn. As the quantity of B increases, the quantity of A decreases at an increasing rate.

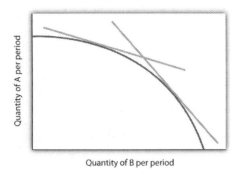

3. USING GRAPHS AND CHARTS TO SHOW VALUES OF VARIABLES

LEARNING OBJECTIVE

1. **Understand and use time-series graphs, tables, pie charts, and bar charts to illustrate data and relationships among variables.**

You often see pictures representing numerical information. These pictures may take the form of graphs that show how a particular variable has changed over time, or charts that show values of a particular variable at a single point in time. We will close our introduction to graphs by looking at both ways of conveying information.

3.1 Time-Series Graphs

One of the most common types of graphs used in economics is called a time-series graph. A **time-series graph** shows how the value of a particular variable or variables has changed over some period of time. One of the variables in a time-series graph is time itself. Time is typically placed on the horizontal axis in time-series graphs. The other axis can represent any variable whose value changes over time.

The table in Panel (a) of Figure 19.13 shows annual values of the unemployment rate, a measure of the percentage of workers who are looking for and available for work but are not working, in the United States from 1998 to 2007. The grid with which these values are plotted is given in Panel (b). Notice that the vertical axis is scaled from 3 to 8%, instead of beginning with zero. Time-series graphs are often presented with the vertical axis scaled over a certain range. The result is the same as introducing a break in the vertical axis, as we did in Figure 19.5

The values for the U.S. unemployment rate are plotted in Panel (b) of Figure 19.13. The points plotted are then connected with a line in Panel (c).

time-series graph

A graph that shows how the value of a particular variable or variables has changed over some period of time.

FIGURE 19.13 A Time-Series Graph

Panel (a) gives values of the U.S. unemployment rate from 1998 to 2010. These points are then plotted in Panel (b). To draw a time-series graph, we connect these points, as in Panel (c).

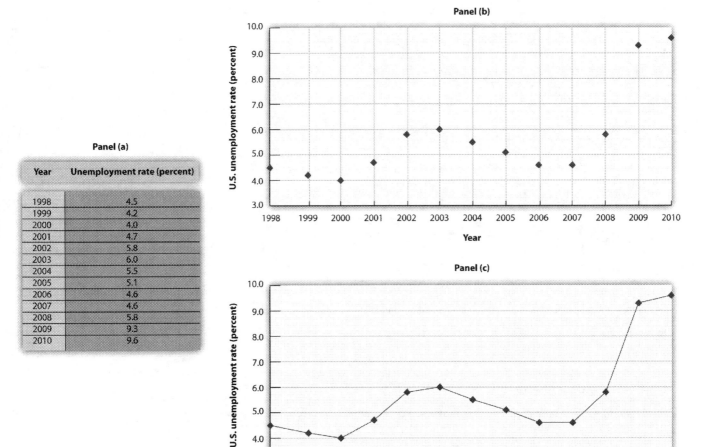

Panel (a)

Year	Unemployment rate (percent)
1998	4.5
1999	4.2
2000	4.0
2001	4.7
2002	5.8
2003	6.0
2004	5.5
2005	5.1
2006	4.6
2007	4.6
2008	5.8
2009	9.3
2010	9.6

Scaling the Vertical Axis in Time-Series Graphs

The scaling of the vertical axis in time-series graphs can give very different views of economic data. We can make a variable appear to change a great deal, or almost not at all, depending on how we scale the axis. For that reason, it is important to note carefully how the vertical axis in a time-series graph is scaled.

Consider, for example, the issue of whether an increase or decrease in income tax rates has a significant effect on federal government revenues. This became a big issue in 1993, when President Clinton proposed an increase in income tax rates. The measure was intended to boost federal revenues. Critics of the president's proposal argued that changes in tax rates have little or no effect on federal revenues. Higher tax rates, they said, would cause some people to scale back their income-earning efforts and thus produce only a small gain—or even a loss—in revenues. Op-ed essays in *The Wall Street Journal*, for example, often showed a graph very much like that presented in Panel (a) of Figure 19.14. It shows federal revenues as a percentage of gross domestic product (GDP), a measure of total income in the economy, since 1960. Various tax reductions and increases were enacted during that period, but Panel (a) appears to show they had little effect on federal revenues relative to total income.

FIGURE 19.14 Two Tales of Taxes and Income

A graph of federal revenues as a percentage of GDP emphasizes the stability of the relationship when plotted with the vertical axis scaled from 0 to 100, as in Panel (a). Scaling the vertical axis from 16 to 21%, as in Panel (b), stresses the short-term variability of the percentage and suggests that major tax rate changes have affected federal revenues.

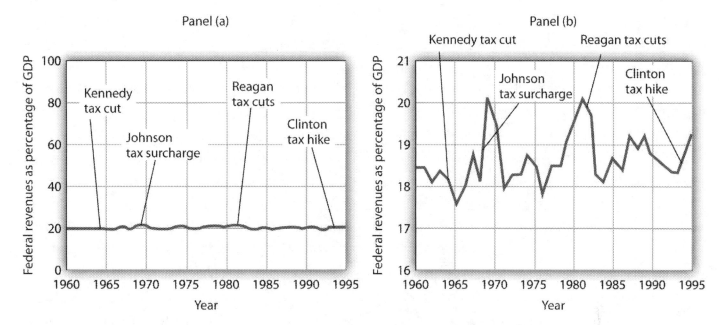

Laura Tyson, then President Clinton's chief economic adviser, charged that those graphs were misleading. In a *Wall Street Journal* piece, she noted the scaling of the vertical axis used by the president's critics. She argued that a more reasonable scaling of the axis shows that federal revenues tend to increase relative to total income in the economy and that cuts in taxes reduce the federal government's share. Her alternative version of these events does, indeed, suggest that federal receipts have tended to rise and fall with changes in tax policy, as shown in Panel (b) of Figure 19.14.

Which version is correct? Both are. Both graphs show the same data. It is certainly true that federal revenues, relative to economic activity, have been remarkably stable over the past several decades, as emphasized by the scaling in Panel (a). But it is also true that the federal share has varied between about 17 and 20%. And a small change in the federal share translates into a large amount of tax revenue.

It is easy to be misled by time-series graphs. Large changes can be made to appear trivial and trivial changes to appear large through an artful scaling of the axes. The best advice for a careful consumer of graphical information is to note carefully the range of values shown and then to decide whether the changes are really significant.

Testing Hypotheses with Time-Series Graphs

John Maynard Keynes, one of the most famous economists ever, proposed in 1936 a hypothesis about total spending for consumer goods in the economy. He suggested that this spending was positively related to the income households receive. One way to test such a hypothesis is to draw a time-series graph of both variables to see whether they do, in fact, tend to move together. Figure 19.15 shows the values of consumption spending and disposable income, which is after-tax income received by households. Annual values of consumption and disposable income are plotted for the period 1960–2013. Notice that both variables have tended to move quite closely together. The close relationship between consumption and disposable income is consistent with Keynes's hypothesis that there is a positive relationship between the two variables.

FIGURE 19.15 A Time-Series Graph of Disposable Income and Consumption

Plotted in a time-series graph, disposable income and consumption appear to move together. This is consistent with the hypothesis that the two are directly related.

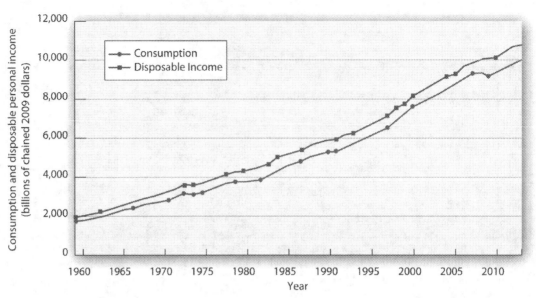

Source: *Department of Commerce*

The fact that two variables tend to move together in a time series does not by itself prove that there is a systematic relationship between the two. Figure 19.16 shows a time-series graph of monthly values in 1987 of the Dow Jones Industrial Average, an index that reflects the movement of the prices of common stock. Notice the steep decline in the index beginning in October, not unlike the steep decline in October 2008.

FIGURE 19.16 Stock Prices and a Mystery Variable

The movement of the monthly average of the Dow Jones Industrial Average, a widely reported index of stock values, corresponded closely to changes in a mystery variable, X. Did the mystery variable contribute to the crash?

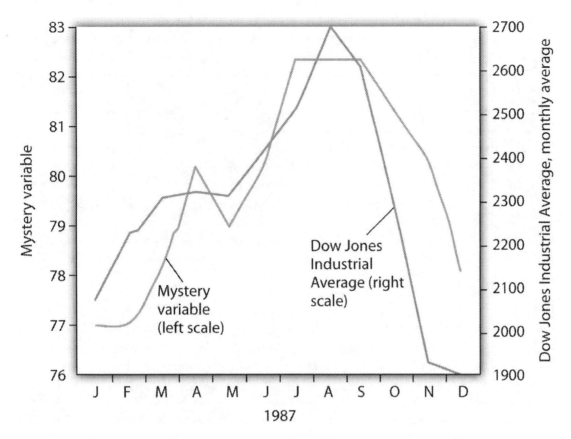

It would be useful, and certainly profitable, to be able to predict such declines. Figure 19.16 also shows the movement of monthly values of a "mystery variable," X, for the same period. The mystery variable and stock prices appear to move closely together. Was the plunge in the mystery variable in October responsible for the stock crash? The answer is: Not likely. The mystery value is monthly average temperatures in San Juan, Puerto Rico. Attributing the stock crash in 1987 to the weather in San Juan would be an example of the fallacy of false cause.

Notice that Figure 19.16 has two vertical axes. The left-hand axis shows values of temperature; the right-hand axis shows values for the Dow Jones Industrial Average. Two axes are used here because the two variables, San Juan temperature and the Dow Jones Industrial Average, are scaled in different units.

3.2 Descriptive Charts

We can use a table to show data. Consider, for example, the information compiled each year by the U.S. National Center for Education Statistics. The table in Panel (a) of Figure 19.17 shows the results of the 2009 survey. In the groupings given, economics is included among the social sciences.

FIGURE 19.17 Bachelor's Degrees Earned by Field, 2009

Panels (a), (b), and (c) show bachelor's degrees earned by field in 2009 in United States. All three panels present the same information. Panel (a) is an example of a table, Panel (b) is an example of a pie chart, and Panel (c) is an example of a vertical bar chart.

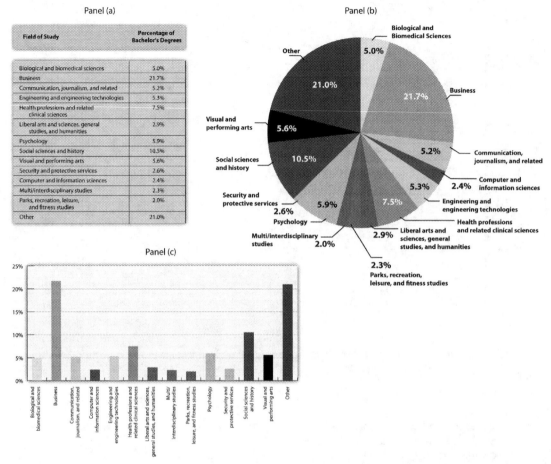

Source: Statistical Abstracts of the United States, 2012, Table 302. Bachelor's Degrees Earned by Field, 1980 to 2009, based on data from U.S. National Center for Education Statistics, Digest of Educational Statistics. Percentages shown are for broad academic areas, each of which includes several majors.

Panels (b) and (c) of Figure 19.17 present the same information in two types of charts. Panel (b) is an example of a pie chart; Panel (c) gives the data in a bar chart. The bars in this chart are horizontal; they may also be drawn as vertical. Either type of graph may be used to provide a picture of numeric information.

KEY TAKEAWAYS

- A time-series graph shows changes in a variable over time; one axis is always measured in units of time.
- One use of time-series graphs is to plot the movement of two or more variables together to see if they tend to move together or not. The fact that two variables move together does not prove that changes in one of the variables cause changes in the other.
- Values of a variable may be illustrated using a table, a pie chart, or a bar chart.

TRY IT!

The table in Panel (a) shows a measure of the inflation rate, the percentage change in the average level of prices below. Panels (b) and (c) provide blank grids. We have already labeled the axes on the grids in Panels (b) and (c). It is up to you to plot the data in Panel (a) on the grids in Panels (b) and (c). Connect the points you have marked in the grid using straight lines between the points. What relationship do you observe? Has the inflation rate generally increased or decreased? What can you say about the trend of inflation over the course of the 1990s? Do you tend to get a different "interpretation" depending on whether you use Panel (b) or Panel (c) to guide you?

Panel (a)

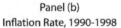

Year	Inflation rate (percent)
1990	6.1
1991	3.1
1992	2.9
1993	2.7
1994	2.7
1995	2.5
1996	3.3
1997	1.7
1998	1.6

Panel (b)
Inflation Rate, 1990-1998

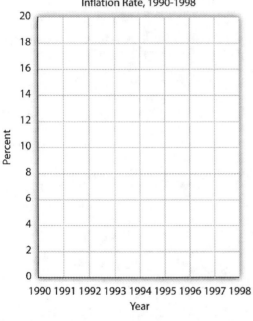

Panel (c)
Inflation Rate, 1990-1998

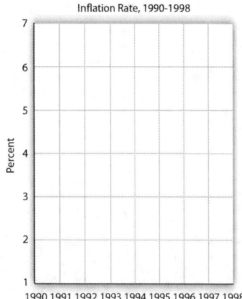

ANSWER TO TRY IT! PROBLEM

Here are the time-series graphs, Panels (b) and (c), for the information in Panel (a). The first thing you should notice is that both graphs show that the inflation rate generally declined throughout the 1990s (with the exception of 1996, when it increased). The generally downward direction of the curve suggests that the trend of inflation was downward. Notice that in this case we do not say negative, since in this instance it is not the slope of the line that matters. Rather, inflation itself is still positive (as indicated by the fact that all the points are above the origin) but is declining. Finally, comparing Panels (b) and (c) suggests that the general downward trend in the inflation rate is emphasized less in Panel (b) than in Panel (c). This impression would be emphasized even more if the numbers on the vertical axis were increased in Panel (b) from 20 to 100. Just as in Figure 19.14, it is possible to make large changes appear trivial by simply changing the scaling of the axes.

Panel (a)

Year	Inflation rate (percent)
1990	6.1
1991	3.1
1992	2.9
1993	2.7
1994	2.7
1995	2.5
1996	3.3
1997	1.7
1998	1.6

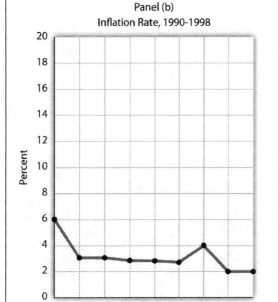

Panel (b)
Inflation Rate, 1990-1998

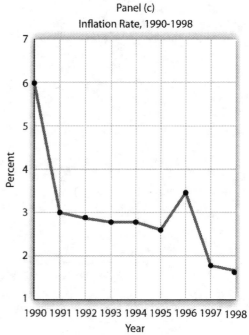

Panel (c)
Inflation Rate, 1990-1998

PROBLEMS

1. Panel (a) shows a graph of a positive relationship; Panel (b) shows a graph of a negative relationship. Decide whether each proposition below demonstrates a positive or negative relationship, and decide which graph you would expect to illustrate each proposition. In each statement, identify which variable is the independent variable and thus goes on the horizontal axis, and which variable is the dependent variable and goes on the vertical axis.

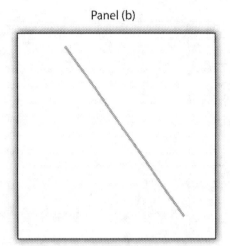

Panel (a)   Panel (b)

   a. An increase in national income in any one year increases the number of people killed in highway accidents.
   b. An increase in the poverty rate causes an increase in the crime rate.
   c. As the income received by households rises, they purchase fewer beans.
   d. As the income received by households rises, they spend more on home entertainment equipment.
   e. The warmer the day, the less soup people consume.

2. Suppose you have a graph showing the results of a survey asking people how many left and right shoes they owned. The results suggest that people with one left shoe had, on average, one right shoe. People with seven left shoes had, on average, seven right shoes. Put left shoes on the vertical axis and right shoes on the horizontal axis; plot the following observations:

Left shoes	1	2	3	4	5	6	7
Right shoes	1	2	3	4	5	6	7

Is this relationship positive or negative? What is the slope of the curve?

3. Suppose your assistant inadvertently reversed the order of numbers for right shoe ownership in the survey above. You thus have the following table of observations:

Left shoes	1	2	3	4	5	6	7
Right shoes	7	6	5	4	3	2	1

Is the relationship between these numbers positive or negative? What's implausible about that?

4. Suppose some of Ms. Alvarez's kitchen equipment breaks down. The following table gives the values of bread output that were shown in Figure 19.9 It also gives the new levels of bread output that Ms. Alvarez's bakers produce following the breakdown. Plot the two curves. What has happened?

	A	B	C	D	E	F	G
Bakers/day	0	1	2	3	4	5	6
Loaves/day	0	400	700	900	1,000	1,050	1,075
Loaves/day after breakdown	0	380	670	860	950	990	1,005

5. Steven Magee has suggested that there is a relationship between the number of lawyers per capita in a country and the country's rate of economic growth. The relationship is described with the following Magee curve.

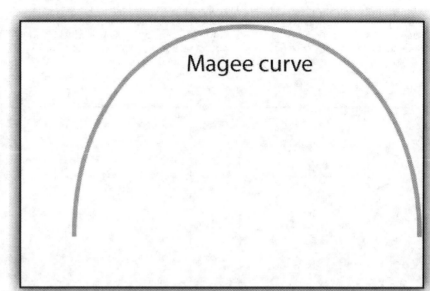

What do you think is the argument made by the curve? What kinds of countries do you think are on the upward- sloping region of the curve? Where would you guess the United States is? Japan? Does the Magee curve seem plausible to you?

6. Draw graphs showing the likely relationship between each of the following pairs of variables. In each case, put the first variable mentioned on the horizontal axis and the second on the vertical axis.

    a. The amount of time a student spends studying economics and the grade he or she receives in the course

    b. Per capita income and total expenditures on health care

    c. Alcohol consumption by teenagers and academic performance

    d. Household income and the likelihood of being the victim of a violent crime

Index